CASES AND MATERIALS ON

Insurance Law

CASES AND MATERIALS ON

Insurance Law

SPENCER L. KIMBALL
Seymour Logan Professor Emeritus
University of Chicago

ASPEN LAW & BUSINESS
Aspen Publishers, Inc.

Library of Congress Catalog Card No. 91-075792

ISBN 0-316-49311-2

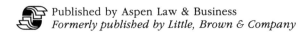 Published by Aspen Law & Business
Formerly published by Little, Brown & Company

Printed in the United States of America

In memory of Kathryn

Summary of Contents

Contents

PART I. *General Doctrines*

CHAPTER 1

Interpretation of Insurance Contracts   *3*

CHAPTER 2

Enforceability of Insurance Contracts   *39*

PART II. *Selected Kinds of Insurance*

CHAPTER 3

Property Insurance 131

CHAPTER 4

Fidelity Insurance   *201*

CHAPTER 6

Life Insurance and Annuities   *407*

Health Insurance   *449*

PART III. *Institutional Problems of Insurance*

CHAPTER 8

Litigation Problems, Especially in Liability Insurance   485

CHAPTER 9

Complex and Unusual Insurance Arrangements 563

CHAPTER 10

Regulation of Insurance 621

Insurance Market Organization: A Primer 681

Preface

There are several ways to approach the teaching of insurance law.

First, the insurance policy is, after all, a contract. Insurance law can be taught as a specialized contracts class. Much of traditional instruction in insurance law took that form. But the doctrines peculiar to insurance contracts are not numerous and few cases turn on them. It is sufficient for the student, if not for the insurance lawyer, to be sensitive to the existence of a few specialized doctrines without knowing about their subtler nuances. Beyond that, the law of contract is equally the law of the insurance contract.

Second, liability insurance increasingly underlies most tort litigation. It is tempting to teachers having a torts orientation to see insurance primarily as the much-prized deep pocket for which tort plaintiffs seek and to be concerned with little else. This approach is no more rewarding than the first.

Third, some might be tempted to focus on the public control of an immensely important enterprise that employs a couple of million Americans, protects the rest, and commands vast and relatively liquid asset portfolios. That would be of special relevance for the increasing group of lawyers that specialize in insurance regulation, as regulators or as other actors. But members of that group are identified only later in life, often long after beginning practice. It would be an atypical study in economic regulation, worthwhile but of uncertain priority for students preparing for an unpredictable legal career.

Nevertheless, the insurance industry purveys such important contracts and is an enterprise so pervasive and so crucial in our time that all lawyers and all judges need to know far more than they characteristically do know about the way insurance works and is used. A surprisingly large share of litigated cases involve insurance, sometimes barely visible behind the nominal parties. Many of the opinions dealing with insurance law problems in the law reports reflect an inadequate understanding of the way the insurance business operates. The average quality of decision-making in insurance cases is low.

In the preparation of this book, it has been my intention to provide materials that will instruct not only about the *legal* aspects of insurance but about the way the business operates. I have sought cases that have both intrinsic interest and that illustrate current problems of importance.

Insurance law has not had a major place in most law school curricula. The materials contained in this book cannot all be covered thoroughly in the time usually allotted to the course. I have adapted them to the limits of time in my own course by (a) omitting completely one or more of Chapters 3, 4, 6, 7, and 8 and (b) omitting selected sections of chapters or even individual cases, depending in the latter case on how the course develops. Chapter 5 on liability insurance is the heart of the book and cannot well be omitted altogether, though certain sections of it can.

Chapter 3 on property insurance can be assigned as a chapter for students to read without having class discussion except perhaps on the materials on causation. Chapter 4 on fidelity insurance, though the subject is of great importance to the financial world, is an apt candidate for omission, especially by relatively new teachers of the subject. Experienced teachers who have not dealt with fidelity insurance before would find the chapter rewarding to them, particularly the part dealing with the financial institution bond. Chapters 6 and 7 are candidates for omission because the treatment in this book is sketchy for subject matters that are very complex and very important. Life insurance, the subject of Chapter 6, is an appropriate subject to be combined with estate planning in a seminar or course. Health insurance, the subject of Chapter 7, when considered together with other aspects of the health care dilemma, needs a full course of its own, and there are teaching materials available for it. The litigation problems dealt with in Chapter 8 may, in particular schools, have received considerable emphasis in procedure courses.

I wish to express my gratitude to the Insurance Services Office and the Surety Association of America for permission to reproduce their policy forms and to the Alliance of American Insurers for cooperation in providing materials. Richard A. Brown has made many useful suggestions. I also wish to thank Michael H. Rudof for helping with the laborious and essential task of checking citations, and to Ms. Shirley Evans for conscientious and skillful assistance in the many clerical tasks connected with producing the manuscript.

Spencer L. Kimball

November 1991

Introduction

There is no good definition of "insurance," for any purpose. This book will not seek to provide one. It is concerned almost solely with mainstream "commercial" insurance, the meaning of which everyone knows.

Most significant assets and nearly all important commercial transactions are undergirded with some, and often many, kinds of insurance. Today no large organization, commercial or nonprofit, can do without its functionary (a risk or insurance manager) to transfer the organization's risks to someone else or to work out ways to deploy the resources of the organization to make that transfer unnecessary. In this book, therefore, doctrinal peculiarities of insurance contract law are subordinated to exploration of the ways in which insurance is used. The objective is to communicate an understanding of the principal kinds of insurance, what they mean, and how they are used. The subject is too vast and intricate for comprehensive coverage, but a close look at some of it should make the rest easier to understand and deal with.

Middle class existence in this society requires insurance of many kinds. Typical coverages include:

- insurance against premature death: life insurance
- insurance to provide for the unproductive years of a long life: social security, private pensions, and annuities
- insurance against unemployment (government provided)
- insurance against disability (through the social security system and through private insurance)
- medical and hospitalization insurance, both private and public

- automobile insurance, which includes: against physical damage to or theft of the car, against medical expenses incurred both by persons using the car and others injured in an accident involving the car, against liability to others as a result of negligence of the driver, against loss from being hit by an uninsured or underinsured motorist
- insurance against fire and other hazards (vandalism, windstorm, flood, earthquake, etc.) to which residences and other real property are subject
- insurance against a wide range of risks of incurring personal liability, now usually combined with fire and extended coverage insurance into a homeowners or tenants policy
- insurance against loss of personal property, sometimes in a homeowners policy and sometimes in a personal property floater
- other kinds of insurance against the risks of particular interests and activities (boating, flying, hunting, making expensive vacation trips)

Commercial activity of any kind requires insurance protection, some kinds paralleling insurance for individuals:

- entrepreneurs need liability insurance for their operations
- most entrepreneurs need business interruption coverage
- professionals (broadly defined) need professional liability insurance
- employers need workers compensation insurance or employers liability insurance or both
- manufacturers need products liability insurance
- contractors need insurance against the risks created by their completed operations (analogous to products liability)
- owners of commercial property need insurance against liability arising from accidents on or adjacent to that property
- shipowners need marine insurance on hulls and against loss of freight charges
- shippers need cargo insurance
- airlines need insurance both on airplane hulls and against liability
- many businesses (as well as individuals) need protection against crime, whether street crime or white collar crime
- lenders like to have and often insist on having the benefit of credit life and disability insurance and often also buy credit insurance against defaults by borrowers
- international traders wish to have insurance against political risks

- lenders on security of real property desire protection against the credit risk in the transaction through mortgage guaranty insurance as well as protection against the loss of the physical security, the latter to be achieved by being named as insureds under the equity owner's fire and extended coverage insurance
- buyers of real property want title insurance, which increasingly takes the place of a lawyer's title opinion
- few people are now willing to serve as officers or directors of corporations, whether profit-seeking or nonprofit, without extensive rights to indemnification by the corporation for personal liability arising out of their activities in that capacity, backed by directors and officers liability insurance (which may give some protection to both the corporation and the directors and officers)
- buyers of municipal bonds will accept a reduced yield if payment of the principal and interest on the bonds is insured

Some illustrations will show the wide range of activities in which insurance is used in our society:

- Columbia Pictures was insured under a cast insurance policy against the death of Samantha Smith, the 13-year-old who gained fame by writing to Yuri Andropov and being invited to the Soviet Union in 1983. When she was killed in August 1985 in an airplane crash in Maine, major adjustments were necessitated in a forthcoming television series, with the costs being shifted in part to the insurer.
- Billy Simms was insured (somewhat unwillingly, it is said) against the risk that his knees would give out under the stress of the professional football game; he was fortunate that his agent insisted on the insurance. Newspaper accounts said a premium of about $100,000 brought him indemnification to the amount of $2 million. The policy was, not surprisingly, written by Underwriters at Lloyd's, London.
- Owners of a stallion put out to stud take out insurance that the horse will not be sterile. That insurance too will probably be written by Underwriters at Lloyd's.
- Horse mortality insurance is common, again dominated by Lloyd's. But a local Kentucky horse owner has acquired a 25 percent share of the thoroughbred insurance business, through his Kirk Horse Insurance Company, taking much of that business from Lloyd's. Swasy, *Racehorse Insurer Proves to Be Good on a Fast Track*, Wall St. J., Feb. 23, 1989, at B2.
- Kidnap insurance dates from shortly after the kidnapping of the Lindbergh baby in the 1930s. Long a sleepy branch of insur-

ance, it has recently had a resurgence and now generates $125 million yearly in premiums, mostly from corporations. The Miniboom in Kidnapping Coverage, Bus. Week, Mar. 19, 1990 at 100.

- A recent entry in the catalog, the viability of which is still uncertain, is insurance against the cost to patent holders of suing for patent infringement.
- Rain insurance can operate in two directions. Promoters of exhibitions, outdoor concerts, games, and the like may wish to insure *against* rain, or an excessive amount of it, that requires cancellation of the event or reduces its revenues. But farmers may wish *for* rain, and insure against inadequate amounts of it. A recent program of commercial insurance against inadequate rainfall during the midwestern drought of the 1980s had a harmful effect on the insurer. The latter authorized a managing general agent* to underwrite such a program for the insurer in a strictly limited amount. The MGA ignored the limits and underwrote an immense program, far in excess of the amount authorized. Then it failed to rain. Though the "agent" had clearly exceeded its authority, leading to considerable uncertainty about the liability of the insurer on policies underwritten, heavy pressure from the insurance commissioners of midwestern farm states led the insurer, a company of excellent reputation, to pay without testing its liability. Its good name in the industry and with regulators was at stake. The agent would perhaps be liable over to the insurer or even directly to policyholders but might not have the resources to pay, unless adequately covered by agent's errors and omissions insurance.
- Another leading insurer issued a similar policy, calling it "efficacy" insurance, to the owners of a dam built for hydroelectric power. The insurance was against inadequate water for the power plant. Again, it didn't rain!
- The list continues. New varieties keep appearing, and some survive to become regular listings in the catalog. As the ultimate example, there even exists (or has recently existed) insurance against insurance company nonperformance of insurance contracts, though it has not had an enthusiastic reception in the market. Why should it? A double layering of insurance does seem a bit much. Yet a currently existing system of guaranty funds (analogous to FDIC and FSLIC), under which solvent insurers pay assessments to fund payment of claimants against insolvent insurers, provides similar protection and could be

---

*The Appendix contains a description of the insurance market, including managing general agents (MGAs).

called a system of public insurance against insurance company nonperformance.

- Finally, primary insurers "reinsure" their risks with other insurance companies whenever they have an insufficiently diversified or excessively large portfolio (or book) of business or individual risks of a size greater than they wish to retain for their own accounts or sometimes to improve the appearance of the balance sheet for regulatory purposes. Reinsurers often *reinsure* (or *retrocede**) part of *their* risks to still other reinsurers (or retrocessionaires). Reinsurance (and retrocession) protects only the reinsured (or ceding) company, not the primary insureds (at least not directly). The reinsuring companies may be "professional" reinsurers that do nothing but reinsure or may be the reinsurance departments of primary carriers. Reinsurance arrangements can be incredibly complicated. Chapter 9 treats some aspects of reinsurance.

These course materials are organized to try primarily to communicate some "feel" for the main lines of insurance in an operating industry; in addition to but subordinate to the primary goal, the materials will expose students to the more important substantive legal doctrines. The materials are structured in three parts.

The first part introduces important doctrines that differ, at least in emphasis, from similar doctrines applying to other contracts. A first chapter introduces the peculiarities of insurance contract interpretation. The second chapter deals with the enforceability of insurance contracts, with special emphasis on warranties, misrepresentations, and concealment as defenses for the insurer, often then overcome by waiver, estoppel, or election. It also deals with the requirement of insurable interest, a pervasive and peculiar doctrine of doubtful merit.

The second part treats major kinds of insurance, which are defined with convenience in view rather than rigor of analysis. Part II focuses on coverage problems and a few doctrines limited to those branches of insurance. The topics are property insurance (centrally insurance against fire), fidelity (or dishonesty or crime insurance, a major part of which could have been classified as property insurance instead), liability, life, and health. Ocean marine, historically and conceptually important but in the contemporary world relatively unimportant in premium volume, is treated only incidentally. It is older than

---

*To retrocede is simply to reinsure the reinsurance one insurer has written for other insurers. The process may go on for any number of transactions, in sequence. It is said that one major American insurer, after having declined to insure the old McCormick Place in Chicago, still found itself liable for a portion of the $100 million loss from the fire through a sequence of retrocessions that had circled the world.

the others; much of insurance contract law developed in connection with marine insurance.

The third part deals with what might be termed institutional problems of insurance. One chapter is mainly about liability insurance, with an emphasis on special litigation problems. A further chapter deals with complicated and sometimes esoteric ways of insuring, including especially surplus lines, excess coverage, and reinsurance. A final chapter on a few selected contemporary problems in insurance regulation concludes the main part of the book.

The Appendix sketches the main outlines of the complicated insurance marketplace. It should be read at the outset and periodically thereafter to provide essential background information. It is intended to provide a sense of the way the insurance institution works.

Citations to cases, to cases within cases, footnotes, and other quoted material have sometimes been eliminated without indication.

CASES AND MATERIALS ON

Insurance Law

PART I

General Doctrines

CHAPTER 1

The Interpretation of Insurance Contracts

A. The Function of Insurance

An element of risk or chance pervades human life. Weather is unpredictable, the length of one's life is unpredictable, whether one's house will burn is unpredictable. Throughout history various social and economic institutions have developed to deal with the economic consequences of such uncertainties. William Graham Sumner regarded insurance as the genus of the species. He even considered religion to be but a form of "insurance," which he described as

> a generic conception covering the methods of attaining security, of which the modern devices are but specific, highly elaborated, and scientifically tested examples. . . .
>
> Insurance is a grand device and is now a highly technical process; but its roots go farther back than one would think, offhand. Man on earth, having always had an eye to the avoidance of ill luck, has tried in all ages somehow to insure himself — to take out a "policy" of some sort on which he has paid regular premiums in some form of self-denial or sacrifice. [Sumner & Keller, The Science of Society 749 (1927-33).]

The early institutions that Sumner would regard as species of insurance included kinship obligations, age-cohort loyalties, secret society affiliations, and the intricate web of interpersonal relationships in feudal society. In modern times, the principal one of the "specific, highly elaborated, and scientifically tested examples" is the contract issued by an insurance company. It exists to give both security and a feeling of security earlier provided in other ways.

One way to define insurance is as a scheme for the transfer of risk from those individuals subject to it to an insurer, which in turn distributes that risk over a large number of persons subject to similar risks, with a view to replacing each individual's uncertain risk of a large loss by a predictable and much smaller cost in the form of a premium. The definition has inadequacies but is sufficient for our purposes.

It is common to explain the basic mechanism of insurance by a homely example from fire insurance. Suppose 10,000 homeowners each have identical houses worth $100,000 each. Further suppose that previous experience shows that about 20 of those houses will burn each year, and that all will be total losses. Each householder then has a risk of .002 that his or her house will burn during the year. The probability of loss to each homeowner is small but the magnitude of the possible loss is great. A risk-averse person is certain to want "insurance" against that possible loss from fire. To provide protection against such loss to householders an insurer will need a pool of $2,000,000 to reimburse the few unfortunate losers. To provide that sum each householder will have to contribute $200 to the pool. That is the loss portion of the premium for the insurance policy.

While the insurer expects, and charges a premium appropriate to, 20 fires, the number that actually occur may be larger than that. That is the insurer's risk in operating the pool. The insurer will *load* the premium with a charge for bearing that risk, to pay for the necessary commitment of capital to the enterprise to keep the insurer financially sound in case the burning ratio does exceed 2 per 1000 in a given year or series of years. The insurer also may seek to lessen its own uncertainty or risk (and need for capital) by converting part of that risk into predictable cost through the purchase of reinsurance from another insurer. See Chapter 9 for discussion of reinsurance.

Of course the foregoing ignores such complications as the uncertainty of the information about the probable future burning ratio, differences in the values of houses and in the degree of risk to which each is subject, transaction costs (which tend to be high), income from invested funds, and any loading for hoped-for profit.

The premium rate for a given insurance policy is based on anticipated experience in the class of insurance to which the policy belongs, which in turn is ordinarily based on the assumption that the future will be much like the past. The calculations are sometimes intricate and always uncertain, for there is no way to be sure how similar the future will be to the past. The variation from the expected loss may be in either direction. In certain lines of insurance, however, the loss experience has been sharply and steadily upward in recent decades, as a result of changes in the law (e.g., in products liability), of changes in patterns of jury verdicts (e.g., in liability generally), or of changes in social patterns (e.g., an increasing level of property crime or of health care costs). The instability of that experience, and especially its upward trend, has contributed mightily to recent insurance "crises."

One of the factors in premium rate calculation is the anticipated income from investments.* The sharp decline in interest rates a decade ago created serious problems for some insurers that had anticipated and unwisely depended on a level of earnings from invested funds that became unrealistic.

B. An Introductory Look at Policy Interpretation

An insurance law course needs to focus first on the interpretation of insurance contracts. In no other respect does insurance law differ so much in real life application from general contract law, even though in abstract doctrinal terms the formal law of insurance contract interpretation is similar, if not identical, to that of general contracts.

Academic discourse sometimes treats the judicial interpretation of insurance contracts as an aspect of the regulation of insurance. As a backdrop for an understanding of what the courts do when they interpret insurance policies, some teachers would begin the insurance law course with an introduction to the objectives and methods of legislative and administrative insurance regulation. In this book systematic introduction to the latter has been placed in Chapter 10 because of the belief that regulation can only be understood adequately after there is considerable knowledge of the insurance business and what it does. But it is true that in a limited way judicial interpretation does have a regulatory role. For the author's own views on that subject, see Kimball & Pfennigstorf, Legislative and Judicial Control of the Terms of Insurance Contracts: A Comparative Study of American and European Practice, 39 Ind. L.J. 675, 699-704 (1964). See also the provocative views of Karl Llewellyn in Book Review, 52 Harv. L. Rev. 700, 703 (1939) and the classical treatment by Friedrich Kessler, Contracts of Adhesion — Some Thoughts About Freedom of Contract, 43 Colum. L. Rev. 629 (1943).

Two fundamental principles underlie the interpretation of insur-

---

*In classes of insurance for which rates are regulated, income from investments has traditionally not been taken explicitly into account, but it clearly does enter into the decisions actually made by regulators. If rates are unregulated, income from investments makes its way directly into rate calculations in all competitive situations. In most lines of insurance, intense competition raises the policy question of whether rates are high enough to keep insurers financially sound. There have been an immense number of insurer insolvencies in recent years, many of which are attributable to inadequate rates in certain volatile lines of insurance.

ance contracts. Though in theory they are reconcilable, they point in different directions and are in constant tension. First, an insurance policy is a contract, and as with other contracts, whenever its meaning is clear, and unless by its terms it contravenes some public policy, it should be (and by most courts will be) interpreted to mean what it says.

The second principle of contract interpretation is the *contra proferentem* principle, as stated in the Restatement (Second) of Contracts §206 (1981):

§206. *Interpretation Against the Draftsman*

In choosing among the reasonable meanings of a promise or agreement or a term thereof, that meaning is generally preferred which operates against the party who supplies the words or from whom a writing otherwise proceeds.

Many courts (possibly even most courts) try to interpret insurance contracts in accordance with the general principles of contract interpretation using in a balanced way the clear meaning rule and the *contra proferentem* doctrine. But as will be apparent as the cases in this book are read, many American courts tend to find multiple "reasonable meanings," that is, ambiguity, in insurance provisions which, when read with a careful eye and with the help of a blue pencil, have only one reasonable meaning. At the extreme, a few courts treat insurance contracts with a degree of suspicion that borders on overt hostility and give readings to the language that would amaze a detached reader seeking the true meaning, which is itself sometimes difficult to ascertain.

In the face of what in some cases appears to be intentional misinterpretation, it is hard to design an insurance contract that will with assurance achieve in the eyes of *all* courts what the drafter wishes. It adds greatly to drafting difficulty when it is necessary to draft, as Sir Frederick Pollock is reputed to have said about statutes, not so that a court reading in good faith can understand but so that a court reading in bad faith cannot misunderstand.

Several factors are at the root of the problem. First, the insurance contract is a technical and complex contract that does not always lend itself to easy interpretation even after generous blue-penciling, though it is not as complex as, for example, major securities transactions.

Second, it is common for the insured to not actually see the written contract until some time after its inception. This tends to prejudice courts in the insured's favor, despite the fact that the contract terms would always be available in advance if requested, and that unless otherwise agreed they will be the company's standard terms, which are often terms standard for the insurance industry as well.

Third, in recent decades the public image of insurance companies has suffered severe blows for a variety of reasons, not every one of which is the fault of the insurance industry. They include such disparate reasons as the tendency of premiums to rise steadily (which may often be a result of inflation or of changing social patterns) and a common practice of cancelling or not renewing whole classes of policies without regard to the characteristics of individual policyholders or individual risks.

Finally, and related to the previous factor, some courts seem subject to half-conscious misconceptions of the insurance institution and therefore of the proper application of the insurance contract that is shared with much of the general population. By the nature of their business, healthy insurers have a copious cash flow and therefore tend to be perceived erroneously as money trees, rather than in their true nature as conduits by which money is transferred from a large class of premium payers to a smaller class of claimants.

Everything (except for investment earnings) received by claimants comes from premium payers, including the money needed to pay the high transaction costs that go with the transfer and the money needed to provide for a hoped-for profit for the insurer-conduits. Insurers are not inexhaustible sources of costless funds. Rational interpretation would be aided by recognition that very often the true contesting parties, at least in the long run, are the claimant class versus the premium paying class, rather than individual claimants versus individual insurers. Every judge really does know that, but too often fails to keep it in mind in deciding cases.

Interpretation would be aided, too, if judges would study how insurance contracts are constructed and, in interpreting an insurance provision, would think themselves into the position of the drafter. After a little practice most insurance contracts are not difficult to understand.

In particular, one elementary lesson judges might profitably learn is the fallacy of the hoary saying that coverage clauses are written in generous terms in large print and placed at the beginning of the contract explicitly to enable insurers to insert later in the contract exclusions in fine print that surreptitiously disembowel what the reasonable buyer of insurance thinks has been bought.

To the contrary, the insured receives a considerable advantage from a general grant of coverage followed by exclusions, in contrast to the converse way of constructing a contract by listing the coverages without exclusions. Brief reflection should show why that is so. Even the cliché of fine print is not real: While the print may often be too fine for easy reading, ordinarily the print size is the same throughout the contract. Further, it is instructive to compare the print size of an insurance contract with that of a municipal or corporate bond, among many other common contracts.

C. Approaches to Interpretation

Some courts apply the two general principles of interpretation mentioned above in a conservative manner; that is, they strive to ascertain the meaning of the language and apply it, resorting to interpretation against the drafter only if the insurance policy language truly has multiple legitimate meanings. Other courts go to the opposite extreme and not only find ambiguity readily, but even manufacture it where it does not exist. Both approaches, and various gradations in between, will be seen in the cases in this book.

1. *Contra Proferentem* and Adhesion

It is established law, not only for insurance contracts but for all contracts, that an ambiguous provision, that is, one with more than one reasonable interpretation, will be interpreted most favorably to the party who did not draft it. Restatement (Second) of Contracts §206 (1981). This is the rule of interpretation *contra proferentem.*

The inclination of many courts to hold against the insurer in case of ambiguity is often said to be based, in part at least, on the ground that the contract is one of *adhesion.* That is, the insurer creates the policy form, to which the insured can only adhere or decline. The notion of the adhesion contract gives added strength to the *contra proferentem* principle because of the perception that advantage is being taken of a stronger market position. The principle may be applied, however, even when the contract is not strictly one of adhesion.

For a good student discussion of the problem, see Note, Insurance as Contract: The Argument for Abandoning the Ambiguity Doctrine, 88 Colum. L. Rev. 1849 (1988).

2. Objectively Reasonable Expectations

The classic academic treatment of modern insurance contract interpretation is a two-part article. Keeton, Insurance Law Rights at Variance with Policy Provisions, 83 Harv. L. Rev. 961, 1261 (1970), also found (with some changes) as Chapter 6 of Keeton & Widiss, Insurance Law: Student Edition (1988). Professor (now Judge) Keeton's seminal article has had unusual generative power. It has often been cited by courts, some of them using it to change the law in their jurisdictions. The article will repay study in view of its continuing influence on the courts. See also Keeton, Reasonable Expectations in the Second Decade, 12 Forum 275 (1976).

Keeton's thesis is that two important principles that go beyond the *contra proferentem* rule and the adhesion contract rationale have often resulted (and should often result) in decisions overriding the unambiguous meaning of the insurance contract. The first is that the courts will often disallow *unconscionable advantage* that an insurer has taken of the insured. Most of the cases on which he bases this view of the law can be found in litigation between an insurer and an ordinary consumer. Should the same approach be followed for large corporate insureds?

Keeton's second principle is that the courts do (and should) honor *objectively reasonable expectations* of the insured, whatever the contract may say. Should this approach prevail if it can be established that the insured actually expected less than the contract language would give? See Restatement (Second) of Contracts §206 comment (1981).

To these two basic principles, Keeton would add *detrimental reliance* as a third principle of interpretation. This notion is inconsistent with the traditional doctrine that estoppel cannot increase insurance coverage, but see the cases on that subject in Chapter 2, which show that the traditional doctrine is not without its qualifications, at least in the *results* of litigated cases.

The title of the Keeton article suggests that insureds may have rights beyond those expressed in the contracts. See Abraham, Distributing Risk: Insurance, Legal Theory, and Public Policy, Ch. 5 (1986), which is derivative of the Keeton work but provides some additional insights. Abraham uses the expression "judge-made insurance" to reflect the useful thought that courts do not merely interpret contracts but sometimes manufacture coverage out of whole cloth. This can certainly be regarded as judicial regulation of the insurance business.

The Iowa Supreme Court recently pronounced its rather conservative view on reasonable expectations, approving the following statement by a trial court:

> The doctrine of reasonable expectations obligates the Court to ignore a policy exclusion if the exclusion: (1) is bizarre or oppressive; (2) eviscerates terms explicitly agreed to; or (3) eliminates the dominant purpose of the transaction. [Cairns v. Grinnell Mut. Reins. Co., 398 N.W.2d 821 (Iowa 1987).]

The decision in *Cairns* was a unanimous one by a five judge panel of a nine judge court. That is important, for *Cairns* is inconsistent with C & J Fertilizer, Inc. v. Allied Mut. Ins. Co., 227 N.W.2d 169 (Iowa 1975), where by a 5-4 vote the Iowa Supreme Court, using a reasonable expectations rationale, held unconscionable and void a requirement of visible external marks of force or violence on property as prerequisite to recovery under a burglary policy. In a vehement majority opinion the court emphasized the fine print of the requirement, how it was "buried" in the definition of burglary and was not in its "logical" place in the exclusions portion of the policy, and how the insured and the insurance agent were both surprised to discover that the burglary was not covered merely because there were no visible marks on the outside door. There seems to have been clear evidence that a burglary had occurred — tire marks in the driveway mud and breaking of an inside door lock. See also Farm Bureau Mut. Ins. Co. v. Sandbulte, 302 N.W.2d 104 (Iowa 1981), a split decision retreating substantially from *C & J Fertilizer.*

In Markline Co., Inc. v. The Travelers Ins. Co., 384 Mass. 139, 424 N.E.2d 464 (1981), the Supreme Judicial Court of Massachusetts reached a result opposite to *C & J Fertilizer,* with a 4-1 vote. The lone dissenter depended heavily on *C & J Fertilizer.*

Most academic writing seems to have approved the reasonable expectations doctrine, though a recent exception is a thoughtful student note. Note, A Critique of the Reasonable Expectations Doctrine, 56 U. Chi. L. Rev. 1461 (1989).

The following case anticipates some of Keeton's analysis. Keeton discusses the case but arguably gives it less credit than it deserves in forecasting the "modern approach." The policy in the case provides personal liability coverage of the kind that would now normally be provided by the homeowner's policy. It is not an automobile liability policy.

As will appear in Chapter 5, in liability insurance the insurer has a dual obligation: to assume the insured's covered liabilities and to defend the insured. The issue in the principal case is how broad the duty of defense is. In understanding the case it is important to note that the duty to defend exists "even if any of the allegations of the suit are groundless, false, or fraudulent."

GRAY v. ZURICH INS. CO.

65 Cal. 2d 263, 419 P.2d 168, 54 Cal. Rptr. 104 (1966)

Tobriner, Justice.

This is an action by an insured against his insurer for failure to defend an action filed against him which stemmed from a complaint alleging that he had committed an assault. The main issue turns on the argument of the insurer that an exclusionary clause of the policy excuses its defense of an action in which a plaintiff alleges that the insured intentionally caused the bodily injury. Yet the language of the policy does not clearly define the application of the exclusionary clause to the duty to defend. Since in that event we test the meaning of the policy according to the insured's reasonable expectation of coverage and since the language of the policy would lead the insured here to expect defense of the third party suit, we cannot exonerate the carrier from the rendition of such protection.

Plaintiff, Dr. Vernon D. Gray, is the named insured under an insurance policy issued by defendant. A "Comprehensive Personal Liability Endorsement" in the policy states, under a paragraph designated "Coverage L," that the insurer agrees "[T]o pay on behalf of the insured all sums which the insured shall become legally obligated to pay as damages because of bodily injury or property damage, and the company shall defend any suit against the insured alleging such bodily injury or property damage and seeking damages which are payable under the terms of this endorsement, even if any of the allegations are groundless, false or fraudulent; but the company may make such investigation and settlement of any claim or suit as it deems expedient." The policy contains a provision that "[T]his endorsement does not apply" to a series of specified exclusions set forth under separate headings, including a paragraph (c) which reads, "under coverages L and M, to bodily injury or property damages caused intentionally by or at the direction of the insured."

The suit which Dr. Gray contends Zurich should have defended arose out of an altercation between him and a Mr. John R. Jones.[1] Jones filed a complaint in Missouri alleging that Dr. Gray "wilfully, maliciously, brutally and intentionally assaulted" him; he prayed for actual damages of $50,000 and punitive damages of $50,000. Dr. Gray notified defendant of the suit, stating that he had acted in self-defense, and requested that the company defend. Defendant refused on the ground that the complaint alleged an intentional tort which fell outside the coverage of the policy. Dr. Gray thereafter unsuccessfully defended on the theory of self-defense; he suffered a judgment of $6,000 actual damages although the jury refused to award punitive damages.

Dr. Gray then filed the instant action charging defendant with breach of its duty to defend. Defendant answered, admitting the execution of the policy but denying any such obligation. . . . [T]he court rendered judgment in favor of defendant. We must decide whether or not defendant bore the obligation to defend plaintiff in the Missouri action.

Defendant argues that it need not defend an action in which the complaint reveals on its face that the claimed bodily injury does not

---

1. Immediately preceding the altercation Dr. Gray had been driving an automobile on a residential street when another automobile narrowly missed colliding with his car. Jones, the driver of the other car, left his vehicle, approached Dr. Gray's car in a menacing manner and jerked open the door. At that point Dr. Gray, fearing physical harm to himself and his passengers, rose from his seat and struck Jones.

fall within the indemnification coverage; that here the Jones complaint alleged that the insured committed an assault, which fell outside such coverage. Defendant urges, as a second answer to plaintiff's contention, that the contract, if construed to require defense of the insured, would violate the public policy of the state and that, indeed, the judgment in the third party suit upholding the claim of an intentional bodily injury operates to estop the insured from recovery. Defendant thirdly contends that any requirement that it defend the Jones suit would embroil it in a hopeless conflict of interest. Finally it submits that, even if it should have defended the third party suit, the damages against it should encompass only the insured's expenses of defense and not the judgment against him.

We shall explain our reasons for concluding that defendant was obligated to defend the Jones suit, and our grounds for rejecting defendant's remaining propositions. Since the policy sets forth the duty to defend as a primary one and since the insurer attempts to avoid it only by an unclear exclusionary clause, the insured would reasonably expect, and is legally entitled to, such protection. As an alternative but secondary ground for our ruling we accept, for purposes of argument, defendant's contention that the duty to defend arises only if the third party suit involves a liability for which the insurer would be required to indemnify the insured, and, even upon this basis, we find a duty to defend.

In interpreting an insurance policy we apply the general principle that doubts as to meaning must be resolved against the insurer and that any exception to the performance of the basic underlying obligation must be so stated as clearly to apprise the insured of its effect.

These principles of interpretation of insurance contracts have found new and vivid restatement in the doctrine of the adhesion contract. . . .

Although courts have long followed the basic precept that they would look to the words of the contract to find the meaning which the parties expected from them,[5] they have also applied the doctrine of the adhesion contract to insurance policies, holding that in view of the disparate bargaining status of the parties we must ascertain that meaning of the contract which the insured would reasonably expect.[7] Thus

---

5. The traditional rules of construction for contracts require the courts to take cognizance of the expectations of the parties. "If the court is convinced that it knows the purposes of the parties, the intended legal result, however vaguely expressed and poorly analyzed, it should be loath to adopt any interpretation of their language that would produce a different result." (3 Corbin on Contracts, p. 164.)

7. Courts have long applied the doctrine of reasonable expectation to the interpretation of insurance contracts. Thus in Coast Mutual B.-L. Assn. v. Security T. I. & G. Co. (1936) 14 Cal. App. 2d 225, 229, 57 P.2d 1392, 1393, the court said: "In the decision of this question we are to be guided by well-established rules relating to the construction of insurance policies. Not only the provisions of the policy as a whole,

as Kessler stated in his classic article on adhesion contracts: "In dealing with standardized contracts courts have to determine what the weaker contracting party could legitimately expect by way of services according to the enterpriser's 'calling', and to what extent the stronger party disappointed reasonable expectations based on the typical life situation." (Kessler, Contracts of Adhesion (1943) 43 Colum. L. Rev. 629, 637.)

Professor Patterson, in describing one characteristic consequence of "the conception of adhesion, whether that term is used or not," writes: "The court interprets the form contract to mean what a reasonable buyer would expect it to mean, and thus protects the weaker party's expectation at the expense of the stronger's. This process of interpretation was used many years ago in interpreting (or construing) insurance contracts. . . ." (Fn. omitted; Patterson, The Interpretation and Construction of Contracts (1964) 64 Colum. L. Rev. 833, 858.) . . .

When we test the instant policy by these principles we find that its provisions as to the obligation to defend are uncertain and undefined; in the light of the reasonable expectation of the insured, they require the performance of that duty. At the threshold we note that the nature of the obligation to defend is itself necessarily uncertain. Although insurers have often insisted that the duty arises only if the insurer is bound to indemnify the insured, this very contention creates a dilemma. No one can determine whether the third party suit does or does not fall within the indemnification coverage of the policy until that suit is resolved; in the instant case, the determination of whether the insured engaged in intentional, negligent or even wrongful conduct depended upon the judgment in the Jones suit, and, indeed, even after that judgment, no one could be positive whether it rested upon a finding of plaintiff's negligent or his intentional conduct. The carrier's obligation to indemnify inevitably will not be defined until the adjudication of the very action which it should have defended. Hence the policy contains its own seeds of uncertainty; the insurer has held out a promise that by its very nature is ambiguous.

Although this uncertainty in the performance of the duty to defend could have been clarified by the language of the policy we find no such specificity here. An examination of the policy discloses that the broadly stated promise to defend is not conspicuously or clearly conditioned solely on a nonintentional bodily injury; instead, the insured could reasonably expect such protection.

The policy is a "comprehensive personal liability" contract; the

---

but also the exceptions to the liability of the insurer, *must be construed so as to give the insured the protection which he reasonably had a right to expect,* and to that end doubts, ambiguities, and uncertainties arising out of the language used in the policy must be resolved in his favor." (Italics added.) . . .

designation in itself connotes general protection for alleged bodily injury caused by the insured. The insurer makes two wide promises: "[1.] To pay on behalf of the insured all sums which the insured shall become legally obligated to pay as damages because of bodily injury or property damage, and [2.] the company shall defend any suit against the insured alleging such bodily injury or property damage and seeking damages which are payable under the terms of this endorsement, even if any of the allegations of the suit are groundless, false, or fraudulent": clearly these promises, without further clarification, would lead the insured reasonably to expect the insurer to defend him against suits seeking damages for bodily injury, whatever the alleged cause of the injury, whether intentional or inadvertent.

But the insurer argues that the third party suit must seek "damages which are *payable* under the terms of this endorsement"; it contends that this limitation *modifies* the general duty to defend by confining the duty only to actions seeking damages within the primary coverage of the policy. Under "Exclusions" the policy provides that it "does not apply . . . under coverage L and M to bodily injury . . . caused intentionally by . . . the insured."

The very first paragraph as to coverage, however, provides that "the company shall defend any such suit against the insured alleging such bodily injury" although the allegations of the suit are groundless, false or fraudulent. This language, in its broad sweep, would lead the insured reasonably to expect defense of *any* suit regardless of merit or cause. The relation of the exclusionary clause to this basic promise is anything but clear. The basic promise would support the insured's reasonable expectation that he had bought the rendition of legal services to defend against a suit for bodily injury which alleged he had caused it, negligently, nonintentionally, intentionally or in any other manner. The doctrines and cases we have set forth tell us that the exclusionary clause must be "conspicuous, plain and clear." (Steven v. Fidelity & Casualty Co., supra, 58 Cal. 2d 862, 878, 27 Cal. Rptr. 172, 377 P.2d 284.) This clause is not "conspicuous" since it appears only after a long and complicated page of fine print, and is itself in fine print; its relation to the remaining clauses of the policy and its effect is surely not "plain and clear." . . .

[The court then dealt with a frivolous argument that the court's position would compel an automobile insurer to defend a suit for negligently maintaining a stairway.]

Our holding that the insurer bore the obligation to defend because the policy led plaintiff reasonably to expect such defense, and because the insurer's exclusionary clause did not exonerate it, cuts across defendant's answering contention that the duty arises only if the pleadings disclose a cause of action for which the insurer must indemnify the insured. Defendant would equate the duty to defend with the complaint that pleaded a liability for which the insurer was bound to indemnify the insured. Yet even if we accept defendant's premises, and define the duty to defend by measuring the allegations in the Jones case against the carrier's liability to indemnify, defendant's position still fails. We proceed to discuss this alternative ground of liability of the insurer, accepting for such purpose the insurer's argument that we must test the third party suit against the indemnification coverage of the policy. We point out that the carrier must defend a suit which *potentially* seeks damages within the coverage of the policy; the Jones action was such a suit.

Defendant cannot construct a formal fortress of the third party's pleadings and retreat behind its walls. The pleadings are malleable, changeable and amendable. . . .

To restrict the defense obligation of the insurer to the precise language of the pleading would not only ignore the thrust of the cases but would create an anomaly for the insured. Obviously . . . the complainant in the third party action drafts his complaint in the broadest terms; he may very well stretch the action which lies in only nonintentional conduct to the dramatic complaint that alleges intentional misconduct. In light of the likely overstatement of the complaint and of the plasticity of modern pleading, we should hardly designate the third party as the arbiter of the policy's coverage.

Since modern procedural rules focus on the facts of a case rather than the theory of recovery in the complaint, the duty to defend should be fixed by the facts which the insurer learns from the complaint, the insured, or other sources. An insurer, therefore, bears a duty to defend its insured whenever it ascertains facts which give rise to the potential of liability under the policy. In the instant case the complaint itself, as well as the facts known to the insurer, sufficiently apprised the insurer of these possibilities; hence we need not set out when and upon what other occasions the duty of the insurer to ascertain such possibilities otherwise arises.

Jones' complaint clearly presented the possibility that he might obtain damages that were covered by the indemnity provisions of the policy. Even conduct that is traditionally classified as "intentional" or "wilful" has been held to fall within indemnification coverage. Moreover, despite Jones' pleading of intentional and wilful conduct, he could have amended his complaint to allege merely negligent conduct. Further, plaintiff might have been able to show that in physically defending himself, even if he exceeded the reasonable bounds of self-defense, he did not commit wilful and intended injury, but engaged only in nonintentional tortious conduct. Thus, even accepting the insurer's premise that it had no obligation to defend actions seeking damages not within the indemnification coverage, we find, upon proper measurement of the third party action against the insurer's liability to indemnify, it should have defended because the loss could have fallen within that liability. . . .

We have explained that the insured would reasonably expect a defense by the insurer in all personal injury actions against him. If he is to be required to finance his own defense and then, only if successful, hold the insurer to its promise by means of a second suit for reimbursement, we defeat the basic reason for the purchase of the insurance. In purchasing his insurance the insured would reasonably expect that he would stand a better chance of vindication if supported by the resources and expertise of his insurer than if compelled to handle and finance the presentation of his case. He would, moreover, expect to be able to avoid the time, uncertainty and capital outlay in finding and retaining an attorney of his own. "The courts will not sanction a construction of the insurer's language that will defeat the very purpose or object of the insurance." (Ritchie v. Anchor Casualty Co., supra, 135 Cal. App. 2d 245, 257, 286 P.2d 1000, 1007.)

[The court then dealt with the insurer's contention that the court's holding would embroil it in a conflict of interests. That difficult subject is treated in Chapter 9.]

Finally, defendant urges that our holding should require only the reimbursement of the insured's expenses in defending the third party action but not the payment of the judgment. Defendant acknowledges the general rule that an insurer that wrongfully refuses to defend is liable on the judgment against the insured. (Arenson v. National Auto. & Cas. Ins. Co. (1955) 45 Cal. 2d 81, 84, 286 P.2d 816; Civ. Code, §2778.) Defendant argues, however, that the instant situation should be distinguished from that case because here the judgment has not necessarily been rendered on a theory within the policy coverage. Thus defendant would limit the insured's recovery to the expenses of the third party suit.

We rejected a similar proposal in Tomerlin v. Canadian Indemnity Co., supra, 61 Cal. 2d 638, 649-650, 39 Cal. Rptr. 731, 394 P.2d 571. In that case, as we have noted, the insurer's obligation to defend arose out of estoppel. The insurer contended that we should apply a "tort" theory of damages to its wrongful refusal to defend. Such a theory, we explained, would impose upon the insured "the impossible burden" of proving the extent of the loss caused by the insurer's breach. As this court said in an analogous situation in Arenson v. National Auto. & Cas. Ins. Co. (1957) 48 Cal. 2d 528, 539, 310 P.2d 961, 968: "Having defaulted such agreement the company is manifestly bound to reimburse its insured for the full amount of any obligation reasonably incurred by him. It will not be allowed to defeat or whittle down its obligation on the theory that plaintiff himself was of such limited financial ability that he could not afford to employ able counsel, or to present every reasonable defense, or to carry his cause to the highest court having jurisdiction. . . . Sustaining such a theory . . . would tend . . . to encourage insurance companies to similar disavowals of responsibility with everything to gain and nothing to lose."

In summary, the individual consumer in the highly organized and integrated society of today must necessarily rely upon institutions devoted to the public service to perform the basic functions which they undertake. At the same time the consumer does not occupy a sufficiently strong economic position to bargain with such institutions as to specific clauses of their contracts of performance, and, in any event, piecemeal negotiation would sacrifice the advantage of uniformity. Hence the courts in the field of insurance contracts have tended to require that the insurer render the basic insurance protection which it has held out to the insured. This obligation becomes especially manifest in the case in which the insurer has attempted to limit the principal coverage by an unclear exclusionary clause. We test the alleged limitation in the light of the insured's reasonable expectation of coverage; that test compels the indicated outcome of the present litigation.

The judgment is reversed and the trial court instructed to take evidence solely on the issue of damages alleged in plaintiff's complaint including the amount of the judgment in the Jones suit, and the costs, expenses and attorney's fees incurred in defending such suit.

TRAYNOR, C.J., and PETERS, PEEK, MOSK and BURKE, JJ., concur.

Dissenting Opinion

McCOMB, Justice.

I dissent. I would affirm the judgment for the reasons expressed by Mr. Justice Fox in the opinion prepared by him for the District Court of Appeal in Gray v. Zurich Ins. Co. (Cal. App.) 49 Cal. Rptr. 271.

Notes and Questions

1. The *Gray* court said that the "duty to defend should be fixed by the facts which the insurer learns from the complaint, the insured, or other sources." If the insurer, after careful investigation of all those sources, were to conclude that the insured was clearly guilty of an unprovoked assault and battery, would there still be a duty to defend? That is, can the "facts" be used defensively as well as offensively? Tobin v. Aetna Casualty & Surety Co., 174 Mich. App. 516, 436 N.W.2d 402 (1988), thought so "where a complaint is merely an attempt to trigger insurance coverage. . . ."

2. An insurer is initially obligated to defend because of the terms of the complaint made against its insured. The insurer files a declaratory judgment suit to determine whether the policy provides coverage. The court in its discretion, as permitted by the jurisdiction's procedural rules, allows the declaratory judgment proceeding to go forward first. That establishes that there is no coverage. Should the duty to defend cease? Fireman's Fund Ins. Co. v. Chasson, 207 Cal. App. 2d 801, 24 Cal. Rptr. 726 (1962) held that the duty ceased prospectively but not retroactively. What does that mean, in practice?

3. In *Gray* the court relied heavily on the notion of the adhesion contract, on a reasonable expectations doctrine, and (somewhat less clearly) on a doctrine of unconscionability. What would have been the result in the case had the court simply interpreted the language with nothing to aid it except the *contra proferentem* doctrine?

4. The intent requisite for liability for battery is only the intent to invade the interest in bodily integrity, not the intent to cause harm. What intention should trigger the exclusion in the insurance policy? Why?

5. *Gray* imposed a duty to defend if the defendant's conduct might *possibly* be negligent rather than intentional. Suppose the insured admits intentional shooting but claims self-defense. Is there an obligation to defend? To indemnify? Preferred Mut. Ins. Co. v. Thompson, 23 Ohio St. 3d 78, 491 N.E.2d 688 (1986) held both obligations existed. Was its decision sound?

6. Is an insured who pleads guilty to voluntary manslaughter collaterally estopped to deny intentional action for purposes of the liability provisions of a homeowners policy? Country Mut. Ins. Co. v. Duncan, 794 F.2d 1211 (7th Cir. 1986) held it was not.

7. In interpreting an insurance contract, should it be relevant:

a. That unlike Gray, the insured is a large corporation with substantially greater assets than the insurer? See the note about the Tylenol recall case, McNeilab, Inc. v. North River Ins. Co., infra.

b. That the insured was advised in the purchase of the insurance by its own risk manager or by a major broker?

c. That the insurance policy involved premiums in seven figures?

d. That the policy was negotiated and was a "manuscript" policy, not a standard form? Would it matter that, though the policy was a manuscript policy, the particular language at issue tracked closely the language of the insurer's form policies?

e. That when the premium was set, no one even contemplated claims like those being made, so that the premium was seriously inadequate for the coverage now asserted? This was the case, for example, with asbestos claims. In Industrial Risk Insurers v. New Orleans Public Service, Inc., 666 F. Supp. 874 (E.D. La. 1987), the court gave considerable weight to the premium paid in determining what the parties intended to have covered. Should it have done so?

Each of the above facts is true of some insurance policies the meanings of which are currently in litigation.

CALIFORNIA STATE AUTO ASSN. INTER-INS. BUREAU v. WARWICK

17 Cal. 3d 190, 550 P.2d 1056, 130 Cal. Rptr. 520 (1976)

Mosk, Justice.

In this action for declaratory relief, the trial court ordered judgment for the plaintiff insurance carrier on the ground that the insurance contract did not provide coverage for defendant Harry C. Warwick (hereinafter Warwick) in regard to the personal injury liability claims of his wife, defendant Bernice C. Warwick. The court declared that the insurer did not have a duty to defend or indemnify Warwick. Defendants appeal from the judgment. We affirm.

The facts are not in dispute. The insurer issued an automobile insurance policy to Warwick covering a 1969 Volvo station wagon for the period February 7, 1972, through February 7, 1973. On September 22, 1972, during the policy period, Bernice Warwick sustained personal injuries resulting from an accident which occurred while she was a passenger in the insured Volvo. She filed suit against Warwick, who was driving the vehicle, alleging that his negligent operation of the car caused the accident. At the time of the accident, Bernice and Harry Warwick were wife and husband residing in the same household.

The pertinent portions of the insurance policy which are applicable to this case are as follows:

INSURING AGREEMENTS. Part I — Liability.

BODILY INJURY LIABILITY: To pay on behalf of the insured all sums which the insured shall become legally obligated to pay as damages, other than punitive damages, because of:

(a) bodily injury, including death resulting therefrom, hereinafter called "bodily injury" sustained by any person;

DEFINITIONS: "Named insured" means the individual named in Item 1 of the declaration and also includes his spouse; if a resident of the same household;

"Insured" means a person or organization described under "Persons Insured";

PERSONS INSURED: The following are insureds under Part I:

(a) With respect to the owned automobile,

(1) the named insured, and if the named insured is an individual or husband and wife, a relative,

(2) any other person using such automobile with the permission of the named insured, provided his actual operation or (if he is not operating) his other actual use thereof is within the scope of such permission.

EXCLUSIONS: This policy does not apply under Part I: . . .

(k) to liability to [*sic*] bodily injury to any insured.

To insurer's basic contention is that it has no duty to indemnify Warwick in the event his wife recovers judgment against him because of the accident. It reasons that the provision of the policy which precludes indemnification for liability to "any insured" covers Bernice Warwick's claim against her husband since, under the definition in the policy, she is a "named insured."

We observe at the outset that the exclusion involved in this case is authorized by subdivision (c) of section 11580.1 of the Insurance Code. That provision states:

(c) In addition to any exclusion as provided in paragraph (3) of subdivision (b), the insurance afforded by any such policy of automobile liability insurance to which subdivision (a) applies may, by appropriate policy provision, be made inapplicable to any or all of the following: . . .

(5) Liability for bodily injury to an insured. . . .

The term "the insured" . . . shall mean only that insured under the policy against whom the particular claim is made or suit brought. The term "an insured" as used in paragraphs (5) and (6) of this subdivision shall mean any insured under the policy.

Because the exclusion clause is permitted by section 11580.1, the determinative issue is whether its language is sufficiently clear to put the policyholder on notice that it is intended to apply to liability for injuries to *any and all* insured persons who are injured while driving or occupying the insured vehicle.[2] Subdivision (b) of section 11580.1 expressly requires that the insurer designate "by explicit description . . . the purposes for which coverage for such motor vehicles is specifically excluded." The Insurance Code thus incorporates the well-established rule that an exclusion clause in an insurance policy cannot be upheld unless the clause is phrased in clear and unmistakable language. (State Farm Mut. Auto Ins. Co. v. Jacober (1973) 10 Cal. 3d 193, 201-202, 110 Cal. Rptr. 1, 514 P.2d 953.)

Defendants contend that the exclusion clause is misleading; they invoke the principle that if coverage is available under any reasonable

2. An ambiguous policy provision would obviously not meet the requirements of subdivision (c) that the enumerated exclusions may be provided "by appropriate policy provision"; only a clearly worded exclusion clause is an "appropriate" provision.

interpretation of an ambiguous clause of an insurance policy, the insurer cannot escape its obligations. (Continental Cas. Co. v. Phoenix Constr. Co. (1956) 46 Cal. 2d 423, 437, 296 P.2d 801.) They argue that the exclusion of coverage for injury to "any insured" can be interpreted reasonably as excluding only injuries sustained by the insured driver. Under this interpretation of the exclusion clause, any person insured under the policy would be entitled to indemnity if he sustained injury while riding as a passenger in the insured vehicle.

Defendants rely on State Farm Mut. Auto. Ins. Co. v. Jacober (1973) supra, 10 Cal. 3d 193, 110 Cal. Rptr. 1, 514 P.2d 953. In that case the owner of the insured vehicle was injured while riding in his car, which was being driven by a permissive user. There, as here, the policy protected the named insured and permissive users of the insured automobile against liability to "other persons." We stated that from the driver's point of view, the automobile owner was clearly among the "other persons" against whom the driver might reasonably expect and claim protection. Unlike the present case, the policy in *Jacober* excluded indemnification for injury to "*the insured.*" We held that this exclusionary language was not sufficiently clear to permit the insurer to exclude recovery for injuries sustained by the owner of the insured vehicle while he was a passenger in the car because the provision could be reasonably interpreted as excluding only injuries sustained by the insured driver himself.

In our view, *Jacober* is distinguishable because its exclusion clause refers to injuries to "*the* insured" while the present policy refers to injuries sustained by "*any* insured." The term "any insured" has a plural connotation, unlike "the insured."[3] Webster defines the word "any" to mean "one indifferently out of more than two"; "one or another"; and "one, no matter what one." (Webster's New Internat. Dict. (3d ed. 1961) p. 97.) From the earliest days of statehood we have interpreted "any" to be broad, general and all embracing. In Davidson v. Dallas (1857) 8 Cal. 227, 239, this court declared the "word 'any' means every, and the expression 'for these purposes or any of them' in effect reads: 'for the foregoing purposes and every of them.' " (To the same general effect are Estate of Wyman (1962) 208 Cal. App. 2d 489, 492, 25 Cal. Rptr. 280; Emmolo v. Southern Pacific Co. (1949) 91 Cal. App. 2d 87, 92, 204 P.2d 427; Coelho v. Truckell (1935) 9 Cal. App. 2d 47, 59, 48 P.2d 697.)

In view of the popular and accepted meaning of the word "any," the term "any insured" unmistakably refers to any person insured

---

3. The definitions provided in section 11580.1 support this semantic distinction. The code provides that for the purpose of subdivision (c) of section 11580.1, the term "the insured" is used in a *singular* sense to mean "only that insured . . . against whom the particular claim is made or suit brought."

under the policy, whether such person is a named or unnamed insured, a driver or a passenger. We conclude that the exclusion clause in the policy is susceptible to only one interpretation by the lay reader: that the insurer would not pay indemnity for injuries suffered by Bernice Warwick while she was riding as a passenger in the insured vehicle.

The judgment is affirmed.

Notes and Questions

1. Why would the insurer wish to insert exclusion (k) in its policy? It is often called the "family exclusion clause."

2. Are there public policy considerations that might have produced the opposite result in *Warwick*? For a discussion of the family exclusion clause, see Chapter 5.

GAUNT v. JOHN HANCOCK MUTUAL LIFE INS. CO.

160 F.2d 599 (2d Cir.), *cert. denied,* 331 U.S. 849 (1947)

L. Hand, Circuit Judge.

The plaintiff appeals from a judgment, dismissing her complaint after a trial to the judge, in an action, brought as beneficiary, to recover upon a contract of life insurance upon her son's life. There are only two questions: first, whether the defendant insured the son at all; and second, if so, whether he was intentionally shot, in which event a provision for "double indemnity" did not apply. The judge made detailed findings, the substance of which, so far as they are material to this appeal, is as follows. One, Kelman, a solicitor for the defendant authorized to take applications from prospective customers and to give receipts for first premiums, after two preliminary interviews with Gaunt, the insured, on August 3d, procured from him the signed "application," which is the subject of the action. This was a printed document of considerable length and much detail, the only passage in which here relevant we quote in full in the margin.[1] The important words were: "if the Company is satisfied that on the date of the

_____

1. "If the first premium or installment thereof above stated was paid when this application was signed, and if the Company is satisfied that on the date of the completion of Part B of this application I was insurable in accordance with the Company's rules for the amount and on the plan applied for without modification, and if this application, including said Part B, is, prior to my death, approved by the Company at its Home Office, the insurance applied for shall be in force as of the date of completion of said Part B, but, if this application so provides, such insurance shall be in force as of the date of issue of the policy."

completion of Part B of this application I was insurable . . . and if this application . . . is, prior to my death, approved by the Company at its Home Office, the insurance applied for shall be in force as of the date of completion of said Part B." Number 12 of the answers which the insured was to make in the "application" was in the alternative; it read: "Insurance effective: (Check date desired) Date of Part B □ Dated of issue of Policy □." When Gaunt signed the application he had not checked either of these answers; but after he had delivered it to Kelman, Kelman checked the second, so that, as the "application" read, Gaunt was to be insured only from the issuance of the policy. The judge found that "Both Gaunt and Kelman intended that Gaunt should be covered from the date of the completion of the medical examination"; and that Kelman's checking of the wrong answer "was due to a mutual mistake on the part of Gaunt and Kelman."

At the time of signing the "application" Gaunt paid the full first premium and Kelman gave him a receipt containing the words we have just quoted without substantial change: both the "application" and the receipt were upon forms prepared by the defendant for use by solicitors such as Kelman. On the same day Kelman took Gaunt to the defendant's local examining physician who found him insurable under the rules and who recommended him for acceptance. Kelman delivered the "application" and the premium, and the physician delivered the favorable report, to one, Wholey, the defendant's local agent for Waterbury, Connecticut, who prepared a report recommending acceptance, signed by himself and Kelman, which he sent with the "application" and the physician's report to the "home office," where the documents were received on the 9th. Since it appeared from the papers that Gaunt had been classified as "4F" in the draft because of defective eyesight, the "medical department" at the "home office" required another physical examination in Waterbury. This took place on the 17th; on the same day the local physician wrote to the "home office" again passing Gaunt; and on the 19th "a lay medical examiner" for the "medical department" at the "home office" approved the "application." Nevertheless the "home office" on the 20th wrote to Wholey asking further information as to Gaunt's classification in the draft; Wholey answered satisfactorily on the 24th by a letter received on the 25th; and on the 26th one of the "doctors of the medical department . . . approved" the application "from a medical standpoint." The "home office" received news on that day of Gaunt's death, and never finally approved the "application," although the judge found that, if Gaunt had lived, it would have done so.

Gaunt left Waterbury on August 19th. He was going to the Pacific Coast or to Alaska in search of work; he arrived at Chicago on the 21st; and on the 24th he had reached Montevideo, Minnesota, where he was seen traveling in an "army bus" that had been loaded upon a flat car of a west-bound freight train. The only other occupant of this bus was one, Rasch, about whom nothing was learned except that he was later traced to the wheat fields of Wyoming as a casual worker. On the 25th Gaunt's body was found beside the west-bound track of the railroad at Milbank, South Dakota, with a hole in his head made by a 38 or 45 calibre bullet, which had entered his right jaw near the ear and had come out at the top of his skull; and although the record contains no evidence on the subject, we may take judicial notice that this must have caused substantially instant death. . . .

The first question is whether Gaunt was covered at all at the time of his death. Curiously, neither party has incorporated in the record "Part B," and we do not know what was the date of its "completion." If it was the approval "from a medical standpoint" as "advised by one of the doctors of the medical department," it was not "completed" before Gaunt's death. On the other hand the judge found that "Gaunt was, at the time of the completion of Part B, insurable in accordance with the rules of the defendant company for the plan and the amount applied for," and that is consistent only with the understanding that "completion" was earlier than the 25th. The defendant has not argued to the contrary and we shall so assume. Thus the question becomes whether the words: "if the application, including Part B, is prior to my death, approved by the Company, at its Home Office," must inescapably be read as a condition precedent upon the immediately following promise: "the insurance . . . shall be in force as of the date of the completion of Part B." It is true that if the clause as a whole be read literally, the insured was not covered if he died after "completion of Part B," but before "approval"; and indeed he could not have been because there must always be an insurable interest when the insurance takes effect. Yet what meaning can be given to the words "as of the date of the completion of Part B" if that be true? The defendant suggests six possible "advantages" to the insured which will satisfy the phrase, "the insurance . . . will be in force," (1) The policy would sooner become incontestable. (2) It would earlier reach maturity, with a corresponding acceleration of dividends and cash surrender. (3) It would cover the period after "approval" and before "issue." (4) If the insured became uninsurable between "completion" and "approval" it would still cover the risk. (5) If the insured's birthday was between "completion" and "approval," the premium would be computed at a lower rate. (6) When the policy covers disability, the coverage dates from "completion." An underwriter might so understand the phrase, when read in its context, but the application was not to be submitted to underwriters; it was to go to persons utterly unacquainted with the niceties of life insurance, who would read it colloquially. It is the understanding of such persons that counts; and not one in a hundred would suppose that he would be covered, not "as of the date of completion of Part B," as the defendant promised, but only as of the date of approval. Had that been what the defendant meant, certainly it was easy to say so; and had it in addition meant to make the policy retroactive for some purposes, certainly it was easy to say that too. To demand that persons wholly unfamiliar with insurance shall spell all this out in the very teeth of the language used, is unpardonable. It does indeed some violence to the words not to make actual "approval" always a condition, and to substitute a prospective approval, however inevitable, when the insured has died before approval. But it does greater violence to make the insurance "in force" only from the date of "approval"; for the ordinary applicant who has paid his first premium and has successfully passed his physical examination, would not by the remotest chance understand the clause as leaving him uncovered until the insurer at its leisure approved the risk; he would assume that he was getting immediate coverage for his money. This is confirmed by the alternatives presented in the twelfth question; the insurance was to be "effective," either when the policy issued, or at the "date of Part B"; there was not an inkling of any other date for the inception of the risk. It is true that in Connecticut as elsewhere the business of writing life insurance is not colored with a public interest; yet in that state, again as elsewhere, the canon contra proferentem is more rigorously applied in insurance than in other contracts, in recognition of the difference between the parties in their acquaintance with the subject matter. A man must indeed read what he signs, and he is charged, if he does not; but insurers who seek to impose upon words of common speech an esoteric significance intelligible only to their craft, must bear the burden of any resulting confusion. We can think of few situations where that canon is more appropriate than in such a case as this. . . .

Judgment reversed; judgment to be entered for plaintiff for $15,000.

CLARK, Circuit Judge (concurring).

I agree that the course of negotiations required and controlled by the insurance company was "unpardonable," and am willing to concur in the decision for that reason. But I do not think we can properly or should rest upon the ambiguity of the company's forms of application and receipt. Had this bargaining occurred between parties with equal knowledge of the business and on equal terms, there could be little difficulty in supporting the condition precedent that the "insurance," i.e., the insurance contract or policy, could not "be in force," i.e., take effect, until approved at the home office, and that then it dated back to an earlier time. Moreover, conditions of this general form are unfortunately still too customary for a court to evince too much surprise at them. There have been acute discussions of the legal problems involved; thus, most helpful is the article, Operation of Binding Receipts in Life Insurance, 44 Yale L.J. 1223.[1] There receipts given for the payment of the first premium were held best divisible in two categories, one requiring approval as a condition precedent to the contract, in substance as here, and the other requiring that the company be satisfied that on the date of the medical examination the applicant was an insurable risk, and that the application was otherwise "acceptable" under the company's regulations for the amount and plan of the policy applied for. The first form, it was said, was generally held to prevent the existence of a contract before acceptance, except with a few courts which found the provision too inequitable to support. The second, however, gave no difficulty where its reasonable requirements were afterwards found to have been met. A questionnaire to insurance officials showed an increasing trend towards the second or fairer form — a development warmly supported by the author. There was further the acute observation that use of the former form resulted in continuous litigation in a field of law where certainty was essentially indispensable, since it stimulated judicial interpretation to resolve the "ambiguity" against the company, followed by the latter's renewed attempts to revise and refine the technical words.

Hence a result placed not squarely upon inequity, but upon interpretation, seems sure to produce continuing uncertainty in the law of insurance contracts. Even though for my part I should feel constrained to concede the weight of judicial authority against our view, I think the considerations stated are persuasive to uphold recovery substantially as would occur under the second form of contract stated above. I am somewhat troubled as to the state of local law in view of the stress in Swentusky v. Prudential Ins. Co. of America, 116 Conn. 526, 165 A. 686, upon the absence of unique features to insurance law. But that was actually in another connection, a fact which I think justifies us in not here abdicating our judicial role for that envisioned by Judge Frank in Richardson v. Commissioner of Internal Revenue, 2 Cir., 126 F.2d 562, 567, 140 A.L.R. 705, of "ventriloquist's dummy" as to state law.

Notes and Questions

1. After careful reading, is there any question about the meaning of the language of the conditional receipt? Or about the meaning the insurer intended it to have?

1. Other references might include Kessler, Contracts of Adhesion — Some Thoughts about Freedom of Contract, 43 Col. L. Rev. 629, 631-635; Patterson, The Delivery of a Life Insurance Policy, 33 Harv. L. Rev. 198; Havighurst, Life Insurance Binding Receipts, 33 Ill. L. Rev. 180.

2. Is Judge Hand applying the *contra proferentem* rule or the reasonable expectations doctrine?

3. Between the opinions in *Gaunt* and *Warwick*, which of the two do you prefer? Why? In what respects do they differ?

4. *The contra proferentem rule.* Should the *contra proferentem* rule (or the adhesion contract doctrine) be applied as between two insurers, if one of them drafted the contract?

5. Should the *contra proferentem* rule apply to a contract every word of which is mandated by statute? In Hoekstra v. Farm Bureau Mut. Ins. Co., 382 N.W.2d 100 (Iowa 1986), the court dealt with the statutory standard fire insurance contract. The contract provided that "[t]he insured, as often as may be reasonably required," must produce records for examination. After what the court considered to be "substantial" compliance, the insured resisted further inquiry. The Iowa Supreme Court found substantial compliance sufficient in the face of a provision (a part of the statutorily mandated language) forbidding suit against the company "unless all the requirements of this policy shall have been complied with." Is that result justified? Why?

6. Should the *contra proferentem* rule apply to individual provisions that are mandated by statute when the bulk of the contract is not mandated? Should it apply to standard language drafted by a committee representing insurance companies, then subjected to criticism by brokers, insurance regulators, and other representatives of the public (including self-appointed guardians of the public weal), modified in response to the criticism, and finally approved by the insurance regulators under statutory procedures? To all contracts approved by the Commissioner?

7. Should the *contra proferentem* rule be applied to a contract negotiated between an insurer and a very large insured if the allegedly ambiguous language is standard language used for all policies of the same kind? That is, should ordinary consumers and large, economically powerful and sophisticated policyholders be treated alike with respect to identical language? This problem was addressed in Ostrager & Ichel, Should the Business Insurance Policy Be Construed Against the Insurer? Another Look at the Reasonable Expectations Doctrine, 33 Fed. Ins. Couns. Q. 273 (1983), in Ostrager & Ichel, The Role of Bargaining Power Evidence in the Construction of the Business Insurance Policy: An Update, 18 Forum 577 (1983), and in the following case:

McNeilab, Inc. v. North River Ins. Co., 645 F. Supp. 525, 528, 544-547 (D.N.J. 1986), aff'd without opinion, 831 F.2d 287 (1987): [In a suit claiming the costs of the prompt recall of millions of Tylenol capsules ordered by the plaintiff which amounted to perhaps one hundred million dollars, the court granted the insurers' motion for summary judgment. The court noted that] Johnson & Johnson spent this $100,000,000 to mitigate damages on a liability it has claimed from day one does not exist. Stated somewhat differently, not believing it was liable, Johnson & Johnson could not have believed it was mitigating damages.

[The court's analysis was complex and detailed. As part of it the court addressed the rule of *contra proferentem*.]

But, even were the policy ambiguous, defendants would prevail. Plaintiff argues that if an ambiguity be found, the rule of *contra proferentem* should be strictly applied and that extrinsic evidence, which here goes one way and one way only and which plaintiff seeks to avoid like the plague, should not be allowed to demonstrate the actual intent of the parties. . . .

It has been held that in disputes as to policies between a large corporation and a large insurance company, both of which were advised by competent counsel at the time of the agreement, ordinary rules of contract construction apply. . . .

Although there are no New Jersey cases directly on point, it would seem that the New Jersey courts would decide that insurance policies of large, skilled corporations — and here, I venture to suggest, Johnson & Johnson is larger than its insurers — would be treated as ordinary contracts. . . .

In the present case, there is no question but that the parties were of equal bargaining power and that all that preceded and all that followed the execution of the policy at issue here is reminiscent of the entry into and the living under a treaty between two great nations. . . .

Johnson & Johnson, which ranks fifty-ninth in the Fortune 500, generates annual insurance premiums of approximately $20,000,000 and maintains a Corporate Insurance Department consisting of an expert insurance staff with a legal staff at its disposal. . . .

Concededly a sophisticated insured, Johnson & Johnson cannot seek refuge in the doctrine of *contra proferentem* by pretending it is the corporate equivalent of "Mike" Leebov[, the insured in a case on which Johnson & Johnson relied heavily.]

Thus, even if there were some ambiguity in the instant policy, which there is not, I would be compelled to find in favor of defendants.

8. It is self-evident that the enormous amount of time lavished by Judge Barry on her analysis in *McNeilab* does not make it right. Would you agree with her apparent inclination to decide otherwise identical cases differently depending on whether the insured is "Mike" Leebov or Johnson & Johnson? In particular, Judge Barry suggests above that the contract should be treated as an "ordinary contract," not as an insurance contract. What does this mean in light of Restatement (Sec-

ond) of Contracts §206, quoted at the beginning of this chapter? Is the judge pronouncing a different law for rich and poor?

See also Puerto Rico Elec. Power Auth. v. Phillips, 645 F. Supp. 770 (D.P.R. 1986). *Phillips* was not as strong a case, however, since the policyholder "concedes that its agents drafted the insurance policy and submitted it to defendant for his approval."

9. *Objectively reasonable expectations.* Though some courts do give effect to reasonable expectations, many courts state unequivocally that unless the contract is ambiguous they must enforce it as written. True ambiguity is, they say, a prerequisite to applying the "objectively reasonable expectations" rule advanced by Keeton. They adhere to the traditional rule of contract interpretation stated in Restatement §206 and purport to apply it to insurance contracts, but in fact do not do so in every case. See Note 11 below.

10. In jurisdictions requiring an ambiguity, the first step in interpretation is to ascertain whether there is an ambiguity. For example, the court in Valley Forge Ins. Co. v. Jefferson, 628 F. Supp. 502 (D. Del. 1986), said that

> the doctrine of reasonable expectations [in Delaware] applies only if the policy terms "are ambiguous or conflicting, or if the policy contains a hidden trap or pitfall, or if the fine print takes away what is written in large print." [quoting from a Delaware case.] [Id. at 509.]

11. Some judges who purport to follow the traditional rule on occasion strive mightily to find an ambiguity. *Gaunt* is a remarkable case in which two learned judges gave rights at variance with language that was complicated but, with appropriate use of a blue pencil to eliminate words not relevant to the particular situation, would have become quite clear. Judge Hand seems to have *created* an ambiguity to resolve the case in favor of the insured; Judge Clark, either more candid or more perceptive, expressed in an embryonic way a philosophy of enforcing even those objectively reasonably expectations that were in clear conflict with policy provisions. *Gaunt* was decided two decades before *Gray* and even longer before Keeton's articles.

12. If the court insists on true ambiguity before it will look for objectively reasonable expectations, does the fact that different courts disagree on the meaning of the language establish the ambiguity? Does it matter whether the courts are in the same jurisdiction? Does it establish ambiguity that judges on the same court disagree on the meaning? The latter is not uncommon; sometimes different judges on the same court in the same case may even say the meaning of a contract (or a statute) is clear, but then disagree on its meaning. On these questions see Breed v. Insurance Co. of North America, 46 N.Y.2d 351, 385 N.E.2d 1280, 413 N.Y.S.2d 352 (1978).

13. The Standard Fire Policy provides that "The insured shall give immediate written notice to the Company of any loss. . . ." While some courts are strict, even here, in enforcing such language when expressed as a condition precedent, many other courts would interpret "immediate" to mean "as soon as practicable." The insurance industry has often responded by substituting that more liberal language in policies.

Some courts are inclined to distort the meaning of clear "prompt notice" provisions in favor of insureds. (Keeton's notion of "unconscionable advantage" may sometimes appropriately explain these cases). Yet even the most liberal of courts will not countenance prejudicial delay. The question of when harmless delay becomes prejudicial delay is not always easy, if the state's law requires prejudice.

14. In general, the courts have rather strictly enforced the common contractual provision requiring that action be brought against the company within a period (most often one year) that is shorter than the statute of limitations. This requirement seems to have been much more strictly enforced than the notice requirement. But see Federal Savings and Loan Ins. Corp. v. Aetna Casualty & Surety Co., 701 F. Supp. 1357 (E.D. Tenn. 1988), where the court was more liberal to the insured. It may not be irrelevant that FSLIC was the party that would have been disadvantaged. See the note on Estoppel Against the Government in Chapter 2.

Problems

1. In York v. Sterling Ins. Co., 114 A.D.2d 665, 494 N.Y.S.2d 243, *aff'd,* 67 N.Y.2d 823, 492 N.E.2d 770, 501 N.Y.S.2d 642 (1986), while *E* was riding *P*'s dirt bike with *P*'s permission on residential property insured under *P*'s homeowners policy, *E* lost control of the bike and hit a building outside the property, ten feet over the property line. *E* sued *P*, and the homeowners insurer disclaimed coverage. *P* brought an action for declaratory judgment against the insurer. The policy excluded coverage "away from the residential premises." The court said that was different from "off" the residential premises and that the insurer was obligated to defend. Is the result sound? If it is, at what point does "off" become "away from?"

2. While driving an automobile an insured suffered an acute myocardial infarction and died. His estate sought to recover under a no-fault statute that provided for payment for bodily injury as "a result of an accident while occupying . . . or using an automobile." Must the insurer pay? See Kordell v. Allstate Ins. Co., 230 N.J. Super. 505, 554 A.2d 1 (App. Div.), *cert. denied,* 117 N.J. 43, 563 A.2d 813 (1989) and cases discussed therein.

3. The insured under a life insurance policy paid for a flight in a private plane. The airplane pilot had only a limited license and the flight was against FAA regulations. The policy excluded flight "except as a fare paying passenger." When death resulted, can the beneficiary recover from the life insurance company? See Sutherland v. Great Fidelity Life Ins. Co., 707 S.W.2d 344 (Ky. 1986).

4. In Alliance Ins. Co., Inc. v. Reynolds, 494 So. 2d 609 (Ala. 1986), the insured (a club) originally had a custom-made package policy including liability coverage that provided for the defense of assault and battery claims against it. On renewal the insurer eliminated that portion of the coverage, without notice to the insured beyond the changed terms of the contract. The court held that the coverage continued into the next policy period. Should it have?

D. The Readable Policy

At best, insurance policies are relatively hard to understand. Seldom do they appear at their best. Their language is sometimes archaic, as in the Lloyd's marine policy, where one suggested justification for quaint language is that every word has been interpreted by case law and that any change, even to modern language, would reduce the level of confidence in contracts where large sums may be at stake. In other contexts, where the contract is of more recent vintage and especially where the case law is less extensive, that argument for continuing to use opaque language is less compelling. Yet once language has been interpreted in a way the insurer is willing to live with, there is obvious advantage in leaving the language alone as much as possible.

Much of the difficulty in understanding an insurance policy is a result of its unfamiliarity. Understanding is easier with awareness of what to look for and where to find it, though unfortunately drafters sometimes misplace provisions. It also helps if one understands what the parties are trying to accomplish, which results from knowledge of the business. The leading contributor to the problem, and an unavoidable one, is the plasticity of the English language.

None of this excuses needless opacity, but some judges have unfairly contributed to the image of insurance policies as unnecessarily obscure with opinions sometimes more opaque than the subject policies.

Recently, legislatures have taken a hand, and insurance practitioners who should know better have too readily acquiesced and have written new policies intended to be more easily "readable." The new language does not always solve problems and often creates new ones.

One dangerous aspect of the new readable policies is their tendency to mislead lay persons to believe, incorrectly, that they can now read and interpret them. The new policies, like the old ones, turn out to have precise meanings only to the drafter, who usually starts with the considerable advantage of knowing what the intended meaning is. Without denying that every reasonable effort should be made to write policies clearly, one can safely assert that recent efforts have not always helped.

The recent consumerist movement has been one of the contributors to this drive to compel insurance companies to rewrite policies to make them more readable. It has had considerable effect. In many states, statutes or administrative rules have required most "personal lines" policies to be rewritten in simpler language. Some companies have even put some commercial policies (i.e., policies written for business insureds) in the same type of language. Many cases in this book deal with policies in "plain language"; you will be able to judge the extent of the need for the change and the degree of success achieved.

The National Association of Insurance Commissioners has developed model acts to mandate readability: see the Life and Health Insurance Policy Language Simplification Model Act, in NAIC, Model Laws, Regulations and Guidelines 575-1 to 575-4 (1985), the Property and Casualty Insurance Policy Simplification Model Act (id. 730-1 to 730-3), and a Model Regulation to go with the latter (id. 735-1 to 735-2). Only a handful of states have adopted the model acts, but the movement has proceeded apace with the apparent acquiescence of the insurers in recent years.

Some commentators think the consequences of the movement have been unfortunate. See Farnham, The Untimely Demise of Policy Defenses — New Property Policies and the I.S.O., 14 Forum 177 (1978).

HAYES v. ALLSTATE INS. CO.

722 F.2d 1332 (7th Cir. 1983)

SWYGERT, Senior Circuit Judge.

The plaintiffs-appellants, Jean Hayes and Citizens National Bank, appeal from the district court's order of March 2, 1983 in their contract action against Allstate Insurance Company and Allstate Indemnity Company ("Allstate"). This order granted Allstate's motion to stay the proceedings and ordered the parties to proceed to appraisal. Our jurisdiction is based on 28 U.S.C. §1292(a)(1). Because we believe that the district court erred by ordering appraisal when it was not unambiguously mandated by the terms of the insurance policy in question, we vacate the district court's order and remand the case for further proceedings.

A house owned by Hayes and insured under a policy issued by Allstate was destroyed in a fire on October 18, 1980. After investigating Hayes's claim, Allstate's representative informed Hayes's attorney that Allstate could not agree with the amount stated on Hayes's proof of loss form and, on January 21, 1981, made an offer of $175,967.10 for repair of the house, $159,976.96 for the contents, and $2,000 for restoration of the yard. Several days later, Hayes's attorney spoke with Allstate's representative and stated that his client accepted the offer for the contents but wanted to negotiate further on the amount offered for the fire damage to the house. Hayes's attorney then sent a letter to Allstate's representative on March 19, 1981 stating that he would recommend a settlement of $330,300 (ninety percent of the policy limit for dwelling protection). This recommendation was based on five separate construction reports submitted to Allstate indicating a consensus of opinion that the house had been ninety percent destroyed. Several weeks later, Allstate's representative responded by sending a draft to Hayes's attorney for $175,967.10, the amount of Allstate's original offer on the dwelling claim. The draft was accompanied by a letter explaining that the amount was based on a bid from Ernie Hatfield, a rebuilder of fire-damaged homes frequently engaged by Allstate, to rebuild the house for that price. Hayes's attorney then requested copies of the bid and supporting documents in order to determine whether to recommend settlement to his client. Allstate's representative mailed the requested documents to Hayes's attorney on April 13, 1981. On April 29, Hayes's attorney rejected the offer of $175,967.10 by letter, returned the draft in that amount to Allstate, and filed suit in Sullivan Circuit Court, Sullivan County, Indiana.

Allstate's attorney filed a petition for removal from the circuit court to the federal district court on May 19, 1981. On June 17, Allstate's attorney then made a written demand for appraisal, naming Hatfield as its appraiser and stating that the demand was pursuant to Condition 8 of the policy at issue. Condition 8, entitled "Appraisal," provides in part: "If *you* and *we* fail to agree on the amount of loss, either party may make written demand for an appraisal. Each party will select a competent and disinterested appraiser and notify the other of the appraiser's identity within 20 days after the demand is received." On July 2, 1981, Hayes's attorney rejected Allstate's demand by letter which referred to the last sentence of Condition 7 of the policy. Condition 7, entitled "Our Payment of Loss," provides as follows: "*We* will settle any covered loss with *you*. *We* will pay *you* unless another payee is named in the policy. *We* will pay within 60 days after the amount of loss is finally determined. This amount may be determined by an agreement, between *you* and *us,* a court judgment, or an appraisal award."

Allstate responded by filing a motion to stay and to enforce appraisal procedures. The district court granted Allstate's motion, basing its decision on the language of Conditions 7 and 8 of the insurance contract. The court construed these two conditions as meaning that "although the parties are free at the outset to pursue any remedy provided in Condition 7, once a demand for the appraisal procedures has been made by either party, those procedures become a mandatory condition precedent to bringing suit." The court also found that the time period in which Allstate had made written demand for appraisal was not unreasonable, and therefore rejected Hayes's assertion that Allstate had waived any right to appraisal.

On appeal, Hayes and Citizens National Bank contend that the order compelling appraisal was contrary to the language of the insurance policy and should therefore be vacated. They alternatively assert that the district court erred in concluding that Allstate had not waived any right to appraisal, and that the court's failure to decide several issues, including whether Allstate's appraiser should be disqualified, deprived the appellants of their constitutional rights to due process and equal protection. Because we agree with the first contention, we need not consider the remaining arguments.

In this case, the district court stayed the action and ordered the parties to proceed under the appraisal procedures of Condition 8 in accordance with its determination that the policy required an appraisal. While a court can exercise discretion in deciding whether to stay an action simply for purposes of awaiting the outcome of another pending proceeding, see Voktas, Inc. v. Central Soya Co., Inc., 689 F.2d 103 (7th Cir. 1982); Microsoftware Computer Systems, Inc. v. Ontel Corp., 686 F.2d 531, 537-38 (7th Cir. 1982), the order in this case was not the result of discretionary judgment. There was no other pending proceeding until the court compelled an appraisal, and the purpose of the order was to enforce the policy conditions as interpreted. We therefore review the court's order to determine whether this interpretation was erroneous under Indiana law.

Although the Indiana courts have not construed an insurance policy like the one at issue here, we are guided by several Indiana cases that have articulated general principles for construing the language of insurance policies. First, Indiana courts have held that any ambiguities in insurance contracts must be construed against the insurer and in favor of the insured because the contracts are drafted solely by the insurers and are thus contracts of adhesion. Travelers Indemnity Co. v. Armstrong, 384 N.E.2d 607, 613 (Ind. App. 1979); Freeman v. Commonwealth Life Insurance Co., 149 Ind. App. 211, 271 N.E.2d 177, 181 (1971), *transfer denied,* 259 Ind. 237, 286 N.E.2d 396 (1972). An ambiguity exists "if reasonably intelligent men, upon reading the contract, would honestly differ as to its meaning." *Travelers Indemnity Co.*, supra, 384 N.E.2d at 613. Second, regarding the more specific issue of whether a policy providing for appraisal should be construed as making appraisal a condition precedent to a right of action, an 1895 decision states that the policy should not be so construed unless the condition is actually expressed in the contract or is necessarily implied from its terms. Manchester Fire Assur. Co. v. Koerner, 13 Ind. App. 372, 40 N.E. 1110, 1111 (1895). More recent Indiana cases have discussed the same issue when construing contracts that provide for arbitration and have taken at least as strict an approach as was taken in *Manchester Fire Assur. Co.*, supra. See Kendrick Memorial Hospital, Inc. v. Totten, 408 N.E.2d 130, 135 (Ind. App. 1980); Shahan v. Brinegar, 390 N.E.2d 1036, 1040 (Ind. App. 1979).

Applying these principles to this case, we do not agree that the Allstate policy issued to Hayes conditions a right of action on the completion of an appraisal. The policy does not expressly provide that no action may be maintained upon it until after the amount of loss is determined by appraisal. To the contrary, Condition 7 expressly states that the amount of the loss may be determined by a court judgment. Condition 8 specifies the procedures by which the appraisal is made, but is silent on whether appraisal must precede the action. Condition 12, which provides that no action may be brought against Allstate unless the insured has fully complied with all the terms of the policy, does not expressly apply either since Hayes was in compliance with all the terms when suit was brought.

Nor do the policy conditions, when read together, necessarily imply that the right of action is conditioned on the completion of an appraisal. Under Condition 7, Allstate expressly promises to pay the insured the amount of loss determined by court judgment. While the policy also permits Allstate to demand an appraisal, if the demand is only made after the insured has properly brought suit, nothing in the policy necessarily precludes the court from still determining the loss as specified by Condition 7.

Finally, Allstate also argues that even if appraisal is not a condition precedent to an action, under *Manchester Fire Assur. Co.*, supra, we should view the district court's order as a separate equitable remedy, similar to specific performance, through which the court enforced Allstate's contractual rights. In *Manchester Fire Assur. Co.*, the court held that where appraisal is not a condition precedent to an action, a breach of a policy provision for submitting the amount of loss to arbitration will support a separate action. *Manchester Fire Assur. Co.*, supra, 40 N.E. at 1111. We do not believe, however, that the policy at issue here supported Allstate's request for specific performance. Unlike the Allstate policy, the policy construed in *Manchester Fire*

Assur. Co. expressly made the insurer's payment of a disputed loss contingent on submitting the amount of loss to appraisal. In contrast, the Allstate policy makes payment contingent on determination of the loss by appraisal *or* by court judgment. Where the insured, like Hayes, is properly pursuing determination by court judgment and Allstate subsequently pursues determination by appraisal, the policy is ambiguous as to which method of determination supersedes the other. Under established Indiana law the policy must therefore be construed against Allstate, and enforcement of the appraisal procedure was improper.

For the reasons stated above, the order of the district court is vacated and the case is remanded for further proceedings.

POSNER, Circuit Judge, dissenting.

[The principal ground for dissent, explained at considerable length, was that in Judge Posner's view the case was not ripe for appeal under the Federal Rules.]

On the merits of the appeal, assuming as I do not that we have jurisdiction to decide it, I also find myself in dissent. The insurance contract gave *either party* an unambiguous right to demand appraisal. Because the provision in question does not favor the insurance company over the insured, but creates a right of appraisal equally available to either party, the cases the majority cite that hold that contractual provisions are to be construed against the insurance company are not in point. For all we know we are hurting more insureds than insurance companies by reading the right to demand appraisal out of the contract.

Notes and Questions

1. The language being interpreted in *Hayes* was in Allstate's plain language policy. The traditional language of the Standard Fire Insurance Policy dealt with appraisal, and the date the loss was payable, as follows:

> In case the insured and this Company shall fail to agree as to the actual cash value or the amount of loss, then, on the written demand of either, each shall select a competent and disinterested appraiser [who together shall] select a competent and disinterested umpire. . . . An award [by the appraisers] in writing . . . when filed with this Company shall determine the amount of actual cash value and loss. . . .
>
> The amount of loss for which this Company may be liable shall be payable sixty days after . . . ascertainment of the loss is made either by agreement . . . or by the filing with this Company of an award as herein provided.

In redrafting, the two provisions were restructured in the way that appears in the majority opinion. Which version is preferable and why?

2. Water damage is an element of coverage under some homeowners policies on which insurers have lost heavily from time to time. Consequently some forms of the homeowners policy exclude some kinds of water damage from coverage. In Primm v. State Farm Fire & Casualty Co., 426 So. 2d 356 (La. App. 1983), damage was caused by a gradual leakage of water from a joint in the plumbing for a hot water heater. The policy stated, "We insure for all risks of physical loss to the [residence premises] except for loss caused by . . . leakage or seepage of water or steam unless sudden and accidental from any . . . plumbing system. . . ." The policy was a "plain language" reformulation of the homeowners policy. The court thought "leakage or seepage" was ambiguous when interpreted together with the "sudden and accidental" exception to the exclusion and found for the insured. Subsequently, on similar facts, the same court found for the insurer in Howard v. Commercial Union Ins. Co., 441 So. 2d 466 (La. App. 1983). The language of the policy was different, however. It excluded loss "to the building caused by continuous or repeated seepage or leakage over a period of weeks, months or years. . . ." The court explicitly distinguished *Primm,* holding that the language in *Howard* was not ambiguous. How would you improve the language in the State Farm policy to achieve what the insurer wanted?

3. Apart from legal compulsion, how far is an insurer justified (in its own interest) in voluntarily converting its policies of long standing, complicated though they may be, into documents understandable by a person with an eighth grade education, which is the oft-expressed goal of the plain language advocates?

CHAPTER 2

The Enforceability of Insurance Contracts

In insurance litigation or disputation, a pattern of argument that roughly resembles the dialectic of confession and avoidance in a common law pleading sequence proceeds through the following stages:

First stage. The claim made by the insured falls within the coverage clause of the policy and does not fall within any exclusion. Thus the insured should recover.

Second stage. Although coverage is conceded, recovery is not, because the insured warranted that it would do something it did not do or warranted some fact that is not so or misrepresented a fact that is material to the risk or concealed (failed to disclose) a material fact that the insured knew or should have known was material or a condition precedent to the insurer's liability did not occur. Thus the insured should not recover, despite the conceded coverage.

Third stage. The second stage argument states a defense that would generally be available to the insurer, but the latter has waived the defense or is estopped to assert it or has elected to treat the policy as effective, so the defense is no longer available. Thus, because of the coverage that is provided, and despite the defense that would ordinarily be available, under the circumstances of this case the insured may recover because of the waiver, estoppel, or election.

Although the above dialectic is at law, reformation followed by enforcement is sometimes available to the insured in equity.

New York Cent. Mut. Fire Ins. Co. v. Markowitz, 537 N.Y.S.2d 571, 147 A.D.2d 461 (1989), is a good example of the dialectic. In an action for a declaratory judgment brought by the insurer on a homeowner's policy, the court skipped the first stage, for coverage was clear. The court then concluded that "in delaying approximately seven months in contacting the plaintiff, the defendants failed 'to do every-thing reasonably to be expected of them to ascertain the identity of the insurance carrier or to give it notice of the accident,' " thus providing the insurer with a good defense. Id. at 571, 147 A.D.2d at 462. Never-theless, the insurer was estopped to rely on the defense because it "delayed in informing the defendants of its intent to disclaim coverage for a period of over six and one-half months." Id. at 572, 147 A.D.2d at 462.

This chapter will illustrate some of the implications of this dialec-tic in insurance law, using cases and statutes from several lines of insurance. Although the results may vary somewhat from one line of insurance to another because of differences in context, the process of analysis is the same for all lines of insurance.

A.   Warranties, Misrepresentations, Concealment

The common law of warranties, misrepresentations, and conceal-ment had its origin in marine insurance. By the late eighteenth century, it was a fully developed system, but it has undergone considerable change in nineteenth- and twentieth-century American law.

The first sequence of cases and notes provides some sense of the nature and scope of the eighteenth-century business of marine under-writing at Lloyd's and other coffeehouses and of the crucial doctrines that developed to a considerable extent under the leadership of Wil-liam Murray, Lord Mansfield, Chief Justice of the King's Bench and chief architect of modern commercial law, including insurance law.

The doctrines we celebrate (or perhaps excoriate) in this section have cast a long shadow and remain controversial after two centuries. They have fared differently in different jurisdictions and in different lines of insurance. Cases and statutes as recent as yesterday still reach divergent results, showing how difficult these problems are.

1.   The Eighteenth-Century Doctrine

DeHAHN v. HARTLEY

1 T.R. 344, 99 Eng. Rep. 1130 [K.B. 1786]

This was an action upon promises brought by the plaintiff (an underwriter) to recover back the amount of a loss which he had paid upon a policy of insurance.

Plea the general issue.

The cause was tried before BULLER, J. at the sittings after last Easter term at Guildhall, when the jury found a special verdict; which stated,

That the defendant on the 14th June 1779, at London, gave to one Alexander Anderson, then being an insurance broker, certain instructions in writing to cause an insurance to be made on a certain ship or vessel called the "Juno," which were in the words and figures following; "Please get 2000l. insured on goods as interest may appear; slaves valued at 30l. per head: comwood 40l. per ton; ivory 20l. per hundred-weight; gum copal 5l. per pound; at and from Africa to her discharging port or ports in the British West-Indies; warranted copper-sheathed, and sailed from Liverpool with 14 six-pounders, (exclusive of swivels, &c.) 50 hands or upwards, at 12, not exceeding 15, guineas. 'Juno.' — Beaver. S. Hartley and Company, June 14th, 1779."

That the said Alexander Anderson, in consequence of the said written instructions from the said defendant on the said 14th June 1779, at London aforesaid, &c. did cause a certain writing or policy of assurance to be made on the said ship or vessel called the "Juno" in the words and figures following; (reciting the policy), which was upon any kind of goods and merchandizes, and also upon the body, tackle, apparel, &c. of and in the ship "Juno," at and from Africa to her port or ports of discharge in the British West Indies, at and after the rate of 15l. per cent.

The verdict, after reciting two memoranda, which are not material, then proceeded to state, that in the margin of the said policy were written the words and figures following, "Sailed from Liverpool with 14 six-pounders, swivels, small arms, and 50 hands or upwards; copper-sheathed."

That on the said 14th June 1779, and not before, at London aforesaid, &c. the plaintiff underwrote the said policy for the sum of 200l. and received a premium of 31l. 10s. 0d. as the consideration thereof.

That the said ship or vessel called the "Juno" sailed from Liverpool aforesaid on the 13th October 1778, having then only 46 hands on board her, and arrived at Beaumaris, in the isle of Anglesea, in six hours after her sailing from Liverpool as aforesaid, with the pilot from Liverpool on board her, who did pilot her to Beaumaris on her said voyage; and that at Beaumaris aforesaid the said ship or vessel took in six hands more, and then had, and during the said voyage until the capture thereof hereinafter mentioned, continued to have, 52 hands on board her.

That the said ship or vessel in the said voyage from Liverpool aforesaid to Beaumaris aforesaid, until and when she took in the said six additional hands, was equally safe as if she had had 50 hands on board her for that part of the said voyage.

That divers goods, wares, and merchandizes, of the said defendant of great value, were laden and put on board the said ship or vessel, and remained on board her until and at the time of the capture thereof hereinafter mentioned. And that on the 14th March 1779 the said ship or vessel, while she remained on the coast of Africa, and before her sailing for her port of discharge in the British West India Islands, was, upon the high seas, with the said goods, wares, and merchandizes on board her as aforesaid, met with by certain enemies of our lord the now King, and captured by them, &c. and thereby all the said goods, wares, and merchandizes of the said defendant, so laden on board her as aforesaid, were wholly lost to him.

That when the said plaintiff received an account of the said loss of the said ship or vessel, he paid to the said defendant the said sum of 200l. so insured by him as aforesaid, not having then had any notice that the said ship or vessel had only 46 hands on board her when she sailed from Liverpool as aforesaid. But whether upon the whole matter, &c.

Law, for the plaintiff, was stopped by the Court.

Wood, for the defendant,

Admitted, that a marginal note in a policy of insurance may be a warranty; but contended that this was distinguishable from the case of *Bean v. Stupart* and all the other cases on the subject. In the cases decided, it has always been a warranty of a fact relating to the voyage insured: but in the present case, that which is written in the margin has no relation whatever to the voyage, for it relates merely to the force of the ship at Liverpool, before the voyage commenced, and is totally unconnected with the risk insured. The insurance is "at and from Africa to her port of discharge in the British West Indies;" and the warranty is from Liverpool; which is antecedent to the voyage insured, and is merely a representation of the state of the ship when she set out on her voyage from Liverpool. Then if it be only a representation, it is immaterial whether complied with or not, because it is found by the verdict that the ship was equally safe with the number of hands she had on board, as if she had had the whole number contained in the warranty. The warranty then can only relate to her being copper-sheathed: that part indeed was extremely material, because otherwise the risk would have been considerably increased; and that extended to the voyage insured: but the other part of the marginal note was merely a representation, because the manner of sailing from Liverpool was unconnected with the risk insured.

But even if the Court should consider the whole as a warranty, it has been substantially complied with.

Lord Mansfield, Ch.J. There is a material distinction between a warranty and a representation. A representation may be equitably and substantially answered: but a warranty must be strictly complied with. Supposing a warranty to sail on the 1st of August, and the ship did not sail till the 2d, the warranty would not be complied with. A warranty in a policy of insurance is a condition or a contingency, and unless that be performed, there is no contract. It is perfectly immaterial for what purpose a warranty is introduced; but, being inserted, the contract does not exist unless it be literally complied with. Now in the present case, the condition was the sailing of the ship with a certain number of men; which not being complied with, the policy is void.

Ashhurst, J. The very meaning of a warranty is to preclude all questions whether it has been substantially complied with; it must be literally so.

Buller, J. It is impossible to divide the words written in the margin in the manner which has been attempted; that that part of it which relates to the copper sheathing should be a warranty, and not the remaining part. But the whole forms one entire contract, and must be complied with throughout.

Judgment for the plaintiff.

MacDOWALL v. FRASER

1 Dougl. 259, 99 Eng. Rep. 170 (1779)

This was an action upon a policy of insurance on the ship the " 'Mary and Hannah,' from New York to Philadelphia." At the time when the insurance was made, which was in London, on the 30th of January, the broker represented the situation of the ship to the underwriter as follows: " 'The Mary and Hannah,' a tight vessel, sailed with several armed ships, and was seen safe in the Delaware on the 11th of December, by a ship which arrived at New York." In fact, the vessel was lost on the 9th of December, by running against a *chevaux de frise** placed across the river. The cause came on to be tried before Lord Mansfield, at the last sittings at Guildhall. The defence was founded on the misrepresentation as to the time when the ship was seen; and the representation and the day of the loss being proved, the jury found for the defendant. On Monday, the 8th of November, Dunning obtained a rule to shew cause, why there should not be a new trial, which came on to be argued this day.

The Solicitor General, and Dunning, for the plaintiff. — Lee and Davenport, for the defendant.

On the part of the plaintiff, the difference between a warranty and a representation was much enlarged upon. It was admitted, that

---

*A *chevaux de frise* is "a piece of timber or an iron barrel traversed with iron-pointed spikes or spears, or pointed poles, five or six feet long, used to defend a passage, stop a breach or impede cavalry, etc." Webster's Second New International Dictionary 462 (2d ed. 1952).

the representation in this case was false in point of fact, though the insured, at the time, believed it to be true. It was also admitted, that a representation, if false, in a material point, annuls the contract. But it was contended, that the particular day when the ship had been seen in the Delaware was not material. That the meaning of the representation was to inform the underwriter, that the ship had got safe through two thirds of her voyage from New York, and beyond the reach of capture. What was stated as to that material part was perfectly true, and that was all that was necessary, as was decided in the cases on the insurance of the "Julius Cæsar." If the representation had been, that she had been seen on the 8th or 9th in the Delaware, it would have made no difference in the premium. There might have been circumstances which would have rendered the day material, as a bad storm on the 9th or 10th; but there was nothing of that sort in this case. An intentional misrepresentation was not imputed to the insured. The manner in which the mistake arose was this the captain who had met the ship said, that he had seen her on the fifth day after her departure from New York. It seems a ship is said to sail from New York indifferently either when she sails from the quay at New York, or from Sandy Hook. When the captain mentioned her departure from New York, he was understood to mean from Sandy Hook, and it was known that she had sailed from thence on the 6th; but it turned out that he meant to speak of her departure from the quay, which was some days before.

For the defendant, it was urged, that the materiality of the fact misrepresented was before the jury, and that they had exercised their judgment upon it, and determined by their verdict, that it was material.

LORD MANSFIELD — The distinction between a warranty and a representation is perfectly well settled. A representation must be fair and true. It should be true as to all that the insured knows: and, if he represent facts to the underwriter, without knowing the truth, he takes the risk upon himself. But the difference between the fact as it turns out, and as represented, must be material. The case of the "Julius Cæsar" was very different from this. The ship, there, was only fitting out when the insurance was made. No guns nor men were put on board. It was only said what was meant to be done, and what was done, though different, was as advantageous, or more so, than what had been represented. There was no evidence of actual fraud in the present case, and no question of that sort seemed to be made. But there was a positive averment, that the ship was seen in the Delaware, on the 11th of December. The underwriter was deceived as to that fact, and entered into the contract under that deception. There was no evidence at the trial when she was seen in the Delaware, or in what condition; but, suppose the fact had been explained in the manner now suggested, why did the insured take upon him to compute the day of the month on which she had been seen? Why did he not mention exactly what his information was, and leave the underwriter to make the computation? In insurances on ships at a great distance, their being safe up to a certain day, is always considered as a very important circumstance. I am of opinion, that the representation concerning the day was material.

WILLES, Justice — This is certainly only a representation; but, in an insurance on so short a voyage, it might have made a material difference whether the ship was known to be safe two days sooner or later. It ought to have been shewn, on the part of the plaintiff, that it was not material, but there was no evidence that the ship was met on the 9th, or any other day. The materiality was proper for the consideration of the jury.

ASHHURST, Justice — The distinction which the Court has made in the cases on the "Julius Cæsar," and some others, between a representation and a warranty, is extremely just. There is no imputation of fraud in this case; but the insured should have been more cautious. In the former cases the representation was of what was intended; here, it was of a fact, stated as having happened within the knowledge of the insured. He should have made the representation in the same words in which the intelligence is said to have been communicated to him.

BULLER, Justice — We cannot say the difference of the day was not material. The safety of the ship is the most material fact of any, in cases of insurance. The plaintiff admits, that the place where she was met in safety was material. Why was not the time equally so? There was no intentional deceit, and it is perhaps unfortunate that the insured made the mistake; but I think the verdict right.

The rule discharged.

Notes and Questions

1. *DeHahn* and *MacDowall* accurately capsulize the eighteenth-century law of warranties and representations, which is the starting point for our present law. The law remains much the same in England, at least for marine insurance, but has changed a great deal in the United States.

2. How do you know whether you are dealing with a representation or a warranty?

3. Is there any policy justification for the fact that the effect of a breach of warranty does not depend on any special relation between the risk the insurer assumed and the fact warranted or the conduct promised nor on any causal connection between the fact or conduct warranted and the loss? That is, if there is a breach of warranty the policy will be voidable (or void?) whether or not the warranty is of any significance: Under the common law, warranties must be strictly accu-

rate if they are matters of fact and strictly complied with if they are promises. All of these statements can be capsulized by saying that materiality was irrelevant with respect to warranties. Should that be regarded as unfair in the context of eighteenth-century marine insurance? If not, why not?

4. *MacDowall* shows that the rule was gentler with respect to misrepresentations. Why should that be so? In a leading case, Pawson v. Watson, 2 Cowp. 785, 98 Eng. Rep. 1361 (K.B. 1778), which was decided the year before *MacDowall*, much of the foregoing doctrine is stated, but in that case Lord Mansfield assumed also that a misrepresentation would have effect only if it were fraudulent as well as material. *MacDowall* jettisoned the need for fraud. Was that a desirable change?

5. In Bize v. Fletcher, 1 Dougl. 284, 99 Eng. Rep. 185 (1779), a ship was insured for a voyage to the Far East, including "all ports and places, and until her safe arrival, back at her last port of discharge in France." The insured represented that the ship was to go "to Madeira, the Isles of France, Pondicherry, China, the Isles of France, and L'Orient." The last named port (Lorient on current maps) was the original port of departure in France. Instead of going to China, the ship traded slowly up the coast of the Indian subcontinent from Pondicherry to Bengal and then back to Pondicherry. Then, en route back to Europe, she was taken by a privateer. How should Lord Mansfield instruct the jury in an action on the policy?

CARTER v. BOEHM

3 Burr. 1905, 97 Eng. Rep. 1162 (1766)

[An insurance policy protected the governor of Fort Marlborough on the island of Sumatra against loss of the fort to a foreign enemy. In this context "foreign" meant "European." The fort was really a trading post (or "factory") and the loss of the fort meant loss of the governor's trading stock. The underwriters defended on the theory that the policy was void because the governor did not disclose to the underwriters the weakness of the fort (which was fortified only against the natives of Sumatra), that he did not disclose the likelihood that the French might attack the fort, and that he did not disclose a letter received some time earlier from which it did indeed seem that the French had such an intention.]

Lord Mansfield now delivered the resolution of the court. . . .

1st. It may be proper to say something, in general, of concealments which avoid a policy.

2dly. To state particularly the case now under consideration.

3dly. To examine whether the verdict, which finds this policy good although the particulars objected were not mentioned, is well founded.

First. Insurance is a contract upon speculation.

The special facts, upon which the contingent chance is to be computed, lie most commonly in the knowledge of the insured only: the under-writer trusts to his representation, and proceeds upon confidence that he does not keep back any circumstance in his knowledge, to mislead the under-writer into a belief that the circumstance does not exist, and to induce him to estimate the risque, as if it did not exist.

The keeping back such circumstance is a fraud, and therefore the policy is void. Although the suppression should happen through mistake, without any fraudulent intention; yet still the under-writer is deceived, and the policy is void; because the risque run is really different from the risque understood and intended to be run, at the time of the agreement.

The policy would equally be void, against the under-writer, if he concealed; as, if he insured a ship on her voyage, which he privately knew to be arrived: and an action would lie to recover the premium.

The governing principle is applicable to all contracts and dealings.

Good faith forbids either party by concealing what he privately knows, to draw the other into a bargain, from his ignorance of that fact, and his believing the contrary.

But either party may be innocently silent, as to grounds open to both, to exercise their judgment upon.

[The verdict at trial before Lord Mansfield had been for the insured; the insurer had then moved for a new trial. After extensive discussion of the evidence and the political background, Lord Mansfield said that] we are all clear that the verdict is well founded: and there ought not to be a new trial. . . .

Notes and Questions

1. The full opinion is worth reading for its illumination of the underlying assumptions of insurance law. The last paragraphs quoted from the opinion set forth the doctrine *uberrimae fidei* — of utmost good faith — that lies at the root of much modern insurance law, though now considerably transformed. For the last survival (and the imminent demise) of the notion in its original form, see the section on Reinsurance in Chapter 9.

2. Note that this is a case of nondisclosure (called "concealment" in the insurance cases), rather than one of active misrepresentation. Is there a difference between active concealment and simple nondisclosure? Between concealment or nondisclosure and misrepresentation? Is it reasonable for an insurer to expect disclosure of facts about which

no questions have been asked? Should that depend on the kind of insurance?

3. Two facts were probably important in producing the eighteenth-century doctrines of warranty, misrepresentation, and concealment. The first was that the losses in all the leading cases so far mentioned, and in many others, were losses from war risks. The second was the slow pace of communication. Note when the insurance was effected in the preceding cases in relation to the period of coverage. Why should these two facts have tended toward the creation of the harsh law of those cases?

4. In England, marine insurance law, particularly that which deals with warranties, representations, and concealment, has not been left solely to case law. The 1906 Marine Insurance Act, a codifying statute based more or less on the continental model, restates the preexisting law of marine insurance. The prior case law is useful mainly to help interpret that Act. Ivamy, Marine Insurance (2d ed. 1974), a standard British treatise, treats *DeHahn, MacDowall,* and *Carter* as still good authority, but *Bize* is not listed in Ivamy's Table of Cases.

2. Implied Warranties

Given the stringency of the doctrines developed by Lord Mansfield concerning express warranties, it is a little surprising that the courts sometimes go even further and subject insureds to equally severe treatment without an express warranty. The best example is the implied warranty of seaworthiness of vessels that will be subjected to the "perils of the seas." The importance of seaworthiness is evident to anyone who has ever experienced a violent storm at sea, even vicariously through the graphic descriptions of typhoons by experienced mariners such as Joseph Conrad. Section 39 of the Marine Insurance Act of 1906 codifies prior case law and makes seaworthiness a statutory implied warranty.

Whether a ship is seaworthy is often a difficult factual question; making that determination *after* the ship's damage or loss is especially difficult. In Insurance Co. of North America v. Lanasa Shrimp Co., 726 F.2d 688 (11th Cir. 1984), a shrimping vessel left Key West headed for the Dry Tortugas. Though weather conditions were good in the area, the ship never returned to port. The owner sought to recover under a "perils of the seas" clause. The trial court judge found, on "ample evidence," that the vessel sailed in a seaworthy condition. On appeal, the court remarked that in "unexplained sinking" cases, there was a rebuttable presumption of unseaworthiness, but once seaworthiness is established by evidence, there is a counter presumption that an unexplained sinking results from "perils of the seas," which the court applied.

Notes and Questions

1. *Lanasa Shrimp* was not an unexplained *sinking* case but a mysterious *disappearance* case, with other possible explanations than sinking (such as piracy or marine fraud). If you were the trial judge, would you apply the second presumption in a mysterious disappearance case off the Florida keys, in good weather, in the 1980s? If you were on the appeals court, would you reverse the trial court?

2. The "missing vessel" problem first became acute in World War I when commercial hull underwriters and war risk insurers each sought to escape liability in missing vessel cases by trying to lay the risk on the other. How would you decide such a case in wartime? Should a showing of seaworthiness of a ship going into waters where enemy aircraft, submarines, or mines might be encountered still lead to a counter presumption that a mysterious disappearance was due to "perils of the seas"? If the rules are modified when there are substantial war risks, when should the ordinary rules again apply? Long after World War II ships were still being lost because of unexpected rogue mines. Separating perils of the seas from war risks is a recurring problem, as appears from the recent conflicts in the Persian Gulf.

3. The Meaning of Materiality

Section 18(2) of the 1906 Marine Insurance Act, in discussing the insured's obligation of disclosure to the insurer, states that "[e]very circumstance is material which would influence the judgment of a prudent insurer in fixing the premium, or determining whether he will take the risk." The provision respecting representations is essentially the same. For warranty, the Act provides (as Lord Mansfield did in *DeHahn*) that materiality is irrelevant.

Notes and Questions

1. If an otherwise operative misrepresentation makes it appear to the insurer that the risk is greater than it would have appeared to be if the truth were told, would the insurer have a defense?

2. In the 1906 Marine Insurance Act, materiality turns on the standard of a "prudent insurer." Should an insurer with more conservative underwriting practices than the minimally prudent insurer be entitled to insist on its own standards of materiality?

3. How would you prove materiality?

4. In its application to renew its hull and machinery policy, Eagle Steamship Company did not report two recent losses that would have

changed its previous year's results from a 92.5 percent loss ratio to one of over 300 percent. Part of the coverage was bound orally by a lead underwriter* at Lloyd's and the rest subsequently by plaintiffs (Puritan Insurance Company and others). At the last minute, information about the occurrence of one of the losses (but apparently not about its extent) was conveyed to the lead underwriter at Lloyd's, who agreed not to take that belatedly reported loss into account. There was a conflict in testimony about a possible telephone call transmitting the same information to plaintiff insurers' underwriting agents. An updated binder issued by Eagle's broker and signed by the underwriters' agents said, under "Information to Underwriters," that "As per leaders agreement 'IRINIO' Machinery Damage Claim March 1980 not taken into account this renewal." Puritan and other insurers, claiming not to have noticed the reference to the IRINIO loss, sued for a declaratory judgment that the policy was void for nondisclosure and that they had relied on the information provided, and for damages. On the disputed facts the trial court decided for Eagle. The appellate court affirmed over a strong dissent. Puritan Ins. Co. v. Eagle Steamship Co., 779 F.2d 866 (2d Cir. 1985). Both prevailing and dissenting opinions adhere verbally to traditional doctrine but the majority *seems* to exhibit a more generous attitude toward insureds than can be found in the old cases. It also seems to be satisfied with the supplying of less than complete information by the insureds on the ground that if insurers are put on notice they should ask for additional information if they want it. It is hard to think Lord Mansfield would have decided the case in the same way on the facts as they are reported in the opinions. Have circumstances changed enough to justify the apparent change in results from two centuries ago?

5. The standard for materiality for property insurance is no different in principle from that for marine insurance.

KNIGHT v. U.S. FIRE INS. CO.

804 F.2d 9 (2d Cir. 1986), *cert. denied*, 480 U.S. 932 (1987)

FEINBERG, Chief Judge:

Frederick W.A. Knight appeals from an order of the United States District Court for the Southern District of New York, Constance Baker Motley, Ch. J., granting summary judgment to defendant insurance companies. Knight argues that summary judgment was inappro-

---

*The lead underwriter decides what the premium rate and policy conditions shall be; other underwriters then decide whether to subscribe or not to subscribe, and if the former, for what percentage of the risk.

priate because several genuine issues of material fact remain unresolved. Upon review, we conclude that no such issues are present. Therefore, we affirm the holding of the district court.

I. Facts

The relevant facts are as follows: Between 1976 and 1979, Knight purchased in Thailand 222 antique stone and bronze statues for approximately $65,000. In 1980, an appraiser hired by Knight valued the collection at $20,205,000. The same appraiser revised his estimate to $27,000,000 in April 1981 and then to $30,307,500 in September 1981, the month in which he died. The appraiser was to receive for his services 5% of the proceeds from the eventual sale of the statues.

Meanwhile, Knight had transported the statuary from Thailand to Singapore. In February 1981, Knight obtained through the insurance brokerage firm of Hogg Robinson & Gardner Mountain (Marine) Ltd. (Hogg Robinson) coverage of $20,205,000 from London underwriters for shipment of the collection from Singapore to Holland. In May 1981, after receiving the first revised estimate from his appraiser, Knight requested and obtained through Hogg Robinson an additional $10,000,000 coverage for the voyage.

In June 1981, however, after the approximately $30 million risk had been placed, Robert Jensen, Knight's broker at Hogg Robinson, received two anonymous phone calls reporting that Knight was planning to perpetrate a fraud. Jensen conveyed this information to the lead London underwriters who, in response, ordered their own appraisal of the statuary. A few days later, Jensen sent a telex to Knight informing him that the underwriters had voided his policy because of his material nondisclosures and misrepresentations regarding his collection. Jensen stated in the telex that, based on their appraiser's inspection of some of the statues, the underwriters believed that the collection was "grossly overvalued and, in some, if not all cases, replicas. . . . The evidence currently available to underwriters suggests that the proper value of the consignment is nominal only (possibly approximately 1 pct of the value declared)." . . .

In October 1982, Knight approached Yerkes & Associates to reinstate his $30 million of coverage, claiming that he was preparing to ship the statues to a purchaser in Greece. The brokers succeeded in placing $30,630,750 of risk for the voyage from Singapore to Greece with several American insurance companies. Many of these insurers had agreed to insure the earlier projected voyage from Singapore to France. These are the policies contested in this lawsuit. For convenience, we will refer to them hereafter as one policy (the New York policy).

In January 1983, the statues were loaded on board a vessel for the voyage from Singapore to Greece. On February 7, 1983, the ship sank in the Indian Ocean and the statues were lost.

After the loss of his statues, Knight attempted to collect on the insurance provided by defendant underwriters. Defendants refused and, instead, voided the New York policy *ab initio* because of Knight's alleged material nondisclosures and misrepresentations. Thereafter, Knight brought this lawsuit. Defendants moved for summary judgment before Judge Motley, and she granted the motion in a 16-page memorandum opinion. This appeal followed.

II.   Summary Judgment . . .

A

In evaluating whether particular facts are material, we must turn to the substantive law governing marine insurance. It is well-established under the doctrine of *uberrimae fidei* that the parties to a marine insurance policy must accord each other the highest degree of good faith. Puritan Ins. Co. v. Eagle S.S. Co. S.A., 779 F.2d 866, 870 (2d Cir. 1985). This stringent doctrine requires the assured to disclose to the insurer all known circumstances that materially affect the risk being insured. Since the assured is in the best position to know of any circumstances material to the risk, he must reveal those facts to the underwriter, rather than wait for the underwriter to inquire. Id. The standard for disclosure is an objective one, that is, whether a reasonable person in the assured's position would know that the particular fact is material. Btesh v. Royal Ins. Co., 49 F.2d 720, 721 (2d Cir. 1931). To be material, the fact must be "something which would have controlled the underwriter's decision" to accept the risk. Id. The assured's failure to meet this standard entitles the underwriter to void the policy *ab initio. Puritan Ins. Co.,* 779 F.2d at 870–871.

Knight contends, however, that an assured's duty to disclose a prior cancellation is not triggered where the cancellation was based on fictitious or false information. He relies on the testimony of Leslie J. Buglass, an expert in marine insurance, that false information cannot materially affect risk. Arguing that his prior cancellation was caused by anonymous phone calls that were entirely groundless and an inspection that was performed by an unqualified appraiser, Knight maintains that it was error for Judge Motley to dismiss his allegations as irrelevant and to grant summary judgment.

The fact of the prior cancellation and the stated reasons for the cancellation are not disputed. In light of these circumstances, Judge Motley stated:

> [A]s a matter of indisputable fact a prior underwriter's voidance of a thirty million dollar insurance policy on antiquities of dubious origin on the grounds that the goods were "grossly over-valued" and inauthentic would have been material to any subsequent underwriter's decision to accept the risk. . . . No reasonable juror could conclude, under the facts of this case, that defendants would not have declined to embrace plaintiff's requested thirty million dollar policy had they known of the prior London cancellation and of the incriminating contents of the telex from the London broker — at least not without subsequent opportunity for defendants to make their own investigation and perhaps adjust . . . the amount insured. . . .

We have also considered Knight's argument that a cancellation of prior insurance may be concealed, based on British cases holding that it is not necessary to disclose a prior refusal by another marine insurer to write a policy. . . .

In any event, we are unpersuaded by the analogy. A refusal to write a policy is not the same as a cancellation, particularly when the latter resulted from the insurer's belief that the goods insured were overvalued and inauthentic. . . .

B

Knight claims that another genuine issue is whether defendants had knowledge, either actual or constructive, of the prior cancellation and the reasons for the cancellation. Such knowledge would defeat defendants' claim that the prior cancellation was not disclosed. . . .

In view of the high burden of disclosure on the assured in the field of marine insurance, we conclude that this information falls short of providing sufficient notice so as to shift the obligation to defendants to inquire about a prior cancellation. . . .

IV. Conclusion

We conclude that Judge Motley's grant of summary judgment was appropriate since Knight has not shown any genuine issue as to a material fact. The justifiability of the prior cancellation is not a material fact and defendants' knowledge of the prior cancellation is not a genuine issue. Therefore, we affirm Judge Motley's decision to grant summary judgment and to dismiss the case.

Notes and Questions

1. For a statement of the *uberrimae fidei* principle, *Knight* cites and relies on *Eagle,* in which the insured won. Can the two cases be reconciled?

2. If it is not necessary to disclose a prior refusal to insure, why is it necessary to disclose a prior cancellation?

3. What kind of conduct by the insurer might violate the *uberimmae fidei* standard and justify recovery by the insured?

4. Modifications by Case Law and Statute

The above materials have dealt mainly with the doctrines of warranties, representations, and concealment in the law of ocean marine insurance. They have not been substantially altered in that line of insurance.

Although originally applicable to all lines of insurance, the doctrines through which the eighteenth-century underwriters of marine insurance controlled the risks they accepted proved less suitable to other lines of insurance. In the former context, information about a risk was ordinarily within the possession of the insured alone, and there was usually parity of economic power and sometimes considerable negotiation between the underwriters and the insureds. In contrast, underwriters of other lines are more often than not in possession of as much information about the risk as their insureds (and sometimes of even more) and can frequently dictate to the insured not only the terms of the insurance transaction but sometimes even relevant aspects of the insured's business conduct. Standardized insurance contracts make negotiation of terms less frequent and less important, though it does still exist in some commercial insurance transactions. Moreover, outside of marine insurance, the pace of communication has always been less important and information easier to acquire.

Even for ocean marine insurance there has been considerable modification of the harsh eighteenth-century doctrines, in the United States if not in the United Kingdom. In Wilburn Boat Co. v. Fireman's Fund Ins. Co., 348 U.S. 310 (1955), the Supreme Court decided by a divided vote that the Texas statute on warranties applied to the marine insurance policy involved in the case. The Court noted that article III, section 2 of the United States Constitution provides that "[t]he judicial power shall extend . . . to all cases of admiralty and maritime jurisdiction." That clause, together with the commerce clause in article I, section 8, gives Congress plenary power to legislate with respect to maritime matters. Justice Black, writing for the majority, said:

Congress has not taken over the regulation of marine insurance contracts and has not dealt with the effect of marine insurance warranties at all; hence there is no possible question here of conflict between state law and any federal statute. But this does not answer the questions presented, since in the absence of controlling Acts of Congress this Court has fashioned a large part of the existing rules that govern admiralty. And States can no more override such judicial rules validly fashioned than they can override Acts of Congress. See, e.g., Garrett v. Moore-McCormack Co., 317 U.S. 239. Consequently the crucial questions in this case narrow down to these: (1) Is there a judicially established federal admiralty rule governing these warranties? (2) If not, should we fashion one? [Id. at 314.]

The court answered both questions negatively, remarking that the law governing insurance had been essentially left to the states. As a result, the appropriate state law, in this case the Texas statute, governed. Though there have been Fifth and Eleventh Circuit decisions and some state cases that have seemed, on their face, to ignore *Wilburn Boat*, as well as some academic criticism at the time that naively predicted that chaos in marine insurance would result from the Court's ruling, most cases have followed it, and it is still good law. Thus, whatever ameliorating doctrines the states have developed and applied to marine insurance have full effect.

For lines other than ocean marine insurance, all three doctrines have been modified by statutes and case law, with diverse results. Sometimes only life insurance is affected; sometimes other specified lines; sometimes all lines. Consider how relevant the following factors should be in setting contemporary public policy either by statute or by case law:

- line of insurance*
- comparative size and sophistication of insurer and insured
- tightness of the relevant insurance market
- degree to which premium rates and policy terms are actually or potentially controlled by regulators
- the diversity of and the quality of relevant regulation among the states
- the importance of the subject of the warranty or representation (does materiality come in degrees?)
- the extent of the deviation (for example, does it matter whether the *Juno* was undermanned by four sailors during an unin-

---

*For adequate or inadequate reasons, the doctrines, or at least the results in reported cases, do vary by line of insurance. For one illustration, see Hoens, When Can the Bankers Blanket Bond Be Rescinded for Fraud or Misrepresentation?, 16 Forum 1102 (1981).

sured part of the voyage in protected waters (DeHahn v. Hartley) or by ten on that leg of the voyage or by four (or ten)
during the insured part of the voyage across the South Atlantic?)
- the duration of the deviation
- the cause of the deviation

Can either the legislature or the courts distinguish among the infinite
variety of factual situations with enough information and expertise to
justify a refined rather than a crude set of doctrines in this area? If
doctrines are to be crude, how should they be formulated?

The materials on this subject can be looked at from several per-
spectives: that of the insurer trying to define and control its book of
business, that of the insured trying to get the purchased protection
without an insurer having arbitrary power over the decision whether to
pay a claim, and that of the court or other arbiter (sometimes the
regulator) seeking to balance the legitimate interests of the other two.
For a summary of a major part of the field, with a review of many of
the leading cases, see Farnham, Application Misrepresentation and
Concealment in Property Insurance — The Elusive Elements of the
Defense, 20 Forum 299 (1985), and Brennan & Hanson, Misrepresentation in the Application as the Basis for Rescission of a Property
Insurance Policy, 21 Tort & Ins. L.J. 451 (1986).

a.   Changes by Case Law

The following case illustrates the way American courts have dealt
with the problems of warranties, representations, and concealment
even in the absence of statutes. Because changes have largely been
made through the interaction of statutes and case law, examples of
statutes then follow, with illustrations of the glosses U.S. courts have
put on them.

WOOD v. HARTFORD FIRE INS. CO.

13 Conn. 533 (1840)

[Action on a fire insurance policy on the undivided half of a paper
mill owned by the plaintiff. It was operated as such at the time the
policy was taken out. Plaintiff's lessee added some millstones for
grinding grain without removing any of the existing machinery except
a rag-cutter and duster. The operation of what was now a grist mill

then continued until the fire, which was not caused by the operation of the mill. The defense was breach of a warranty.]

SHERMAN, J. It is not necessary to advert to all the points which have been discussed in this case, by the learned counsel. The general rule in regard to what constitutes a warranty, in a contract of insurance, is well settled. Any statement or description, or any undertaking on the part of the insured, on the face of the policy, which relates to the risk, is a warranty. Whether this is declared to be a warranty *totidem verbis*, or is ascertained to be such, by construction, is immaterial. In either case, it is an *express* warranty, and a condition precedent. If a house be insured against fire, and is described in the policy as being "copper roofed," it is as express a warranty, as if the language had been, "*warranted* to be copper roofed;" and its truth is as essential to the obligation of the policy, in one case as in the other. In either case, it must be strictly observed. There may often be much difficulty in ascertaining from the construction of the policy, whether a fact, quality or circumstance specified, relates to the risk, or is inserted for some other purpose — as to shew the identity of the article insured, &c. This must be settled, before the rule can be applied. But when it is once ascertained, that it relates to the risk, and was inserted in reference to that, it must be strictly observed and kept, or the insurance is void. The word "warranted" dispels all ambiguity, and supersedes the necessity of construction. . . . Parties may contract as they please. When a condition precedent is adopted, the court cannot enquire as to its wisdom or folly, but must exact its strict observance. An entry on the margin of the policy, or across the lines, or on a separate paper, expressly referred to in the policy, will be construed a warranty, if it relates to the risk; that is, if it defines, or, in any respect, limits, the risk assumed. . . .

It is immaterial whether the non-performance or violation of the warranty, be with, or without, the consent or fault of the insured. Its strict observance is exacted, by law; and no reason or necessity will dispense with it.

The argument of the defendants is, therefore, conclusive, if the policy warrants this building to be and continue a paper-mill, and it was not one, at the time of the loss.

In the policy, this establishment is described as "the one undivided half of the paper-mill, which they [the insured] own at Westville, together with the half of the machinery wheels, gearing, &c.; the other half being owned by *William Buddington.*" If this relates to the risk, it is a warranty. That it does, is evident from the memorandum in the conditions of the policy, where "paper-mills" are enumerated among those articles which "will be insured at special rates of premium;" that is, a paper-mill is the subject of peculiar risks, and is to be insured upon special stipulations. Therefore, the description of this, in the policy, as a "paper-mill," relates to the risk, and is, consequently, a warranty. It is the only subject of insurance; and if it was not a paper-mill, at the time of the loss, the warranty was not kept, and the plaintiffs cannot recover, although the change may have diminished the hazard, and been effected without their knowledge, or against their will.

It is contended, that the paper-mill had become converted into a grist-mill. The policy is dated in February, 1837. In the August, following, the use of the paper-mill was discontinued, and a pair of mill-stones were added, for grinding grain. They were located in the place previously occupied by the rag-cutter and duster; and were moved by the same gearing, and by the power of the same water-wheel. No other machinery was used for the grindstones. All remained as it was, except the rag-cutter and duster — which were dismounted — and all the other machinery might, at any time, have been employed in making paper. It was, to all intents and purposes, a paper-mill, ready for use. The character of the establishment was no more altered, than if a grindstone had been attached, by a band, to the water-wheel and all the other machinery left at rest. The warranty was duly kept.

It has been further contended, that the defendants are absolved from their obligations, by reason of the increased hazard resulting from the use of the mill-stones. In most cases of insurance, circumstances occur, which increase the hazard; but whether they impair the policy, must depend on its construction, or on the general principles of the law of insurance. The jury have found, that by the use of the mill-stones the risk is greater than it would have been if no use were made of the premises, but not greater than if the paper-mill only was in full operation; but that they were not the cause of the loss. Admitting that, as the facts were, the hazard was increased, by the use of the mill-stones; yet, to this claim of the defendants, the policy itself furnishes a satisfactory answer. It provides, that if, without the written agreement of the company, the building shall be appropriated for carrying on any trade, business or vocation, or for the storing of any articles, "denominated hazardous or extra-hazardous," in the annexed conditions, the insurance shall be of no effect, so long as the same shall be so appropriated. In the conditions annexed, grist-mills are not denominated hazardous or extra-hazardous, but enumerated in the memorandum relating to special rates of premium. They were under the consideration of the parties, and advisedly omitted from that class, which should affect the validity of the insurance. An effect of the memorandum is, to exclude from insurance the articles which it embraces, unless specially provided for in the policy; but they are purposely distinguished from those which affect its validity.

It is admitted, that the loss has happened, by the risk insured against; and that all the preliminary steps, to entitle the defendants to the benefit of the policy, have been taken. The property insured has not been changed; the warranty has been kept; and the obligations of the defendants have not been impaired, by any increase of hazard, resulting from the alterations in the mill.

We advise that judgment be entered for the plaintiffs.

In this opinion the other Judges concurred, except WILLIAMS, Ch. J., who gave no opinion, being nearly related to one of the stockholders in The Hartford Fire Insurance Company.

Judgment for plaintiffs.

Notes and Questions

1. For treatment of the "increase of hazard" problem, see Chapter 3.

2. Does *Wood* change anything in the eighteenth-century doctrine of breach of warranty?

3. Should the result in *Wood* depend at all on the relative premium rates charged for grist mills and for paper mills? Does it matter which are higher?

b. Changes by Statute

In the United States, warranty and representation doctrines have been modified by statute in a variety of ways. Those statutes have then been further modified (interpreted) by the courts. Concealment has less often received statutory attention. The statutes vary greatly, both as to the lines of insurance covered and as to the way in which the law is changed.

IOWA CODE §515.101

Iowa Code Ann. §515.101 (West 1988)

Any condition or stipulation in an application, policy, or contract of insurance, making the policy void before the loss occurs, shall not prevent recovery thereon by the insured, if it shall be shown by the plaintiff that the failure to observe such provision or the violation thereof did not contribute to the loss.

MASSACHUSETTS GENERAL LAWS CH. 175, §186

Mass. Ann. Laws ch. 175, §186 (Law Co-op. 1987)

No oral or written misrepresentation or warranty made in the negotiation of a policy of insurance by the insured or in his behalf shall be deemed material or defeat or avoid the policy or prevent its attaching unless such misrepresentation or warranty is made with actual intent to deceive, or unless the matter misrepresented or made a warranty increased the risk of loss.

FLORIDA STATUTES §627.409(1)

Fla. Stat. Ann. §627.409(1) (West 1984)

All statements and descriptions in any application for an insurance policy or annuity contract, or in negotiations therefor, by or in behalf of the insured or annuitant, shall be deemed to be representations and not warranties. Misrepresentations, omissions, concealment of facts, and incorrect statements shall not prevent a recovery under the policy or contract unless:

(a) They are fraudulent;

(b) They are material either to the acceptance of the risk or to the hazard assumed by the insurer; or

(c) The insurer in good faith would either not have issued the policy or contract, would not have issued it at the same premium rate, would not have issued a policy or contract in as large an amount, or would not have provided coverage with respect to the hazard resulting in the loss, if the true facts had been made known to the insurer as required either by the application for the policy or contract or otherwise.

NEW YORK INSURANCE LAW §3106

N.Y. Ins. Law §3106 (McKinney 1985)

§3106. Warranty Defined; Effect of Breach

(a) In this section "warranty" means any provision of an insurance contract which has the effect of requiring, as a condition precedent of the taking effect of such contract or as a condition precedent of the insurer's liability thereunder, the existence of a fact which tends to diminish, or the non-existence of a fact which tends to increase, the risk of the occurrence of any loss, damage, or injury within the coverage of the contract. The term "occurrence of loss, damage, or injury" includes the occurrence of death, disability, injury, or any other contingency insured against, and the term "risk" includes both physical and moral hazards.

(b) A breach of warranty shall not avoid an insurance contract or defeat recovery thereunder unless such breach materially increases the risk of loss, damage or injury within the coverage of the contract. If the insurance contract specified two or more distinct kinds of loss, damage or injury which are within its coverage, a breach of warranty shall not avoid such contract or defeat recovery thereunder with respect to any kind or kinds of loss, damage or injury other than the kind or kinds to which such warranty relates and the risk of which is materially increased by the breach of such warranty.

(c) This section shall not affect the express or implied warranties under a contract of marine insurance in respect to, appertaining to or in connection with any and all risks or perils of navigation, transit, or transportation, including war risks, on, over or under any seas or inland waters, nor shall it affect any provision in an insurance contract requiring notice, proof or other conduct of the insured after the occurrence of loss, damage or injury.

Notes and Questions

1. The New York statute is unusual in defining warranty in terms of the effect of its breach. Is the definition circular?

2. Many other statutes, such as that of Massachusetts, do not define warranty. How would you describe the effect of the Massachusetts statute on common law doctrine?

3. What has the Florida statute done to the common law doctrines of warranty and representation? In Home Guar. Ins. Corp. v. Numerica Financial Services, Inc., 835 F.2d 1354 (11th Cir. 1988), HGIC issued mortgage guaranty insurance* policies to Numerica, relying on representations in documents supplied by Numerica. One set of documents stated that the construction of the property was complete and that the borrowers had made a cash down payment of $17,000, when in fact the construction had not been finished and no down payment had been made. Comparable misrepresentations were made in another instance. HGIC sought to avoid the policies for material misrepresentation, based on the statute reproduced above. The trial court

---

*Mortgage guaranty insurance protects lenders who have loaned money on real property with a mortgage as security, against losses from borrower defaults. Characteristically, the insurer protects itself by insisting on a reasonably substantial down payment and may also evaluate the borrower's credit rating and the lender's loan underwriting practices as well. In many cases, however, the pressures of competition lead the insurer to rely on the lender to do most of the underwriting. The incentive of the lender to underwrite its loans carefully is reduced, however, by the protection against bad loans afforded by the insurance. Recently this has led in a number of cases to serious losses by insurers, and to consequent threatened insolvency.

found that the Florida statute did not apply to mortgage guaranty insurance because a separate part of the insurance code, to which the misrepresentation statute did not apply, governed it instead.* The court said:

> In addition, mortgage guaranty insurance companies *also* do not require the protection provided by Section 627.409. Section 627.409 lets insurance companies void policies when material misrepresentations have been made. This protects insurers who reasonably relied on misrepresentations made in application for insurance. [The court then discussed the documentation supplied with the application in mortgage guaranty insurance, enabling the insurer to engage in careful underwriting of the risk.] Because of their unique ability to evaluate the documentation, mortgage guaranty insurance companies are on a more equal footing with mortgage lenders and need not rely on Section 627.409 for protection.
>
> Thus, we find that the legislature's policy is to exclude Section 627.409 from Chapter 635. [Id. at 1358–1359.]

Is the court's reasoning persuasive?

4. In a written proposal to an insurer for a Jeweler's Block Policy,† the applicant stated, in response to Question 14B of the proposal form, that the value of jewelry to be displayed in the shop window would not exceed certain specified amounts. The policy expressly made the proposal part of the policy and then stated that "[i]t is a condition of this insurance precedent to any recovery hereunder that the values of property displayed will not exceed the amount represented in answer to Question 14B of the Proposal form attached to this policy." Sure enough, the jeweler displayed too much jewelry in the window and the insurer declined to pay anything when a loss occurred. Under Massachusetts law the case was decided for the insurer. Why? How would the case have been decided had it been in New York? See Charles, Henry & Crowley Co. v. Home Ins. Co., 349 Mass. 723, 212 N.E.2d 240 (1965).

5. What relevance does *Charles, Henry* have for the drafting of a warranty statute?

6. In another Jeweler's Block Policy, the proposal form asked the maximum value of jewelry that would be displayed in the window

---

*The first modern statute authorizing mortgage guaranty insurance seems to have been 1957 Wis. Laws ch. 417. See also Kimball, Insurance and Public Policy 12-13 (1960). Under the statute, Mortgage Guaranty Insurance Corporation was organized in Milwaukee, as the first of the modern mortgage guaranty insurers. Its subsequent career has been checkered, and very interesting, but the story is too long and complex to be discussed here.

†A Jeweler's Block Policy is property coverage classified under the rubric "inland marine insurance."

when the premises were open for business. The answer was $5,000. Statements in the proposal were expressly made warranties. Two armed men entered the store during business hours and robbed the store of about $11,000 of jewelry, $8,000 from the window and $3,000 from the vault. The window was neither cut nor smashed. The insurer denied the claim. How should the case be decided in the absence of a statute? Under the New York statute? Those of Massachusetts and Iowa? See Diesinger v. American & Foreign Ins. Co., 138 F.2d 91 (3d Cir. 1943).

7. In Mutual Fire, Marine and Inland Ins. Co. v. Costa, 789 F.2d 83 (1st Cir. 1986), the court had to deal with ocean or "wet" marine insurance against claims for liability to passengers. Under "Description of Hazards" the policy stated "Max. # of Passengers: 100." The vessel was carrying 118 passengers when it was struck by the wake from a freighter. Three passengers were injured and filed suit. The insurer initiated a declaratory judgment to determine whether it was on the risk, and moved for summary judgment. How do you think the court should rule if it is to apply Massachusetts law? How should it rule if it is to apply the New York warranty law?

NEW YORK INSURANCE LAW §3105

N.Y. Ins. Law §3105 (McKinney 1985)

§3105. Representations by the Insured

(a) A representation is a statement as to past or present fact, made to the insurer by, or by the authority of, the applicant for insurance or the prospective insured, at or before the making of the insurance contract as an inducement to the making thereof. A misrepresentation is a false representation, and the facts misrepresented are those facts which make the representation false.

(b) No misrepresentation shall avoid any contract of insurance or defeat recovery thereunder unless such misrepresentation was material. No misrepresentation shall be deemed material unless knowledge by the insurer of the facts misrepresented would have led to a refusal by the insurer to make such contract.

(c) In determining the question of materiality, evidence of the practice of the insurer which made such contract with respect to the acceptance or rejection of similar risks shall be admissible.

(d) A misrepresentation that an applicant for life or accident and health insurance has not had previous medical treatment, consultation or observation, or has not had previous treatment or care in a hospital or other like institution, shall be deemed, for the purpose of determining its materiality, a misrepresentation that the applicant has not had the disease, ailment or other medical impairment for which such treatment or care was given or which was discovered by any licensed medical practitioner as a result of such consultation or observation. If in any action to rescind any such contract or to recover thereon, any such misrepresentation is proved by the insurer, and the insured or any other person having or claiming a right under such contract shall prevent full disclosure and proof of the nature of such medical impairment, such misrepresentation shall be presumed to have been material.

Notes and Questions

1. How does the New York statute on representations change the common law? On the merits, which is preferable, the Iowa, New York, or Massachusetts law?

2. The above statutes are conspicuously silent about the common law doctrine of concealment. Does that mean that the doctrine remains unaltered? In Galvan v. Cameron Mut. Ins., 733 S.W.2d 771 (Mo. App. 1987), the court states that "[d]efendant submitted to the jury two alternative material misrepresentations in the application." It then appears that the "misrepresentations" were (1) a failure to reveal prior insurance losses within recent years, including total loss of a home, and (2) an incorrect negative answer to the question whether the husband was the "Galvan" in jail awaiting trial for robbery. How should the case be decided in principle? How under the above statutes?

3. Is it possible to regard concealment as a variety of misrepresentation and assimilate it both to the common law and to the statutory treatment of misrepresentation?

4. Some of the above statutes would seem to make the policy voidable if there was *either* fraud *or* materiality. Might a court read the "or" as "and", requiring both fraud *and* materiality? See, for example, Hoffpauir v. Time Ins. Co., 536 So. 2d 699 (La. App. 1988), interpreting La. Rev. Stat. Ann. §22:619B, which bars recovery on a policy if the false statement "was made with actual intent to deceive or . . . materially affected either the acceptance of the risk or the hazard assumed by the insurer." Section 22:619B applied to life and health or accident insurance. The result may have been influenced by the fact that §22:619A, applying to other kinds of insurance, specifically required the "intent to deceive." Yet the distinction in language between the two companion provisions should have indicated to the court an intended difference in meaning. It may be difficult for the insurer to prove intent to deceive. But Darby v. Safeco Ins. Co., 545 So. 2d 1022 (La. 1989), while finding that there was no intent to

deceive in the particular case, did say that the requirements of proof by the insurer had been relaxed so that intent was to be proved by considering the surrounding circumstances. Under the New York statute, scienter is not required, only materiality. Slevin v. Amex Life Assurance Co., 695 F. Supp. 712 (E.D.N.Y. 1988).

B. Waiver, Estoppel, Election, Reformation

Even an otherwise operative breach of warranty, failure of condition, or misrepresentation does not necessarily conclude the argument. In particular there must usually be reliance by the insurer, which is impossible if the insurer is charged with knowledge of the facts.

A full illustration of the detailed working out of the dialectic discussed at the beginning of this chapter with all its nuances requires a great deal of case law. The first stage is treated at length in this book in the various chapters on the coverage of various kinds of policies. The second stage has already been treated in a number of cases and will appear from time to time in others. The third stage is treated in the following cases, which demonstrate some factors that have seemed relevant to the courts as they decided whether to find that an insured could recover despite a presumptively good defense.

CANAL INS. CO. v. ALDRICH

489 F. Supp. 157 (S.D. Ga. 1980)

Bowen, District Judge.

[The plaintiff moved for summary judgment in its action for declaratory judgment as to collision coverage.]

The plaintiff issued an automobile insurance contract to the defendant Haldean Aldrich, d/b/a Aldrich and Hendrix on February 4, 1977. The language of the policy limits coverage to events taking place within a 300-mile radius of defendants' place of business in Brooklet, Georgia. On May 17 or May 18, 1977, Aldrich called Carl Reddick, the soliciting insurance agent to request that the mileage limitation be removed. Reddick notified plaintiff's general agent, C. A. Hottell & Associates, and a change endorsement was issued effective May 31, 1977 at 5:05 p.m.

Approximately two hours prior to the effective time of this change, one of defendant's vehicles covered by the policy was involved in a collision in North Carolina, beyond the 300-mile radius. Defendants contend that this accident was covered under the terms of the policy as modified by the conversation with Reddick. Plaintiff maintains that the request for extended coverage did not effectuate such coverage until authorized by C. A. Hottel & Associates by written endorsement. Thus, the issue involved in this case is a simple one: when did unlimited mileage coverage become a part of the insurance contract?

Georgia Code Section 56-2420(1) states:

> Binders or other contracts for temporary insurance may be made orally or in writing, and shall be deemed to include all the usual terms of the policy as to which the binder was given together with such applicable endorsements as are designated in the binder, except as superseded by the clear and express terms of the binder.

The Georgia Court of Appeals has held that oral orders by an insured for a change of coverage is in the nature of a binder and enforceable under this code section. See Allstate Insurance Company v. Reynolds, 138 Ga. App. 582, 227 S.E.2d 77 (1976). However, the policy issued on February 4, 1977, in this case contained the following paragraph:

> *Changes:* Notice to any agent or knowledge possessed by any agent or by any other person shall not effect a waiver or a change in any part of this policy or estop the company from asserting any right under the terms of this policy; nor shall the terms of this policy be waived or changed except by endorsement issued to form a part of this policy.

Provisions of this sort have been addressed by the Georgia courts in several cases. . . .

Under the principles cited in these Georgia cases, Reddick had no power to orally modify the terms of the insurance policy. According to the conditions set forth in the policy itself, any change required the issuance of an endorsement. The endorsement providing extended mileage coverage did not become effective until two hours after the collision. The 300-mile radius limitation was in effect at the time.

The courts have no more right or power to extend coverage of a policy or to make it more beneficial to the insured than they do to rewrite the contract and increase the coverage. Prudential Insurance Company v. Kellar, 213 Ga. 453, 99 S.E.2d 823 (1957). There was no coverage under the terms of the policy in effect at the time of the collision. Accordingly, plaintiff's motion for summary judgment is hereby granted. . . .

Notes and Questions

1. Is there anything incongruous in the result in *Aldrich* when the agent had the power to bind the company orally?

2. Why would the insurer give such broad power to the agent and then limit it by the nonwaiver clause?

REPUBLIC INS. CO. v. SILVERTON ELEVATORS

493 S.W.2d 748 (Tex. 1973)

DANIEL, Justice.

This suit was brought by Respondents, Silverton Elevators, Inc. and Carl L. Tidwell, against Petitioner, Republic Insurance Company, to recover under a Texas Standard Fire Policy issued to Silverton Elevators by Republic covering a residential dwelling and household goods contained therein. In a non-jury trial, Silverton was awarded $3,000 "for the use and benefit" of Carl L. Tidwell for the loss of the household goods. The Court of Civil Appeals affirmed. 477 S.W.2d 336. We affirm.

Carl L. Tidwell was at all times material to this controversy, an officer, director and the general manager of Silverton Elevators, Inc. Silverton owned and furnished to Tidwell a house near its elevators, together with the insurance on the house and on Tidwell's household goods, as part of his compensation as general manager. Since 1964, Republic's local agent had issued and renewed insurance policies in the name of Silverton covering the dwelling and its household goods. It is undisputed that the local agent, who had authority to issue the policies and receive the premiums, knew that the household goods belonged to Tidwell and that Silverton was carrying the insurance for the benefit of Tidwell. On April 17, 1970, a tornado destroyed the house and the household goods.

On the date of the tornado there was in effect a Texas Standard Fire Policy with Extended Coverage on DWELLING & HOUSEHOLD GOODS in the sum of $10,000 issued by Republic to Silverton for the period of April 20, 1969 to April 20, 1972, insuring against loss from windstorm the specifically described "occupied dwelling" for $7,000 and "household goods . . . while in the described building" for $3,000.00. It is undisputed that Silverton paid the $227.00 premium, and the local agent admitted that at the time he issued the policy he knew the facts heretofore mentioned with respect to actual ownership of the insured property. He testified that he wrote the policy to cover Tidwell's household goods located in the dwelling which Tidwell and his family occupied; that he knew Silverton was carrying the policy on the household goods for the benefit of Tidwell; that when he issued the policy he did not think it made any difference that it was in the name of Silverton because "they were paying the premium;" and that he told Tidwell that the policy covered his household goods both before and after the tornado.

Republic acknowledged coverage on the house and paid Silverton $7,000 for its damage, but it denied any liability to Silverton or Tidwell on the household goods. Thereupon, Silverton and Tidwell brought this suit against Republic claiming coverage to the limit of the policy ($3,000) on the household goods owned by Tidwell. Republic defended on the grounds that Silverton had no ownership and therefore no insurable interest in the household goods and that the policy as written was limited by its terms to household goods owned by Silverton Elevators, Inc., the named insured.

Silverton and Tidwell's pleadings asserted that they both had insurable interests; that the insurance was purchased by Silverton and extended to Tidwell as part of his compensation as manager and as "a legal representative of Silverton Elevators, Inc.;" and that when Republic issued its policy and accepted premiums with full knowledge of the true ownership and relations between Silverton and Tidwell, it waived the right to complain about any lack of ownership or insurable interest of the named insured and was estopped from denying coverage on behalf of Tidwell. As heretofore indicated, the trial court awarded Silverton Elevators $3,000 "for the use and benefit of Carl L. Tidwell."

Since the policy refers to and clearly purports to cover the household goods located in the specifically described dwelling, we agree with the Court of Civil Appeals that the knowledge of Tidwell's ownership of the household goods by Republic's local agent and his actions with respect thereto were imputed to and binding upon Republic. Issuance of the policy and collection of the premiums with such knowledge operates as a waiver of any requirement that the named insured own or possess a beneficial interest in the insured property.

In the above cases, the named insureds were not the owners or sole owners of the insured properties. In each case, the true owner was known to the insurance agent and was allowed direct recovery, or recovery for his benefit, on the grounds that the insurance company had waived warranties of sole ownership or lack of insurable interest. There is no conflict between the above cases and those which hold that waiver and estoppel cannot operate to bring within the terms of a policy liabilities or benefits which were expressly excepted therefrom, such as liability from injuries due to gunshot wounds in Washington Natl. Ins. Co. v. Craddock, 130 Tex. 251, 109 S.W.2d 165 (1937); loss for injuries while in military service in time of war, as in Ruddock v. Detroit Life Ins. Co., 209 Mich. 638, 177 N.W. 242 (1920); or payment of benefits beyond a specified termination date at age 65, as in Great

American Reserve Ins. Co. v. Mitchell, 335 S.W.2d 707 (Tex. Civ. App. 1960, writ ref.). The latter cases recognize that waiver and estoppel may operate to avoid forfeiture of coverage and benefits stated in the policy, but not to add specifically excluded risks or to enlarge the benefits or risks therein set forth. In the present case, plaintiffs seek to recover only on the risk assumed by Republic under the terms of the written policy. Republic's policy insured against the destruction of precisely the same household goods identified in its policy and for which it collected its premiums. There is no evidence that its risk was enlarged because the household goods were owned by Tidwell rather than Silverton. . . .

[We] hold that the portion of the clause relating to limitation of liability to "the interest of the insured" falls within the category of ownership provisions which may be waived; the insurer may be estopped from denying liability to the true owner on policies issued in the names of third parties covering the risks on identified property with full knowledge by the company that the property is actually owned by the one for whose benefit the policy was written or maintained.

Republic insists that reformation of the policy is the only proper remedy, if any, for recovery by Silverton on behalf of Tidwell, because of failure of the written policy to identify the household goods as belonging to Tidwell. We disagree. As heretofore indicated, under the undisputed facts, the household goods described in the policy belonged to Tidwell and were insured by Silverton for his benefit in a policy drawn by Republic's agent for such purpose, with assurances from the agent that it would cover Tidwell's furniture. If this was a mistake, it was made by Republic's agent, and it was mutual, because Tidwell and Silverton took the agent's word that it expressed the true agreement. With this evidence being fully developed in the present record, there is no reason to require another trial for reformation of the written policy. It has been held that even without a plea for reformation, when the facts show the true agreement intended and a mutual mistake, or mistake of the agent, in preparing the written policy, the agreement intended will be enforced without going through the formal proceedings of reformation.

Silverton and Tidwell made every proof in this case that would entitle recovery on the policy as written. [T]he trial court and Court of Civil Appeals have properly held that Silverton is entitled to recover for the benefit of Tidwell on the written policy without seeking a reformation thereof.

Accordingly, the judgments of the lower courts are affirmed. . . .

WALKER, Justice (dissenting). . . .

The net effect of the majority holding is to extend the policy coverage and create an entirely different contract by waiver or estoppel. That is contrary, of course, to the established rule in Texas and most other jurisdictions.

As pointed out by the Supreme Court of Michigan in Ruddock v. Detroit Life Ins. Co., 209 Mich. 638, 177 N.W. 242, "to apply the doctrine of estoppel and waiver here would make this contract of insurance cover a loss it never covered by its terms, to create a liability not created by the contract and never assumed by the defendant under the terms of the policy." Neither doctrine can properly be made to serve that purpose. In Great American Reserve Ins. Co. v. Mitchell, Tex. Civ. App., 335 S.W.2d 707 (wr. ref.), the court reviewed the authorities and correctly stated the Texas rule as follows. . . .

> Waiver and estoppel may operate to avoid a forfeiture of a policy, but they have consistently been denied operative force to change, re-write and enlarge the risks covered by a policy. In other words, waiver and estoppel can not create a new and different contract with respect to risks covered by the policy. This has been the settled law in Texas since the decision in Washington Nat. Ins. Co. v. Craddock, 130 Tex. 251, 109 S.W.2d 165, 113 A.L.R. 854.

None of the cases cited in support of the waiver holding is pertinent here. Most of them involved the so-called sole and unconditional ownership clause, which provided that the entire policy would be void if the interest of the insured was other than sole and unconditional ownership* Others involved a stipulation that the policy would be void in case of a change of ownership† unless otherwise provided by agreement endorsed on the policy. . . .

It is my opinion that respondents are not entitled to recover on the policy as written, and that is all they have attempted to do thus far. Tidwell may show his right to recover by offering evidence and obtaining findings that establish mutual mistake and the terms of the true agreement. See Aetna Ins. Co. v. Brannon, 99 Tex. 391, 89 S.W. 1057. The trial court would then be in position to enter a judgment based on the coverage actually agreed upon and intended by the parties. It would also be in position to insure that petitioner receives the appropriate premium for the risk actually assumed. I would reverse the judgments of the courts below and remand the cause in the interest of justice.

GREENHILL, C. J., and POPE and REAVLEY, JJ., join in this dissent.

Notes and Questions

1. The dissent in *Silverton Elevators* says that "[t]he net effect of the majority holding is to extend the policy coverage and create an

---

*For discussion of this "moral hazard" clause, see Chapter 3.
†This clause had the same history as the "sole and unconditional ownership" clause.

entirely different contract by waiver or estoppel. That is contrary, of course, to the established rule in Texas and most other jurisdictions." If the established rule is what the dissent says it is, can the majority decision be right?

2. Is your answer to the previous question a way to reconcile *Aldrich* and *Silverton Elevators?*

3. Difficult policy questions are raised by the roles of agents and brokers in insurance transactions. See the Appendix for a description of the various relationships between companies and marketing intermediaries. A question that repeatedly arises in insurance litigation is how far the insurance company is bound by the words and acts of an agent who has exceeded his or her authority. (Obviously, no problem arises if the agent is acting within the bounds of the authority granted by the company.) Stating general principles or rules is difficult, but some attempt should be made to establish patterns in the cases you see.

HARR v. ALLSTATE INS. CO.

54 N.J. 287, 255 A.2d 208 (1969)

HALL, J.

This is an action against an insurer to recover for water damage to certain business merchandise stored in the basement of plaintiffs' dwelling. Their theory is that, although neither a homeowner's policy nor a fire insurance policy issued by defendant covered the peril causing the loss, the insurer is estopped to deny coverage under the fire policy by reason of a contrary representation made by its agent and relied on by plaintiffs to their detriment.

The trial court, sitting without a jury, granted defendant's motion for involuntary dismissal at the end of plaintiffs' proofs as to liability, holding that in a suit at law, as distinct from an action in equity to reform a policy, statements made by the insurer's agent at the inception of the contract, which had been received in evidence, could not be considered to broaden the coverage of the policy because of the parol evidence rule. The Appellate Division affirmed, 99 N.J. Super. 90, 238 A.2d 688 (1968), although on a different basis. It decided that a defense of non-coverage could be barred by the doctrine of equitable estoppel on appropriate facts, in which event the parol evidence rule would be irrelevant. It found, however, upon exercise of its fact-finding appellate jurisdiction, that there was insufficient proof both of representation of coverage by the agent and of reliance by plaintiffs. . . .

Mr. Harr was in the business of selling and servicing beer and soft drink dispensing equipment and for some years had conducted that business from his home in Essex Fells. In connection with it, he stored in the basement mixing valves, refrigeration equipment, regulators, syrup tanks, cooling plates and the like for replacement parts. In the middle of January 1963, he went to Florida for a vacation and was away from home six or seven weeks. During February a water pipe in the basement of the house burst, cascading some 90,000 gallons of water through that area, and seriously damaging the structure, certain household and personal effects, and the stored merchandise. A claim was made upon the defendant for the entire loss, and it finally paid $12,062.13 under the homeowner's policy for damage to the building and the household and personal effects, but denied liability under either policy for damage to the merchandise on the ground of non-coverage.

In 1961 Mr. Harr had changed insurance agents and, to replace a homeowner's policy that was expiring in another company, procured a similar contract from defendant through a Mr. Meinsohn, who, it was stipulated, was its agent. . . .

The day before Mr. Harr left for Florida in January 1963, he telephoned Mr. Meinsohn and asked whether he could "cover" the merchandise in the basement, which he described, in the amount of $15,000. Meinsohn replied that he would find out and would call plaintiff back. He did so the same day and, according to Harr's testimony Meinsohn said "Mr. Harr, we can cover you for $7500 and you are *fully covered*. Go to Florida . . . and have a good time." (Emphasis supplied). Mr. Meinsohn told him the amount of the premium and asked for a check, which was immediately sent. Harr did not receive the contract — the fire insurance policy previously referred to — before he left for Florida, but testified that he took Meinsohn's word that he was "fully covered" because "I felt I had confidence in him."

There is nothing in the evidence to indicate that the two men discussed or even mentioned what perils the policy insured against. Mr. Harr was not asked, as he might well have been, what he expected or what he understood was meant by Mr. Meinsohn's assertion that he was "fully covered." We think it a fair inference, however, that he would expect, and reasonably so, coverage for the same perils of physical damage included in the homeowner's policy, and that he could justifiably construe "fully covered" as so indicating. We further believe that Mr. Meinsohn should be held to have understood that his use of the phrase "fully covered" would convey that impression to Mr. Harr, in absence of an express statement by him that this peril was not covered, since he had written the homeowner's policy and also must be said to realize that the possibility of water damage from bursting pipes to personal property in a basement is a common peril against which protection would be desired and expected. . . .

The fire policy, while not as lengthy as the homeowner's contract, would nevertheless be confusing and abstruse to the average person. The heading "Fire Insurance Policy" is itself something of a misnomer these days, when almost all such contracts, including this one, insure against, and are generally known to cover, some additional perils. The general insuring clause on the first page insurers ". . . against all Direct Loss by Fire, Lightning and by Removal from Premises Endangered by the Perils Insured Against In this Policy, Except as Hereinafter Provided." Confusion as to coverage begins with the next sentence, which reads

> INSURANCE IS PROVIDED AGAINST ONLY THOSE PERILS AND FOR ONLY THOSE COVERAGES INDICATED BELOW BY A PRE-MIUM CHARGE AND AGAINST OTHER PERILS AND FOR OTHER COVERAGES ONLY WHEN ENDORSED HEREON OR ADDED HERETO. . . .

The only reference to bursting water pipes is a negative one, found in similar language on both sides of the sheet in the paragraphs defining losses covered by explosion. It is stated that rupture or bursting of water pipes is not an explosion within the intent and meaning of the explosion provisions. Ambiguity arises, however, because another paragraph in the extended coverage endorsement entitled "WATER EXCLUSION CLAUSE" declares that the company shall not be liable for loss occasioned by various specified kinds of water occurrences (unless loss by fire or explosion ensues) and water from bursting pipes is not listed as one of the excluded occurrences. A person could conceivably believe that loss from other water occurrences, including bursting pipes, was covered. While thorough examination of all the attached sheet provisions convinces us that there is no coverage in such event, we do not believe that the average person, if he could struggle through the fine print and uncommon verbiage, could reasonably be said to be so alerted. . . .

II

We turn to the principal legal question in the case — whether, in an action at law on an insurance policy, equitable estoppel may operate to bring within its coverage risks or perils which are not provided for, or which are expressly excluded.

The courts of this state early held that estoppel was not available at law if the estopping conduct occurred before or at the inception of the contract. While the complete separation between law and equity, which remained in this state until 1948, undoubtedly contributed to this view, the main thesis of the cases was that an insurance policy was no different from any other integrated written contract between knowledgeable and sophisticated parties, and the parol evidence rule was thus held a bar to proofs which would vary the terms of the instrument. . . .

The idea of estoppel *in pais* was cast aside as nothing more than a mere evasion of the parol evidence rule. . . .

New Jersey insureds have therefore been largely remitted to the rather strict remedy of reformation where the estopping conduct arose before or at the inception of the contract or perhaps, before 1948 as indicated in one case, to a collateral proceeding in chancery to enjoin the insurer from setting up the claimed breach at law by reason of its inequitable conduct. See Giammares v. Allemania Fire Insurance Co., 89 N.J. Eq. 460, 105 A. 611 (Ch. 1918), *rev'd on factual grounds*, 91 N.J. Eq. 114, 108 A. 237 (E. & A. 1919). But reformation, with its rigid requirements, including among other things that the proofs be clear, convincing and free from doubt, is frequently of no help, even though parol evidence is admissible in such cases. Again [Vance, Handbook on the Law of Insurance (3d ed. 1951)], referring as examples to the opinion of the Court of Errors and Appeals in *Giammares*, and Koch v. Commonwealth Ins. Co., 87 N.J. Eq. 90, 99 A. 920 (Ch. 1917), *affirmed o. b.* 88 N.J. Eq. 344, 102 A. 1053 (E. & A. 1917), succinctly summarized the difficulty:

> The equitable remedy of reformation is not sufficiently broad to be available in securing the results arrived at under the rule of equitable estoppel. It frequently happens that evidence, that is sufficient to show clearly such inequitable conduct on the part of the insurer as to estop him from setting up a breach of condition, falls short of that certainty that is required to prove the terms of a contract which a court of equity is asked to substitute, by reformation, in place of the one actually executed. . . . It is not at all impossible that the insurer intended to make the contract exactly as written, though knowing that as so written it imposed no enforceable duty upon him and that he was taking the insured's premium money without rendering any consideration therefor. Upon proof of such a state of facts, there is no intended agreement which the court can substitute for that executed. But there is an estoppel which will preclude the insurer from profiting by his fraud. . . ." (Id. at p.471, n.3).

Professor Clarence Morris penetratingly analyzed the reason for the development of equitable estoppel, as well as waiver, in the insurance field in his article, Waiver and Estoppel in Insurance Policy Litigation, 105 U. Pa. L. Rev. 925 (1957):

> Indexes to the great nineteenth century insurance texts do not list waiver and estoppel. But times have changed. The 1951 third edition of

Vance on Insurance enfolds an excellent and important seventy-six page 'Waiver & Estoppel' chapter — about a fourteenth of the book's bulk. What has fostered this growth in the last hundred years? My thesis is that waiver and estoppel are two of several guises that cloak the courts' part in changing insurance from a service safely bought only by sophisticated businessmen to a commodity bought with confidence by untrained consumers. Judges, at the urging of policyholders' advocates, have used waiver and estoppel to convert insurance from a custom-made document designed in part by knowing buyers to a brand-name staple sold over the counter by mine-run salesmen to the trusting public.

Seventeenth and eighteenth century marine insurance contracts were handwritten; hull and cargo owners and their brokers knew insurance as thoroughly as the underwriters. When a marine policy buyer entertained a proposal of a warranty, he bargained for important premium concessions and knew the courts would construe the warranty strictly against him. American draftsmen-lawyers, sometimes in the hire of fly-by-night companies, proliferated fine print in the nineteenth century fire and life insurance policies. Companies, spurred by competition, debased their product (as the Germans did their linen). Restrictions on coverage, not noticed or not understood by policyholders at the time of issue, became painfully clear after uncovered losses which policyholders would have paid to cover. The insurance market might have soured had not the law stepped in and afforded consumer protection greater than companies intended to sell.

Of course this process of favoring consumers can be carried too far. Insurance companies need and are entitled to reasonable limits on their responsibilities; the public is prejudiced when company liabilities are by generous caprice stretched over risks that cannot be profitably underwritten at a just premium. By and large, however, the courts have not been overgenerous to the public. Judges have limited their use of the doctrines of waiver and estoppel because of their awareness of important underwriting realities. (Id. at pp. 925-926).

It is clear that this court's approach to defenses to claims on insurance contracts has changed very substantially in recent years. Our expressions have come in a variety of issues and contexts, but all have indicated as their keystone the goal of greater protection to the ordinary policyholder untutored in the intricacies of insurance. We have realistically faced up to the fact that insurance policies are complex contracts of adhesion, prepared by the insurer, not subject to negotiation, in the case of the average person, as to terms and provisions and quite unintelligible to the insured even were he to attempt to read and understand their unfamiliar and technical language and awkward and unclear arrangement. Recognition is given to the usual and justifiable reliance by the purchaser on the agent, because of his special knowledge, to obtain the protection he desires and needs, and on the agent's representations, whether that agent be a so-called "independent" but authorized representative of the insurer, or only an employee. We have stressed, among other things, the aim that average purchasers of insurance are entitled to the broad measure of protection necessary to fulfill their reasonable expectations; that it is the insurer's burden to obtain, through its representatives, all information pertinent to the risk and the desired coverage before the contract is issued; and that it is likewise its obligation to make policy provisions, especially those relating to coverage, exclusions and vital conditions, plain, clear and prominent to the layman. . . .

Although we have not previously passed upon the question here involved, we have no hesitation in deciding, in line with the rationale just outlined, that, speaking broadly, equitable estoppel is available to bar a defense in an action on a policy even where the estopping conduct arose before or at the inception of the contract, and that the parol evidence rule does not apply in such situations. The contrary holding of Dewees v. Manhattan Insurance Co., [35 N.J.L. 366 (Sup. Ct. 1872)] and Franklin Fire Insurance Co. v. Martin, [40 N.J.L. 568 (E. & A. 1878)] and their progeny can no longer be considered to be the law of this state.

However, many jurisdictions which have long followed this view nevertheless hold that equitable estoppel is not available to broaden the *coverage* of a policy so as to protect the insured against risks not included therein or expressly excluded therefrom, as distinct from alleviation of other limitations or conditions of the contract. . . .

While there is a clear split of authority, with the decisions holding estoppel not available to broaden coverage presently representing the majority view, many of the cases so stating are confusing and not clear cut. Estoppel and waiver are often interchangeably and improperly used, and in many cases where estoppel is held unavailable the necessary elements have not been made out anyway, or the insured by reason of his own conduct is clearly not entitled to relief. The reasons generally advanced in support of the majority view are that a court cannot create a new contract for the parties, that an insurer should not be required by estoppel to pay a loss for which it charged no premium, and perhaps that a risk or peril should not be imposed upon an insurer which it might have declined.

We are more impressed with the decisions in those jurisdictions which hold that equitable estoppel is utilizable to bar a defense of noncoverage of the loss claimed, i.e., the minority rule. The following cases, arising in various contexts, are illustrative. . . .

These decisions all proceed on the thesis that where an insurer or its agent misrepresents, even though innocently, the coverage of an insurance contract, or the exclusions therefrom, to an insured before or at the inception of the contract, and the insured reasonably relies thereupon to his ultimate detriment, the insurer is estopped to deny coverage after a loss on a risk or from a peril actually not covered by the terms of the policy. The proposition is one of elementary and simple justice. By justifiably relying on the insurer's superior knowledge, the insured has been prevented from procuring the desired coverage elsewhere. To reject this approach because a new contract is thereby made for the parties would be an unfortunate triumph of form over substance. The fact that the insurer has received no premium for the risk or peril as to which the loss ensued is no obstacle. Any additional premium due can be deducted from the amount of the loss. If the insurer is saddled with coverage it may not have intended or desired, it is of its own making, because of its responsibility for the acts and representations of its employees and agents. It alone has the capacity to guard against such a result by the proper selection, training and supervision of its representatives. Of course, the burden of proof of equitable estoppel rests on the insured and, since evidence of representations is almost always oral, a trial court must be convinced that the requisite elements have been established by reliable proof and that the insured has met his burden by a fair preponderance of the evidence. . . .

III

In the light of what has just been said, we shall now consider the precise issue before us: Whether plaintiffs made out a sufficient case of equitable estoppel to withstand the motion for involuntary dismissal and to require defendant to go forward with its proofs. . . .

[U]nder the proofs and inferences as they exist at this posture of the case, we conclude plaintiffs made a sufficient showing of reliance to defeat the dismissal motion. That such reliance was to their detriment is obvious. All the elements of equitable estoppel were consequently *prima facie* established.

The judgment of the Appellate Division which is the subject of the cross-appeal is affirmed; its judgment on the main appeal is reversed and the case is remanded to the Law Division for a new trial.

Notes and Questions

1. Professor Clarence Morris, quoted in *Harr*, says that "Companies, spurred by competition, debased their product (as the Germans did their linen)." Does that statement accurately describe the way competition works in a well-functioning market? In any event, the factual accuracy of his premise is doubtful. There came to be no

competition at all on policy terms (and little on premiums) when standard fire insurance policies were enacted by all legislatures in the late nineteenth century and little variation from state to state, since New York's version of the policy was adopted in all but a few states.

2. Professor Morris talks of waiver and estoppel converting a custom-made document into a brand name staple. Isn't the opposite true? Reflect on the posture of the ordinary consumer arguing that the insurer has "waived" a provision of its policy that has been carefully drafted for mass consumption or is "estopped" to assert a defense contained in that same policy.

3. In this much cited article, Professor Morris has, however, made the case for the difficulty of rationalizing waiver and estoppel cases across policy lines and infinitely differing circumstances.

McCOLLUM v. CONTINENTAL CASUALTY CO.

151 Ariz. 492, 728 P.2d 1242 (1986)

CORCORAN, Judge.

[After deciding that the insurer's defense was not effective to avoid the policy in any event, the Arizona Supreme Court went on to discuss, in dictum, the possible applicability of waiver and estoppel.]

Even if we were to hold that Battersby had a legal duty to disclose the McCollums' suit to Continental once he learned of its existence, the doctrines of waiver and estoppel would prevent Continental from prevailing in this action.

> Waiver, either express or implied, has been defined as the voluntary and intentional relinquishment or abandonment of a known right. It is unilateral in that it arises out of either action or nonaction on the part of the insurer or its duly authorized agents and rests upon circumstances indicating or inferring that the relinquishment of the right was voluntarily intended by the insurer with full knowledge of all of the facts pertaining thereto.
>
> Estoppel, on the other hand, refers to a preclusion from asserting a right by an insurer where it would be inequitable to permit the assertion. It arises by operation of law, and rests upon acts, statements or conduct on the part of the insurer or its agents which lead or induce the insured, in justifiable reliance thereon, to act or forbear to act to his prejudice. Abatement of the right or privilege involved by way of estoppel need not be intentionally, voluntarily or purposely effected by or on the part of the insurer.

Buchanan v. Switzerland Gen. Ins. Co., 76 Wash. 2d 100, 108, 455 P.2d 344, 349 (1969) (citations omitted). Despite these generally recognizable distinctions between waiver and estoppel, the two terms are often employed in insurance law as synonyms and used indiscriminately. American Natl. Ins. Co. v. Cooper, 169 Colo. 420, 425, 458 P.2d 257, 260 (1969).

Continental learned of the McCollums' suit in June 1981, and yet it retained and continued to accept premiums from Battersby. When an insurer has knowledge of facts allegedly justifying a denial of coverage or the forfeiture of a policy previously issued, an unequivocal act that recognizes the continued existence of the policy or an act wholly inconsistent with a prior denial of coverage constitutes a waiver thereof. See Greber v. Equitable Life Assur. Socy., 43 Ariz. 1, 28 P.2d 817 (1934). Continental's retention of Battersby's premiums was such an act. See Glens Falls Indem. Co. v. D.A. Swanstrom Co., 203 Minn. 68, 73, 279 N.W. 845, 847 (1938); 16C J. Appleman, Insurance Law and Practice §9303 (rev. ed. 1981); 45 C.J.S. Insurance §716(b) (1946).

An insurer cannot treat a policy as void for the purpose of denying coverage, and at the same time treat it as valid for the purpose of retaining premiums collected thereon. See Collier v. General Exch. Ins. Corp., 58 Ariz. 122, 118 P.2d 74 (1941); *Glens Falls Indem. Co.*, 203 Minn. at 73, 279 N.W. at 847 (the insurer is "not privileged 'to run with the hare and hold with the hounds' until such time as it should become plain on which side its advantage lay"). Continental is barred by both waiver and estoppel from avoiding its obligations under the policy. . . .

Judgment affirmed.

Notes and Questions

1. *Election* is sometimes a useful alternative to either waiver or estoppel. If an insurer must choose between two inconsistent courses of action, one recognizing that a contract is effective and the other denying it, taking the former action can be called an election and should bind the insurer. Could the insurer's conduct in *McCollum* usefully be called an election? For another case in which acceptance of late premiums kept a policy in force, see Cormier v. Lone Star Life Ins. Co., 500 So. 2d 431 (La. App. 1986). But see American Crown Life Ins. Co. v. Dickson, 748 F. Supp. 184 (S.D.N.Y. 1990) for a case in which subsequent acceptance of a late premium did not constitute waiver (or election).

2. In Gulf Trading, Inc. v. New Hampshire Ins. Co., 521 N.Y.S.2d 417, 135 A.D.2d 356 (as amended 1988), the insurer insisted on an extensive investigation of goods lost from a warehouse, pursuant to the contract. The court said that "by exercising a right granted by the

policy, that is, an extensive investigation of the claim, defendant New Hampshire recognized the validity of the policy itself and was estopped to deny its validity." Id. at 418, 135 A.D.2d at 357. Perhaps the court might better have called this election, but the case shows the overlapping of these concepts.

3. The problems of waiver, estoppel, and related doctrines come in almost infinite variety. Initially results were based on technical contract doctrine, but in the insurance context doctrine has been subordinated to policy, as Morris's seminal article quoted in *Harr* points out. What is the doctrinal framework on which waiver and estoppel cases were originally hung? How significantly does doctrine constrain courts deciding waiver and estoppel cases? Does the addition of election and reformation to the court's arsenal expand its power to produce desired results? Despite the fact-sensitivity of the cases and the difficulty of manipulating the doctrines, some generalizations may be possible, based on large numbers of cases.

4. The proposition that neither waiver nor estoppel can *create* coverage is sometimes ignored but is still good law, at least in general. What does that mean? Was coverage created in any of the preceding cases? Standard Fire Ins. Co. v. Marine Contracting and Towing Co., 392 S.E.2d 460 (S.C. 1990), held on a motion for summary judgment that coverage could be created by estoppel if the insurer misled the policyholder into thinking there was coverage.

5. If misrepresentation of full coverage by an agent does not suffice to create coverage under the policy, as is often true, it still may make the *agent* liable even if the misrepresentation is merely negligent. See Runia v. Marguth Agency, Inc., 437 N.W.2d 45 (Minn. 1989). This is less favorable to the plaintiff than a doctrine permitting recovery from the insurer, for agents are less likely to be able to satisfy large judgments. But they often do have professional liability insurance (errors and omissions insurance).

6. Estoppel is delictual; it depends on reliance. Waiver is consensual, if not contractual. In Cameron v. Frances Slocum Bank & Trust Co., 628 F. Supp. 966 (N.D. Ind. 1986), the court, applying Indiana law, held that there must be consideration for an effective waiver, thus making it a matter of contract. The insurer had disclaimed coverage under a fire policy because the building had been unoccupied and vacant for more than 60 days at the time of the fire, which under the language of the standard fire insurance policy suspended the coverage. The claimed ground for waiver or estoppel was that the company's agent, knowing the true facts, filled out the application and recommended issuing the policy. There was no consideration to support waiver, nor was there reliance or changed position to support estoppel. An alleged waiver given so little scope seems no more than an incipient

estoppel, awaiting reliance to become effective. The trial court gave summary judgment to the insurer. The reviewing court reversed on the ground that there were controverted facts essential to the decision; the question whether waiver requires consideration was not mentioned. Id., 824 F.2d 570 (7th Cir. 1987).

7. The willingness of courts to find an effective waiver or estoppel seems to depend in part on the importance of the provision waived. Certain requirements in the policy are treated cavalierly by the courts. The requirement of prompt notice of loss is often excused unless the insurer is prejudiced. Is that akin to waiver or estoppel? The result is often cast as a matter of policy interpretation. See Chapter 1. But the usual requirement that any suit against the insurer must be brought within a specified period, most often 12 months, is less frequently excused. Aldalali v. Underwriters at Lloyd's, London, 174 Mich. App. 395, 435 N.W.2d 498 (1989), while saying that the insured "must strictly comply with time periods set out in an insurance policy for filing notice of a claim and proof of loss" would toll the limitation period "from the date that the insured gives notice of the loss until liability is formally denied by the insurance company." The statement was dictum but there is no reason not to give it credence.

Problem

Under the contemporary "bad faith" doctrine (see Chapter 8), the stakes have suddenly become larger in cases involving warranty and misrepresentation, as well as waiver and estoppel. A homeowners insurer declined to pay a fire loss on the insured's home when it discovered that the insured responded "no" to the question "have you . . . ever been convicted of a crime?", despite convictions of ten crimes in the prior eight years, seven of which were property crimes involving dishonesty. The insured responded with a suit for damages, including punitive damages for a bad faith refusal to pay. The underwriter who approved the issuance of the policy testified that he would have declined the application had he known of the crime. The jury found for the insured on the basis of evidence that the company had issued an automobile policy to the insured despite knowledge of a DWI (or DUI) conviction, even though the insured had denied any arrests for offenses other than traffic violations. The jury awarded damages on the contract plus $20,000 in punitive damages. The federal district court denied a motion for judgment n.o.v. How should the court rule on appeal? See Conner v. Shelter Mut. Ins. Co., 779 F.2d 335 (6th Cir. 1985), *cert. denied*, 476 U.S. 1117 (1986).

C.   The Doctrines in Life and Health Insurance

The application of the common law of misrepresentation, breach of warranty, and concealment to life and health insurance differs strikingly from its application to other lines for several reasons. One reason is the different extent to which legislatures have intervened. Another is the incontestable clause, which is applied universally in life insurance and often in health insurance. A third is the greater difficulty in achieving precision in making statements about the condition of one's health, about which misrepresentations would most often have to be made in order to be material. (Sometimes occupation or avocation might also be material, as in the case of structural steel workers and recreational flyers, but the majority of cases deal with misstatements about or concealment of facts relating to the insured's health.) During the contestable period the traditional doctrines would presumptively apply, subject to modification by applicable statute and case law. Statutes need to be examined carefully for applicability. For the incontestable clause, see *infra*, this chapter.

The countervailing doctrines of estoppel, warranty, election, and reformation apply in much the same way as in property insurance, though with differences reflecting the nature of the information represented.

1.   Misrepresentations in Life and Health Insurance

USLIFE CREDIT LIFE INS. CO. v. McAFEE

29 Wash. App. 574, 630 P.2d 450 (1981)

ANDERSEN, Judge.

Facts of Case

Gerald D. McAfee, beneficiary of insurance on his late wife's life, appeals from a judgment rescinding certain insurance policies and certificates on her life on the basis of fraud.

McAfee, an insurance agent, learned that his wife was suffering from terminal cancer. Thereupon he bought a number of credit life insurance policies and certificates insuring her life (as well as his own) in insurance companies which did not require a good health statement or health information of any kind from prospective insureds. Two of the certificates were written in a company at a time when he was an insurance agent for the company.

Following a trial to the court, detailed findings of fact and conclusions of law were entered. In its findings, the trial court explained credit life insurance as follows:

> Credit Life Insurance is life insurance issued on the life of the debtor. It is normally sold by a lending institution or a retail outlet. It requires that there be a valid debt, and that the debtor-insured has not reached his 65th birthday, and is generally issued up to the limits of between $12,500 and $15,000 without any medical questions or medical examination. The premium paid by the insured under a credit life policy is shared by the lending institution or retail outlet (which gets 40%) and the insurance carrier (which receives 60%). There would be no substantial cost or effort to credit life insurance carriers to have a written application include one question as to health which will allow complete protection to the carriers in the form of post-claim underwriting. A question of this type was in use at all material times in Washington by plaintiff Pacific Standard Life Insurance Company on its credit life insurance policies for amounts exceeding $15,000. [Finding of fact No. 33.]

Between July 15, 1974 and February 21, 1975, Mr. and Mrs. McAfee were involved in a series of credit transactions, including vehicle leases, for which they obtained credit life insurance coverage. Premiums on this insurance were paid. Each policy was a joint level term policy under which payment was to be made on the death of either party. Mrs. McAfee died of cancer on June 30, 1975.

Most of the 17 transactions at issue in this case involved a loan of money by a bank to the McAfees, the immediate deposit by them of the loan proceeds in a blocked savings account in the same bank as security for the loan and their election of credit life insurance coverage on each loan transaction. Most of the credit life policies were group policies though a few were individual policies. One loan was covered by other collateral and there were three vehicle leases with credit life insurance coverage. Insurance totalling $188,459 was involved in the 17 policies here in issue.

Essentially it was the trial court's conclusion in this case that McAfee had a duty to disclose his wife's terminal illness at the time he purchased the credit life insurance policies and certificates and his failure to do so constituted fraud. On this basis, the monies paid to Mr. McAfee by one insurer were ordered repaid and he was denied the right to recover from the other insurers.

This appeal presents two principal issues.

Issues

ISSUE ONE. Does an applicant for life insurance have a duty to volunteer information to the insurer concerning the applicant's poor health?

ISSUE TWO. Where the applicant for life insurance is at the time an agent for the life insurance company to which application is made, does the applicant in that case have a duty to volunteer information concerning poor health to the prospective insurer?

Decision

Issue One

CONCLUSION. Absent an insurer's request for health information or a statement of good health, a prospective insured is under no duty to volunteer it.

It is the general rule that "when the insurer asks no information in regard to a certain matter, it is a fair assumption that it regards the matter as immaterial." 43 Am. Jur. 2d Insurance §730, at 717 (1969). Accord, 45 C.J.S. Insurance §473(3), at 153 (1946). While it might seem facetious to presume that a life insurer would regard a prospective insured's terminal illness as immaterial, it is not unreasonable to assume that a life insurer which does no underwriting of the risks it insures expects a certain percentage of such poor risks and has adjusted its premiums to compensate for insuring them. Indeed where, as here, the insurers insured any debtor up to age 65 who paid a premium (whether that person was personally seen by the agent or not), and where the premium is the same for everybody regardless of age or health, no other conclusion seems reasonable. Furthermore, it cannot be deemed particularly surprising that a person in poor health would seek out insurance companies that see fit to write life (or health) insurance without having good health requirements of some kind.

Here the trial court's findings are silent as to any health inquiries having been made to the insureds. Numerous authorities stand for the proposition succinctly stated in Graham v. Aetna Ins. Co., 243 S.C. 108, 132 S.E.2d 273, 275, 100 A.L.R.2d 1352 (1963):

> Mere silence on the part of the assured as to a matter not inquired of is not to be considered such a concealment as to avoid the policy. *Aliud est celare, aliud tacere.*

See 9 G. Couch, Insurance §38:72 (2d ed. 1962); 12 J. Appleman, Insurance §7276 (1943); 43 Am. Jur. 2d Insurance §731 (1969).

In upholding coverage under a group insurance policy issued to a quadriplegic who died 14 months after his certificate was written, the Supreme Court of Wisconsin quoted with approval from 9 G. Couch, Insurance §38:58 (2d ed. 1962):

> The insured is not obligated to volunteer statements of every circumstance which anybody may subsequently deem important as affecting the risk upon his life, for it is requisite only that he answer all questions truly, make no untrue statements, and submit himself to a full examination.

Southard v. Occidental Life Ins. Co., 31 Wis. 2d 351, 142 N.W.2d 844, 848 (1966). . . .

Three sections of this state's insurance code are directly pertinent to the issue before us.

One section which pertains specifically to credit life policies and certificates required that a description of the coverage, including the amount and terms thereof, be set out in such policies and certificates along with any exceptions, limitations and restrictions thereto. RCW 48.34.090(2). No health exceptions, limitations or restrictions were set out in any of the policies and certificates in this case.

Another section of the insurance code which pertains to group life insurance (as most of the policies and certificates were in this case) required the insurers to state any conditions under which they reserved the right to require evidence of individual insurability, RCW 48.24.140, and if such evidence was required, provided that it had to appear in a written statement signed by the insured or else it could not be used to contest the validity of the insurance, RCW 48.24.120. No such conditions were stated in the group policies and certificates before us and no signed health statements were requested or given.

Based on the reciprocal obligations of insured and insurer to act in good faith, RCW 48.01.030,[1] the insurers in effect ask that we declare that there is a legal obligation on all life insurance applicants to fully disclose the state of their health to a prospective insurer when the insurer makes no inquiry concerning it.

While the adoption of such a principle might impart a semblance of fairness in a case as unsympathetic appearing as this one, where the husband obtained 17 credit life insurance policies and certificates (totaling $188,459) on his wife's life after learning of her terminal illness, it would, in fact, establish a precedent destructive of much of

---

1. "Public interest. The business of insurance is one affected by the public interest, requiring that all persons be actuated by good faith, abstain from deception, and practice honesty and equity in all insurance matters. Upon the insurer, the insured, and their representatives rests the duty of preserving inviolate the integrity of insurance." RCW 48.01.030.

the insurance consumer protective legislation that has been adopted in this state. Some of these protective statutes are discussed above. Others provide, for example, that insurance applications cannot be admitted in evidence unless attached to the policies so the insured will be sure to see them, RCW 48.18.080, and that no representation by an insured will defeat coverage under a policy unless the representation is material and made with an intent to deceive, RCW 48.18.090.

In short, to impose a duty on every insurance applicant to fully disclose the state of his or her health where the insurer does not request that information would be to build a trap for all purchasers of life and health insurance. Such a holding would be precedent allowing any life or health insurer so inclined, whenever a claim is presented, to use the 20-20 vision of hindsight to seek out prior health problems in order to try and defeat the claim. That is precisely the kind of post-claim underwriting which the statutes herein discussed were designed to prevent. See RCW 48.18.080-.090; RCW 48.24.120; RCW 48.24.140; RCW 48.34.090(2). An insured has the right to have any application or health statement before him or her in order to review or correct it, if necessary, Lundmark v. Mutual of Omaha Ins. Co., 80 Wash. 2d 804, 807, 498 P.2d 867 (1972); and an insurer must require evidence of insurability before the insured's death, not after, Ryan v. Cuna Mut. Ins. Socy., 84 Wash. 2d 612, 615-16, 529 P.2d 7 (1974).

Based on the foregoing principles, and on the credit life insurance policies and certificates in question, we conclude that absent a request for health information or a statement of good health by an insurer, the insured has no duty to provide it. There was no request for such information here, therefore, Mr. and Mrs. McAfee were under no duty to provide it. It follows that the McAfees' failure to provide such health information to the insurers cannot be deemed fraudulent.

Issue Two

CONCLUSION. When the prospective insured or beneficiary is an agent for the insurer at the time the insurance is written, the agency relationship imposes an affirmative duty on the agent to provide full health particulars to that insurer.

[Based on this proposition, the court held two of the certificates invalid because McAfee was an agent for the companies. The remaining certificates were effective.]

Unigard Olympic Life Insurance Company's money judgment and the judgment rescinding its credit life insurance certificates Nos. 896035 and 919070 are affirmed and the remaining portions of the judgment and supplemental judgment are reversed.

RINGOLD and DURHAM, JJ., concur.

Notes and Questions

1. Readey, Cancer Cases — The Achilles Heel of Credit Life Insurance, 50 Ins. Couns. J. 241 (1983), deals with the *McAfee* "problem" from the insurance company perspective. See also Swain v. Life Insurance Co. of Louisiana, 537 So. 2d 1297 (La. App. 1989), *cert. denied*, 541 So. 2d 895 (La. 1989), also a credit life insurance case.

2. The court in *McAfee* talked about "post-claim underwriting." What do you understand to be the meaning and significance of that term? To what extent is it legitimate?

3. Are there any characteristics of credit life insurance that would explain the apparent disappearance there of the concealment doctrine? That would justify its disappearance? Should it also be abandoned in ordinary life insurance? If not, should it be modified there? In health insurance? Should it be treated differently in group and in individual insurance, whether life or health?

4. In. Cohen v. Mutual Benefit Life Ins. Co., 638 F. Supp. 695 (E.D.N.Y. 1986), the insured responded to certain questions in the application as follows:

> 3. Have you ever had, or been told you had, or been treated for (Circle illness, injury, or complaint to which each "Yes" answer refers.)
>   a. heart trouble, high blood pressure, or pain about the heart or chest? Yes ["heart trouble" circled].
>   b. diabetes; presence of albumin, blood, or sugar in urine; . . . ? No. . . .
>   d. any injuries or other illnesses? No. . . .
> 13. Remarks. <u>Myocardial Infarction 1976 — 3 weeks — Booth Mem. Hosp. — 10 weeks — home — no recurrence — Dr. Safrin.</u>

After the insured's death, investigation revealed the undisputed information that six months before the application, the applicant was diagnosed "as suffering from advanced coronary disease, severe ventricular failure, angina pectoris, papillary muscle dysfunction and complete left bundle branch block, for which he took five types of medication twice a day." There was also disputed evidence that the insured suffered from diabetes. The court granted the defendant's motion for summary judgment; the plaintiff's contentions that the questions were answered "in good faith and [the insured] did not understand the nature of his condition are unavailing and do not create an issue of fact for trial." Id. at 696. This is, so far at least, consistent with traditional doctrine. Is it consistent with *McAfee*? Is *Cohen* a concealment or a misrepresentation case?

5. In Waxse v. Reserve Life Ins. Co., 809 P.2d 533 (Kan. 1991), the

insured's estate sued the insurer for refusal to pay major medical benefits. The insurer sought rescission for material misrepresentation,
asserting that the insured did not disclose positive results of a test for
the HIV virus. The Kansas Supreme Court reversed the lower court
because the insured had answered each question on the application
honestly and with literal accuracy. Is the result sound?

6. As a legislator, how would you react to a proposal to require
intent to deceive before a misrepresentation would be a defense to a
policy? Would your answer be the same for property insurance, for
health insurance, and for life insurance? Why or why not?

7. Some statutes require that an application for life insurance be
attached to the policy; if it is not, no misrepresentation thereon may be
used by the insurer in defense. A recent case that applied that statutory
rule is Wise v. Mutual Life Ins. Co., 714 F. Supp. 822 (E.D. Tex. 1989),
applying Texas law. The decision was reversed by 894 F.2d 140 (5th
Cir. 1990), based on a different reading of the Texas statute and cases.

STIPCICH v. METROPOLITAN LIFE INS. CO.

277 U.S. 311 (1928)

Mr. Justice STONE delivered the opinion of the Court.

The plaintiff brought this action in the circuit court for Clatsop
County, Oregon, as beneficiary of a policy by which the defendant had
insured the life of her husband, Anton Stipcich. The case was removed
for diversity of citizenship to the United States district court for Oregon. The company defended principally on the ground that Stipcich,
after applying for the insurance and before the delivery of the policy
and payment of the first premium, had suffered a recurrence of a
duodenal ulcer, which later caused his death, and that he failed to
reveal this information to the company.

It was shown on the trial by uncontradicted evidence that after his
application Stipcich consulted two physicians and that they told him
that an operation for the removal of the ulcer was necessary. Plaintiff
then made tender of evidence to the effect that Stipcich had communicated this information to Coblentz, the defendant's agent who had
solicited the policy, and that the visit to the second doctor was made at
Coblentz' request to confirm the diagnosis of the first.

The proffered evidence was excluded and, at the close of the
whole case and over plaintiff's objection, the court directed a verdict
for the defendant, stating that it did so because Stipcich was under a
duty to inform the defendant of his knowledge of the serious ailment
of which he had learned after making application for insurance; and
that he had failed in that duty since his communication of the facts to

Coblentz did not amount to notice of them to the insurance company. The case was taken on writ of error to the court of appeals for the ninth circuit. That court certified to this, certain questions of law presented by the case. Jud. Code, §239. Without answering, we ordered the entire record to be sent up and the case is here as though on writ of error.

An insurer may of course assume the risk of such changes in the insured's health as may occur between the date of application and the date of the issuance of a policy. Where the parties contract exclusively on the basis of conditions as they existed at the date of the application; the failure of the insured to divulge any later known changes in health may well not affect the policy. Insurance Co. v. Higginbotham, 95 U.S. 380; see New York Life Insurance Co. v. Moats, 207 Fed. 481; Grier v. Insurance Co., 132 N.C. 542; compare Gardner v. North State Mutual Life Insurance Co., 163 N.C. 367. But there is no contention here that the parties contracted exclusively on the basis of conditions at the time of the application. Here both by the terms of the application and familiar rules governing the formation of contracts no contract came into existence until the delivery of the policy, and at that time the insured had learned of conditions gravely affecting his health, unknown at the time of making his application.

Insurance policies are traditionally contracts *uberrimae fidei* and a failure by the insured to disclose conditions affecting the risk, of which he is aware, makes the contract voidable at the insurer's option. Carter v. Boehm, 3 Burrows, 1905; Livingston v. Maryland Insurance Co., 6 Cranch, 274; McLanahan v. Universal Insurance Co., 1 Pet. 170; Phoenix Life Insurance Co. v. Raddin, 120 U.S. 183, 189; Hardman v. Firemen's Insurance Co., 20 Fed. 594.

Concededly, the modern practice of requiring the applicant for life insurance to answer questions prepared by the insurer has relaxed this rule to some extent, since information not asked for is presumably deemed immaterial. Penn Mutual Life Insurance Co. v. Mechanics' Savings Bank & Trust Co., 72 Fed. 413, 435-441. See Clark v. Manufacturer's Insurance Co., 8 How. 235, 248-249; compare Phoenix Life Insurance Co. v. Raddin, 120 U.S. 183, 190.

But the reason for the rule still obtains, and with added force, as to changes materially affecting the risk which come to the knowledge of the insured after the application and before delivery of the policy. For, even the most unsophisticated person must know that in answering the questionnaire and submitting it to the insurer he is furnishing the data on the basis of which the company will decide whether, by issuing a policy, it wishes to insure him. If, while the company deliberates, he discovers facts which make portions of his application no longer true, the most elementary spirit of fair dealing would seem to require him to make a full disclosure. If he fails to do so the company may, despite its acceptance of the application, decline to issue a policy, Canning v. Farquhar, 16 Q.B.D. 727; McKenzie v. Northwestern Mutual Life Insurance Co., 26 Ga. App. 225, or if a policy has been issued, it has a valid defense to a suit upon it. Equitable Life Assurance Society v. McElroy, 83 Fed. 631, 636, 637. Compare Traill v. Baring, 4 DeG. J. & S. 318; Allis-Chalmers Co. v. Fidelity & Deposit Co. of Maryland, 114 L.T. 433; compare Piedmont and Arlington Life Insurance Co. v. Ewing, 92 U.S. 377.

This generally recognized rule, in the absence of authoritative local decision, we take to be the law of Oregon. Its application here is not affected by Oregon Laws, §6426(1) c, which provides that the policy shall set forth the entire contract between the parties. The defendant in insisting that Stipcich was under an obligation to disclose his discovery to it is not attempting to add another term to the contract. The obligation was not one stipulated for by the parties, but is one imposed by law as a result of the relationship assumed by them and because of the peculiar character of the insurance contract. The necessity for complying with it is not dispensed with by the failure of the insurer to stipulate in the policy for such disclosure.

The evidence proffered and rejected tended to show that the insured, in good faith, made the required disclosure to Coblentz who, for some purposes, admittedly represented the defendant. If he represented it for this purpose the evidence should have been received. . . .

In communicating to him the information as to his changed condition of health Stipcich acted only in what must have appeared to him the most natural and obvious way to supplement the information already given in his written application.

Defendant relies on the established rule, here expressed in part at least in the printed clause of the application, incorporated in the policy and printed in the margin,[2] that the authority of a soliciting agent to receive the application and transmit it to the company and to deliver the policy when issued, does not include power to vary the terms of the contract, to waive conditions or to receive information sought by questions in the application other than that embodied in it. But Coblentz, when the insured communicated the information to him, did not purport to vary any term or waive any condition of the proposed insurance contract; he did not acquiesce in a variation of the application; nor in connection with the preparation of the written application did he receive any information not written into it. The insured merely communicated information, supplementing the application, to the des-

---

2. "2. That no agent, medical examiner, or any other person except the Officers at the Home Office of the Company, have power on behalf of the Company; (a) to make, modify or discharge any contract of insurance, (b) to bind the Company by making any promises respecting any benefits under any policy issued hereunder."

ignated agent of the company for the transaction of business in the state, as the most natural and appropriate channel of communication to the company.

In insisting that it was entitled to information of the insured's change of health after the application, but that such information could not be effectively communicated to its agent to receive the application and transact business with insured preliminary to the acceptance of the risk, defendant is not aided by the stipulations of the policy and any doubts as to the agent's implied authority to receive it must be resolved in the light of the Oregon statutes. Oregon Laws §6435 reads as follows:

> Any person who shall solicit and procure an application for life insurance shall, in all matters relating to such application for insurance and the policy issued in consequence thereof, be regarded as the agent of the company issuing the policy and not the agent of the insured, and all provisions in the application and policy to the contrary are void and of no effect whatever.

Provisions of this character are controlling when inconsistent with the terms of a policy issued after their enactment. National Union Fire Insurance Co. v. Wanberg, 260 U.S. 71; Continental Life Insurance Co. v. Chamberlain, 132 U.S. 304; Whitfield v. Aetna Life Insurance Co., 205 U.S. 489. Here the statute does more than provide that the soliciting agent in matters relating to the application and policy does not represent the insured. In connection with those matters it makes him the agent of the company, a phrase which would be meaningless unless the statute when applied to the facts of the case indicated in what respects he represented the company. Here the statute in terms defines the scope of his agency to the extent that he is stated to represent the company "in all matters relating to the application and the policy issued in consequence" of it. We need not inquire what are the outer limits of that authority, but we think this language plainly makes him the representative of the company in connection with all those matters which, in the usual course of effecting insurance, are incidental to the application and the delivery of the policy. . . .

Reversed.

Notes and Questions

1. In dictum, the court in *Stipcich* says that, because of the modern practice of requiring answers to detailed questions, "information not asked for is presumably deemed immaterial." Is that true irrespective of the nature of the information not asked for and not disclosed?

To put an extreme case, suppose the insured had previously had a kidney removed and was living on one kidney, but no question in the application called for such information. If the applicant did not volunteer the information, would the nondisclosure (concealment) be a valid defense to a claim under the policy?

2. On November 15, Miller was solicited for life insurance and signed an application stating that he was in "good health." No question arises with respect to that statement. Between November 29 and December 4 he experienced three events characterized by a neurologist as "strange thoughts." The neurologist declined to call them hallucinations. On December 4, he paid the first premium and obtained a conditional receipt that would make the insurance effective if he was "insurable" on that day. On December 5 he went to a doctor who, thinking he might have a brain tumor, suggested further testing. A neurologist performed tests that revealed one. Miller was operated on and later died. The insurer denied the application, relying on Miller's failure to disclose on December 4 the three events that followed the application. Should Miller's widow, the beneficiary, recover from the insurer? See Miller v. Republic Natl. Life Ins. Co., 789 F.2d 1336 (9th Cir. 1986).

2. Waiver and Estoppel in Life and Health Insurance

REPUBLIC-VANGUARD LIFE INS. CO. v. WALTERS

728 S.W.2d 415 (Tex. App. 1987)

WARREN, Justice.

The appellee sued on a contract insuring the life of her deceased husband. Appellant's main defense to the suit was that the insured made material misrepresentations in his application for insurance, and that if it had known the true facts it would not have written the policy.

Judgment was rendered for appellee, based on the jury's finding that the appellant insurer knew facts that would have caused a prudent person to inquire about and discover material facts intentionally omitted by the decedent in his application for the policy.

The main question on appeal is whether, in seeking to avoid a policy on the basis of misrepresentations by the insured, an insurer may justifiably rely on representations that were obviously false at the time they were made.

In 1981, the decedent, James B. Walters, applied to the appellant for mortgage protection life insurance. In the application, which he received in a mail solicitation, he stated that he knew of no impairment to his health, and that he had visited a doctor during the previous two years for treatment of a sprained and bruised back.

At the appellant's request, Mr. Walters consented to an examination by a registered nurse. She completed a form detailing his personal history, in which he reported that he had been hospitalized within the previous five years for hernia repair and back treatment; that he had been treated in 1957 for a lung ailment; that he had gained 50 pounds in the previous year "due to beer drinking"; that he had been wounded in Vietnam; and that he underwent an annual electrocardiogram at the Marine Hospital in Galveston.

When the nurse asked whether he had any "[i]mpaired sight or hearing; other physical impairment, sickness, mental illness, injury; cancer; growth; rupture; syphilis," Mr. Walters said he did not. In addition to the Galveston Marine Hospital, he provided the names and addresses of Dr. Minyard, of Dr. P. Cunningham, who also treated his back, and of St. Mary's Hospital in Galveston.

The appellant's underwriter requested a copy of Dr. Minyard's records for the hernia and back treatment, but requested no other information from the decedent or his doctors. On November 1, 1981, the appellant issued a mortgage protection life insurance policy, with an initial death benefit of $42,900.

In the early morning hours of December 23, 1982, the appellee shot and killed her husband during the course of a violent struggle that also involved her 19-year-old son, the decedent's stepson. The appellee testified that her husband had a drinking problem; that he had become drunk and beaten her on previous occasions, causing her to call the police; and that he had earlier ripped their telephone from the wall to prevent her from calling again for assistance.

On the night of his death, she further testified, the decedent had broken her glasses, beaten her, attempted to gouge her face with a wire clothesline, and bloodied her nose; that when her son came to her aid, the decedent began choking him; that she retrieved a revolver and fired it, intending to frighten the decedent; that two bullets struck and killed him; and that she called the police after locating and plugging in a new telephone she had hidden from the decedent.

As the death occurred within two years of the policy's issuance, under the policy's terms the appellant was allowed to contest claims on the basis of misrepresentations by the insured. See Tex. Ins. Code Ann. art. 3.44 §3, art. 21.35 (Vernon 1981).* After the insured's death, the appellant requested all of the decedent's medical records and conducted a thorough investigation of the claim.

---

* After a period of one or two years, a life insurance policy becomes incontestable, that is, defenses previously available to the insurer cease to be available to it. See Section C(3) for a discussion of incontestable clauses. — ED.

The investigation revealed that the decedent had been treated for depression, beginning in 1977; that he was hospitalized from September 30 to November 28 of that year, and from January 19 to January 30, 1979; and that in February 1979, he was hospitalized after he had taken an overdose of a drug prescribed for his depression. Because Mr. Walters had represented a history free of mental illness, the appellant declared the policy void from its inception and refunded the premiums paid, in a letter to the appellee dated May 18, 1983.

In response to special issues, the jury found that (1) the decedent had intentionally misrepresented material facts in his application for the policy; (2) that the appellant insurer relied on those misrepresentations in issuing the policy; (3) that the appellant knew facts that would have caused a prudent person to inquire further, and that such an inquiry would have disclosed omissions in the application; and that the appellee did not intentionally and illegally bring about the death of her husband. . . .

As the appellee observes, no Texas court has squarely addressed the question of whether an insurer's reliance must be reasonable, in light of facts discovered during an investigation, but the question has been answered affirmatively in other contexts. . . .

The appellant argues that it did not know of facts that would put a prudent person on notice that further inquiry was required. Although the medical examination revealed inconsistencies between the insurance application, which stated that the decedent's only medical problem had been a sprained and bruised back, and the decedent's actual history of a hernia, excessive weight gain, and annual electrocardiograms, Mr. Walters gave no indication that he suffered from mental illness. He did not name the physician, Dr. Towler, who treated his depression, or the hospital, the University of Texas Medical Branch, where he was treated.

The appellee cites the evidence that the medical examination revealed a range of other medical problems and a list of four other health care providers. She contends that these facts created a duty to investigate, even though they did not indicate mental illness, and that the medical records from the providers listed by Mr. Walters would have revealed the problems that the insurer did not discover until its final investigation of the claim. The Galveston Marine Hospital records referred to Mr. Walters's treatments for depression at the University of Texas Medical Branch, and were available to appellant had it decided to obtain them prior to issuing the policy. . . .

In [Jefferson Amusement Co. v. Lincoln Natl. Life Ins. Co., 409 F.2d 644 (1969)], as here, a medical examination revealed information that was inconsistent with the initial application. In his application, the decedent in *Jefferson* had failed to list the names of three doctors who had treated him, including one who had treated him for chest pains.

The insured died after a heart attack. The court held that the facts supported a finding that the insurer waived its right to rely on the false representations because, at the examination, the insured had given the names of two of the previously unreported doctors; a reading of their records would have identified the third doctor, who knew of the chest pains. The court stated that the insurer failed to make a prudent inquiry because "[i]t did not follow up all its leads which would have revealed all that it knows now except the results of the post-mortem." Id. at 649.

In our case, the appellant learned, from the nurse's examination, of a number of medical problems that Mr. Walters failed to report on his initial application. He supplied the name of a hospital whose records, if read, would have informed the appellant of his treatment for depression. Based on these facts, it might reasonably be expected that the insurer would have ordered and read medical records that would have fully informed it of the details behind the decedent's excessive weight gain, his back surgery by Dr. Cunningham, and his annual electrocardiograms. The evidence supported the submission of an issue, and, regardless of insurance industry custom, the question of whether the appellant's investigation met the standard required of a prudent person was within the province of the jury. See Air Control Engg., Inc. v. Hogan, 477 S.W.2d 941, 946 (Tex. Civ. App. — Dallas 1972, no writ) (whether standard of care was met is jury question); Restatement (Second) of Torts §328C (1965).

The judgment of the trial court is affirmed.

Notes and Questions

1. Based on the facts reported in the application, would you as an underwriter have made further inquiry? Would that inquiry have led you to a knowledge that the decedent was prone to violence? If not, would that have made a difference in the result of the case?

2. Koral Industries v. Security-Connecticut Life Ins. Co., 788 S.W.2d 136 (Tex. App. 1990), declined to follow *Republic-Vanguard*, saying that it was inconsistent with the bulk of Texas case law. Which is the sounder view?

3. Does it matter that the policy, a "mortgage protection life insurance policy," is a declining term policy, so that the company's exposure decreases over time?

4. Ordinarily, the smaller the amount at stake the more risk insurers are willing to take without detailed underwriting, and compensate for the higher average risk with higher premiums. Would your answers to the above questions be affected by the amount at stake?

ROBERTS v. NATIONAL LIBERTY GROUP
OF COMPANIES

159 Ill. App. 3d 706, 512 N.E.2d 792, 111 Ill. Dec. 403 (1987)

Justice WOMBACHER delivered the opinion of the court:

In Spring of 1982, Plaintiff Paul Roberts called Defendant Veteran's Life Insurance Company (administered by National Liberty Group of Companies) in response to a television ad. Mr. Roberts applied for a $30,000.00 life insurance policy which was only available to individuals under the age of 60 years. Mr. Roberts' original application, submitted prior to his 60th birthday was either lost or misplaced by the defendant insurance company. A second application exists which is signed by Mr. Roberts and his wife Dolores under the date of April 7, 1982. A notation on the application indicates receipt by the defendant's mailing room of November 23, 1982. The parties stipulated that the application and the policy itself were backdated so that the 60 year limitation of insurance liability could be avoided. The issued policy was backdated to April 11, 1982. Mr. Roberts' sixtieth birthday occurred in April of 1982.

On the insurance application, Mr. Roberts had reported that he had been treated for an ulcer; however, he marked "no" on the question of treatment for high blood pressure. In fact, the record indicates that in 1979 and 1980 Mr. Roberts was tested for blood pressure at the office of his family physician, Dr. Hetherington. Various readings were slightly elevated, and eventually medication was prescribed in June 1979. No testing appears from December of 1980 through May of 1982. According to the defendant's corporate records, a call was made to the Roberts' residence on November 23, 1982, asking about the prior treatment for ulcers. There had been no surgery for the ulcers and no current medication.

Cancer was diagnosed in Mr. Roberts in October of 1982, and he died of cancer on June 5, 1983. A claim was duly processed by Mr. Roberts' wife, Dolores (listed beneficiary), at which time the defendant denied the claim and mailed Mrs. Roberts a premium refund check totaling $818.62.

Mrs. Roberts was appointed Administrator of her husband's estate by the circuit court of Vermilion County, IL. She filed suit against the defendant demanding the $30,000.00 together with interest thereon. The trial court found for the plaintiff.

Upon appeal the defendant contends that the false answer on the application regarding high blood pressure treatment constituted a misrepresentation which allows them to avoid the policy. Additionally, the defendant asserts that the failure to disclose the cancer prior to the policy being issued allows them to avoid the policy.

Under Illinois law, a false statement in an application for insurance is not in itself a ground for avoiding the insurance policy. The insurer must prove that the statements were made with intent to deceive or involved matters materially affecting the acceptance of the risk. (Ill. Rev. Stat. 1985, ch. 73, par. 766.) The statute is to be read in the disjunctive and an insurer need not show both the materiality of the misrepresentation and an actual intent to deceive, but satisfies its burden if it establishes either a material misrepresentation or an intent to deceive. Campbell v. Prudential Ins. Co. of America, 15 Ill. 2d 308, 155 N.E.2d 9 (1958).

A "misrepresentation" is a false representation of a material fact by one party to an insurance contract to the other party, tending directly to induce the other party to enter into a contract of insurance. Jung v. Siegal, 314 Ill. App. 67, 40 N.E.2d 840 (1942). The trial court, as the fact-finder, found that the evidence of previous medical attentions, the method of completing the form and the disclosure of the ulcer condition, required a finding of lack of intent to deceive. The trial court's findings are presumed to be correct. Gillespie v. Gillespie, 70 Ill. App. 2d 38, 216 N.E.2d 462 (1966). We agree with the trial court. The omission in reporting the high blood pressure does not reflect a concerted effort to deceive the insurance company when viewed in light of the totality of the circumstances. Furthermore, Mr. Roberts' doctor believed the elevated pressure was slight and was technically stress-related hypertension rather than a physical condition constituting high blood pressure. . . .

Lastly, the defendant contends that the failure to disclose the cancer prior to the issuance of the policy in November of 1982 voided the policy. The cancer was diagnosed one month prior to the receipt of the application by the defendant. However, the policy which was issued predates by six months the date that the cancer was diagnosed. The trial court held that the backdating of the policy estopped the defendant from asserting the defense of nondisclosure.

"Estoppel" is a term applied to a situation where, a party is denied the right to plead or prove an otherwise important fact, because of something which he has done or omitted to do. Jennings v. Bituminous Casualty Corp., 47 Ill. App. 2d 243, 197 N.E.2d 513 (1964). If a party's conduct has reasonably induced another to follow a course of action that otherwise would not have been followed, and which would be to the latter's detriment if he could not later repudiate such course of action, an estoppel will arise to prevent injustice or fraud. Sabath v. Morris Handler Co., 102 Ill. App. 2d 218, 243 N.E.2d 723 (1968). The test of estoppel is whether, considering all the circumstances of the case, conscience and honest dealing require that the defendant be estopped. Lincoln-Way Community High School Dist. 210 v. Village of Frankfort, 51 Ill. App. 3d 602, 9 Ill. Dec. 884,

367 N.E.2d 318 (1977). Estoppel generally is based upon an insurance carrier's conduct and/or representations which mislead an insured to his detriment. DeGraw v. State Security Insurance Co., 40 Ill. App. 3d 26, 351 N.E.2d 302, *appeal denied,* 64 Ill.2d 595 (1976). We agree with the trial court. The defendant may not now adopt an inconsistent position or course of conduct to the loss of the plaintiff. Indeed, had the policy not been backdated then no policy would exist because Mr. Roberts' sixtieth birthday occurred in April 1982. The insurance coverage in question was only available to individuals under 60 years of age. Equity requires that due to the defendants' action of backdating the application and policy, they now be barred from asserting the nondisclosure defense.

For all of the foregoing reasons the judgment of the Circuit Court of Vermilion County is affirmed.

Affirmed.

Question

1. In *Roberts*, as a result of backdating the policy, the insured would be paying premium from the backdated inception of the policy. Might that have had any effect on the decision?

3. Incontestability Clauses

Most life insurance policies contain a clause such as the following:

> This Policy shall be incontestable after it has been in force during the lifetime of the Insured for a period of two years from the date of issue, except for non-payment of premiums.

Notes and Questions

1. An insurer backdated a policy to December 4, 1981, in accordance with the insurer's "customary practices" to enable the insured to take advantage of a lower premium rate. That date was called the "date of issue." The policy provided that its "effective date" was February 25, 1982. After what date is it too late to contest the policy, under the above clause?

2. An unusual group of cases decided together in 1984 in the Federal District Court for the Northern District of Georgia involved the application of the incontestability clause, among other issues. Kristofer Lee Wood died in 1982 at the age of 22 from respiratory failure

resulting from muscular dystrophy, from which he had suffered from the age of six. By the time of his death, about fifteen life insurance companies had issued life insurance to cover Wood in an amount aggregating over half a million dollars. The policies were issued from about 1977 on into 1981. The policies presented a wide range of problems.

For some of them the contestable period had not yet run. They were easily avoided because of blatant misrepresentations in the applications. For many of the others, however, the contestable period had run, so simple avoidance or rescission was not available. That problem was solved by a decision that the policies were void ab initio: The insured had neither signed the applications nor consented to the insurance in writing, as required by statute for individual life insurance policies. In some cases, however, there was a technical barrier to that neat disposition. In those cases certificates had been issued under group policies issued to two organizations of which Wood became a member* and the requirement of signature by the insured or written consent did not apply to group policies. The group policies provided, however, for individual underwriting and sale of the policies; the court decided that despite the appellation "group" they were really "franchise" policies, not true group, for they were sold in the same way as individual policies. Thus the court interpreted the consent requirement as applying to them after all. They too could therefore be regarded as void ab initio.

The great difficulty these cases occasioned is suggested by the appearance of a group of opinions, dated 1984, in volumes of the reporters not issued until 1986. The cases reported in that group are Delaware Am. Intl. Life Ins. Co. v. Wood, 630 F. Supp. 364 (N.D. Ga. 1984); Wood v. New York Life Ins. Co., 631 F. Supp. 3 (1984); Wood v. National Benefit Life Ins. Co., 631 F. Supp. 6 (1984); Connecticut Gen. Life Ins. Co. v. Wood, 631 F. Supp. 9 (1984); Guarantee Trust Life Ins. Co. v. Wood, 631 F. Supp. 15 (1984); and Northwestern Natl. Life Ins. Co. v. Wood, 631 F. Supp. 22 (1984).

3. The incontestability clause was interpreted by Chief Judge Cardozo in Metropolitan Life Ins. Co. v. Conway, 252 N.Y. 449, 169 N.E. 642 (1930), to apply only to conditions and warranties and not to operate to expand coverage beyond that defined by the policy. In *Conway*, the insurance company applied to the New York Insurance Superintendent for approval of a clause denying coverage for death as a result of travel or service in an aircraft, except for fare-paying passengers. The Superintendent refused to approve the clause, contending that it was contrary to a statutorily mandated two year incontestability clause. Judge Cardozo found the conflict nonexistent:

*There is no explanation of how he managed to join.

The provision that a policy shall be incontestable after it has been in force during the lifetime of the insured for a period of two years is not a mandate as to coverage, a definition of the hazards to be borne by the insurer. It means only this, that within the limits of the coverage the policy shall stand, unaffected by any defense that it was invalid in its inception, or thereafter became invalid by reason of a condition broken. . . . "A provision for incontestability does not have the effect of converting a promise to pay on the happening of a stated contingency into a promise to pay whether such contingency does or does not happen." [Citations omitted.] Where there has been no assumption of the risk, there can be no liability. . . . The kind of insurance one has at the beginning, that, but no more, one retains until the end. [Id. at 452, 169 N.E. at 642.]

This interpretation, which has been almost universally accepted, has not fully solved the problem. It now becomes one of determining whether a certain provision is a condition, warranty, or representation or whether it defines the scope of coverage. The incontestability clause prevents the insurer from raising the defense that the insured has not complied with all of the policy conditions. On the other hand, the insurer will not have to pay the insured if the loss was outside of the policy coverage, regardless of the clause's existence. But many terms can be written formally in either fashion. Try your hand at converting a warranty into a coverage provision to take advantage of the *Conway* doctrine. Do you think a court would give effect to your effort to evade the incontestability clause?

4. Is the way a policy characterizes a provision important? Can an insurer always (or ever) eliminate the effect of the incontestability clause by redesignating as matters of coverage terms that would normally be warranties, representations, and conditions? If the terminology is not the deciding factor, what criteria should the court use in determining whether a provision is to be treated as a condition or as a coverage provision? Should it simply apply the *contra proferentem* rule to lean in favor of applying the incontestability clause?

5. The problem has been most acute in group insurance connected with employment. Most group life insurance policies issued to an employer for the benefit of the employees require that the insured be an employee of the employer-policyholder. If the insured misrepresents his own status to be that of an employee, can the insurer assert, after the contestable period has run, that the insured was not an employee in order to avoid paying on the policy? The courts have been hopelessly split on this issue, with both sides contending that they are following *Conway*. In Simpson v. Phoenix Mut. Life Ins. Co., 24 N.Y.2d 262, 247 N.E.2d 655, 299 N.Y.S.2d 835 (1969), the New York Court of Appeals held that employment was a condition of the insurance and therefore, since the insurer did not contest the employee's

eligibility within the period of contestability, it was barred from raising it as a defense to the beneficiary's claim. It also held a provision to be a coverage limitation if its applicability could not be ascertained by the insurer by investigation at the time the policy was issued. If the insurer could have discovered the fact at the time the policy was issued, the insurer cannot dispute that fact after the time specified by the incontestability clause. Thus, according to *Simpson*, because employment status is discoverable at issuance, it is a condition and, under the *Conway* standard, the insurer cannot dispute it after the contestable period has run.

The other view of the matter is illustrated by Crawford v. Equitable Life Assurance Socy., 56 Ill. 2d 41, 305 N.E.2d 144 (1973). The Illinois Supreme Court determined the crucial distinction to be between a fact affecting the policy's validity, to which the incontestability clause applies, and the risk assumed, to which it does not. The court went on to find the group policy valid but the insurance did not cover nonemployed individuals. The court emphasized the fluctuating situation of a business with employees coming and going and moving from full-time to part-time or the reverse. If the incontestability clause would bar any challenge to the insured's status after a one- or two-year period, an insured could leave the employ of the policyholder after the contestable period had elapsed and still be insured by the group policy. That would be absurd.

Cases on the question of whether employment status goes to coverage or is a condition are collected in Annot., 26 A.L.R.3d 632 (1969).

6. Is the *Simpson* "discoverability" test or the *Crawford* "realistic view of the business" test more consistent with *Conway*? Which best achieves the legitimate goals of life insurers? Should some other test be used? A thoughtful essay dealing with the problems illustrated by the *Simpson* and *Crawford* cases is Works, Coverage Clauses and Incontestable Statutes: The Regulation of Post-Claim Underwriting, 1979 U. of Ill. L. Forum 809.

Similar questions exist of whether the age of the insured (see Annot., 135 A.L.R. 439 (1941)), the identity of the insured (see Annot., 98 A.L.R. 710 (1935)), the occupation of the insured (see Annot., 85 A.L.R. 317 (1933)), the existence of other insurance on the life of the insured (see Annot., 22 A.L.R.2d 809 (1952)), the marital status of the insured (see Jackson v. Continental Casualty Co., 402 So. 2d 175 (La. App. 1981)), a clerical error in the policy resulting in greater policy limits (see Mutual Life Ins. Co. v. Simon, 151 F. Supp. 408 (S.D.N.Y. 1957)), or the existence of preexisting disease (see Annot., 13 A.L.R.3d 1392 (1967)), can be the basis of a challenge by the insurer after the contestable period has run. How should these questions be answered?

7. If there must be a "contest" to stop the running of the period,

what constitutes a "contest"? In general, it is a pleading, either a complaint or an answer. The New York Court of Appeals held in Berkshire Life Ins. Co. v. Fernandez, 71 N.Y.2d 874, 522 N.E.2d 1049, 527 N.Y.S.2d 751 (1988) that delivery of a copy of a summons to the sheriff of the defendants' county of residence within the two-year period was sufficient if the summons was thereafter served on defendant within 60 days after the two year period had expired. The court noted that the contestable period had not been *tolled* but that the requirement had been *met*.

8. What is the significance of the words "during the lifetime of the insured?"

9. Incontestable clauses are sometimes used in health insurance. They produce the same results, terminating defenses of misrepresentation at the end of the contestable period. See Button v. Connecticut Gen. Life Ins. Co., 847 F.2d 584 (9th Cir. 1988), *cert. denied*, 488 U.S. 909 (1988), applying Arizona law. The court believed "that the better-reasoned view is that the incontestability clause relates to the validity of the contract and not to the construction of policy provisions." Id. at 588.

4.   The Agent's Conduct as a Factor

The conduct of the agent is more often decisive in life and health insurance than in other lines. Characteristically the application (or that portion not to be filled out by the doctor when a physical examination is called for) is filled out by the agent during the interview with the applicant. It is not uncommon for the agent to misreport some of the applicant's answers, sometimes intentionally, and sometimes only because the agent hears what he or she wants to hear rather than because of outright dishonesty. If the misreporting is intentional, what are the likely motivations? How should that affect the court's handling of the problem?

TIDELANDS LIFE INS. CO. v. FRANCO

711 S.W.2d 728 (Tex. App. 1986)

Nye, Chief Justice.

This is an action under the Deceptive Trade Practices-Consumer Protection Act. Appellee Linda Franco sued appellant Tidelands Life Insurance Company (United International Life Insurance Company, by the time of trial), claiming damages for Tidelands' failure to pay her expenses for gall bladder surgery. After a non-jury trial, the trial court rendered judgment in favor of appellee. . . .

Only two witnesses testified at trial: Linda Franco (the appellee) and an executive of appellant insurance company. Ms. Franco testified that she was at her place of business when one Alvin Choate approached her and introduced himself as an agent of appellant company. She was interested in the terms of the policy he offered, but told him she was already covered by a health policy. Furthermore, she told him, she had been diagnosed as having a gall bladder problem. Mr. Choate nevertheless assured her she would be covered under the insurance policy he proposed to sell her. He filled out an application for her, adding a note that she had a pre-existing gall bladder problem but was 100% recovered. He then had her sign the application. The application contained at least three references to Choate as agent. Over a year later, appellee was required to have gall bladder surgery, and appellant refused coverage.

The insurance company contends that Choate had no authority to bind the insurance company as a matter of law because he was a "soliciting agent" as opposed to a "local recording agent." See Royal Globe Insurance Co. v. Bar Consultants, Inc., 577 S.W.2d 688, 692 (Tex. 1979). We rejected the same argument by the same appellant in Tidelands Life Insurance Co. v. Harris, 675 S.W.2d 224, 227 (Tex. App. — Corpus Christi 1984, writ ref'd n.r.e.). As in that case, Choate orally held himself out as a Tidelands agent, and the insurance application form referred to him as their agent. The finding of the trial court that Choate acted with actual, apparent, and implied authority has ample support in the record. . . .

Appellee testified that she was interested in the policy, but thought she could not be covered. Choate, acting as appellant's agent, assured her that the policy would cover her, and filled out the application himself. He put in the statement that she was fully recovered from her gall bladder condition specifically to assure her that she would be covered. A fair inference from this testimony is that appellant's agent, Choate, misrepresented the coverage of the policy and then answered questions on the application himself, in such a way that the application would be accepted. The falsity of some of the answers was admittedly known by the appellee. This false statement is immaterial to the outcome of this case. The suit was brought under the DTPA, and judgment was rendered on the theory that appellant insurance company, through its agent, Choate, misrepresented the coverage of the policy which appellee bought, thereby causing the insurance company to refuse to pay her medical expenses.

Accordingly, we modify the judgment to award appellee Linda Franco treble damages of $12,181.65. As modified, the judgment of the trial court is affirmed.

Notes and Questions

1. *Franco* makes reference to a Texas statute, and awards treble damages, without much analysis. Chitsey v. National Lloyds Ins. Co., 738 S.W.2d 641 (Tex. 1987), and Vail v. Texas Farm Bureau Mut. Ins. Co., 754 S.W.2d 129 (Tex. 1988), deal with the question whether and how the convoluted statute provides for treble damages in such cases.

2. In a case recently settled without trial, an agent represented a limited coverage major medical policy to a prospect as being "the best on the market." In fact, it was narrower in coverage than the one the applicant already had in place. After the policy had been issued, the insured had an accident as a result of which he became a quadriplegic, only to find out that certain costs important in that circumstance were not covered by the new policy, though they would have been by the policy the insured had given up. In defense of the insured's bad faith claim against the insurer for denying *full* coverage (the insurer had paid large sums pursuant to its policy obligations), the latter produced an application signed by the insured in which, just above the signature, in large print, are plain language warnings both about the limited authority of the agent and about the limitations in coverage of the policy. How would you decide the case?

3. Insured had been operated on for cancer. She already had insurance from another company which had been paying for her visits to the doctor's office. An agent who knew of the cancer operation from previous business relations with the insured (not involving insurance) induced her to apply for insurance with his company. After the new policy was issued the insured dropped the prior insurance. The agent filled out crucial questions in the application form incorrectly and the insured signed them without reading them. The policy provided for payment for medical expenses resulting from sickness "which first manifests itself more than 15 days after this policy is in force." The insurer refused to pay for medical expenses because of the misrepresentations in the application. The insured's response was based on an estoppel theory because of the complete knowledge of the agent and the incorrect recording of the information. The court discussed at length the creation of coverage by estoppel, *Harr* (Section B), and the article by Professor Clarence Morris therein. The court held "that the doctrine of estoppel was available for appellee's use in this case . . . ," and found the company was estopped to deny coverage. Time Ins. Co. v. Graves, 21 Ark. App. 273, 734 S.W.2d 213 (1987). Is this the creation of coverage by estoppel? Is the result sound? But compare Fishel v. American Security Life Ins. Co., 835 F.2d 613 (5th Cir. 1988), applying Missis-

sippi law, which held that waiver and estoppel could not be used to reform a group employee policy in order to create liability of the insurer for death of a former employee who had terminated the employment, when the policy did not cover persons not directly employed.

4. The insurer in Guy v. Commonwealth Life Ins. Co., 894 F.2d 1407 (1990), sought to rescind a policy ab initio for failure of the insured to inform the insurer of a gall bladder problem. The court, believing the insured's testimony that she had fully informed the agent, declined to permit rescission. Mississippi law was applied.

D. Insurable Interest

An insurable interest is a prerequisite to a valid insurance contract. As a venerable hornbook put it:

> The requirement of an insurable interest to support a contract of insurance is based upon considerations of public policy, which condemn as wagers all agreements for insurance of any subject in which the contracting parties have no such interest. [Vance, Handbook on the Law of Insurance 156 (Anderson 3d ed. 1951).]

That much is easy to say, but what it really means and what the absence of insurable interest does is a lot less clear than the black letter statements assume.

In England the doctrine of insurable interest was, at least initially, the product of statutes, some of which are reproduced below. The same doctrines developed in the United States, but largely without the benefit of express American statutes. The Marine Insurance Act of 1746 and the Statute 14 George III, ch. 48 (1774), establishing the doctrine of insurable interest in life insurance, may have been "received" in some states, however.*

Whether the American doctrine was initially the result of the application of English statutes to American cases or a case law development, many states later reduced insurable interest doctrine to statutory form. Some of the American statutes, too, are reproduced below.

---

*The "reception" of English law in the United States is a complicated matter. For a brief selection of materials relating to that reception, see Kimball, Historical Introduction to the Legal System 263-309 (1966).

1.   Marine Insurance

STATUTE ON INSURABLE INTEREST IN MARINE INSURANCE

19 Geo. II, ch. 37 (1746)

An act to regulate insurance on ships belonging to the subjects of Great Britain, and on merchandizes or effects laden thereon.

WHEREAS it hath been found by experience, that the making assurances, interest or no interest, or without further proof of interest than the policy, hath been productive of many pernicious practices, whereby great numbers of ships, with their cargoes, have either been fraudulently lost and destroyed, or taken by the enemy in time of war; and such assurances have encouraged the exportation of wooll, and the carrying on many other prohibited and clandestine trades, which by means of such assurances have been concealed, and the parties concerned secured from loss, as well to the diminution of the publick revenue, as to the great detriment of fair traders: and by introducing a mischievous kind of gaming or wagering, under the pretence of assuring the risque on shipping, and fair trade, the institution and laudable design of making assurances, hath been perverted; and that which was intended for the encouragement of trade and navigation, has in many instances, become hurtful of, and destructive to the same: for remedy whereof, be it enacted by the King's most excellent majesty, by and with the advice and consent of the lords spiritual and temporal, and commons, in this present parliament assembled, and by the authority of the same, That from and after the first day of August, one thousand seven hundred and forty-six, no assurance or assurances shall be made by any person or persons, bodies corporate or politick, on any ship, or ships belonging to his Majesty, or any of his subjects, or on any goods, merchandizes, or effects, laden or to be laden on board of any such ship or ships, interest or no interest, or without further proof of interest than the policy, or by way of gaming or wagering, or without benefit of salvage to the assurer; and that every such assurance shall be null and void to all intents and purposes.

Notes and Questions

1. The learning of the original statute as glossed by case law was reproduced in §§4 and 5 of the Marine Insurance Act of 1906:

4. Avoidance of wagering or gaming contracts —

(1) Every contract of marine insurance by way of gaming or wagering is void.

(2) A contract of marine insurance is deemed to be a gaming or wagering contract —

> a. where the assured has not an insurable interest as defined by this Act, and the contract is entered into with no expectation of acquiring such an interest; or

> b. where the policy is made "interest or no interest" or "without further proof of interest than the policy itself" or "without benefit of salvage to the insurer" or subject to any other like term:

Provided that, where there is no possibility of salvage, a policy may be effected without benefit of salvage to the insurer.

5. Insurable interest defined —

(1) Subject to the provisions of this Act, every person has an insurable interest who is interested in a marine adventure.

(2) In particular a person is interested in a marine adventure where he stands in any legal or equitable relation to the adventure or to any insurable property at risk therein, in consequence of which he may benefit by the safety or due arrival of insurable property, or may be prejudiced by its loss, or by damage thereto, or by the detention thereof, or may incur liability in respect thereof.

2. By The Marine Insurance (Gambling Policies) Act of 1909, Parliament amended the criminal law to support the public policy enunciated in the Act of 1906.

3. Prior to the 1746 statute, the courts enforced on behalf of the insureds many policies written "interest or no interest." Examination of a collection of such cases found in footnotes to Fitzgerald v. Pole, 4 Bro. Parl. Cas. 439, 445-447 (1754), suggests that the clause may have served mostly the convenience of the parties, and that most plaintiffs did in fact have an insurable interest. No doubt that was not always true. In any event, for good or for ill, the statute made such contracts null and void for all purposes.

4. Despite the statutory prohibition, it remains common in British marine insurance practice to issue "interest or no interest" policies, often using the language "In the event of loss the production of this policy to be deemed a sufficient proof of interest" (a P.P.I., or policy proof of interest clause). A P.P.I. policy is also called an *honour policy* because under English law the insured must rely on the honor of the insurer; the policy is void under the 1906 Act. Strikingly, the statute was so strictly interpreted that a P.P.I. policy was void even if the insured did in fact have an insurable interest. Cheshire v. Vaughan, 3

K.B. 240 (1920). Sometimes a policy is issued with a detachable P.P.I. clause: When claim is made, the insured detaches the clause if there is insurable interest at the crucial time. Yet even these policies have been held void on the ground that the crucial time to judge the validity of the policy is the time of issue. Re London County Com. Reins. Office, Ltd., 2 Ch. 67 (1922).

5. American policies, too, contain similar P.P.I. clauses, sometimes referred to as F.I.A. (full interest admitted) clauses. The American doctrine is apparently less rigorous than the English, and the policy will be enforced, it seems, if there is in fact an insurable interest. There is not much American authority on the point, but see Cabaud v. Federal Ins. Co., 37 F.2d 23 (2d Cir. 1930). In the United States, unlike Britain, the doctrine of insurable interest is mainly a product of case law, not of statute, though later many states reduced the doctrine to statutory form.

6. Sometimes parties to honour policies need a decision on an issue having nothing to do with the validity of the policy, and it would be well for the decision to be made by a court. English courts seem to have occasionally decided such questions while keeping a blind eye toward the fact that the contract was null and void for all purposes. Chorley, Liberal Trends in Present-day Commercial Law, 3 Mod. L. Rev. 272, 279 (1940). When and why would insurers pay under "honour" policies without taking advantage of their voidness? When and why would they contest liability without taking advantage of the voidness?

7. Suppose an action is brought on a policy and the insurer seeks to raise for the first time at the appellate stage the defense of lack of insurable interest. Can it do so or has it waived the defense? In Moss v. Union Mut. Ins. Co. of Providence, 11 Mich. App. 334, 161 N.W.2d 158 (1968), that question arose on an inland marine policy and the court answered that it can do so. A dissent noted that "this is the first Michigan case in over 75 years to declare a policy of property insurance invalid because the insured did not have an insurable interest." Id. at 346, n.6., 161 N.W.2d at 164, n.6. If the insurer had not raised the defense, as in the cases discussed in the previous note, could the court raise the issue sua sponte?

8. Another clause that raised comparable problems about the traditional doctrine is the "lost or not lost" clause. Arguably, if the subject of the insurance had been lost before the policy was written, the contract would fail under the doctrine of impossibility or of frustration, or alternatively of lack of insurable interest. But if neither insurer nor insured knew that the subject was lost, there is no common sense reason not to enforce the policy. Uniformly such policies have been enforced. The Marine Insurance Act of 1906, Rule 1 of the First Schedule, continued that doctrine. The possibility of valid insurance

lost or not lost was especially important in the days when communication was by ship, not by telegraph, telephone, or wireless communication. In those days, by the time intelligence reached London as to a projected voyage with a request that insurance be written for it, many months might have passed and the ship have been long since sunk or captured. If the insured's interest was only acquired after the loss, is the interest sufficient to sustain a lost or not lost policy? Section 6 of the Act answered the question in the affirmative if the insured did not know of the loss when the insurance was effected.

2. Property Insurance

a. Definition and Enforcement

The standard form of fire policy in use in the United States reads as follows:

> In consideration of the provisions and stipulations herein or added hereto and of the premium above specified, this Company . . . does insure the insured named above and legal representatives, to the extent of the actual cash value of the property at the time of loss but not exceeding [various other limitations] nor in any event for more than the interest of the insured, against all DIRECT LOSS BY FIRE. . . .

This language states an "indemnity" principle, as do most other nonlife policies, usually quite expressly. If the insurance contract states such a principle and if it is not contrary to public policy (about which there can surely be no doubt), is there any need for or value in a separate public policy doctrine that imposes the same or similar limits on the insured's recovery?

Whether or not there is need for such a doctrine, one is found in a multitude of statutes.

CALIFORNIA INSURANCE CODE §§280-287

Cal. Ins. Code §§280-287 (West 1972)

§280. If the insured has no insurable interest, the contract is void.

§281. Every interest in the property, or any relation thereto, or liability in respect thereof, of such a nature that a contemplated peril might directly damnify the insured, is an insurable interest.

§282. An insurable interest in property may consist in:

1. An existing interest.

2. An inchoate interest founded on an existing interest; or

3. An expectancy, coupled with an existing interest in that out of which the expectancy arises.

§283. A mere contingent or expectant interest in anything, not founded on an actual right to the thing, nor upon any valid contract for it, is not insurable.

§284. Except in the case of property held by the insured as a carrier or depositary the measure of an insurable interest in property is the extent to which the insured might be damnified by loss or injury thereof.

§285. A carrier or depositary of any kind has an insurable interest in a thing held by him as such to the extent of its value.

§286. An interest in property insured must exist when the insurance takes effect, and when the loss occurs, but need not exist in the meantime.

§287. Every stipulation in a policy of insurance for the payment of loss whether the person insured has or has not any interest in the property insured, or that the policy shall be received as proof of such interest, is void.

NEW YORK INSURANCE LAW §3401

N.Y. Ins. Law §3401 (McKinney 1985)

(A) Insurable interest in property. No contract or policy of insurance on property made or issued in this state, or made or issued upon any property in this state, shall be enforceable except for the benefit of some person having an insurable interest in the property insured. In this article, "insurable interest" shall include any lawful and substantial economic interest in the safety or preservation of property from loss, destruction or pecuniary damage.

(B) Insurable interest and consent

(1) Insurable interest. No insurer may knowingly issue a policy to a person without an insurable interest in the subject of the insurance.

(2) Consent in life and disability insurance. [omitted]

Notes and Questions

1. Under the New York statute, does a mortgagee have an insurable interest? If a mortgagee insures property for its actual cash value (which is in excess of the amount due under the mortgage) and the property is a total loss, how much may the insured recover under the

statute? How much under the above-quoted standard policy language? Does the statute add anything?

If the mortgage includes equity participation under which the mortgagee receives some percentage of profits or revenue from the use of the property or some share of its increased value on subsequent sale, how much may the mortgagee recover if the property is totally destroyed by fire?

2. A company owned a toll road or turnpike. Two segments of it were connected by a wooden bridge owned by the county. The company insured the bridge, which burned. Is the company entitled to collect on the insurance, and if so, how much? Under New York law? Under California law? See Farmers' Mut. Ins. Co. v. New Holland Turnpike Road Co., 122 Pa. 37, 15 A. 563 (1888). If a court were to hold that the insurance was void for lack of insurable interest, would there be any way for the owner of the toll road to protect its obvious economic interest in the continued existence of the bridge?

3. An insured purchased a policy that recited a contract under which John Ellis & Co. was to pay royalties to the insured on oil refined in a reducing and filtering plant owned by Ellis, for the use of insured's patent. If the insurance were expressly stated to be insurance on the plant, which belongs to Ellis, not the insured, can the insured recover when the plant burns? If so, how much? Under the New York statute? Under the California statute? If instead the cover is written "on royalties payable to insured from the business of John Ellis & Co.," can the insured recover and if so how much? If the result would be different in the two cases, why would that be the case? Does that suggest a solution to the problem of the turnpike owner in *New Holland*? See National Filtering Oil Co. v. Citizens' Ins. Co., 106 N.Y. 535, 13 N.E. 337 (1887).

4. The basic fire insurance policy insures against loss of the property, for actual cash value. If the insurance is for more — for replacement cost — does that raise insurable interest problems? Other practical or legal problems? An owner of property can also insure against consequential damages through "business interruption" insurance (formerly called "use and occupancy" or "U & O" insurance). Does that raise insurable interest or other legal problems? What are they?

5. If the insurance in *National Filtering Oil* is held valid, it might be called "contingent business interruption" insurance, or more recently insurance on "business income from dependent properties." Would a sound public policy permit such insurance? Would a wise underwriter sell it?

6. Suppose in a case analogous to *National Filtering Oil* there is no contract as a basis for the insured's claim to have insurable interest in another's property. For example, a small business is dependent for its

viability on the continued operation of a great neighboring resort hotel. Can the small business owner acquire insurance protection against loss from destruction of the hotel, despite lack of any legal or equitable interest of any kind? If so, on what terms? How much could the insured recover?

7. Note the time at which an insurable interest must exist under the California statute. What problems does that create for the protection of legitimate business interests? How would you alter the time requirement to correct the error, if it is one? There have been almost no appellate cases in California in which the problem has even been raised, and those few do not tell us much. In an important commercial state, why is that so after the provision has been on the books for over a century?

UNIFORM COMMERCIAL CODE §2 — 501

§2—501. Insurable Interest in Goods; Manner of Identification of Goods

(1) The buyer obtains a special property and an insurable interest in goods by identification of existing goods as goods to which the contract refers even though the goods so identified are non-conforming and he has an option to return or reject them. Such identification can be made at any time and in any manner explicitly agreed to by the parties. In the absence of explicit agreement identification occurs

(a) when the contract is made if it is for the sale of goods already existing and identified;

(b) if the contract is for the sale of future goods other than those described in paragraph (c), when goods are shipped, marked or otherwise designated by the seller as goods to which the contract refers;

(c) when the crops are planted or otherwise become growing crops or the young are conceived if the contract is for the sale of unborn young to be born within twelve months after contracting or for the sale of crops to be harvested within twelve months or the next normal harvest season after contracting whichever is longer.

(2) The seller retains an insurable interest in goods so long as title to or any security interest in the goods remains in him and where the identification is by the seller alone he may until default or insolvency or notification to the buyer that the identification is final substitute other goods for those identified.

(3) Nothing in this section impairs any insurable interest recognized under any other statute or rule of law.

Notes and Questions

1. If a buyer of goods takes out insurance on goods described generically, before identification, and the goods burn after identification, can the buyer recover under the policy? If the seller does not cancel his or her insurance after identification and the goods burn, can the seller recover under the policy? If so, how much?

2. The owner of a hardware store seeks to establish insurable interest in inventory it does not own. Franchisees own the inventory, but pay the rental and franchise fees to the store owner out of the proceeds of the sale of the inventory. The store owner is also co-obligor or guarantor on a note with the owners of the inventory, repayment of which is to be funded out of the proceeds of sales. Does the store owner have insurable interest in the inventory despite the lack of any legal or equitable interest? See Seals, Inc. v. Tioga County Grange Mut. Ins. Co., 359 Pa. Super. 606, 519 A.2d 951 (1986).

3. In *Silverton Elevators*, supra Section B, one of the defenses urged was lack of insurable interest. The court seems to have considered that defect subject to waiver by the insurer. If the insurer raises the issue of insurable interest for the first time on appeal, what should be the result? If the courts were to take a cue from the marine insurance statute of 19 Geo. II or its modern incarnation in the Marine Insurance Act of 1906, should the defense of lack of insurable interest be subject to waiver? If your answer is affirmative, is there any way to prevent an insurer from paying on the policy? Who might want that result?

4. If the insurer declines to pay on other grounds, without raising lack of insurable interest, and the claimant makes a good case apart from insurable interest, can and should the trial court raise and apply the doctrine *sua sponte*? If the trial court does not, should the appellate court do so?

5. Why might an insurer not want to pay on an insurance policy but also want to avoid raising the insurable interest defense?

b. Merits of the Doctrine

The merits of the insurable interest doctrine have seldom been questioned. The Wisconsin insurance code, however, does not accept the doctrine as useful. The relevant part of the Wisconsin statute is reproduced here, with the accompanying committee comment. Is this minority view tenable?

1975 WISCONSIN LAWS CH. 375, §41

1975 Wis. Laws ch. 375, §41

631.07 Insurable interest and consent.

(1) INSURABLE INTEREST. No insurer may knowingly issue a policy to a person without an insurable interest in the subject of the insurance.

(2) CONSENT IN LIFE AND DISABILITY INSURANCE. Except under sub. (3), no insurer may knowingly issue an individual life or disability insurance policy to a person other than the one whose life or health is at risk unless the latter has given written consent to the issuance of the policy. Consent may be expressed by knowingly signing the application for the insurance with knowledge of the nature of the document, or in any other reasonable way.

(3) CASES WHERE CONSENT IS UNNECESSARY OR MAY BE GIVEN BY ANOTHER. (a) *Consent unnecessary.* A life or disability insurance policy may be taken out without consent in the following cases: . . . [This subsection states some narrow exceptions to the general rule of subsection (2). Note that subsection (1) applies to all insurance, subsection (2) only to life and disability insurance.]

(4) EFFECT OF LACK OF INSURABLE INTEREST OR CONSENT. No insurance policy is invalid merely because the policyholder lacks insurable interest or because consent has not been given, but a court with appropriate jurisdiction may order the proceeds to be paid to someone other than the person to whom the policy is designated to be payable, who is equitably entitled thereto, or may create a constructive trust in the proceeds or a part thereof, subject to terms and conditions of the policy other than those relating to insurable interest or consent.

NOTE: Insurable interest makes sense as an underwriting restriction but not as a prerequisite to the validity of an insurance policy. If viewed as a disincentive to deliberate loss-causing it is largely ineffective; most known cases of homicide or of arson for insurance proceeds were committed by persons with a clear insurable interest. If viewed as a disincentive to gambling, it need only be pointed out that the house's cut is smaller in Las Vegas or at the local racetrack. The best way to discourage insurers from issuing insurance policies to persons without insurable interest is to make them pay if they do, not to permit them freely to issue such policies knowing that they have a good public policy defense that lets them off the hook whenever a loss occurs. The court should have power to order the proceeds paid as justice dictates.

Consent of the person at risk is the preferable device for protecting him in personal insurance. Some exceptions are necessary. It should be noted that lack of consent, too, does not invalidate the policy but makes it possible for a court to decide that the proceeds should go to someone other than as provided by the contract.

Note

Though few cases nowadays turn on the presence or absence of insurable interest, the requirement still lives on. A recent application of the doctrine resulted in denial of recovery. Puritan Ins. Co. v. Yarber, 723 S.W.2d 98 (Mo. App. 1987). The result *could* have been reached on other grounds. Further, in a subsequent case, G.M. Battery & Boat Co. v. L.K.N. Corp., 747 S.W.2d 624 (Mo. 1988), the Supreme Court of Missouri enforced an insurance contract that had been challenged for lack of insurable interest, though the insured got a windfall as a result of the state's valued policy law (see Chapter 3). In *G.M. Battery* the court could simply have overruled *Yarber* but instead distinguished it as one of a line of cases holding that only the holder of a certificate of title had an insurable interest in a motor vehicle.

3. Insurable Interest in Life

In life insurance, most of the significance of the insurable interest doctrine is at once negated by the division of life insurance policies into two categories: those in which the person whose life is insured is the moving party, and those in which someone else is the moving party. For the former the statement is made *ad nauseum* that every person has an unlimited insurable interest in his or her own life and may designate anyone at all as beneficiary. Inasmuch as most life insurance is taken out by the person whose life is insured, the insurable interest doctrine is at once relegated to a small corner of the field of life insurance — to those cases where someone other than the person whose life is insured is the moving party.

Interesting problems are concealed in the expression *moving party*, however, as the following cases show.

BROMLEY'S ADMR. v. WASHINGTON LIFE INS. CO.

122 Ky. 402, 92 S.W. 17 (1906)

HOBSON, C.J. In December, 1900, George Bromley made an arrangement with Otis Bates by which he was to have his life insured for $1,000, and Bates was to pay the premiums and pay him $50 for the policy, which was to be assigned to Bates by Bromley. He made the application for the policy in Washington Life Insurance Company, which issued the policy on January 29, 1901, the policy being payable to his estate. Bromley and Bates then came to the office of the local agent. Bates was fixing to pay the premium and Bromley asked him if he would not take another $1,000 on the same terms. He agreed to pay the premiums and pay him $25 for another policy of like amount. Bromley then applied for another policy and the application was sent on, the agent retaining the policy which had come and Bates giving the agent a check for $127.64, the premium on the two policies. On February 18, 1901, Bates gave Bromley a check for $75 for the two policies as promised. The policies were assigned by Bromley to Bates. The assignment on the policies is dated March 25, 1901. The policies were never delivered to Bromley, but remained in the hands of the insurance agent until the assignment was put on them and he then delivered them to Bates. When the subsequent premiums fell due on the policies they were paid by Bates; after this Bromley died and this suit was brought by his administrator to recover on the policies. Bates was made a defendant and by his answer set up that the policies belonged to him. The insurance company pleaded the facts above stated, insisting that the policies were a wagering contract and void. On final hearing, the court dismissed the petition of the administrator and he appeals.

The proof shows clearly that Bates had no insurable interest in the life of Bromley, and while the assignment on the policies is dated March 25, 1901, the proof is clear that the policies were taken out by Bromley for the purpose of assigning them to Bates, under the arrangement that Bates was to pay him $75 for them and pay the premiums. In other words, the arrangement was simply that Bromley was to get $75 for having his life insured for Bates' benefit, Bates to pay the premiums on the policies. It is conceded that if the policies under this arrangement had been made payable to Bates they would have been void, as he had no insurable interest in the life of Bromley. But it is insisted that as they were made payable to Bromley's estate and were assigned by him to Bates, only the assignment is void, and that his administrator may recover of the insurance company. There would be force in this, if the policies had been delivered to Bromley and the assignment to Bates had been a subsequent and independent transaction. But the proof leaves no doubt that Bromley did not contemplate insuring his life for the benefit of his estate at any time. He contemplated simply getting $75 out of the arrangement. The policies were never intended to be delivered to Bromley. Bates was to pay the premiums and get the policies. The policies did not become effective until the first premium was paid. Bates paid the premium upon the idea that the policies were to be assigned to him and for this reason they were left in the hands of the insurance agent until the assignment was made, the delay in closing up the matter being due to the fact that the parties had to wait for the second policy to come. To hold such an arrangement good would be to shut our eyes to the truth and to enforce a mere form. The law does not allow one who has no insurable interest in the life of another, to insure it for his benefit, for the reason that it is a mere wager and holds out a temptation to fraud, the insurer having no interest in the life of the assured and having a direct interest in his death. Basye v. Adams, 81 Ky. 368; Warnock v. Davis, 104 U.S. 779, 26 L. Ed. 924; Keystone Association v. Norris, 115 Pa. 446, 8 Atl. 638, 2 Am. St. Rep. 572; Steinback v. Diepenbrock, 158 N.Y. 24, 52 N.E. 662, 44 L.R.A. 417, 70 Am. St. Rep. 424. In the latter case the court said: "The insured, instead of taking out a policy payable to a person having no insurable interest in his life, can take it out to himself, and at once assign it to such person. But such an attempt would not prove successful, for a policy issued and assigned under such circumstances, would be none the less a wagering policy, because of the form of it. The intention of the parties procuring the policy would determine its character, which the court would unhesitatingly declare in accordance with the facts, reading the policy and the assignment together, as forming part of one transaction." The cases of Prudential Life Insurance Company v. Cummins' Admr., 44 S.W. 431, 19 Ky. Law Rep. 1770, New York Life Insurance Company v. Brown's Adm'r, 66 S.W. 613, 23 Ky. Law Rep. 2070, and Griffin's Administrator v. Equitable Assurance Society, 84 S.W. 1164, 27 Ky. Law Rep. 313, may be distinguished from this case. In the first case, there was no assignment of the policy to the person who paid the premiums and the court simply held that the fact that a stranger paid the premiums did not invalidate the policy. In the second case, the assignee testified that he had no interest in the policy until it was assigned to him subsequent to the delivery. In the last case the insurance company had paid the money to the persons to whom the policies were payable and after this was sued by the administrator of the assured. The court in deciding that the insurance company was not liable used this language: "The transaction as to each policy was clearly a speculation upon the hazard of human life, and consequently a gambling scheme, pure and simple, which rendered the policies void, because against public policy; and, if void, no cause of action against appellee exists in favor of Griffin's administrator for the recovery of the proceeds."

It is also insisted for the plaintiff that as the policies contain a clause to the effect that they are incontestable after one year, the company cannot rely upon this defense. But the incontestable clause is no less a part of the contract than any other provision of it. If the contract is against public policy the court will not lend its aid to its enforcement. The defense need not be pleaded. If at any time it appears in the process of the action that the contract sued upon is one which the law forbids, the court will refuse relief. The parties to an illegal contract cannot by stipulating that it shall be incontestable, tie the hands of the court and compel it to enforce contracts which are illegal and void. If this were allowed, then the law might be evaded in all cases and the aid of the court might be secured in aid of its infraction. In Hall v. Coppell, 7 Wall. 559, 19 L.Ed. 244, the United States Supreme Court said: "The defense is allowed, not for the sake of the defendant, but of the law itself. The principle is indispensable to the purity of its administration. It will not enforce what it has forbidden and denounced. The maxim, 'Ex dolo malo non oritur actio,' is limited by no such qualification. The proposition to the contrary strikes us as hardly worthy of serious refutation. Whenever the illegality appears, whether the evidence comes from one side or the other, the disclosure is fatal to the case. No consent of the defendant can neutralize its effect. . . .

Judgment affirmed.

GRIGSBY v. RUSSELL

222 U.S. 149 (1911)

Mr. Justice HOLMES delivered the opinion of the court.

This is a bill of interpleader brought by an insurance company to determine whether a policy of insurance issued to John C. Burchard, now deceased, upon his life, shall be paid to his administrators or to an assignee, the company having turned the amount into court. The material facts are that after he had paid two premiums and a third was overdue, Burchard, being in want and needing money for a surgical operation, asked Dr. Grigsby to buy the policy and sold it to him in consideration of one hundred dollars and Grigsby's undertaking to pay the premiums due or to become due; and that Grigsby had no interest in the life of the assured. The Circuit Court of Appeals in deference to some intimations of this court held the assignment valid only to the extent of the money actually given for it and the premiums subsequently paid. 168 Fed. Rep. 577, 94 C.C.A. 61.

Of course the ground suggested for denying the validity of an assignment to a person having no interest in the life insured is the public policy that refuses to allow insurance to be taken out by such persons in the first place. A contract of insurance upon a life in which the insured has no interest is a pure wager that gives the insured a sinister counter interest in having the life come to an end. And although that counter interest always exists, as early was emphasized for England in the famous case of Wainewright (Janus Weathercock), the chance that in some cases it may prove a sufficient motive for crime is greatly enhanced if the whole world of the unscrupulous are free to bet on what life they choose. The very meaning of an insurable interest is an interest in having the life continue and so one that is opposed to crime. And, what perhaps is more important, the existence of such an interest makes a roughly selected class of persons who by their general relations with the person whose life is insured are less likely than criminals at large to attempt to compass his death.

But when the question arises upon an assignment it is assumed that the objection to the insurance as a wager is out of the case. In the present instance the policy was perfectly good. There was a faint suggestion in argument that it had become void by the failure of Burchard to pay the third premium *ad diem,* and that when Grigsby paid he was making a new contract. But a condition in a policy that it shall be void if premiums are not paid when due, means only that it shall be voidable at the option of the company. Knickerbocker Life Ins. Co. v. Norton, 96 U.S. 234; Oakes v. Manufacturers' Fire & Marine Ins. Co., 135 Massachusetts, 248. The company waived the breach, if there was one, and the original contract with Burchard remained on foot. No question as to the character of that contract is before us. It has been performed and the money is in court. But this being so, not only does the objection to wagers disappear, but also the principle of public policy referred to, at least in its most convincing form. The danger that might arise from a general license to all to insure whom they like does not exist. Obviously it is a very different thing from granting such a general license, to allow the holder of a valid insurance upon his own life to transfer it to one whom he, the party most concerned, is not afraid to trust. The law has no universal cynic fear of the temptation opened by a pecuniary benefit accruing upon a death. It shows no prejudice against remainders after life estates, even by the rule in *Shelley's Case.* Indeed, the ground of the objection to life insurance without interest in the earlier English cases was not the temptation to murder but the fact that such wagers came to be regarded as a mischievous kind of gaming. St. 14 George III, c.48.

On the other hand, life insurance has become in our days one of the best recognized forms of investment and self-compelled saving. So far as reasonable safety permits, it is desirable to give to life policies the ordinary characteristics of property. This is recognized by the Bankruptcy Law, §70, which provides that unless the cash surrender value of a policy like the one before us is secured to the trustee within thirty days after it has been stated the policy shall pass to the trustee as assets. Of course the trustee may have no interest in the bankrupt's life. To deny the right to sell except to persons having such an interest is to diminish appreciably the value of the contract in the owner's hands. The collateral difficulty that arose from regarding life insurance as a contract of indemnity only, Godsall v. Boldero, 9 East, 72, long has disappeared. Phoenix Mutual Life Ins. Co. v. Bailey, 13 Wall. 616. And cases in which a person having an interest lends himself to one without any as a cloak to what is in its inception a wager have no similarity to those where an honest contract is sold in good faith.

Coming to the authorities in this court, it is true that there are intimations in favor of the result come to by the Circuit Court of Appeals. But the case in which the strongest of them occur was one of the type just referred to, the policy having been taken out for the purpose of allowing a stranger association to pay the premiums and receive the greater part of the benefit, and having been assigned to it at once. Warnock v. Davis, 104 U.S. 775. On the other hand it has been decided that a valid policy is not avoided by the cessation of the insurable interest, even as against the insurer, unless so provided by the policy itself. Connecticut Mutual Life Ins. Co. v. Schaefer, 94 U.S. 457. And expressions more or less in favor of the doctrine that we adopt are to be found also in Ætna Life Ins. Co. v. France, 94 U.S. 561. Mutual Life Ins. Co. v. Armstrong, 117 U.S. 591. It is enough to say that while the court below might hesitate to decide against the language of *Warnock v. Davis*, there has been no decision that precludes us from exercising our own judgment upon this much debated point. It is at least satisfactory to learn from the decision below that in Tennessee, where this assignment was made, although there has been much division of opinion, the Supreme Court of that State came to the conclusion that we adopt, in an unreported case, Lewis v. Edwards, December 14, 1903. The law in England and the preponderance of decisions in our state courts are on the same side.

Some reference was made to a clause in the policy that "any claim against the company arising under any assignment of the policy shall be subject to proof of interest." But it rightly was assumed below that if there was no rule of law to that effect and the company saw fit to pay, the clause did not diminish the rights of Grigsby as against the administrators of Burchard's estate.

Decree reversed.

Notes and Questions

1. What jurisdiction's law was applied in *Grigsby*? Under present doctrine, what law should have governed the case?

2. Justice Holmes distinguished *Grigsby* from *Warnock* on the facts, but *Warnock* stated the broader doctrine that "assignment of a policy to a party not having an insurable interest is as objectionable as the taking out of a policy in his name." If *Warnock* stands for the broader doctrine, which rule is preferable? What social policies should the insurable interest doctrine try to implement?

STATUTE ON INSURABLE INTEREST
IN LIFE INSURANCE

14 George III, ch. 48 (1774)

AN ACT *for regulating Insurances upon Lives, and for prohibiting all such Insurances except in cases where the Persons insuring shall have an Interest in the Life or Death of the Persons insured.*

WHEREAS it hath been found by experience that the making insurances on lives or other events wherein the assured shall have no interest hath introduced a mischievous kind of gaming: For remedy whereof, be it enacted by the King's most excellent Majesty, by and with the advice and consent of the lords spiritual and temporal, and commons, in this present Parliament assembled, and by the authority of the same, that from and after the passing of this Act no insurance shall be made by any person or persons, bodies politick or corporate, on the life or lives of any person or persons, or on any other event or events whatsoever, wherein the person or persons for whose use, benefit, or on whose account such policy or policies shall be made, shall have no interest, or by way of gaming or wagering; and that every assurance made contrary to the true intent and meaning hereof shall be null and void to all intents and purposes whatsoever.

[II.] AND be it further enacted, that it shall not be lawful to make any policy or policies on the life or lives of any person or persons, or other event or events, without inserting in such policy or policies the person or persons name or names interested therein, or for whose use, benefit, or on whose account such policy is so made or underwrote.

[III.] AND be it further enacted, that in all cases where the insured hath interest in such life or lives, event or events, no greater sum shall be recovered or received from the insurer or insurers than the amount or value of the interest of the insured in such life or lives, or other event or events.

NEW YORK INSURANCE LAW §3205

N.Y. Ins. Law §3205 (McKinney 1985)

§3205. Insurable interest in the person; consent required; exceptions

(a) In this section:

(1) The term, "insurable interest" means:

(A) in the case of persons closely related by blood or by law, a substantial interest engendered by love and affection;

(B) in the case of other persons, a lawful and substantial economic interest in the continued life, health or bodily safety of the person insured, as distinguished from an interest which would arise only by, or would be enhanced in value by, the death, disablement or injury of the insured.

(2) The term "contract of insurance upon the person" includes any policy of life insurance and any policy of accident and health insurance.

(3) The term "person insured" means the natural person, or persons, whose life, health or bodily safety is insured.

(b)(1) Any person of lawful age may on his own initiative procure or effect a contract of insurance upon his own person for the benefit of any person, firm, association or corporation.

(2) No person shall procure or cause to be procured, directly or by assignment or otherwise any contract of insurance upon the person of another unless the benefits under such contract are payable to the person insured or his personal representatives, or to a person having, at the time when such contract is made, an insurable interest in the person insured.

(3) If the beneficiary, assignee or other payee under any contract made in violation of this subsection receives from the insurer any benefits thereunder accruing upon the death, disablement or injury of the person insured, the person insured or his executor or administrator may maintain an action to recover such benefits from the person receiving them.

(c) No contract of insurance upon the person, except a policy of group life insurance, group or blanket accident and health insurance, or family insurance, as defined in this chapter, shall be made or effectuated unless at or before the making of such contract the person insured, being of lawful age or competent to contract therefor, applies for or consents in writing to the making of the contract, except in the following cases:

(1) A wife or a husband may effectuate insurance upon the person of the other.

(2) Any person having an insurable interest in the life of a minor under the age of fourteen years and six months or any person upon whom such minor is dependent for support and maintenance, may effectuate a contract of insurance upon the life of such minor, in an amount which shall not exceed the limits specified in section three thousand two hundred seven of this article.

Notes and Questions

1. In New York (and many other states), an insurable interest in a life can be based upon either love and affection (§3205(a)(1)(A)) or a substantial economic interest (§3205(a)(1)(A)). The love and affection

required need not be real. But in the absence of a pecuniary interest, the relationship must be close, by marriage or blood. That suffices, however unfriendly the personal relationships may actually be. Insurable interest generally exists between husband and wife, parent and child, and among siblings. The following relationships, however, have been found not to be close enough for an insurable interest to exist: cousin and cousin, aunt or uncle and niece or nephew, and stepdaughter and stepfather. See Keeton & Widiss, Insurance Law: Student Edition 181-183 (1988). Mutual Savings Life Ins. Co. v. Noah, 291 Ala. 444, 282 So. 2d 271 (1973). See also Best, Defining Insurable Interest in Lives, 22 Tort & Ins. L.J. 104 (1986). Is it sensible to assume for the purpose of validating insurance policies that all parents and children, or all siblings, or all married couples do feel love and affection for one another?

2. The rationale behind the insurable interest doctrine in life insurance is two-fold: (1) that if insurable interest exists the contract is not a wagering contract, and (2) that so long as an insurable interest exists the policyholder will usually prefer to have the insured alive rather than dead. Theoretically the latter will neutralize any monetary incentive to terminate the insured's life for the policy benefits, but it is surely safe to say that only a small proportion of all the cases of homicide for insurance proceeds, which may be much more numerous than those that are detected, is committed by persons without an insurable interest. If that is a correct statement, why would it be so?

3. Should insurable interest be found to exist if two people in fact feel love and affection for one another, even if their relationship falls outside of the traditional categories? That is, should the validity of an insurance policy depend on actual love and affection or only on a presumption that it exists? If on a presumption, should it be rebuttable or conclusive? Should such a presumption exist for unmarried heterosexual couples living together in a putatively permanent relationship? If insurable interest (or a presumption of it) were extended to such heterosexual couples, should it also be extended to putatively permanent homosexual couples? If the answer to either of the two previous questions is yes, then how do you determine, in the absence of a legal ceremony, whether a relationship is putatively permanent?

4. Whatever the merits of the insurable interest doctrine, it surely rests in public policy. New England Mut. Life Ins. Co. v. Caruso, 73 N.Y.2d 74, 535 N.E.2d 270, 538 N.Y.S.2d 217 (1989), held that in New York the passage of the contestable period makes the policy invulnerable to the defense of lack of insurable interest. Is that a sound result?

5. The choice of law rule for life insurance is stated in Restatement of Conflicts Second §192, as follows:

> The validity of a life insurance contract and the rights created thereby are determined by the local law of the state where the insured was

domiciled at the time the policy was issued, unless, with respect to the particular issue, some other state has a more significant relationship to the transaction and the parties, in which event the local law of the other state will be applied.

Comment (a) makes it clear that §192 applies to insurable interest.

6. On some points, the choice of law may be important. For example, Texas long stood virtually alone on the basis of the doctrine illustrated by the following case. Somewhat later, Texas by statute joined the rest of the states on this point.

CHEEVES v. ANDERS

87 Tex. 287, 28 S.W. 274 (1894)

BROWN, J. J. H. Anders, as administrator of L. B. Chilton, brought this suit in the district court of Falls county to recover the amount of a policy issued by the New York Life Insurance Company for $10,000, payable to Cheeves & Chilton, or their administrators or assigns, making the insurance company and Cheeves defendants. The insurance company did not deny liability, and the contest was between the plaintiff and Cheeves as to the right to receive the proceeds from the policy. Cheeves filed an answer in which he pleaded that he was entitled to the proceeds of the policy, as against the company and plaintiff, because at the time of issuing the said policy, on the 17th day of May, 1889, he and the deceased. L. B. Chilton, were partners engaged in mercantile business in Falls county, and that the said partnership procured the issuance of the said policy of insurance upon the life of the said Chilton, and paid the premium thereon, $590, out of and with the money and assets of said firm, and that thereafter, on April 23, 1890, the said firm paid out of its assets another premium of $590 upon said policy, which kept it in force until the death of Chilton. It is alleged in the answer that at the same time another policy was issued by the said insurance company, payable to Cheeves & Chilton, or their administrators or assigns, upon the death of T. A. Cheeves, and for the like sum of $10,000, upon which premiums were paid out of the assets of the said firm amounting to an equal sum to that paid upon the policy in suit; that on the 23d day of September, 1890, the firm of Cheeves & Chilton was dissolved, and Chilton, for a consideration of about $20,500, by writing, conveyed to Cheeves all his right and claim in and to all of the partnership property and rights of every kind, the language being set out broadly enough to include all interest that the firm had in the policy at the time of the transfer. Chilton died November 7, 1890, and proofs of loss were duly furnished. Cheeves claims that he was interested in the life of Chilton, as his partner, at the time the policy was issued, and also that Chilton transferred the policy to him. He closed his answer with a prayer for general relief. There is no allegation in the answer that L. B. Chilton was indebted to the firm of Cheeves & Chilton or to Cheeves, or in what respect Cheeves had any interest in the life of Chilton, except simply that he was a partner when the policy was issued. Plaintiff filed a general demurrer to the answer, which the court sustained, and, upon trial without a jury, gave judgment for the plaintiff against both defendants for the whole amount of the policy, which judgment was by the court of civil appeals affirmed.

It is against the public policy of this state to allow any one who has no insurable interest to be the owner of a policy of insurance upon the life of a human being. Price v. Supreme Lodge, 68 Tex. 361, 4 S.W. 633; Schonfield v. Turner, 75 Tex. 329, 12 S.W. 626; Insurance Co. v. Hazlewood, 75 Tex. 351, 12 S.W. 621. In some states it is held that an element of wagering likewise enters into such contracts, which has led, as we believe, to inconsistencies in the decisions in some of the courts. Our court has placed the inhibition against such contracts upon the higher and sounder ground that the public, independent of the consent or concurrence of the parties, has an interest that no inducement shall be offered to one man to take the life of another. Making this the test in every phase of such cases, there can be no inconsistency in our decisions, and the public good will be better guarded. . . .

A man may insure his own life, making the policy payable to his legal representatives, and afterwards assign it to any one, or he may procure such policy, and make it payable to any person that he may name; but in either case, if the person to whom it is assigned or who is named in the policy has no insurable interest, he will hold the proceeds as a trustee for the benefit of those entitled by law to receive it. Price v. Supreme Lodge, and Schonfield v. Turner, cited above. The law permits one who is interested in the life of another to become the owner of insurance upon the life of such other person, either by contracting with the insurance company, or by contract made by the party whose life is insured, or by assignment of the policy after it is issued. If, however, the interest is of a definite character, as that of a creditor of the insured, or of one who may, from the life of the insured, reap some pecuniary advantage of a definite nature, the interest of the holder of such policy will be limited to the amount of such liability at the death of the insured, together with such amount as he has paid to preserve the policy, with interest thereon, and the remainder will be given to the estate of the party insured. Price v. Supreme Lodge, 68 Tex. 361, 4 S.W. 633; Schonfield v. Turner, 75 Tex. 324, 12 S.W. 626; Insurance Co. v. Hazlewood, 75 Tex. 338, 12 S.W. 621; Goldbaum v. Blum, 79 Tex. 638, 15 S.W. 564. If the interest of the policy holder should cease before the death of the insured, as if the debt should be paid and premiums advanced, then the whole of the policy will go to the estate of the insured.

When an insurance company has issued a policy upon the life of a person, payable to one who has no insurable interest in the life insured, or when a policy has been assigned to one having no such interest, the insurance company must nevertheless pay the full amount of the policy, if otherwise liable, because it has so contracted; and it is no concern of the insurer as to who gets the proceeds, except to see that it is paid to the proper parties, under its agreement. It is simply required to perform its contract, and the law will dispose of the money according to the rights of the parties. Insurance Co. v. Williams, 79 Tex. 637, 15 S.W. 478, and authorities cited. This rule does no wrong to the insurance company. It, having agreed to pay the money upon the death of a named person, ought not to be permitted to avoid liability upon its contract upon the ground that it has made an unlawful agreement, when that contract can be enforced in favor of a person who is in no wise concerned in the unlawful part of the transaction. . . .

It has, however, been held that where the interest existed at the time of making the contract, but ceased before death, the person to whom the policy is made payable may recover and hold the entire amount of the policy, as against the claim of the representatives of the insured. Scott v. Dickson, 108 Pa. St. 6; Ritter v. Smith, 70 Md. 261, 16 Atl. 890; Amick v. Butler, 111 Ind. 578, 12 N.E. 518. This we regard as opposed to the paramount reason for holding such insurance to be unlawful; that is, the danger in offering an inducement to destroy human life. If the inhibition against such transactions be that they are considered wagering contracts, as appears to be the ground upon which the decisions cited are placed, it is consistent to hold as in the cases quoted. If, however, the making of such agreements be placed upon the ground that it is against public policy for one to be interested in the death of another when he has no interest in the continuance of his life, the decisions cannot be sustained upon principle. The want of insurable interest is just as absolute where it has ceased as where it never existed, and the inducement to destroy the life insured for gain is just as strong in the one case as in the other. We cannot disregard the sound principles established by our courts, and follow another line of decisions, however eminent the courts or numerous the cases. We therefore hold that in this case the interest which Cheeves may have had in the policy as partner, aside from his interest which was joint with Chilton, and therefore belonged to partnership, ceased at the dissolution of the firm, and will not sustain his claim to the proceeds of this policy. . . .

The judgments of both courts are reversed as to plaintiff J. H. Anders, administrator of L. B. Chilton, and defendant Cheeves, and this cause is remanded to the district court for further proceedings in accordance with this opinion, to ascertain the rights of the said Anders, administrator, and Cheeves, in the proceeds of said policy.

Notes and Questions

1. Which is preferable: the traditional Texas approach or the majority doctrine? Why?

2. Reexamine 1975 Wis. Laws, ch. 375, §41, supra, and the comments on it. The author did not succeed in getting the whole of what he proposed in earlier versions of the draft, as the comments make clear. The second (unenacted) draft stated, "No insurance policy is invalid because the policyholder lacks insurable interest in the risk insured." Id., §631.07(1). Would this unenacted provision have been sound for life insurance? For fire insurance? If you think not, what is the case for adhering to traditional insurable interest doctrine, apart from the fact that it represents the received wisdom?

3. How would you structure rules that would minimize the incentives to commit homicide for life insurance proceeds? To commit arson?

4. Would it make sense to recognize a right of action in tort for wrongful death against an insurance company that issues a policy when there is no insurable interest, if homicide results? See Liberty Nat. Life Ins. Co. v. Weldon, 267 Ala. 171, 100 So. 2d 696 (1957). Is there a significant difference between that result and the result produced by the old Texas doctrine?

5. None of the above is intended to minimize the horror of murder for insurance proceeds, nor to suggest it is not important to deal with it: The question is *how* to deal with it most effectively. Penn, Deadly Policies: Murder for Insurance, A Crime Hard to Solve, Seems to Be Growing, Wall St. J., Jan. 14, 1988, at 1, suggests that the problem is increasingly serious. Penn quoted a vice president of a medium sized life insurance company as saying the company "had 30 homicide cases last year in which beneficiaries are suspect. Five years earlier, we didn't have more than 10 or 11." The article remarks elsewhere that there is no way of knowing how many "champagne sippers and caviar nibblers" are giggling over the old saw that "crime doesn't pay." The article described a number of the *detected* cases of homicide for insurance proceeds. In all those described, there clearly *was* insurable interest, which may say something about the utility of the doctrine as it now stands.

PART II

Selected Kinds of Insurance

CHAPTER 3

Property Insurance

A. Introduction

Insurance may be classified in many ways, depending on the purpose of the classification: The one used here names as broad categories (1) property, (2) fidelity, (3) liability, (4) life, (5) health, and (6) "other" coverages, including suretyship, financial guaranty insurance, title insurance, and credit insurance. This book deals only incidentally with the "other" category. Marine insurance, too, is incidentally treated here, though for some purposes it would be a main category. The most interesting part of marine insurance is property insurance, though marine liability coverage also exists. It has great intrinsic interest and historical importance, but comparatively few lawyers now deal with it.

Insurance against crimes could be treated as an independent category, but protection from offenses against property is also property insurance and is not dealt with independently. White collar crime is treated in this book under fidelity bonds.

Marine insurance, the oldest branch of insurance, still bears the marks of its antiquity. Life insurance is nearly as old as marine but needs to be treated in close connection with health insurance, which is very modern. Fire insurance, coming next in time after life insurance, is subsumed here under the broader rubric of property insurance, along with many later developing coverages. Liability insurance and insurance against crime are relatively recent in origin and are now of massive significance.

This chapter deals with selected problems in property insurance.

Some doctrines that affect property insurance, such as insurable interest, warranties, representations, and concealment derive from those applicable to marine insurance but are more modern. They were covered in Chapter 2. To a considerable extent the same doctrines also apply, *mutatis mutandis,* to liability insurance and even to life and health insurance and the miscellaneous coverages.

Measured by premium volume, the most important kinds of property insurance are insurance against automobile physical damage and against fire.

Automobile physical damage coverage will get summary treatment because of its general familiarity and also because today it appears relatively infrequently in appellate litigation, considering its economic importance. In general, the stakes in individual cases are too small to justify pressing litigation to the appellate level. Moreover, the doctrines are relatively well established, though there is often a dispute on the facts.

There are two branches of automobile physical damage insurance. *Collision* is, in monetary terms, the more important. *Comprehensive* coverage includes fire insurance on the car as one element; theft is the second most important element under that heading. There are also lesser components, such as insurance against falling objects.

In addition to its appearance as a risk covered by automobile and marine insurance, fire insurance can be found both in a pure form and in multiple peril policies (homeowners, farmowners, commercial multiline). In marine and auto, coverage against the fire risk is supplementary and produces a small premium volume, but the multiple peril policies start from a base of fire insurance protection with liability and theft as the supplementary coverages. Homeowners policies appear in this chapter for their fire and other property coverage and in Chapter 5 for their liability coverage.

Compared to fire and automobile physical damage, other kinds of property insurance produce a relatively small premium volume. Among the other property coverages, protection against theft and related crimes is probably the largest.

Until about 1800 marine insurance was the most important branch of insurance. After that it took second place to fire insurance, though it still accounted for about 30 percent of the world's premium volume. It continued to grow slowly in absolute terms, increasing to about $10.5 billion worldwide in 1980, but simultaneously it steadily decreased in relative importance until by 1900 its share of world premium volume was about eight percent. By 1925 it was only two percent.

Other property coverages, such as earthquake, flood, and livestock morbidity and mortality, among others, receive only passing mention here. But no coverage is unimportant to the person who needs it nor to the insurer that makes a market in it.

The heydey of fire insurance *litigation* was the nineteenth century. Today, most basic problems of doctrine and contract interpretation have been settled, so litigation about fire insurance has become relatively uncommon. Property insurance can involve large sums of money, though the litigation problems tend to be less complex than those of liability insurance.

For an impression of the patterns of litigation flow in insurance, based on a study of fire and automobile insurance, see Kimball, The Role of the Court in the Development of Insurance Law, 1957 Wis. L. Rev. 520, 562. The article suggests an elementary theory of insurance litigation, and should make it clear why property insurance litigation is not now an active part of insurance law.

Examples of major property losses include any hurricane that hits a heavily populated area along the coast of the United States, the $2.7 billion storm loss of 1987 in Britain and Western Europe, and two *more* "once-in-a-lifetime" storms in the same areas in 1990. Of the latter storms, the first is currently estimated to have cost insurers $1.6 billion and the second is too recent to estimate at this writing but may be comparable to the 1987 storm. Some early estimates of insured damage from 1989's Hurricane Hugo exceed $4 billion, while the final numbers may be even larger. The insured losses from the 1989 San Francisco earthquake cannot yet be estimated with precision: early estimates ranged from about $1 billion to $4 billion, with the lower ones being more probable. The $1.2-1.5 billion marine insurance loss at the Piper Alpha drilling rig in the North Sea in 1989 was a catastrophic property loss. Except for Piper Alpha, these property losses are individually small; it is only in the aggregate that they are massive. Yet there are numerous cases of single property insurance claims in nine figures.

For lawyers, much of the "action" in insurance is now in the newer liability fields as an outgrowth of the recent explosive developments in tort law. Partly, too, the action is there because of the complexity of the cases and the large stakes involved in individual cases. Some individual cases involve many hundreds of millions of dollars: Unlike a good many of the tort cases underlying them, the *ad damnums* tend to be fairly realistic estimates of possible recoveries rather than the absurdly exaggerated claims common to tort complaints.

The fact that a class of insurance policies has ceased to appear frequently in reported cases because the doctrines have become relatively settled does not make the class unimportant for the lawyer. It instead means that cases of even substantial magnitude are settled rather than litigated. But they are still the stuff of the law!

B.   Moral Hazard Clauses

1.   In General

If there is any reason the insured might prefer that an insured loss occur, or be inclined to be less careful to avoid the loss, there is said to be a *moral hazard*. The existence of moral hazards is one of the primary concerns in underwriting insurance policies; insurers try to avoid significant moral hazard through policy design, or if it cannot be avoided they may decline to write the risks or may qualify their promises.

The problem exists in all lines of insurance, and takes different forms in different situations. At the extreme, one can be tempted to commit homicide (or even suicide) for life insurance proceeds, to commit arson for fire insurance proceeds, or to stage accidents fraudulently to collect under automobile insurance policies. In some lines of insurance, notably liability insurance, the very existence of the insurance is thought to be a disincentive, though not always a major one, to the exercise of the degree of care the insurer would hope for.

Clauses seeking to minimize moral hazard have an especially interesting history in fire insurance. In the 1887 New York Standard Fire Insurance Policy* there are fourteen moral hazard clauses, each providing for avoidance of the contract on breach of the condition stated in the clause. In 1918 a new standard fire policy reduced to five the number of clauses that made the policy void; the other moral hazard clauses only suspended it. Finally, all the moral hazard clauses but three were eliminated from the 1943 New York Standard Fire Policy; the surviving three, including the increase of hazard clause, only suspended coverage. This step-by-step liberalizing of restrictive clauses (together with a broadening of coverage clauses) occurred over the long term in most lines of insurance, as experience with the coverage reduced underwriters' fears and competition worked its magic.

The liberalizing of restrictive clauses has not proceeded at a uniform pace everywhere. One of the original moral hazard clauses was the "sole and unconditional ownership" clause, which avoided the policy if the named insured(s) did not have sole and unconditional ownership of the insured property. The most frequent consequence of this clause, if given literal effect, would be to invalidate insurance on property owned by spouses in joint tenancy or in tenancy by the entireties but insured in the name of only one spouse.

---

*The standard fire insurance policy has a long history. Massachusetts adopted one in 1873, and the New York standard policy, which eventually dominated the country, was first adopted in 1887. The standard fire insurance policies found their way into the statute books; the resulting rigidity complicated such innovations as homeowners insurance.

In 1936, Professor George Goble sampled policies in Champaign-Urbana, Illinois, and found that 28 percent of all those on real property and 55 percent of all those on jointly owned real property were void under the terms of the policy, as interpreted by the Illinois Supreme Court in Pollock v. Connecticut Fire Ins. Co., 362 Ill. 313, 199 N.E. 816 (1935). How often and under what circumstances would insurance companies actually rely on the sole and unconditional ownership clause to avoid paying a loss? Obviously they sometimes did: *vide Pollock.* Goble's findings were published in The Moral Hazard Clauses of the Standard Fire Insurance Policy, 37 Colum. L. Rev. 410, 418 (1937). The clause was deleted in the 1943 New York standard fire insurance policy. It is a matter of speculation whether Goble's article produced that result or whether the long-term tendency to liberalize coverage was sufficient by itself. A professor who writes articles would like to believe the former.

The sole and unconditional ownership clause has long since been abandoned in most states. It was recently given effect to make a policy void, however, in National Security Fire & Casualty Co. v. London, 180 Ga. App. 198, 348 S.E.2d 580 (1986). Several family members had inherited interests in common in the insured property but only some of them were named insureds, thus violating the clause. In another recent case, Old Reliable Fire Ins. Co. v. Alduro-Raynes Arabians, Inc., 717 S.W.2d 124 (Tex. App. 1986), a sole ownership clause, designated in the policy as a warranty *and* as a condition precedent, voided an animal mortality policy on a horse. The court noted that §21.16 of the Texas Insurance Code, which applies to all insurance policies, deals only with misrepresentations, not with conditions or warranties. The court did not mention the more sweeping §6.14, which deals with "any warranty, condition or provision" in a policy or in an application for one, but applies only to fire insurance on personal property. Although animal mortality insurance is insurance on personal property, §6.14 would only be relevant if the death were caused by fire. The opinion does not mention the cause of death, but assuming good lawyering in the case, it must not have been by fire. Compare *Alduro-Raynes* with *Charles, Henry,* Chapter 2, Section A(4)(b), and consider how it would have fared under each of the statutes quoted there.

Another of the original moral hazard clauses forbade "other insurance." Mister v. Highlands Ins. Co., 650 F. Supp. 428 (N.D. Miss. 1986) gave effect to a strict version of that clause, applying Mississippi law in Zepponi v. Home Ins. Co., 248 Miss. 828, 161 So. 2d 524 (1964). "Other insurance" is now generally dealt with differently.

Despite the long-term tendency to liberalize coverage, some moves in the opposite direction also occur, at least for the short term. Homeowners insurance illustrates both. Its very existence reflects the liberalizing tendency. After it came into vogue, however, some insurance companies initially suffered heavy losses. On the basis of perverted "insurance" logic they supposed at first that they had found the perpetual motion machine — that they could provide broader coverage for a global premium that was less than the previous aggregate cost of providing lesser coverage through separate policies. After this misplaced optimism was tempered by experience, they retreated to more realistic pricing and coverage terms. Only then did homeowners insurance become a permanent and successful part of the insurance landscape.

2.   Increase of Hazard

The standard fire insurance policy now in use contains a clause that states, "Unless otherwise provided in writing added hereto this Company shall not be liable for loss occurring (a) while the hazard is increased by any means within the control or knowledge of the insured." This increase of hazard clause has been greatly liberalized from its original formulation. The 1887 New York Standard Fire Policy said, "This entire policy . . . shall be void if . . . the hazard be increased by any means within the control or knowledge of the insured."

The effect of an increase of hazard in the current policy — the one first quoted — is to suspend coverage. Use of the conjunction "while" seems decisive on that point.

Notes and Questions

1. Should an increase of hazard clause be treated as a warranty? Is the decision whether to apply the clause a matter of degree, that is, of how much the hazard is increased? If so, how much of an increase (defined verbally, not in numbers) should make the clause operative?

2. What is meant by having the increase be within the knowledge or control of the insured? Is it enough that it is within the insured's control if the insured is not aware of it? The language seems to say so. Would the various statutes in Chapter 2, Section A(4), have any effect on the answer to the last question? What constitutes control and what constitutes knowledge?

3.   Illustrative Cases on the Increase of Hazard

In which of the following cases should the increase of hazard clause preclude recovery by the insured?

a. *Bringing explosives or dangerous chemicals onto the insured premises.* Compare Continental W. Fire Ins. Co. v. Poly Industries, 349 N.W.2d 606 (Minn. App. 1984) (bringing ethylene oxide (boiling point 51°F, coming in pressurized containers, and dangerously reactive) onto premises where isopropyl alcohol, methyl alcohol, and toluene (all flammable) were stored for use in making soaps and detergents was an increase of hazard) with Alabama Farm Bureau Mut. Casualty Ins. Co. v. Moore, 435 So. 2d 712 (Ala. 1983), *aff'd,* 452 So. 2d 712 (Ala. 1984) (having several boxes of fireworks in insured house for P's children at Christmas time is not an increase of hazard). Should it be relevant in *Poly Industries* that the ethylene oxide was not intended for use in soap making but for experimenting with a new product? Contrast *Moore* with Heron v. Phoenix Mut. Fire Ins. Co., 180 Pa. 257, 36 A. 740 (1897), where an earlier increase of hazard clause specifically forbade keeping fireworks on the premises.

b. *Turning the sprinkler system off.* Charles Stores, Inc. v. Aetna Ins. Co., 428 F.2d 989 (5th Cir. 1970), held that the failure to maintain the sprinkler system was an increase in hazard, as was the failure to maintain a fire alarm system. The "source of the fire appears to have been an incendiary device," however, allegedly placed by a vice president of the plaintiff. In Adams Machine & Tool Co. v. MFB Mut. Ins. Co., 479 F.2d 439 (5th Cir. 1973), the sprinkler system had been turned off. The case turned on complex evidentiary questions, but the court seemed to regard the turning off of the system as an increase in hazard. Again, arson was suspected. In Vicksburg Furniture Mfg., Ltd. v. Aetna Casualty & Surety Co., 625 F.2d 1167 (5th Cir. 1980), the court held that turning a sprinkler system off was an increase in hazard that suspended coverage even though it was done because a sprinkler head was leaking onto merchandise and there may not yet have been an opportunity to repair the system. Again there was suspicion of arson. What does the suspicion of arson in these cases suggest about the utility of technical clauses in adjusting claims? Should the result be different if there were no reasonable suspicion of arson?

c. *Allowing the building to deteriorate.* Compare Imperial Ins. Co. v. National Homes Acceptance Corp., 626 S.W.2d 327 (Tex. App. 1981) (allowing electricity and water to be disconnected, having tenant move out, letting squatter remain, and permitting building to remain in need of painting and screens do not make out a substantial or material increase in hazard, suspending coverage) with Bass v. Illinois FAIR Plan Assn.,* 98 Ill. App. 3d 549, 424 N.E.2d 908, 54 Ill. Dec. 158 (1981) (when insured premises were abandoned after previous fires, failing to keep them fully boarded up plus allowing easy access increased the hazard and suspended coverage).

d. *Using insured premises for an illegal purpose.* In Frisby v. Central Mut. Ins. Co., 238 Miss. 538, 119 So. 2d 382 (1960), insured premises described as a grocery were used for illegal sale of liquor. It was held to be a jury question whether there was an increase in hazard. The jury found for the defendant insurer. In Good v. Continental Ins. Co., 277 S.C. 569, 291 S.E.2d 198 (1982) the court reversed a jury verdict for plaintiff, finding that operating an illegal still in the attic of the insured premises was an increase of hazard. Should the illegality be dispositive? Relevant? It was mentioned, even emphasized, in both cases.

e. *Change in occupancy.* In Simpson v. Millers Natl. Ins. Co., 175 Colo. 197, 486 P.2d 12 (1971), the insured rented a building previously classified as a general warehouse to a tenant who processed cotton for mattresses. That was held to be a substantial increase in the hazard. Compare with *Wood,* Chapter 2.

f. *Termination of operation and of heating.* In Newmont Mines Ltd. v. Hanover Ins. Co., 784 F.2d 127 (2d Cir. 1986), the insured property was an enormous concentrator building at a British Columbia mine. The annual snowfall was as much as 1,200 inches, "the highest annual snowfall in the world." Snow removal was effected by heating the steeply sloping roof enough

---

*The mid-1960s were troubled years for urban American society. In the major cities riots destroyed large amounts of property and made the market for fire insurance tight or, in many central city areas, even nonexistent. In July 1967, President Johnson appointed a National Advisory Commission on Civil Disorders to investigate the causes of the disorders and to recommend corrective measures. Because insurance was a crucial factor in the solution of the problem, a supplementary National Advisory Panel on Insurance in Riot-Affected Areas was appointed in the following month. The result was "Meeting the Insurance Crisis of our Cities," an extensive and (for governmental studies) good report on the problem. Thereafter the Urban Property and Reinsurance Act of 1968, 82 Stat. 555 (1968), created the basis for Fair Access to Insurance Requirements (FAIR) plans which were subsequently enacted in about half the states. The plans provided for inspection of property that could not be insured in the private market and then assignment of the property through a central placement facility to participating insurers. Each FAIR plan that met certain standards could buy federal riot reinsurance.

For a detailed statement of the background leading to the FAIR plans, see the above named report; for a brief sketch of their operation, see G. Rejda, Principles of Insurance 153–154 (1982).

for it to act as a giant snowslide. When the mine ceased to be operated, no arrangements were made for snow removal and portions of the roof collapsed. The jury found the absence of heat was not a *material* change in the risk; the appellate court found the evidence sufficient to uphold that finding on appeal.

C. Coverage Problems

The multiplicity of kinds of property insurance and the variation among policy forms even within individual lines provide too much grist for an all-purpose mill to grind. The selection of problems to be discussed here depends in part on their value as illustrations, but also in part on the accidents of litigation, for a great many difficult problems have not yet been litigated; indeed, many are yet to be perceived as problems. The ingenuity of good lawyers in discerning latent ambiguities in contract language when they have unusual incidents to spur them on, their inability to anticipate the occurrence of all those incidents when they are drafting policy language, and the inexhaustible diversity in the human predicament make it certain that the possibilities will not all be revealed before the end of time.

1. All Risk v. Specified Perils Coverage

In both marine and property insurance, coverage can be either against all risks or only against specified perils. An article on all risk insurance begins with the statement:

> In addition to the exclusions that are named in the policy itself, every "all risk" contract of insurance contains an unnamed exclusion — the loss must be *fortuitous* in nature. This may be termed the fortuity doctrine. Even "all risk" coverage extends only to *risks*; an insurance carrier simply does not undertake to reimburse its insured for loss that is certain or expected to occur.
> Fortuity is not, in fact, an exclusion, but something inherent in the concept of "all risk" itself. As a result, the burden of proof with respect to a loss within coverage rests, as usual, on the shoulders of the insured. [Cozen & Bennett, Fortuity: The Unnamed Exclusion, 20 Forum 222 (1985).]

Avis v. Hartford Fire Ins. Co., 283 N.C. 142, 195 S.E.2d 545 (1973), stated four conditions for coverage under an all risk policy: (1) that the loss be fortuitous; (2) that the loss not result from an inherent quality or defect; (3) that the loss not result from intentional misconduct or fraud of the insured; and (4) that the risk be lawful. Essex House v. St. Paul Fire & Marine Ins. Co., 404 F. Supp. 978 (S.D. Ohio 1975), applied the fortuity test to "brick failure" on a building and found the loss fortuitous.

In Harbor House Condo. Assn. v. Massachusetts Bay Ins. Co., 703 F. Supp. 1313 (N.D. Ill. 1988), the insured could not recover for failure to show that part of the damage to a heating system claimed by the insured was caused by a fortuitous event.

Despite such cases and many dicta supporting the fortuity doctrine, Cozen and Bennett conclude that however valid the doctrine, "it has been emasculated by the courts." Supra at 248. Emasculation may not be an apt description of what has happened. Courts are reluctant to find that a particular loss is nonfortuitous; indeed, there seem to be few cases that have so held, *Harbor House* notwithstanding. Perhaps the inquiry should instead be whether the so-called fortuity doctrine means anything more than that a policy that covers *all* risks covers only *risks*. Despite the doctrine, there are cases where nonfortuitous loss is covered. A good example is suicide, which is covered after a period of noncoverage at the inception of the policy. There are also cases in liability insurance where a policy covers losses that have already occurred *and are known to have occurred* though their precise dimensions may not yet be known. Are such losses fortuitous?

Though it seems that courts have not entirely emasculated the fortuity doctrine, and though many authors even regard the doctrine as a basic principle of insurance law, it is doubtful that it really rises to that level. But few policies would be written to cover events that are not fortuitous. A more extensive discussion of fortuity and its application in insurance is found in Keeton & Widiss, Insurance Law: Student Edition §5.3(a) (1988).

Notes and Questions

1. In Peters Township School Dist. v. Hartford Accident & Indem. Co., 643 F. Supp. 518 (W.D. Pa. 1986), an all risk policy excluded:

> D. Loss caused by, resulting from, contributed to or aggravated by any of the following:
>
> > 1. earth movement, including but not limited to earthquake, landslide, mudflow, earth sinking, earth rising or shifting; . . .
>
> unless fire or explosion as insured against ensues, and then this Company shall be liable for only loss caused by the ensuing fire or explosion. . . .

The two insured buildings were allegedly damaged by mine subsidence. The mining operations had been terminated forty and fifty years earlier, respectively. The trial court noted that the sites were considered safe for building and said that the earth movement exclusion seemed to have had its origin after the San Francisco earthquake and was intended to exclude natural calamities such as those listed (making the *eiusdem generis* rule appropriate). The trial court concluded that mine subsidence caused by human mining activity that was terminated so long ago must be classed with natural events, not human activities, and found for the insurer. On appeal, however, the court said it was irrelevant how long ago the mining activity was terminated: Mine subsidence was not the natural kind of earth movement that was excluded. Since for one building there was no argument with respect to causation, the appellate court held for the insured, while for the other building a dispute over causation led that part of the case to be remanded for further proceedings. Id., 833 F.2d 32 (3d Cir. 1987). Were the losses fortuitous?

2. Having been as generous as it was to the insurer in *Peters Township School District,* the trial court felt justified in offering the insurer some advice:

> We suggest, however, in the interest of minimizing future widespread litigation, that the insurers in future policies insert a specific exclusion for "subsidence" if that is a particular peril which they do not wish to insure against. [Id., 643 F. Supp. 518, 523 (W.D. Pa. 1986).]

Though the trial court by its decision briefly made it appear less necessary to follow the advice (until after the decision on appeal), it seems on its face to be good advice. The differing facts of the next case to come along, or a different composition of the court, might lead to a different result (as the latter factor did here on appeal). On the other hand, even if the decision of the trial court had held up on appeal, is there not a risk that changing the terms of the contract will result in the loss of similar cases that arise on the old contract, on the ground that making the change was an admission of ambiguity? Would following the advice be wiser for property insurance, in which claims tend to be made and settled quickly, than for liability insurance, in which cases governed by the old language may not be initiated until long after the change in policy terms?

3. In Insurance Co. of North America v. United States Gypsum Co., 678 F. Supp. 138 (W.D. Va. 1988), the insured's gypsum processing plant subsided as a result of earlier mining activity. The insurance was all risk with no relevant express exclusion. The court focused on whether the subsidence was fortuitous and held it was, since if it were not there would have been an implied exception or exclusion. "The court finds a non-fortuitous loss is one that must have been intended

and expected from the standpoint of the insured." Id. at 144. Does this mean that only deliberate loss-causing is to be considered non-fortuitous?

4. All risk coverage does not cover *all* causes of loss. See Hecker & Goode, Wear and Tear, Inherent Vice, Deterioration, Etc.: The Multi-Faceted All-Risk Exclusions, 21 Tort & Ins. L.J. 634 (1986). Is the preferable explanation of all these exceptions or exclusions that the losses are not *fortuitous,* or that they are not *risks?*

5. In Puerto Rico Elec. Power Auth. v. Philipps, 645 F. Supp. 770 (D.P.R. 1986), the insured had an all-risk policy with Lloyd's, with a deductible of $1 million (for the kind of loss at issue) and a limit of $5 million *per loss*. There was also an "Application of Deductibles" clause providing that "[a] series of losses arising from the same event shall be treated as a single loss in the application of the deductibles." The Authority suffered a strike by its employees, during which 238 separate acts of sabotage or vandalism against its property were committed. How many "events" were there, and how many "losses"?

2. Causation, Sequential and Concurrent

Causation problems frequently surface in interpreting property insurance policy language. Sometimes there is a single significant causal relationship. If there is more than one such cause, sometimes those causes are sequential and sometimes they are concurrent. The considerations taken into account in dealing with these different cases vary.

One elementary causation problem arises out of an exclusion that has often (but not always) been inserted in aircraft policies. It seeks to exclude coverage for aircraft not complying with certain federal regulations. In O'Connor v. Proprietors Ins. Co., 696 P.2d 282 (Colo. 1985), the policy excluded "loss occurring while the aircraft is operated in violation of the terms of its Federal Aviation Airworthiness Certificate or Operational Record." The FAA certification required both annual and 100-hour inspections; the annual inspections had to be more thorough and be performed by a more highly rated inspector. There had been an annual inspection 15 months before the accident and a 100-hour inspection less than 12 months (and less than 100 logged hours) earlier. The insurer denied liability under the policy for lack of a required inspection. There was no evidence of what *caused* the accident. Should the owner recover? If there were conclusive evidence that the accident was caused by something that could not have been detected by an inspection, however thorough (such as pilot error), would the insurer be liable?

The parallel of airworthiness to seaworthiness is apparent, but while possession of a certificate correlates with airworthiness, certification and airworthiness are not the same. The similarity of the lack of a certificate to some of the breaches of warranty seen in the early ocean marine cases is almost equally apparent. Would not the natural form of the inspection provision be a warranty or a condition precedent? Although the provision is cast in coverage language, its similarity to breach of warranty leads to the question of what effect a "contribute to the loss" statute would have on the result. Texas Insurance Code §6.14 is typical. It requires a causal relationship before "breach or violation by the insured of any warranty, condition *or provision* of any fire insurance policy, contract of insurance, or applications therefor, upon personal property" would be a defense to the insurer (emphasis added). Compare Security Mut. Casualty Co. v. O'Brien, 99 N.M. 638, 662 P.2d 639 (1983) (no coverage) with Puckett v. U.S. Fire Ins. Co., 678 S.W.2d 936 (Tex. 1984) (coverage). The New Mexico case asked only whether the language was ambiguous. The Texas case glossed over the distinction between coverage provisions and breach of warranty or condition by speaking of the statute as an "anti-technicality" statute that indicated the public policy of the state. Florida had a statute similar to that of Texas except that the test was not contribution to the loss but "increase of the hazard by any means within the control of the insured." Pickett v. Woods, 404 So. 2d 1152 (Fla. App. 1981) reached the same result as did Texas. The fairly numerous cases are divided, with the New Mexico result probably representing the majority position. Comment, Aviation Insurance Exclusions — Should a Causal Connection Between the Loss and Exclusion be Required to Deny Coverage?, 52 J. Air L. & Com. 451 (1986) reviews the authorities. See also Oldham & Dillingham, Developments and Trends in Aviation Insurance, 21 Tort & Ins. L.J., 44, 45 (1985).

a. Sequential Causation

A series of cases in the state of Washington point up some of the problems arising out of sequential causation. In the first case, a driver lost control of an automobile and skidded while rounding a mountain curve, went off the road, after some distance collided with a stump, and then rolled until the car was a total loss. The automobile insurance included collision but excluded comprehensive. Ploe v. International Indem. Co., 128 Wash. 480, 223 P. 327 (1924), said that the skidding was the proximate cause of the loss, not the collision with the stump nor that with the earth. The trial court judgment for the insured was reversed on appeal.

In Bruener v. Twin City Fire Ins. Co., 37 Wash. 2d 181, 222 P.2d

833 (1950), the coverage was reversed, with comprehensive being included and collision excluded. The plaintiff skidded on an icy road, left the road and collided with an embankment. The court said, "The rule of the *Ploe* case . . . is that the hazards which are covered and excluded from coverage by the terms of an insurance policy are the proximate causes of accidents, not the accidents themselves." It pointed out that the purpose of reaching back of the accident to an earlier proximate cause in tort cases was to establish liability for a culpable act, but that insurance coverage cases are concerned not with culpability as a basis for liability but "only with the nature of the injury and how it happened." The loss in *Bruener* was therefore a collision loss, not one from skidding. The trial court's decision for the insured, following the *Ploe* reasoning, was reversed, *Ploe* was overruled and judgment was given for the insurer.

GRAHAM v. PUBLIC EMPLOYEES MUT. INS. CO.

98 Wash. 2d 533, 656 P.2d 1077 (1983)

DORE, Justice.

This appeal arises from a dispute which erupted between two insurance companies and their insureds following the May 18, 1980 explosion of Mt. St. Helens. The early pyroclastic flows from the eruption, along with hot ash and debris, began melting the snow and ice flanking the mountain and the broken glacial ice blocks within the Toutle River valley. This water, combined with torrential rains from the eruption cloud, existing ground water, water displaced from Spirit Lake, and ash and debris, created mudflows which began moving down the valley shortly after the eruption began. This process continued throughout the day of May 18.

At some point, a large mudflow developed in the upper reaches of the south fork of the valley from the Toutle and Talus glaciers. The mudflow gouged and filled the land into new forms as it moved, damaging or destroying many homes within its path. Approximately 10 hours after the eruption began, the appellants' homes, 20-25 miles away from Mt. St. Helens, were destroyed by a mudflow or a combination of mudflows preceded by water damage from flooding.

At the time of the eruption, homeowners insurance policies issued by Public Employees Mutual Insurance Company (hereafter PEMCO) to appellants Graham and Campbell, and a policy issued by Pennsylvania General Insurance Company (hereafter PGI) to appellants Fotheringill were in effect. All three policies provided in pertinent part as follows:

Section 1 — Exclusions

We do not cover loss resulting directly or indirectly from: . . .

2. Earth Movement. Direct loss by fire, explosion, theft, or breakage of glass or safety glazing materials resulting from earth movement is covered.

3. Water damage, meaning:
    a. flood, . . .

Of the seven exclusions listed in the PEMCO policy, "earth movement" is the only one not specifically defined in the policy.

Prior to March 1980, PEMCO utilized insurance forms containing this exclusionary language:

This policy does not insure against loss: . . .

2. caused by, resulting from, contributed to or aggravated by any earth movement, including but not limited to earthquake, volcanic eruption, landslide, mudflow, earth sinking, rising or shifting; unless loss by fire, explosion or breakage of glass constituting a part of the building(s) covered hereunder, including glass in storm doors and storm windows, ensues, and this Company shall then be liable only for such ensuing loss, but this exclusion does not apply to loss by theft;

This language was deleted by PEMCO in an overall effort to simplify the policy language.

The homeowners filed claims against the insurance companies under their homeowners policies, but the insurance companies rejected their claims on the basis that the damage was excludable as "earth movement" in the form of mudflows or a combination of earth movement and water damage. The Grahams and Campbells then commenced this action against PEMCO in Cowlitz County Superior Court. On April 10, 1981, the trial court granted PEMCO's motion for summary judgment, dismissing the homeowners' complaint. . . .

For the purpose of ruling on the summary judgment motion, the trial court assumed the movement of Mt. St. Helens to be an "explosion" within the terms of the insurance policies. The trial court noted this issue was a factual issue to be determined by a jury. We agree, as the true meaning of "explosion" in each case must be settled by the common experience of jurors. Oroville Cordell Fruit Growers, Inc. v. Minneapolis Fire & Marine Ins. Co., 68 Wash. 2d 117, 122, 411 P.2d 873 (1966). Because direct loss from an explosion resulting from earth movement is not excluded from coverage, the jury must also determine the factual issue of whether the earth movements were caused by the earthquakes and harmonic tremors which preceded the eruption.

If the jury determines the volcanic eruption was an explosion resulting from earth movement, it will then be necessary to reach the issue of whether the loss was a direct result of the eruption. The trial court held that the causation analysis of Bruener v. Twin City Fire Ins. Co., 37 Wash. 2d 181, 222 P.2d 833 (1950) precluded the plaintiffs' claims.

[*Ploe, Bruener,* and another case were discussed.]

In reviewing the foregoing cases, we conclude the immediate physical cause analysis is no longer appropriate and should be discarded. The *Bruener* rule is an anomaly, inconsistent with the rule in the majority of other jurisdictions.[1] We have defined "proximate cause" as that cause "which, in a natural and continuous sequence, unbroken by any new, independent cause, produces the event, and without which that event would not have occurred." Stoneman v. Wick Constr. Co., 55 Wash. 2d 639, 643, 349 P.2d 215 (1960). Where a peril specifically insured against sets other causes in motion which, in an unbroken sequence and connection between the act and final loss, produce the result for which recovery is sought, the insured peril is regarded as the "proximate cause" of the entire loss.

It is the efficient or predominant cause which sets into motion the chain of events producing the loss which is regarded as the proximate cause, not necessarily the last act in a chain of events. The mechanical simplicity of the *Bruener* rule does not allow inquiry into the intent and expectations of the parties to the insurance contract. Sears, Roebuck & Co. v. Hartford Accident & Indem. Co., 50 Wash. 2d 443, 313 P.2d 347 (1957). We now specifically overrule the *Bruener* case.

The determination of proximate cause is well established in this state. As a general rule, the question of proximate cause is for the jury, and it is only when the facts are undisputed and the inferences therefrom are plain and incapable of reasonable doubt or difference of opinion that it may be a question of law for the court.

In the present case, the mudflows which destroyed the appellants' homes would not have occurred without the eruption of Mt. St. Helens. The eruption displaced water from Spirit Lake, and set into motion the melting of the snow and ice flanking the mountain. A jury could reasonably determine the water displacement, melting snow and ice and mudflows were mere manifestations of the eruption, finding that the eruption of Mt. St. Helens was the proximate cause of the damage to appellants' homes. This issue is not a question of law but a question of fact, to be determined by the trier of facts.

---

1. 18 G. Couch, Insurance §74:693 (2d ed. 1968) states the majority rule as: "When loss is sustained by the insured it is necessary that the loss be proximately, rather than remotely, caused by the peril insured against."

Conclusion

The *Bruener* decision is hereby overruled. We remand to the trial court for a jury determination of whether the movement of Mt. St. Helens was an "explosion" within the terms of the insurance policies; whether that "explosion" was preceded by earth movement, and whether appellants' damages were proximately caused by the eruption of Mt. St. Helens on May 18, 1980.

ROSELLINI, STAFFORD, UTTER, WILLIAMS and PEARSON, JJ., concur.

BRACHTENBACH, Chief Justice (dissenting).

In its ardour to explain the relationship of proximate cause to insurance law the majority strays from the basic issues presented by this case. First, what are the express terms of the policy? Second, are any of those terms ambiguous? Third, if the terms of the policy are unambiguous, would application of those terms result in coverage? The majority fails to apply such a step by step analysis. Consequently, it neglects a clear provision of the policy that requires that we affirm the trial court's grant of summary judgment. I therefore dissent.

This court has long recognized that insurance policies are private contracts. See Sears, Roebuck & Co. v. Hartford Accident & Indem. Co., 50 Wash. 2d 443, 449, 313 P.2d 347 (1957). As a private contractor, the insurer is ordinarily permitted to limit its liability unless inconsistent with public policy or some statutory provision. Mutual of Enumclaw Ins. Co. v. Wiscomb, 97 Wash. 2d 203, 210, 643 P.2d 441 (1982). Thus the court's initial task here is to identify fully the terms of this contract. Here the homeowner's policy provided for coverage, against *inter alia,* fire and explosion. In addition, however, the policy contained an exclusion for earth movement which in turn contained its own exception. That exclusion and exception provide:

> We do not cover loss resulting directly or indirectly from:
> 2. Earth movement. Direct loss by fire, explosion, theft, or breakage of glass or safety glazing materials resulting from earth movement is covered.

The next step is to determine whether any of these provisions are ambiguous. Although this issue was raised by the parties the majority chooses to ignore it and proceeds instead to analyze the case as if it were a question of proximate cause. It then determines that that issue is a question of fact for the jury and reverses summary judgment.

The obvious flaw in the majority's opinion is that it improperly applies the terms of the policy to the chain of events. The facts of this case reveal the following possible chain of events which should result in a denial of coverage regardless of proximate cause analysis. As suggested by the majority, on May 18, 1980, earthquakes and moving lava caused earth to move, which caused an eruption (explosion?), which caused earth movement in the form of mudflows. The majority concludes that the exclusion operates to exclude the initial earth movement which preceded the eruption but that the exception for explosion contained in the exclusion brings the incident back within the potential terms of the policy. But if that result is correct, the majority neglects a necessary additional inquiry — that is — should the earth movement exclusion be applied a second time to exclude coverage for mudflows? This last question presents strictly a legal issue involving the proper interpretation of policy terms. I submit that the only logical resolution of this issue is that the earth movement exclusion must be considered a second time. This answer requires, unfortunately, that we deny coverage. To do otherwise, however, would be to use proximate cause analysis to circumvent the clear terms of the policy. In addition, the majority appears to stop its inquiry at a point on the causation chain where coverage would be provided. The majority's analysis requires that we ignore clear provisions in the insurance contract. This we cannot do. As we have said in the past:

> Since an insurance policy is merely a written contract between an insurer and the insured, courts cannot rule out of the contract any language which the parties thereto have put into it; cannot revise the contract under the theory of constructing it; and neither abstract justice nor any rule of construction can create a contract for the parties which they did not make for themselves.

Sears, Roebuck & Co. v. Hartford Accident & Indem. Co., 50 Wash. 2d 443, 449, 313 P.2d 347 (1957).

The interpretation I suggest is necessary to give effect to the expectations that the parties had at the time they contracted for insurance coverage.[1] I would therefore deny coverage and affirm the trial court.

DOLLIVER and DIMMICK, JJ., concur.

Notes and Questions

1. If a house had collapsed as a direct result of the earth movement that preceded the eruption, would the damage have been covered?

---

1. The fact that the Grahams made a claim and recovered under their Federal Flood Insurance policy for this damage demonstrates that they at least viewed the primary cause of the damage as unrelated to the explosion. Transcript at 43.

2. Would the court have reached a different result under the language of the policy PEMCO used prior to March 1980?

3. In Villella v. Public Employees Mut. Ins. Co., 106 Wash. 2d 806, 725 P.2d 957 (1986), a contractor was negligent in building a drainage system for insured's house. The filled soil under the house became saturated and soil destabilization caused the foundation to sink. The insurer was the same as in *Graham*; the same earth movement exclusion was involved. The court held for the insured, following the "efficient proximate cause" theory. Safeco Ins. Co. of America v. Hirschmann, 112 Wash. 2d 621, 773 P.2d 413 (1989), also says that *Graham* announces an "efficient proximate cause" rule.

4. The "causes" in *Graham* were sequential. Was each an "efficient proximate cause" of the harm? If so, and if a single one of such causes is covered and all others are excluded, should the insurer always have to pay? See Withers, Proximate Cause and Multiple Causation in First-Party Insurance Cases, 20 Forum 256 (1985), for a summary of the various rules applied in different jurisdictions.

5. Earth movement cases, if they are decided like *Graham,* present additional problems when the actual loss spans multiple policy periods. One problem is created by annual policy limits, another by changes in insurers. See Hook, Multiple Policy Period Losses Under First-Party Policies, 21 Tort & Ins. L.J. 393 (1986). A recent California case dealt with the problem of allocating the losses among insurers and decided that the insurer on the risk when the damage first manifests itself must pay it all. Home Ins. Co. v. Landmark Ins. Co., 205 Cal. App. 3d 1388, 253 Cal. Rptr. 277 (1988).

6. The paradigm case of sequential causation is fire resulting from an earthquake. If an insurance contract covers fire but excludes coverage for "loss caused directly or indirectly by invasion, insurrection, riot [and other similar events]; for loss or damage occasioned by or through any volcano, earthquake, or hurricane, or other eruption, convulsion, or disturbance," should an insured recover for a fire resulting from the 1989 San Francisco earthquake? Pacific Heating & Ventilating Co. v. Williamsburgh City Fire Ins. Co., 158 Cal. 367, 111 P. 4 (1910) held the insurer whose policy contained the above exclusion liable on the policy. Was the court right? If you were redrafting the *Pacific Heating* policy for the insurer and wished to exclude earthquake-caused fire, what changes would you make?

b. Concurrent Causation

Where the causation is concurrent, the cases are complicated by the tendency of courts to analogize first party (property) insurance with third party (liability) insurance cases. Many interesting cases in liability insurance involve the distressingly common phenomenon of a negligent shooting linked in time and space, and often in causation, with the use of a car. The liability insurance case most often cited on this point is State Farm Mut. Auto. Ins. Co. v. Partridge, 10 Cal. 3d 94, 514 P.2d 123, 109 Cal. Rptr. 811 (1973). See Chapter 5.

Many of those liability insurance cases might, on slightly altered facts, have involved property insurance. The problem with using those multiple cause liability insurance cases as authority for first-party cases is that coverage in liability insurance is inextricably tied up with liability in tort. When using them in first-party cases, there is a tendency to confuse the causation required to establish liability in tort with the requirements for coverage under an insurance contract. The considerations are not the same.

Partridge is sufficiently summarized in *Garvey,* which follows.

GARVEY v. STATE FARM FIRE & CASUALTY CO.

48 Cal. 3d 395, 770 P.2d 704, 257 Cal. Rptr. 292 (1989)

Lucas, Chief Justice.

We granted review to consider the Court of Appeal's reversal of a directed verdict of coverage in favor of Jack and Rita Garvey (hereafter plaintiffs). We sought to resolve some of the confusion that has arisen regarding insurance coverage under the "all-risk" section of a homeowner's insurance policy when loss to an insured's property can be attributed to two causes, one of which is a nonexcluded peril, and the other an excluded peril.

In recent years, some courts have misinterpreted and misapplied our decisions in Sabella v. Wisler (1963) 59 Cal. 2d 21, 27 Cal. Rptr. 689, 377 P.2d 889, and State Farm Mut. Auto Ins. Co. v. Partridge (1973) 10 Cal. 3d 94, 109 Cal. Rptr. 811, 514 P.2d 123. In so doing, they have allowed coverage in first-party property damage cases under our holding in *Partridge* by inappropriately using the *Partridge* concurrent causation approach as an alternative to *Sabella*'s efficient proximate cause analysis. This extension of the analysis in *Partridge,* a third-party *liability* case, allows coverage under a first-party *property* insurance policy whenever a covered peril is a concurrent proximate cause of the loss, without regard to the application of specific policy exclusion clauses. Such reasoning ignores the criteria set forth in Insurance Code sections 530 and 532, the relevant analysis in *Sabella* and the important distinction between property loss coverage under a first-party property policy and tort liability coverage under a third-party liability insurance policy. Indeed, because a covered peril usually can be asserted to exist somewhere in the chain of causation in cases involving multiple causes, applying the *Partridge* approach to coverage in first-party cases effectively nullifies policy exclusions in "all risk" homeowner's property loss policies, thereby essentially abrogating the limiting terms of insurance contracts in such cases. We cannot believe *Partridge* intended such a sweeping result in first-party property loss cases. To the contrary, as we explain below, we must put *Partridge*, in its proper perspective, i.e., that decision should be utilized only in *liability* cases in which true concurrent causes, each originating from an independent act of negligence, simultaneously join together to produce injury. Therefore, as will appear, we conclude this case should be remanded to the Court of Appeal with directions to remand to the trial court for a jury determination of causation pursuant to *Sabella*, supra, 59 Cal. 2d 21, 27 Cal. Rptr. 689, 377 P.2d 889.

I. Facts

Plaintiffs bought their house in the mid-1970's. In 1977, plaintiffs purchased from State Farm Fire and Casualty Company (hereafter defendant) an "all risk" homeowner's policy of insurance which was in effect at all times relevant. Section I of the policy in question provided coverage for "all risks of physical loss to the property covered" except as otherwise excluded or limited. Losses excluded by this portion of the policy included those "caused by, resulting from, contributed to or aggravated by any earth movement, including but not limited to earthquake, volcanic eruption, landslide, mudflow, earth sinking, rising or shifting," and losses caused "by . . . settling, cracking, shrinkage, bulging or expansion of pavements, patios, foundations, walls, floors, roofs or ceilings. . . ."

In August 1978, plaintiffs noticed that a house addition, built in the early 1960's, had begun to pull away from the main structure. They also discovered damage to a deck and garden wall. There ensued numerous phone calls, letters, meetings and investigations as plaintiffs tried to determine from defendant whether the damage was covered by their homeowner's property insurance policy.

[The insurer unsuccessfully sought a settlement and the insured sued.]

Defendant rested on the 12th day of trial, and the court granted a directed verdict for plaintiffs on the coverage issue. The court informed the parties it was following the decisions in *Partridge*, supra, 10 Cal. 3d 94, 109 Cal. Rptr. 811, 514 P.2d 123, and *Sabella*, supra, 59 Cal. 2d 21, 27 Cal. Rptr. 689, 377 P.2d 889, and that plaintiffs were covered under the policy because negligent construction, a covered risk, was a concurrent proximate cause of the damage. Specifically, the trial court stated: "[The Supreme Court] told me in *Sabella* that negligent construction can be a proximate cause. They told me in *Partridge* there may be coverage whenever an insured risk constitutes simply a concurrent proximate cause of the injuries. [¶] Now, to me that is crystal clear, putting those two causes together, that if negligent construction is a concurrent proximate cause of the loss, there is coverage." The court continued, "The key witness for the defense, Mr. Nelson, conceded in his testimony, as I heard it and understood it, that the negligent construction was a cause of the room falling away. He did not use the word 'proximate.' He said a causative factor at one time. I don't recall the exact language when he answered the question. In substance, that it was a cause on another occasion. As a matter of law, based upon the evidence, it was a proximate cause."

The jury subsequently found defendant liable for $47,000 in policy benefits and general damages, and $1 million in punitive damages. The court denied defendant's motions for judgment notwithstanding the verdict and for a new trial, and declined to issue a remittitur with respect to the punitive damages award. The court entered judgment in accordance with the verdict. Defendant appealed, and the Court of Appeal reversed the judgment in a divided opinion. Before reviewing the Court of Appeal holding, and in order to provide sufficient background information that will aid in the understanding of this case, we first discuss the development of multiple and concurrent causation insurance analyses, and the important distinction between property and liability policies.

II. Discussion

A. Development of Multiple Causation Insurance Coverage Analyses

1. The Efficient Proximate Cause Standard

Our courts have long struggled to enunciate principles that determine whether coverage exists when excluded and covered perils interact to cause a loss. Initially, the courts attempted to reconcile section 530 (which provides for coverage when a peril insured against was the "proximate cause" of loss) with section 532 (which provides, that "If a peril is specifically excepted in a contract of insurance, and there is a loss which would not have occurred but for such peril, such loss is thereby excepted [from coverage] even though the immediate cause of the loss was a peril which was not excepted").

In our 1963 *Sabella* decision, supra, 59 Cal. 2d 21, 27 Cal. Rptr.

689, 377 P.2d 889, we faced a difficult property loss coverage question arising after a building contractor constructed a house on uncompacted fill and negligently installed a sewer line; negligent installation was a covered peril. Eventually, the sewer line ruptured causing water to saturate the ground surrounding the insured's house, resulting in subsidence, an excluded peril. The insureds brought a first-party action against their insurer, seeking recovery for property loss under their homeowner's property policy. (Id., at p. 26, 27 Cal. Rptr. 689, 377 P.2d 889.) The trial court found the loss was not covered because subsidence was a specifically excluded peril under the policy. The insureds appealed this ruling and we reversed.

On its face, section 532 would have precluded coverage because the loss would not have occurred "but for" the excluded peril of subsidence. We recognized, however, that such a result would be absurd because it would deny coverage even though an insured peril "proximately" caused the loss simply because a subsequent, excepted peril was also part of the chain of causation. We reasoned that sections 530 and 532 were not intended to deny coverage for losses whenever "an excepted peril operated to any extent in the chain of causation so that the resulting harm would not have occurred 'but for' the excepted peril's operation. . . ." (*Sabella*, supra, 59 Cal. 2d at p. 33, 27 Cal. Rptr. 689, 377 P.2d 889.) Rather, we explained that when section 532 is read along with section 530, the "but for" clause of section 532 necessarily refers to a "proximate cause" of the loss, and the "immediate cause" refers to the cause most immediate in time to the damage. (Id., at pp. 33-34, 27 Cal. Rptr. 689, 377 P.2d 889.)

Thus, *Sabella* held that:

> [I]n determining whether a loss is within an exception in a policy, where there is a concurrence of different causes, the efficient cause — the one that sets others in motion — is the cause to which the loss is to be attributed, though the other causes may follow it, and operate more immediately in producing the disaster. (Id., at pp. 31-32, 27 Cal. Rptr. 689, 377 P.2d 889, quoting from Couch on Insurance (1930) §1466; Houser & Kent, Concurrent Causation in First-Party Insurance Claims: Consumers Cannot Afford Concurrent Causation (1986) Tort & Ins. L.J. 573, 575.)

Furthermore, in characterizing the "but for" clause of section 532 as referring to the efficient proximate cause of the loss, we impliedly recognized that coverage would not exist if the covered risk was simply a *remote* cause of the loss, or if an excluded risk was the efficient proximate (meaning predominant) cause of the loss. On the other hand, the fact that an excluded risk contributed to the loss would not preclude coverage if such a risk was a remote cause of the loss. . . .

2. The Doctrine of Concurrent Causation

In 1973, we were faced with a third-party tort liability situation that presented a "novel question of insurance coverage" and did not fit the *Sabella* analysis because no single peril could be labeled the predominant cause of the loss. In *Partridge,* supra, 10 Cal. 3d 94, 109 Cal. Rptr. 811, 514 P.2d 123, the insured was covered under both an automobile liability policy and a homeowner's *liability* policy with comprehensive personal liability coverage. (The latter liability policy excluded losses "arising out of the use" of a motor vehicle.) The insured, after filing the trigger mechanism of his pistol to create a "hair-trigger" action (such negligence was a covered risk under the homeowner's property policy), hunted jackrabbits at night from his vehicle. As he drove over rough terrain while waving the gun in his hand (negligent driving was an excluded risk under homeowner's liability policy), the gun fired and injured a passenger.

First-party property coverage issues were not involved. The case concerned the personal *liability* of the insured who was sued by his injured passenger. Both policies were issued by the same insurer, which conceded the accident was covered under the automobile liability policy. The parties, however, disputed whether coverage was also afforded under the homeowner's liability policy, which excluded coverage for injuries "arising out of the use of motor vehicles." As in *Sabella,* supra, 59 Cal. 2d 21, 27 Cal. Rptr. 689, 377 P.2d 889, we relied on *Brooks,* supra, 27 Cal. 2d 305, at pages 309-310, 163 P.2d 689, to find coverage under the homeowner's policy. In analyzing the liability coverage, we explicitly recognized

> the "efficient cause" language [of *Sabella*] is not very helpful, for here both causes were independent of each other: the filing of the trigger did not "cause" the careless driving, nor vice versa. Both, however, caused the injury. . . . If committed by separate individuals, both actors would be joint tortfeasors fully liable for the resulting injuries. Moreover, the fact that both acts were committed by a single person does not alter their nature as concurrent proximate causes. (Cf., Flournoy v. State of California (1969) 275 Cal. App. 2d 806, 811 [80 Cal. Rptr. 485]. *Partridge,* supra, 10 Cal. 3d at p. 104, fn. 10, 109 Cal. Rptr. 811, 514 P.2d 123.)

We concluded by stating,

> Although there may be some question whether either of the two causes in the instant case can be properly characterized as *the* "prime," "moving" or "efficient" cause of the accident we believe that *coverage under a liability insurance policy* is equally available to an insured whenever an insured risk constitutes simply *a* concurrent proximate cause of the

injuries. (Id. at pp. 104-105, 109 Cal. Rptr. 811, 514 P.2d 123, fns. omitted, second italics added.)

Because *Partridge* dealt with causation in the context of third-party liability insurance, we did not address, nor did we contemplate, the application of our decision to the determination of coverage in the first-party property insurance context. Indeed, *Partridge* asserted only that the "concurrent cause" standard was "consistent with Insurance Code sections 530 and 532, as authoritatively construed in *Sabella v. Wisler.* . . ." (*Partridge,* supra, at p. 105, fn. 11, 109 Cal. Rptr. 811, 514 P.2d 123.)

Furthermore, *Partridge* never considered in what manner concurrent causation could apply in the first-party property insurance context. Rather, by recognizing in *Partridge* the "novel question" of liability coverage presented because two separate acts of negligence simultaneously joined together to cause an injury, we also impliedly recognized the limited scope of our holding. We did not extend our holding to first-party property insurance cases. Accordingly, we should not apply the decision to such cases merely because it appears to simplify the coverage analysis.

B. The Distinction Between Liability and Property Insurance. . . .

The scope of coverage and the operation of the exclusion clauses, however, are different in the separate policy portions and should be treated as such. As one commentator has recently stated: "Liability and corresponding coverage under a third-party insurance policy must be carefully distinguished from the coverage analysis applied in a first-party property contract. Property insurance, unlike liability insurance, is unconcerned with establishing negligence or otherwise assessing tort liability." (Bragg, Concurrent Causation and the Art of Policy Drafting: New Perils for Property Insurers (1985) 20 Forum 385, 386.)

For these reasons it is important to separate the causation analysis necessary in a first-party property loss case from that which must be undertaken in a third-party tort liability case. The following quotation summarizes the distinction that must be drawn:

> Property insurance . . . is an agreement, a contract, in which the insurer agrees to indemnify the insured in the event that the insured property suffers a covered loss. Coverage, in turn, is commonly provided by reference to causation, e.g., "loss caused by . . ." certain enumerated perils.
>
> The term "perils" in traditional property insurance parlance refers to fortuitous, active, physical forces such as lightning, wind, and explo-

sion, which bring about the loss. *Thus, the "cause" of loss in the context of a property insurance contract is totally different from that in a liability policy.* This distinction is critical to the resolution of losses involving multiple causes.

Frequently property losses occur which involve more than one peril that might be considered legally significant. If one of the causes (perils) arguably falls within the coverage grant — commonly either because it is specifically insured (as in a named peril policy) or not specifically excepted or excluded (as in an "all risks" policy) — disputes over coverage can arise. The task becomes one of identifying the most important cause of the loss and attributing the loss to that cause. (Bragg, supra, 20 Forum at pp. 386-387, italics added.)

On the other hand, the right to coverage in the third-party liability insurance context draws on traditional tort concepts of fault, proximate cause and duty. This liability analysis differs substantially from the coverage analysis in the property insurance context, which draws on the relationship between perils that are either covered or excluded in the contract. In liability insurance, by insuring for personal liability, and agreeing to cover the insured for his own negligence, the insurer agrees to cover the insured for a broader spectrum of risks. In order to further demonstrate the differences between property loss and liability coverage, we compare two sections of a typical homeowner's policy — the all-risk property loss coverage section of the policy in this case and the personal liability section at issue in *Partridge*. . . .

This case presents a classic *Sabella* situation. Coverage should be determined by a jury under an efficient proximate cause analysis. Accordingly, bearing in mind the facts here, we conclude the question of causation is for the jury to decide. If the earth movement was the efficient proximate cause of the loss, then coverage would be denied under *Sabella,* supra, 59 Cal. 2d 21, 27 Cal. Rptr. 689, 377 P.2d 889. On the other hand, if negligence was the efficient proximate cause of the loss, then coverage exists under *Sabella*. These issues were jury questions because sufficient evidence was introduced to support both possibilities.

The judgment of the Court of Appeal is affirmed with directions to remand the cause to the trial court for further proceedings consistent with the opinion of this court.

KAUFMAN, Justice, concurring: . . .

While I recognize important differences between property damage insurance and liability insurance and first-party and third-party cases, I am doubtful that those differences compel or warrant two separate and entirely different rules for ascertaining the coverage provided by the two kinds of policies. In my view, the confusion in this area of the law results primarily from two major flaws in the *Partridge* decision which have made it all but impossible to reconcile with *Sabella* and which ought to be recognized and disapproved.

The first flaw in *Partridge* is, as the majority suggests, that it imported into the determination of coverage, concepts and rules of tort law inapplicable to the contractual question of the coverage afforded by an insurance policy, and based on them, adopted the tort rule of concurrent causation to determine coverage. One of the principal rationalizations for the rule announced in *Partridge* was that if two different persons had separately performed the two negligent acts involved therein, ((1) filing down the gun's trigger to a hair trigger and (2) driving the vehicle off the road over rough terrain with the gun pointed at the passenger), each actor as a joint tortfeasor would have been liable. Therefore, if the trigger filer had a homeowner's policy including personal liability coverage and the vehicle driver had auto liability insurance, both insurers would have been obliged to indemnify their respective insureds in respect to a judgment against them.

That rationalization accurately reflected tort law, but it failed entirely to recognize that the problem before the court in *Partridge* was not the joint and several liability of joint tortfeasors, but the interpretation of a homeowner's policy owned by the single tortfeasor, which expressly excluded any injury arising out of the use of a motor vehicle. One might ask what the situation would have been if there were in fact two tortfeasors but the vehicle driver had only a homeowner's policy and the trigger filer had only an automobile liability insurance policy. Both tortfeasors would still have been liable under tort law, but neither policy would have afforded coverage for the conduct of the insured and neither insurer would have had any liability. The point is that tort liability on the part of the insured does not establish liability on the part of the insurer unless the policy affords coverage for the conduct of the insured and that is to be determined by contract principles, not tort principles, in both first-party and third-party cases.

[The opinion goes on to discuss other "flaws" in *Partridge,* and concludes:]

Thus, while I would not say there is no case in which an independent concurrent causation rule similar to that set forth in *Partridge* might be useful or helpful, I find *Partridge* fundamentally flawed in the several respects mentioned and would overrule it to the extent it is inconsistent with the views here expressed.

[In a long dissent, MOSK, Justice, defended *Partridge.* BROUSSARD, Justice, also dissented, separately.]

Notes and Questions

1. How would the *Garvey* court have decided *Graham?*

2. In an earlier context, we saw the U.S. government, acting as insurer, treated more generously than a commercial insurer would have been in that it could not be estopped. In the sequential causation case Sodowski v. National Flood Insurance Program of the Federal Emergency Management Agency, 834 F.2d 653 (7th Cir. 1987), *cert. denied,* 486 U.S. 1043 (1988), the insurance was against flood with all earth movement excluded "except such mudslide or erosion as is covered under the peril of flood." When the Illinois River overflowed, plaintiff's home was flooded, and structural damage resulted from the settling of the ground under the house. The court held there was no coverage. Would the decision have been the same if the insurance had been written by a commercial insurer? In *Sodowski,* the law to be applied was federal law, because the insurance was pursuant to a federal statute.

3. The multiple cause situation, whether the causes are concurrent or sequential, creates a dilemma for the insurer. The insurer may either pay whenever any covered cause is involved, whether or not it is thought to be the efficient proximate cause, or may resist the claim and take chances on a claim for bad faith and punitive damages if it loses. See Chapter 8, which deals with bad faith claims.

For further discussion on this knotty problem in California property insurance cases, see Comment, Farmers Insurance Exchange v. Adams: Concurrent Causation and the All-Risk Homeowner's Policy, 20 Loyola L.A.L. Rev. 841 (1987); Schauble, Garvey v. State Farm: California's New Approach to Concurrent Causation, 23 Idaho L. Rev. 419 (1986-1987). Houser & Kent, Concurrent Causation in First-Party Insurance Claims: Consumers Cannot Afford Concurrent Causation, 21 Tort & Ins. L.J. 573 (1986), dealt with California doctrine while *Garvey* was pending in the California Supreme Court.

4. An insured was covered against windstorm. The insurer denied payment for collapse of the roof because the wind was not the sole cause of the harm. The other causes were bad construction of the roof and an accumulation of weight by successive build-ups of the roof. How should the case be decided? See Koory v. Western Casualty and Surety Co., 153 Ariz. 412, 737 P.2d 388 (1987), reversing and remanding the case as reported in 153 Ariz. 408, 737 P.2d 384 (Ariz. App. 1986).

3. Implied Exceptions

It is widely thought, or at least often said, that insurance policies consist of a general grant of coverage in large print that is then emasculated by exceptions or exclusions in fine print. There is just enough truth in this notion to make it a misleading caricature. The characteristic insurance policy tends to state coverage, whether it be all risk or specified perils, more broadly than the coverage desired in order to avoid unintended gaps and then qualifies that grant of coverage by carefully stated exclusions. Sometimes the risks excluded are uninsurable; sometimes they are insured either separately by other policies or by an endorsement for which an extra premium is charged. The exclusions are seldom arbitrary and unconscionable limitations of coverage. They are merely priced and sold separately if they are considered insurable.

It may come as a surprise to one both long instructed in the persistent myth of small print exclusions and aware of the frequent judicial hostility to insurers in the interpretation of policies to learn that in a number of situations there is yet a further subtraction from coverage by *implied* exceptions. They are established by industry practice and when challenged are considered fair by the courts, despite the *contra proferentem* rule and the dislike of courts for even *express* exclusions. Examples include seaworthiness in marine insurance and fortuity in all risk policies. The next few cases deal with two illustrations from fire insurance: arson and the friendly fire doctrine.

Sometimes an express exception or exclusion would be implied even if it were not expressed in the policy. The difference is important. Implied exceptions implement public policy while express exceptions or exclusions are subject to the *contra proferentem* doctrine. If courts generally treat an explicit exclusion favorably to the insurer, it suggests either unusual clarity of language or public policy considerations driving the analysis and supporting the contract language. Some of the following cases illustrate this tendency.

a. Arson

The cost of arson to the American public is immense. About 97,000 incendiary or suspicious structure fires were reported in 1989. The estimated property loss from incendiary fires was about $1.6 billion, a fifth of the total property loss. Over 600 non-fire-fighters were killed, 13 percent of all deaths in structure fires. There were an estimated 46,000 vehicle fires of incendiary or suspicious nature. Arson Continues Decline in 1989, National Underwriter (Property and Casualty/Employee Benefits Edition), Nov. 26, 1990, at 34. The decline through 1989 probably reflected the long period of prosperity in the 1980s. It would be reasonable to expect the 1990 figures to begin to show worsening results, for arson is correlated with the business cycle.

Not surprisingly arson frequently appears (or is hinted at) in reported cases. See the discussion of increase of hazard under case b, Section 3(b).

CORA PUB, INC. v. CONTINENTAL CASUALTY CO.

619 F.2d 482 (5th Cir. 1980)

Lewis R. Morgan, Circuit Judge:

The Coral Way Pub of Miami, Florida was totally destroyed by fire in May 1975. Continental Casualty Co., the insurer, suspected arson by the lessee and refused to pay any claim on the loss. Subsequently the lessee of the restaurant, Cora Pub, Inc., instituted this action against Continental on the policy. Other parties having an interest in the property and insurance policy joined the action seeking their share of any insurance proceeds.

The district court directed a verdict against Continental's arson defense and submitted the issue of damages to the jury, which returned an award of $409,000 in favor of Cora Pub and the intervenors. On appeal, Continental contends that the evidence that Cora Pub committed arson was sufficient to create a question for the jury, and that a directed verdict against the arson defense was improper. Cora Pub argues in reply that the evidence was sufficient neither to prove that there was arson nor to prove that arson was committed by any individual whose actions could be imputed to the corporation. . . .

I.   The Arson Defense . . .

The Coral Way Pub was a 27 year old restaurant owned by Moss and Son, Inc., and leased and managed by numerous different parties over its life. In November 1974, Cora Pub acquired the lease and continued to manage the restaurant until it was destroyed half a year later. [The court went on to describe the evidence of the restaurant's financial difficulties.]

At 2:00 a.m. on the night of the fire that led to this claim, a passer-by noticed smoke coming from the restaurant, and then observed an unidentified man walk from the parking lot behind the restaurant to a car parked at a nearby gas station, and drive away. The passer-by immediately notified the fire department, but the building burned rapidly to ruin after several explosions. A fireman who arrived at the scene found the doors to the building unlocked.

Julian Kirsch — general manager, secretary, and treasurer of Cora Pub — was the last person to leave the restaurant on the night of the fire, although he testified that he had locked and left the building at

11:00P.M. and was home with a girl when the fire started. Earlier, the burglar alarm system for the restaurant had been disconnected, and although Kirsch had been informed of this fact, he gave a statement after the fire that he had set the alarm before leaving the restaurant.

All of Cora Pub's business records, including much important evidence of the actual financial loss suffered, have vanished. Kirsch testified at trial that the records were destroyed in the blaze, but a fireman who had been at the scene testified that the fire never reached the office where the books and records were kept. . . .

Though the case for arson is wholly circumstantial, we cannot deny that reasonable men might draw the inferences necessary for Continental's arson defense. . . .

Cora Pub's second line of defense, and the district court's alternative ground for directed verdict, is that even if Kirsch kindled the fire that destroyed the building, his criminal act cannot legally be imputed to the insured corporation. This argument seems to confuse two entirely separate issues, one being whether there is sufficient circumstantial evidence of corporate complicity to require a jury verdict, and the other being whether Kirsch's actions must be regarded as those of the corporation as a matter of law.

In no case can arson be attributed to a corporation unless it is established that the perpetrator acted with the corporation's assent. Owl & Turtle, Inc. v. Travelers Indemnity Co., 554 F.2d 196 (5th Cir. 1977). Of course, since the corporation has no physical existence, it can only act through its officers and agents. Moreover, proof of corporate assent to arson, like proof of any other conspiracy, is not likely to be found in the archives of the corporation. Hence, courts have permitted insurers to attribute arson to a corporation by a variety of methods other than proof of a formal grant of authority to the arsonist.

Where the individual arsonist owns all or substantially all of the stock of the corporation courts have pierced the corporate veil to treat the actions of the individual as those of the corporation. E.g., General Electric Credit Corp. v. Aetna Cas. & Surety Co., 437 Pa. 463, 263 A.2d 448 (1970). Where arson was committed for the benefit of the corporation by an officer or general manager who dominated corporate affairs, courts have often imputed the arson of the individual to the corporation, on the ground that when the owners entrust the business to one person, they should be bound by his actions. E.g., Kimball Ice Co. v. Hartford, 18 F.2d 563 (4th Cir. 1927). This theory of the law was repudiated in *Owl & Turtle,* a diversity case governed by Florida law.

In a third category of cases, courts have permitted the jury to decide from circumstantial evidence that the arsonist acted at the request or with the approval of the insured corporation.

These cases typically involve closely-held corporations in which principal officers, stockholders or general managers are implicated in the fraud. In *Crown Colony,* for example, a panel of this circuit upheld a jury verdict finding a corporation responsible for the arson based on the financial plight of the corporation, overinsurance of the building, and circumstantial evidence linking the manager and the son of the president to the fire and to an attempted destruction of corporate records.

Cora Pub cites *Owl & Turtle* as a comparable case in which the court held that as a matter of law, arson could not be attributed to the corporation. In that case, however, the insurer stipulated that the sole stockholder was completely innocent of the attempted fraud, and alleged only that the stockholder's son, who dominated corporate affairs, had procured the burning of the building. In the case before us, there is no stipulation of the owner's innocence. To the contrary, Continental implicated the owner by introducing evidence of his effort to withdraw from the business. There is also evidence of intentional destruction of corporate records, and of the corporation's financial suffering. While Kirsch's relationship to the corporation and the owner do not require that we hold as a matter of law that he personified the corporation, the fact that arson was committed by an agent and officer of the corporation is evidence of the corporation's complicity. 2 Wigmore on Evidence §280, at 128-31 (3d ed. 1940). . . .

Reversed and remanded.

Notes and Questions

1. Is there any question that arson should be an implied exception or exclusion even in the absence of an explicit policy provision? Look in *Hedtcke,* which follows, for possibly relevant policy provisions. Do they in themselves create an "arson defense?" Should it matter whether the information leading to the suspicion of arson was available to the insurer prior to its letter denying coverage? The court in State ex rel. Shelter Mut. Ins. Co. v. Crouch, 714 S.W.2d 827 (Mo. App. 1986) thought it did. The issue is whether the arson defense can be waived and what will constitute waiver.

2. Arson is an affirmative defense, and both the burden of going forward and the risk of nonpersuasion are on the insurer. What standard of proof should apply? Compare Palace Entertainment, Inc. v. Bituminous Casualty Corp., 793 F.2d 842 (7th Cir. 1986) (preponderance of the evidence under Indiana law) with McGory v. Allstate Ins. Co., 527 So. 2d 632 (Miss. 1988) (clear and convincing evidence). Which standard is preferable?

3. In Owl & Turtle, Inc. v. Travelers Indem. Corp., 554 F.2d 196 (5th Cir. 1977), the son of the sole shareholder of the plaintiff corporation was accused of setting fire to the plaintiff's nightclub. The trial court instructed the jury that the action of the son, who was alleged to be "the dominant force directing the club's business activities," could be imputed to the corporation (thus defeating coverage) if the son "set or caused to be set the fire or fires for the purpose of advantaging the plaintiff." The Fifth Circuit reversed, confidently asserting what Florida law would be even though there was no Florida case on point. The crucial question was not the son's intent, it held, but whether the corporation or its sole shareholder had consented to the arson. "If an individual, not in control of the corporate affairs, wilfully set fire to the premises without the complicity of the corporation the insurance would still remain valid." Id. at 199, *quoting from* Charles Stores, Inc. v. Aetna Ins. Co., 428 F.2d 989, 992 (5th Cir. 1970). The court did not find sufficient evidence to attribute the son's act to the insured and held that there should have been a directed verdict for the insured. The fact that the son was general manager does not impute all of his actions to the corporation. Given his position as general manager plus his relationship to the sole shareholder, was the decision sound?

4. Would the result have been the same in *Owl & Turtle* if the son had owned some shares in the plaintiff corporation? How large a financial interest in the insured corporation must the individual actor have before his or her acts can be imputed to the corporation on that ground? In Kimball Ice Co. v. Hartford Fire Ins. Co., 18 F.2d 563 (4th Cir. 1927) (arising in West Virginia but applying general common law with no special attention to West Virginia cases), the arsonist owned one fourth of an insolvent company's shares, managed the company, took out the insurance, and was a major creditor of the company. The court upheld an instruction that the jury might find for the defendant if "the burning was at the instance of Kaufman, a stockholder and general manager of the plaintiff." Can a sharp line be drawn between *Owl & Turtle* and *Kimball Ice*?

5. Is the arson defense waived if its possible availability is known but not mentioned in the communication denying the claim? See State of Missouri ex rel. Shelter Mut. Ins. Co. v. Crouch, 714 S.W.2d 827 (Mo. App. 1986) (defense is waived); A & E Supply Co. v. Nationwide Mut. Fire Ins. Co., 589 F. Supp. 428 (W.D. Va. 1984) (defense is waived); Lawndale Natl. Bank, Under Trust No. 4846 v. American Casualty Co., 489 F.2d 1384 (7th Cir. 1973) (defense is not waived). Hoey, Property Insurance: Annual Survey of Property Insurance Law 405, 418, 23 Tort & Ins. L.J. 405, 418 (1988) expressed the view that public policy favored the "no" result. What do you think?

6. The defense of arson has its counterpart in other lines of insur-

ance, and is sometimes called the "barn burning" defense. See, for example, in the context of fidelity bonds, Witten, "Barn Burning" and What Can Be Done to Prevent It, 22 Tort & Ins. L.J. 511 (1987).

HEDTCKE v. SENTRY INS. CO.

109 Wis. 2d 461, 326 N.W.2d 727 (1982)

ABRAHAMSON, Justice. . . .

The facts relevant to the review of both issues are not in dispute. On July 27, 1980, Judith A. Hedtcke commenced this action against Sentry to recover proceeds under a fire insurance policy. Her complaint alleges that, on December 13, 1976, Sentry issued a three-year policy covering any loss or damage resulting from a fire on the residential property owned jointly by Hedtcke and her husband. The language of the insurance policy is incorporated into the complaint by reference. The policy lists both Judith A. Hedtcke and her husband, Ronald E. Hedtcke, under the designation "named insured." The complaint further alleges that a fire destroyed the property on November 20, 1979, at which time her husband, not she, occupied the home. The complaint further alleges that, although Hedtcke had complied with all obligations established by the policy, she had not received the proceeds forthcoming under the insurance policy. . . .

Sentry filed its answer on September 15, 1980, denying coverage on the ground that the policy relieved Sentry of liability if an insured caused the damage and that Hedtcke's husband was wholly or partially responsible for the fire which caused the damage. . . .

The circuit court granted Sentry's motion to dismiss the complaint on its merits on the basis of the pleadings, briefs, and arguments of counsel. The circuit court found that Judith and Ronald Hedtcke were joint owners of the home which at the time of the fire was insured by Sentry under a fire insurance policy naming both spouses as insured parties; that the policy contained a standard provision absolving Sentry of liability for damage if it was "caused directly or indirectly, by . . . neglect of the insured to use all reasonable means to save and preserve the property at and after a loss" or if "the hazard is increased by any means within the control or knowledge of the insured"; that by the time of the fire Judith Hedtcke had left the home, had initiated divorce proceedings, and had obtained a court order directing her husband to vacate the premises by November 23, 1979; that the insured property was destroyed by fire on November 20, 1979, and that Ronald Hedtcke had pleaded guilty to the crime of arson for his part in setting fire to the Hedtcke home. . . .

In Bellman v. Home Ins. Co. of N.Y., 178 Wis. 349, 189 N.W.

1028 (1922), an "innocent" partner sought to recover on fire insurance policies insuring partnership property which one of the partners had wilfully destroyed. The policy provided that the insurer would "not be liable for loss or damage caused directly or indirectly by . . . neglect of the insured to use all reasonable means to save and preserve the property at and after a fire." The court began its analysis by stating the basic proposition that to allow an arsonist to recover insurance proceeds would "reward crime and shock the most fundamental notions of justice." Id., 178 Wis. at 350, 189 N.W. 1028. Without citing supporting authority, the court concluded that to permit a recovery by either the partnership or an innocent partner where one of the partners has wilfully set fire to the insured property "is likewise repugnant to an intuitive sense of justice." Id., 178 Wis. at 350, 189 N.W. 1028. The court then went on to explain the result it reached by referring to what it regarded as "fundamental principles." The court said that the nature of the partnership relation spawned the joint obligation that each partner would on his own behalf and on behalf of his partners "use all reasonable means to save and preserve the property." Thus when one partner sets fire to the property, held the court, the arson constitutes a breach of the policy by all partners, and the insurer is relieved of all liability under the policy. The *Bellman* court did not state whether its reasoning was limited to those cases in which a partnership is the insured.

This court further discussed the rights of an innocent insured in Klemens v. Badger Mut. Ins. Co., 8 Wis. 2d 565, 99 N.W.2d 865 (1959). . . .

Under the *Bellman* and *Klemens* decisions, the rights of the innocent insured turn on whether the interests and obligations of the insureds are considered joint or several. If the interests and obligations of the insureds are joint, the misconduct of one insured is considered the misconduct of the other, and neither may recover under the policy. If the interests and obligations of the insureds are several, then each insured's recovery depends on his or her conduct, not that of the other insured. . . .

Courts in other jurisdictions, on examining the principles underlying this court's analysis in *Bellman, Klemens,* and [Shearer v. Dunn County Farmers Mut. Ins. Co., 39 Wis. 2d 240, 159 N.W.2d 89 (1968)], have concluded that these principles require rejection of the rule denying recovery by innocent insureds. These courts focus, as we did in *Klemens,* on the contract of insurance rather than the nature of property ownership. These courts recognize the fundamental principle of individual responsibility for wrongdoing, as this court did in *Shearer*. These courts address, as we did in *Bellman,* the issue of the innocent insured's recovery with scrupulous care to prevent the guilty arsonist from reaping financial benefit from the arson. For the reasons we set forth below, we conclude that the modern rule adopted by courts in other jurisdictions permitting recovery by innocent insureds preserves the essence of the legal principles recognized in the *Bellman, Klemens,* and *Shearer* cases and produces an equitable result, and we adopt the modern rule.

Courts adopting the modern rule focus on the contract of insurance rather than the interests and obligations arising from the nature of the property ownership. In *Klemens* this court concluded without analysis that if there are several insureds, the joint nature of the insurance contract gives rise to joint interests and obligations on the part of each policyholder. The courts following the modern rule discard this conclusory maxim and turn instead to the language of the policy to determine whether the rights of the insureds are joint or several.

One court justified this mode of analysis by noting that one who owns an undivided interest in property may insure his or her interest under a separate insurance policy or under a joint policy with the other co-owners. In the former case, arson perpetrated by one owner would not influence the right of the innocent owner to recover under his or her own separate policy; in the latter case, the innocent owner would confront an absolute bar to recovery. The court implied that these disparate results should not rest on whether there was one policy or several policies. Hoyt v. New Hampshire Fire Ins. Co., 92 N.H. 242, 29 A.2d 121, 123 (1942). . . .

Courts adopting the modern rule recognize the need to deter arsonists but also recognize the fundamental principle of individual responsibility for wrongdoing. A legal principle denying coverage to an innocent party implicitly imputes the guilt of the arsonist to the innocent insured. Contrary to our basic notions of fair play and justice, the *Bellman* rule punishes the innocent victim. An absolute bar to recovery by an innocent insured is particularly harsh in a case in which the arson appears to be retribution against the innocent insured. Having lost the property, the innocent insured is victimized once again by the denial of the proceeds forthcoming under the fire insurance policy. American Economy Ins. Co. v. Liggett, Ind. App., 426 N.E.2d 136, 140, n. 1, 140 (1981). Focusing on the nature of the individual responsibility for wrongdoing, we hold that the obligations of the insurer under the insurance policy in this case should be considered several as to each person insured.

Finally, courts adopting the modern rule have fashioned it to effectuate the public policy that guilty persons must not profit from their own wrongdoing. As one court said: "the arsonist whose business is failing and who cannot sell his property must not be permitted, as a matter of public policy, to find a way out of his dilemma by setting a fire. It may also be appropriate to prevent the depressed, jealous, murderous or even insane spouse from profiting by setting a fire by denying that spouse any recovery from an insurance carrier." American Economy Ins. Co. v. Liggett, Ind. App., 426 N.E.2d 136, 140 (1981).

We conclude, as have the courts adopting the modern rule, that the absolute bar embodied in the *Bellman* rule is an inappropriate method of deterring crime and preventing a wrongdoer from profiting from his or her own wrong. These valid public policy concerns can be vindicated by the trial court if it tailors the recovery permitted the innocent insured to guard against the possibility that the arsonist might receive financial benefit as a result of the arson. For example, the arsonist may be denied all recovery while the innocent insured may recover a pro rata share of the insurance proceeds, according to his or her interest in the property. Indirect profit and insurance fraud may also be avoided without recourse to an absolute bar on the recovery of the innocent insured. The possibility that an arsonist may profit through the co-mingling of funds with the innocent insured or otherwise is a factual issue properly resolved by the fact-finder.

On reexamination of the *Bellman* rule we are persuaded that imputing the incendiary actions of an insured to the innocent insured and creating an absolute bar to recovery by the innocent insured, produces inequitable results. We therefore conclude that the *Bellman* rule should no longer be followed in this state, and accordingly we overrule *Bellman* and *Klemens*. We reverse the circuit court's order in the case at bar dismissing this complaint on the merits. . . . The decision of the court of appeals is reversed; the judgment of the circuit court is reversed, and the cause is remanded to the circuit court for further proceedings consistent with this opinion.

Notes and Questions

1. In *Hedtcke,* the quoted standard provisions both talked of *the* insured. McCauley Enterprises, Inc. v. New Hampshire Ins. Co., 716 F. Supp. 718 (D. Conn. 1989), purporting to apply Connecticut law, distinguished between real and personal property on the basis of policy language. The innocent coinsured could recover on real property because the increase of hazard clause talked of "the" insured, but recovery on personal property was barred by the act of *any* insured. Would you make the same distinction? The court in Vance v. Pekin Ins. Co., 457 N.W.2d 589 (Iowa 1990), did. Finding that a policy excluded coverage for the intentional act of "an insured," the court denied recovery to an innocent coinsured whose spouse was convicted of burning down the insured property.

2. The *Hedtcke* result was also reached in Commercial Union Ins. Co. v. State Farm Fire & Casualty Co., 546 F. Supp. 543 (D. Colo. 1982). The policy at issue was a "plain language" homeowners policy

containing an exclusion for "neglect" in language essentially the same as that quoted in *Hedtcke* and a "severability of insurance" clause which stated, "This insurance applies separately to each insured. This condition shall not increase our limit of liability for any one occurrence."

Unlike *Hedtcke,* which relied almost exclusively on Wisconsin cases, *Commercial Union* cited authorities from across the country and followed the majority rule. Essentially, the court gave the innocent spouse half the recovery the couple would have had in combination if both had been innocent.

3. The Supreme Court of Colorado recently reached the same result in Republic Ins. Co. v. Jernigan, 753 P.2d 229 (Colo. 1988). The court relied on *Hedtcke* and also expressly approved *Commercial Union.* The federal court in Haynes v. Hanover Ins. Cos., 783 F.2d 136 (8th Cir. 1986), thought that Missouri would decide in favor of the innocent spouse, though the Missouri Court had not yet spoken. See also Reed v. Federal Ins. Co., 71 N.Y.2d 581, 523 N.E.2d 480, 528 N.Y.S.2d 355 (1988), where the innocent coinsured was a daughter to whom the guilty father had transferred the property without consideration when she was 18.

4. The trend of the cases seems to favor the innocent coinsured, especially a spouse. See McCann & Hall, Innocent Spouse Doctrine — New Fire in an Old Issue, 51 Ins. Coun. J. 86 (1984), which found six jurisdictions following the older, more restrictive doctrine, and twenty following the more liberal one. In the case of coinsureds there is always, of course, the substantial risk of undetected collusion. For an article opposing the trend and suggesting the redrafting of policies to preclude such recovery, see Butler & Freemon, The Innocent Coinsured: He Burns It, She Claims — Windfall or Technical Injustice?, 17 Forum 187 (1981). See also Comment, The Problem of the Innocent Co-Insured Spouse: Three Theories of Recovery, 17 Val. U.L. Rev. 849 (1983).

5. In Short v. Oklahoma Farmers Union Ins. Co., 619 P.2d 588 (Okla. 1980), the court came down on the other side by a 4-3 decision and denied recovery to the innocent spouse, holding that as both spouses were "Insureds" within the policy definition, the clause excluding coverage for fires caused by "neglect of the insured to use all reasonable means to save and preserve the property at and after a loss" was a "joint obligation." Id. at 590. The majority opinion also emphasized the policy ground that "[a]rson is a crime whose threat to the public is general. . . . To allow recovery . . . where the arsonist has been proven to be a joint insured would allow funds to be acquired by the entity of which the arsonist is a member and is flatly against public policy." Id. Sales v. State Farm Fire and Casualty Co., 849 F.2d 1383 (11th Cir. 1988) (applying Georgia law) agrees with *Short.*

6. In a case almost on all fours with *Short,* the Supreme Court of Texas allowed the innocent spouse to recover half the loss, overruling prior Texas authority. Kulubis v. Texas Farm Bureau Underwriters Ins. Co., 706 S.W.2d 953 (Tex. 1986). The reach of *Kulubis* was tested in Norman v. State Farm Fire & Casualty Co., 804 F.2d 1365 (5th Cir. 1986). In *Kulubis* the property had been "separate property held in undivided interests by a husband and wife"; in *Norman* the burned property was community property. The court was not willing to extend *Kulubis* that far in the absence of definitive Texas action. Was the federal court unduly cautious? The more difficult question is whether the *Kulubis* result should be reached if the parties continue to live together as husband and wife after the unsuccessful attempt at criminal fraud. See Casenote on *Kulubis,* 22 Tort & Ins. L.J. 486 (1987).

7. Hoyt v. New Hampshire Fire Ins. Co., 92 N.H. 242, 29 A.2d 121 (1942), apparently the first case to find for the innocent co-owner, distinguished *Bellman* (see discussion in *Hedtcke*) as involving a partnership in which the interests were joint. Should the nature of the relationship of the owners matter if one party is truly innocent? The court in McCracken v. Government Employees Ins. Co., 284 S.C. 66, 325 S.E.2d 62 (1985), did not think so, absent a statute or specific policy language to the contrary.

8. In Hogs Unlimited v. Farm Bureau Mut. Ins. Co., 401 N.W.2d 381 (Minn. 1987), one of three partners intentionally killed the insured hogs by suffocating them with anhydrous ammonia. A policy clause would have avoided coverage for fraudulent concealment either before or after loss. The guilty partner joined in submitting the proof of loss statement. The fraud was held to bar only the guilty partner; the others recovered their proportionate share. For partnership situations, is this case or *Bellman* the better result?

b. The Friendly Fire Doctrine

Austin v. Drew, 4 Camp. 360 (1815), was the first case to recognize the so-called *friendly fire doctrine.* Sugar being refined in plaintiff's factory was damaged by excessive heat and smoke. The sugar was contained in various rooms of an eight-story building through which ran a flue supplying the heat for the refining process. At the top of the flue was a register normally kept open when the fire was high. An employee started the fire without opening the register. The fire overheated, smoking up the rooms containing the sugar and causing the damage complained of. The court denied recovery.

Despite vigorous criticism, most jurisdictions treat a "friendly" fire as an implied exception. See Vance, Friendly Fires, 1 Conn. B.J.

284 (1927); Ingram, The Friendly Fire Doctrine: Judicial Misconstruction Run Amok, 22 Tort & Ins. L.J. 312 (1987).

In Engel v. Redwood County Farmers Mut. Ins. Co., 281 N.W.2d 331, 332 (Minn. 1979), the doctrine was stated as follows:

> [T]he rule generally states that a fire which is intentionally kindled and which remains at all times confined to the place where it was intended to be will be characterized as friendly and will not subject the insurer to any liability for the resulting loss.

In *Engel,* the plaintiff constructed and obtained insurance on a hog barn heated by a furnace, which was controlled by a thermostat to keep the internal temperature at 75°F. A short rendered the thermostat inoperable, and the temperature inside the barn reached 120°F, resulting in the death of 15 sows. At all times the fire inside the furnace produced heat at its usual rate and was confined within the furnace, causing no damage to the barn or to the furnace and producing no soot or other foreign material. The Supreme Court of Minnesota nevertheless allowed recovery, holding that the fire had become "hostile." A fire "which causes damage by burning for a greater length of time than intended is no less uncontrolled merely because it continues to burn at its usual rate." Id. at 333.

Engel illustrates a recent trend to limit the friendly fire exception. See also Karadontes v. Continental Ins. Co., 139 N.J. Super. 599, 354 A.2d 696 (1976) (insured's boiler damaged when low water cut-off valve failed, allowing boiler to crack); Schulze and Burch Biscuit Co. v. American Protection Ins. Co., 96 Ill. App. 3d 350, 421 N.E.2d 331, 51 Ill. Dec. 823 (1981) (oven damaged by overheating). In *Schulze,* the court said, "While we are mindful of the long-standing doctrine of 'friendly' versus 'hostile' fires, to apply such a principle in this case would be to further alienate the judicial principle of policy construction."

Notes and Questions

1. With the weakening of the friendly fire doctrine by cases like *Engel* and *Schulze,* can you argue effectively that any fire that does damage is hostile? Should the *contra proferentem* rule and other rules of construction favorable to the insured have any effect on that argument?

2. Perhaps the most common, though not the most serious, fire damage is the cigarette burn on a rug, coffee table, or couch. Is it caused by a "fire?" A friendly one or a hostile one? See Swerling v. Connecticut Fire Ins. Co., 55 R.I. 252, 180 A. 343 (1935), for the only

reported case found. Why should that be so when rugs and furniture are frequently damaged by fire and are often expensive?

3. The friendly fire doctrine could sometimes be treated as a problem in determining the meaning of "fire." In Washington State Hop Producers, Inc. v. Harbor Ins. Co., 34 Wash. App. 257, 660 P.2d 768 (1983), the insured produced hops and insured the warehoused hops against fire. "Browning," caused by heat which "is indicative of a chemical oxidation" similar to being "charred," damaged 253 bales of hops. The insurer denied that the hops were "destroyed by fire." The court took the definition of fire from Webster's dictionary, as "the phenomenon of combustion as manifested in light, flame, and heat," and required "some visible indication of fire such as flame, glow, or light." Id. at 259-260, 660 P.2d at 769. With no evidence of flame or glow, the court denied recovery. Is the decision sound?

4. Is an explosion a fire? In Bird v. St. Paul Fire & Marine Ins. Co., 224 N.Y. 47, 120 N.E. 86 (1918), a fire caused an explosion, which caused another fire, which in turn caused another explosion, the concussion from which caused damage to the plaintiff's boat (at a considerable distance from either fire). The plaintiff sought recovery under a marine insurance contract insuring against fire, but the court held the damage was not proximately caused by the fires. There was no express exclusion of explosion in the policy: Why wasn't the last explosion itself a fire, disposing of the "cause" question in the plaintiff's favor?

4. Multiple or Limited Interests in Property

One of the most important and tricky of the many clusters of property insurance law problems is that concerning multiple (or limited) interests in property. The assumption from which a business planner or personal adviser should start is that every person with an interest in property stands alone and needs separate insurance. That is not always true, of course, and it is wasteful to have duplicate coverage of the same risks, but until you are confident your jurisdiction's law is otherwise for the particular relationship it is safer to assume that separate insurance should be purchased. Fire insurance is considerably cheaper than a house!

The difficulty stems in large part from the traditional view of the insurance contract as a personal contract. The policy insures the policyholder's interest in property, not the property, and cannot be assigned without the consent of the insurer. For example, Service America Corporation, a concessionaire at the Arlington Park Racetrack in the northwestern Chicago suburbs, was a subsidiary of City Investing Company, which had insurance covering "City Investing

Company and/or any affiliated or subsidiary organization." City sold SAC to Allegheny Beverage Corporation. Ten weeks later the Arlington Park Racetrack fire occurred, and SAC claimed under City's policy for loss to its concessions. The court held there was no coverage under the policy, although when the policy was issued the racetrack was part of the property explicitly covered. Home Ins. Co. v. Service America Corp., 662 F. Supp. 964 (N.D. Ill. 1987).

One alternative that is frequently available is having the client named as an additional insured on the policy that was taken out by the person with the other interest in the property. Despite the personal nature of the contract, the insurer usually bases its premium rates primarily on the value and characteristics of the property, not on the nature of the interest in the property. If the insurer has no concern about extra hazard because of the split interests, or because of the identity of the additional party, it will probably include the extra insured at no charge or a nominal charge.

For a case showing that an insurance agent (and on some possible facts a lawyer) may be liable for failure to get a client named as an additional insured, see Zitelman v. Metropolitan Ins. Agency, 482 A.2d 426 (D.C. App. 1984).

This solution is not fail-safe because it is possible that the insurer may raise defenses based on the conduct of the principal insured, such as misrepresentation on the application or failure to proceed properly after loss. Complete assurance of protection depends on one's own control over any conduct that may defeat the coverage. Although it can be argued that such defenses should not bar recovery to a person designated as an additional insured, the joint ownership arson cases show that this argument, however plausible, will not necessarily prevail. Still, that particular difficulty can sometimes be overcome. See Section 4(b) on mortgagor and mortgagee.

In addition to concern about subjection to defenses that are out of the client's control, it is also necessary that the terms of the policy meet the client's own particular needs.

This solution (at least partial) to the multiple party problem is illustrated in the context of construction contracts by provisions of the standard form construction contract of the American Institute of Architects. The 1987 edition of this important contract may be found in 4 Stein, Construction Law, Appendix of Forms at App.-33 et seq. The provision has sometimes been called the *name and waive* provision.

The contract requires the Owner to purchase and maintain property insurance to the full value of the contract on a replacement cost basis. There are detailed provisions about the terms of the insurance. The contract further provides that the Owner and the Contractor "waive all rights against (1) each other and any of their subcontractors

. . . and (2) the Architect. . . ." Losses under the policy are to be adjusted with the Owner as fiduciary for the other named insureds. Id. at §§11.3.1 to 11.3.11.

Should such a clause, if in a construction contract, create any concern in an insurance underwriter's mind? What steps might an underwriter wish to take because of the existence of such a contract? Would such a contract provision have any direct effect on the meaning of the insurance policy if the contract is implemented? For a concrete application in a case, see Tokio Marine & Fire Ins. Co. v. Employers Ins. of Wausau, 786 F.2d 101 (2d Cir. 1986).

a. Vendor and Purchaser of Realty

Of all multiple interest problems, the worst "trap for the unwary" concerns vendors and purchasers of realty. In some jurisdictions, the insurance taken out by the vendor protects only the vendor, cannot be assigned without the consent of the insurer (see Carle Place Plaza Corp. v. Excelsior Ins. Co., 534 N.Y.S.2d 397 (A.D. 1988)), does not run with the land, and leaves the unwary buyer unprotected if the latter is depending on coverage by the existing insurance after the risk of loss of the property passes. Under the Uniform Vendor and Purchaser Risk Act, the risk shifts to the purchaser after either title or possession is transferred. The many jurisdictions without that Act differ as to when the risk shifts. The matter should be dealt with in the land sale contract and the insurance handled accordingly. Except when the insurer wants to get off the risk altogether, it will probably endorse the policy to cover both interests at no, or a nominal, extra charge. The caveats mentioned above about subjection to defenses apply here also.

The problems that have resulted when the parties have fallen into the trap are interesting and complex, but can be omitted here. Access to the relevant material is easy, through standard texts and treatises such as Appleman, Couch, and Keeton and Widiss. For a brief introduction to the problem, see Bixby, The Vendor-Vendee Problem: How Do We Slice the Insurance Pie?, 19 Forum 112 (1983).

Comparable problems arise in connection with the sale of goods, but here the Uniform Commercial Code gives considerable direction. See §§2-509(3) and 2-510. See also Stockton, An Analysis of Insurable Interest Under Article Two of the Uniform Commercial Code, 17 Vand. L. Rev. 815 (1964); R. Alderman, A Transactional Guide to the U.C.C. 170-188 (2d ed. 1983). Jason's Foods v. Peter Eckrich & Sons, Inc., 774 F.2d 214 (7th Cir. 1985), lucidly illustrates the application of the UCC.

Should automobile insurance coverage "run with the property," on sale of the car? Colonial Ins. Co. of Cal. v. Blankenship, 231 Mont. 469, 753 P.2d 880 (1988), discusses this issue, and concludes, "no."

b.   Mortgagor and Mortgagee

In at least one area, the problem of the person with the second interest in a policy (that is, being subject to policy defenses over which he has no control) has been neatly solved. A standard clause protecting institutional lenders has long been used, typically reading somewhat as follows:

> Loss or damage, if any, under this policy, shall be payable to the mortgagee (or trustee), named on the first page of this policy, as interest may appear . . . and this insurance, as to the interest of the mortgagee (or trustee) only therein, shall not be invalidated by any act or neglect of the mortgagor or owner . . . ; provided, that in case the mortgagor or owner shall neglect to pay any premium due under this policy, the mortgagee (or trustee) shall, on demand, pay the same.

Does such a clause have a different effect than adding the mortgagee as an "additional insured?" If so, in what respect and why?

A second mortgagee is also protected by the clause. See State Farm Fire and Casualty Co. v. Folger, 677 F. Supp. 844 (E.D.N.C. 1988).

In Grange Mutual Casualty Co. v. Central Trust Co., N.A., 774 S.W.2d 838 (Ky. App. 1989), the court reached an interesting result on the theory that the mortgagee under a standard mortgage clause was an independent contracting party, not a third party beneficiary. Though the fire-damaged property had been restored to its former condition, the mortgagee was still able to recover from the insurer. Is that a sound result?

Although fire insurance is the natural habitat of the standard mortgage clause, there is nothing to preclude its utilization in other property insurance. For automobile collision coverage, see International Surplus Lines Ins. Co. v. Associates Commercial Corp., 514 So. 2d 1326 (Ala. 1987); for theft coverage in a marine insurance policy, see Ingersoll-Rand Fin. Corp. v. Employers Ins. of Wausau, 637 F. Supp. 642 (E.D. La. 1984); for protection to the mortgagee in a marine policy against scuttling by the mortgagor, see Zurich Ins. Co. v. Wheeler, 838 F.2d 338 (9th Cir. 1988). In Aetna Casualty & Surety Co. v. Roland, 47 Ohio App. 3d 93, 547 N.E.2d 379 (1988), a similar clause in a property policy on an airplane was called a "standard breach of warranty endorsement."

For a general treatment of this topic, see Dwyer & Barney, Analysis of Standard Mortgage Clause and Selected Provisions of the New York Standard Fire Policy, 19 Forum 639 (1984), and Connally, Mortgagor-Mortgagee Problems and the Standard Mortgage Clause, 13 Forum 786 (1978).

Notes and Questions

1. A more traditional "loss payable" clause overcomes the personal contract difficulty by making the additional party a designated third-party beneficiary (if not more), but it does not overcome the problem of defenses. It often reads (though the language is not standardized), "Loss, if any, hereunder shall be adjusted with the Insured and be payable to the Insured and [mortgagee] as their respective interests may appear." It is often called an *open mortgage clause*. Under classic contract law, a creditor third-party beneficiary may not have a vested right under the contract. But Perfect Investments, Inc. v. Underwriters at Lloyd's, London, 782 P.2d 932 (Okla. 1989), held that a simple loss payee's right against the insurer could not be defeated by settlement between insured and insurer without the knowledge and consent of the loss payee. Is the result sound under traditional contract doctrine?

2. Does a standard mortgage clause make the mortgagee a third party beneficiary or an independent contracting party? State Farm Fire and Casualty Co. v. Folger, 677 F. Supp. 844 (E.D.N.C. 1988), applying North Carolina law, says the independent contract conceptualization is "well settled." See also May v. Market Ins. Co., 387 So. 2d 1081 (La. 1980); World of Tires, Inc. v. American Ins. Co., 360 Pa. Super. 514, 520 A.2d 1388 (1987). What technical difficulties accompany each conceptualization? Which is the better view?

3. Can it be argued that the effectiveness of the standard mortgage clause depends on the existence of a valid contract, and that either breach of an affirmative warranty or misrepresentations by the insured in applying for the policy would preclude recovery by the mortgagee under a standard mortgage clause?

4. If an insurer has paid the mortgagee despite the mortgagor's breach of warranty or the failure of a condition, what recourse does the insurer have? See Northwest Farm Bureau Ins. Co. v. Althauser, 90 Or. App. 13, 750 P.2d 1166 (1988).

5. Can the coverage of the mortgagee be broader than that of the mortgagor? General Motors Acceptance Corp. v. Western Fire Ins. Co., 457 S.W.2d 234 (Mo. App. 1970), held it could not. Quoting Appleman, a much used multivolume treatise on Insurance Law, the

court said that though the standard mortgage clause operates as an independent contract between insurer and mortgagee, "the policy terms are themselves not nullified by a standard mortgage clause. It is, rather, that a new contract containing those provisions is made with the mortgagee personally." Id. at 237. But Southwestern Funding Corp. v. Motors Ins. Corp., 59 Cal. 2d 91, 378 P.2d 361, 28 Cal. Rptr. 161 (1963), held that, notwithstanding the usual geographical policy limit to the United States and Canada, as to the mortgagee an automobile policy with a standard mortgage clause would apply also in Mexico.

6. In a certain jurisdiction where the independent contract theory is followed, the Small Business Administration became a mortgagee by assignment. The policy had a standard mortgage clause. Three years after loss but within the otherwise applicable statute of limitations, the SBA sued the insurer which pleaded among its defenses the policy's one year limitation period for bringing suit. How should the court rule on that defense? See United States v. Commercial Union Ins. Cos., 821 F.2d 164 (2d Cir. 1987).

7. In Dalrymple v. Royal-Globe Ins. Co., 280 Ark. 514, 659 S.W.2d 938 (1983), Dalrymple was the builder of an apartment and, after its sale, the mortgagee-loss payee under the buyer's insurance contract. The insurer paid Dalrymple, then tried to recover the payment on learning that the cause of the fire was defective wiring for which Dalrymple was responsible. The court recognized the cliché that an insurer has no subrogation* against an insured but said Dalrymple was not *really* an insured and upheld the trial court's granting of summary judgment to the insurer. It is not clear from the opinion whether the loss payee clause was an open mortgage clause or a standard mortgage clause. Should that matter? The same result was reached in Rocky Mountain Helicopters Inc. v. Bell Helicopters Textron, 805 F.2d 907 (10th Cir. 1986), applying Texas law. *Rocky Mountain* recognizes the complexity of the problem and discusses various cases reaching different results.

8. The relationships of parties can get complicated in real property transactions. In In re S.P.G. of Schenectady, Inc., 833 F.2d 413 (2d Cir. 1987), a restaurant was mortgaged and then twice sold, resulting in three successive mortgages on the property. The new owner got into financial difficulty and could not keep the property insured. Two of the mortgagees took out fire insurance policies to protect their own interests when the equity owner filed a Chapter 11 bankruptcy petition. The individual mortgagees were the only named insureds. When one of the insurers paid on its policy after a fire, it sought to be

---

*For a discussion of subrogation, see Section E.

subrogated to the mortgagee's lien against the equity owner. The court held

> that *all* insurance policies taken out by a mortgagee pursuant to §254(4) [New York Real Property Law] are automatically "dual interest" policies. A close reading of the text of §254(4) points persuasively toward this finding. First, §254(4) provides that if the mortgagor defaults in insuring the premises, the mortgagee "may make *such insurance* from year to year." If the mortgagor had insured the premises himself, he undoubtedly would have benefited from the policy. It follows that the mortgagee's acquisition of "such insurance" is — absent compelling evidence to the contrary — similarly intended to benefit the mortgagor. (Emphasis in original). [Id. at 417.]

9. An automobile policy with collision coverage contained the following clause:

> We will pay the lienholder for a loss under this policy even though you have violated the terms of the policy by something you have done or failed to do. However, we will not pay for any loss caused by conversion, embezzlement or secretion by you or anyone acting on your behalf. [Chrysler Credit Corp. v. Dairyland Ins. Co., 491 So. 2d 402, 403 (La. App. 1986), *cert. denied,* 494 So. 2d 1178 (La. 1986).]

The insured had an accident. The insurer issued a draft to the insured but stopped payment on learning that the insured had settled with the tortfeasor's insurer. Can the lienholder recover from the insurer?

10. In First Natl. Bank in Sioux City v. Watts, 462 N.W.2d 922 (Iowa 1990), an automobile collision policy provided that the loss payee's protection "shall not be invalidated by any act or neglect of the . . . Owner of the . . . automobile." The insurer renewed policies only after payment of the renewal premium. The court held the provision in the policy did not help the loss payee when the insured did not pay at renewal time. Would you reach the same result?

11. Under the physical damage portion of an automobile policy, "loss" was defined as "direct and accidental loss of or damage to the INSURED CAR, including its equipment." The lienholder's protection (in a loss payable clause) "shall not be invalidated by any act or neglect of the . . . Owner." Allegedly, the owner intentionally burned the car. Should the lienholder recover under the policy? Boyd v. General Motors Acceptance Corp., 162 Mich. App. 446, 413 N.W.2d 683 (1987), followed by General Motors Acceptance Corp. v. Auto Club Ins. Assn., 168 Mich. App. 733, 425 N.W.2d 157 (1988) held the lienholder could not recover. Can you reproduce the line of analysis of the courts? To check your reasoning, see *Boyd* rather than *GMAC.*

c.   Lessor and Lessee

The problems here are more complicated in some ways, for they involve not simultaneous but successive interests in the property. Consider the plight of a lessee who, losing a place from which to do business, *is* insured but under the indemnity principle embedded in the contract (see Section E regarding measurement of losses) receives only the value of the leasehold interest. The problem may be especially poignant for the lessee who has spent large sums in improving the leased property, in reliance on a long-term lease subject to termination on destruction by fire. For the lessee caught in this situation, business interruption insurance is at least as important as pure property insurance. Attention should be given in the transaction documents to insurance needs and their satisfaction, and appropriate coverage negotiated.

An illustration of a lessor's failure to protect himself appears in Simon v. Truck Ins. Exch., 757 P.2d 1123 (Colo. App. 1988). Under the lease the lessee was obligated to insure and have the lessor named as a beneficiary. The lessee insured, but only for himself. Despite the fact that there had been discussion with the agent about adding the lessor as an insured, the court declined to reform the contract for lack of adequate evidence of mutual mistake.

A frequently recurring and more homely problem arises when a renter of property who has no fire insurance is negligently responsible for damages to the premises. In Ford v. Jennings, 70 Ill. App. 3d 219, 387 N.E.2d 1125, 26 Ill. Dec. 295 (1979), a *yield up clause* in a written lease required the tenant to yield up the premises in a condition as good as when they were obtained, "loss by fire or inevitable accident, and ordinary wear excepted." The property burned while in the possession of a sublessee without privity with the landlord. The court held the lessor could recover from the sublessee for the latter's negligence. Should the yield up clause protect the lessee against the sublessee's potential liability for negligence? Safeco Ins. Cos. v. Weisgerber, 115 Idaho 428, 767 P.2d 271 (1989), says it would.

In Anderson v. Peters, 142 Ill. App. 3d 182, 491 N.E.2d 768, 96 Ill. Dec. 489 (1986), the insurer sought to be subrogated against a *tenant* under an oral lease for the tenant's negligence in causing a fire. The court considered from a public policy perspective the heavy burden on *lessees* without either insurance or the protection of an exculpatory yield up clause and ruled in favor of the tenant, considering the tenant the coinsured of the owner. The opposite result was reached in Fire Ins. Exch. v. Geekie, 179 Ill. App. 3d 679, 534 N.E.2d 1061, 128 Ill. Dec. 616 (1989) and in Regent Ins. Co. v. Economy Preferred Ins. Co., 749 F. Supp. 191 (C.D. Ill. 1990), the latter predicting that the Illinois Supreme Court would follow *Geekie*. See also unfavorable comment on the result in *Anderson* and a discussion of related cases by

Hoey, Property Insurance: Annual Survey of Property Insurance Law, 23 Tort & Ins. L.J. 405, 427-434 (1988).

A lessor of heavy construction equipment obtained an agreement from the lessee to maintain insurance on the equipment. The lessee insured the equipment but the policy did not name the lessor as an insured or a loss payee. The Washington Supreme Court held in Postlewait Constr., Inc. v. Great American Ins. Cos., 106 Wash. 2d 96, 720 P.2d 805 (1986), that the lessor was not a third-party beneficiary under the policy and could not recover under it. Is the lessor without remedy? If there is one, what is it? Would the end result be different?

If the lease contains a provision that both lessor and lessee agree to release each other from any claim that could be insured against, would the lessor's insurer have a subrogation claim against the lessee for negligently causing the fire? Alliance Ins. Co. v. First Tape, Inc., 713 S.W.2d 718 (Tex. App. 1986), held it would not. Do you agree?

d. Life Tenant and Remainderman

This dual interest situation presents interesting problems. If the life tenant has the normal fire insurance policy (under which payment for loss is at actual cash value and in any event for no more than the interest of the insured), the payment to the life tenant after a total loss will neither replace the property nor buy equivalent property. Indeed, the payment might be trivial in the case of an elderly life tenant of a residence. The life tenant needs to join forces with the remainderman and insure both interests as well as buy replacement cost coverage, so that the life tenant will have an equivalent place to sleep and eat. The analogue of business interruption insurance is also available to pay living costs during reconstruction. But suppose the remainderman, for any or no reason, won't cooperate? Is it possible for the life tenant who is acting alone to acquire adequate protection? Suppose the life tenant obtains replacement cost coverage for the full value of the building and the remainderman also insures, separately, to the extent of his remainder interest. Who should pay how much to whom?

e. Bailor and Bailee

Finally, we have the multiple interest situation with the most interesting legal problems: that of bailor and bailee. There is a multitude of policy forms; some purport to protect customers (that is, bailors) and some do not. Often those that do not directly protect the bailor's interest do protect the bailee against liability to customers, which may provide some measure of indirect protection to bailors. Are the results equivalent?

Solutions for this, as of other limited or multiple interest problems, result from the interplay of the principle of indemnity (or a contractual provision for indemnity only) generally applicable to property insurance, the principle that insurance is a "personal" contract, the principle that neither insurer nor insured should be unjustly enriched, and the principle (in jurisdictions where it is applicable) that reasonable expectations should be honored. The conflict of and the interplay among these principles results in great complexity and much interstate disagreement on specific rules. It is harder to generalize for the whole country with respect to these problems than for most.

For bailments related to sales, see the Uniform Commercial Code, §§2-509(1) and (2). See also Alderman, A Transactional Guide to the UCC 178-181 (2d ed. 1983).

FOLGER COFFEE CO. v. GREAT AMERICAN INS. CO.

333 F. Supp. 1272 (W.D. Mo. 1971)

William H. Becker, Chief Judge. . . .

The following facts, pertinent to the issue under consideration, have been admitted by the parties:

> On or about September 14, 1966, defendant made and delivered its policy of insurance, number 1-00-91-31 to Ar-Ka-Mo Sporting Goods, Inc., a Missouri corporation. . . .
> In June and July, 1969, Ar-Ka-Mo Sporting Goods, Inc., was a warehouseman of property owned by the plaintiff and others.
> On or about the date set out in plaintiff's Complaint, the plaintiff did sustain damage to certain of its property which was warehoused and bailed with Ar-Ka-Mo Sporting Goods, Inc., however, the extent of that loss is not admitted. . . .

According to the true copy of the insurance policy attached to the complaint herein, the following is the clause which is relied upon by plaintiff as bringing its losses within the coverage of the policy:

III. Property covered
The policy covers:
    A. Personal property usual to the conduct of the Insured's business, consisting principally of Premiums for Prizes, the property of the Insured, or similar property of others held by the insured *for which the insured is liable,* except as provided elsewhere in this policy." (Emphasis added.)

Defendant relies on the emphasized language, contending that the word "liable" in the provision means "legally liable" and that plaintiff must therefore show the negligence of the bailee Ar-Ka-Mo Sporting Goods, Inc., before it can recover under the policy.

In cases like that at bar, however, the courts have almost uniformly held that if, from the contract construed in its entirety, the fair interpretation and construction of the insurance contract is that it was intended primarily to cover the property held by the insured, then "liable," as used within the policy, does not refer to any fixed legal liability of the insured to respond in damages, but should be construed more broadly to mean "responsible." . . .

In the *Globe & Rutgers* case, [104 F. Supp. 632 (N.D. Texas 1952), aff'd, 202 F.2d 696 (5th Cir. 1953)], the Government sued the defendant insurance companies for the loss of certain cotton seed which was destroyed by fire at the premises of the McCoy Gin Company, Inc., on November 18, 1949. The policies sued upon all contained the following provision, concerning the property insured:

> On cotton, ginned and unginned, baled and unbaled, seed cotton, cotton seed, supplies of sacks and other packaging material containing or to contain cotton seed, and bagging and ties, their own, and provided the insured is legally liable therefor, this policy shall also cover such property sold but not delivered, held in trust, or on consignment or for storage.

The Government sued for the loss of cotton seed which it had contracted to buy under price support programs and which was destroyed by fire. In holding that the Government could recover without any showing of negligence on the part of the McCoy Gin Company, Inc., the Court stated as follows:

> The contention of the defendants is that the plaintiff cannot recover under the present policies without showing that the insured is legally liable for the fire loss of the cotton seed. That view is quite arguable. The pertinent provision of the policies has been quoted in full above and the central phrase thereof reads "provided the insured is legally liable therefor." The words "liability" and "liable" have manifold meanings in law and that nuance makes "liable" fit as well in respect to one bound to respond in duty as to one bound to respond in damages. The gin company under its caretaker duty as bailee for hire certainly was responsible for the cotton seed and obligated to keep and deliver same safely, subject to exoneration only if performance be prevented without negligence on its part. That was a present and positive liability, and in fact no other liability ever supervened. In other words that liability in being was complete, and adequately answers the terms of the policy provision. Nothing novel is being stated. In the typical instance of bailment relationship a proper delivery of the property thereupon satisfies

the right of the bailor and discharges the liability of the bailee, but that does not gainsay the fact that the bailee bore a legal liability during the period of the bailment.

Of course when construing flexible language the best key usually is the context. The entire language of the relevant policy provision in its ordinary sense consistently points to insurance on *property,* not on the insured's *liability* for a fire loss on such property. A strained construction is required to say that "legally liable therefor" in the central phrase defines the thing insured. Instead the more natural reading is that it defines a selective condition on the thing being insured. A simpler statement perhaps is that said central phrase is really some of the descriptive language identifying the property insured. This viewpoint may draw question on the theory that it renders such phrase sterile, presupposing the insured would necessarily and without more be legally liable in the sense herein stressed for all property "held in trust or on consignment or for storage," but for one thing that contention would overlook the frequent tendency of bailees to attempt contractual stipulations against their common law liability. [Emphasis in original.]

If the policy provision in fact read "on the liability" of the insured then to be sure it could only mean liability for fire loss of the property, and the plaintiff would fail in the suit. This is true for the simple reason that a fire insurance policy, like many forms of insurance, is a contract of pecuniary indemnity. Its subject matter must have a money measure. Such insurance on *liability* cannot become payable apart from an incurred liability of the insured for money damages or at least a pecuniary obligation. The present policies however plainly purport to insure *property,* not only property of the specified kinds belonging to the insured, but also property of like kind, for which insured is liable, belonging to another owner, and the reasonable construction of the insurance contract is that the central phrase of the policy provisions means liability of the insured already present and not contingent liability ushered in by a fortuitous fire. If the contrary meaning had been intended it would have been easy to state same in unmistakable terms. This construction makes for certainty instead of contingency. The protection of the bailor is on a dependable footing. Bailor and bailee are spared the vexation of controversy as to liability of the bailee for the fire loss. No violence is done to the language of the policies. Even any fair doubt should be resolved in favor of the insured. The plaintiff has a good claim under the policies. [Emphasis in original.] [104 F. Supp. at 634-635.]

. . . See the following analysis in Anno., Fire Insurance — Insured's Bailor, 67 A.L.R.2d at 1244:

At one extreme are the decisions in which clauses covering property contained in specific places and for which the insured "is," "are," "may be," or "shall be" liable, used independently of trust and commission provisions, have been held to insure the property of others while in the insured's custody and control, the courts stating that the word "liable," as used in the provision, refers not to a particular fixed legal liability to respond in pecuniary damages, but may instead be equated with "responsibility," since a bailee is "responsible" for the goods of the bailor. Thus, they have held that it is not necessary that there be a showing of the insured's contractual or tort liability to the owner in order to recover the full value of customers' or bailor's property when it is damaged or destroyed by fire while in the insured's building, warehouse, or other location specified in or covered by the policy.

At the other extreme are decisions in which the fire policy covered insured's "interest in and legal liability for" property of others, or property held in trust, on commission, on storage, or otherwise. Here the courts have generally held that the policy was one of indemnity only, that it insured not property but only the liability of the insured with respect to property, and that there could be no recovery from the insurer for customers' or bailors' goods unless the insured himself had incurred legal liability, or at least a pecuniary obligation, because the loss was due to negligence for which he was responsible or because he had contractually assumed liability for loss of the property.

Both of these views would seem to be correct, for it is apparently recognized as a rule of construction that if the primary intention of the policy is to insure property, then the property of others will be included, but that when the intent is only to insure against liability, and not to insure property, then only the legal liability of the insured with respect to the property will be covered. (Emphasis added.) . . .

In the case at bar, the true meaning of the contract, properly construed in light of the admitted facts, is that it covers *property* rather than *liability*. Under the law of Missouri, as under the law generally, as noted above, this has the effect of including property of others possessed by the insured. Thus, in Ferguson v. Pekin Plow Company, 141 Mo. 161, 42 S.W. 711, a policy provision insuring property of the insureds "or held by them in trust or on commission or sold, but not removed" was held to cover goods held on commission even though there was some evidence of an intent to restrict coverage to the goods of those with whom the insured had contracts at the date of the issuance of the policies. . . . Similarly, in the case at bar, the terms of the policy must prevail over any parol evidence which would tend to vary its terms. . . .

It is therefore adjudged that judgment be, and it is hereby, entered for plaintiff and against defendant on the issue of defendant's liability to plaintiff on the insurance policy of defendant numbered 1-00-19-31. . . .

Notes and Questions

1. The policy in Sid's, Inc. v. Continental Ins. Co., 540 A.2d 119 (Me. 1988), reads, "This policy covers [t]he legal liability of the Insured

as a motor carrier, as such liability is defined, limited and set forth in the bill of lading. . . ." A load of live lobsters was hijacked from the insured's truck. Can the insured recover their value from the insurer in the absence of any lawsuit or even formal claim against the insured? The question arose on a motion of the insurer for summary judgment.

2. If the bailee advertises that customers are fully insured in bailee's warehouse (or truck), should that be decisive irrespective of policy wording? Would such advertising lead to liability under the policy in *Sid's, Inc.*?

3. If in the *Folger* situation the bailor had itself also insured its interest in its own property, who would have owed how much to whom?

D. Subrogation

1. Basic Principles

If property is insured by a contract of indemnity and loss occurs as the result of a tort or breach of contract by a third party, there are three ways to treat the tripartite relationship in which the parties find themselves, each of which appears, at least at first look, to be unsatisfactory.

a.   The insured may recover in tort (or for breach of contract) as well as on the insurance contract, and thus receive a windfall. This solution produces a result for insured property loss parallel to that produced by the collateral source rule for bodily injury.

b.   The third party may be excused from payment on the ground that the insured has already been indemnified. This would give the third party the benefit of the insurance and would appear to be a windfall to the third party. Yet, if the third party and the insured are engaged in business relations, the third party may often be named as an additional insured with no or nominal additional premium, thus effecting protection of all interests at the least cost. And as the material in this chapter shows, the same result is sometimes produced by an agreement to insure.

c.   The insurer may, *after payment to the insured,** be subrogated to the insured's claim against the third party, that is, be put in

*See Union Ins. Socy. v. Consolidated Ice Co., 261 Mich. 35, 245 N.W. 563 (1933), for an early statement of the rule that the insured must first be made whole before the subrogee may recover from the third party. There are cases that seem to

the position of the insured for that claim. At first look, this seems to give a windfall to the insurer which appears to have received a premium for protection against a loss for which it does not have to pay.

In general the third solution is adopted for property insurance. Contrary to superficial appearance, the insurer gets no windfall. The insurer has promised only *indemnity* and has thus fulfilled its promise, for the property owner suffers no loss if there is recovery from a third person. The insurer has promised to protect the third person only if the insured has made that third person a named insured or intended beneficiary or (sometimes) if the insured and the third person have made an agreement that the insured will do so. And despite mistaken statements to the contrary by people who should know better, subrogation recoveries *are* taken into account in premium rates (usually a year or two belatedly under a rate regulatory regime but promptly in a competitive environment such as exists in most places at most times in commercial property insurance). The insured gets what is paid for, which is indemnity — being made whole. The insured did not buy a promise of payment irrespective of actual loss.

In some lines, notably ocean marine and automobile collision insurance, subrogation recoveries are important in the economics of the business. In Meyers, Subrogation Rights and Recoveries, 9 Forum 83, 85 (1973), subrogation recoveries for ocean marine have been estimated at 14 to 15 percent of paid loss and 8.56 percent of paid loss for automobile physical damage claims. In others, such as fire insurance, insurers tend to pursue subrogation recoveries with vigor only when large sums are involved. Meyer said there was a net recovery of only .68 percent[†] of paid loss for fire insurance. But there is a contracyclical tendency by speakers at industry gatherings to encourage pursuit of subrogation recoveries. Pursuit of subrogation recoveries seems much more attractive in that part of the insurance cycle when insurers are trying desperately to move into the black, and seems much less useful in the other part of the cycle. This is not surprising, for in the generality of cases, at most times, the pursuit of subrogation recoveries

---

apply different rules but most of them can be explained by the presence of contractual provisions that vary the rights of the parties from those they would have in the absence of such provisions. For a compact treatment of the various possible rules, see Keeton & Widiss, Insurance Law §3.10(b)(1) (1988).

[†]Although his figure for automobile physical damage claims is based on his own company's experience, Meyers does not explain the illusory precision of his numbers for it and for fire insurance; one wonders whether the numbers he provides for ocean marine insurance are any more reliable. But perhaps it can be assumed that they indicate sufficiently the general magnitude of subrogation recoveries in various lines of insurance.

in many lines is not worthwhile, or only marginally so, for rational maximizers.

In automobile collision insurance, subrogation recoveries may be economically important mainly because of regulation. In some other parts of the world, automobile insurers tend not to pursue subrogation, relying instead on *knock for knock agreements* that stipulate against subrogation on the reasonable assumption that over time the recoveries thus foregone will be about the same in both directions. In the United States such agreements have been regarded with disfavor by regulators as unfair to the nonnegligent policyholder whose claim to recoup the deductible would thus be sacrificed. When insurers recover pursuant to subrogation, the insured is generally entitled to receive his or her deductible as the first part of the recovery.

2.   Subrogation in Property Insurance

Insurance subrogation is not complex if it is seen to be (1) the product of equitable principles and (2) a corollary of the indemnity character of the insurance contract. The following case illustrates the application of subrogation doctrine in property insurance.

ALLSTATE INS. CO. v. MEEK

489 N.E.2d 530 (Ind. App. 1986)

SHIELDS, Judge.

This is an interlocutory appeal by Allstate Insurance Company from the trial court's denial of its motion for summary judgment in an action brought against it by an insured, Leslie A. Meek. We reverse.

Facts

On July 29, 1979, Leslie A. Meek sustained injuries to her person and damage to her car as the result of the collision of her automobile with that of Richard Bruce. On May 22, 1980, Meek filed suit against Bruce seeking compensation for damage to her vehicle, loss of its use, and for her personal injuries. On or about March 9, 1983, Meek settled her suit with Bruce. As a part of the settlement, Meek executed a release which barred any further action by her against Bruce.

At the time of the accident, Meek was insured with Allstate Insurance Company under a comprehensive automobile insurance policy which included collision coverage. The record is unclear as to when, or if, Meek made a claim against Allstate under her policy. However, at some point in time, Allstate apparently denied coverage for loss of use of the vehicle and for towing expenses and refused to pay for damages to the vehicle on the grounds Meek's release prejudiced Allstate's right of subrogation. Meek then brought this suit against Allstate on the insurance contract.

Allstate moved for summary judgment against Meek on the grounds of: (1) no coverage for two items of damage; and (2) the release, as a matter of law, prejudiced Allstate's contractual right of subrogation, and thus released Allstate's contractual obligations. The trial court denied the motion and certified its interlocutory order for appeal. Subsequently, this court accepted jurisdiction of the interlocutory appeal pursuant to Indiana Rules of Procedure, Appellate Rule 4(B)(6).

Issue

The issue presented for our review is whether Meek's release prejudiced Allstate's right of subrogation and thus, under the terms of the contract, relieved Allstate of its obligation to pay.

We reverse.

Discussion . . .

The contract for insurance between Allstate and Meek contains the following relevant provisions: . . . .

General Conditions

4. Action Against Allstate
No action shall be [brought] against Allstate until after full compliance with all the terms of this policy. . . .

9. Assistance and Cooperation
The insured shall cooperate with Allstate . . . in enforcing any right of contribution or indemnity. . . .

10. Subrogation
Upon payment under Section I, Section III, or Part 1 of Section IV, Allstate shall be subrogated to the extent of such payment to all of the insured's rights of recovery therefore. The insured shall do whatever is necessary to secure such rights and do nothing before or after the loss to prejudice such rights.

Record at 69, 74, 75.

The policy imposes upon Allstate a duty to pay for damage to Meek's automobile, regardless of whether the insured or a third party causes the damage. However, if a third party causes the damage, the policy contract gives Allstate a right of subrogation after payment to the insured and also imposes a duty upon the insured to refrain from taking any action which prejudices that right. Finally, the insured cannot maintain an action against the insurer if the insured fails to comply with his obligations under the contract.

The undisputed facts reveal Meek executed a full and unconditional release of her rights against the alleged tortfeasor Bruce prior to Allstate's payment on the policy. On these facts Allstate argues Meek's act in releasing Bruce bars any recovery on her policy with Allstate citing Hockelberg v. Farm Bureau Insurance Company (1980) Ind. App., 407 N.E.2d 1160 and Auto Owner's Protective Exchange of Kankakee, Ill. v. Edwards (1922), 82 Ind. App. 558, 136 N.E. 577. These cases hold an insured's right of action on his policy is destroyed if he releases the tortfeasor prior to receiving payment on his policy. The rationale is that because the insurer possesses only the rights of its insured, the insured's release of the tortfeasor deprives the insurer of its subrogation rights granted by the policy.

Meek, on the other hand, argues Allstate's right of subrogation is not prejudiced by the release because Meek did not receive full compensation for her loss. Meek contends that until the insured receives full compensation any rights of subrogation are not prejudiced by the release. Citing Capps v. Klebs (1979) Ind. App., 382 N.E.2d 947, and Willard v. Automobile Underwriters Inc. (1980) Ind. App., 407 N.E.2d 1192, Meek asserts a factual dispute exists precluding summary judgment over whether the $35,000 settlement she received from tortfeasor Bruce constitutes payment in full of her loss.

Capps and *Willard* hold an insurer's right of action against its own insured to recover payments the insurer has made under its policy does not mature until and unless the insured's debt, i.e. loss, is paid in full. A casual reading of these two cases would seem to contradict, if not overrule, *Hockelberg* and *Edwards*. However, in fact, the cases are critically distinguishable. In *Capps* and *Willard*,[2] the insurer's contrac-

---

2. In *Capps* the insured pursued the tortfeasor through judgment and, accordingly, a release or other conduct of the insured was not an issue. In *Willard* the insurer had given notice to the alleged tortfeasor of its payment to its insured. Therefore, the insurer's right of subrogation was fully protected even though the insured subsequently released the tortfeasor. Indiana courts have held, "if the tortfeasor, with knowledge that the insurer has already made payment to the insured, makes settlement with him and thus obtains a release, it will not be a defense as against the insurer in enforcing its rights as subrogee." Hockelberg v. Farm Bureau Insurance, supra at 1161, quoting American Automobile Fire Insurance Co. v. Spieker (1933), 97 Ind. App. 533,

tual right of subrogation continued although it was held in abeyance until insured received full compensation. In *Hockelberg* and *Edwards,* the insurer's contractual right of subrogation was destroyed. Thus, the two lines of cases are not in conflict but rather are entirely consistent.

In summary, an insured who destroys the insurer's contractual subrogation rights breaches the insurance contract and, as a result, extinguishes his right of action on the policy. An insured destroys the insurer's contractual subrogation right by releasing the tortfeasor prior to settling with the insurer because it is that very settlement which enables the insurer to protect its subrogation right by giving notice thereof to the tortfeasor. In this case Meek executed a release prior to settling with Allstate; therefore, as a matter of law, Allstate's right of subrogation was prejudiced, i.e., destroyed, and Meek's right of action on the policy is destroyed.

Judgment reversed and cause remanded with instructions to enter judgment for Allstate.

BUCHANAN, C.J., and SULLIVAN J., concur.

Notes and Questions

1. The policy in *Meek* contains an express subrogation clause, but there would have been subrogation even without the clause because subrogation has its origin in equity. Within limits it can be modified by agreement. These two sources of subrogation rights are described as *legal* (properly *equitable*) and *conventional* subrogation. The latter is most important in health insurance. For historical reasons there is no subrogation to claims for bodily injury in the absence of a specific agreement. See Chapter 7.

2. An insurer is subrogated not only to tort claims against third party tortfeasors, but also to some contract claims, such as rights under mortgages on the property. See Garrison v. Great Southwest Ins. Co., 809 F.2d 500 (8th Cir. 1987).

3. Examine the name and waive provisions of the standard form construction contract of the American Institute of Architects, supra. Various possible situations can arise. The insurance policy obtained to satisfy the requirement of §11.3.1 may either predate or postdate the construction contract, and it may either say nothing relevant to subrogation or it may contain a relevant provision, for example, which reads, "Subrogation — This insurance shall not be invalidated should the Insured waive in writing prior to a loss any or all right of recovery against any party for loss occurring to the property described herein."

---

187 N.E.2d 355, at 366; Pittsburg C.C. & St. Louis Ry. Co. v. Home Insurance Co. of New York (1915), 183 Ind. 355, 108 N.E. 525, 531.

If a covered loss occurs and the insurer pays the owner, is the insurer subrogated to claims against a tortfeasor who falls within one of the classes mentioned in the AIA standard contract? For two cases exploring the matter, see Haemonetics Corp. v. Brophy & Phillips Co., 23 Mass. App. Ct. 254, 501 N.E.2d 524 (1986); United States Fidelity and Guaranty Co. v. Farrar's Plumbing and Heating Co., 158 Ariz. 354, 762 P.2d 641 (Ariz. App. 1988).

4. A cliché that is oft-repeated in discussion of subrogation is that the insurer can not be subrogated against its own insured. Is this circular? Who is an insured? If a waiver of subrogation clause is included in the policy, any person given the advantage of that clause is, indeed, an insured *at least for subrogation purposes*. It is a harder case if the claimed subrogation is against an ordinary loss payee for the latter's negligence. This problem arises in connection with the standard mortgage clause (see Section 4(b)).

5. In Control Specialists Co. v. State Farm Mut. Auto. Ins. Co., 228 Neb. 642, 423 N.W.2d 775 (1988), State Farm insured both automobiles that were involved in an accident. The company paid the innocent driver pursuant to the liability coverage of the other driver but then refused to pay again under the collision coverage of the innocent driver. The latter sued. What should be the result?

6. An insurer of property is entitled to subrogation against a tortfeasor who has been released by the insured if before the release the tortfeasor has notice of the subrogation rights. Leader Natl. Ins. Co. v. Torres, 113 Wash. 2d 366, 779 P.2d 722 (1989). The same is true if the tortfeasor's insurer has such notice. Dickhans v. Missouri Property Ins. Placement Facility, 705 S.W.2d 104 (Mo. App. 1986).

7. Under a homeowners policy, an insured suffered damage from a construction company's blasting. The insurer declined to pay a claim for the damage. The insured then settled the claim with the construction company. Does the insurer now have a defense because the insured has destroyed its subrogation rights? See Berry v. Nationwide Mut. Fire Ins. Co., 381 S.E.2d 367 (W. Va. 1989).

3. Loan Receipts

If an insurer is subrogated to the rights of its insured and pursues them in its own name, it may be subject to the prejudice jurors are thought to have against insurance companies. Insurers are therefore wont to believe it advantageous for actions to be brought in the names of insureds so that they can remain in the background. This is difficult in a jurisdiction with a real party in interest statute.

One device often used to try to solve the problem is the loan receipt. Under it the insurer makes a no-interest loan to the insured, usually in the amount of the loss, to be repaid out of the proceeds of a lawsuit the insured is to bring against the tortfeasor, with the insurer financing and controlling the lawsuit. In addition to its utility in concealing the presence of the insurer, at least in some jurisdictions, it is a device that may be used to avoid certain technical difficulties based on common law doctrines (the nonassignability of a personal injury cause of action, for example) or statutory limitations. For an introduction to the loan receipt as used in insurance, see Kenney, The Loan Receipt and Its Use by Insurers: Considerations and Suggestions, 10 Forum 920 (1975).

E. Measurement of Losses

The amount to be paid the insured after a loss is a matter for contractual agreement, except to the extent that the indemnity principle (or the insurable interest requirement) rises to the level of a public policy to be given effect irrespective of contract terms.

The standard fire policy provides in its insuring clause that it insures to an amount not exceeding the amount specified on the policy face,

> to the extent of the actual cash value of the property at the time of loss, but not exceeding the amount which it would cost to repair or replace the property with material of like kind and quality within a reasonable time after such loss, without allowance for any increased cost of repair or reconstruction by reason of any ordinance or law regulating construction of repair, and without compensation for loss resulting from interruption of business or manufacture, nor in any event for more than the interest of the insured.

Notes and Questions

1. What are the reasons for the insertion of each limiting phrase in the insuring clause, all of which must be satisfied?

2. The cases have established that actual cash value (ACV) is, at least presumptively, replacement cost less depreciation (sometimes known as the Pennsylvania rule) or the difference in market value before and after the insured event (sometimes known as the California rule). The former seems to be more widely adopted; it is certainly the easier rule to apply, but sometimes other factors should be taken into

account. In the leading case of McAnarney v. Newark Fire Ins. Co., 247 N.Y. 176, 159 N.E. 902 (1928), the building that burned was formerly used to manufacture malt. The jury found the intrinsic or depreciated structural value of the building to be $55,000. But because malt could no longer be manufactured in the building because of Prohibition, the most recent bid and asked figures in efforts to sell the building were $6,000 and $15,000. The principle of indemnity led the court of appeals to establish what has since been called the "broad evidence rule" (sometimes known as the New York rule), which permitted evidence of the statute-created obsolescence of the building in order to establish ACV. It is, of course, consistent with the other two, if limited to unusual circumstances. A broad evidence rule would also permit evidence of special factors *enhancing* value, if any, but most often it permits evidence of obsolescence. Not every jurisdiction has adopted the broad evidence rule and some that have apply it only to certain kinds of property.

Suppose McAnarney believed, and could prove he believed, that the country was on the verge of eliminating national prohibition, so that the building would again be worth $55,000. Is there any good reason McAnarney should not be able to insure the building for that amount as a stipulated value and collect it from the insurer?

3. If you determine ACV on a straightforward replacement cost less depreciation basis, how should the depreciation be calculated?

4. The ACV measure of recovery leaves the insured without the funds to replace an old and depreciated but perfectly satisfactory building with an equivalent one in the same location. Replacement cost insurance is generally available to replace the old building with an equivalent new one. There is a "moral hazard" attached to such insurance, because payment under it leaves the insured better off than before the fire. Are there simple methods by which an insurer can reduce that moral hazard?

5. Is it unreasonable to believe that many lay persons buying fire insurance simply assume the proceeds will replace their homes if they burn? Would the reasonable expectations doctrine produce that result despite the language of the policy? Would an insurance agent be liable to an applicant for failing to explain the difference between ACV coverage and replacement cost coverage? See Stokes v. Harrell, 289 Ark. 179, 711 S.W.2d 755 (1986).

6. If the loss is partial, not total, as is true of most losses, how should the payment to the insured be calculated under the ACV measure? Can you make a case that actual replacement cost is the proper measure of ACV for partial losses? Does it matter whether the insured actually replaces, and whether the materials are new or used? Should a distinction be taken between cost of materials and labor cost? Note, Functional Value vs. Actual Cash Value in Partial Loss Settlements, 50 Ins. Coun. J. 332 (1983) explores the partial loss problem.

1. The Valued Policy Law

It is common for agents to encourage overinsurance by insureds, ostensibly as a precaution against inflation, and for insureds to agree to the overinsurance because of a natural tendency to put an optimistic (that is, excessive) value on their treasured property. (Automatic escalation for inflation is now optional; taken together with depreciation, it would also produce overvaluation.) Of course, any insured contemplating fraud needs no encouragement to overvalue property.

Because fire insurance premiums are calculated on the basis of a rate per hundred dollars of coverage, overinsurance results in an excessive premium (and simultaneously an extra commission to the agent). As we've seen, the normal measure of damages for fire loss (and by extension for other property losses) is its ACV at the time of the fire, even if more coverage was paid for. About half the states have responded to this perceived problem of "gouging" by enacting a *valued policy law*. Such statutes vary considerably, but in general they provide that when there is a total loss of a dwelling (or sometimes of any real property) without criminal fault of the insured, the face amount of the policy shall be paid to the insured without regard to the actual cash value. The statute was intended to alter incentives. In what way?

When the author of this book revised the Wisconsin Insurance Code, he proposed and secured repeal of the Wisconsin valued policy law. (It was the first of its kind when it was initially enacted in 1874. It was repealed in 1915, but reenacted in 1917.) Following is the author's successful proposal for repeal, together with the provision that preceded the repeal.

WISCONSIN VALUED POLICY LAW*

Preliminary Comment to Possible Section 632.01.

The valued policy law (s. 203.21), first enacted in 1874, was intended to prevent "greedy and unscrupulous" insurers and agents from overinsuring property and receiving unjustifiably high premiums and commissions thereon. The indemnity principle in fire insurance limited a policyholder's recovery to the amount of his loss, even if he had paid a premium based on a much larger sum. The obvious unfair-

---

*This excerpt is taken from the Fourth Draft of "Insurance Contracts," which later became 1975 Wis. Laws ch. 375. This passage did not need to appear in the final bill because the recommendation was adopted by the Insurance Laws Revision Committee.

ness of this situation led the legislature to require payment of the face amount of the policy in most cases of total loss. It was hoped the law would induce companies to force their agents into careful and realistic evaluations of insured property, to develop institutional controls against over-insurance. On the other hand, the companies argued that it encouraged arson.

In the first decades after its initial enactment, there was constant effort to repeal the statute, which succeeded in 1915. It was reenacted in identical terms in 1917. During several decades the valued policy law was a national issue, then called "The Wisconsin Problem." The statute fell short of its objectives; it is also doubtful if the law ever made much difference in the Wisconsin arson rate. [The story is told in detail in S. Kimball, Insurance and Public Policy 240-246 (1960). — ED.]

Better construction of premises and improved firefighting methods have probably led to a decline in the number of total losses; the law does not apply to partial ones. On the other hand, building codes sometimes artificially create a total loss by forbidding reconstruction. Under those circumstances, and with the deterioration of the slum areas of big cities, there is a new incentive to arson on the part of "slumlords." The problem is undoubtedly less serious in Wisconsin than in states with larger and more badly deteriorated cities.

The section should be repealed and the issue of the measure of recovery left to free contract, but the provision is included virtually unchanged here so that it will not be repealed inadvertently.

Possible Section 632.01 — Valued Policy Law

Whenever any fire insurance policy insures real property and the insured property is wholly destroyed, without criminal fault on the part of an insured or his assigns, the amount of the policy shall be taken conclusively to be the value of the property when insured and the amount of loss when destroyed.

Notes and Questions

1. Does the valued policy law reflect a sound public policy?

2. In a state with a valued policy law, the city's building inspector required complete demolition of a building after a fire. How much should the insured receive from the insurer? For such a case with somewhat more complicated facts, see Algernon Blair Group, Inc. v. U.S. Fidelity & Guaranty Co., 821 F.2d 597 (11th Cir. 1987). The

village ordinance that was quoted in Stahlberg v. Travelers Indem. Co., 568 S.W.2d 79 (Mo. App. 1978), forbade restoration except in accordance with district regulations if the building was damaged by fire to the extent of more than 60 percent of its *assessed* value. The court said that contract provisions limiting liability for loss when such ordinances are in effect would be held to be invalid.

3. Valued policies, even when not statutorily required, are common in a number of settings. In business interruption insurance, for example, it is common to specify the per diem rate the insurer will pay for total interruption of the business. For example, a policy insuring a railway against business interruption for blockage of its tracks from flood, mudslide, or other insured risk would be likely to specify separately the per diem payment to be made for interruption of operations on each of its segments. If detouring is possible, either on its own lines or by arrangement with another line, adjustments will have to be made, though such adjustments may be provided for in advance in setting the per diem payments and the premium rates.

4. The most common arena for valued policies is marine insurance, where a pure indemnity contract is uncommon. Why should that be so?

5. A variation on the valued policy is sometimes called *stated amount insurance.* A natural place for it to appear is in automobile collision insurance, especially if the insured car is old but well preserved, if it has been rebuilt, or if it has value as an antique. In normal cases calculation of the ACV would start with the "Bluebook" value, which might be grossly inadequate compensation for the loss of a real treasure. In Meier v. Aetna Life & Casualty Standard Fire Ins. Co., 149 Ill. App. 3d 932, 500 N.E.2d 1096, 103 Ill. Dec. 25 (1986), an insured bought such insurance on a 1962 Chevrolet which had a new engine and a new paint job. The stated amount was supported by photographs and an appraisal. The court's opinion is not clear about why the insurer sought to pay less than half the stated amount, but in any case the court held for the insured. There was also a bad faith issue that was dealt with pursuant to Illinois Insurance Code §155 (see Chapter 8).

6. Another place one regularly finds "stated amount" coverage is in livestock mortality insurance, especially in insurance of thoroughbred horses. For such a policy, where a horse was held not to be covered because it was not in sound health at the time of writing the insurance, see Tate v. Charles Aguillard Ins. & Real Estate, Inc., 508 So. 2d 1371 (La. 1987). The case also involved conditions precedent to liability as well as waiver.

Serious problems of moral hazard have made their appearance in livestock mortality insurance recently. A precipitous decline in the value of thoroughbreds has led to more frequent unexplained deaths of horses. In one case, a dentist with syringes in his socks, allegedly about to administer a lethal injection to a thoroughbred, was arrested and charged in a "scheme to kill horses for insurance." Chicago Trib., Feb. 27, 1990, §4, at 5. An associate claimed the man had been involved in killing other horses for insurance proceeds. The extent of this practice obviously remains conjectural.

2. Coinsurance

How much the deterrent effect of possible loss is lessened by the existence of an insurance policy will vary from person to person, from one line of insurance to another, and depending on the relationship of coverage and value, from one policy to another. Various devices have been developed by insurers to counter the temptation to cause loss deliberately or to be less careful.

Sometimes the insurance company will insist that the insured coinsure the risk (that is, absorb a share of the loss), and couple the coinsurance requirement with a deductible provision or a *franchise clause* which is like a deductible, except that once the loss passes a specified level, the deductible no longer applies. Sometimes maximum limits will be imposed on coverage. When would you use each of these various devices?

Coinsurance has different meanings in health insurance and in fire insurance. In the former, a coinsurance clause provides a formula for sharing the loss between insurer and insured, but in the latter sharing does not necessarily result. In fire insurance, the objective is to encourage insurance to full value. Compare the objective of the valued policy law: the coinsurance clause forces insurance to full value, or nearly full value; the valued policy law seeks to prevent insurers from allowing or encouraging overinsurance.

Notes and Questions

1. Fire insurance premium rates have traditionally been quoted as $x per $100 of insurance coverage. Thus, if the rate were $.43, a fire insurance policy for $100,000 of coverage on a building would cost $430; $200,000 of coverage on the same building would cost $860. In areas with fire departments, a total loss is relatively rare, which creates a considerable incentive for some persons to insure for only a part of the property's value.

The automobile liability policy premium is calculated for different limits of coverage in a different way. In automobile liability insurance, if the base rates are set for $5/10,000 limits, $10/20,000 limits might cost 115 percent of the base rate, $25/50,000 limits 127 percent of the base rates, and so forth. These numbers, though of the right order of magnitude, have been selected arbitrarily and do not necessarily represent any schedule currently in force.

2. The following is a fire insurance coinsurance clause:

Coinsurance Claims

Coinsurance: _____ %

   This Company shall not be liable for a greater proportion of any loss to the property covered than the amount of insurance under this policy for such property bears to the amount produced by multiplying the actual cash value of such property at the time of the loss by the coinsurance percentage applicable (specified above or on the first page of this policy).

   In the event that the aggregate claim for any loss is both less than $10,000 and less than 5% of the total amount of insurance applicable to the property involved at the time such loss occurs, no special inventory or appraisement of the undamaged property shall be required, providing that nothing herein shall be construed to waive the application of the first paragraph of this clause.

   If this policy covers on two or more items, the provisions of this clause shall apply to each item separately.

   The value of property covered under Extensions of Coverage if any, and the cost of the removal of debris, shall not be considered in the determination of actual cash value when applying the Coinsurance Clause.

The "percentage specified" is usually 80 or 90 percent. Assuming the former, the formula would be:

$$\frac{\text{AMOUNT OF INSURANCE}}{80\% \text{ OF ACV}} \times \text{AMOUNT OF LOSS} = \text{AMOUNT PAYABLE}$$

Of course the amount payable never exceeds the face of the policy, placing an upper boundary on the formula. If the face of the policy is $50,000, the ACV is $100,000, and the loss is $8,000:

$$\frac{\$50,000}{\$80,000} \text{ or } \frac{5}{8} \times \$8,000 = \$5,000$$

3. Why would fire insurers wish to force policyholders to participate in the risk — to coinsure — only when property is insured at less

than 80 percent (or 90 or 100 percent) of replacement cost? Is this merely a heavyhanded attempt to force the payment of more premium?

4. Some legislatures have prohibited the use of coinsurance clauses on policies covering residential property, while permitting it for commercial property. Is there merit in such a statute? Others have permitted coinsurance clauses only if there is a premium reduction from the rate without the clause. See Missouri Annotated Statutes §379.160(3) (Vernon Supp. 1981). Still others have required that a policy with a coinsurance clause must have stamped on the front such words as "Coinsurance Contract," in a fashion and with a size of type approved by the Insurance Commissioner. Surrant v. Grain Dealers Mut. Ins. Co., 74 N.C. App. 288, 328 S.E.2d 16 (1985), illustrates the latter form of statute. It also provides a good overview of the whole problem of coinsurance in fire insurance.

5. If there are legitimate objections to the use of coinsurance clauses, are there other ways of dealing with the problem the clauses attack than those mentioned so far? Does the way premiums are calculated suggest any alternatives? Are they practicable?

6. In what other lines of insurance might one expect the insurers to require (or otherwise encourage) coinsurance? Would the insurer's motivation be the same?

7. The 1947 Texas City explosion, which you may have met in connection with the Federal Tort Claims Act (see Dalehite v. United States, 346 U.S. 15 (1953)), resulted in other important litigation, including a famous case interpreting the interrelationship of a coinsurance clause and a bailee's "in trust or on commission" coverage. In this case, the policy covering the contents of the plaintiff's warehouse contained a 90 percent coinsurance clause. The coverage clause covered "the interest of the assured in and/or liability for similar property belonging in whole or in part to others, and held by the assured either sold but not removed on storage or for repairs, or otherwise held." Property owned by the plaintiff and covered by the policy had an ACV of about $4.5 million; property of others in storage was worth $19.6 million. The policy was written for $2.3 million. What percentage should the plaintiff recover? See Texas City Terminal Ry. Co. v. American Equitable Assurance Co. of New York, 130 F. Supp. 843 (S.D. Tex. 1955).

8. In periods with a high inflation rate, the fixed face amount of the insurance policy rapidly decreases as a percentage of value of the property as the latter increases. How can an insured be protected against the adverse effect of underinsurance resulting from the terms of a coinsurance clause?

9. Carley Capital Group v. Fireman's Fund Ins. Co., 877 F.2d 78 (D.C. Cir. 1989), applying Pennsylvania law, showed that problems in interpreting the clause still occur. There was a total loss by fire of a

building in course of construction. The policy covered replacement cost. The coinsurance clause provided for payment of no greater proportion of the loss than the face amount bore to the "projected value" at the date of completion. The face amount was $20 million, the estimated replacement cost upon completion was $22 million, and the replacement cost at the time of loss was $13 million. Should the insured recover $13 million or 10/11 of $13 million?

CHAPTER 4

Fidelity Insurance

The forms of insurance used to protect policyholders against the financial consequences of the dishonest acts of others are as varied as the ways in which dishonesty may appear in a complex society. Such insurance may sometimes protect also against conduct that is not actually dishonest or at least not technically criminal. Insurance against dishonesty shades into insurance of creditworthiness and thence into financial guaranty insurance of various kinds.

Much insurance against dishonesty is a part of multiple risk insurance covering specified property. There is protection against theft in the comprehensive coverage of an automobile insurance policy, in the marine open cargo insurance policy, and in the homeowners policy, among others. Though numerous difficult problems arise in these forms of insurance against theft committed by strangers, they can be treated only incidentally in this book.

This chapter deals centrally with insurance against loss from conduct that would, at common law, have been called embezzlement. As elsewhere, however, insurance contracts have developed to fit perceived markets, not to conform to legal categories. The chapter concentrates on blanket bonds, which insure against dishonesty in transactions rather than against theft of property. They also extend outward to provide other coverages.

A. *Fidelity Bonds and Employee Dishonesty*

In a complex commercial society dishonesty by employees is a problem at least as important as theft by strangers. While some employee dishonesty would be covered under property insurance policies that include coverage against theft, more of it would not. Much employee dishonesty appears in the form of embezzlement. Simply stated, embezzlement occurs when an employee who acquires from a third person possession of property intended for the employer converts it to his or her own use. The nice distinctions of the historical criminal law cases turning on who has possession at the time criminal intent is formed and how the criminal intent is manifested in action are irrelevant to the design of practical insurance devices for protecting the owner. For a very short collection of materials illustrating the rise of embezzlement as a punishable crime, see S. Kimball, Historical Introduction to the Legal System 254-259 (1966).

In the 1980s, the advertisements of large insurance companies selling fidelity bonds made the point of how hard white collar crimes are to discover — much harder than they are to solve. The recent disclosures about the Bank of Credit and Commerce International (BCCI) make that point clearly.

Some of the advertisements noted that catching a thief depended more on chance than on skillful security work. One told the story of an executive who took well over a million dollars to cover horseracing debts: His "amateurish" embezzling was discovered only by chance when his name was found among his bookie's records after a police raid. In another case, a small town bookkeeper got away with over $2 million by keeping two sets of books before she was discovered, only because of the large size of the deficit compared to the size of the bank. Reported employee losses, of the order of $2 billion or more, are probably only a small fraction of the true total.

It is obvious that insurance cannot help with undetected embezzlement, but it can help lessen the exposure of a business to employee dishonesty. The device most often used to protect against the financial losses resulting from employee dishonesty is the *fidelity bond,* sometimes called "dishonesty insurance." It covers all criminal activity of the employee directed at the employer's property, not just embezzlement.

Three basic types of fidelity bonds have appeared. The earliest and most basic was the *individual bond,* issued to cover a named employee in favor of a named employer (the insured) up to a specified dollar amount. The employer was thus protected from dishonest activities by the bonded employee. The individual bond was a cumbersome device for both the employer and the insurer, however, when there were numbers of employees to be bonded.

The individual bond was followed and largely replaced by the *name schedule bond,* whereby several employees could be covered by name on the same bond, and those employees would be covered regardless of position simply by filing a "Change Notice" with the insurer. A burden still existed but it was a lesser one; the bond might have to be changed frequently as new employees came and old ones left. Failure to file a change notice might leave a crucial employee uncovered. To overcome this problem, the *position schedule bond* was developed; coverage in it applied to the current occupants of listed positions. Thus, *any* person who was the treasurer of the company, for instance, would be covered.

The name schedule bond differed from the position schedule bond in one important respect: While the name schedule bond covered listed employees when occupying any position in the service of the insured, it was essential under a position schedule bond to prove that the loss-causing employee occupied a bonded position at the time of causing the loss.

Individual and schedule bonds have been largely replaced by *blanket bonds,* which are issued to a business to cover *all* employees, regardless of position. Employee changes do not necessitate special notice to the insurer. The blanket bond, despite its sweeping title, is not all-risk insurance but covers only specified types of losses incurred during the policy period. It is blanket with respect to employees, not with respect to coverage.

Close attention must be given to the scope of bond coverage. For example, officers of labor unions must be bonded if they handle funds in excess of $5,000. 29 U.S.C. §502 (a). The law earlier required bonding for "faithful performance of duty," but in 1965 it was amended to require bonding only against "fraud and dishonesty" because of the cost of the broader coverage. Air traffic controllers who did not join the 1981 strike sued the bonding company for the illegal action of the leaders of Professional Air Traffic Controllers Organization (PATCO) in calling the strike. Skirlick v. Fidelity & Deposit Co., 271 App. D.C. 409, 852 F.2d 1376 (D.C. Cir. 1988), *cert. denied,* 488 U.S. 1007 (1989). The court found for the bonding company because the bond was a "fraud or dishonesty" bond, not one covering faithful discharge of duty, although there were also other grounds on which the decision could (and may in part) have turned.

The dishonest employee is not an insured under the policy. Indeed, the insurer is subrogated to the insured's claims and may recover from the employee if it is thought worthwhile to make the effort. In Home Indem. Co. v. Boe, 499 So. 2d 1301 (La. App. 1986), the dishonest employee put ghosts on the payroll. The insurer was held entitled to recover from the employee the amount of the loss paid to the insured.

B. Blanket Crime Policies

One blanket crime policy is the Three-D policy (for dishonesty, disappearance, and destruction). It covers much more than employee dishonesty, though that is still a primary focus. In breadth of coverage it approaches the coverage of the Bankers Blanket Bond (now the Financial Institution Bond), which will be examined in detail later.

NORTHWEST AIRLINES, INC. v. GLOBE INDEM. CO.

303 Minn. 16, 225 N.W.2d 831 (1975)

YETKA, Justice.

Plaintiff brought an action in the District Court of Hennepin County, seeking recovery under an insurance policy issued it by defendant for losses sustained as the result of criminal acts of an unknown person perpetrated in the states of Washington and Oregon during an airline flight. From the judgment of the district court determining that plaintiff was entitled to recovery, defendant appeals. We affirm.

On September 29, 1965, defendant (insurer) and plaintiff (insured) executed an insurance agreement entitled "Blanket Crime Policy" and providing indemnity for covered losses not to exceed $250,000, with a $20,000 deductible clause. This policy was in effect at the time of the alleged loss.

On November 24, 1971, plaintiff, in the normal course of its air carrier business, was operating Flight 305, originating at Minneapolis, Minnesota, terminating at Seattle, Washington, with intermediate stops, including Portland, Oregon.

A male passenger, ticketed under the name of D. B. Cooper, boarded Flight 305 at Portland, Oregon, carrying a briefcase. Cooper took a seat in the tourist section at the rear of the passenger cabin. At or near the time of takeoff, at approximately 3P.M., he proceeded to "hijack" Flight 305 by threatening to detonate what appeared to be a bomb concealed in his briefcase unless the following demands were met:

(1) $200,000 in cash, to be delivered to the plane at Seattle.
(2) Four parachutes, to be delivered with the money.
(3) No police interference.
(4) Refueling of the plane at Seattle.

The above demands were communicated to the pilot, Captain William A. Scott, who, in turn, radioed plaintiff's headquarters at Minneapolis-St. Paul, and advised the company officials of Cooper's demands. As a result of discussions with other crew members, Captain Scott decided to cooperate with the hijacker. [Money was obtained from a Seattle bank and transferred to an official of the insured within the insured's air freight terminal ("premises" within the meaning of the policy). It was then delivered to the hijacker in the airplane by an employee of the insured. The plane took off and Cooper jumped from the plane by parachute between Seattle and Portland. He was never seen again.]

The "Blanket Crime Policy" underlying this appeal provides coverage as set forth in five insuring agreements, which may be described in general terms as follows:

(1) Employee dishonesty coverage.
(2) Loss inside the premises coverage.
(3) Loss outside the premises coverage.
(4) Money orders and counterfeit paper currency coverage.
(5) Depositor's forgery coverage.

Plaintiff seeks recovery under the following insuring agreements, which state in relevant part:

Loss Inside the Premises Coverage

II. Loss of Money and Securities by the actual destruction, disappearance or *wrongful abstraction* thereof *within the Premises* or within any Banking Premises or similar recognized places of safe deposit.

Loss Outside the Premises Coverage

III. Loss of Money and Securities by the actual destruction, disappearance or *wrongful abstraction* thereof outside the Premises while being conveyed by a *Messenger* or any armored motor vehicle company, or while within the living quarters in the home of any Messenger.

Section 3 of the conditions and limitations of the policy provides the following definitions of terms relevant to the issues presented in this appeal:

"Messenger" means the Insured or a partner of the Insured or any Employee who is duly authorized by the Insured to have the care and custody of the insured property outside the Premises.

The trial court determined that there was a wrongful abstraction of money from within plaintiff's premises or from within plaintiff's bank premises, and also outside the premises while the money was being conveyed by a messenger as defined in the policy. From judgment for plaintiff in the amount of $180,000 plus interest and costs and disbursements, defendant appeals.

To recover, defendant correctly states that plaintiff must establish:

(1) That it suffered a loss of money.
(2) That the loss resulted from the actual wrongful abstraction thereof.
(3) That the wrongful abstraction is a risk covered in the policy. . . .

Defendant maintains that the insuring agreement was intended to cover only specific money that plaintiff might have on its premises at any particular time from ticket sales and other receipts, and could not include borrowed money and that, therefore, the money taken really did not belong to Northwest Airlines. However, we see little reason for a distinction between money which plaintiff has on hand itself, which it borrowed, or which it could readily borrow.

The second requisite element, wrongful abstraction, is not defined in the policy and the parties agree that said term is unambiguous. . . .

Defendant contends that wrongful abstraction cannot occur when the taking is consented to by the owner, citing in support of this contention Farmers & Merchants State Bank v. National Surety Co., 163 Minn. 257, 203 N.W. 969 (1925). We reject this argument also. To say that, in the circumstances of this case, plaintiff in any way consented to its $200,000 loss is contra to logic as well as to law.

In summary, it is fair to state that the term "wrongful abstraction" is as broad in scope as it is possible to envision. . . .

Defendant contends the third requisite element for coverage under Insuring Agreement II, wrongful abstraction within the premises, has not been fulfilled. It argues that the wrongful abstraction took place when Cooper assumed control of the airplane. Thus, it concludes that, since the $200,000 was not at the covered premises *at that moment,* there was no loss of money due to wrongful abstraction. This argument, too, must fail in the cold light of the fact that the hijacking consisted of a continuing course of related events beginning with the takeover of the airplane and culminating with the hijacker's successful escape with the money which was, *when taken,* owned by plaintiff.

[The plaintiffs were in error in considering the airplane to be "premises" within the meaning of the policy.] However, the decision of the trial court was not reached on the erroneous interpretation that the airplane was the "premises."

In continuation of the above argument, defendant concludes that since the wrongful taking did not occur until the hijacker first exercised dominion over the money (i.e., when the money was delivered to him aboard the airplane) the wrongful taking did not occur within "premises" as defined in the policy. The authority cited in support of this theory is Saks v. St. Paul Mercury Ind. Co., 308 Mich. 719, 724, 14 N.W.2d 547, 549 (1944), which held that "the crime of robbery is consummated only when the victim is deprived of dominion over his money or property."

However, the Saks case deals with robbery. Plaintiff has cited two recent extortion cases which are more closely analogous to the facts and insurance policy now at issue. The first of these cases is The University Nat. Bank of Fort Collins v. Insurance Co. of North America, No. C-3603 Civil, June 5, 1972 (unreported memorandum decision by Chief Judge Alfred A. Arraj, D. Colo.), which involved a successful extortion scheme directed against a bank president who was led to believe that his wife and daughter were in the custody of a kidnapper. Pursuant to the demands of the extortionist, the bank president took a large sum of money from the bank and delivered it to a designated "drop site" outside the bank premises from which the money was thereafter taken, presumably by the extortionist. . . .

The insurer denied coverage, alleging the loss took place at the drop site and thus did not occur within the premises. The court rejected this argument by stating:

> . . . We find this argument unpersuasive, because under the agreed facts *the thief had effectively asserted control over the funds as of the time that Farnham* [the bank president] *decided to comply with the instructions.*
> . . . Rather, it seems obvious to us that once having determined the threat was viable and compliance called for, Farnham became an unwilling agent of the thief in effectuating the actual removal. Consequently, we find that the loss occurred at the moment Farnham took possession of the money with the purpose of depriving the bank of it. [Italics supplied.] [Unreported memorandum decision, p. 3.]

It is apparent that much of the argument in the instant litigation was addressed to the meaning of the allegedly "clear" language of the policy at issue.

When that policy is read as a whole, we find it to be in the nature of a blanket or all-risk policy, as opposed to one which covers only specified risks. As defendant's counsel admitted in oral argument, mere unforeseeability of the manner in which the loss was sustained will not *per se* constitute grounds for the insurer to deny coverage. In the present case, where there is blanket coverage and the risk at issue was not excluded, the insurer must fulfill its contractual obligation to indemnify the insured.

Notes and Questions

1. In Eagle Indem. Co. v. Cherry, 182 F.2d 298 (5th Cir. 1950), the court held that a fidelity bond provided coverage when an employee diverted business from his employer and shared the profit with the person to whom it was diverted. The opinion gives no indication of what state's law was applied, if any. In the same year, the Court of Appeals of Maryland, in Levy v. American Mut. Liab. Ins. Co., 195 Md. 537, 73 A.2d 892 (1950), decided the contrary under a Three-D policy. Loss of profits did not fall within the meaning of "loss of property" in the policy.

2. The uncertainty over lost profits led to an exclusion in the Three-D policy in Diversified Group, Inc. v. Van Tassel, 806 F.2d 1275 (5th Cir. 1987), which stated, "Potential income, including but not limited to interest and dividends, not realized by the Insured because of a loss covered under this policy." Employees, knowing the bid their employer had made for a military contract, successfully underbid the employer through corporations they owned surreptitiously. The court held the employer was not protected by the policy against loss of profits. See also Lentz, Profit and the Potential Income Exclusion, 19 Forum 694 (1984).

3. The Three-D policy, while broader than the fidelity bond, is narrower than the Bankers Blanket Bond (BBB), which follows. The BBB also contains the potential income exclusion. In particular, the Three-D policy is narrower than the BBB in being limited to loss of property. King, Coverage Under Fidelity Bonds for Third-Party Claims Not Involving Loss of Property, 13 Forum 507 (1978), discusses the coverage of the Three-D policy. In Portland Federal Employees Credit Union v. Cumis Ins. Socy., 894 F.2d 1101 (9th Cir. 1990), "property" was interpreted broadly to limit the effect of the exclusion.

4. An employee leaks a trade secret to a competitor, costing the employer substantial revenue. Can the employer recover under the Three-D policy or other similar policies? United States Gypsum Co. v.

Insurance Co. of North America, 813 F.2d 856 (7th Cir. 1987), held not. Can you make a persuasive argument to the contrary?

Problem

Consider the effect of the potential income exclusion, if any, on the following fact situation. The employee engages in an embezzlement scheme in which fictitious notes are created to support withdrawals by the employee. As the notes come due, new fictitious notes are created to pay off the old ones, with a pyramiding effect. The bank's practice is to discount the notes, that is, to deduct the interest on the front end. When the scheme is discovered, how much should the insurer pay?

To make the problem concrete, suppose the initial note is for $100,000 of which the employee gets $90,000 after the note is discounted for interest. When the note comes due, another loan is made to repay the first, this time for $111,000, of which $11,000 is discounted interest and the remainder of which pays off the first note. The employee gets no additional money. The next day the scheme is discovered. Should the insurer have to pay $90,000, $100,000 or $111,000, or some other amount? See St. Paul Fire & Marine Ins. Co. v. Branch Banking and Trust Co., 643 F. Supp. 648 (E.D.N.C. 1986), aff'd, 834 F.2d 416 (4th Cir. 1987); Bank of Huntingdon v. Smothers, 626 S.W.2d 267 (Tenn. App. 1981) (a less than satisfactory opinion); Lentz, Profit and the Potential Income Exclusion, 19 Forum 694 (1984).

C. Bankers Blanket Bond (Financial Institution Bond)

1. Form of Banker's Blanket Bond (Financial Institution Bond)

The most important bond that is in substantial part a fidelity bond is the Bankers Blanket Bond (BBB). Since 1986 it has been called the Financial Institution Bond, so the terms will be used interchangeably here. Most reported cases still involve the BBB. Like the blanket crime policy, the BBB covers much more than employee defalcations; it covers six separate enumerated types of losses:

(1) loss resulting from the dishonest conduct of an employee (the traditional fidelity bond coverage)

(2)   loss resulting from robbery, burglary, disappearance, theft, etc. while the property is located within the insured premises and damage to the premises
(3)   loss resulting from robbery, larceny, disappearance, etc. while property is in the hands of a messenger in transit
(4)   loss resulting from forgery or alteration of any negotiable instrument and various other business documents
(5)   loss resulting from acting upon the basis of lost, stolen, forged, or altered securities
(6)   loss resulting from the receipt of counterfeit or altered U.S. or Canadian currency

While dishonesty is the core of this coverage, there is a good deal of coverage unrelated to dishonesty of an employee, and occasionally even coverage that need not involve dishonesty at all.

Similar blanket bonds are available for certain other businesses, but most do not have the broad coverage of the financial institution bond; on the whole they cover mainly employee dishonesty. There is no inherent reason why blanket bonds with comparably broad coverage should not be developed and used. Bonds essentially as broad are used for securities brokers, for example. See Barbagallo, Violations of Antifraud Provisions of Federal Securities Laws and the Stockbrokers Blanket Bond, Form 14, 18 Forum 417 (1983); Sullivan, The Trading Exclusion in the Broker's Blanket Bond, 15 Forum 297 (1979); Weiner & David, The Credit Union Discovery Bond and the Directors and Officers Policy: Elements of an Attorney's Conflict of Interest, 15 Forum 321 (1979).

We will focus on the Bankers Blanket Bond (Financial Institution Bond), considering each part of the agreement. See pp. 214-225, infra.

A useful compact treatment of the BBB is found in Howard, The Swan Song of a Dishonest Duck: A Prototype for Analyzing Coverage Under the Bankers Blanket Bond, 20 Loy. U. Chi. L.J. 81 (1988). See also A.B.A. Tort and Ins. Prac. Sec., Annotated Bankers Blanket Bond (1980); A.B.A. Tort and Ins. Prac. Sec., Financial Institution Bond Litigation: A Case Study for Bankers, Sureties, Insurers, and Attorneys (1988).

a.   Insuring Agreements

The first page of the bond is the declaration page. The next part (and first substantive part) of the BBB consists of the six insuring agreements, stated in considerably more detail than in the above summary description. The bond is not an all-risk policy but one of enumerated risks. For the policyholder to receive payment on a claim the loss must be one of those specifically covered. Moreover, the limits and deductibles (as well as some other terms) may differ from one coverage to another. The following materials show some of the difficulties in dealing with the BBB and others similar to it, such as the Brokers Blanket Bond.

Additional coverage may be purchased and embodied in endorsements. One frequent addition is the Servicing Contractors Endorsement, which protects against the dishonesty of persons not officers or employees of the insured but who, under contract with the insured, collect and record payments on real estate mortgage or home improvement loans, manage real property, and perform similar acts.

The specification respecting the intent of the employee contained in the second paragraph of Coverage A was at first an optional rider. See Skillern, The New Definition of Dishonesty in Financial Institution Bonds, 14 Forum 339 (1978). It was added to the 1980 version of the BBB and further elaborated in the 1986 version. Why should insurers wish to restrict the fidelity coverage in the bond to cases where employees have a narrowly defined intent? There is nothing inherently disadvantageous to insurers in broader coverage; to the contrary, the broader the coverage, the larger the premium that can appropriately be charged, leading to a larger aggregate premium volume and perhaps a larger profit. On the other hand, if coverage is very broad and the premium is correspondingly high, some insureds with no need for certain kinds of protection may be paying for it anyway, ultimately providing a cross-subsidy to those who do need the coverage. One solution to that problem is to offer narrower basic coverage, with endorsements providing extra coverage for extra premium, sold only to those who need it.

FINANCIAL INSTITUTION BOND

Standard Form No. 24, Revised to January, 1986

Bond No.

(Herein called Underwriter)

DECLARATIONS

Item 1. Name of Insured (herein called Insured):

Principal Address:

Item 2. Bond Period: from 12:01 a.m. on _____ to 12:01 a.m. on _____
(MONTH, DAY, YEAR) (MONTH, DAY, YEAR)

Item 3. The Aggregate Liability of the Underwriter during the Bond Period shall be
$ _____

Item 4. Subject to Sections 4 and 11 hereof,
the Single Loss Limit of Liability is $
and the Single Loss Deductible is $

Provided, however, that if any amounts are inserted below opposite specified Insuring Agreements or Coverage, those amounts shall be controlling. Any amount set forth below shall be part of and not in addition to amounts set forth above. (If an Insuring Agreement or Coverage is to be deleted, insert "Not Covered.")

	Single Loss Limit of Liability	Single Loss Deductible
Amount applicable to:		
Insuring Agreement (D)—FORGERY OR ALTERATION	$	$
Insuring Agreement (E)—SECURITIES	$	$
Optional Insuring Agreements and Coverages:	$	$

If "Not Covered" is inserted above opposite any specified Insuring Agreement or Coverage, such Insuring Agreement or Coverage and any other reference thereto in this bond shall be deemed to be deleted therefrom.

Item 5. The liability of the Underwriter is subject to the terms of the following riders attached hereto:

Item 6. The Insured by the acceptance of this bond gives notice to the Underwriter terminating or canceling prior bond(s) or policy(ies) No.(s)
such termination or cancelation to be effective as of the time this bond becomes effective.

TSB 5018d

213

The Underwriter, in consideration of an agreed premium, and in reliance upon all statements made and information furnished to the Underwriter by the Insured in applying for this bond, and subject to the Declarations, Insuring Agreements, General Agreements, Conditions and Limitations and other terms hereof, agrees to indemnify the Insured for:

INSURING AGREEMENTS

FIDELITY

(A) Loss resulting directly from dishonest or fraudulent acts committed by an Employee acting alone or in collusion with others.

Such dishonest or fraudulent acts must be committed by the Employee with the manifest intent:

(a) to cause the Insured to sustain such loss; and
(b) to obtain financial benefit for the Employee or another person or entity.

However, if some or all of the Insured's loss results directly or indirectly from Loans, that portion of the loss is not covered unless the Employee was in collusion with one or more parties to the transactions and has received, in connection therewith, a financial benefit with a value of at least $2,500.

As used throughout this Insuring Agreement, financial benefit does not include any employee benefits earned in the normal course of employment, including: salaries, commissions, fees, bonuses, promotions, awards, profit sharing or pensions.

ON PREMISES

(B) (1) Loss of Property resulting directly from
  (a) robbery, burglary, misplacement, mysterious unexplainable disappearance and damage thereto or destruction thereof, or
  (b) theft, false pretenses, common-law or statutory larceny, committed by a person present in an office or on the premises of the Insured.
  while the Property is lodged or deposited within offices or premises located anywhere.
(2) Loss of or damage to
  (a) furnishings, fixtures, supplies or equipment within an office of the Insured covered under this bond resulting directly from larceny or theft in, or by burglary or robbery of, such office, or attempt thereat, or by vandalism or malicious mischief, or

Coverage under this Insuring Agreement begins immediately upon the receipt of such Property by the natural person or Transportation Company and ends immediately upon delivery to the designated recipient or its agent.

FORGERY OR ALTERATION

(D) Loss resulting directly from
(1) Forgery or alteration of, on or in any Negotiable Instrument (except an Evidence of Debt), Acceptance, Withdrawal Order, receipt for the withdrawal of Property, Certificate of Deposit or Letter of Credit,
(2) transferring, paying or delivering any funds or Property or establishing any credit or giving any value on the faith of any written instructions or advices directed to the Insured and authorizing or acknowledging the transfer, payment, delivery or receipt of funds or Property, which instructions or advices purport to have been signed or endorsed by any customer of the Insured or by any banking institution but which instructions or advices either bear a signature which is a Forgery or have been altered without the knowledge and consent of such customer or banking institution. Telegraphic, cable or teletype instructions or advices, as aforesaid, exclusive of transmissions of electronic funds transfer systems, sent by a person other than the said customer or banking institution purporting to send such instructions or advices shall be deemed to bear a signature which is a Forgery.

A mechanically reproduced facsimile signature is treated the same as a handwritten signature.

SECURITIES

(E) Loss resulting directly from the Insured having, in good faith, for its own account or for the account of others,
(1) acquired, sold or delivered, or given value, extended credit or assumed liability, on the faith of, any original
  (a) Certificated Security,
  (b) Document of Title,
  (c) deed, mortgage or other instrument conveying title to, or creating or discharging a lien upon, real property,

214

(b) such office resulting from larceny or theft in, or by burglary or robbery of such office or attempt thereat, or to the interior of such office by vandalism or malicious mischief,

provided that

(i) the Insured is the owner of such furnishings, fixtures, supplies, equipment, or office or is liable for such loss or damage, and

(ii) the loss is not caused by fire.

IN TRANSIT

(C) Loss of Property resulting directly from robbery, common-law or statutory larceny, theft, misplacement, mysterious unexplainable disappearance, being lost or made away with, and damage thereto or destruction thereof, while the Property is in transit anywhere in the custody of

(a) a natural person acting as a messenger of the Insured (or another natural person acting as messenger or custodian during an emergency arising from the incapacity of the original messenger), or

(b) a Transportation Company and being transported in an armored motor vehicle, or

(c) a Transportation Company and being transported in a conveyance other than an armored motor vehicle provided that covered Property transported in such manner is limited to the following:

(i) records, whether recorded in writing or electronically, and

(ii) Certificated Securities issued in registered form and not endorsed, or with restrictive endorsements, and

(iii) Negotiable Instruments not payable to bearer, or not endorsed, or with restrictive endorsements.

(d) Certificate of Origin or Title,

(e) Evidence of Debt,

(f) corporate, partnership or personal Guarantee,

(g) Security Agreement,

(h) Instruction to a Federal Reserve Bank of the United States, or

(i) Statement of Uncertificated Security of any Federal Reserve Bank of the United States

which

(i) bears a signature of any maker, drawer, issuer, endorser, assignor, lessee, transfer agent, registrar, acceptor, surety, guarantor, or of any person signing in any other capacity which is a Forgery, or

(ii) is altered, or

(iii) is lost or stolen;

(2) guaranteed in writing or witnessed any signature upon any transfer, assignment, bill of sale, power of attorney, Guarantee, endorsement or any items listed in (a) through (h) above;

(3) acquired, sold or delivered, or given value, extended credit or assumed liability, on the faith of any item listed in (a) through (d) above which is a Counterfeit.

Actual physical possession of the items listed in (a) through (i) above by the Insured, its correspondent bank or other authorized representative, is a condition precedent to the Insured's having relied on the faith of such items.

A mechanically reproduced facsimile signature is treated the same as a handwritten signature.

COUNTERFEIT CURRENCY

(F) Loss resulting directly from the receipt by the Insured, in good faith, of any Counterfeit Money of the United States of America, Canada or of any other country in which the Insured maintains a branch office.

GENERAL AGREEMENTS

NOMINEES

A. Loss sustained by any nominee organized by the Insured for the purpose of handling certain of its business transactions and composed exclusively of its Employees shall, for all the purposes of this bond and whether or not any partner of such nominee is implicated in such loss, be deemed to be loss sustained by the Insured.

ADDITIONAL OFFICES OR EMPLOYEES—CONSOLIDATION, MERGER OR PURCHASE OF ASSETS—NOTICE

B. If the Insured shall, while this bond is in force, establish any additional offices, other than by consolidation or merger with, or purchase or acquisition of assets or liabilities of, another institution, such offices shall be automatically covered hereunder from the date of such

the first named Insured of loss sustained by any Insured shall fully release the Underwriter on account of such loss. If the first named Insured ceases to be covered under this bond, the Insured next named shall thereafter be considered as the first named Insured. Knowledge possessed or discovery made by any Insured shall constitute knowledge or discovery by all Insureds for all purposes of this bond. The liability of the Underwriter for loss or losses sustained by all Insureds shall not exceed the amount for which the Underwriter would have been liable had all such loss or losses been sustained by one Insured.

NOTICE OF LEGAL PROCEEDINGS AGAINST INSURED—ELECTION TO DEFEND

F. The Insured shall notify the Underwriter at the earliest practicable moment, not to exceed 30 days after notice thereof, of any legal proceeding brought to determine the Insured's liability for any loss, claim or damage, which, if established, would constitute a collectible loss under this bond. Concurrently, the Insured shall furnish copies of all pleadings and pertinent papers to the Underwriter.

The Underwriter, at its sole option, may elect to conduct the defense of such legal proceeding, in whole or in part. The defense by the Underwriter shall be in the Insured's name through attorneys selected by the Underwriter. The Insured shall provide all reasonable information and assistance required by the Underwriter for such defense.

If the Underwriter elects to defend the Insured, in whole or in part, any judgment against the Insured on those counts or causes of action which the Underwriter defended on behalf of the Insured or any settlement in which the Underwriter participates and all attorneys' fees, costs and expenses incurred by the Underwriter in the defense of the litigation shall be a loss covered by this bond.

If the Insured does not give the notices required in subsection (a) of Section 5 of this bond and in the first paragraph of this General Agreement, or if the Underwriter elects not to defend any causes of action, neither a judgment against the Insured, nor a settlement of any legal proceeding by the Insured, shall determine the existence, extent or amount of coverage under this bond for loss sustained by the Insured, and the Underwriter shall not be liable for any attorneys' fees, costs and expenses incurred by the Insured.

With respect to this General Agreement, subsections (b) and (d) of Section 5 of this bond apply upon the entry of such judgment or the

establishment without the requirement of notice to the Underwriter or the payment of additional premium for the remainder of the premium period.

If the Insured shall, while this bond is in force, consolidate or merge with, or purchase or acquire assets or liabilities of, another institution, the Insured shall not have such coverage as is afforded under this bond for loss which

(a) has occurred or will occur in offices or premises, or
(b) has been caused or will be caused by an employee or employees of such institution, or
(c) has arisen or will arise out of the assets or liabilities

acquired by the Insured as a result of such consolidation, merger or purchase or acquisition of assets or liabilities unless the Insured shall

(i) give the Underwriter written notice of the proposed consolidation, merger or purchase or acquisition of assets or liabilities prior to the proposed effective date of such action and

(ii) obtain the written consent of the Underwriter to extend the coverage provided by this bond to such additional offices or premises, Employees and other exposures, and

(iii) upon obtaining such consent, pay to the Underwriter an additional premium.

CHANGE OF CONTROL—NOTICE

C. When the Insured learns of a change in control, it shall give written notice to the Underwriter.

As used in this General Agreement, control means the power to determine the management or policy of a controlling holding company or the Insured by virtue of voting stock ownership. A change in ownership of voting stock which results in direct or indirect ownership by a stockholder or an affiliated group of stockholders of ten percent (10%) or more of such stock shall be presumed to result in a change of control for the purpose of the required notice.

Failure to give the required notice shall result in termination of coverage for any loss involving a transferee, to be effective upon the date of the stock transfer.

REPRESENTATION OF INSURED

D. The Insured represents that the information furnished in the application for this bond is complete, true and correct. Such application constitutes part of this bond.

Any misrepresentation, omission, concealment or any incorrect statement of a material fact, in the application or otherwise, shall be grounds for the rescission of this bond.

JOINT INSURED

E. If two or more Insureds are covered under this bond, the first named Insured shall act for all Insureds. Payment by the Underwriter to

occurrence of such settlement instead of upon discovery of loss. In addition, the Insured must notify the Underwriter within 30 days after such judgment is entered against it or after the Insured settles such legal proceeding, and, subject to subsection (e) of Section 5, the Insured may not bring legal proceedings for the recovery of such loss after the expiration of 24 months from the date of such final judgment or settlement.

CONDITIONS AND LIMITATIONS

(g) Employee means
(1) an officer or other employee of the Insured, while employed in, at, or by any of the Insured's offices or premises covered hereunder, and a guest student pursuing studies or duties in any of said offices or premises;
(2) an attorney retained by the Insured and an employee of such attorney while either is performing legal services for the Insured;
(3) a person provided by an employment contractor to perform employee duties for the Insured under the Insured's supervision at any of the Insured's offices or premises covered hereunder;
(4) an employee of an institution merged or consolidated with the Insured prior to the effective date of this bond; and
(5) each natural person, partnership or corporation authorized by the Insured to perform services as data processor of checks or other accounting records of the Insured (not including preparation or modification of computer software or programs), herein called Processor. (Each such Processor, and the partners, officers and employees of such Processor shall, collectively, be deemed to be one Employee for all the purposes of this bond, excepting, however, the second paragraph of Section 12. A Federal Reserve Bank or clearing house shall not be construed to be a processor.)

(h) Evidence of Debt means an instrument, including a Negotiable Instrument, executed by a customer of the Insured and held by the Insured which in the regular course of business is treated as evidencing the customer's debt to the Insured.

(i) Forgery means the signing of the name of another person or organization with intent to deceive; it does not mean a signature which consists in whole or in part of one's own name signed with or without authority, in any capacity, for any purpose.

DEFINITIONS

Section 1. As used in this bond:
(a) Acceptance means a draft which the drawee has, by signature written thereon, engaged to honor as presented.
(b) Certificate of Deposit means an acknowledgment in writing by a financial institution of receipt of Money with an engagement to repay it.
(c) Certificate of Origin or Title means a document issued by a manufacturer of personal property or a governmental agency evidencing the ownership of the personal property and by which ownership is transferred.
(d) Certificated Security means a share, participation or other interest in property of or an enterprise of the issuer or an obligation of the issuer, which is:
(1) represented by an instrument issued in bearer or registered form;
(2) of a type commonly dealt in on securities exchanges or markets or commonly recognized in any area in which it is issued or dealt in as a medium for investment; and
(3) either one of a class or series or by its terms divisible into a class or series of shares, participations, interests or obligations.
(e) Counterfeit means an imitation which is intended to deceive and to be taken as an original.
(f) Document of Title means a bill of lading, dock warrant, dock receipt, warehouse receipt or order for the delivery of goods, and also any other document which in the regular course of business or financing is treated as adequately evidencing that the person in possession of it is entitled to receive, hold and dispose of the document and the goods it covers and must purport to be issued by or addressed to a bailee and purport to cover goods in the bailee's possession which are either identified or are fungible portions of an identified mass.

(i) Guarantee means a written undertaking obligating the signer to pay the debt of another to the Insured or its assignee or to a financial institution from which the Insured has purchased participation in the debt, if the debt is not paid in accordance with its terms.

(k) Instruction means a written order to the issuer of an Uncertificated Security requesting that the transfer, pledge, or release from pledge of the Uncertificated Security specified be registered.

(l) Letter of Credit means an engagement in writing by a bank or other person made at the request of a customer that the bank or other person will honor drafts or other demands for payment upon compliance with the conditions specified in the Letter of Credit.

(m) Loan means all extensions of credit by the Insured and all transactions creating a creditor relationship in favor of the Insured and all transactions by which the Insured assumes an existing creditor relationship.

(n) Money means a medium of exchange in current use authorized or adopted by a domestic or foreign government as a part of its currency.

(o) Negotiable Instrument means any writing
(1) signed by the maker or drawer; and
(2) containing any unconditional promise or order to pay a sum certain in Money and no other promise, order, obligation or power given by the maker or drawer; and
(3) is payable on demand or at a definite time; and
(4) is payable to order or bearer.

(p) Property means Money, Certificated Securities, Uncertificated Securities of any Federal Reserve Bank of the United States, Negotiable Instruments, Certificates of Deposit, Documents of Title, Acceptances, Evidences of Debt, Security Agreements, Withdrawal Orders, Certificates of Origin or Title, Letters of Credit, insurance policies, abstracts of title, deeds and mortgages on real estate, revenue and other stamps, tokens, unsold state lottery tickets, books of account and other records whether recorded in writing or electronically, gems, jewelry, precious metals in bars or ingots, and tangible items of personal property which are not hereinbefore enumerated.

(q) Security Agreement means an agreement which creates an interest in personal property or fixtures and which secures payment or performance of an obligation.

(r) Statement of Uncertificated Security means a written statement of the issuer of an Uncertificated Security containing:
(1) A description of the Issue of which the Uncertificated Security is a part;

(b) loss due to riot or civil commotion outside the United States of America and Canada; or loss due to military, naval or usurped power, war or insurrection unless such loss occurs in transit in the circumstances recited in Insuring Agreement (C), and unless, when such transit was initiated, there was no knowledge of such riot, civil commotion, military, naval or usurped power, war or insurrection on the part of any person acting for the Insured in initiating such transit;

(c) loss resulting directly or indirectly from the effects of nuclear fission or fusion or radioactivity; provided, however, that this paragraph shall not apply to loss resulting from industrial uses of nuclear energy;

(d) loss resulting directly or indirectly from any acts of any director of the Insured other than one employed as a salaried, pensioned or elected official or an Employee of the Insured, except when performing acts coming within the scope of the usual duties of an Employee, or while acting as a member of any committee duly elected or appointed by resolution of the board of directors of the Insured to perform specific, as distinguished from general, directorial acts on behalf of the Insured;

(e) loss resulting directly or indirectly from the complete or partial nonpayment of, or default upon, any Loan or transaction involving the Insured as a lender or borrower, or extension of credit, including the purchase, discounting or other acquisition of false or genuine accounts, invoices, notes, agreements or Evidences of Debt, whether such Loan, transaction or extension was procured in good faith or through trick, artifice, fraud or false pretenses, except when covered under Insuring Agreements (A), (D) or (E);

(f) loss of Property contained in customers' safe deposit boxes, except when the Insured is legally liable therefor and the loss is covered under Insuring Agreement (A);

(g) loss through cashing or paying forged or altered travelers' checks or travelers' checks bearing forged endorsements, except when covered under Insuring Agreement (A); or loss of unsold travelers' checks or unsold money orders placed in the custody of the Insured with authority to sell, unless (a) the Insured is legally liable for such loss and (b) such checks or money orders are later paid or honored by the drawer thereof, except when covered under Insuring Agreement (A);

(h) loss caused by an Employee, except when covered under Insuring Agreement (A) or when covered under Insuring Agreement (B) or (C) and resulting directly from misplacement, mysterious unexplainable disappearance or destruction of or damage to Property;

(i) loss resulting directly or indirectly from trading, with or without the knowledge of the Insured, whether or not represented by any indebtedness or balance shown to be due the Insured on any customer's account, actual or fictitious, and notwithstanding any act or omission on the part of any Employee in connection with any account relating to such trading, indebtedness, or balance, except when covered under Insuring Agreements (D) or (E);

(j) shortage in any teller's cash due to error, regardless of the amount of such shortage, and any shortage in any teller's cash which is not in excess of the normal shortage in the tellers' cash in the office where such shortage shall occur shall be presumed to be due to error;

(k) loss resulting directly or indirectly from the use or purported use of credit, debit, charge, access, convenience, identification or other cards

(1) in obtaining credit or funds, or
(2) in gaining access to automated mechanical devices which, on behalf of the Insured, disburse Money, accept deposits, cash checks, drafts or similar written instruments or make credit card loans, or
(3) in gaining access to point of sale terminals, customer-bank communication terminals, or similar electronic terminals of electronic funds transfer systems,

whether such cards were issued, or purport to have been issued, by the Insured or by anyone other than the Insured, except when covered under Insuring Agreement (A);

(l) loss involving automated mechanical devices which, on behalf of the Insured, disburse Money, accept deposits, cash checks, drafts or similar written instruments or make credit card loans, unless such automated mechanical devices are situated within an office of the Insured which is permanently staffed by an Employee whose duties are those usually assigned to a bank teller, even though public access is from outside the confines of such office, but in no event shall the Underwriter be liable for loss (including loss of Property)

(1) as a result of damage to such automated mechanical devices from vandalism or malicious mischief perpetrated from outside such office, or
(2) as a result of failure of such automated mechanical devices to function properly, or
(3) through misplacement or mysterious unexplainable disappearance while such Property is located within any such automated mechanical devices,

except when covered under Insuring Agreement (A).

(m) loss through the surrender of Property away from an office of the Insured as a result of a threat

(2) the number of shares or units:
(a) transferred to the registered owner;
(b) pledged by the registered owner to the registered pledgee;
(c) released from pledge by the registered pledgee;
(d) registered in the name of the registered owner on the date of the statement; or
(e) subject to pledge on the date of the statement;
(3) the name and address of the registered owner and registered pledgee;
(4) a notation of any liens and restrictions of the issuer and any adverse claims to which the Uncertificated Security is or may be subject or a statement that there are none of those liens, restrictions or adverse claims; and
(5) the date:
(a) the transfer of the shares or units to the new registered owner of the shares or units was registered;
(b) the pledge of the registered pledgee was registered, or
(c) of the statement, if it is a periodic or annual statement.

(s) Transportation Company means any organization which provides its own or leased vehicles for transportation or which provides freight forwarding or air express services.

(t) Uncertificated Security means a share, participation or other interest in property of or an enterprise of the issuer or an obligation of the issuer, which is:
(1) not represented by an instrument and the transfer of which is registered upon books maintained for that purpose by or on behalf of the issuer;
(2) of a type commonly dealt in on securities exchanges or markets; and
(3) either one of a class or series or by its terms divisible into a class or series of shares, participations, interests or obligations.

(u) Withdrawal Order means a non-negotiable instrument, other than an Instruction, signed by a customer of the Insured authorizing the Insured to debit the customer's account in the amount of funds stated therein.

EXCLUSIONS

Section 2. This bond does not cover:
(a) loss resulting directly or indirectly from forgery or alteration, except when covered under Insuring Agreements (A), (D), (E) or (F);

219

(1) to do bodily harm to any person, except loss of Property in transit in the custody of any person acting as messenger provided that when such transit was initiated there was no knowledge by the Insured of any such threat, or

(2) to do damage to the premises or property of the Insured, except when covered under Insuring Agreement (A).

(n) loss resulting directly or indirectly from payments made or withdrawals from a depositor's account involving erroneous credits to such account, unless such payments or withdrawals are physically received by such depositor or representative of such depositor who is within the office of the Insured at the time of such payment or withdrawal, or except when covered under Insuring Agreement (A);

(o) loss resulting directly or indirectly from payments made or withdrawals from a depositor's account involving items of deposit which are not finally paid for any reason, including but not limited to Forgery or any other fraud, except when covered under Insuring Agreement (A);

(p) loss resulting directly or indirectly from counterfeiting, except when covered under Insuring Agreements (A), (E) or (F);

(q) loss of any tangible item of personal property which is not specifically enumerated in the paragraph defining Property and for which the Insured is legally liable, if such property is specifically insured by other insurance of any kind and in any amount obtained by the Insured, and in any event, loss of such property occurring more than 60 days after the Insured shall have become aware that it is liable for the safekeeping of such property, except when covered under Insuring Agreements (A) or (B)(2);

(r) loss of Property while
   (1) in the mail, or
   (2) in the custody of any Transportation Company, unless covered under Insuring Agreement (C) except when covered under Insuring Agreement (A);

(s) potential income, including but not limited to interest and dividends, not realized by the Insured;

(t) damages of any type for which the Insured is legally liable, except compensatory damages, but not multiples thereof, arising directly from a loss covered under this bond;

(u) all fees, costs and expenses incurred by the Insured
   (1) in establishing the existence of or amount of loss covered under this bond, or
   (2) as a party to any legal proceeding whether or not such legal proceeding exposes the Insured to loss covered by this bond;

(v) indirect or consequential loss of any nature;

LIMIT OF LIABILITY

Section 4.   Aggregate Limit of Liability

The Underwriter's total liability for all losses discovered during the Bond Period shown in Item 2 of the Declarations shall not exceed the Aggregate Limit of Liability shown in Item 3 of the Declarations. The Aggregate Limit of Liability shall be reduced by the amount of any payment made under the terms of this bond.

Upon exhaustion of the Aggregate Limit of Liability by such payments

(a) The Underwriter shall have no further liability for loss or losses regardless of when discovered and whether or not previously reported to the Underwriter, and

(b) The Underwriter shall have no obligation under General Agreement F to continue the defense of the Insured, and upon notice by the Underwriter to the Insured that the Aggregate Limit of Liability has been exhausted, the Insured shall assume all responsibility for its defense at its own cost.

The Aggregate Limit of Liability shall not be increased or reinstated by any recovery made and applied in accordance with subsections (a), (b) and (c) of Section 7. In the event that a loss of Property is settled by the Underwriter through the use of a lost instrument bond, such loss shall not reduce the Aggregate Limit of Liability.

Single Loss Limit of Liability

Subject to the Aggregate Limit of Liability, the Underwriter's liability for each Single Loss shall not exceed the applicable Single Loss Limit of Liability shown in Item 4 of the Declarations. If a Single Loss is covered under more than one Insuring Agreement or Coverage, the maximum payable shall not exceed the largest applicable Single Loss Limit of Liability.

Single Loss Defined

Single Loss means all covered loss, including court costs and attorneys' fees incurred by the Underwriter under General Agreement F, resulting from

(a) any one act or series of related acts of burglary, robbery or attempt thereat, in which no Employee is implicated, or

(b) any one act or series of related unintentional or negligent acts or omissions on the part of any person (whether an Employee or not) resulting in damage to or destruction or misplacement of Property, or

(w) loss resulting from any violation by the Insured or by any Employee

(1) of law regulating (i) the issuance, purchase or sale of securities, (ii) securities transactions upon security exchanges or over the counter market, (iii) investment companies, or (iv) investment advisers, or

(2) of any rule or regulation made pursuant to any such law, unless it is established by the Insured that the act or acts which caused the said loss involved fraudulent or dishonest conduct which would have caused a loss to the Insured in a similar amount in the absence of such laws, rules or regulations;

(x) loss resulting directly or indirectly from the failure of a financial or depository institution, or its receiver or liquidator, to pay or deliver, on demand of the Insured, funds or Property of the Insured held by it in any capacity, except when covered under Insuring Agreements (A) or (B)(1)(a);

(y) loss involving any Uncertificated Security except an Uncertificated Security of any Federal Reserve Bank of the United States or when covered under Insuring Agreement (A);

(z) damages resulting from any civil, criminal or other legal proceeding in which the Insured is alleged to have engaged in racketeering activity except when the Insured establishes that the act or acts giving rise to such damages were committed by an Employee under circumstances which result directly in a loss to the Insured covered by Insuring Agreement (A). For the purposes of this exclusion, "racketeering activity" is defined in 18 United States Code 1961 et seq., as amended.

DISCOVERY

Section 3. This bond applies to loss discovered by the Insured during the Bond Period. Discovery occurs when the Insured first becomes aware of facts which would cause a reasonable person to assume that a loss of a type covered by this bond has been or will be incurred, regardless of when the act or acts causing or contributing to such loss occurred, even though the exact amount or details of loss may not then be known.

Discovery also occurs when the Insured receives notice of an actual or potential claim in which it is alleged that the Insured is liable to a third party under circumstances which, if true, would constitute a loss under this bond.

(c) all acts or omissions other than those specified in (a) and (b) preceding, caused by any person (whether an Employee or not) or in which such person is implicated, or

(d) any one casualty or event not specified in (a), (b) or (c) preceding.

NOTICE / PROOF – LEGAL PROCEEDINGS AGAINST UNDERWRITER

Section 5.

(a) At the earliest practicable moment, not to exceed 30 days, after discovery of loss, the Insured shall give the Underwriter notice thereof.

(b) Within 6 months after such discovery, the Insured shall furnish to the Underwriter proof of loss, duly sworn to, with full particulars.

(c) Lost Certificated Securities listed in a proof of loss shall be identified by certificate or bond numbers if such securities were issued therewith.

(d) Legal proceedings for the recovery of any loss hereunder shall not be brought prior to the expiration of 60 days after the original proof of loss is filed with the Underwriter or after the expiration of 24 months from the discovery of such loss.

(e) If any limitation embodied in this bond is prohibited by any law controlling the construction hereof, such limitation shall be deemed to be amended so as to equal the minimum period of limitation provided by such law.

(f) This bond affords coverage only in favor of the Insured. No suit, action or legal proceedings shall be brought hereunder by any one other than the named Insured.

VALUATION

Section 6. Any loss of Money, or loss payable in Money, shall be paid, at the option of the Insured, in the Money of the country in which the loss was sustained or in the United States of America dollar equivalent thereof determined at the rate of exchange at the time of payment of such loss.

Securities

The Underwriter shall settle in kind its liability under this bond on account of a loss of any securities or, at the option of the Insured, shall pay to the Insured the cost of replacing such securities, determined by the market value thereof at the time of such settlement. In case of a loss of subscription, conversion or redemption privileges through the misplacement or loss of securities, the amount of such loss shall be the value of such privileges immediately preceding the expiration thereof. If such securities cannot be replaced or have no quoted market value, or if such privileges have no quoted market value, their value shall be determined by agreement or arbitration.

If the applicable coverage of this bond is subject to a Deductible Amount and/or is not sufficient in amount to indemnify the Insured in full for the loss of securities for which claim is made hereunder, the liability of the Underwriter under this bond is limited to the payment for, or the duplication of, so much of such securities as has a value equal to the amount of such applicable coverage.

Books of Account and Other Records

In case of loss of, or damage to, any books of account or other records used by the Insured in its business, the Underwriter shall be liable under this bond only if such books or records are actually reproduced and then for not more than the cost of the blank books, blank pages or other materials plus the cost of labor for the actual transcription or copying of data which shall have been furnished by the Insured in order to reproduce such books and other records.

Property other than Money, Securities or Records

In case of loss of, or damage to, any Property other than Money, securities, books of account or other records, or damage covered under Insuring Agreement (B)(2), the Underwriter shall not be liable for more than the actual cash value of such Property, or of items covered under Insuring Agreement (B)(2). The Underwriter may, at its election, pay the actual cash value of, replace or repair such property. Disagreement between the Underwriter and the Insured as to the cash value or as to the adequacy of repair or replacement shall be resolved by arbitration.

ASSIGNMENT – SUBROGATION – RECOVERY – COOPERATION

Section 7.

(a) In the event of payment under this bond, the Insured shall deliver, if so requested by the Underwriter, an assignment of such of the Insured's rights, title and interest and causes of action as it has against any person or entity to the extent of the loss payment.

(b) In the event of payment under this bond, the Underwriter shall be subrogated to all of the Insured's rights of recovery therefor against any person or entity to the extent of such payment.

(c) Recoveries, whether effected by the Underwriter or by the Insured, shall be applied net of the expense of such recovery first to the satisfaction of the Insured's loss which would otherwise have been paid but for the fact that it is in excess of either the Single or Aggregate Limit

total liability of the Underwriter under this bond and under such other bonds or policies shall not exceed, in the aggregate, the amount carried hereunder on such loss or the amount available to the Insured under such other bonds or policies, as limited by the terms and conditions thereof, for any such loss if the latter amount be the larger.

If the coverage of this bond supersedes in whole or in part the coverage of any other bond or policy of insurance issued by an Insurer other than the Underwriter and terminated, canceled or allowed to expire, the Underwriter, with respect to any loss sustained prior to such termination, cancelation or expiration and discovered within the period permitted under such other bond or policy for the discovery of loss thereunder, shall be liable under this bond only for that part of such loss covered by this bond as is in excess of the amount recoverable or recovered on account of such loss under such other bond or policy, anything to the contrary in such other bond or policy notwithstanding.

OTHER INSURANCE OR INDEMNITY

Section 9. Coverage afforded hereunder shall apply only as excess over any valid and collectible insurance or indemnity obtained by the Insured, or by one other than the Insured on Property subject to exclusion (q) or by a Transportation Company, or by another entity on whose premises the loss occurred or which employed the person causing the loss or the messenger conveying the Property involved.

OWNERSHIP

Section 10. This bond shall apply to loss of Property (1) owned by the Insured, (2) held by the Insured in any capacity, or (3) for which the Insured is legally liable. This bond shall be for the sole use and benefit of the Insured named in the Declarations.

DEDUCTIBLE AMOUNT

Section 11. The Underwriter shall be liable hereunder only for the amount by which any single loss, as defined in Section 4, exceeds the Single Loss Deductible amount for the Insuring Agreement or Coverage applicable to such loss, subject to the Aggregate Limit of Liability and the applicable Single Loss Limit of Liability.

The Insured shall, in the time and in the manner prescribed in this bond, give the Underwriter notice of any loss of the kind covered by the terms of this bond, whether or not the Underwriter is liable therefor, and upon the request of the Underwriter shall file with it a brief statement giving the particulars concerning such loss.

of Liability, secondly, to the Underwriter as reimbursement of amounts paid in settlement of the Insured's claim, and thirdly, to the Insured in satisfaction of any Deductible Amount. Recovery on account of loss of securities as set forth in the second paragraph of Section 6 or recovery from reinsurance and/or indemnity of the Underwriter shall not be deemed a recovery as used herein.

(d) Upon the Underwriter's request and at reasonable times and places designated by the Underwriter the Insured shall

   (1) submit to examination by the Underwriter and subscribe to the same under oath; and

   (2) produce for the Underwriter's examination all pertinent records; and

   (3) cooperate with the Underwriter in all matters pertaining to the loss.

(e) The Insured shall execute all papers and render assistance to secure to the Underwriter the rights and causes of action provided for herein. The Insured shall do nothing after discovery of loss to prejudice such rights or causes of action.

LIMIT OF LIABILITY UNDER THIS BOND AND PRIOR INSURANCE

Section 8. With respect to any loss set forth in sub-section (c) of Section 4 of this bond which is recoverable or recovered in whole or in part under any other bonds or policies issued by the Underwriter to the Insured or to any predecessor in interest of the Insured and terminated or canceled or allowed to expire and in which the period for discovery has not expired at the time any such loss thereunder is discovered, the

TERMINATION OR CANCELATION

Section 12. This bond terminates as an entirety upon occurrence of any of the following:—(a) 60 days after the receipt by the Insured of a written notice from the Underwriter of its desire to cancel this bond, or (b) immediately upon the receipt by the Underwriter of a written notice from the Insured of its desire to cancel this bond, or (c) immediately upon the taking over of the Insured by a receiver or other liquidator or by State or Federal officals, or (d) immediately upon the taking over of the Insured by another institution, or (e) immediately upon exhaustion of the Aggregate Limit of Liability, or (f) immediately upon expiration of the Bond Period as set forth in Item 2 of the Declarations.

This bond terminates as to any Employee or any partner, officer or employee of any Processor—(a) as soon as any Insured, or any director or officer not in collusion with such person, learns of any dishonest or fraudulent act committed by such person at any time, whether in the employment of the Insured or otherwise, whether or not of the type covered under Insuring Agreement (A), against the Insured or any other person or entity, without prejudice to the loss of any Property then in transit in the custody of such person, or (b) 15 days after the receipt by the Insured of a written notice from the Underwriter of its desire to cancel this bond as to such person.

Termination of the bond as to any Insured terminates liability for any loss sustained by such Insured which is discovered after the effective date of such termination.

In witness whereof, the Underwriter has caused this bond to be executed on the Declarations page.

223

Notes and Questions

1. Mortell v. Insurance Co. of North America, 120 Ill. App. 3d 1016, 458 N.E.2d 922, 76 Ill. Dec. 268 (1983), examined the effect of the change in the definition of dishonesty. The insured was a licensed futures commodity merchant; the bond was a *Brokers* Blanket Bond. The case nicely illustrates the underwriting problems that exist in the brokerage field, for the claims were based on high pressure sales practices of the sales personnel in connection with London commodity futures.

2. The 1980 form incorporated a number of changes that had been added by endorsement in the late 1970s. For a discussion of some of those changes, including the one in the definition of dishonesty, see Clore, Suits Against Financial Institutions: Coverage and Considerations, 20 Forum 84 (1984).

3. In some lines of insurance there is real competition with respect to coverage. Contrary to the suggestion of Professor Morris in his waiver article, quoted in Chapter 2, the currency does not always tend to be debased, at least not when dealing with customers as sophisticated as banks are.

4. A life insurance company purchased a fidelity bond that provided coverage similar to Coverage A of the BBB. The company paid to its agents large commissions on life insurance, sometimes exceeding the first year premiums. Two agents independently devised similar fraudulent charitable contribution schemes to take advantage of the high commissions. They would advance money for a cashier's check in the name of an applicant whose employer matched charitable contributions. Then the cashier's check and the employee's matching gift form would be used to pay the initial premiums on policies on key executives of certain universities. The employees were told they could take a tax deduction; the policies generated commissions substantially in excess of the agent's investment. The schemes ultimately cost the insurance company large sums which they sought to recover from the fidelity insurer. With what result? See Hartford Accident & Indem. Co. v. Washington Natl. Ins. Co., 638 F. Supp. 78 (N.D. Ill. 1986). *Mortell* was one of the cases relied on by the federal judge to inform her on applicable Illinois law.

5. Should the actions of a loan officer in issuing unauthorized letters of credit or making unauthorized loans be considered a dishonest act within the meaning of the BBB? In Rock Island Bank v. Aetna Casualty & Surety Co., 706 F.2d 219 (7th Cir. 1983), the issue was whether Kearney, the president of the insured bank, acted dishonestly when he issued letters of credit in the amount of $1.05 million to Silver, a wealthy local businessman, in violation of the limit on his authority to make loans only in the amount of $50,000 or less. There

was no indication that Kearney received any personal compensation or had any interest in the business ventures benefitted, nor was there evidence that he tried to conceal the issuance of the letters. The financial standing of Silver was investigated and it was found that he had an open line of credit with another bank in the amount of $100,000, and had been loaned $3.5 million for a construction project by a third bank. Silver's personal net worth was estimated at $5 million. The district court found that Kearney's actions were dishonest because he acted contrary to a resolution of the loan committee. The appellate court reversed, finding that there was a material issue of fact as to whether Kearney acted dishonestly. Kearney explained his failure to inform the loan committee as resting on his belief that he did not have to inform the Loan Committee when no funds were to be disbursed. The court examined the conflicting case law and decided that "each case must be analyzed on its own facts and a per se rule that unauthorized loans are dishonest is unwarranted. A person may exceed his or her authority without a dishonest purpose." Id. at 223.

6. Should an insured ever be able to recover if the dishonest employee does not expect to profit financially from his wrongdoing or at least have someone else benefit? Might the personal benefit be personal satisfaction from causing one's hated employer to lose money? Why should it be necessary for the employee to benefit when the purpose of the bond is to protect the employer from loss?

UNITED BANK OF PUEBLO v. HARTFORD ACCIDENT AND INDEM. CO.

529 F.2d 490 (10th Cir. 1976)

Lewis, Chief Judge.

This case arose from Hartford's denial of coverage under a banker's blanket bond issued to the United Bank of Pueblo (Pueblo bank) for a cash letter stolen while being transported to the United Bank of Denver (Denver bank). The district court for the District of Colorado held that the loss was covered by insurance and entered judgment against Hartford for $51,963.37, later reduced by $2,500.00, the amount of the bond's deductible.

The case was submitted on stipulated facts. On August 24, 1970, the Pueblo bank prepared a cash letter of around 2,200 checks worth $891,228.32 for delivery to the Denver bank. Prior to sending the cash letter, a transit letter deposit slip, filled out in triplicate, was addressed: "To: Check Processing Center, United Bank of Denver National Association, P.O. Box 5848, Denver, Colorado 80217." The Pueblo bank retained one copy of the deposit slip, sealed the other two in the bag with the cash letter, and delivered the bag to Continental Trailways in Pueblo, for shipment to the "Denver U.S. National Bank, Denver, Colorado" as consignee.

When the sealed bag arrived at the Continental Trailways' office in Denver, employees of the bus line notified the Denver bank of its presence. The Denver bank sent Mr. Blinde, an employee in the bank's mail room, to retrieve the bag. . . .

After executing a receipt to the bus company, Blinde commenced his return to the bank via the bank's outdoor mall. Since it was approximately 11:00P.M., the only entrance open was the Lincoln Street entrance. Before reaching this entrance, Blinde was assaulted by two unknown men who stole the cash letter. While the cash letter was never recovered, the Pueblo bank was able to reduce its loss to $46,931.71, expending $5,031.66 to do so.

The issue before the trial court which is the subject of this appeal was:

> [W]ere the checks, at the time they were stolen, in the custody of a person acting as a messenger, as required by the "In Transit" clause, as Plaintiff contends, or, as contended by the Defendant, did the delivery of the checks at the bus station to Mr. Blinde, a mail room employee of the Denver U.S. National Bank, constitute a delivery of the checks "at destination", and, at that point, terminate the policy liability?

In response to this issue, the trial court made the following conclusion of law:

> 2. At the time the checks were stolen they were "in transit" within the meaning of the policy. The transit letter (Exhibit "C") stated the destination for delivery to be "Check Processing Center" of the Denver United States National Bank. The checks never reached the processing center and the delivery of the checks to a mail room employee of the Denver U.S. National Bank was a delivery to him as a messenger and cannot properly be construed as a delivery "at destination."

The main question raised by Hartford on this appeal is whether the district court properly interpreted the meaning of the "in transit" clause of the banker's blanket bond, specifically the meaning of "messenger" and "delivery at destination." The "in transit" clause provided for the following coverage:

> (C) Any loss of Property (occurring with or without negligence) through robbery, common-law or statutory larceny, theft, hold-up, misplacement, mysterious unexplainable disappearance, being lost or otherwise made away with, damage thereto or destruction thereof, and any loss of subscription, conversion, redemption or deposit privileges through the

misplacement or loss of Property, *while the Property is in transit anywhere in the custody* of any of the Employees or partners of the Insured *or of any other person or persons acting as messenger,* except while in the mail or with a carrier for hire other than an armored motor vehicle company for the purpose of transportation, such transit to begin immediately upon receipt of such Property by the transporting Employee or partner or such other person, and *to end immediately upon delivery thereof at destination.* (Emphasis added.) . . .

We must review the trial court's interpretation of two terms in the United Bank of Pueblo's banker's blanket bond — "delivery at destination" and "messenger." "Delivery" is a legal term of art, but its legal meaning in this instance has been qualified by the accompanying phrase "at destination." Under Colorado law, the words used in an insurance contract should be interpreted according to their ordinary and obvious meaning absent a showing of ambiguity. Reed v. United States Fidelity & Guar. Co., 176 Colo. 568, 491 P.2d 1377, 1379.

"Destination" is an unambiguous, ordinary word susceptible to a dictionary definition: "A place which is set for the end of a journey or to which something is sent; place or point aimed at. . . ." Webster's Third New International Dictionary (1971). While the meaning of "destination" is clear, in the present case the intended journey's end is somewhat uncertain. The district court determined that the destination of the cash letter was the check processing center of the Denver bank. . . .

[The court held that the destination was the interior of the Bank's building.]

Even though delivery had not yet occurred, the loss was not covered unless the lost property was "in the custody of any of the Employees or partners of the Insured [United Bank of Pueblo] or of any other person or persons acting as messenger. . . ." The trial court concluded that Mr. Blinde, the Denver bank mail room employee, was a messenger for the purposes of the "in transit" clause and therefore the loss was covered by the blanket bond. . . .

The apparent purpose of the "in transit" clause was to protect the bank against loss of property while being transported from the bank to a designated destination, but the coverage specifically excluded the time while the property was in the mail or in the custody of a carrier for hire. In other words, the clause was intended to cover possible gaps in the transportation of the property — intervals when the property, while still in transit, was not in the possession of a carrier or in the mail. The instant case is an example of one such possible gap — the loss occurred after the carrier relinquished possession of the property, but prior to the arrival of the cash letter at its specified destination.

However, the property must not only be lost in one of these gaps prior to delivery at destination, but it must be lost while in the "custody" of an employee or partner of the insured or "any other person or persons acting as messenger. . . ." The main problem with defining "messenger" is that it is not a legal term of art representing a special, recognized legal status such as the words "agent" or "bailee." Using a process of definition through elimination, we can determine that because the policy specifically covered employees and partners, one can be a messenger without being an employee or partner. Likewise, if the insurance company had intended that a "messenger" must be an agent or bailee of the insured, it would have employed such a term of art to describe the relationship. It is reasonable, therefore, to conclude that the insurance company employed a general term like "messenger" to describe the many possible persons who might have "custody" of the "in transit" property during one of the gaps in the transportation process. In this context, Blinde, even though an employee of the Denver bank, may also be considered a person acting as a messenger for the Pueblo bank in completing the delivery of the cash letter.

In sum, after reviewing the ordinary meaning of "destination," the context in which "destination" and "messenger" were employed, and the intended scope of the "in transit" coverage, we conclude that the district court did not err in holding that the loss of the cash letter was insured.

Judgment affirmed.

BREMEN STATE BANK v. HARTFORD ACCIDENT AND INDEM. CO.

427 F.2d 425 (7th Cir. 1970)

SWYGERT, Chief Judge.

Plaintiff, Bremen State Bank, brought this diversity action in the district court to recover $10,342.03, which sum was lost during a move by the bank from one location to another within the village of Tinley Park, Illinois. On the day before the move the bank instructed its tellers to put their money at the end of the day in canvas bags on the floor of the vault rather than in metal lockers inside the vault, the usual practice. One teller, Mrs. Laucke, did not receive these instructions and thus put her cash drawer money, $10,342.03, in her metal locker instead of on the vault floor.

Arrangements had been made for the Tinley Park police to move the bank's money and for defendant, Bekins Van & Storage Company, to move the office equipment, including the metal lockers, inside the vault. After the police, under guard, had moved the money from the vault floor to the new location, Bekins' employees entered the bank and began their job. While removing some of the metal lockers from the vault, one of Bekins' employees, Danny Francis, noticed that something was inside one of the lockers. After placing them in a van, he opened the locker used by Mrs. Laucke and discovered the money. Francis finished working that day and later absconded with the $10,342.03, none of which was ever recovered.

Plaintiff's complaint contained two counts: Count I sought recovery against Hartford Accident and Indemnity Company on a "Banker's Blanket Bond" issued by Hartford to the bank; Count II sought recovery in the alternative against Bekins on the theory of respondeat superior. The district court granted summary judgment against the bank on both counts and this appeal followed. We reverse as to Count I and affirm as to Count II.

I

The banker's blanket bond issued by Hartford contained the following relevant clauses:

On Premises

(B) Any loss of Property through robbery, burglary, common-law or statutory larceny, theft, false pretenses, hold-up, misplacement, mysterious unexplainable disappearance, damage thereto or destruction thereof, whether effected with or without violence or with or without negligence on the part of any of the Employees, and any loss of subscription, conversion, redemption or deposit privileges through the misplacement or loss of Property, while the Property is (or is supposed to be) lodged or deposited within any offices or premises located anywhere, except in an office hereinafter excluded or in the mail or with a carrier for hire, other than an armored motor vehicle company, for the purpose of transportation.

In Transit

(C) Any loss of Property (occurring with or without negligence) through robbery, common-law or statutory larceny, theft, hold-up, misplacement, mysterious unexplainable disappearance, being lost or otherwise made away with, damage thereto or destruction thereof, and any loss of subscription, conversion, redemption or deposit privileges through the misplacement or loss of Property, while the Property is in transit anywhere in the custody of any of the Employees or partners of the Insured or of any other person or persons acting as messenger except while in the mail or with a carrier for hire other than an armored motor vehicle company for the purpose of transportation, such transit to begin immediately upon receipt of such Property by the transporting Employee or partner or such other person, and to end immediately upon delivery thereof at destination.

The bank claims coverage only under Clause B, arguing that the loss was occasioned through "misplacement" of the money. Hartford contends that although the money was misplaced "in a loose sense," the loss resulted through theft after the money had left the bank premises, and was therefore not covered by the bond. The fallacy of Hartford's argument lies in its reliance on the events which occurred after the money had been misplaced. We think it is plain from the language of the bond that a loss resulting from misplacement of money, regardless of subsequent events, was contemplated as being covered. Surely the bank's loss in the instant case would not have been suffered had it not been for Mrs. Laucke's misplacement of the money. The subsequent theft by Danny Francis resulted from that misplacement and does not take the loss out of the coverage of the bond.

To hold against coverage in this case would fly in the face of the intention of the parties when the blanket bond was purchased. It is well settled under the law of Illinois, as well as most other jurisdictions, that if an insurer does not intend to insure against a risk which is likely to be inherent in the business of the insured, it should specifically exclude such risk from the coverage of the policy. Canadian Radium & Uranium Corp. v. Indemnity Insurance Co., 411 Ill. 325, 334-335, 104 N.E.2d 250 (1952). This complements the general rule that contracts of insurance should be liberally construed in favor of the insured and against the insurer. Farber v. Great American Insurance Co., 406 F.2d 1228, 1230 (7th Cir. 1969). We conclude that in the absence of specific language to the contrary, plaintiff's loss was occasioned by misplacement of the money as covered by the bond.

Hartford also argues that the exclusion contained in Clause B of the bond precludes recovery by the bank. The clause in question provides that property is not covered when it is placed "with a carrier for hire, other than an armored motor vehicle company, for the purpose of transportation." Since Bekins was a carrier, but not an armored car company, Hartford claims that the exclusion applies. We disagree.

The clause, by its own terms, does not apply to money which comes into the possession of a carrier unless it was so placed "for the purpose of transportation." There is no contention that the bank gave any money to Bekins for that purpose. Rather, the money in question was placed in Bekins' possession purely by accident and without the knowledge of anyone except Francis. Hartford's argument over the meaning of the language, "for the purpose of transportation," is directed more to Clause C than to Clause B, under which the plaintiff's claim is made. Of course, any ambiguity in the terms of the bond must be resolved in favor of the insured.

We conclude that the exclusion in Clause B applies only when property is placed with a carrier for the purpose of transportation and such carrier is not an armored car company. Accordingly, summary judgment should have been granted in favor of the plaintiff against Hartford. . . .

Notes and Questions

1. The BBB is highly structured. There are definite coverage areas, and within each, there are specific exclusions from and limitations on coverage. This structure is important when it is difficult to ascertain the facts in a case, and then to establish whether those facts bring the loss (a) within a coverage category and (b) within an exclusion to the coverage. The insured has the burden of proof to show that the loss sustained resulted from a covered act. If the insured sustains this burden the onus then falls on the insurer to show the loss to be within one of the policy exclusions.

2. Would *United Bank of Pueblo* be decided the same way under the 1986 provision of the bond? Would *Bremen State Bank?* What was the industry probably trying to achieve with the recent amendments?

3. "Mysterious, unexplainable disappearance" is covered under both Coverage B and Coverage C of the BBB. Palmer, Is There a Mystery to Mysterious, Unexplainable Disappearance Coverage?," 16 Forum 988 (1981), discusses the coverage and provides citations to cases and articles on the subject.

4. When a bond covers an employer against dishonesty of an employee, the insurer will be subrogated to the insured's rights against the employee. Ordinarily the subrogation right is not worth much. If the employee is an officer, or if the bond insures against the dishonesty of a director, the subrogation right may have value, for such persons may not be judgment-proof. The matter is explored in Wisner & Leo, Subrogation Rights of Surety on a Fidelity Bond Against Officers and Directors of Insured Corporation, 18 Forum 320 (1983), and Rizk, Bank Directors' Liability to Fidelity Insurers: How "Bad" is Bad Faith?, 19 Forum 481 (1984). If a fidelity insurer pays a bank for losses from embezzlement by an employee, the insurer will be subrogated to the bank's claim against its directors only if the latter have been guilty of more than mere negligence. This limitation on subrogation is based on the equitable character of subrogation doctrine. For a recent application of this doctrine, see Home Indem. Co. v. Shaffer, 860 F.2d 186 (6th Cir. 1988).

5. A problem of potentially overlapping insurance coverage exists in the situation discussed in note 4. If subrogation is allowed against the director who is, in the particular case, protected by Directors and

Officers Liability Insurance, the allowance of subrogation would ultimately result in a claim against the directors' D & O carrier. See
Chapter 5 for a treatment of D & O insurance.

MERCHANTS NATL. BANK v. TRANSAMERICA INS. CO.

408 N.W.2d 651 (Minn. Ct. App. 1987)

CRIPPEN, Judge.

In this declaratory judgment action, appellant The Merchants
National Bank of Winona challenges the trial court's determination
that fictitious construction contracts containing forged signatures,
which were assigned to the bank as a condition of obtaining loans, are
neither "evidence of debt" nor "security agreements" as defined by an
insurance policy issued to the bank by respondent Transamerica Insurance Company. We affirm.

Facts

Between 1975 and 1982, Merchants National made several commercial loans to the GHK Construction Company. Acting through
Larry A. Hoppe, its principal owner, GHK used the loan proceeds to
purchase construction materials. As a condition of issuing the loans,
Merchants National often required Hoppe to present it with fully
executed construction contracts and to assign to the bank all proceeds
that GHK was entitled to receive under the construction contracts.

In 1980, in connection with a $50,000 loan, Hoppe assigned to
Merchants National a fictitious construction contract bearing the
forged signature of Allyn Jarvinson. For a $70,000 loan in 1981, Hoppe
assigned to the bank a second fictitious construction contract bearing
the forged signature of Mark Oium. In each instance, the assignment
language was stamped directly onto the face of the construction contracts.

When GHK later defaulted on the loans, appellant filed a claim
with its insurer, respondent Transamerica Insurance Company, asking
for indemnification for the loss under its Bankers Blanket Bond policy.
The policy generally excluded coverage for losses resulting from loan
defaults. However, Coverage E of the policy provided coverage for
losses that resulted directly from the insured having "extended credit
. . . on the faith of, or otherwise acted upon" certain counterfeit documents and certain documents bearing a forged signature, including
documents of title, securities, deeds, mortgages, guarantees, evidences
of debt, and security agreements. The bond policy also stated these
definitions:

"Evidence of debt" means an instrument, including a Negotiable Instrument, executed by a customer of the Insured and held by the Insured which in the regular course of business is treated as evidencing the customer's debt to the Insured.

"Security Agreement" means an agreement which creates an interest in personal property or fixtures and which secures payment or performance of an obligation.

Transamerica denied coverage on the grounds that the documents listed in Coverage E and defined by the policy did not include the forged construction contracts assigned to Merchants National by GHK. The bank brought this action, asking the trial court to declare that the construction contracts constituted either evidence of debt, or security agreements, or both.

The trial court found that appellant extended credit to GHK on the faith of the forged construction contracts. The court observed that the bank "acknowledges that the contracts involved here are not primary evidences of debt such as promissory notes or checks," but that the bank "argues the definition of Evidence of Debt contained in the Policy is broad enough to include instruments which banks treat as evidences of debt in the regular course of business even though such instruments might not traditionally be viewed as evidence of debt."

Upon review of the documents listed in Coverage E, the court found they are all "items which in themselves have value or are the embodiment of the debt or obligation itself," while, in contrast, the "contracts submitted by Hoppe do not in themselves have any real value [but are] merely evidences of a contract between Hoppe and his customers." Thus, the court found the contracts neither evidenced GHK's debt to Merchants National nor constituted a "security agreement as that term is defined in the policy. . . ."

The trial court acknowledged its duty to construe any ambiguities in the insurance contract in favor of the insured, but found no ambiguity. Hypothesizing that there were ambiguities in the term "evidence of debt," the trial court nevertheless found the evidence did not support appellant's broad view of the meaning of that term. The court concluded: "It is clear from an overall reading of Coverage E that contracts of this nature are not the type of instruments intended to be covered by the policy." The trial court entered judgment for respondent Transamerica, and the bank appeals.

Issue

Did the trial court err in finding that the construction contracts did not constitute evidence of debt or security agreements as defined by the insurance policy? . . .

Appellant claims the construction contracts are evidence of debt as defined by the insurance policy. The trial court concluded that contracts such as those submitted to appellant by GHK are not, "in the regular course of business," "treated as evidencing the customer's debt to the Insured." The court's determination was partially based on opinion testimony on accepted banking practices.

. . . The trial court's conclusion is supported by the nature of the documents covered by the policy and by the testimony of record. "Evidence of debt" refers to primary indicia of debt, such as promissory notes or other instruments that reflect a customer's debt to the bank. Under this standard, the construction contracts do not constitute evidence of GHK's debt to Merchants National. Given the trial court's opportunity to judge the credibility of witnesses' testimony on the meaning of "the regular course of business," we find no basis for reversing the trial court's finding in this regard.

2. Security agreement

The trial court determined that Coverage E necessarily refers only to documents that have real value to the insured bank in the event of the borrower's default. We agree. The policy definition of security agreement refers to the creation of an interest in property. In contrast to documents listed in Coverage E that create an interest in property, the construction contracts here, absent performance by GHK, were of no value.

Appellant argues the trial court erred by viewing the construction contracts separately from the assignment clauses stamped onto the face of the contracts. Appellant claims the construction contracts are an integral part of the security agreements, because each assignment clause specifically refers to and incorporates by reference the construction contract and because the assignment clause is meaningless without the underlying forged contract. The trial court concluded that although the assignment clause might be evidence of a security agreement, the "assignment clause is something entirely separate from the contracts themselves." The court observed that the "assignments themselves are not forged and thus are not covered by any of the Bankers Bond policy provisions."

We reach no conclusion on whether the construction contracts are part of the instruments of assignment. Even assuming integration of the contracts and the assignment clauses, however, we do not find significance in the two instruments. Absent Hoppe's performance under the contract, neither the contract nor the assignment clause are of value.

Finally, appellant urges consideration of language contained in an earlier bond policy, which provided coverage for "securities, documents or other written instruments" that contained a forgery. That language was significantly changed in 1980 to the current provisions and definitions and is not relevant to the present determination of rights under the insurance contract.

In sum, the fact that the bank took the construction contracts as security for its loans to GHK does not mean the contracts are security agreements within the definition in the policy.

Decision

The trial court properly determined that appellant's loss is not covered by the provisions of the insurance policy issued to appellant by respondent.

Affirmed.

Notes and Questions

1. Would *Merchants National Bank* have been decided differently under the pre-1980 language discussed near the end of the opinion?

2. National City Bank v. St. Paul Fire & Marine Ins. Co., 447 N.W.2d 171 (Minn. 1989) established that, for there to be a counterfeit under Insuring Agreement E, there must be a real document of which the counterfeit is an imitation. Further, under Agreement E, the counterfeit document must be in the actual physical possession of the insured bank before making the loan.

3. The importance of the allocations of the burden of proof of coverage and exclusion is clearly seen in another case involving Insuring Agreement E. In Farmers Bank & Trust Co. v. Transamerica Ins. Co., 674 F.2d 548 (6th Cir. 1982), *cert. denied,* 459 U.S. 943 (1982), the insured bank suffered a $355,000 loss as a result of an almost successful bank fraud (the perpetrators were caught). The main perpetrator, Robert Herring, purportedly sold three pieces of heavy equipment (two Caterpillar bulldozers and a Caterpillar loader) to Standard Leasing Corporation, then leased the equipment back again for $8,000 per month for 60 months. Standard then assigned the leasing contract to the insured bank for $363,317. Standard provided the bank, among other documents, with a bill of sale from David Hill to Herring, reciting that Hill had sold Herring the equipment two months earlier. Herring defaulted on the lease after paying $9,000, and the bank then discovered that Herring did not own the three pieces of equipment because no such equipment existed. The signature of Hill turned out to have been written by Herring himself.

The bank claimed under Insuring Agreement E of its Blanket Bond, arguing that it had financed purchase of the equipment and given value on the faith of a written instrument that had been counterfeited or forged as to the signature of the maker. The insurer denied that the signature was a forgery, arguing that a person who signs another's name with the authority to do so is not guilty of forgery. The question thus became who had to show the existence or nonexistence of Herring's authority to sign for Hill. The burden of proof would determine the outcome because Hill had been murdered shortly before trial. Hill's wife testified that she did not know whether the necessary authority existed. The notary testified he would not have notarized the document without Hill's authority. Herring was in prison for fraud and had invoked his fifth amendment privilege against self-incrimination. Whether there was any way to obtain his testimony was not discussed.

The court held that the initial burden of proving the loss came within the coverage of the policy was on the claimant: The insurer then has the burden of proving the applicability of an exclusion. Under Agreement E, forgery was expressly covered, but the bank had to first show that one occurred. The insurer must then show there was no coverage because of exclusion (e), which said

> This bond does not cover loss resulting from default upon any transaction in the nature of a loan made by the insured or agreement or other evidence of debt assigned or sold to the insured, whether procured in good faith or through trick, artifice, fraud or false pretenses unless such loss is covered under section (E).

(Note the changed wording in the 1986 version.) Because the exclusion did not come into play until the bank had first shown that there was coverage, the bank had to show that the signature was a forgery (i.e., that Herring had no authority to sign Hill's signature). This it could not do.

4. See University Natl. Bank of Fort Collins v. Insurance Co. of North America, discussed in *Northwest Airlines,* Section B. Should an act of extortion against a bank's president, on facts like those of *Fort Collins,* be covered by the 1986 bond? If so, under which of the insuring agreements? The policy language quoted in *Fort Collins* is not the same as but is similar to some of the 1986 Financial Institution Bond language. See United States Fire Ins. Co. v. First State Bank, 538 S.W.2d 209 (Tex. Civ. App. 1976).

5. Montgomery, The Alter Ego Type Defenses Reconsidered, 13 Forum 528 (1978), deals with the problem of coverage when the knowledge or action of the bad actor can be imputed to the insured, that is, when the employee in question is the alter ego of the insured.

b. General Agreements

The second major portion of the BBB is entitled "General Agreements." It sets forth the rights and duties of the parties as they relate to the insured's business operations and the insurer's duties with respect to court costs and attorneys' fees.

For instance, the insured is allowed to open branch offices without notifying the insurer or paying a higher premium for the remainder of the premium period. If the insured merges or consolidates with or purchases the assets of another institution, however, the insured must inform and obtain the consent of the insurer and pay such additional premiums as may be assessed. This condition is surely reasonable, for unlike the case where the business is merely growing naturally, the insurer should have the opportunity to evaluate the new business acquired or merged with, and to evaluate its business operations and accounting practices.

The general agreements portion also includes a provision that terminates coverage in the event of a change of control of the insured unless the insured gives written notice to the underwriter. The standard BBB says that

> A change in ownership of voting stock which results in direct or indirect ownership by a stockholder or an affiliated group of stockholders of ten percent (10%) or more of such stock shall be presumed to result in a change of control for the purpose of the required notice.

In Kelly Associates, Inc. v. Aetna Casualty & Surety Co., 662 S.W.2d 777 (Tex. App. 1983), *rev'd*, 681 S.W.2d 593 (Tex. 1984), the Texas Supreme Court had occasion to interpret a clause in a stockbrokers blanket bond which read, "This bond shall be deemed terminated or cancelled as an entirety . . . immediately upon the taking over of the Insured by another business entity." The words "taking over" were not defined nor had any Texas case interpreted them. The insured, a stock brokerage firm, sold all or substantially all of its assets to another brokerage firm. Two months later the insured discovered a loss of over $200,000 caused by an employee's misappropriations. The insured gave notice of discovery three weeks later. The appellate court held that the bond was not in force at the time of the discovery because the business had been taken over prior to that discovery, and gave judgment to the insurer. The crucial facts establishing a takeover were the assumption of control of general management, the sale of the assets, and the hiring of the insured's employees by the new owner. The Texas Supreme Court reversed. The insured was a limited partnership and continued to exist after the sale for the purpose of "winding up" its affairs. The court held the coverage continued through this last phase of the partnership's existence.

The general agreements part also includes a provision that the insurer will indemnify the insured for court costs and attorneys' fees incurred in defense of actions on account of a loss which if proven would be covered under the policy. This is similar to the supplementary payments provision in liability insurance providing for defense of the insured by the insurer, which is often more valuable to the policyholder than the indemnification itself. See Chapter 5.

c. Conditions and Limitations

After the general agreements part of the bond comes a part entitled "Conditions and Limitations." The conditions and limitations of the bond (or policy) are numerous. This section sets forth the definitions used in the bond, specifies the exclusions (which are described separately below to the extent that they have not already appeared), describes limits on liability, and provides for notice, proof of loss, legal proceedings, valuation, subrogation, other insurance, and various other matters. Murray, Conditions to Recovery Under the Bankers Blanket Bond, 50 Ins. Coun. J. 617 (1983), deals in detail with some of the Conditions and Limitations of the BBB. First Natl. Bank of Bowie v. Fidelity & Casualty Co., 634 F.2d 1000 (5th Cir. 1981), illustrates the application of the timely proof of loss condition.

d. Exclusions

An important part of the bankers blanket bond provides for "Exclusions." In the 1986 revised bond, it is Section 2 of the Conditions and Limitations. In that version, there are 26 separate exclusion clauses, exhausting the alphabet. Most are straightforward and some are too new to have generated litigation. Only clauses (d), (e), (i), and (o) have generated enough to justify a closer look.

The directors exclusion, (d) in the BBB, excludes losses suffered by reason of fraud, dishonesty, or breach of fiduciary duty when the board of directors had knowledge of, or condoned, acquiesced, or participated in such a loss. The board of directors is the embodiment of the bank, and any acts of the directors are deemed to be the acts of the insured. If there were not such an exclusion the bank would be insured against its own dishonesty.

In Farmers & Merchants State Bank v. St. Paul Fire & Marine Ins. Co., 309 Minn. 14, 242 N.W.2d 840 (1976), the directors of the insured bank were found to have breached a fiduciary duty intentionally. A customer asked for a loan to purchase a local building at auction in order to build an apartment building. Upon hearing of the building's availability, the bank's directors entered a bid they knew was higher. The customer sued the bank and the bank's fidelity insurer declined to defend. The bank settled the action, incurring $5,730 in attorney's fees. The court rejected the bank's demand for reimbursement; the director exclusion removed the underlying suit from the coverage.

The second exclusion in the BBB that has generated litigation is (e), which attempts to exclude credit risks. The bond is intended to protect the insured bank from losses over which it has relatively little control, such as employee dishonesty and forgeries, not from bad decisionmaking in the extension of credit, which is the normal business of a bank. A bank cannot recover under the fidelity bond if a loan is not paid back and there are no assets to secure the loan, even if the applicant for the loan intentionally lied on the loan application and stated that certain assets did exist. It is the bank's business to verify the existence of the assets. This situation is to be distinguished from cases where a stock certificate or certificate of deposit is counterfeited, in which case the loss would be recoverable under Coverage E.

Courts have often had to address the question whether a certain transaction is an extension of credit. The question arises most frequently when the defrauder is engaging in a *check-kiting* scheme, which is

> a process whereby a person with a checking account in two banks can create an illusion of money in his accounts. A check drawn on the first bank is deposited with the second bank. Before the check reaches the first bank for payment, a check drawn on the second bank is deposited in the first bank. If the bank is willing to give credit in the interim, and many banks are if the person is a regular customer, the person can use the bank's money without first providing collateral and without paying interest. The scheme can go on as long as the person keeps on depositing checks in both banks and as long as the banks believe that there is money behind the checks. [Calcasieu-Marine Natl. Bank v. American Employer's Ins. Co., 533 F.2d 290, 294 n.3 (5th Cir.), *cert. denied*, 429 U.S. 922 (1976)]

In *Calcasieu*, the court considered check-kiting not to be a loan or loans, though the more complex schemes with which the court was dealing in that case were held to be loans and therefore were excluded from coverage. The difference was between expectation of repayment in the normal course of business (in check-kiting) and the unaccepted drafts involved in *Calcasieu*, where repayment in the normal course of business was not assured until acceptance. Application of the exclusion depends on the particular facts. Check-kiting was considered a loan in Citizens Natl. Bank v. Travelers Indem. Co., 296 F. Supp. 300 (M.D. Fla. 1967), but not in Hartford Accident & Indem. Co. v. Federal Deposit Ins. Corp., 204 F.2d 933 (8th Cir. 1953).

The "trading" exclusion appears also in the *brokers* blanket bond, where it is more obviously relevant. It excludes "loss resulting directly or indirectly from trading . . . except when covered under Insuring Agreements (D) or (E)." See Exclusion (i) in the BBB reproduced above. In Insurance Co. of North America v. Gibralco, Inc., 847 F.2d 530 (9th Cir. 1988), the insurer contended that dishonesty of the employee would not be covered if at any point the employee used trading to further the dishonest scheme. The court held for the insured; the trading loss was not a central part of the dishonest scheme.

Another new exclusion in the 1980 version of the BBB is (o), dealing with withdrawals from uncollected deposits. This is a useful exclusion if the insurer wishes to avoid covering check-kiting cases. In the 1980 version it contained an exception, "unless such payments or withdrawals are physically received by such depositor . . . who is within the office of the insured at the time of such payment or withdrawal. . . ." In Bradley Bank v. Hartford Accident & Indem. Co., 557 F. Supp. 243 (W.D. Wis. 1983), *aff'd,* 737 F.2d 657 (7th Cir. 1984), a check-kiting scheme was found not covered by the bank's fidelity bond. Schnabel maintained a checking account at Bradley Bank and another at a bank in the next county. Bradley's policy was to credit Schnabel's account immediately upon deposit of checks. By a scheme like that described in the quotation from *Calcasieu,* Schnabel floated checks from one bank to the other, and when the bubble burst, Bradley Bank was stuck with $45,270 in NSF checks written upon the other bank.

The trial court said that the loss was within coverage (B), which included, *inter alia,* loss of property through false pretenses. The loss was not through a loan and therefore was not within exclusion (e). The court next examined an exclusion added by rider, later included as a standard part of the policy for the first time in 1980, as standard exclusion (o). The loss occurred because Schnabel's account had been credited with uncollected items of deposit not covered by funds in Schnabel's other bank account. The phrase "within the office of the insured" was not ambiguous, and Schnabel was not within the bank at the time of the withdrawals (though the insured contended that he was *constructively* there). On the basis of exclusion (o), the court held that the bank could not recover for the check-kiting loss; the exclusion applied but the exception to it did not.

The word "physically" had been added to modify "received" in exclusion (o) *after* these events, and the bank argued that the addition conceded prior ambiguity. The court disagreed.

See also Mitsui Mfrs. Bank v. Federal Ins. Co., 795 F.2d 827 (9th Cir. 1986); Fidelity & Deposit Co. v. Reliance Federal Savings and Loan Assn., 795 F.2d 42 (7th Cir. 1986); Bay Area Bank v. Fidelity & Deposit Co., 629 F. Supp. 693 (N.D. Cal. 1986). In the last named case, the bank made a "desperation" argument, trying to obtain application of the California concurrent cause doctrine. But that doctrine does not expand coverage without limit.

The new exclusion (s), excluding coverage for lost income, was also added in 1980.

The BBB has been modified through the years to incorporate technological development and changes in business practice. For example, the 1986 revision of the standard bond specifically excludes "loss involving automated mechanical devices which . . . disburse Money, accept deposits, cash checks . . ." unless located in a permanently staffed office, and in no event is the underwriter liable for loss as a result of vandalism, machine malfunction, or mysterious disappearance while the property is within the device. This automated teller machine exclusion was not part of the standard 1969 bankers blanket bond, although a rider to the same effect was available as of 1974. Considerable change was made between the 1980 and 1986 versions.

2. Variations on a Theme

There will probably be no early end to the creation of new varieties of bonds to meet new needs. The Employee Retirement Income Security Act (ERISA), sometimes known only half facetiously as the Lawyers Full Employment Act of 1974, created new categories of fiduciaries who were at risk if they failed to perform their tasks properly as judged post hoc by a court. Sokolowski v. Aetna Life & Casualty Co., 670 F. Supp. 1199 (S.D.N.Y. 1987), illustrates the application of the Aetna's Fiduciary Responsibility Insurance Policy, designed "to provide fiduciary liability insurance coverage to the trustees of employee benefit plans." While the duties of the fiduciaries are based on ERISA, the insurance law applications do not differ greatly from those already seen in connection with other bonds. These bonds, too, cover mainly dishonesty but extend their reach beyond that area.

D. Credit Insurance

Earlier discussion focused on the distinction between the credit risk and the risk of dishonesty. It is quite clear that in selling the Financial Institutions Bond insurers are not seeking to sell credit insurance of any kind. Rather, they seem to be trying to avoid it like the plague.

Both banks and insurance companies deal in the assumption of risk. Until recently, the kinds of risk appropriate for them were fairly sharply differentiated. Assuming credit risk has in general been regarded as banking business and outside the normal range of insurer activity. Nevertheless, there has long been a minor line of insurance called credit insurance. It amounts to a kind of excess of loss coverage on the insured's accounts receivable. It is not available to retail firms. See Rejda, Principles of Insurance 258-259 (1982), for a brief description.

E. Financial Guaranty Insurance

Always looking for new worlds to conquer, insurance entrepreneurs have lately gone into a special kind of credit risk business in a substantial way.

Mortgage guaranty insurance has been important in the marketplace since the 1950s, although it has a long history prior to that. Offered in the private market as early as 1855, that branch of insurance collapsed in the Great Depression. Since 1934 the business has been a conspicuous feature of the public sector, notably through the Federal Housing Administration (FHA). By 1970 FHA insurance covered a third of all new homes. As interest rates climbed in the 1950s and 1960s, however, statutory limitations on interest rates for FHA-guaranteed loans opened a window of opportunity for private insurers. Mortgage Guaranty Insurance Company of Milwaukee was the first company organized to take advantage of the opening; other companies followed, though it remained the dominant company in that line of insurance for a considerable time. Since then the business has operated soundly and profitably most of the time, in competition with FHA and other parallel governmental programs. Mortgage guaranty insurance is now big business, despite the continued presence of government guaranteed insurance, but for the last few years it has been a troubled business.

The risk in mortgage guaranty insurance is closely related to economic cycles and depends relatively little on individual creditworthiness, so the spreading of risks by an insurer can be difficult. As a result most states require it to be sold by a monoline company. The top layer of the coverage is the most risky because it is least sheltered by the policyholder's equity in the real estate; it is common underwriting practice now for the insurer to insist that the mortgagor have an equity interest of perhaps 20 percent or more. That rule is generally relaxed somewhat in the case of owner-occupied residential property, but the collapse of the real estate markets in parts of the Southwest due to the oil recession of the 1980s led to the liquidation of some mortgage guaranty insurance companies. See, for example, Hughes & Hilder, Liquidation of TMIC Insurance Sought in Court Filing by California Regulators, Wall St. J., Feb. 22, 1988, at 5.

The practice of at least some mortgage guaranty insurers is to issue master contracts to institutional lenders, who then are empowered by company commitments to issue certificates of coverage for individual borrowers. The institutional lender is the real insured, however. The existence of this kind of insurance is useful, making possible a nationwide flow of capital for investment in mortgages through a secondary (and nationwide) market facilitated by the insurance, and making it unnecessary for investors to investigate the creditworthiness of the ultimate borrowers.

The issuance of such master contracts is not without risk to the insurer. The institutional lender does not share the insurer's incentive to exercise caution in issuing certificates of coverage, leading to recent complicated lawsuits between insurers and institutional lenders, with the insurers seeking rescission of the contracts for material misrepresentation. One such case is Firstier Mortgage Co. v. Investors Mortgage Ins. Co., 930 F.2d 1508 (10th Cir. 1991).

For more details on the development of mortgage guaranty insurance, see Greene & Serbein, Risk Management: Text and Cases, 322-324 (1978).

Another instance of financial guaranty insurance rather like mortgage guaranty insurance has been used in the purchase of automobiles where the customary down payment is beyond the means of an otherwise creditworthy buyer. Though it closely parallels mortgage guaranty insurance in form, its merit is more questionable. For a description of the insurance and the question of its coverage under state guaranty funds, see Guaranty Bank & Trust Co. v. Ideal Mut. Ins. Co., 526 So. 2d 1094 (La. 1988).

Insurance companies have recently gotten deeply involved in still other kinds of financial guaranty insurance, such as guarantees of payment of municipal bonds. Another, which contributed significantly to a major insurance insolvency now in process, is the guaranty of the debts of limited partners to lending institutions that advanced the money, or part of it, for investment in the partnerships. Inasmuch as the partnerships themselves tended to be driven by tax advantages and were often quite speculative, this kind of credit insurance seems particularly questionable.

The traditional line of demarcation between insurance and banking is getting quite fuzzy. These kinds of financial guaranty insurance represent assumptions of what has traditionally been banking-type risks. When insurers cover the risk of payment of mortgages (mortgage

guaranty insurance — a well established branch) or guarantee municipal bonds (a newer line of insurance), insurance companies have
crossed the line. The issues of whether they should be allowed to do
so, and if so, what special regulations (if any) should be imposed on
them is much discussed nowadays in regulatory circles. In Note, Financial Guaranty Insurance: Is It "The Business of Insurance?", 1988
Colum. Bus. L. Rev. 855, 868 (1988), it is argued that such instruments,
if they are insurance at all, should be simultaneously regulated by the
S.E.C. because "[f]inancial guaranty insurance has a strong investment
orientation. The overwhelming objective of the instrument is to ele-
vate the credit status of the underlying financial instrument thereby
reducing borrowing costs."

On the other side, there is much talk of banks crossing the line in
the opposite direction by being freed to engage in the insurance business. Although that extension of banking powers seems unlikely, the
bare possibility has been an emotionally charged issue, with insurance
agents and even some companies fighting it as if the fate of the world
turned on the outcome. One must distinguish the *underwriting* of
insurance by banks from the *sale* of insurance by banks as agents,
because the issues involved are quite distinct. It is fair to ask whether
the latter is a nonproblem. By federal statutes, banks in small towns
have long been permitted to sell insurance as agents, and no serious
problems seem to have emerged. The possibility of tie-ins with loans is
perhaps the only legitimate basis for concern. Statutes in most if not all
the states forbid such tying arrangements. Would such statutes adequately solve whatever problems there are?

If banks only underwrite insurance through subsidiaries, there
may be no more objection to that arrangement than to any other
conglomerate holding company. But there has been considerable concern about such holding companies, too.

F.   Political Risk Insurance

As an outgrowth of the post-World War II Marshall Plan the
United States actively encouraged investment and trade abroad, especially for reconstruction of Western Europe. Later the program was
extended to less developed countries. As part of that activity, it was
necessary to provide insurance to American businesses engaged
abroad. The principal risk insured against was currency nonconvertibility.

The Agency for International Development (AID) was formed in 1961 and took over both assistance to foreign governments and insurance. A separate agency, the Overseas Private Investment Corporation (OPIC), took over the insurance function from AID in 1969. By that time the insurance coverage had been expanded to include coverage against expropriation. When Chile expropriated Anaconda Copper and International Telephone and Telegraph, among others, the resulting claims of between $350 and $400 million led to two problems: (1) the possible need for a bailout of OPIC by the taxpayer, and (2) the probable involvement of a government agency in subrogation claims against the government of Chile (and potentially other governments). The prospects of unseemly international controversy, plus hope that the insurance program could become self-supporting, led Congress to mandate the privatization of OPIC by 1980. Though a limited private market did develop, it was not adequate, and OPIC's government-backed insurance activities still continue. In 1989 OPIC was reported to have provided coverage for about 25 projects in China, with exposure of about $95 million. Garcia, Political Risk Insurance Turns Scarce in China, Wall St. J., June 16, 1989, at A3E. The opening up of Eastern Europe also provides new opportunities for both OPIC and private insurers.

Three basic political risks are insured against: expropriation, currency nonconvertibility, and war. Though these coverages are not the usual subjects of insurance contracts, they present no insurmountable underwriting problems. The risk of most contemporary significance is of currency nonconvertibility. Insurers protect themselves against adverse selection by requiring substantial coinsurance (20 to 25 percent) and a substantial waiting period (usually 18 to 30 months) after default before the losses must be paid. Because no interest is paid by the insurer on the loss for the waiting period, the insured's coinsurance participation is more nearly one third. Apart from those two provisions the policies are not unusual.

The Persian Gulf crisis of 1990 threw an interesting light on political risk insurance. Potential losses from political risks in Kuwait could reach billions of dollars, but little of it was insured because of Kuwait's supposed stability and creditworthiness. Potential claims for losses resulting from trade with Iraq will likely be substantial, but less than might be expected because the premium rate for trades with Iraq were running in the range of 15 percent of contract value, compared with 2 to 4 percent for most countries. In addition, many companies stopped writing political risk insurance for Iraqi deals to avoid undue concentration there. Thus for opposite reasons, much of the potential loss in trading with Iraq and Kuwait has not been insured. See Political Risk Insurers Fear Crisis Escalation, Bus. Ins., Aug. 13, 1990, at 1.

G.   Surety Bonds

He that is surety for a stranger shall smart for it: and he that hateth suretiship is sure.

Proverbs 11:15

Up to this point this book has been discussing insurance. Fidelity bonds provide dishonesty insurance and do not differ in principle from other kinds of insurance. Other classes of bonds sold by insurers present altogether different problems. Insurance policies are two-party contracts, under which the insurer promises to indemnify or pay a specific or determinable sum to the insured in certain events. Surety bonds are three-party contracts in which the *surety* (the insurance company) promises to pay the *obligee* (a third party) a debt or perform some other obligation owed by the *obligor* (the insured) in the event the obligor does not pay or perform. Individuals may be and often are accommodation sureties for others. If surety bonds are issued as a business, however, by statutory definition they constitute insurance and must be issued by licensed insurers, most of which also sell other kinds of insurance. See, for example, N.Y. Ins. Law §1101(b)(1)(B) (McKinney 1985).

Surety bonds exist in great variety. Public official bonds, construction contract bonds, other contract bonds, lost document bonds, license and permit bonds, and judicial bonds are the most common. The principal difference from insurance (in the narrower sense) is that the professional surety expects very few losses: to protect itself against loss, the surety is likely to require collateral or other security from the bonded principal, if it has any doubt about the principal's responsibility.

It has seemed convenient to exclude surety bonds from all but the most superficial mention in this book, in deference to limitations on the endurance of the reader. The subject is important, and it would be wrong to say that it is uncomplicated. Specialized treatment may be found in both the lawbooks and the books dealing with insurance economics and practice.

Liability Insurance: The Duties to Defend and Indemnify

A. Introduction

Liability insurance is essentially a product of the twentieth century. It grew apace with the development of novel and powerful physical instruments, materials, and techniques through which harm could be inflicted and, especially after the middle of the century, with the expansion of liability in tort. It is not surprising that liability insurance covering the use of automobiles is today by far the largest branch of liability insurance, accounting for over a quarter of all insurance premiums other than life and health.*

Workers compensation statutes date from the 1920s. Workers compensation insurance ranks second in premium volume among the branches of liability insurance, producing about half as much premium as automobile liability. Because of the peculiarities of its statutory foundation, workers compensation insurance stands apart from other branches of liability insurance; because the employer must pay regardless of fault, it is sometimes not considered to be liability insurance at all.

General liability insurance covers mostly commercial risks. Some of its components originated long ago but it has become especially important in recent decades. It produces a little over five percent of total property-liability premiums. Premiums for personal liability cannot easily be separated from those for dissimilar coverages like fire insurance that are combined with liability in the multiple peril policies, such as homeowners and farmowners, but it produces perhaps another

---

*The numerical relationships in the first three paragraphs of this chapter come from Insurance Information Institute, 1988-89 Property/Casualty Fact Book, at 19. The relationships change little over short periods of time.

five percent or more. Medical malpractice insurance produces about two percent. In the aggregate, liability insurance premiums (including workers compensation) approach half of all premiums other than life and health.

1. Comprehensive Liability

This chapter concentrates on general liability insurance sold as a package, though the law relevant to other liability insurance contracts is similar. General liability insurance comprehends a number of coverages that developed at various times. The covered risks varied greatly and the forms that had evolved did not necessarily dovetail accurately, leaving gaps or producing overlapping coverage. In the 1930s, the insurance industry began to develop *comprehensive* liability coverage to minimize the gaps and overlapping. Sometimes the resulting product was truly comprehensive, including automobile; sometimes it was only comprehensive *general* liability, excluding automobile. In either case it was usually limited to liability for bodily injury and property damage, although it could be and sometimes was extended by endorsement to include *personal injury liability.* In many currently issued general liability policies, including the one reproduced in this chapter, personal injury liability is included as an integral part of the coverage, without the necessity of endorsing the basic form.

"Personal injury" in insurance terminology usually refers to liability based on some intentional torts that ordinarily do *not* involve harm to the body, including liability for false arrest, libel, and wrongful entry and eviction. What is often termed "personal injury" in the law of torts is designated as "bodily injury" in liability insurance policies. The names of the torts added by personal injury liability coverage themselves suggest the settings in which such coverage would be commercially useful and feasible. This chapter deals only incidentally with personal injury liability insurance.

Workers compensation is based on special state statutes and the underlying liability claims are administered by state administrative agencies; in contrast most liability policies insure against common law-created and judge-administered liabilities (though sometimes with statutory modifications). For those and other reasons, such as market differences, it is uncommon to find workers compensation coverage combined with other liability insurance in the same policy (except with employers liability coverage, which provides for liability to employees that is outside the scope of the workers compensation statutes). Workers compensation insurance is, however, often sold to an employer by the same insurer that provides the employer's other coverages, so that it forms part of a single account, with important consequences for pricing and other marketing practices.

Whether written with or without automobile liability coverage, comprehensive liability insurance may cover all risks of liability for bodily injury and property damage, yet it is usually written in schedule form, listing individually designated coverages. The coverages are still broad and it is not inappropriate to describe the policies as comprehensive. There are also specifically expressed and usually narrow exclusions. Even when exclusions are numerous most of them are irrelevant for particular insureds. For example, the watercraft exclusion is not relevant to the insured who neither owns nor uses a boat. Whether a policy is in a schedule or a comprehensive form is important to the burden of proof: Some cases turn on it.

This chapter deals mainly with questions of coverage. It is useful, therefore, to list the main categories of risk within comprehensive general liability. They are:

1. *Premises and operations.* Historically, this appeared in two parallel forms with minor differences in terms. They were (1) owners', landlords', and tenants' coverage (O.L.&T.) and (2) manufacturers' and contractors' coverage (M.&C.). Each could be written separately as well as within a general liability policy. A single policyholder would need both only if the policyholder's activities were broad-ranging and diverse. The nature of the insured's activity determined which should be purchased; the names of the coverages suggest their appropriate uses.

2. *Elevator liability.*

3. *Construction and alterations.* Liability that arises from ordinary maintenance and repair is covered under premises and operations, but liability from new construction and from major alterations is not, except for policyholders whose normal activity is construction.

4. *Liability for independent contractors.*

5. *Products/completed operations.* The products hazard is well known. The completed operations hazard is analogous to products: It exists where the insured has been operating away from the insured's own premises and has placed third persons at risk there. The coverage applies to cases arising after the operations are completed or abandoned, and thus complements the O.L.&T. and M.&C. coverages. Products and completed operations may be covered either together or separately.

There is no magic in the above listing. Some comprehensive liability policies contain errors and omissions (professional liability, malpractice) insurance as well, though usually errors and omissions insurance is separately written. Personal injury coverage, applying to intentional torts not involving bodily injury or property damage, can also be added by endorsement or be included within the same basic contract.

2. Standardized Policies

Two standardized policies, the fire insurance policy* and the Bankers Blanket Bond,† have already been discussed in this book.

Standardized liability insurance policies date from the 1930s and originated in automobile liability insurance. Both the idea of standardization and some specific provisions were readily adaptable to other coverages. Standard liability policies were not generally mandated by statute, however, as the fire policies were. In consequence there has always been some variation among companies, mainly in premiums or limits but sometimes in policy provisions. This is especially true in commercial insurance, where the premiums are large enough to stimulate considerable competition among insurers.

A collision on the highway was the paradigm insured event for the drafters of the automobile policy. One driver is allegedly negligent and is sued by the other for bodily injury or property damage. Under the policy the insurance company is obligated to defend the insured and provide indemnity for any adverse judgment. Other types of liability insurance had similar simple paradigms: the slip and fall case in O.L.&T. coverage, or the collapse of a wooden wheel in products liability. The result was the *accident form,* protecting the insured against the liability resulting from an accident within the policy period.

Problems with the accident form led ultimately to the *occurrence policy,* which was created by endorsement in the early 1960s and became standard after 1966. See Beryllium Corp. v. American Mut. Liab. Ins. Co., Section B. Interesting questions are whether and, if so, in what ways the drafters were successful in their attempts to improve the product. The occurrence form intentionally enlarged both the coverage the insurers had *intended* to provide under the accident form and, to a lesser degree, the coverage the courts decided the accident policies had *actually* provided. The occurrence form was the standard for over two decades and is still extensively used.

---

*The fire insurance policy is mandated by statute. For further discussion, see Chapter 3. Standardized provisions in health and life insurance are frequently mandated by statute as well. It should not be surprising that insurance industry organizations have had much to do with the development of the wording, and sometimes (though not always) have provided the impetus for the enactment. Other standard policies are developed by industry organizations and then widely used, but are not required by law. Standardized policies contribute to what the Germans call *Markttransparenz* and provide a useful way to concentrate competition on less opaque factors than policy wording.

†See Chapter 4.

It is possible that despite consumer and regulatory resistance, the *claims-made policy* will replace the occurrence policy as the industry standard form, at least in commercial settings. It has been used for some time in a few policies, and some cases in these materials will illustrate it. Because claims-made has inherent problems, however, it may not displace the occurrence policy except in limited situations such as medical malpractice.

3.   The Dual Obligation

The liability insurer normally has two duties to the insured: to indemnify and to defend. The latter duty is considerably broader than the former. The relationship between the two is illustrated by the following case.

GRAY v. ZURICH INS. CO.

65 Cal. 2d 263, 419 P.2d 168, 54 Cal. Rptr. 104 (1966)

[The text of this opinion is found in Chapter 1, Section C.]

Originally liability policies placed no dollar limits on the duty to defend. The 1955 standard comprehensive general liability (CGL) policy stated, so far as relevant to this question:

> With respect to such insurance as is afforded by this policy, the company shall:
>
> (a) defend any suit against the insured alleging such injury, sickness, disease or destruction and seeking damages on account thereof, even if such suit is groundless, false or fraudulent; but the company may make such investigation, negotiation and settlement of any claim or suit as it deems expedient; . . . and the amounts so incurred, except settlements of claims and suits, are payable by the company in addition to the applicable limit of liability of this policy.

Insurers have argued that the duty to defend under the 1955 policy derives from the duty to indemnify and automatically ceases once the limits of the policy have been paid out in judgments or settlements. Insureds, on the other hand, have argued that the duty to defend is sufficiently independent to continue despite the exhaustion of the liability limits. In many important cases, the result chosen by the courts will be crucial, for defense costs often loom larger than the cost of indemnity. If defense costs on a claim can be allocated to a policy based on the 1955 form, it might be advantageous to an insured if the result advocated by insureds prevails, for although indemnity limits were low the language quoted above gave hope of unlimited payment of defense costs.

The insurance crisis of the 1980s involved some large groups of cases, such as the asbestos cases, in which defense costs tended to be greater than indemnification costs. The problem has long existed, though with lesser intensity. Recognition of this problem led insurers to try to protect themselves in the future against the potentially unlimited liability for defense costs found in the 1955 policy. One step was to insert in the 1966 GCL policy the language, "but the company shall not be obligated . . . to defend any suit after the applicable limit of the company's liability has been exhausted by payment of judgments or settlements."

The question of whether defense costs under the 1955 policy were potentially unlimited was decided for Illinois in the *Raymark* case, an excerpt from which appears below. The remainder of the case is reproduced later.

The next step, already applied by some companies to some policies (for example, the commercial umbrella policy), will be to include defense costs within the policy limits. Regulated insurers have not yet succeeded in primary insurance in achieving that change to any considerable extent. If there were soon another crisis on the scale of that of the 1980s, however, such a change might occur as a product of the growing cost of litigation in our system.

ZURICH INS. CO. v. RAYMARK INDUS., INC.

118 Ill. 2d 23, 514 N.E.2d 150, 112 Ill. Dec. 684 (1987)

[The court first describes the facts and the course of the motion practice in the case, then deals with the events that trigger coverage and their timing. For that part of the case see Section E(2). The court then proceeds to the duty to defend under the pre-1967 policies and the post-1966 policies — ED.]

II. Do the Terms of Raymark's Pre-1967 Policies Require the Primary Insurers to Defend New Actions and to Continue to Defend Actions Pending Against Raymark After the Limits of Liability Under Those Policies Have Been Exhausted by the Payment of Judgments or Settlements?

As cross-appellant, Raymark contends that its pre-1967 insurers have a duty to continue to pay defense costs in all asbestos-related lawsuits, whether currently pending or subsequently commenced against Raymark, even after the indemnity limits of their various policies have been exhausted by payment of judgments or settlements. The insurer's duty to defend its insured arises from the undertaking to defend as stated in the contract of insurance. (Conway v. Country Casualty Insurance Co. (1982), 92 Ill. 2d 388, 394, 65 Ill. Dec. 934, 442 N.E.2d 245.) Raymark contends that its pre-1967 policies contain no language limiting the insurers' duty to defend. To determine the scope of the insurers' duty to defend under these policies, we turn to the policy language.

The introductory sentence of each of the policies issued to Raymark before September 26, 1967, provides that the insurer "agrees with the insured . . . subject to the limits of liability . . . and other terms of this policy." Immediately following this sentence, and under the title "Insuring Agreements," the policies set forth the various insuring agreements. Insuring Agreement I provides various coverages, including coverage for bodily injury liability. Insuring Agreement II in Federal's policies provides:

II. Defense, Settlement, Supplementary Payments.

With respect to such insurance as is afforded by this policy, the company shall:

(a) defend any suit against the insured alleging such injury, sickness, disease . . . and seeking damages on account thereof, even if such suit is groundless, false or fraudulent; but the company may make such investigation, negotiation and settlement of any claim or suit as it deems expedient.

. . . and the amounts so incurred, except settlements of claim and suits, are payable by the company in addition to the applicable limit of liability of this policy.

The defense insuring agreements contained in Commercial Union's policies are nearly identical to those included in Federal's policies.

The appellate court concluded that the introductory sentence of the policies specifically rendered each of the insuring agreements, including the duty to defend, subject to the policy's indemnity limits. (145 Ill. App. 3d 175, 192-193, 98 Ill. Dec. 512, 494 N.E.2d 634.) Accordingly, the court held that an insurer's duty to defend is discharged after its duty to indemnify has been fully discharged by the payment of judgments or settlements to the extent of its policy limits and it has made an orderly withdrawal from Raymark's defense. (145 Ill. App. 3d 175, 193-194, 98 Ill. Dec. 512, 494 N.E.2d 634.) Raymark argues that the appellate court erred in concluding that the phrase "subject to the limits of liability" confines the duty to defend as provided in Insuring Agreement II. According to Raymark's construction of the plain and unambiguous language of the policies, the phrase "subject to the limits of liability" somehow qualifies only the duty to indemnify set forth in Insuring Agreement I. We find this argument to be without merit. The introductory phrase, "subject to the limits of liability," clearly means that all rights and duties — including the duty to defend — are subject to liability limits of the policy. Moreover, Raymark's own interpretation of the introductory sentence belies the construction it urges us to accept. As explained below, it contends that a different phrase contained in the introductory sentence applies to the defense provision of Insuring Agreement II.

Raymark argues that the appellate court improperly focused its attention on the phrase "subject to the limits of liability," and notes that the policy's introductory sentence also renders the insuring agreements "subject to the . . . other terms of this policy." Raymark then notes that Insuring Agreement II contains an "other term" that provides that defense costs are to be paid "in addition to the applicable limit of liability." Therefore, Raymark concludes, according to the unambiguous language of the policy, the duty to defend pursuant to Insuring Agreement II is not "subject to the limits of liability" If we were to consider only those provisions of the policy quoted by Raymark to the exclusion of other policy language, the duty to defend would appear to be unlimited. An insurance contract must, however, be interpreted from an examination of the complete document and not an isolated part. Western Casualty & Surety Co. v. Brochu (1985), 105 Ill. 2d 486, 493, 86 Ill. Dec. 493, 475 N.E.2d 872.

The introductory phrase contained in Insuring Agreement II of Federal's policies states that the insurer will provide a defense "[w]ith respect to such insurance as is afforded by this policy." Commercial Union's policies contain a nearly identical provision. The parties agree that the quoted language limits the insurer's obligation to defend. They differ as to whether the duty to defend is limited only to the type of coverage afforded by the policy or to both the type and amount of coverage afforded. . . .

We believe that the only reasonable interpretation of the language in question limits the duty to defend to the amount of coverage as well as to the type of coverage provided. . . .

Raymark seeks to avoid this conclusion by arguing that the duty to defend is an independent undertaking of the insurer that exists in addition to the duty to indemnify. Raymark's argument is premised on this court's statement that "an insurer's duty to defend and its duty to indemnify are separate and distinct and . . . the former duty is broader than the latter." (Conway v. Country Casualty Insurance Co. (1982), 92 Ill. 2d 388, 394, 65 Ill. Dec. 934, 442 N.E.2d 245.) The duty to indemnify arises only when the insured becomes legally obligated to pay damages in the underlying action that gives rise to a claim under the policy. The duty to defend an action brought against the insured, on the other hand, is determined solely by reference to the allegations of the complaint. If the complaint alleges facts which bring the claim within the potential indemnity coverage of the policy, the insurer is obligated to defend the action. (Thornton v. Paul (1978), 74 Ill. 2d 132, 144, 23 Ill. Dec. 541, 384 N.E.2d 335; Maryland Casualty Co. v.

Peppers (1976), 64 Ill. 2d 187, 193-194, 355 N.E.2d 24.) Thus, the insurer must defend an action even though it *may not* ultimately be obligated to indemnify the insured. Where the insurer has exhausted its indemnity limits, however, the insurer *cannot* ultimately be obligated to indemnify the insured. Thus, the duty to defend is broader than the duty to indemnify only when the insurer has the potential obligation to indemnify. But when, as here, the insurer has no potential obligation to indemnify it has no duty to defend. . . .

III. Do the Terms of Raymark's Post-1967 Policies Require Zurich to Continue to Defend Actions Pending Against Raymark After the Limits of Those Policies Have Been Exhausted by the Payment of Judgments or Settlements?

We turn now to the question of the extent of Zurich's duty to defend claims against Raymark pursuant to the terms of its policies issued after September 26, 1967. Raymark concedes that the defense provision in those policies terminates Zurich's defense obligation with respect to cases that are filed after the indemnity limits of those policies are exhausted. With regard to cases that are pending at the time of exhaustion, however, Raymark contends that Zurich's duty to defend continues until another insurer assumes the defense.

The defense clause of Zurich's policies provides:

> [T]he company shall have the right and duty to defend any suit against the insured seeking damages on account of such bodily injury . . . but the company shall not be obligated . . . to defend any suit after the applicable limit of the company's liability has been exhausted by payment of judgments or settlements.

The circuit court found that this provision was clear and unambiguous. It initially concluded, however, that this provision required the insurer to continue to defend and to absorb the costs of those cases that it had already undertaken to defend prior to the exhaustion of the indemnity limits. Zurich moved to modify the court's order to permit it to withdraw from pending cases unconditionally once its policy limits were exhausted. On rehearing, the court modified its order to provide that an insurer, upon exhaustion of its policy limits, is not obligated to continue to defend cases then pending against Raymark if another insurer is also obligated to defend Raymark in those cases. In that event, the court ruled, Raymark must tender the cases to the other carrier. The court then held that the first insurer is entitled to cease defending those cases once the new carrier assumes their defense. The appellate court held that Zurich's duty to defend pending cases terminates upon the exhaustion of the policy limits and, accordingly, modified the circuit court's order. 145 Ill. App. 3d 175, 196, 98 Ill. Dec. 512, 494 N.E.2d 634.

. . . This language clearly and explicitly manifests the parties' intention to limit Zurich's obligation to defend all actions, including pending actions, to the period of time prior to the time when its obligation to indemnify is discharged by the payment of judgments or settlements. We therefore affirm the judgment of the appellate court to the extent that it held that Zurich is not obligated to continue to defend actions pending against Raymark after the limits of its policies are exhausted by the payment of judgments or settlements.

Notes and Questions

1. Justice Simon dissented in part, expressing the view that the relieving clause applies only to the defense of suits *filed* after liability limits have been exhausted, not to pending suits. Are you persuaded to the opposite view by the majority's opinion?

2. In an omitted passage, the opinion rejects Raymark's contention that the 1966 amendment establishes that the earlier policy contains an unqualified promise to pay defense costs. Do you agree?

3. The Third Circuit, in trying to anticipate what the Pennsylvania Supreme Court would do, held as did the *Raymark* court that the duty to defend ceased when the duty to indemnify did, subject to the insurer's obligation to make an orderly transfer of the defense to whoever was to take it up. Commercial Union Ins. Co. v. Pittsburgh Corning Corp., 789 F.2d 214 (3d Cir. 1986). The court also discussed conflict of interest problems that would arise. Those questions are dealt with more fully in Chapter 8.

4. A discharged school director brought a §1983 action against the school board, alleging as damages mental distress, hypertension, and assorted other physical ills. The school board had a policy insuring against bodily injury (*not* personal injury, which would have included some tort damages not involving bodily injury); the policy had the traditional dual obligation. The court held that the insurer must defend, even if the plaintiff's case looked shaky. See Kufalk v. Hart, 636 F. Supp. 309 (N.D. Ill. 1986).

5. Even when the complaint does not allege facts that if proved would require indemnification, the insurer may also be obligated to defend if it knows facts (or perhaps even in the course of a reasonable investigation would have learned facts) that would ground a duty to indemnify. See Annot., 50 A.L.R.2d 458, 500-505 (1956). But, however surely the insurer knows that the true facts will not support a duty to indemnify, most cases hold that it must still defend if the complaint is framed broadly enough. Are these asymmetrical rules fair to the insurer? Do they represent sound social policy? Among the few excep-

tional cases are State Farm Fire & Casualty Co. v. Moss, 182 Mich. App. 559, 452 N.W.2d 816 (1989) (prior conviction of insured for assault on police officer negated duty to defend); Millers Mut. Ins. Assn. of Illinois v. Ainsworth Seed Co., 194 Ill. App. 3d 888, 552 N.E.2d 254, 141 Ill. Dec. 886 (1990) (affidavit accompanying the complaint for a declaratory judgment negated duty to defend). The latter court also mentioned as another example cases where there was collusion between the insured and a third party complainant.

6. Because appropriately stated claims can bring the defendant's insurer to the rescue, the insurer is available with its moneybags to help fund a settlement, whether the claim could be proved or not. The influence that can have on the strategy of claimants should be apparent.

7. Is there any public policy reason to preclude an insurer from agreeing to defend but not to indemnify? It might be called "legal defense" insurance: Are there reasons an insured might wish to have such insurance?

8. In the asbestos litigation, manufacturer-insureds often had insurance policies with low limits for (sometimes many) years preceding 1966, followed for years by 1966 standard policies with increasing limits. Once asbestos litigation became a serious threat, they held policies with substantial self-insured retentions and (sometimes) a considerable reduction in limits. Asbestos coverage has recently been hard to obtain on any terms.

Where the old policies might have had per occurrence and aggregate limits of, say, $1 million or so, the intermediate ones might have limits of $50 or $100 million or even more. Not all of the coverage need be in primary policies. Much of it was in excess layers, of which there were sometimes several. The companies along the line, from the primary carrier to the topmost excess carrier, were likely to reinsure all or part of the risk they had written. For a discussion of excess coverage and reinsurance, see Chapter 9. The key issue is whether the pre-1966 policies, though having low limits, might be interpreted to have unlimited defense obligations.

The question of whether the duty to defend under the old policies ceases when coverage is exhausted must be regarded as still open, despite recent decisions in some very important asbestos cases. See *Raymark* and *Pittsburgh Corning,* supra note 3.

B. The Accident Policy

The original form of liability insurance was triggered by the happening of an "accident," the meaning of which was thought clear enough that no definition was needed in the policy. In due time, the courts, aided by the ingenuity of plaintiffs' lawyers, taught the insurance companies that they suffered from an illusion; and thus the policy was reworked. The recasting took place in the 1966 standard policy, which changed to the occurrence form. The present state of tort law, however, is such that the earlier accident policies are still relevant in some very important litigation.

BERYLLIUM CORP. v. AMERICAN MUT. LIAB. INS. CO.

223 F.2d 71 (3d Cir. 1955)

McLaughlin, Circuit Judge.

An assured under a comprehensive general liability policy sued its insurer on the policy in the district court and obtained judgment in its favor. The insurance company appeals. Pennsylvania law governs this diversity action.

The policy in suit is a "Comprehensive General Liability Policy." Its pertinent clause is designated "Coverage A — Bodily Injury Liability." It reads:

> To pay on behalf of the insured all sums which the insured shall become obligated to pay by reason of the liability imposed upon him by law, or assumed by him under contract as defined herein, for damages, including damages for care and loss of services, because of *bodily injury, sickness or disease,* including death at any time resulting therefrom, sustained by any person or persons and *caused by accident.* (Emphasis supplied).

Plaintiff appellee is a producer of the mineral beryllium.[1] It is agreed that the wife of one of its employees and the daughter of another died of beryllium poisoning contracted through handling the employees' work clothes during periods of five and eight years respectively. Suits were brought against the Beryllium Corporation on behalf of the decedents. The insurance company disclaimed. The corporation settled the claims directly and sued in the present action for the amount of the settlements and counsel fees.

Appellant argues that though the deaths were accidental, i.e. unintentional, they were not the result of an accidental cause. It is contended that in each instance there must be a single unexpected distinctive event for the particular death in order to come within the policy. . . .

There is no mystery about the facts. The minute particles of beryllium which had adhered to the clothing of the employees con-

---

1. A hard, light, steel-gray metallic element used chiefly in copper alloys.

cerned became detached and entered the lungs of decedents setting up conditions which resulted fatally to them. It is accepted by appellant that the Beryllium Corporation negligently failed to warn its employees of the danger and to provide proper safeguards against it; further that the two employees were ignorant of the existing menace of beryllium poisoning. . . .

This brings us to the main point in this appeal. While these deaths clearly resulted from accidental causes it was not just one but a series of causes which produced them. Appellant contends that this defeats the claims. Its theory as we have mentioned is that the policy contemplated that the accidental means must be an isolated occurrence.

The policy may have so contemplated but if that were its purpose it is not easy to explain why it did not say so. If restriction to covering accidents resulting from a single accidental cause was part, and an important part, of the protection furnished; entered into the premium income, cost, etc., it seems curious that it was not plainly stated so that the insurance purchaser would know the limitations of his policy and at least have the opportunity of safeguarding himself with more complete insurance.

By the contract in suit the company agrees to pay the arising damages from death "caused by accident." If this clause was confined to one accident, if the word "an" had been inserted so that the language read "caused by an accident", there would be some justification for the argument now made. With full knowledge, we must assume, of a basic principle of insurance law that ambiguity in the company drawn policy will be resolved against the insurer, the drafter of the agreement inserts this at least ambiguous phrase and it is now used in an effort to defeat these serious claims. We are unable to accept such contention. As we read the clause it does not bar the accidental deaths before us caused as they were "by accident."

. . . [T]he Pennsylvania decisions that deal with accidental deaths caused by inhaling formaldehyde vapor, McCarron v. John Hancock Mut. Life Ins. Co., [156 Pa. Super. 287, 40 A.2d 118 (1944)], by inhaling carbon monoxide gas, Urian v. Equitable Life Assurance Society, [310 Pa. 342, 165 A. 388 (1933)], and by mistakenly taking soluble salts of barium instead of barium sulphate, Bloom v. Brotherhood Accident Co., [85 Pa. Super 398 (1925)], are more helpful in determining pertinent Pennsylvania law. In the present state of the Pennsylvania law we would be unjustified in assuming that the Pennsylvania courts when confronted not with a statute but with an insurance contract which indemnifies the insured for damages paid for "bodily injury, sickness or disease . . . caused by accident," would restrict such broad language to only those injuries caused by an identifiable event, particularly in view of the well-established principle applied in Pennsylvania as elsewhere, that an ambiguity must be construed against the insurer.

The judgment of the district court will be affirmed.

Notes and Questions

1. If there are no relevant exclusions, would the accident policy in *Beryllium* provide coverage for the alleged liability of a supplier of asbestos for the asbestosis or mesothelioma that results from the long-term exposure of a claimant to dust containing asbestos fibers?

2. With no relevant exclusions, would it provide coverage to a waste disposal dump operator for the leaching of toxic chemicals from the dump into the underground drinking water supply of neighbors?

3. Would it provide coverage for the owner of an underground gasoline storage tank that was leaking into the underground drinking water supply? The EPA estimates that from 50,000 to 200,000 out of 1.4 million regulated tanks are leaking. (Millions more are unregulated.) The earlier generations of such tanks were made of bare steel, which in 15 to 20 years corrodes enough for gasoline to leak into aquifers. Even if made with materials that do not corrode, there is still risk from the installation, piping, maintenance of fittings, and disturbance by earth tremors which occur in all states. For a journalistic treatment of this problem, see Leavenworth, L.U.S.T., [1987] Ins. Rev. 20 (March 1987). Despite bad experience with storage tanks, some insurers currently believe they can profitably insure the new generation of noncorroding underground tanks.

C. The Occurrence Policy

1. The 1966 Occurrence Policy

After more than six years of work, committees from insurance industry organizations proposed a new standard policy, changing the insured event from an "accident" to an "occurrence." For another year, the new policy was subjected to intense scrutiny by regulators and other interested groups. The result was the 1966 occurrence policy. In due course it was replaced by the 1973 occurrence policy.

Prior to 1966 an optional endorsement was used by some companies that merely substituted the word "occurrence" for "accident." Would that change the meaning of the policy?

Consider the following excerpts from 1966 Standard CGL Policy:

"bodily injury" means bodily injury, sickness or disease sustained by any person. . . .

"damages" includes damages for death and for care and loss of services resulting from *bodily injury* and damages for loss of use of property resulting from *property damage*. . . .

"**occurrence**" means an accident, including injurious exposure to conditions, which results, during the policy period,* in *bodily injury* or *property damage* neither expected nor intended from the standpoint of the *insured*. . . .

"**property damage**" means injury to or destruction of tangible property. . . .

The company will pay on behalf of the *insured* all sums which the *insured* shall become legally obligated to pay as *damages* because of

A. *bodily injury* or
B. *property damage*

to which this insurance applies, caused by an *occurrence*. . . .

One of the participants in the development of the 1966 policy, Roland Wendorff of Employers of Wausau, made an informative presentation about the development to the ABA Section of Insurance, Negligence and Compensation Law. Wendorff, The New Standard Comprehensive General Liability Insurance Policy, A.B.A. Sec. Ins., Neg. & Comp. L. Proc. 250 (1966). The following paragraphs summarize the important points in his presentation:

1. The format of the 1966 policy was new.
2. The new policy uses definitions more extensively than did previous policies.[†] "A defined word or phrase will mean the same thing in the statement of coverage as it does in the exclusions." Id. at 250.
3. The exclusions are brought into closer proximity to the coverage language in an effort to overcome judicial hostility reflected in the perception that fine print on the last page takes away what bold print on the front page gives.
4. The insured event was broadened from an undefined "accident" to a defined "occurrence." The historical conception of an accident was a sudden and unexpected event identifiable in time and place, the paradigm case being a highway accident. He noted further that the new basis of liability had been anticipated by the interpretation many courts had given to "accident," which led to an inconsistency in the settling of claims. Id. at 253. The inconsistency could be eliminated by broadening the *intended* coverage.

*In the 1973 version of the occurrence policy the phrase "during the policy period" was no longer part of the definition of "occurrence" but was part of the definitions of "bodily injury" and "property damage." In the policy reproduced below, it is a separate clause in the Insuring Agreement. Consider in due course whether these variations change the policy's coverage. — ED.

†Defined words are usually underlined, italicized or enclosed in quotation marks in contemporary policies.

5. Under the new policy the trigger of coverage "is clearly set forth as the time when the bodily injury or property damage occurs." This should correct the erroneous interpretation of some courts that the negligent act is the trigger.
6. The new policy seeks to correct the tendency of some courts to examine the state of mind of the injured person, rather than that of the insured, in determining whether an event was an "accident."

Notes and Questions

1. Was Wendorff right in his statement quoted in paragraph 2?
2. He says that the coverage has been broadened. In what respects would the definition of occurrence broaden the coverage given by the accident policy?
3. Based on the policy language, was Wendorff right about the "triggering" of coverage? Cases later in this chapter will explore that problem.
4. Is there coverage for economic loss when a court imposes that liability in the law of products liability? That problem will reappear later.

2. The 1973 Occurrence Policy

The 1973 policy will be the principal general liability policy involved in litigation for the next decade or more. Long after it is replaced by a new policy it will remain important for those cases in which the coverage is particularly "long-tailed." For such very long-tailed coverage as products liability and some professional liability, the 1966 policy and even the pre-1966 policies are still relevant for some cases. Some recent asbestos coverage cases have involved policies written as far back as the 1940s.

In the 1973 standard form of the CGL policy, like the 1966 policy, there was first a general declarations page, showing the advance premiums* for each coverage included within the policy. After the declarations page came the part of the agreement that applied no matter what the specific coverages might be, including (most importantly) the definitions. Then a smorgasbord of material was available

---

*The final premium for most commercial liability policies is determined by audits of the insured's records. For products liability coverage, for example, the premium may be calculated as $x per $100 of sales, for workers compensation as $y per $100 of payroll, rated separately for jobs of different riskiness. The premium formula varies from coverage to coverage.

for selective inclusion. If the comprehensive general liability coverage was chosen, there was another declarations page with space for detailed premium calculations, followed by a page of contractual items applicable to the comprehensive general liability coverage. If, instead of comprehensive, specific scheduled coverages were elected, there would be a similar declarations page or part page and a page or part page of coverage-specific contract provisions for each elected coverage. (These other pages are similarly structured and have similar terms.) Finally, a multitude of endorsements, some of them following standard forms and some specially negotiated, would be included to complete the contract. The general material would always remain. These various pages in combination, together with any special endorsements, make up the liability policy.

Tinker, Comprehensive General Liability Insurance — Perspective and Overview, 25 Fed. of Ins. Counsel Q. 217 (1975), seeks to give a comprehensive overview of the 1973 policy, and may prove useful for some purposes.

The following excerpts from the 1973 Standard GCL policy should be compared with those from the 1966 policy. Section C(1). Note that "damages" is no longer defined. Should it be?

> **"bodily injury"** means bodily injury, sickness or disease sustained by any person which occurs during the policy period.
>
> **"damages"** [is not defined].
>
> **"occurrence"** means an accident, including continuous or repeated exposure to conditions, which results in bodily injury or property damage neither expected nor intended from the standpoint of the insured.
>
> **"property damage"** means (1) physical injury to or destruction of tangible property which occurs during the policy period, including the loss of use thereof at any time resulting therefrom, or (2) loss of use of tangible property which has not been physically injured or destroyed provided such loss of use is caused by an occurrence during the policy period.

The coverage language is the same as in the 1966 policy. Additional changes in policy forms have been made since 1973 to respond to difficulties the cases have made apparent. The following contemporary CGL policy is included as an example of those likely to appear more and more in new litigation. This one is based generally on the 1973 policy but with numerous and major changes. It will be useful to study the entire form, noting in particular the changes made in the crucial definitions and key clauses. The form should be referred to repeatedly as the cases in this chapter are read, to see if this particular form would have resulted in a different decision in each case.

COMMERCIAL GENERAL LIABILITY DECLARATIONS

POLICY NO. _____

COMPANY NAME AREA	PRODUCER NAME AREA

NAMED INSURED _____

MAILING ADDRESS _____

POLICY PERIOD: From _____ to _____ at _____

12:01 A.M. Standard Time at your mailing address shown above.

IN RETURN FOR THE PAYMENT OF THE PREMIUM, AND SUBJECT TO ALL THE TERMS OF THIS POLICY, WE AGREE WITH YOU TO PROVIDE THE INSURANCE AS STATED IN THIS POLICY.

LIMITS OF INSURANCE

GENERAL AGGREGATE LIMIT (Other Than Products—Completed Operations)	$ _____
PRODUCTS-COMPLETED OPERATIONS AGGREGATE LIMIT	$ _____
PERSONAL & ADVERTISING INJURY LIMIT	$ _____
EACH OCCURRENCE LIMIT	$ _____
FIRE DAMAGE LIMIT	$ _____ ANY ONE FIRE
MEDICAL EXPENSE LIMIT	$ _____ ANY ONE PERSON

RETROACTIVE DATE (CG 00 02 only)

Coverage A of this insurance does not apply to "bodily injury" or "property damage" which occurs before the Retroactive Date, if any, shown below

Retroactive Date: _____

(Enter Date or "None" if no Retroactive Date applies.)

Form of Business:

☐ Individual
☐ Joint Venture
☐ Partnership
☐ Organization (Other than Partnership or Joint Venture)

Business Description:

Location of All Premises You Own, Rent or Occupy:

CLASSIFICATION	CODE NO.	PREMIUM BASIS	RATE	ADVANCE PREMIUM	
				PR/CO	ALL OTHER
				$	$
			TOTAL	$	$

Premium shown is payable: $ _____ at inception.

ENDORSEMENTS ATTACHED TO THIS POLICY: IL 00 21 11 85 — Broad Form Nuclear Exclusion

COUNTERSIGNED _____ **BY** _____

(Date)   (Authorized Representative)

NOTE: OFFICERS' FACSIMILE SIGNATURES MAY BE INSERTED HERE, ON THE POLICY COVER OR ELSEWHERE AT THE COMPANY'S OPTION

COMMERCIAL GENERAL LIABILITY COVERAGE FORM

Various provisions in this policy restrict coverage. Read the entire policy carefully to determine rights, duties and what is and is not covered.

Throughout this policy the words "you" and "your" refer to the Named Insured shown in the Declarations, and any other person or organization qualifying as a Named Insured under this policy. The words "we," "us" and "our" refer to the company providing this insurance.

The word "insured" means any person or organization qualifying as such under WHO IS AN INSURED (SECTION II).

Other words and phrases that appear in quotation marks have special meaning. Refer to DEFINITIONS (SECTION V).

SECTION I - COVERAGES

COVERAGE A. BODILY INJURY AND PROPERTY DAMAGE LIABILITY

1. Insuring Agreement.

a. We will pay those sums that the insured becomes legally obligated to pay as damages because of "bodily injury" or "property damage" to which this insurance applies. We will have the right and duty to defend any "suit" seeking those damages. We may at our discretion investigate any "occurrence" and settle any claim or "suit" that may result. But:

c. Damages because of "bodily injury" include damages claimed by any person or organization for care, loss of services or death resulting at any time from the "bodily injury."

2. Exclusions.

This insurance does not apply to:

a. "Bodily injury" or "property damage" expected or intended from the standpoint of the insured. This exclusion does not apply to "bodily injury" resulting from the use of reasonable force to protect persons or property.

b. "Bodily injury" or "property damage" for which the insured is obligated to pay damages by reason of the assumption of liability in a contract or agreement. This exclusion does not apply to liability for damages:

(1) Assumed in a contract or agreement that is an "insured contract," provided the "bodily injury" or "property damage" occurs subsequent to the execution of the contract or agreement; or

(2) That the insured would have in the absence of the contract or agreement.

c. "Bodily injury" or "property damage" for which any insured may be held liable by reason of:

266

(1) The amount we will pay for damages is limited as described in LIMITS OF INSURANCE (SECTION III); and

(2) Our right and duty to defend end when we have used up the applicable limit of insurance in the payment of judgments or settlements under Coverages A or B or medical expenses under Coverage C.

No other obligation or liability to pay sums or perform acts or services is covered unless explicitly provided for under SUPPLEMENTARY PAYMENTS - COVERAGES A AND B.

b. This insurance applies to "bodily injury" and "property damage" only if:

(1) The "bodily injury" or "property damage" is caused by an "occurrence" that takes place in the "coverage territory;" and

(2) The "bodily injury" or "property damage" occurs during the policy period.

(1) Causing or contributing to the intoxication of any person;

(2) The furnishing of alcoholic beverages to a person under the legal drinking age or under the influence of alcohol; or

(3) Any statute, ordinance or regulation relating to the sale, gift, distribution or use of alcoholic beverages.

This exclusion applies only if you are in the business of manufacturing, distributing, selling, serving or furnishing alcoholic beverages.

d. Any obligation of the insured under a workers' compensation, disability benefits or unemployment compensation law or any similar law.

e. "Bodily injury" to:

(1) An employee of the insured arising out of and in the course of employment by the insured; or

(2) The spouse, child, parent, brother or sister of that employee as a consequence of (1) above.

This exclusion applies:

(1) Whether the insured may be liable as an employer or in any other capacity; and

(2) To any obligation to share damages with or repay someone else who must pay damages because of the injury.

This exclusion does not apply to liability assumed by the insured under an "insured contract."

f. (1) "Bodily injury" or "property damage" arising out of the actual, alleged or threatened discharge, dispersal, seepage, migration, release or escape of pollutants:

(d) At or from any premises, site or location on which any insured or any contractors or subcontractors working directly or indirectly on any insured's behalf are performing operations:

(i) if the pollutants are brought on or to the premises, site or location in connection with such operations by such insured, contractor or subcontractor; or

(ii) if the operations are to test for, monitor, clean up, remove, contain, treat, detoxify or neutralize, or in any way respond to, or assess the effects of pollutants.

Subparagraphs (a) and (d)(i) do not apply to "bodily injury" or "property damage" arising out of heat, smoke or fumes from a hostile fire.

As used in this exclusion, a hostile fire means one which becomes uncontrollable or breaks out from where it was intended to be.

(2) Any loss, cost or expense arising out of any:

(a) At or from any premises, site or location which is or was at any time owned or occupied by, or rented or loaned to, any insured;

(b) At or from any premises, site or location which is or was at any time used by or for any insured or others for the handling, storage, disposal, processing or treatment of waste;

(c) Which are or were at any time transported, handled, stored, treated, disposed of, or processed as waste by or for any insured or any person or organization for whom you may be legally responsible; or

(a) Request, demand or order that any insured or others test for, monitor, clean up, remove, contain, treat, detoxify or neutralize, or in any way respond to, or assess the effects of pollutants; or

(b) Claim or suit by or on behalf of a governmental authority for damages because of testing for, monitoring, cleaning up, removing, containing, treating, detoxifying or neutralizing, or in any way responding to, or assessing the effects of pollutants.

Pollutants means any solid, liquid, gaseous or thermal irritant or contaminant, including smoke, vapor, soot, fumes, acids, alkalis, chemicals and waste. Waste includes materials to be recycled, reconditioned or reclaimed.

g. "Bodily injury" or "property damage" arising out of the ownership, maintenance, use or entrustment to others of any aircraft, "auto" or watercraft owned or operated by or rented or loaned to any insured. Use includes operation and "loading or unloading."

This exclusion does not apply to:

(1) A watercraft while ashore on premises you own or rent;

(2) A watercraft you do not own that is:

  (a) Less than 26 feet long; and

  (b) Not being used to carry persons or property for a charge;

(3) Parking an "auto" on, or on the ways next to, premises you own or rent, provided the "auto" is not owned by or rented or loaned to you or the insured;

(4) Liability assumed under any "insured contract" for the ownership, maintenance or use of aircraft or watercraft; or

(5) "Bodily injury" or "property damage" arising out of the operation of any of the equipment listed in paragraph f.(2) or f.(3) of the definition of "mobile equipment" (Section V.8.).

h. "Bodily injury" or "property damage" arising out of:

(1) The transportation of "mobile equipment" by an "auto" owned or operated by or rented or loaned to any insured; or

(5) That particular part of real property on which you or any contractors or subcontractors working directly or indirectly on your behalf are performing operations, if the "property damage" arises out of those operations; or

(6) That particular part of any property that must be restored, repaired or replaced because "your work" was incorrectly performed on it.

Paragraph (2) of this exclusion does not apply if the premises are "your work" and were never occupied, rented or held for rental by you.

Paragraphs (3), (4), (5) and (6) of this exclusion do not apply to liability assumed under a sidetrack agreement.

Paragraph (6) of this exclusion does not apply to "property damage" included in the "products-completed operations hazard."

k. "Property damage" to "your product" arising out of it or any part of it.

l. "Property damage" to "your work" arising out of it or any part of it and included in the "products-completed operations hazard."

(2) The use of "mobile equipment" in, or while in practice or preparation for, a prearranged racing, speed or demolition contest or in any stunting activity.

i. "Bodily injury" or "property damage" due to war, whether or not declared, or any act or condition incident to war. War includes civil war, insurrection, rebellion or revolution. This exclusion applies only to liability assumed under a contract or agreement.

j. "Property damage" to:

(1) Property you own, rent, or occupy;

(2) Premises you sell, give away or abandon, if the "property damage" arises out of any part of those premises;

(3) Property loaned to you;

(4) Personal property in the care, custody or control of the insured;

This exclusion does not apply if the damaged work or the work out of which the damage arises was performed on your behalf by a subcontractor.

m. "Property damage" to "impaired property" or property that has not been physically injured, arising out of:

(1) A defect, deficiency, inadequacy or dangerous condition in "your product" or "your work;" or

(2) A delay or failure by you or anyone acting on your behalf to perform a contract or agreement in accordance with its terms.

This exclusion does not apply to the loss of use of other property arising out of sudden and accidental physical injury to "your product" or "your work" after it has been put to its intended use.

n. Damages claimed for any loss, cost or expense incurred by you or others for the loss of use, withdrawal, recall, inspection, repair, replacement, adjustment, removal or disposal of:

271

(1) "Your product;"

(2) "Your work;" or

(3) "Impaired property;"

if such product, work, or property is withdrawn or recalled from the market or from use by any person or organization because of a known or suspected defect, deficiency, inadequacy or dangerous condition in it.

Exclusions c. through n. do not apply to damage by fire to premises rented to you. A separate limit of insurance applies to this coverage as described in LIMITS OF INSURANCE (SECTION III).

COVERAGE B. PERSONAL AND ADVERTISING INJURY LIABILITY

1. Insuring Agreement.

a. We will pay those sums that the insured becomes legally obligated to pay as damages because of "personal injury" or "advertising injury" to which this coverage part applies. We will have the right and duty to defend any "suit" seeking those damages. We may at our discretion investigate any "occurrence" or offense and settle any claim or "suit" that may result. But:

(1) The amount we will pay for damages is

b. This insurance applies to:

(1) "Personal injury" caused by an offense arising out of your business, excluding advertising, publishing, broadcasting or telecasting done by or for you;

(2) "Advertising injury" caused by an offense committed in the course of advertising your goods, products or services;

but only if the offense was committed in the "coverage territory" during the policy period.

2. Exclusions.

This insurance does not apply to:

a. "Personal injury" or "advertising injury:"

(1) Arising out of oral or written publication of material, if done by or at the direction of the insured with knowledge of its falsity;

(2) Arising out of oral or written publication of material whose first publication took place before the beginning of the policy period;

(3) Arising out of the willful violation of a penal statute or ordinance committed by or with the consent of the insured; or

(4) For which the insured has assumed liability

limited as described in LIMITS OF IN-SURANCE (SECTION III); and

(2) Our right and duty to defend end when we have used up the applicable limit of insurance in the payment of judgments or settlements under Coverage A or B or medical expenses under Coverage C.

No other obligation or liability to pay sums or perform acts or services is covered unless explicitly provided for under SUPPLEMENTARY PAYMENTS - COVERAGES A AND B.

in a contract or agreement. This exclusion does not apply to liability for damages that the insured would have in the absence of the contract or agreement.

b. "Advertising injury" arising out of:

(1) Breach of contract, other than misappropriation of advertising ideas under an implied contract;

CG 00 01 11 88

□

273

(2) The failure of goods, products or services to conform with advertised quality or performance;

(3) The wrong description of the price of goods, products or services; or

(4) An offense committed by an insured whose business is advertising, broadcasting, publishing or telecasting.

COVERAGE C. MEDICAL PAYMENTS

1. Insuring Agreement.

a. We will pay medical expenses as described below for "bodily injury" caused by an accident:

(1) On premises you own or rent;

(2) On ways next to premises you own or rent; or

(3) Because of your operations;

provided that:

(1) The accident takes place in the "coverage territory" and during the policy period;

(2) The expenses are incurred and reported to us within one year of the date of the accident; and

(3) The injured person submits to examination,

(3) Necessary ambulance, hospital, professional nursing and funeral services.

2. Exclusions.

We will not pay expenses for "bodily injury:"

a. To any insured.

b. To a person hired to do work for or on behalf of any insured or a tenant of any insured.

c. To a person injured on that part of premises you own or rent that the person normally occupies.

d. To a person, whether or not an employee of any insured, if benefits for the "bodily injury" are payable or must be provided under a workers' compensation or disability benefits law or a similar law.

e. To a person injured while taking part in athletics.

f. Included within the "products-completed operations hazard."

g. Excluded under Coverage A.

h. Due to war, whether or not declared, or any act or condition incident to war. War includes civil war, insurrection, rebellion or revolution.

SUPPLEMENTARY PAYMENTS - COVERAGES A AND B

274

at our expense, by physicians of our choice as often as we reasonably require.

b. We will make these payments regardless of fault. These payments will not exceed the applicable limit of insurance. We will pay reasonable expenses for:

(1) First aid at the time of an accident;

(2) Necessary medical, surgical, x-ray and dental services, including prosthetic devices; and

We will pay, with respect to any claim or "suit" we defend:

1. All expenses we incur.

2. Up to $250 for cost of bail bonds required because of accidents or traffic law violations arising out of the use of any vehicle to which the Bodily Injury Liability Coverage applies. We do not have to furnish these bonds.

3. The cost of bonds to release attachments, but only for bond amounts within the applicable limit of insurance. We do not have to furnish these bonds.

CG 00 01 11 88

□ □

275

COMMERCIAL GENERAL LIABILITY
COVERAGE FORM

4. All reasonable expenses incurred by the insured at our request to assist us in the investigation or defense of the claim or "suit," including actual loss of earnings up to $100 a day because of time off from work.

5. All costs taxed against the insured in the "suit."

6. Prejudgment interest awarded against the insured on that part of the judgment we pay. If we make an offer to pay the applicable limit of insurance, we will not pay any prejudgment interest based on that period of time after the offer.

7. All interest on the full amount of any judgment that accrues after entry of the judgment and before we have paid, offered to pay, or deposited in court the part of the judgment that is within the applicable limit of insurance.

These payments will not reduce the limits of insurance.

SECTION II - WHO IS AN INSURED

1. If you are designated in the Declarations as:

a. An individual, you and your spouse are insureds, but only with respect to the conduct of a business of which you are the sole owner.

b. A partnership or joint venture, you are an insured. Your members, your partners, and their spouses are also insureds, but only with re-

provide professional health care services; or

(3) "Property damage" to property owned or occupied by or rented or loaned to that employee, any of your other employees, or any of your partners or members (if you are a partnership or joint venture).

b. Any person (other than your employee), or any organization while acting as your real estate manager.

c. Any person or organization having proper temporary custody of your property if you die, but only:

(1) With respect to liability arising out of the maintenance or use of that property; and

(2) Until your legal representative has been appointed.

d. Your legal representative if you die, but only with respect to duties as such. That representative will have all your rights and duties under this Coverage Part.

3. With respect to "mobile equipment" registered in your name under any motor vehicle registration law, any person is an insured while driving such equipment along a public highway with your permission. Any other person or organization re-

276

spect to the conduct of your business.

c. An organization other than a partnership or joint venture, you are an insured. Your executive officers and directors are insureds, but only with respect to their duties as your officers or directors. Your stockholders are also insureds, but only with respect to their liability as stockholders.

2. Each of the following is also an insured:

a. Your employees, other than your executive officers, but only for acts within the scope of their employment by you. However, no employee is an insured for:

(1) "Bodily injury" or "personal injury" to you or to a co-employee while in the course of his or her employment, or the spouse, child, parent, brother or sister of that co-employee as a consequence of such "bodily injury" or "personal injury," or for any obligation to share damages with or repay someone else who must pay damages because of the injury; or

(2) "Bodily injury" or "personal injury" arising out of his or her providing or failing to

sponsible for the conduct of such person is also an insured, but only with respect to liability arising out of the operation of the equipment, and only if no other insurance of any kind is available to that person or organization for this liability. However, no person or organization is an insured with respect to:

a. "Bodily injury" to a co-employee of the person driving the equipment; or

b. "Property damage" to property owned by, rented to, in the charge of or occupied by you or the employer of any person who is an insured under this provision.

4. Any organization you newly acquire or form, other than a partnership or joint venture, and over which you maintain ownership or majority interest, will qualify as a Named Insured if there is no other similar insurance available to that organization. However:

a. Coverage under this provision is afforded only until the 90th day after you acquire or form the organization or the end of the policy period, whichever is earlier;

       CG 00 01 11 88   □

277

b. Coverage A does not apply to "bodily injury" or "property damage" that occurred before you acquired or formed the organization; and

c. Coverage B does not apply to "personal injury" or "advertising injury" arising out of an offense committed before you acquired or formed the organization.

No person or organization is an insured with respect to the conduct of any current or past partnership or joint venture that is not shown as a Named Insured in the Declarations.

SECTION III - LIMITS OF INSURANCE

1. The Limits of Insurance shown in the Declarations and the rules below fix the most we will pay regardless of the number of:

   a. Insureds;

   b. Claims made or "suits" brought; or

   c. Persons or organizations making claims or bringing "suits."

2. The General Aggregate Limit is the most we will pay for the sum of:

   a. Medical expenses under Coverage C;

   b. Damages under Coverage A, except damages because of "bodily injury" or "property damage" included in the "products-completed

6. Subject to 5. above, the Fire Damage Limit is the most we will pay under Coverage A for damages because of "property damage" to premises rented to you arising out of any one fire.

7. Subject to 5. above, the Medical Expense Limit is the most we will pay under Coverage C for all medical expenses because of "bodily injury" sustained by any one person.

The limits of this Coverage Part apply separately to each consecutive annual period and to any remaining period of less than 12 months, starting with the beginning of the policy period shown in the Declarations, unless the policy period is extended after issuance for an additional period of less than 12 months. In that case, the additional period will be deemed part of the last preceding period for purposes of determining the Limits of Insurance.

SECTION IV - COMMERCIAL GENERAL LIABILITY CONDITIONS

1. **Bankruptcy.**

   Bankruptcy or insolvency of the insured or of the insured's estate will not relieve us of our obligations under this Coverage Part.

2. **Duties In The Event Of Occurrence, Claim Or Suit.**

278

operations hazard;" and

c. Damages under Coverage B.

3. The Products-Completed Operations Aggregate Limit is the most we will pay under Coverage A for damages because of "bodily injury" and "property damage" included in the "products-completed operations hazard."

4. Subject to 2. above, the Personal and Advertising Injury Limit is the most we will pay under Coverage B for the sum of all damages because of all "personal injury" and all "advertising injury" sustained by any one person or organization.

5. Subject to 2. or 3. above, whichever applies, the Each Occurrence Limit is the most we will pay for the sum of:

a. Damages under Coverage A; and

b. Medical expenses under Coverage C

because of all "bodily injury" and "property damage" arising out of any one "occurrence."

a. You must see to it that we are notified as soon as practicable of an "occurrence" or an offense which may result in a claim. To the extent possible, notice should include:

(1) How, when and where the "occurrence" or offense took place;

(2) The names and addresses of any injured persons and witnesses; and

(3) The nature and location of any injury or damage arising out of the "occurrence" or offense.

b. If a claim is made or "suit" is brought against any insured, you must:

(1) Immediately record the specifics of the claim or "suit" and the date received; and

(2) Notify us as soon as practicable.

You must see to it that we receive written notice of the claim or "suit" as soon as practicable.

COMMERCIAL GENERAL LIABILITY
COVERAGE FORM

c. You and any other involved insured must:

(1) Immediately send us copies of any demands, notices, summonses or legal papers received in connection with the claim or "suit;"

(2) Authorize us to obtain records and other information;

(3) Cooperate with us in the investigation, settlement or defense of the claim or "suit;" and

(4) Assist us, upon our request, in the enforcement of any right against any person or organization which may be liable to the insured because of injury or damage to which this insurance may also apply.

d. No insureds will, except at their own cost, voluntarily make a payment, assume any obligation, or incur any expense, other than for first aid, without our consent.

3. Legal Action Against Us.

No person or organization has a right under this Coverage Part:

a. To join us as a party or otherwise bring us into a "suit" asking for damages from an insured; or

unless any of the other insurance is also primary. Then, we will share with all that other insurance by the method described in c. below.

b. Excess Insurance

This insurance is excess over any of the other insurance, whether primary, excess, contingent or on any other basis:

(1) That is Fire, Extended Coverage, Builder's Risk, Installation Risk or similar coverage for "your work;"

(2) That is Fire insurance for premises rented to you; or

(3) If the loss arises out of the maintenance or use of aircraft, "autos" or watercraft to the extent not subject to Exclusion g. of Coverage A (Section I).

When this insurance is excess, we will have no duty under Coverage A or B to defend any claim or "suit" that any other insurer has a duty to defend. If no other insurer defends, we will undertake to do so, but we will be entitled to the insured's rights against all those other insurers.

When this insurance is excess over other in-

280

b. To sue us on this Coverage Part unless all of its terms have been fully complied with.

A person or organization may sue us to recover on an agreed settlement or on a final judgment against an insured obtained after an actual trial; but we will not be liable for damages that are not payable under the terms of this Coverage Part or that are in excess of the applicable limit of insurance. An agreed settlement means a settlement and release of liability signed by us, the insured and the claimant or the claimant's legal representative.

4. **Other Insurance.**

If other valid and collectible insurance is available to the insured for a loss we cover under Coverages A or B of this Coverage Part, our obligations are limited as follows:

a. Primary Insurance

This insurance is primary except when b. below applies. If this insurance is primary, our obligations are not affected

surance, we will pay only our share of the amount of the loss, if any, that exceeds the sum of:

(1) The total amount that all such other insurance would pay for the loss in the absence of this insurance; and

(2) The total of all deductible and self-insured amounts under all that other insurance.

We will share the remaining loss, if any, with any other insurance that is not described in this Excess Insurance provision and was not bought specifically to apply in excess of the Limits of Insurance shown in the Declarations of this Coverage Part.

c. Method of Sharing

If all of the other insurance permits contribution by equal shares, we will follow this method also. Under this approach each insurer contributes equal amounts until it has paid its applicable limit of insurance or none of the loss remains, whichever comes first.

If any of the other insurance does not permit contribution by equal shares, we will contribute by limits. Under this method, each insurer's share is based on the ratio of its applicable limit of insurance to the total applicable limits of insurance of all insurers.

5. Premium Audit.

a. We will compute all premiums for this Coverage Part in accordance with our rules and rates.

b. Premium shown in this Coverage Part as advance premium is a deposit premium only. At the close of each audit period we will compute the earned premium for that period. Audit premiums are due and payable on notice to the first Named Insured. If the sum of the advance and audit premiums paid for the policy term is greater than the earned premium, we will return the excess to the first Named Insured.

c. The first Named Insured must keep records of the information we need for premium computation, and send us copies at such times as we may request.

6. Representations.

By accepting this policy, you agree:

Part, those rights are transferred to us. The insured must do nothing after loss to impair them. At our request, the insured will bring "suit" or transfer those rights to us and help us enforce them.

9. When We Do Not Renew.

If we decide not to renew this Coverage Part, we will mail or deliver to the first Named Insured shown in the Declarations written notice of the nonrenewal not less than 30 days before the expiration date.

If notice is mailed, proof of mailing will be sufficient proof of notice.

SECTION V - DEFINITIONS

1. "Advertising injury" means injury arising out of one or more of the following offenses:

a. Oral or written publication of material that slanders or libels a person or organization or disparages a person's or organization's goods, products or services;

b. Oral or written publication of material that violates a person's right of privacy;

c. Misappropriation of advertising ideas or style of doing business; or

d. Infringement of copyright, title or slogan.

282

a. The statements in the Declarations are accurate and complete;

b. Those statements are based upon representations you made to us; and

c. We have issued this policy in reliance upon your representations.

7. Separation Of Insureds.

Except with respect to the Limits of Insurance, and any rights or duties specifically assigned in this Coverage Part to the first Named Insured, this insurance applies:

a. As if each Named Insured were the only Named Insured; and

b. Separately to each insured against whom claim is made or "suit" is brought.

8. Transfer Of Rights Of Recovery Against Others To Us.

If the insured has rights to recover all or part of any payment we have made under this Coverage

2. "Auto" means a land motor vehicle, trailer or semitrailer designed for travel on public roads, including any attached machinery or equipment. But "auto" does not include "mobile equipment."

3. "Bodily injury" means bodily injury, sickness or disease sustained by a person, including death resulting from any of these at any time.

4. "Coverage territory" means:

a. The United States of America (including its territories and possessions), Puerto Rico and Canada;

b. International waters or airspace, provided the injury or damage does not occur in the course of travel or transportation to or from any place not included in a. above; or

c. All parts of the world if:

(1) The injury or damage arises out of:

(a) Goods or products made or sold by you in the territory described in a. above; or

(b) The activities of a person whose home is in the territory described in a. above, but is away for a short time on your business; and

(2) The insured's responsibility to pay damages is determined in a "suit" on the merits, in the territory described in a. above or in a settlement we agree to.

5. "Impaired property" means tangible property, other than "your product" or "your work," that cannot be used or is less useful because:

a. It incorporates "your product" or "your work" that is known or thought to be defective, deficient, inadequate or dangerous; or

b. You have failed to fulfill the terms of a contract or agreement;

if such property can be restored to use by:

a. The repair, replacement, adjustment or removal of "your product" or "your work;" or

b. Your fulfilling the terms of the contract or agreement.

6. "Insured contract" means:

a. A lease of premises;

An "insured contract" does not include that part of any contract or agreement:

a. That indemnifies any person or organization for "bodily injury" or "property damage" arising out of construction or demolition operations, within 50 feet of any railroad property and affecting any railroad bridge or trestle, tracks, road-beds, tunnel, underpass or crossing;

b. That indemnifies an architect, engineer or surveyor for injury or damage arising out of:

(1) Preparing, approving or failing to prepare or approve maps, drawings, opinions, reports, surveys, change orders, designs or specifications; or

(2) Giving directions or instructions, or failing to give them, if that is the primary cause of the injury or damage;

c. Under which the insured, if an architect, engineer or surveyor, assumes liability for an injury or damage arising out of the insured's rendering or failure to render professional services, including those listed in b. above and supervisory, inspection or engineering services; or

b. A sidetrack agreement;

c. Any easement or license agreement, except in connection with construction or demolition operations on or within 50 feet of a railroad;

d. An obligation, as required by ordinance, to indemnify a municipality, except in connection with work for a municipality;

e. An elevator maintenance agreement;

f. That part of any other contract or agreement pertaining to your business (including an indemnification of a municipality in connection with work performed for a municipality) under which you assume the tort liability of another party to pay for "bodily injury" or "property damage" to a third person or organization. Tort liability means a liability that would be imposed by law in the absence of any contract or agreement.

d. That indemnifies any person or organization for damage by fire to premises rented or loaned to you.

7. "Loading or unloading" means the handling of property:

a. After it is moved from the place where it is accepted for movement into or onto an aircraft, watercraft or "auto;"

b. While it is in or on an aircraft, watercraft or "auto;" or

c. While it is being moved from an aircraft, watercraft or "auto" to the place where it is finally delivered;

but "loading or unloading" does not include the movement of property by means of a mechanical device, other than a hand truck, that is not attached to the aircraft, watercraft or "auto."

8. "Mobile equipment" means any of the following types of land vehicles, including any attached machinery or equipment:

CG 00 01 11 88

285

a. Bulldozers, farm machinery, forklifts and other vehicles designed for use principally off public roads;

b. Vehicles maintained for use solely on or next to premises you own or rent;

c. Vehicles that travel on crawler treads;

d. Vehicles, whether self-propelled or not, maintained primarily to provide mobility to permanently mounted:

(1) Power cranes, shovels, loaders, diggers or drills; or

(2) Road construction or resurfacing equipment such as graders, scrapers or rollers;

e. Vehicles not described in a., b., c. or d. above that are not self-propelled and are maintained primarily to provide mobility to permanently attached equipment of the following types:

(1) Air compressors, pumps and generators, including spraying, welding, building cleaning, geophysical exploration, lighting and well servicing equipment; or

(2) Cherry pickers and similar devices used to raise or lower workers;

f. Vehicles not described in a., b., c. or d. above maintained primarily for purposes other than

10. "Personal injury" means injury, other than "bodily injury," arising out of one or more of the following offenses:

a. False arrest, detention or imprisonment;

b. Malicious prosecution;

c. The wrongful eviction from, wrongful entry into, or invasion of the right of private occupancy of a room, dwelling or premises that a person occupies by or on behalf of its owner, landlord or lessor;

d. Oral or written publication of material that slanders or libels a person or organization or disparages a person's or organization's goods, products or services; or

e. Oral or written publication of material that violates a person's right of privacy.

11. a. "Products-completed operations hazard" includes all "bodily injury" and "property damage" occurring away from premises you own or rent and arising out of "your product" or "your work" except:

(1) Products that are still in your physical possession; or

(2) Work that has not yet been completed or abandoned.

the transportation of persons or cargo.

However, self-propelled vehicles with the following types of permanently attached equipment are not "mobile equipment" but will be considered "autos:"

(1) Equipment designed primarily for:

(a) Snow removal;

(b) Road maintenance, but not construction or resurfacing;

(c) Street cleaning;

(2) Cherry pickers and similar devices mounted on automobile or truck chassis and used to raise or lower workers; and

(3) Air compressors, pumps and generators, including spraying, welding, building cleaning, geophysical exploration, lighting and well servicing equipment.

9. "Occurrence" means an accident, including continuous or repeated exposure to substantially the same general harmful conditions.

b. "Your work" will be deemed completed at the earliest of the following times:

(1) When all of the work called for in your contract has been completed.

(2) When all of the work to be done at the site has been completed if your contract calls for work at more than one site.

(3) When that part of the work done at a job site has been put to its intended use by any person or organization other than another contractor or subcontractor working on the same project.

Work that may need service, maintenance, correction, repair or replacement, but which is otherwise complete, will be treated as completed.

c. This hazard does not include "bodily injury" or "property damage" arising out of:

    (1) The transportation of property, unless the injury or damage arises out of a condition in or on a vehicle created by the "loading or unloading" of it;

    (2) The existence of tools, uninstalled equipment or abandoned or unused materials;

    (3) Products or operations for which the classification in this Coverage Part or in our manual of rules includes products or completed operations.

12. "Property damage" means:

  a. Physical injury to tangible property, including all resulting loss of use of that property. All such loss of use shall be deemed to occur at the time of the physical injury that caused it; or

  b. Loss of use of tangible property that is not physically injured. All such loss shall be deemed to occur at the time of the "occurrence" that caused it.

13. "Suit" means a civil proceeding in which damage because of "bodily injury," "property damage," "personal injury" or "advertising injury" to which this insurance applies are alleged. "Suit" includes:

  a. An arbitration proceeding in which such

  a. Any goods or products, other than real property, manufactured, sold, handled, distributed or disposed of by:

    (1) You;

    (2) Others trading under your name; or

    (3) A person or organization whose business or assets you have acquired; and

  b. Containers (other than vehicles), materials, parts or equipment furnished in connection with such goods or products.

"Your product" includes:

  a. Warranties or representations made at any time with respect to the fitness, quality, durability, performance or use of "your product;" and

  b. The providing of or failure to provide warnings or instructions.

"Your product" does not include vending machines or other property rented to or located for the use of others but not sold.

15. "Your work" means:

  a. Work or operations performed by you or on your behalf; and

  b. Materials, parts or equipment furnished in

damages are claimed and to which you must submit or do submit with our consent; or

b. Any other alternative dispute resolution proceeding in which such damages are claimed and to which you submit with our consent.

14. "Your product" means:

connection with such work or operations.

"Your work" includes:

a. Warranties or representations made at any time with respect to the fitness, quality, durability, performance or use of "your work;" and

b. The providing of or failure to provide warnings or instructions.

CG 00 01 11 88   □

D.   The Claims-Made Policy

The latest development in the evolution of the liability insurance policy is the *claims-made policy,* which in its simplest form insures against claims that are made during the policy period, no matter when the accident or occurrence and the damage resulting from it may have taken place. Ordinarily the detailed features vary somewhat from that simple model. For example, the policy may be written in terms of discovery of a potential claim (and provision of notice to the insurer) rather than the actual filing of a claim. Claims covered may be limited to those arising out of occurrences after a set date prior to inception, which is called the *retroactive date.* The retroactive date chosen is apt to be the date on which the present insurer originally went on the risk.

The most difficult problems yet encountered with the claims-made policy concern its linkage with the occurrence coverage that may have preceded it, and the problems for the insured if there is subsequently a voluntary or involuntary discontinuance of coverage, a shift back to an occurrence policy, or a change of insurer. Some of the problems termination would create can be solved or at least reduced by a provision allowing the policyholder to purchase *tail coverage,* which would cover claims made for a specified period into the future that arise out of occurrences before termination. Such coverage would be necessary, for example, for a professional such as a doctor who is terminating a practice and does not need coverage for on-going activity. Because of the discovery rule in applying the statute of limitations, claims in medical (and other) malpractice may be latent for decades. Even so, there would probably be few cases in which the doctor would not know fairly soon that "something" had happened that might someday produce a claim. The doctor might therefore be adequately protected under a discovery policy, plus reasonable tail coverage, rather than strict claims-made policy.

If an occurrence policy is followed by a claims-made policy issued by a different insurer, and a claim made after the change is based on an occurrence prior to or about the time of the change, controversy may arise between the two insurers. Imprecision in dating an occurrence is likely to be especially common in medical malpractice cases, where claims-made policies are particularly common. For an example, see St. Paul Fire & Marine Ins. Co. v. Vigilant Ins. Co., 724 F. Supp. 1173 (M.D.N.C. 1989).

SPARKS v. ST. PAUL INS. CO.

100 N.J. 325, 495 A.2d 406 (1985)

STEIN, J.

In this case, as in Zuckerman v. National Union Fire Ins. Co., 100 N.J. 304, 495 A.2d 395 (1985), which the Court also decides today, we consider the enforceability of certain coverage limitations contained in a "claims made" professional liability insurance policy issued by appellant St. Paul Insurance Company (St. Paul). The trial court and the Appellate Division refused to enforce the policy provision limiting coverage to claims and potential claims reported to St. Paul during the policy period. We granted the insurance company's petition for certification, 99 N.J. 211, 491 A.2d 706 (1984), in order to resolve the apparent conflict between the unreported Appellate Division decision in this case and the Appellate Division decision in *Zuckerman,* supra, 194 N.J. Super. 206, 476 A.2d 820 (1984), enforcing a similar provision in the "claims made" policy at issue in that case.

I

The material facts are not in dispute. In November, 1978, respondents, John and Carolyn Sparks, retained A. Raymond Guarriello, a New Jersey attorney, to represent them in connection with the sale of their residence. That transaction resulted in litigation between respondents and the prospective purchasers. In the course of that litigation, apparently due to Guarriello's negligence, Mr. and Mrs. Sparks failed to answer interrogatories. This resulted in an order entered in mid-October, 1979, suppressing the Sparks' answer and counter-claim. A default judgment for specific performance was entered against Mr. and Mrs. Sparks in February, 1980, and a money judgment for $18,899.08 was entered against them in May, 1981. It is not disputed that Guarriello's negligence was the proximate cause of the judgments against Mr. and Mrs. Sparks.

On November 6, 1976, appellant, St. Paul, issued Guarriello a one-year professional malpractice policy that was renewed for successive one-year periods, terminating on November 6, 1979. On September 27, 1979, St. Paul issued a substitute policy for one additional year that was to take effect on November 6, 1979. Guarriello failed to pay the premium and appellant sent Guarriello a notice cancelling the substitute policy, effective January 21, 1980. Between June and August of 1980, substituted counsel for respondents notified St. Paul of the underlying facts and demanded that the insurance company provide malpractice coverage with respect to Guarriello's negligence.

The policy issued to Guarriello in 1976 was denominated a "claims made" policy. A "Schedule" attached to the declaration page of the policy bore the following notice:

To Our Policyholders

This is a "claims made" Coverage Form. It only covers claims arising from the performance of professional services *subsequent to the retroactive date indicated* and then only to claims first made within the provisions of the Policy while this Coverage Form is in force. No coverage is afforded for claims first made after the termination of this insurance unless and to the extent that Reporting Endorsements are purchased in accordance with Condition 3 of this Coverage Form. Please review the Policy carefully. [Emphasis added.]

The retroactive date set forth in the policy was November 6, 1976, the same date as the effective date of coverage. Therefore, unlike the standard "claims made" policy that was involved in our decision in *Zuckerman,* supra, 100 N.J. at 307-309, 495 A.2d 395, St. Paul's policy provided no retroactive coverage whatsoever during its first year. In that year, the coverage provided by the policy applied only to errors and omissions that occurred during the policy year and were reported to the company within the policy year. During the two renewal years beginning November 6, 1977 and November 6, 1978, the policy afforded "retroactive" coverage for negligence that occurred subsequent to November 6, 1976.

In April, 1981, St. Paul rejected respondent's demand that it provide coverage for Guarriello's malpractice since the company received notice of the claim after the termination of the second renewal policy in November, 1979 and after the January, 1980 cancellation of the replacement policy for nonpayment of the premium. In June, 1981, Mr. and Mrs. Sparks obtained a $42,968.08 judgment against Guarriello based upon his malpractice.

The present action commenced in October, 1981. Mr. and Mrs. Sparks sought a declaratory judgment that the liability insurance policy issued by St. Paul was valid and enforceable to pay the judgment obtained against Guarriello. In August, 1983, St. Paul's motion for summary judgment was denied and in September, 1983, summary judgment was granted in favor of Mr. and Mrs. Sparks. That judgment was affirmed by the Appellate Division, which held "claims made" policies to be unenforceable as violative of public policy. . . .

In *Zuckerman,* supra, 100 N.J. at 311-313, 495 A.2d at 399, we discussed in detail the significant social utility of the "claims made" policy that has led to its supplanting the occurrence policy in the professional liability field. We noted that since the insurance company that issues an "occurrence" policy is exposed to a "tail" — that is, the lapse of time between the occurrence and the date on which the claim is made — there is considerable difficulty in accurately calculating underwriting risks and premiums with respect to perils that typically lead to long tail exposure. Moreover, claims asserted in the fields of professional malpractice, products liability, and environmental law often present the added difficulty of determining precisely when the actuating event "occurred" for the purpose of defining coverage. From the standpoint of the insured, there is the danger of inadequate coverage in cases in which claims are asserted long after the error or omission occurred, because inflationary factors lead to judgments that are higher than those originally contemplated when coverage was purchased years earlier. Id., 100 N.J. at 311-313, 495 A.2d at 399.

From the insurer's perspective, the clear advantage derived from a "claims made" policy is the limitation of liability to claims asserted during the policy period. This limitation enables insurers to calculate risks and premiums with greater precision. Although "claims made" policies provide coverage for errors and omissions occurring prior to the policy's inception, the elimination of exposure to claims filed after the policy expiration date enables companies to issue these policies at reduced premiums. *Zuckerman,* supra, 100 N.J. at 312-313, 495 A.2d at 399-400; J. Parker, "The Untimely Demise of the 'Claims Made' Insurance Form? A Critique of Stine v. Continental Casualty Co.," 1983 Det. C. L. Rev. 25, 73.

In *Zuckerman,* we observed that Courts throughout the country have upheld the validity of "claims made" policies. 100 N.J. at 313-314, 495 A.2d at 400. Although "claims made" policies have regularly been challenged on public policy grounds, the vast majority of courts that have considered these challenges have enforced the policies as written. . . .

We also reviewed in *Zuckerman,* supra, the commercial utility of "claims made" policies and scrutinized the terms of the policy at issue in that case. 100 N.J. at 311-313, 319, 495 A.2d at 399, 403. We concluded that there were "no considerations of public policy that would inhibit . . . enforcement of the 'claims made' policy issued to appellant [Zuckerman]." Id. at 321, 495 A.2d at 404. Similarly, we would not hesitate to enforce St. Paul's policy in this case if it comported with the generally accepted expectations of "claims made" insurance. The coverage provided by St. Paul's policy, however, materially diverges from customary "claims made" coverage in terms of its retroactive protection. It provides neither the prospective coverage typical of an "occurrence" policy, nor the retroactive coverage typical of a "claims made" policy. During the first policy year, coverage was limited to acts of malpractice that occurred, were discovered, and were reported to the insurance company during the same year. Although there was slight retroactive coverage during the second and third renewal years of the policy, the retroactive coverage was significantly more limited than that contemplated in the standard "claims made" policy. See S. Kroll, supra, 13 Forum at 843, 850, 854 (1978); D. Shand, " 'Claims Made' vs. 'Occurrence,' " 27 Int'l Ins. Monitor 269, 270, 273 (1974); D. Shand, "Is Your Policy on a 'Claims Made' Basis?," The Weekly Underwriter, Sept. 15, 1973, at 8; J. Parker, supra, 1983 Det. C. L. Rev. 25, 27 & n.3. . . .

We find that the contract of insurance sold by St. Paul to Guarriello does not conform to the objectively reasonable expectations of the insured and is violative of the public policy of this State. Although we held today in Zuckerman v. National Union Fire Ins. Co., supra, 100 N.J 304, 495 A.2d 395 (1985), that a "claims made" policy that fulfills the reasonable expectations of the insured with respect to the scope of coverage is valid and enforceable, the policy at issue here is substantially different from the standard "claims made" policy. Indeed, St. Paul's policy combines the worst features of "occurrence" and "claims made" policies and the best of neither. It provides neither the prospective coverage typical of an "occurrence" policy, nor the "retroactive" coverage typical of a "claims made" policy. During the first year that the policy was in force, it provided no retroactive coverage for occurrences prior to the effective date of the policy. Thus, it afforded the insured only minimal protection against professional liability claims. Only claims asserted during the policy year, based on negligence that occurred during the policy year, and that were subsequently communicated to the company during the policy year were under the umbrella of coverage.

The realities of professional malpractice, however, suggest that it would be the rare instance in which an error occurred and was discovered with sufficient time to report it to the insurance company, all within a twelve-month period. The victims of professional malpractice are frequently unaware of any negligence until their injury becomes manifest long after the error or omission was committed.

Our review of the use of "claims made" policies in the professional liability field demonstrates that a policy that defines the scope of coverage so narrowly is incompatible with the objectively reasonable expectations of purchasers of professional liability coverage. We assume that there are vast numbers of professionals covered by "claims made" policies who are unaware of the basic distinction between their policies and the traditional "occurrence" policy. See Middle Dept. Inspection Agency v. Home Ins. Co., 154 N.J. Super. 49, 55-56, 380 A.2d 1165 (App. Div. 1977), *cert. denied*, 76 N.J. 234, 386 A.2d 858 (1978). However, those professionals covered by "claims made" policies who do understand how their policies differ from "occurrence" policies would expect that in return for the loss of prospective coverage provided by "occurrence" policies, they would be afforded reasonable retroactive coverage by their "claims made" policies. A leading proponent of "claims made" coverage has characterized this *quid pro quo* — the relinquishment of prospective coverage in return for retroactive coverage — as *"the essential* trade-off inherent in the concept of 'claims-made' insurance." S. Kroll, supra, 13 Forum at 854 (emphasis added); see J. Parker, supra, 1983 Det. C. L. Rev. at 27 & n.3.

We do not decide in this case the precise standard by which the reasonableness of retroactive coverage is to be measured. We hold, however, that where there has been no proof of factual circumstances that would render such limited retroactive coverage both reasonable and expected,[4] a "claims made" policy that affords no retroactive coverage whatsoever during its initial year of issuance does not accord with the objectively reasonable expectations of the purchasers of professional liability insurance. The fact that subsequent renewals of that policy provide minimal retroactive coverage, i.e., to the effective date of the original policy, does not cure the significant deficiency inherent in the underlying policy. . . .

Accordingly, we hold that under these circumstances, the claim asserted by respondents against Guarriello, to the extent that it is based upon negligence that occurred during the policy period, is within the coverage afforded by appellant's policy. The notice to appellant between June and August, 1980, is sufficient to invoke that coverage. Accordingly, we modify and affirm the judgment of the Appellate Division and remand the matter to the trial court to consider, in accordance with the principles set forth in this opinion, any unresolved issues with respect to the specific coverage afforded by St. Paul's policy for the money judgment recovered against Guarriello. We do not retain jurisdiction.

Notes and Questions

1. Note that New Jersey follows the reasonable expectations doctrine.

2. If you were sitting on the *Sparks* case *in New Jersey,* would you join the opinion of Justice Stein, or would you dissent? If the latter, on

---

4. "Claims made" policies with no retroactive coverage might be appropriate in certain contexts. For example, such policies might properly be offered at a reduced premium to the professional in his very first year of practice, or to the professional who changes from "occurrence" to "claims made" protection. Nothing in the record before us suggests that this is such a case.

what grounds would you dissent? If not, what additional facts would change your vote?

3. Oettle & Howard, *Zuckerman* and *Sparks:* The Validity of "Claims Made" Insurance Policies as a Function of Retroactive Coverage, 21 Tort & Ins. L.J. 659 (1986), is a casenote reviewing those two cases.

4. For an explanation of the sequence of coverages in *Sparks,* written by counsel who represented the St. Paul, see Catenacci, *Sparks* Revisited: Sparks v. St. Paul Insurance Co., 23 Tort & Ins. L.J. 707 (1988). The most important facts apparently not known to the Supreme Court in *Sparks* are (1) that the plaintiff had had a St. Paul occurrence policy for six continuous years prior to the issuance of the claims-made policy, and (2) that the St. Paul offered different degrees of retroactive coverage for different premium rates, in five different rate steps.

5. If an insurer is hemorrhaging from inadequately priced professional liability insurance sold over a long period, can it better stem its losses by changing from an occurrence to a claims-made form, or by withdrawing from the line of insurance?

6. On what terms should an insurer be willing to agree to a retroactive date that is earlier than the date it went on the risk? If the insured was previously covered by an occurrence policy written by a different company, what would be the result of insertion of a retroactive date that preceded the date the new company went on the risk?

E.   Coverage Provisions

The coverage of comprehensive general liability is broad but far from unlimited. The policy applies only to bodily injury and property damage, not to other kinds of harms. Special endorsements, or such scheduled coverages as personal injury liability, may broaden the coverage. The latter adds coverage for libel and false imprisonment, for example. In the policy reproduced above, personal injury liability is included as an integral part of the coverage.

A number of exclusions follow. Automobile liability is carefully excluded by Exclusion (g). A separate policy is then necessary to provide automobile liability coverage. Workers compensation is excluded by Exclusion (e) because it too is issued in a separate policy. The other exclusions, though narrower, are also important for any policyholder exposed to the excluded hazards. Some of them can be insured specially.

1. The Meaning of "Occurrence"

The 1966 and 1973 policy provisions should be examined to ascertain what must happen within the policy period in order for there to be an occurrence identified with that period. If the buyer of a product manufactured during the policy period is injured after the policy period expires, is the injury covered by the 1966 policy? By the 1973 policy? Evanston Ins. Co. v. International Mfg. Co., 641 F. Supp. 733 (D. Wyo. 1986), illustrates the problem. Purporting to follow California law, the federal court held that the insurance covered the manufacturer, even though the injury occurred after the policy period had expired. Did the court read the policy correctly? If the policyholder has insurance both at the time of manufacture and of injury, but in different companies at the two times, which insurer must defend and indemnify? If the manufacture and the sale are in different policy periods, how should the result differ, if at all?

TRANSPORT INS. CO. v. LEE WAY MOTOR FREIGHT

487 F. Supp. 1325 (N.D. Tex. 1980)

SANDERS, District Judge.

Plaintiff Transport Insurance Company ("Transport") sues its insured, Defendant Lee Way Motor Freight, Inc. ("Lee Way"), for declaratory judgment pursuant to Title 28, United States Code §2201 in order to determine the extent of Transport's liability under excess umbrella insurance policies that provide coverage for damages that Lee Way must pay on account of discrimination.

In a previous suit, *United States v. Lee Way*, Lee Way was found to have engaged in a pattern and practice of race discrimination and ordered to pay over $1.8 million in damages to individual discriminatees. In the present case Transport asks this Court to determine (1) whether the liability imposed upon Lee Way in the previous suit resulted from a single occurrence, a separate occurrence as to each of the four terminal locations involved, or a separate occurrence as to each of the individual discriminatees, (2) whether certain back-pay awards imposed upon Lee Way fell within or outside of the applicable policy coverages, and (3) whether (and how) Lee Way's costs of defending the discrimination suit should be apportioned between Transport and Lee Way.

The Court finds and concludes (1) that the pattern and practice of discrimination found by the court in *United States v. Lee Way* constitutes "one occurrence" as that term is used in the insurance policies; (2) that back pay for the period prior to the inception of the policies on

January 1, 1967, is not covered by the policies but back pay for all discriminatees after January 1, 1967, is within the policy coverage; and (3) that Lee Way's defense costs in *United States v. Lee Way* are fully reimbursable and should not be apportioned.

I. Background

A. *United States v. Lee Way*

In June of 1972, the United States filed suit against Lee Way and two labor unions, alleging that they had engaged in and were engaging in a pattern and practice of discrimination in employment. United States v. Lee Way Motor Freight, Inc., et al., W.D. Okla., Civil Action No. 72-445. Following several months of trial, the district court issued its findings and conclusions December 27, 1973, in which it found and concluded that Lee Way had engaged in a pattern and practice of employment discrimination. The court determined that Lee Way had discriminated on the grounds of race in its hiring practices and in its promotion and transfer policies, all of which operated to restrict black employees to the poorest paying and least desirable jobs. The court noted that certain practices, although neutral on their face, operated to freeze the status quo of prior discriminatory practices and thus could not be lawfully maintained.

After referring the case to a special master for determination of individual entitlement to relief, the trial court entered its final judgment October 11, 1977, wherein it ordered Lee Way to pay the sum of $1,818,191.33 as damages in the form of forty-seven individual back-pay awards, ranging from $3,000 to $138,000. The judgment was appealed, and in September 1979, the Tenth Circuit Court of Appeals affirmed the district court's judgment but remanded the case for consideration of additional damages.

B. The Insurance Policies

For many years prior to the filing of *United States v. Lee Way,* Lee Way had purchased all its insurance coverage from Transport. In January 1967, Lee Way purchased from Transport additional insurance in the form of a series of eight excess umbrella insurance policies which afforded substantially higher limits of liability and broader coverages than the underlying Transport policies. This excess umbrella coverage (in the form of annually renewed policies) was in effect from January 1, 1967, through early 1978. The first five policies (those in effect from January 1, 1967, until mid-1972) expressly provided coverage for discrimination. However, in late August or early September 1972, Transport rewrote the umbrella policy then in effect with an endorsement excluding any future coverage for discrimination. Consequently, in this action the Court is only concerned with the five umbrella policies which were in effect from January 1, 1967, through late August or early September, 1972.

The parties have stipulated that a specimen policy (admitted into evidence) contains the language relevant to all the policies in question. The general coverage provision says that Transport will indemnify Lee Way

> for all sums which [Lee Way] shall be obligated to pay by reason of the liability imposed upon [Lee Way] by law . . . for damages, . . . on account of personal injuries . . . caused by or arising out of each occurrence happening anywhere in the world.

The term "personal injuries" is separately defined and includes discrimination as one kind of personal injury. Also defined is "occurrence":

> The term "occurrence" means an accident or a happening or event or a continuous or repeated exposure to conditions which unexpectedly and unintentionally results in personal injury, property damage or advertising liability during the policy period. All such exposure to substantially the same general conditions existing at or emanating from one premises location shall be deemed one occurrence.

The declarations of the policies in question provide for a deductible amount to be borne by Lee Way of $25,000 *per occurrence.*

Thus, if Lee Way's discriminatory conduct constituted one occurrence, then Lee Way bears only one $25,000 deductible amount. If Lee Way's conduct as to each individual discriminatee constituted a separate occurrence as to each, then Lee Way must bear the first $25,000 of each back-pay award.

II. Single vs. Multiple Occurrence

The Court is unable to find another case that has addressed this precise issue. The question of what constitutes a single "accident" or "occurrence", as the terms are used within liability policies to limit an insurer's liability to a specified amount, has been addressed in numerous cases and is the subject of one annotation. 55 A.L.R.2d 1300; see also, 8 Appleman's Insurance Law and Practice §4891 and Long, The Law of Liability Insurance §§2.12-2.14. The cases indicate that a court should "examine the policies in light of the business purposes sought to be achieved by the parties and the plain meaning of the words chosen by them to effect those purposes." Champion International Corp. v. Continental Casualty Co., 546 F.2d 502, 505 (2nd Cir. 1976); see also, Union Carbide Corp. v. Travelers Indemnity Co., 399 F. Supp. 12, 17 (W. D. Pa. 1975). The district court in *Union Carbide v. Travelers,* supra, explained that a term such as "occurrence" should be construed in the light of the hazard insured against. Id.

In this case the hazard insured against is discrimination. In the prior litigation, Lee Way was found to have engaged in a "pattern and practice" of discrimination. "Pattern and practice" actions have the following characteristics:

1. A pattern and practice of discrimination exists only where the defendant routinely follows generalized policies, procedures or practices which have a discriminatory effect. Individual instances of discrimination are not a pattern and practice.
2. A pattern and practice of discrimination is ordinarily proven through the use of statistics and other evidence of a general nature. Proof of individual instances of discrimination alone is not proof of a pattern and practice.
3. In a pattern and practice case, the cause of action belongs to the Government and not to the individuals affected. However, once the defendant's liability is established, the Government can obtain equitable relief (including back pay) for those specific individuals found to have been affected by the pattern and practice.
4. Intent to discriminate is irrelevant in a pattern and practice case. Instead, the Government must merely show that the defendant's policies, procedures or practices were not accidental or inadvertent.
5. In a pattern and practice case, the defendant's policies, procedures and practices need not themselves be discriminatory. Rather, if they are facially neutral but have the effect of perpetuating past discrimination, the defendant is nevertheless liable.

The findings and conclusions of the district court in *United States v. Lee Way* indicate that these same characteristics existed at Lee Way. . . .

When the language of the Transport policies is construed in light of the particular hazard insured against (see authorities cited supra), the inevitable conclusion is that the discrimination suffered by Lee Way's employees constituted a single "occurrence" as that term is used in the policies. . . .

The first sentence of the definition standing alone indicates that the discrimination here constituted one "occurrence". Lee Way's employees were subject to a "continuous or repeated exposure to conditions," viz., company-wide discriminatory policies and practices, which resulted in "personal injury," i.e. discrimination. The prior judgment (as well as relevant case law) shows that the pattern and practice of discrimination found to have occurred consisted of generalized discriminatory policies routinely followed. Minority employees suffered a "continuous or repeated exposure" to such discriminatory conditions and thus there was only "one occurrence." . . .

The fact that Lee Way operated four separate trucking terminals (Oklahoma City, Los Angeles, Houston, and San Antonio) is no reason for dividing Lee Way's liability into four separate occurrences — one occurrence at each of the four terminal locations. Exposure to the same general conditions "existing at *or emanating from* one premises location" constitutes a single "occurrence." (Emphasis added.) The court in *United States v. Lee Way* concluded that the pattern and practice of discrimination was a continuous company-wide policy traceable to the decisions and procedures made at Lee Way's headquarter's terminal in Oklahoma City. Lee Way's discriminatory policies originated in Oklahoma City and emanated from its headquarters there; the discriminatory policies thus emanated from one location; it would gild the lily to say more.

The fact that the parties provided for a "per occurrence" deductible, as opposed to a "per claim" deductible, is further indication that the parties intended that Lee Way's discriminatory practices would be deemed a single occurrence. The $25,000 deductible "per occurrence" suggests that the policy was not intended to define coverage on the basis of individual instances of discrimination. In a case involving very similar policy language, the Second Circuit affirmed a district court's holding that the continuous and repeated distribution of defective products constituted but a single "occurrence," even though there were 1400 different claims arising from individual ultimate users. Champion International Corp. v. Continental Casualty Co., 546 F.2d 502, supra. The appellate court considered the insured's selection of a "per occurrence" deduction to be important in interpreting "occurrence". Id. at 505. It regarded the insured's distribution of defective vinyl-covered paneling as one "occurrence" out of which 1400 "claims" arose. Id. at 506. In the instant case, each individual award of back pay should be regarded as a different "claim" arising out of but one "occurrence," viz., the continuous and repeated exposure to discriminatory employment conditions.

Transport could have limited the meaning and scope of discrimination to single, individual acts of discrimination and excluded from coverage a pattern and practice of discrimination; it did not do so. . . .

Finally, although the plain language of the policy alone supports the Court's "single occurrence" conclusion, the analogous case law also upholds this result. The rationale underlying the various decisions which have held that particular events constituted but a single occurrence has been that courts generally look to the *cause* as opposed to the *effect* of such events. The great majority of courts have adopted a "cause" analysis, American Casualty Co. v. Heary, 432 F. Supp. 995, 997 (E.D. Va. 1977), holding that where a single event, process or condition results in injuries, it will be deemed a single occurrence even though the injuries may be widespread in both time and place and may affect a multitude of individuals. . . .

IV. Apportionment of Defense Costs

Finally, Transport argues that the costs of defending the discrimination suit should be apportioned between Transport and Lee Way, since Lee Way was essentially a self-insurer prior to January 1, 1967. Transport suggests either of two methods: (1) apportionment according to the number of years which Lee Way and Transport respectively provided self-insurance or insurance, or (2) apportionment according to the fraction of the total damages awarded for each is responsible in the light of this opinion.

Lee Way counters that apportionment of its defense costs is not feasible and that, in any case, such costs should be fully reimbursed by Transport. Lee Way argues that the bulk of its defense costs were incurred in defending the liability phase of the Government's pattern and practice suit, and that those costs simply cannot be allocated among separate claimants or time periods. Lee Way further argues that its defense costs in the relief phase of the litigation related to general matters — such as disputes regarding computation of back pay and claims by individuals who were not awarded relief by the special master or the court — and are not susceptible to apportionment.

The Court agrees with Lee Way. Neither method of apportionment proposed by Transport seems practicable or justified. The reasons for apportionment of defense costs present in Insurance Company of North America vs. Forty-eight Insulations, Inc., 451 F. Supp. 1230 (E.D. Mich. 1978) are not present here. The Court accordingly concludes that Transport is liable for the full amount of defense costs sustained by Lee Way in defending *United States v. Lee Way.*

In sum, the Court finds and concludes: (1) that the liability imposed upon Lee Way in *United States v. Lee Way* represents a single "occurrence", as that term is used in Transport's excess umbrella policies; (2) that the subject policies provide coverage for all back pay for the period after January 1, 1967; and (3) that the subject policies provide coverage for the full amount of defense costs incurred by Lee Way in defending *United States v. Lee Way.*

Counsel for Lee Way will promptly prepare and submit to the Court a judgment in accordance with this Opinion.

So Ordered.

Notes and Questions

1. In Appalachian Ins. Co. v. Liberty Mut. Ins. Corp., 507 F. Supp. 59 (W.D. Pa. 1981), *aff'd,* 676 F.2d 56 (3d Cir. 1982), the court said there was no dispute that gender discrimination by Liberty was covered by the insurance. It held that there was a single occurrence which took place at the time the discriminatory policy was adopted, prior to the policy term. Mead Reinsurance v. Granite State Ins. Co., 873 F.2d 1185 (9th Cir. 1989) held that the alleged policy of condoning police brutality by the City of Richmond, California was a single occurrence. There were eleven complaints based on indifference to use of excessive force. A complaint for police harassment, however, was a separate occurrence.

2. Discrimination appears in two forms: disparate treatment and disparate impact. The latter turns not on identifiable discriminatory acts but the application of a facially neutral pattern or practice that has discriminatory effect. The discrimination in *Lee Way* was based on disparate impact and was proved by statistical evidence. Should it matter in deciding how many occurrences there are whether the theory of the underlying case is based on disparate treatment or disparate impact? *Lee Way* deals with the meaning of the insurance contract. Recent Supreme Court decisions might affect the underlying liability issue, but that does not seem relevant to the insurance questions.

3. Note the *Lee Way* court's emphasis on "cause" instead of "effect" in defining "an occurrence." Compare with the analysis of cause in the property cases in Chapter 3.

4. In *Lee Way* the discriminatory practice began before there was insurance. In an omitted passage the court held that the damages prior to inception were not covered. Is the court right in holding that nevertheless the insurer must pay the entire cost of defending? Would the result be different if there is a break in the chain of coverage, so that for one or more years after coverage began Lee Way was self-insured (or more properly, merely uninsured)?

5. Suppose the facts were the same as in *Lee Way* but the policy differed in that there was no deductible but there was a per occurrence limit of $100,000 with an aggregate limit of $1 million. Now the pocketbook interests of the parties would be reversed with respect to the number of occurrences. Would the result change? Would it matter which of the two fact situations first surfaced in litigation?

6. For a discussion of the utilization of excess umbrella policies, see Chapter 9.

7. Between 1948 and 1958 Owens-Illinois (O-I) manufactured and sold an asbestos-containing thermal insulation product. Thousands of claims were made against O-I alleging exposure to asbestos in that period. O-I was self-insured up to a *retained limit* or *per occurrence deductible* of $100,000 from 1963 to 1971, and of $250,000 from 1971 to 1977, and was insured by Aetna under an excess umbrella policy for the "ultimate net loss" in excess of the self-retained limit. The per occurrence and "aggregate annual" limits in each policy were identical and ranged from $20 million in the early policy years to $50 million in the later ones. How many occurrences would you find? Owens-Illinois, Inc. v. Aetna Casualty & Surety Co., 597 F. Supp. 1515 (D.D.C. 1984), held that there was a single occurrence for purposes of the deductible.

8. Insured's employee, using heavy equipment to clear snow from in front of garage doors in a mini-storage rental facility, injured 98 doors in a four hour period. There was a per-occurrence deductible greater than the damage to any one door. Must the insurer pay? Unigard Ins. Co. v. United States Fidelity & Guaranty Co., 111 Idaho 891, 728 P.2d 780 (1986), held that it must. The court discussed cases in which a painter's employees damaged several windows during a painting job, in which an insured's employees broke 189 light bulbs while repairing 4500 windows at Hunter College, in which 200 dents were put in a ship's deck during a nine-day scrap steel unloading operation, and in which carpeting was damaged in 34 apartments while cleaning them. Would all be decided in the same way? Would the results be the same if the multiple injuries occurred during completely separate jobs, done on different days?

9. Two tour busses operated by the same owner and covered under the same insurance policies were running in tandem, 150 yards apart. Coming over a hill, the first found it necessary to pull off the right side of the road to avoid stopped cars. Having done so, it turned over. The second bus did exactly the same, but did not touch the first bus. Was there one "accident" or were there two? The answer determines whether the primary insurer must pay up to two per accident limits of $500,000, or whether after $500,000 the excess insurer picks up the coverage. Nora v. Grayline Motor Tours, Inc., 499 So. 2d 401 (La. App. 1986).

10. Unlike the general liability policy, the automobile liability policy still insures against liability for accidents, not occurrences. Why? One of the specified policy limits is for "an accident." If an automobile tries to pass a car on a two-lane highway and collides separately with two other automobiles, is there one accident or are there two? There are many such cases. See Kansas Fire and Casualty Co. v. Koelling, 729 S.W.2d 251 (Mo. App. 1987).

MICHIGAN CHEMICAL CORP. v. AMERICAN HOME ASSURANCE CO.

728 F.2d 374 (6th Cir. 1984)

CONTIE, Circuit Judge.

The defendants, American Home Assurance Company (American Home), Aetna Casualty and Surety Company (Aetna) and Insurance Company of North America (INA) have filed an interlocutory appeal in response to a partial summary judgment granted by the district court in favor of the plaintiffs, Michigan Chemical Corporation (MCC) and American Mutual Reinsurance Company (Amreco). Since the district court's order involves a controlling question of law upon which there is substantial ground for difference of opinion, and since an immediate appeal will materially advance the ultimate termination of this litigation, this court has jurisdiction pursuant to 28 U.S.C. §1292(b). We reverse and remand for further proceedings consistent with this opinion.

I

MCC filed a declaratory judgment action in the district court in order to determine how much insurance coverage was available to pay farmers who had sustained property damage resulting from the distribution of contaminated livestock feed throughout Michigan. The record reflects that in early 1973, MCC produced and distributed both a magnesium oxide livestock feed supplement and a flame retardant which contained the toxin polybrominated biphenyl (PBB). These substances were packaged in nearly identical brown fifty-pound bags. The sole difference between the magnesium oxide and PBB bags was the stenciled trade names of the respective products, "Nutrimaster" and "Firemaster."

The district court found that MCC accidentally shipped PBB rather than magnesium oxide to Farm Bureau Services on May 2, 1973. The court did not determine whether any other accidental shipments occurred. Farm Bureau Services then mixed the PBB with regular feed and sold the resulting product to dairy farmers. In October of 1973, the farmers began complaining that some animals were rejecting the feed and that ingestion caused decreased milk production. After Farm Bureau Services and state authorities discovered that the feed was contaminated, 28,679 cattle, 4,612 swine, 1,399 sheep and over 6,000 chickens and other farm animals were destroyed. Their owners filed hundreds of claims against MCC and Farm Bureau Services.

MCC possessed five liability indemnity insurance policies during

1973-1974, the time period in which the property damage took place. Travelers Indemnity Company (Travelers) provided the primary coverage of $1 million per "occurrence," subject to an annual aggregate limit of $1 million. If losses exceeded these limits, excess layers of insurance provided further coverage. Lloyd's of London (Lloyd's) contracted to pay the next $2 million per occurrence, subject to an annual aggregate limit of $2 million. American Home provided an additional $15 million of coverage per occurrence with an annual aggregate limit of $15 million. Midland Insurance Company reinsured some of American Home's potential liability. Amreco reinsured Midland. Finally, Aetna and INA agreed to share equally any further MCC liability up to $10 million per occurrence, subject to an annual aggregate limit of $10 million. The American Home and Aetna policies tracked the other terms and conditions of the Lloyd's policy; the INA policy adopted those of the Travelers' policy. MCC's total liability coverage for property damage during the relevant time period therefore was $28 million per occurrence.

MCC and Amreco have contended throughout this litigation that each claim filed against MCC constitutes an "occurrence" within the meaning of the insurance policies. They argue that there can be no occurrence until injury takes place because an indemnifiable event stems not from an insured's abstract act of negligence, but arises only when damage is suffered. The plaintiffs therefore assert that the five insurers are liable for $28 million per filed claim, subject to the $28 million aggregate annual limit of all the policies combined. Since all of the property damage took place in 1973 and 1974, the plaintiffs argue that MCC's total liability coverage is $56 million.

Conversely, American Home, Aetna and INA contend that the only "occurrence" was the May 2, 1973 accidental shipment of PBB. Although injury must be suffered before the insured becomes liable, the timing of the injury only determines the policy year to which that injury is assigned. The *number of occurrences* is said to be governed by the cause of the accident rather than its effects. Since the cause of the property damage in this case allegedly was a single mis-shipment of PBB, the defendants conclude that MCC's maximum coverage is $28 million.

To date, MCC and Farm Bureau Services have paid over $45 million in claims. The five insurers have acknowledged that one occurrence took place and have contributed $28 million to the settlement of these claims. In consideration for being dismissed from this suit, Travelers has paid an additional $1 million and Lloyd's has paid an additional $2 million. Travelers has received a refund of over $960,000 in deductibles. Lloyd's will not receive such a refund.

The plaintiffs raised one additional issue before the district court. Since Amreco's obligations expired on December 31, 1973, it is in

Amreco's interest to have as many damages fall in the 1974 policy year as possible. Consequently, Amreco argued before the district court that particular damage claims should be assigned to the year in which injury to the affected animal became manifest as opposed to the year in which exposure to the contaminated feed took place. MCC, however, argued for the exposure theory.

The district court found the definitions of "occurrence" in the insurance policies to be ambiguous and therefore construed the policies against the defendants. Hence, MCC's argument that the number of occurrences equals the number of claims was held to be reasonable. The district court held in abeyance the plaintiffs' motions concerning whether the manifestation theory or the exposure theory would determine the policy year to which particular damages would be assigned. . . .

[The court decided Illinois contract law applied and went on to state its principles at length.]

III

This interlocutory appeal presents the question of what constitutes a separate "occurrence" under each of the five insurance policies. The Lloyd's policy, which controls the liability of defendants American Home and Aetna, contains the following definition:

> The term "Occurrence" wherever used herein shall mean *an accident or a happening or event* or a continuous or repeated exposure to conditions *which unexpectedly and unintentionally results in* personal injury, *property damage* or advertising liability *during the policy period*. All such exposure to substantially the same general conditions existing at or emanating from one premises location shall be deemed one occurrence. [Emphasis supplied.]

The Travelers' policy, which governs the liability of INA, contains a similar definition. . . .

The parties agree that the minor differences in the wording of these provisions are immaterial. . . .

A

The vast majority of courts (including two courts which have interpreted the precise language of the definition of occurrence in the Lloyd's policy) have concluded that although injury must be suffered before an insured can be held liable, the number of occurrences for purposes of applying coverage limitations is determined by referring to the cause or causes of the damage and not to the number of injuries or claims. The number and timing of injuries is relevant in addressing the distinct question of the policy period to which each injury will be assigned. See [Appalachian Ins. Co. v. Liberty Mut. Ins. Co., 676 F.2d 56, 61-62 (3d Cir. 1982).]

The definitions of "occurrence" in the present insurance policies reflect this approach. First, these provisions in essence refer to an "accident" which results in injury during the policy period. The language makes the accident constituting the occurrence logically distinct from the injuries which later take place. Second, the insurance policies under review afford coverage on an "occurrence" rather than on a "claim" basis. The use of the former term "indicates that the polic[ies were] not intended to gauge coverage on the basis of individual accidents giving rise to claims, but rather on the underlying circumstances which resulted in the claim[s] for damages." Champion International Corp. v. Continental Casualty Co., 546 F.2d 502, 505-06 (2d Cir. 1976), *cert. denied,* 434 U.S. 819, 98 S. Ct. 59, 54 L. Ed. 2d 75 (1977); see also *Lee Way,* 487 F. Supp. at 1329. We hold that where the courts over such an extended period of time have reached virtually a uniform result in interpreting the term "occurrence" (including two courts which have interpreted the exact language of the Lloyd's policy), and where the policy language reflects this approach, the policy terms admit of only one reasonable interpretation. The terms therefore are unambiguous and require no further construction.

We are aware of only one case which calculated the number of occurrences by referring to the number of injuries rather than to the cause or causes of those injuries. See Elston-Richards Storage Co. v. Indemnity Insurance Co. of North America, 194 F. Supp. 673, 678-82 (W.D. Mich. 1960), *aff'd,* 291 F.2d 627 (6th Cir. 1961). Although this court decided *Elston-Richards,* the holding is not binding because the current litigation involves Illinois law. We are persuaded that if the Illinois courts were presented with the current case, they would follow the overwhelming majority of decisions which have held that the number of occurrences is determined by examining the cause or causes of the damage.

B

The plaintiffs attempt to distinguish the cases upon which the defendants rely by arguing that in most of the cited cases, injuries or damages were suffered immediately after the causal event took place. This scenario contrasts with the present situation in which several months elapsed between the mis-shipment or mis-shipments of PBB and the resulting property damage. One commentator has suggested that if a single cause and numerous injuries are closely linked in time and space, then there has been one occurrence, but if a cause and its effects are temporally removed, then each injury constitutes an occurrence. See Annot., 55 A.L.R.2d 1300, 1304 (1957). This argument, however, was considered and rejected by the Third Circuit in the *Appalachian Insurance* case:

> The fact that there were multiple injuries and that they were of different magnitudes *and that injuries extended over a period of time* does not alter our conclusion that there was a single occurrence. . . . Indeed, the definition of the term "occurrence" in the Appalachian policy contemplates that one occurrence may have multiple and disparate impacts on individuals *and that injuries may extend over a period of time.* [Emphasis supplied.]

676 F.2d at 61. See also *Lee Way,* 487 F. Supp. at 1330. In addition, the fact patterns of the *Champion, Pincoffs* and *Union Carbide* cases* demonstrate that the number of injuries or claims, even if temporally removed from their causes, are irrelevant when determining the number of occurrences.[7]

[The court distinguished the asbestos cases as being concerned with assigning a claim to a policy period rather than determining the number of occurrences.]

IV

The plaintiffs also argue that if the number of occurrences is calculated by examining the cause or causes of injury, then the definitions of products liability contained in the policies under review make

---

*Maurice Pincoffs Co. v. St. Paul Fire & Marine Ins. Co., 477 F.2d 204 (5th Cir. 1971); Union Carbide Corp. v. Traveler's Indem. Co., 399 F. Supp. 12 (W.D. Pa. 1975). — ED.

7. The district court distinguished [*Champion, Lee Way* and E.B. Michaels v. Mutual Marine Office, Inc., 472 F. Supp. 26 (S.D.N.Y. 1979)] on the ground that the courts in those cases limited the number of occurrences so that the insured parties would not have to pay multiple per occurrence deductibles. The district court implied that this approach was consistent with the Illinois rule that an ambiguous insurance contract is to be construed against the insurer who drafted it. In the present case, however, applying those cases to limit the number of occurrences would disadvantage the insured party.

The problem with this argument is that once courts establish a legal rule, such as how the number of occurrences is to be determined, any party is entitled to rely upon that rule in future litigation. Our jurisprudence is not so result oriented that it will permit court holdings to be relied upon only if such holdings benefit a particular party. . . .

no sense. If the plaintiffs are correct, then our interpretation of the contract violates the general rule that an agreement is to be construed as a whole in order to effectuate all of its provisions. See, e.g., *Joseph*, 106 Ill. App. 3d at 991, 62 Ill. Dec. 637, 436 N.E.2d 663. The Lloyd's policy defines the term "Products Liability" as:

> Liability arising out of goods or products manufactured, sold, handled or distributed by the Assured . . . if the occurrence occurs after possession of such goods or products has been relinquished to others by the Assured . . . and if such occurrence occurs away from premises owned, rented or controlled by the Assured. . . .

The Travelers' policy contains the following language: . . .

The plaintiffs contend that under these definitions, an "occurrence" must take place: (1) after the insured has relinquished control of the product and (2) away from the latter's premises. They argue that under the cause theory, however, occurrences such as mis-shipments or defects in construction and design normally will happen at the insured's facility. The plaintiffs therefore conclude that if this court adopts the cause theory, then the products liability coverage provided in the policies will be nullified.

We disagree. First, the defendants have admitted in their briefs and during oral argument that the present case involves products liability under the provisions of the policies in question. Second, the products liability definitions stipulate *when* and *where* an occurrence must take place for products liability coverage to exist. The cause standard, however, governs only the *number* of occurrences; it is irrelevant in determining when and where an occurrence happens. See *Appalachian Insurance*, 676 F.2d at 61-62. Consequently, using the cause test in order to calculate the number of occurrences is perfectly consistent with looking to the time and place of injury in order to decide when and where an occurrence or occurrences takes place for purposes of either applying a product liability provision or assigning a claim to a particular policy period. . . .

V

Since the relevant language of the insurance policies is plain and unambiguous, this court may not resort to parol evidence or to the rule of strict construction against the insurer in order to ascertain the parties' intent. We hold that under the language of these contracts, the number of occurrences must be determined by examining the cause of the property damage, i.e., the mis-shipment or mis-shipments of PBB.

As has been indicated, the district court did not decide whether only one mis-shipment of PBB occurred. We nevertheless emphasize that each shipment would constitute a separate occurrence under these policies. In the *Pincoffs* case, the insured made sales of contaminated birdseed to eight dealers who in turn sold the seed to pet owners. Many birds died after eating the seed. One insurer contended that the sole "occurrence" was the contamination of the seed. The court rejected this argument and held that each of the eight sales constituted an occurrence because the sales, rather than the mere possession of contaminated seed, created the exposure to liability. Id., 447 F.2d at 206-07.

The present case is highly analogous. So long as MCC retained possession of the PBB, no liability could result. The shipment of the substance constituted the act from which liability arose. Other shipments, if any took place, created additional exposure to liability and therefore were separate occurrences. In such a situation, there would not have been one uninterrupted and continuing cause, *Appalachian Insurance*, 676 F.2d at 61, but several distinct acts from which liability would have resulted.[10]

The district court therefore is instructed to determine how many shipments of PBB occurred. It also must determine whether the manifestation theory or the exposure theory shall apply in this case. We express no view on either issue. The judgment of the district court is REVERSED and the case is REMANDED for further proceedings consistent with this opinion. The appellants shall recover costs on appeal, except for those costs associated with the inclusion in the appendix of materials which we have previously held to be unnecessary.

KEITH, Circuit Judge, dissenting.

I dissent from the majority's holding that the number of occurrences for purposes of applying coverage limitations is determined by referring to the cause of the damage. In my view, the district court was correct to construe an occurrence as taking place at the time that damage resulted.

The occurrence definition in the insurance policies is composed of one sentence containing two conjunctive elements. The first element is an "accident," "happening" or "event" or a "continuous or repeated exposure to conditions". The second element is "property damage resulting during the policy period". Thus, the sentence reads

10. The facts of the *Champion* case are not persuasive on this point. The insured in that case sold defective vinyl to twenty-six recreational vehicle manufacturers who in turn used the vinyl in 1,400 vehicles. The court held that one occurrence, not 1,400, had taken place. 546 F.2d at 505-06. The *Pincoffs* court, however, would have ruled that 26 occurrences had happened. We follow the *Pincoffs* approach because the court in *Champion* did not advert to the possibility that 26 occurrences had taken place.

that an accident does not take place until it results in damage or injury. The majority's interpretation, which makes these two elements distinct, contravenes both insurance and tort law and is contrary to a plain reading of the sentence. It is well established that liability does not result until harm occurs. In Steinheider & Sons, Inc. v. Iowa Kemper Ins. Co., 204 Neb. 156, 281 N.W.2d 539 (1979), a case relied upon by the district court and involving an incident of negligent misdelivery, the court said "there could be no indemnifiable occurrence if a truck delivering a wrong chemical had simply turned over before it got to the customer, the negligent act must have resulted in damage." 281 N.W.2d at 543-44. Thus an indemnifiable event does not arise at the time of some abstract act of negligence, but rather at the time it results in injury or harm.

The district court's interpretation of occurrence also finds support in Elston-Richards Storage Co. v. Indemnity Ins. Co. of North America, 194 F. Supp. 673, 678-82 (W.D. Mich. 1960), *aff'd*, 291 F.2d 627 (6th Cir. 1961). This Court in *Elston-Richards* was presented with the identical insurance policy construction issue now before it: whether the term "occurrence" in an indemnity insurance policy is defined by reference to the negligent act of the insured, or by actual events which inflict injury that follow the initial negligent act. Our Court affirmed the trial judge's holding that each separate incident of damage constituted a separate "occurrence".

Although the majority acknowledged the holding in *Elston-Richards,* it found the case to be inapposite because it involved Michigan law and the current litigation involves questioned governed by Illinois law. At 380. This ground for distinction is woefully inadequate since the majority relies upon a multitude of cases which are not governed by the law of Illinois.

I find particularly troubling the majority's reliance in this case upon Appalachian Ins. Co. v. Liberty Mutual Ins. Co., 676 F.2d 56 (3d Cir. 1982) and Transport Ins. Co. v. Lee Way Motor Freight, Inc., 487 F. Supp. 1325 (N.D. Tex. 1980) because neither case involved products liability but instead concerned issues of employment discrimination. In fact, a footnote in the *Appalachian* opinion indicates that the case may be inapplicable in the products liability arena. The footnote reads: "[T]his is not a case where an insured commits a tortious act and then after a lapse of time a claimant is injured by the act." The majority's attempt to discount this footnote on grounds that it concerned a discussion of when an occurrence takes place as opposed to the number of occurrences is wholly unconvincing. The footnote makes no bright line distinction between "when" and "how many" and in any event the principles underlying an analysis of when an occurrence takes place would be instructive in a determination of how many occurrences took place.

Finally, the majority's opinion fails to recognize the time honored principle that an insurance policy is interpreted in such a way that it makes sense as a whole. 3A Corbin, Contracts §549 (Supp. 1971). An examination of the definition of products liability in the instant policy makes it apparent that the majority's interpretation of occurrence runs contrary to this principle. Indeed, the majority's interpretation deprives the policy's products liability section of any reasonable meaning. This section provides:

> The term "Products Liability" means . . . liability arising out of goods or products manufactured, sold, handled or distributed by the Assured . . . if the occurrence occurs after possession of such goods or products has been relinquished to others by the Assured . . . and if such occurrence occurs away from premises owned, rented or controlled by the Assured.

Thus, products liability coverage only applies to occurrences which occur away from the insured's premises and after the goods have been transferred. Yet, if occurrence means the misshipment or cause of injury, then there could not be liability in this case because neither occurred away from the plant. In contrast, the district court's interpretation gives reasonable meaning to this section. As the district court stated, "if an occurrence occurs when damage appears during the policy period, then almost all products liability actions are covered by the products liability portion of the insurance policy which is presumably what the drafters intended." 530 F. Supp. at 152.

At most, an examination of the policy language and consideration of arguments as to its intended merits lead to a conclusion that occurrence should be construed as taking place at the time injury results. At the very least, one must find the terms ambiguous. Illinois' law as do most states, recognize that an ambiguous contract should be construed against the insurer who drafted it. Therefore, the district court's decision, interpreting the contract in favor of the insured, was not clearly erroneous and I would affirm.

Notes and Questions

1. On remand, the District Court found there was only one shipment. See Michigan Chemical Corp. v. Travelers Indem. Co., 644 F. Supp. 239 (W.D. Mich. 1986).

2. If it is plausible to argue that each claim is an occurrence, is it not equally plausible to make each animal destroyed an occurrence?

3. Are you persuaded by the court's parsing of the products hazard definitions? Do you agree that the "relevant language of the insurance policies is plain and unambiguous?"

4. Is the dissent plausible? In particular, are you troubled by the point that the negligent act(s) took place on the insured's premises?

5. If cases were brought against the retail dealers on the facts of any of these cases, how many occurrences would there be?

6. Would you decide *Champion International* as the Second Circuit did (supra, n.10.)? The *Champion* case cited in *Michigan Chemical* was decided in 1976. Champion was still litigating about its insurance coverage on the same events and with respect to some of the same issues over a decade later. See Champion Intl. Corp. v. Liberty Mut. Ins. Co. v. Aetna Casualty & Surety Co., 128 F.R.D. 608 (S.D.N.Y. 1989).

7. Uniroyal, Inc. v. Home Ins. Co., 707 F. Supp. 1368 (E.D.N.Y. 1988), deals with the meaning and number of occurrences (and other issues) in the context of the Agent Orange settlement.

8. Under current products liability doctrine, several persons in the chain of manufacture and sale may be strictly liable under Restatement (Second) of Torts §402A. Does the definition (and the number) of the occurrences differ depending on who the defendant is?

2. The Meaning of Bodily Injury

The insurer has no duty under the liability policy unless an occurrence results in bodily injury (or property damage). The meaning and timing of bodily injury have been the focus of many important recent insurance cases. For a general overview, see Kahn, Looking for "Bodily Injury": What Triggers Coverage Under a Standard Comprehensive General Liability Insurance Policy?, 19 Forum 532 (1984).

The most interesting cases arose out of the liability of manufacturers for disease caused by their products made of or containing asbestos. The key case was Borel v. Fibreboard Paper Products Corp., 493 F.2d 1076 (5th Cir. 1973). Applying the law of Texas, Judge Wisdom held defendant manufacturers jointly and severally liable. This case unleashed a flood of claims for injury caused by asbestosis, mesothelioma, and lung cancer resulting from exposure to asbestos in the workplace or elsewhere.

It was a short step to the next level of litigation, based on claims by manufacturers against their comprehensive general liability insurers. Two competing theories were initially advanced: that bodily injury occurred and coverage was "triggered" when the body was exposed to asbestos fibers, and that coverage was "triggered" by a manifestation of bodily injury.

Insurance Co. of North America v. Forty-Eight Installations, 633 F.2d 1212 (6th Cir. 1980), *aff'd on reh'g*, 657 F.2d 814 (6th Cir. 1981), purporting to apply Illinois and New Jersey law, said that it was the overwhelming of the body's defenses from the buildup of asbestos fibers in the lungs that was "bodily injury" within the meaning of the policy. To avoid the cost of making the "Solomonian interpretation" involved in determining exactly when that happened, the court opted for the practical solution of making exposure to asbestos fibers the trigger of coverage, that is, the point at which there was bodily injury. 633 F.2d at 1218. Porter v. American Optical Corp., 641 F.2d 1128 (5th Cir. 1981), applying Louisiana law, followed the lead of *Forty-Eight Installations.*

Eagle-Picher Industries, Inc. v. Liberty Mut. Ins. Co., 682 F.2d 12 (1st Cir. 1982), took the other route, finding no bodily injury until it was manifest. The court considered that there was "no true conflict among all potentially applicable laws," which appear to have included Ohio, Illinois, and England.

Meanwhile, another asbestos case was proceeding toward decision in the federal courts in the District of Columbia. A number of insurers were on the risk in sequence and took different views: some urged the exposure theory and some the manifestation theory. On appeal the District of Columbia Circuit pronounced the most cited and influential of the asbestos coverage cases. Keene Corp. v. Insurance Co. of North America, 215 App. D.C. 156, 667 F.2d 1034 (D.C. Cir. 1981), *cert. denied*, 455 U.S. 1007 (1982). Judge Bazelon emphasized that the purpose of insurance was the purchase of certainty and that the insured would sometimes be deprived of certainty under either the exposure or manifestation theory. He said that "our objective must be to give effect to the policies' dominant purpose of indemnity." 667 F.2d at 1041. In order for the insured's rights under the policy to be secure, and for that purpose to be achieved, the court held that coverage must be triggered by any of inhalation exposure, exposure in residence (that is, while the asbestos fibers are in the lungs, insidiously working their harm), and by manifestation of disease. All insurers on the risk at any of those times must defend or indemnify if called upon to do so. The opinion cited and approved the Keeton articles espousing "reasonable expectations" as a basis for coverage.

The Keene "triple trigger" theory quickly became the favorite of plaintiffs.

Notes and Questions

1. Oshinsky, Comprehensive General Liability Insurance: Trigger and Scope of Coverage in Long-Term Exposure Cases, 17 Forum 1035 (1982), commented on *Keene* with complete approval, as could be expected from a member of the firm that represented Keene. The

article helps set the case in the context of the developing doctrine in the area.

2. The prevailing opinion in *Keene* said the insured could select the insurer to defend and that each insurer is fully liable. May the insured pick one insurer to defend and another to indemnify? If so, that would make it possible for the insured to marshal its coverage for maximum protection. How?

3. One of the insurers in *Keene,* pressing a theory of coverage that would prorate protection in proportion to the periods of insurance coverage provided by the insurers, argued that otherwise an insured would be as well off with one year of coverage as with continuous coverage. The court rejected that argument out of hand but a dissent agreed with it. Which view is preferable?

4. In Abex Corp. v. Maryland Casualty Co., 790 F.2d 119 (D.C. Cir. 1986), Abex manufactured brake linings containing asbestos. Abex chose the District of Columbia for suit, presumably hoping to get the advantage of the *Keene* doctrine, but the D.C. Circuit held that New York law applied and that it must follow the Second Circuit's interpretation of New York law. This was found in American Home Products Corp. v. Liberty Mut. Ins. Co., 748 F.2d 760 (2d Cir. 1984), where the court adopted an "injury-in-fact" trigger.

The disadvantage of this trigger lies in the fact that it is fact-sensitive and requires proof, which impedes the expeditious disposition of litigation. Since it usually precludes summary judgment, it would more often than other triggers require a trial to explore the etiology of particular diseases. In Eli Lilly and Co. v. Home Ins. Co., 653 F. Supp. 1 (D.D.C. 1984), the D.C. District Court was ready to be influenced by *Keene.* It held that Indiana law applied, but finding no Indiana authority, the court relied on external authority and quickly found it in *Keene.* One is entitled to be skeptical about that guess and especially about the facile way it was made.

5. Most asbestos coverage litigation has been in the federal courts, though state law governs. Thus there has been a good bit of guessing about the proper rules. It is beginning now to be possible to get direct information about state law, however. See Zurich Ins. Co. v. Raymark Indus., Inc., the following case. The intermediate appellate court characterized *Keene*'s "triple trigger" theory as a " 'result-oriented' exercise in judicial legislation." *Raymark,* 144 Ill. App. 3d 943, 494 N.E.2d 630, 645, 98 Ill. Dec. 508 (1986). Illinois has rejected the reasonable expectations doctrine that was heavily relied on in *Keene.*

6. More recently, the judge in the Coordination Proceeding of the Asbestos Insurance Coverage Cases, the largest and most fully tried of all the asbestos cases, uttered a cry of despair at the hopelessness of his case, which was then several years in process. Judge Brown admon-

ished insurance companies and asbestos producers for bringing "very difficult" issues to court. "Generations on top of generations of people experienced in the handling of insurance matters" should settle the issues, he said. In a transcript of a hearing on January 12, 1988, he is quoted as saying:

> It is an awesome thing you do to put these decisions on a person who really has no background in insurance law except in this case, and then put that responsibility on three people above me or perhaps, more appropriately, law clerks fresh out of law school who certainly will be taking a crack at the opinion first who have even less experience than I do.
>
> I just wonder if there are no statesmen left out there someplace in your companies who can resolve these issues, who have much more experience, who are much more adept at it than any of us (judges) are at these issues. [Judge Admonishes Execs, Bus. Ins., Mar. 7, 1988, at 2.]

ZURICH INS. CO. v. RAYMARK INDUS., INC.

118 Ill. 2d 23, 514 N.E.2d 150, 112 Ill. Dec. 684 (1987)

Justice THOMAS J. MORAN delivered the opinion of the court:

This declaratory judgment action involves the construction of various comprehensive general liability insurance policies issued to the defendant, Raymark Industries, Inc. (Raymark). In 1978, Zurich Insurance Company (Zurich), one of Raymark's primary insurers, filed this action in the circuit court of Cook County against Raymark and two of Raymark's other primary insurers, Federal Insurance Company (Federal) and Commercial Union Insurance Company (Commercial Union). Zurich sought a declaration of its obligations and the obligations of Federal and Commercial Union to defend and indemnify Raymark in thousands of underlying actions filed by individuals alleging personal injuries or wrongful death resulting from exposure to asbestos-containing products manufactured by Raymark. . . .

[The court described at length the pleadings and the decisions in the trial and intermediate appellate courts, continuing as follows:]

Five issues have been raised in this court: (1) What event or events give rise to the primary insurers' obligation to provide coverage for asbestos-related claims under the standard comprehensive general liability policy, and when do those events occur? . . .

Raymark (formerly Raybestos-Manhatten, Inc.) has manufactured products containing asbestos since the 1920's. Raymark is currently a defendant in more than 30,000 lawsuits pending in both State and Federal courts throughout the United States in which plaintiffs have alleged injuries caused by exposure to asbestos products. The plaintiffs in these underlying actions typically allege that they or their decedents contracted asbestosis, mesothelioma or bronchogenic carcinoma (lung cancer) resulting from exposure to asbestos products, including products manufactured and sold by Raymark, during the 1940's, 1950's and 1960's.

Since 1941, Raymark has been insured under various comprehensive general liability insurance policies issued by the primary insurers in this case. The Employers' Liability Assurance Corporation, the predecessor in interest to Commercial Union, insured Raymark from May 1, 1941, through May 1, 1945, and from February 4, 1947, through February 4, 1950. Federal and its predecessor in interest, United States Guaranty Company, insured Raymark from September 26, 1951, through September 26, 1967. Commercial Union insured Raymark from September 26, 1967, through October 15, 1969. Zurich insured Raymark after October 15, 1969. Northbrook has issued excess policies since 1976.

The circuit court found, as we do, that the policies at issue are identical in all relevant respects and warrant the same interpretation. The language of the policies that Zurich issued to Raymark is typical. Those policies include:

I.   Coverage A — Bodily Injury Liability

The company will pay on behalf of the insured all sums which the insured shall become legally obligated to pay as damages because of Coverage A. bodily injury . . . caused by an occurrence. . . .

The policies also set forth the following definitions:

"bodily injury" means bodily injury, sickness or disease. . . .
"occurrence" means an accident, including injurious exposure to conditions, which results during the policy period, in bodily injury . . . neither expected nor intended from the standpoint of the insured.

When Raymark tendered the asbestos-related actions to its insurance companies for defense, disputes arose among Raymark and its insurance carriers concerning the interpretation of the policies' coverage of asbestos-related claims. Zurich filed this action for declaratory judgment in 1978. Zurich contended that coverage was triggered only when a claimant inhaled asbestos fibers and that the defense and indemnity obligations for each claim are to be allocated among the various insurers who were on the risk during the years when the claimant was exposed to asbestos in proportion to the number of years that each carrier was on the risk throughout the claimant's exposure. Federal and Commercial Union argued that their respective policies provided coverage only for those claims in which the asbestos-related injury first manifested itself during a policy period. Raymark initially advocated the exposure theory advanced by Zurich. In June 1981, Zurich moved for summary judgment, asking the court to declare that coverage was triggered only by exposure to asbestos. Raymark submitted a memorandum in support of Zurich's motion. On October 1, 1981, in an unrelated action construing the comprehensive general liability policy's coverage for asbestos-related diseases, the United States Court of Appeals for the District of Columbia held that each insurer on the risk from a claimant's initial exposure to asbestos through the manifestation of a disease is liable to its insured for the costs of defense and indemnification. (Keene Corp. v. Insurance Co. of North America (D.C. Cir. 1981), 667 F.2d 1034, 1040-41, *cert. denied* (1982), 455 U.S. 1007, 102 S. Ct. 1644, 71 L. Ed. 2d 875.) Less than three weeks later, Raymark withdrew its support for Zurich's motion for summary judgment and argued that the court should apply the *Keene* approach. The circuit court denied the motion for summary judgment, ruling that medical evidence concerning the cause and course of development of asbestos-related diseases was necessary to determine how the policy language applied to asbestos-related diseases.

During a hearing that began on May 2, 1983, and concluded on June 7, 1983, the court heard extensive medical testimony from nine experts who were board certified clinicians or pathologists. The trial court summarized the evidence in a lengthy memorandum opinion and order. . . .

[The court then gave an extensive summary of the etiology of the asbestos-caused diseases, exploring two medical points of view: those of the clinician and the pathologist. They perceive the origin of disease (the trigger for insurance coverage) in different ways. The clinician sees only manifest disease while the pathologist sees the bodily changes in the process of a disease's development. It is a helpful summary for anyone who seeks to understand the medical background of the asbestos cases.]

I. The Coverage Issue — What Event or Events Trigger Coverage Under the Standard Comprehensive General Liability Policy?

The Parties' Arguments

Zurich contends that the appellate court erred in holding that events other than exposure to asbestos give rise to the insurers' obligation to afford coverage. In support of this argument, Zurich maintains that in interpreting the policies at issue, the appropriate focus is not upon the definition of "bodily injury," but upon the definition of "occurrence," and that an "occurrence" is the event that determines the insurers' duties under the policies. According to Zurich's interpretation, an occurrence consists of two elements — an accident, and bodily injury during the policy period. In the case of asbestos-related diseases, exposure to asbestos fibers is an "accident." The medical evidence demonstrates that exposure to asbestos fibers causes immediate bodily injury in the form of cellular damage to the lungs. This bodily injury completes an "occurrence," as defined in the policy, and thus triggers coverage under the policy then in force even though the injury cannot be detected at that time and the cumulative effect of the injury has not yet manifested as a disease.

The compensable damages flowing from a claimant's initial exposure to asbestos may include sickness, disease and ultimately death. Zurich submits that these elements of damage do not, however, trigger additional coverage in the absence of new exposure to asbestos. Each new exposure to asbestos, on the other hand, causes another separate and distinct bodily injury and thus completes another occurrence. That new occurrence, in turn, will trigger coverage under the policy then in effect. . . .

Federal contends that according to the plain and unambiguous language of the policies, an insurer is required to provide coverage only if the claimant's asbestos-related disease manifested itself during the policy period. In support of its position, Federal argues that the proper analysis requires the determination, first, of the nature of the event ostensibly triggering coverage, and second, of when that event occurred. Federal submits that given the ordinary meaning of the terms "injury" and "disease," it is necessary to conclude that asbestosis, mesothelioma and bronchogenic carcinoma are diseases, not injuries. Having reached this conclusion, it is then necessary to determine when, in a given case, the claimant's disease occurred. Federal asserts that asbestosis, mesothelioma and bronchogenic carcinoma occur when the body's defense mechanisms are overcome and can no longer cope with the cellular changes that occur in response to the inhalation of asbestos fibers. At what point in time this happened is a question of fact to be determined on a case-by-case basis. . . .

Federal also argues that its policies were intended to cover only *compensable* injuries. Federal insists that manufacturers insure only against compensable injuries or diseases, not against microscopic changes at the cellular level. . . .

Commercial Union asserts that, unlike the other parties, it does not espouse any of the "coverage theories." Instead, Commercial Union asks this court to hold that the coverage issue must be determined on a case-by-case basis. The insurer's duty to defend is determined by the allegations of the complaint in the underlying action. If the complaint alleges facts within the coverage or the potential coverage of the policy, the insurer has the duty to defend the action. (Maryland Casualty Co. v. Peppers (1976), 64 Ill. 2d 187, 193, 355 N.E.2d 24.) If, on the other hand, the complaint does not seek a recovery which, if obtained, would be paid by the insurer under its duty to indemnify, then the insurer is not obligated to defend the action. Under the various policies Raymark purchased, the insurer's duty to indemnify is limited to bodily injury occurring during the policy period. An action which either alleges no bodily injury during the policy period or seeks no recovery for injuries allegedly sustained during the policy period states no basis for potential indemnity coverage. Consequently, an insurer has no duty to defend such an action. . . .

Raymark interprets the policies as containing three separate and distinct triggers of coverage. As appellee, Raymark urges this court to affirm the circuit court's findings that "bodily injury" encompasses the microscopic and clinically undetectable damage to lung cells that takes place when asbestos fibers are inhaled and retained in the lung. In response to Federal's argument that coverage is triggered only when an asbestos-related disease manifests itself, Raymark notes that the policy language provides coverage when bodily injury, sickness or disease occurs during the policy period, not when bodily injury, sickness or disease becomes compensable or manifest. In response to Zurich's argument, Raymark notes that the policy language provides coverage when bodily injury, sickness or disease occurs within the policy period, not when the event which causes that bodily injury, sickness or disease occurs. Accordingly, regardless of when the causative event happened, the insurers' obligations under the policies arise when the resulting bodily injury, sickness or disease occur during the policy period. Finally, contrary to Commercial Union's argument, Raymark does not contend that its insurers owe it any duties whatsoever without reference to the underlying tort complaints. Rather, Raymark maintains that the undisputed evidence concerning the pathogenesis of asbestos-related diseases shows that "bodily injury," as defined by the policies at issue, takes place continuously from the time of an alleged exposure to asbestos through the time a claimant files an action alleging an asbestos-related disease. Consequently, any carrier having a policy in effect during that time is obligated to afford coverage.

As cross-appellant, Raymark argues that the circuit court and the appellate court erroneously determined that there is no continuing bodily injury between the time a claimant's exposure to asbestos ceases and the time an asbestos-related disease becomes diagnosable. Raymark insists that every individual who ultimately manifests an asbestos-related disease necessarily continues to sustain microscopic bodily injuries during periods of nonexposure which preceded the clinical onset of an asbestos-related disease. These ongoing bodily injuries, Raymark contends, also trigger coverage. Consequently, Raymark takes the position that each and every carrier whose policy or policies were in effect at any time between a claimant's initial exposure to asbestos and his manifestation of an asbestos-related disease must provide coverage. Raymark submits that the trial court's conclusion, that there may be no progression of disease after exposure ceases, is contrary to the manifest weight of the evidence and inconsistent with the court's other findings.

Analysis

What Events Trigger Coverage?

Contrary to Zurich's argument, the circuit court and the appellate court correctly found that coverage is triggered by "bodily injury," as defined in the policies, which occurs during the policy period. The plain language of Zurich's policies provides that:

> The [insurance] company will pay on behalf of the insured all sums which the insured shall become legally obligated to pay as damages because of . . . *bodily injury* . . . caused by an occurrence. (Emphasis added.)

This language unambiguously provides that "bodily injury" is the event which gives rise to the insurers' obligations under the policies. In addition, the definition of "occurrence" requires that the exposure to conditions result in bodily injury during the policy period. . . .

"Bodily injury," which gives rise to the insurer's duties under the policies, is defined as "bodily injury, sickness, or disease." The circuit court and the appellate court correctly concluded that these terms must be read as separate and distinct triggers of coverage. Thus, under the plain and unambiguous language of the policies, an insurer must provide coverage for a claim if the claimant sustained "bodily injury" or "sickness" or "disease" during the policy period. Having concluded that each of these events triggers coverage, the inquiry becomes when "bodily injury," as defined in the policy, occurs.

When Does "Bodily Injury" Occur?

The circuit court, after hearing extensive expert medical testimony, found that asbestos fibers cause physical and biochemical injuries to the cells of the lung at or shortly after inhalation. Zurich and Northbrook agree that these microscopic injuries, although they cannot be detected, constitute "bodily injury." Federal does not take issue with the circuit court's findings that lung cells are physically and chemically damaged by asbestos fibers.

. . . We therefore conclude that an insurer whose policy was in force at the time a claimant was exposed to asbestos must provide coverage of that claim.

As we have already noted, "sickness" and "disease" are included within the policy definition of "bodily injury," and therefore, also trigger coverage. The circuit court found that the plain meaning of the term "disease" is "a condition of the living animal . . . or one of its parts that impairs the performance of a vital function." The court concluded, on the basis of this definition, that an asbestos-related disease occurs when it progresses to the point at which it significantly impairs the lungs' function. When that point is reached, the disease is ordinarily capable of clinical detection and diagnosis. The appellate court found no reason to disturb the trial court's finding that the manifestation of a disease also triggers coverage. Given the ordinary meaning of the term "disease," we agree that the evidence supports the conclusion that disease occurs, and therefore triggers coverage, when it becomes manifest. The time when a disease is reasonably capable of diagnosis varies depending upon factors unique to each individual. Therefore, as the circuit court correctly held, the question of when a disease became manifest must be resolved in the context of a particular case.

The circuit court also found that the "body's condition is clearly not normal" during the time preceding the manifestation of a disease. The court found that the term "sickness" is defined as "ill health, a disordered, weakened or unsound condition." Given this definition, the court concluded, and the appellate court affirmed, that an individual who "suffers from a disordered, weakened or unsound condition" which has not yet progressed to the point of impairment characteristic of "disease," may be classified as having a "sickness," which would also trigger coverage under the policies. Again, we believe that this conclusion finds ample support in the record. As in cases in which the claimant alleges "disease," when "sickness" occurred is a question of fact to be decided on a case-by-case basis.

We turn now to Raymark's contention that the circuit court and the appellate court erroneously determined that there is no continuing bodily injury between the time a claimant's exposure to asbestos ends and the time an asbestos-related disease becomes diagnosable. Raymark maintains that this finding is contrary to the manifest weight of the evidence and inconsistent with the court's other findings. Given the fact that the tissue of the lungs is injured when asbestos fibers are inhaled, it may seem illogical to conclude that an individual, who is known to have been exposed to asbestos, and who later developed an asbestos-related disease, suffered no "bodily injury" between the cessation of exposure and the diagnosis of the disease. Nevertheless, the expert testimony in the record establishes that asbestos-related disease may or may not progress during periods of nonexposure. The evidence shows that the diseases originate with the inhalation of asbestos fibers, and, the *continued inhalation* of asbestos causes additional injuries which eventually culminate in a disease. As both the circuit court and the appellate court properly concluded, there is no evidence in the record to support Raymark's contention that the disease progresses in every case after exposure ends. In fact, the evidence indicates that there are cases in which the disease progresses during periods of nonexposure and cases in which there is no progression. We therefore conclude that both the circuit court and the appellate court properly rejected Raymark's contention that those who ultimately manifest an asbestos-related disease necessarily sustained "bodily injury" between the time when they were no longer exposed to asbestos and the time when their disease manifested itself.

In summary, we hold that under the plain and unambiguous language of the policies at issue, the insurer must provide coverage of asbestos-related claims if the claimant in the underlying action suffered "bodily injury," "sickness" or "disease" during the policy period. "Bodily injury" takes place at or shortly after the time a claimant was exposed to asbestos and continues throughout a claimant's exposure to asbestos. Thus, an insurer that was on the risk during the time the claimant was exposed to asbestos must provide coverage. "Disease" takes place when it is reasonably capable of clinical detection and diagnosis. The determination of when a claimant's disease was reasonably capable of diagnosis must be made on a case-by-case basis. "Sickness" takes place at any time during which the claimant "suffers from a disordered, weakened or unsound condition" before the clinical manifestation of a disease. Whether and when a claimant suffered "sickness" must be determined on a case-by-case basis. Accordingly, the judgment of the appellate court is affirmed with respect to its determination as the events which give rise to the insurers' obligations to provide coverage of asbestos-related claims.

Notes and Questions

1. *Raymark* is one of the earliest state supreme court cases to state authoritatively the meaning of bodily injury. Many cases on the question preceded it, but nearly all were in the federal courts, which could only guess at the governing state law. There may be many different rules before the results are all in, but for now the few opinions thus far

do not lead to any conclusive trends. *Raymark* may find a considerable following, at least in asbestos cases. Its debt to *Keene* is obvious. Which approach is preferable?

2. In the asbestos cases to date, the courts have generally been able to avoid the thorny problems of allocation among insurers by postponing it to future stages of the cases (which seldom materialize). The court in Ducre v. Mine Safety Appliance Co., 645 F. Supp. 708 (E.D. La. 1986), however, faced the issue squarely in a case concerning an old-fashioned disease — silicosis. It was obligated to follow the exposure theory of Insurance Co. of North America v. Forty-Eight Insulations, 633 F.2d 1212 (6th Cir. 1980), for the Fifth Circuit had followed it in Porter v. American Optical Corp., 641 F.2d 1128 (5th Cir. 1981). The court allocated liability to the insurers on a per year/per person basis, and in the opinion provided an illustration of the calculations.

3. A policy contains the following language, called a *deemer* clause:

> The policy applies only to personal injury and property damage anywhere in the world; *provided personal injury or property damage caused by exposure to injurious conditions over a period of days, weeks, months or longer shall be deemed to occur only on the last day of exposure to such injurious conditions.* Personal injury or property damage caused by such continuous or repeated exposure for which written claim is made against the insured during the policy period shall be deemed to occur only on the last day of the last exposure prior to the date such claim is made. Subject to the foregoing provisions, the policy does not apply to such personal injury or property damage caused by such continuous or repeated exposure, any part of which occurs after the policy period. (Emphasis added by the court.)

How does this deemer clause affect the application of the statute of limitations? How will it affect allocation of coverage to successive insurers when the injurious conditions overlap the times when insurers were changed? Suppose the exposure continues indefinitely: Does this mean there will never be any coverage until it finally terminates? In Abex Corp. v. Maryland Casualty Co., 790 F.2d 119, 122 (D.C. Cir. 1986), the D.C. Circuit noted the above clause for attention on remand, without raising specific questions and without giving any answers.

4. The triple or continuous trigger doctrine developed in *Keene* and other cases implements the underlying goal of many insurance cases — to maximize coverage. But see Howard, "Continuous Trigger" Liability: Application to Toxic Waste Cases and Impact on the Number of "Occurrences," 22 Tort & Ins. L.J. 625 (1987) for a discussion of the doctrine's potential for *reducing* coverage in certain cases.

3.   The Meaning of Property Damage

The 1973 Comprehensive General Liability policy offers the following definition:

> *"property damage"* means (1) physical injury to or destruction of tangible property which occurs during the policy period, including the loss of use thereof at any time resulting therefrom, or (2) loss of use of tangible property which has not been physically injured or destroyed provided such loss of use is caused by an occurrence during the policy period. . . .

The definition of occurrence requires bodily injury or property damage. Is the second part of the definition of property damage circular? How can it be given meaning?

The homeowners and personal automobile policies define it more briefly:

> *"property damage"* means physical injury to, destruction of, or loss of use of tangible property.

Is the definition wider or narrower than that in the CGL policy? In what way?

Some policies have the following definition:

> *"property damage"* means physical injury to or destruction of tangible property, including loss of use of this property.

Is this definition wider or narrower than the others? In what way?

Notes and Questions

1. Property damage to the insured's own property is excluded from coverage by exclusion (k) of the 1973 CGL policy (exclusion (j)(1) of the policy reproduced in Section C). In his discussion of the 1966 CGL policy, Roland Wendorff states the case of "[t]he insured's crane [which] broke down in front of the door of a supermarket and prevented access to the supermarket by its customers." Wendorff, The New Standard Comprehensive General Liability Insurance Policy 254, Section C(1).] He says insurers differed on whether there was liability under pre-1966 policies but that there would be coverage under the 1966 policy. Do you agree that the supermarket's loss of use of its store, without any physical damage except to property of the insured, would be covered under the 1973 policy? Would it be under the 1966 policy? Federal Ins. Co. v. General Machine Corp., 699 F. Supp. 490 (E.D. Pa. 1988), deals with a comparable problem.

2. In Prudential Property and Casualty Ins. Co. v. Lawrence, 45

Wash. App. 111, 724 P.2d 418 (1986), the insureds were sued by neighbors for obstruction of view, breach of the covenant of quiet enjoyment of their property, and emotional distress because the placement of their new home allegedly violated zoning ordinances and restrictive covenants. Under which of the definitions of property damage above would there be coverage?

3. The insured supplied defective couplings for a solar heating and cooling facility. It leaked as soon as it was installed, within the policy period, and could not be used for a time. The insured was sued to judgment. The plaintiff then filed a writ of garnishment against the liability insurer, claiming property damage within the meaning of the policy. The loss of use was after the policy period terminated. Under the 1973 CGL definition of property damage, was there coverage? See University Mech. Contractors, Inc. v. Puritan Ins. Co., 150 Ariz. 299, 723 P.2d 648 (1986).

4. In Lund v. American Motorists Ins. Co., 797 F.2d 544 (7th Cir. 1986), the damage claimed was the 1984 collapse of a building constructed in the early 1960s, when the contractor was covered by an accident policy. The court, purporting to follow Wisconsin law, found the "accident" to be in the negligence (the cause) rather than in the collapse (the result). "[I]f the insurer wanted to limit coverage to accidents that resulted in injury during the policy period it must say so, as the insurers did in some of the later policies." Id. at 547.

5. Accidental erasure of magnetically encoded data on computer disk cartridges was initially held to be property damage within the meaning of the CGL, but it was held not to be on appeal because the data were not "tangible property." Magnetic Data, Inc. v. St. Paul Fire & Marine Ins. Co., 430 N.W.2d 483 (Minn. App. 1988), *rev'd*, 442 N.W.2d 153 (1989).

6. One property damage issue that has been litigated for years has reached partial tentative resolution in Dow Chemical Co. v. Associated Indem. Corp., 724 F. Supp. 474 (E.D. Mich. 1989). Dow produced Sarabond as a mortar additive to give greater strength to masonry structures. Sarabond allegedly caused the steel supports to rust and the structure to crack. In examining the issue of "trigger of coverage" for the property damage situation, the court adopted the *injury in fact* theory (as against either a naked exposure theory, a continuous trigger theory, or a manifestation theory). The court said the record was not sufficient, however, to decide when there was injury in fact.

Problem

Up to this point, most of the asbestos litigation concerned bodily injury, but a new kind of lawsuit is coming to the fore. Manufacturers of various building products containing asbestos — insulation, plaster with special acoustical qualities, etc. — have been sued because of the fear, induced largely by the EPA, that the materials will become friable and release asbestos fibers into the air, and thereby put users of the buildings at risk.* The suits have been brought mostly by school boards, although owners of other buildings have also sued. In early 1986, for example, jury verdicts for $2.4 million and $8.4 million were awarded in suits by Mercer University and by Greenville, South Carolina (the latter for the cost of replacing the suspect material in the City Hall).

When sued, the manufacturers respond by tendering the defense of the cases to their comprehensive general liability insurers under the products liability coverage, claiming that the suits are for property damage.

Is there property damage in these cases? If the claim is not based on property damage, what is its basis? If it is, what property is damaged and how?

If as counsel for the insured you want to argue for maximum insurance protection, how would you analyze the case? An article written from that perspective is Pasich, Insurance Coverage for the Asbestos Building Cases: There's More Than Property Damage, 24 Tort & Ins. L.J. 630 (1989).

4. The Expected or Intended Problem

An "occurrence" exists only when the harm that results is "neither expected nor intended from the standpoint of the insured." In some older policies the same effect was sought by an explicit exclusion of damages "caused intentionally by or at the direction of the insured." Before that the word "accident" was thought (perhaps quite reasonably) to produce the same result, until courts began to interpret "accident" from the viewpoint of the person injured, by whom the damage would seldom be either intended or expected. For the interpretation of "accident," see Annot., 7 A.L.R.3d 1262 (1966). For an overview, see Rynerson, Exclusion of Expected or Intended Personal Injury or Property Damage Under the Occurrence Definition of the Standard Comprehensive General Liability Policy, 19 Forum 513 (1984).

Whether the harm is expected or intended is a question of fact: Who should have the burden of persuasion? Would the answer to that

---

*Removal of asbestos from buildings may itself be a considerable part of the problem of the use of asbestos in building construction, as is indicated by the difficulties of Acmat, a major asbestos removal company. Acmat had such difficulties in obtaining insurance that it created a captive insurance company. See Appendix. Some think that in most situations the risk is minimized if the asbestos is encapsulated and left in place until the building needs rehabilitation or demolition.

question depend on whether the phrase was part of the definition of "occurrence" as in the 1973 policy or was in an explicit exclusion?

The question of what is "expected or intended" is fact-sensitive and can be very difficult. It looms large in important cases where big corporations are sued for damages resulting from exposure to toxic substances. Suppose, for example, the conduct of a manufacturer-insured is such as to justify punitive damages: does that suggest there is no coverage under the "expected or intended" language? Punitive damages themselves might be expressly excluded or uninsurable as a matter of local public policy, but the question raised here is more basic. It is whether coverage for even compensatory damages is foreclosed by the terms of the contract when punitive damages are justified.

The complexity of what might at first glance appear a fairly straightforward problem is illustrated by the emanation of five separate opinions from the Supreme Court of Michigan when it examined the "expected or intended" question in Allstate Ins. Co. v. Freeman, 432 Mich. 656, 443 N.W.2d 734 (1989). The case involved two unrelated incidents, one of shooting and one of stabbing. On remand the Michigan Court of Appeal concluded that

> the presence of expert testimony . . . that plaintiff's insured was either not aware of what he was doing or was unable to control his actions when he embarked on a killing spree established a genuine issue of material fact as to whether the plaintiff's insured acted intentionally. Therefore, summary disposition was improper. [Allstate Ins. Co. v. Miller, 460 N.W.2d 612 (Mich. App. 1990).]

Notes and Questions

1. Defendants, without permission, entered plaintiffs' land, removed trees, installed a cement culvert, and developed a roadway. On the basis of the "expected or intended" exclusion, defendants' insurer declined to defend. Defendants cross-claimed, contending they had an easement. The trial court found specifically that defendants did not intend to injure plaintiffs' property, honestly believed they had an easement, and legitimately believed they were improving the property. The court held the exclusion did not apply because the insured did not intend to cause injury to plaintiff's property. Turner v. Burch, 156 Mich. App. 303, 401 N.W.2d 355 (1986). The contrary result was reached on similar facts in National Farmers Union Property and Casualty Co. v. Kovash, 452 N.W.2d 307 (N.D. 1990). Which result is preferable? Should "intent" have the same meaning for the "expected or intended" clause as it does in the law of intentional torts?

2. In White v. Smith, 440 S.W.2d 497 (Mo. App. 1969), an insured

abattoir operator deposited waste material in a lagoon. Periodically the material escaped and constituted a private nuisance. The court held the insured was covered by an "accident" policy because the damages had not been intentionally inflicted. Would the court reach the same result under an "occurrence" policy, limiting the coverage to cases in which the damage was "neither expected nor intended from the standpoint of the insured?"

3. A homeowners policy excluded "bodily injury . . . which is expected or intended by the insured." The claim against the insured was for battery — for a shooting in a parking lot. If the insured pleads self-defense, does the insurer have an obligation to defend? To indemnify? Western Fire Ins. Co. v. Persons, 393 N.W.2d 234 (Minn. App. 1986), said yes. Should that depend on whether the response of self-defense was reasonable? See Berg v. Fall, 138 Wis. 2d 115, 405 N.W.2d 701 (Wis. App. 1987).

4. A homeowners policy had the usual exclusion of conduct intended or expected. In a state of paranoid schizophrenia the insured, an apparently mild and harmless man, shot a friend because he thought God had ordered him to do so. Must the insurer defend? Indemnify? See Johnson v. Insurance Co. of North America, 232 Va. 340, 350 S.E.2d 616 (1986).

5. See Note, Mental Incapacity and Liability Insurance Exclusionary Clauses: The Effect of Insanity upon Intent, 78 Calif. L. Rev. 1027 (1990), for a lengthy treatment of that subject, together with a proposal for a new test of the requisite intent.

6. One would have thought it obvious that incest would not be covered by the liability policy, and Rodriguez v. Williams, 107 Wash. 2d 381, 729 P.2d 627 (1986) so held. Linebaugh v. Berdish, 144 Mich. App. 750, 376 N.W.2d 400 (1985), held the same for rape. See also Altena v. United Fire and Casualty Co., 422 N.W.2d 485 (Iowa 1988). But see Zordan v. Page, 500 So. 2d 608 (Fla. App. 1986), where a stepgrandfather's sexual fondling of a minor female with no "claim of either penetration or violence or threat thereof" was not excluded from coverage without proof of specific intent to harm. There was, not unexpectedly, a dissent. A like result was reached in MacKinnon v. Hanover Ins. Co., 124 N.H. 456, 471 A.2d 1166 (1984). See State Auto Mut. Ins. Co. v. McIntyre, 652 F. Supp. 1177 (N.D. Ala. 1987), for an exhaustive examination of a great many similar cases.

7. Insurers do eventually respond to stimuli emanating from the courts. In the renewal of the author's homeowners policy effective December 1990 is a new exclusion: "arising out of sexual molestation, corporal punishment, or physical or mental abuse."

8. In an "ordinary" assault and battery case, Breland v. Schilling, 550 So. 2d 609 (La. 1989), the court reached a result like some in the preceding paragraph. The insured hit a third person, intending only

minor injury but breaking the jaw. The court found for the insured despite the intended or expected clause. Allstate Ins. Co. v. Lewis, 732 F. Supp. 1112 (D. Colo. 1990), purporting to apply Colorado law, was somewhat similar. A 17-year-old boy, trying to discourage demonstrations of affection by a 13-year-old girl, pointed at her a gun he thought empty. It wasn't. There was no intention to shoot her but he did. The court denied the insurer's motion for summary judgment on the basis of the intentional act exclusion.

9. In Physicians Ins. Co. v. Swanson, 58 Ohio St. 3d 189, 569 N.E.2d 906 (1991), a teenager shot a BB gun in the vicinity of the opposite side after a fight, intending to scare them. The shot put out the plaintiff's eye. Must the insurer defend? Indemnify?

10. Does "expected" mean the same thing in these insurance cases that "foreseeable" does in tort law in determining whether an insured is negligent and whether there was proximate cause? If the words have different meanings, how would you charge the jury respecting them? If the two words mean the same thing, is there any insurance coverage at all for negligence?

Problem

In developing a drug, one test gives clear indications that the drug may be carcinogenic. From further tests there are indications of carcinogenic properties but, on balance, the findings are favorable to the drug, the use of which has many advantages in treating a serious disease. After F.D.A. approval, the drug is marketed. Some users develop cancer and file suit. The tests are disclosed through discovery and, shouting "smoking gun," the plaintiffs proceed to trial. This is no fanciful scenario for pharmaceutical manufacturers nor for many another product manufacturer. How should the torts case come out? Is there doubt of the insurer's obligation to defend? But if the plaintiff(s) win(s) the tort case(s), must the insurer indemnify?

5. Personal Injury Coverage

Personal injury is of lesser importance in insurance than are bodily injury and property damage, but it presents some especially interesting legal problems.

In Ploen v. Aetna Casualty & Surety Co., 138 Misc. 2d 704, 525 N.Y.S.2d 522 (Sup. Ct. 1988), the plaintiff was president of a union local and was covered by a homeowner's policy that provided protection against suits for libel. The alleged libel was uttered in the course of a political campaign for the union office. The court held the insurer had an obligation to defend. Similarly, Vargas v. Calabrese, 714 F. Supp. 714 (D.N.J. 1989), held that a standard broad form comprehensive general liability policy issued to cover three political organizations required defense of a suit for infringement of the voting rights of minority voters.

In John Deere Ins. Co. v. Shamrock Indust., 696 F. Supp. 434 (D. Minn. 1988), on a motion for summary judgment the court held that an insured's letter to a single customer alleging patent infringement, and thus being potentially libellous, would constitute advertising activity such as to require the insurer to defend an action under a policy covering liability based on advertising activity.

In Davidson v. Cincinnati Ins. Co., 572 N.E.2d 502 (Ind. App. 1991), a landlord in litigation with a tenant about unauthorized removal of fixtures made campaign contributions to the judge sitting on the case. The tenant then sued the landlord; one of the counts was for malicious prosecution. The insurer sought a declaratory judgment to determine whether it was required to defend. The trial court granted summary judgment in favor of the insurer on the ground that the harm to the tenant was intended or expected. The appellate court thought that made the coverage illusory and reversed. One judge dissented.

The range of potential coverage under the personal injury endorsement does seem very broad.

Personal injury coverage raises the threshold question of whether it is contrary to public policy for an insurer to provide defense and indemnity against intentional torts. In Alabama, it is not. Burnham Shoes, Inc. v. West Am. Ins. Co., 504 So. 2d 238 (Ala. 1987). *Should* it be contrary to public policy?

TRANSPORT INS. CO. v. LEE WAY MOTOR FREIGHT

487 F. Supp. 1325 (N.D. Tex. 1980)

[The text of this opinion is found in Section E(1).]

Notes and Questions

1. *Lee Way* involved awards of back pay. In National Union Fire Ins. Co. v. City of Leeds, 530 So. 2d 205 (Ala. 1988), the policy covered discrimination but excluded "injunctive or equitable relief." Is

there any merit to the argument that a back pay award is not "damages for liability" but equitable relief and thus not covered by the policy?

2. The distinction between disparate treatment and disparate impact may make a difference in ways other than in determining the number of occurrences. Solo Cup Co. v. Federal Ins. Co., 619 F.2d 1178 (7th Cir.), *cert. denied,* 449 U.S. 1033 (1980), held the policy obliged the insurer to defend when disparate impact was alleged. In that case the coverage would be in accordance with public policy and might encourage equal treatment by bringing the resources of the insurer to help small insureds prevent claims. The court construed the policy as not covering disparate treatment cases, but did not decide whether it would be contrary to public policy if it had. Should it be? An earlier case at the District Court level, Union Camp Corp. v. Continental Casualty Co., 452 F. Supp. 565 (S.D. Ga. 1978), would uphold even that insurance coverage, saying that the argument that such insurance would encourage violations of civil rights was erroneous. Can you justify on public policy grounds a distinction between insurance coverage of disparate impact and disparate treatment? The insurer's resources *may* be the most reliable source of compensation for the person discriminated against. Willborn, Insurance, Public Policy, and Employment Discrimination, 66 Minn. L. Rev. 1003 (1982), argues that a public policy limitation on insurance against liability for civil rights violations is unsound. Do you agree? Ranger Ins. Co. v. Bal Harbour Club, Inc., 549 So. 2d 1005 (Fla. 1989), held that the public policy of Florida precluded coverage for an intentional act of religious discrimination.

3. If there is a sound argument for considering it contrary to public policy to insure against liability for unlawful discrimination, either of disparate treatment or of all unlawful discrimination, how can the question be raised in those cases, such as *Lee Way,* in which the insurer concedes the coverage but denies that the facts fall within the coverage?

4. Note that the personal injury liability in *Lee Way* is broader than that in the sample policy above, which does not appear to include discrimination. In Z.R.L. Corp. v. Great Central Ins. Co., 156 Ill. App. 3d 856, 510 N.E.2d 102, 109 Ill. Dec. 481 (1987), the policy was a "Restaurant Package Policy" covering against "false arrest, malicious prosecution, detention, imprisonment, libel, slander, defamation of character, invasion of privacy, wrongful eviction or wrongful entry." The restaurant was operated as a private club. A club member brought two black guests who were excluded because they were not members, although at the same time some white guests were permitted to remain. The black guests sued the insured restaurant for racial discrimination. The insurer declined to defend. The insured insisted that the allegation

was of a "wrongful eviction," and therefore was covered. How would you decide the case? The insurer cited to the court a similar prior case (not binding on it) in which "wrongful eviction" had been held not to apply, the earlier court applying the maxim *noscitur a sociis* ("a word is known by its associates") to interpretation of the phrase "wrongful entry or eviction, or other invasion of the right of private occupancy." Do you find that argument persuasive as to *Z.R.L.?*

5. Liberty Mut. Ins. Co. v. Those Certain Underwriters at Lloyds, 650 F. Supp. 1553 (W.D. Pa. 1987) begins as follows:

> This matter has taken us rushing headlong into the past, to events which occurred over twenty years ago and which have now spawned 10 reported decisions in three separate lawsuits. For the reader's sake we will condense that history as best we can.
> Prior to 1965, life was relatively simple in Liberty Mutual's claims departments. Sometime in 1965, the company altered the structure of those offices to create two parallel positions: Claims Representative and Claims Adjuster. The company's hiring for these positions was gender-based, approaching 100% women in claims representative positions, and achieving 100% males in the claims adjuster position, over a 6 year period.

The practice led to a leading case, Appalachian Ins. Co. v. Liberty Mut. Ins. Co., 676 F.2d 56 (3d Cir. 1982), *aff'g* 507 F. Supp. 59 (W.D. Pa. 1981), holding there was a single occurrence that took place upon promulgation of the discriminatory employment policies.

6. Could insurers routinely provide insurance against damages from discriminatory conduct? Is the risk of liability for discrimination an insurable risk? The insured's personal liability coverage included discrimination in *Lee Way Motor Freight,* but the policies at issue covered the period from 1967 to 1972, after which coverage of discrimination was excluded by endorsement. Recently, an intermediate appellate court in Washington held that "personal injury" included "racial discrimination not committed by or at the direction of the insured." Castle & Cooke, Inc. v. Great Am. Ins. Co., 42 Wash. App. 508, 711 P.2d 1108 (1986). The insurer denied coverage on the basis of an exclusion which, when interpreted by the court (probably quite correctly), did not exclude employee claims for race discrimination. The exclusion was for "mental anguish or bodily injury to any employee arising out of and in the course of his employment." Id. at 511, 711 P.2d at 1110. Would there be substantial demand for such coverage? Would it be generally available? John G. Poust argued that resourceful insurers should be able to provide it, in Coverage for Civil Rights Liability — A Great Opportunity for Insurers, 51 Ins. Couns. J. 55 (1984).

F. Exclusions

Broad as the coverage may be in the comprehensive general liability policy, it is far from total coverage. The standard CGL policy of 1973 contains sixteen exclusions. Exclusions for automobile and aircraft, watercraft, and workers compensation are in the policy because those risks are covered under other well-established lines of insurance in separate policies. Many other exclusions can be eliminated from the policy by endorsement for an additional premium, or without additional charge because the insurer wants the insured's overall account, or on an underwriting decision that the risk is inconsequential in the insured's situation.

It is not generally in the interest of an insurance company to minimize its coverage without good reason. First, that would be bad public relations. Second, the broader the coverage, the larger the premiums and (if underwriting is successful) the larger the profits. Exclusions have a more legitimate function.

The purposes of exclusions are perhaps two-fold: (1) to carve out risks that insurers cannot practicably insure, and (2) to distinguish for separate treatment risks that should receive individual underwriting evaluation, including independent rating consideration. The second purpose also prevents double coverage, which is wasteful. Further, failure to exclude or separately charge for the second category of risks will result in the overcharging of insureds who are not subject to those risks and the probable loss of those less risk-subject policyholders to insurers that do use the exclusion. See Bean, The Accident Versus the Occurrence Concept, 440 Ins. L.J. 550 (Sept. 1959), for an insurance executive's view of the principles underlying the designing of coverage. Mr. Bean was Assistant Secretary of the Liberty Mutual Insurance Company.

Some exclusions represent risks that are probably truly uninsurable, although experiments in insuring some of them have been made and some such experiments are still in process, albeit with doubtful continued life.

Of the last named, perhaps the most important is the pollution exclusion. Pollution liability has been the subject of experimental coverage that has not yet proved successful, but is important enough to receive special attention later in this chapter.

1. The Sistership Exclusion

This important exclusion is set forth in the following case, which also briefly describes its origin.

ATLANTIC MUT. INS. CO. v. JUDD COMPANY

380 N.W.2d 122 (Minn. 1986)

AMDAHL, Chief Justice.

This case involves a declaratory judgment action in which appellant, Atlantic Mutual Insurance Company (insurer), sought a determination (1) whether exclusions in a comprehensive general liability (CGL) insurance policy issued to respondent, Judd Company (insured), operate to exclude coverage for certain claims made against insured by a third party, and (2) whether the exclusions also operate to relieve insurer of its obligation under the policy to defend insured against the claims. The trial court determined under stipulated facts that the policy exclusions prevented coverage for the damages claimed against insured but that insurer nonetheless had a duty to defend. The trial court also awarded insured attorney fees of $8,500 in defending the declaratory judgment action. The court of appeals, 367 N.W.2d 609 (Minn. App. 1985), reversed on the issue of coverage, holding that the exclusions in the policy are inapplicable to the damages claimed, and affirmed on the issue of insurer's duty to defend and on the award of attorney fees. We affirm the decision of the court of appeals.

In January 1980, insured, a plumbing and heating supply wholesaler, entered into a contract with a plumbing and heating contractor for a construction project in Austin, Minnesota. Under the contract, insured was to furnish soil pipes and fittings for an underground sewage system. After the contractor had installed a number of the soil pipes and fittings, tests were performed to determine whether the pipes would withstand the pressure required of the sewage system. The tests revealed that some of the fittings leaked and that some of the pipes had hairline cracks. The defects allegedly occurred during the manufacturing process. Although the contractor was supplied new pipes and fittings at no additional charge, it allegedly spent about $116,000 locating the defects and repairing and replacing the pipes.

In August 1981 the contractor commenced suit against insured for expenses incurred in replacing defective pipes and fittings, pleading negligence and breach of express and implied warranties. At the time the defective pipes and fittings were sold to the contractor, insured was covered under a policy of CGL insurance issued by insurer. Pursuant to the policy, insured tendered defense of the lawsuit to insurer.

Insurer investigated the claims brought by the contractor and commenced the present declaratory action, seeking to avoid the obligation to defend Judd in the main action and to ultimately provide coverage for any awarded damages. . . .

The next issue is whether exclusions in the CGL policy operate to preclude coverage for the claims brought against the insured. At trial insurer relied upon several exclusions in the policy. On appeal, however, it argues only with respect to exclusion (p), which provides that the insurance policy does not apply:

(p) to damages claimed for the withdrawal, inspection, repair, replacement, or loss of use of the named insured's products or work completed by or for the named insured or of any property of which such products or work form a part, if such products, work or property are withdrawn from the market or from use because of any known or suspected defect or deficiency therein.

Exclusion (p) is often called the "sistership" exclusion because it originated from an occurrence in the aircraft industry where all airplanes of a certain make were grounded by the federal government after one crashed and the others were suspected of having common structural defects. 2 R. Long, Law of Liability Insurance, App. §15 (1966). The purpose of exclusion (p) has been described in the following manner:

The plain meaning and intent of [the exclusion] is that while the insurance covers damages for bodily injuries and property damage caused by the product that was defective or fails, it was never intended that the insurer would be saddled with the cost of preventing such defects or failure any more than it was intended that the insurer would pay the cost of avoiding the defect in the first place or preventing the first failure of the product to have been discovered to be in a defective or dangerous condition before the occurrence. [2 R. Long, Law of Liability Insurance §11.11 (1983).]

The sole authority which insurer relies upon in support of its argument that exclusion (p) precludes coverage of the claims against the insured is an Alabama case, Commercial Union Assurance Co. v. Glass Lined Pipe Co., 372 So. 2d 1305 (Ala. 1979). In that case the insured, a manufacturer of glass-lined pipe, sought coverage from its insurer to defend a suit brought by the contractor on construction of a sewage disposal plant. The contractor claimed that the lining in pipes supplied by the insured was deficient and that the pipes had to be relined, resulting in damages for expenses incurred in inspecting the pipe and for delay in construction. There was no other damage to the project; no walls were taken down and no damage was done to the pipe itself. Id. at 1308. On these facts, the Alabama Supreme Court held that the insurer's obligation to defend and indemnify the insured was precluded by exclusion (p). Id. at 1309.

Insurer argues that *Glass Lined Pipe* is directly on point with the issues presented here and, therefore, that exclusion (p) precludes coverage. A close reading of the Alabama case reveals, however, that the court addressed only one aspect of exclusion (p) — whether the damages claimed were "for the withdrawal, inspection, repair, replacement, or loss of use of the named insured's products or work completed by the named insured" — and held in the affirmative. See id. at 1308. The court never specifically addressed the question raised here — whether "such products, work or property [were] withdrawn from the market or from use because of any known or suspected defect or deficiency therein."

A majority of courts that have considered the question have adopted the view that repair and replacement of *just* those products that actually failed in use, with no attempt to prevent future failures by removal of other similar suspect products, does not constitute withdrawal. We have also adopted this view. In Ohio Casualty Insurance Co. v. Terrace Enterprises, Inc., 260 N.W.2d 450 (Minn. 1978), the general liability insurer of a construction company brought a declaratory judgment action to determine coverage in regard to the company's liability for damages to an apartment building resulting from defective construction. The insurer asserted, among other things, that a "sistership exclusion" in the policy precluded the insurance company's liability. We held that the exclusion was inapplicable because the "apartment building in question was not withdrawn from the market because of a suspected defect in *another* building. It was withdrawn because it was damaged by defective construction." Id. at 455 (emphasis added).

Applying this view of exclusion (p) to the present case leads to the conclusion that the exclusion does not apply. The record indicates that the only pipes and fittings which were repaired or replaced were those which had actually proven defective after being installed and tested. There is no evidence that other pipes or fittings which had not actually failed were removed or rejected. Accordingly, exclusion (p) is not applicable. . . .

Affirmed.

Notes and Questions

1. After seven people in the Chicago area died from ingesting Tylenol capsules containing cyanide, McNeilab, Inc., a subsidiary of Johnson & Johnson, acted promptly to remove all Tylenol capsules from the market in the United States and seven foreign countries. The costs of the recall have been estimated at from $40 million to $150 million. Does the sistership exclusion prevent McNeilab from recovering? Review the excerpt from *McNeilab* in Chapter 1.

2. If the recall is under compulsion, as it usually is in the automobile recall cases, would there be coverage?

3. See Pillsbury Co. v. National Union Fire Ins. Co., 425 N.W.2d 244 (Minn. App. 1988), for a case involving a Products Integrity Impairment Loss of Revenue and Product Recall Extra Expense Insurance Policy. Pillsbury paid $280,000 for coverage of $150 million in excess of a $20 million deductible. What is the future of such "recall" insurance? Compare the premium with the potential loss in the event of a maximum claim, and consider whether writing such insurance with limits so high will interest many insurers. Such disparity would at least require substantial reinsurance by the primary insurer. See Chapter 9 for a treatment of reinsurance.

4. For a recent case discussing the sistership exclusion and its relation to the business risk exclusion (excluding coverage for damage to an insured's own product) — a problem with some subtleties — see Forest City Dillon, Inc. v. Aetna Casualty & Surety Co., 852 F.2d 168 (6th Cir. 1988).

5. See Annot., Validity and Construction of "Sistership" Clause of Products Liability Insurance Policy Excepting from Coverage Cost of Product Recall or Withdrawal of Product from Market, 32 A.L.R.4th 630 (1984).

2. The Employee Injury Exclusions

Exclusions (i) and (j) of the 1973 standard policy read as follows:

This insurance does not apply:
    (i) to any obligation for which the insured or any carrier as his insurer may be held liable under any workmen's compensation, unemployment compensation or disability benefits law, or under any similar law;
    (j) to bodily injury to any employee of the insured arising out of and in the course of his employment by the insured or to any obligation of the insured to indemnify another because of damages arising out of such injury.

The purpose of exclusion (i) is self-evident. The first part of exclusion (j) is only a more inclusive way of stating (i), but the second part has a less obvious purpose. It deals with the problem for employers created by cases like Dole v. Dow Chemical Co., 30 N.Y.2d 143, 282 N.E.2d 288, 331 N.Y.S.2d 382 (1972), which enable a third party liable for injury to an employee to obtain indemnity or contribution from the employer who was protected from direct tort liability to the employee by the exclusive remedy provision of the workers compensation statutes. For a recent case illustrating the matter, see Granite State Ins. Co. v. Transamerica Ins. Co., 148 Ariz. 111, 713 P.2d 312 (Ariz. App. 1985).

3. The Asbestos Exclusions

By the late 1970s insurance companies could anticipate the possibility of catastrophic losses from asbestos claims. In an effort at damage control, some companies began to insert exclusions in liability policies, disclaiming liability for "claims relating to asbestos," or from "asbestosis," or from "asbestosis-related claims." Do these all mean the same thing?

Litigation is in process, as of this writing, respecting the exclusion for claims for asbestosis. The insurers in question claim that the exclusion covers all the asbestos-related diseases; the insureds contend that the exclusion means what it says and that mesothelioma, lung cancer, and other asbestos-related diseases are covered by the insurance. Full recognition of the detailed nature of the asbestos problem came slowly to insurance underwriters as well as to the general population. Further, in most cases where the more serious diseases, like mesothelioma, develop, there is also asbestosis. Given these facts, how would you argue the case for the insurers? For the insureds? For one resolution of the controversy, see Carey Canada, Inc. v. California Union Ins. Co., 720 F. Supp. 1018 (D.D.C. 1989), purporting to apply Florida and Illinois law.

G. Concurrent Coverage

In many liability insurance situations, there is or arguably may be coverage by two or more separate policies. The cases may be loosely divided into two categories: in some duplicated coverage is reasonably to be expected, in some it is unintended. In the former category (other insurance), the usual problem is one of determining which of the policies is primary and which secondary, or of allocating the coverage between them. In the latter category (the boundary problem), the usual problem is one of ascertaining which, if any, of the policies provides coverage, since occasionally both may.

1. Other Insurance

In automobile insurance, concurrent insurance coverage is routinely expected. For example, the standard automobile policy provides both drive-other-cars (DOC) coverage and omnibus (other drivers) coverage, so that in a substantial percentage of automobile liability cases at least two policies, and often more, are fully available to provide liability protection. When concurrent insurance coverage is expected, each insurer may seek to protect itself with one of the following types of clauses. The precise language used may vary considerably.

1. *Pro rata clause:* If the insured has other insurance against a loss covered by this policy the company shall not be liable under this policy for a greater proportion of such loss than the applicable limit of liability stated in the declarations bears to the total applicable limit of liability of all valid and collectible insurance against such loss.
2. *Excess clause:* This policy is in excess of all other valid and collectible insurance and shall not be called upon in contribution.
3. *Escape clause:* If any person, firm, or corporation other than the Assured . . . is . . . entitled to be indemnified hereunder and is also covered by other valid and collectible insurance, such other person, firm, or corporation shall not be indemnified under this policy.

Notes and Questions

1. If two policies may cover a risk, there are six possible types of pairing of other insurance clauses. If both are pro rata clauses and are identical in wording, the clauses may be given effect and the result achieved seems reasonable. Can the same thing be said if both have excess clauses or both have escape clauses?

2. In Continental Casualty Co. v. New Amsterdam Casualty Co., 28 Ill. App. 2d 489, 171 N.E.2d 406 (1960), both policies had excess other insurance clauses. The court said the clauses were mutually repugnant and prorated the loss between the companies. Is that an appropriate result? If not, how should such a case be decided?

3. If two policies cover the risk, one having an excess clause and the other an escape clause, how should the loss be allocated? New Amsterdam Casualty Co. v. Certain Underwriters at Lloyds, London, 34 Ill. 2d 424, 216 N.E.2d 665 (1966), prorated the coverage, contrary to what the court said was the majority view, which was said to favor the insurer with the excess clause. Is a plausible argument possible for each result?

3. If two policies cover the risk and both have pro rata clauses or excess clauses, but with different limits and premium rates, is a simple proration of the loss appropriate? If one has a self-insured retention and the other does not, or both have such retentions but for different amounts, how should liability be allocated? For a general treatment of other insurance clauses see Keeton & Widiss, Insurance Law: Student

Edition 253-275 (1988). In liability insurance, the problems of allocating indemnity are not the only ones; problems of allocating defense costs also arise. See *Raymark,* supra.

4. An other insurance clause states, "The insurance afforded by this policy does not apply to that portion of the loss for which the insured has other valid and collectible insurance, whether on a primary, excess or contingent basis." Should this clause receive different treatment than the one quoted above?

5. If one liability policy provides primary coverage while the other is an umbrella excess policy, and both policies have excess other insurance clauses, how should liability be allocated? In Illinois Emcasco Ins. Co. v. Continental Casualty Co., 139 Ill. App. 3d 130, 487 N.E.2d 110, 93 Ill. Dec. 666 (1985), the court held the umbrella policy to be excess over the primary policy, despite the similar other insurance clauses in the two policies. In analyzing the problem, the court examined the premiums charged for the two policies. That practice is seldom followed by courts. Should it be? The opinion explicitly disagreed with the Seventh Circuit, which had purported to apply Illinois law in Home Ins. Co. v. Certain Underwriters at Lloyd's London, 729 F.2d 1132 (7th Cir. 1984).

6. A statute will override a contract provision in a subsequent contract. See Canal Ins. Co. v. United States Fidelity and Guaranty Co., 149 Ariz. 578, 720 P.2d 963 (Ariz. App. 1986), referring to a statute providing that "when a vehicle is covered by two or more policies, the policy which describes or rates the vehicle shall be the primary coverage."

7. If a prospective buyer who has insurance on her own car is test-driving a dealer's car which also has insurance, are there considerations other than the clauses the policies contain to help determine which policy is primary and which excess? Should the status of the automobile sale make a difference? See Palladino v. Dunn, 361 Pa. Super. 99, 521 A.2d 946 (1987).

8. The following case, though representing a minority view, provides what to many has seemed an equitable approach to the allocation of responsibility among insurers having inconsistent other insurance clauses.

LAMB-WESTON, INC. v. OREGON AUTO. INS. CO.

219 Or. 110, 341 P.2d 110 (1959)

Perry, Justice.

Defendant appeals from a judgment in the sum of $3,399.23. The case was tried without a jury. There are two assignments of error, the first listing eight subdivisions, and the second, two. The first assignment, in general, challenges rulings of the trial court in denying motions for nonsuit and for judgment for defendant. The second assignment of error raises the question of whether or not the trial court erred in entering judgment against the defendant for the entire loss, instead of prorating the loss between the two insurers.

The essential facts are these: The plaintiff Lamb-Weston, Inc., an insured of the plaintiff St. Paul Fire and Marine Insurance Company, leased a truck from Dick Shafer for its use in connection with its business of canning and freezing peas. This included hauling water to crews in the pea fields. Nathan Cole, employee of Lamb-Weston, Inc., drove the truck. The evening of June 18, 1956, Cole was driving the truck to Elgin, Oregon, where he resided, for repair of faulty brakes and gears, a condition he had noticed for some little time. He had been advised to have the brakes repaired in Elgin. About two miles from Elgin his axle refused to "engage", his engine died, and his brakes would not hold in descending a grade and he lost control of the truck and crashed into and damaged a warehouse of the Union County Grain Growers. The Union County Grain Growers demanded damages and threatened suit. Plaintiff Lamb-Weston, Inc. settled the claim, borrowing the amount paid from its insurer St. Paul Mercury Indemnity Company, a subsidiary of St. Paul Fire & Marine Insurance Company, on a "loan receipt."

Defendant had, prior to this accident, issued its policy of insurance protecting Shafer against liability for property damage resulting from the operation of the leased truck. This policy contained an "omnibus" clause extending the protection afforded Shafer to "any person or organization legally responsible for the use thereof, . . . with Shafer's permission. The insurance contract also contained these provisions:

> . . . if the insured has other insurance against a loss covered by this policy the Company shall not be liable under this policy for a greater proportion of such loss than the applicable limit of liability stated in the declaration bears to the total applicable limit of all valid and collectible insurance against such loss.

Plaintiff Lamb-Weston, Inc. notified defendant of the threatened suit and the latter denied liability and refused to pay or recognize the claim. Thereafter, on July 9, 1956, defendant sent the following letter to plaintiff St. Paul Fire & Marine Insurance Company:

> This will confirm our understanding to the effect that you may settle the property damage claim of Union County Grain Growers for the approximate amount of Thirty-Four Hundred Dollars ($3,400.00),

and that the payment of said sum by you will not be construed to waive in any way your right to contend that our policy of insurance covers the loss.

Acting thereon, plaintiffs settled the claim. The judgment from which this appeal was taken resulted from plaintiffs' effort to collect under the terms of defendant's policy for its payment of damages to the Union County Grain Growers. . . .

It is also argued, the loan receipt arrangement was a "sham and subterfuge." Oregon, however, recognizes these transactions as entirely legal and effective, depending upon the intention of the parties. Furrer v. Yew Creek Logging Co., 206 Or. 382, 292 P.2d 499. Generally, see 29 Am. Jur. 1002, Insurance §1337. Here there is no evidence of intention other than as expressed in the instrument itself. We conclude a valid borrower-lender arrangement was intended and effected.

Referring now to the second issue presented, the trial court in its findings of fact found that defendant was the primary insurer and thereon based its conclusion of law that defendant was liable to indemnify the plaintiffs for their entire loss from the occurrence. The defendant duly excepted to the finding of fact and conclusion of law and proposed a conclusion of law that it was liable for but one-half as its share of the loss.

This issue, which is of first impression in this jurisdiction, presents a question of importance only as between the insuring companies, which bears upon the financial responsibility of each for the accrued loss, for it must be conceded by each insurance company that if the other was not an insurer against this occurrence then it would be liable for the full amount.

For a complete understanding of this issue it is necessary to set forth the provisions of the insuring policies and for convenience in this part of the opinion the plaintiff St. Paul Fire and Marine Insurance Company will be hereinafter referred to as St. Paul, and the defendant Oregon Automobile Insurance Company will be referred to as Oregon.

The St. Paul policy contract, which insured the plaintiff Lamb-Weston, Inc., defines "insured" [in a way that makes the driver an insured.] This policy also provided:

> If the Insured's liability under this policy is covered by any other valid and collectible insurance, then this policy shall act as excess insurance over and above such other insurance.

The Oregon policy, which was purchased by Mr. Shafer, owner of the truck, defines "insured" [in a way that also makes the driver an insured]. With reference to "other insurance," this policy provides as follows:

[I]f the insured has other insurance against a loss covered by this policy the Company shall not be liable under this policy for a greater proportion of such loss than the applicable limit of liability stated in the declarations bears to the total applicable limit of all valid and collectible insurance against such loss. . . .

It is, therefore, at once apparent from a consideration of the above policy provisions that each company by its "other insurance" clause seeks to limit its liability if other insurance is available to pay a part or all of an insured's loss. This is demonstrated by the fact that St. Paul provides that its policy can only be treated as "excess insurance over and above" other "valid and collectible insurance," and the Oregon policy can be treated only as paying a proportionate share if there is other "valid and collectible insurance" against such loss.

It is also clear that as between the companies themselves no determination of whether or not there is other valid and collectible insurance can be established without first deciding which company is primarily and which secondarily liable, for St. Paul says it will pay only the excess after the limits of the Oregon policy are exhausted, and Oregon says, since there is other insurance, it will pay only a proportionate share of the loss.

Thus, in such a situation, the court is faced with determining which company shall be considered primarily liable, or treating the "other insurance" clause in each insurer's policy as so repugnant that they must both be ignored, and apply the rule that the loss shall be equally prorated between them.

The trial court applied the rule of primary and secondary liability, following the general rule set out in 8 Appleman, Insurance Law and Practice 333, §4914, that when it is determined who is the primary insurer "the courts give no application to the other insurance clause in the primary policy, which provides that if the additional insured has other valid and collectible insurance he shall not be covered by the primary policy." The difficulty that is encountered by the courts, however, is not in applying this rule, but in finding sound reasoning upon which to base a determination of primary and secondary liability.

[The court discussed cases both applying and rejecting a rule that the policy issued first in time was primary, and another rule that the policy which was most specific in its coverage was primary. The court then goes on to comment on the second group of cases.]

The reasoning of these cases, however, is not applicable to the facts of this case, because the policy of each insurer specifically covers the operation of the particular truck, describing it in its policy, and the driver of the truck, through which liability arises, is covered only by reason of the additional insured provisions of each policy, generally referred to as "omnibus" clauses.

However, in general, the fallacy of the reasoning of adopting this rule is apparent in the fact that the clear intent of each insurer in the policies is clearly expressed to cover the liability of the tort feasor, whether named or additional, and to escape all or partial liability if there is other insurance applicable to the same occurrence.

The courts have also, in seeking to discover which company under conflicting policy provisions, when involved on the same risk, should be primary and which secondary, resorted to applying a rule that, if a named insured is the primary tort feasor, the company so specifically naming him is primary and the other company secondary.

This doctrine, of course, cannot be applied under the facts of this case, because the primary tort feasor, Cole, the driver of the truck, is not a named insured in either policy, and the coverage attaches in each policy only because of the other driver provisions. If, however, the underlying consideration for this doctrine should be applied to the facts of this case, then Cole, the driver, being at the time the agent of the plaintiff Lamb-Weston, Inc., lessor of the truck and the primary tort feasor, it would seem that St. Paul should be considered the primary insurer. Apart from the facts present, this approach to a determination of such an issue, like all others, fails in logic for each policy does in fact intend to insure the driver of the truck, whether named or not, and thus the intent of both insuring companies is to insure the actual tort feasor under circumstances reasonably to be anticipated by both. It can, therefore, be considered only an arbitrary rule to reach a result. Maryland Casualty Co. v. Employers Mutual Liability Ins. Co., D.C. Conn. 1953, 112 F. Supp. 272.

From an examination of the above-cited cases and others of similar import we believe none can be logically acceptable and it is our view that any attempt to give effect to the "other insurance" provision of one policy while rejecting it in another is like pursuing a will o' the wisp.

In 1952, the United States Circuit Court of Appeals for the 9th Circuit recognized the futility of a sound rule seeking to determine primary and secondary liability between different insurers covering the same risk, and in Oregon Auto. Ins. Co. v. United States Fidelity & Guar. Co., 195 F.2d 958, 959, the Court said:

> We have examined cases in other jurisdictions cited by counsel where closely similar or substantially identical disputes between insurance companies have arisen. These decisions point in all directions. One group indicates that the policy using the word "excess" is secondary and that containing the language of the Oregon policy is primary. Examples of these decisions are cited on the margin. Their reasoning appears to us completely circular, depending, as it were, on which policy one happens to read first. Other cases seem to recognize the truth of the matter,

namely, that the problem is little different from that involved in deciding which came first, the hen or the egg. See remark of Judge Major in Zurich General Accident & Liability Insurance Co. v. Clamor, 7 Cir., 124 F.2d 717, 719. In this dilemma courts have seized upon some relatively arbitrary circumstances to decide which insurer must assume primary responsibility. Thus one group of cases fixes primary liability on the policy which is prior in date. Another group undertakes to decide which policy is the more specific, holding the one thought more specific to be primary. Another solution is represented by Maryland Casualty Co. v. Bankers Indemnity Ins. Co., 51 Ohio App. 323, 200 N.E. 849, where it was held that the policy issued to the person primarily liable for the damage is the primary insurance. In sum, the cases are irreconcilable in respect both of approach and result.

As a result of these observations the Court determined each company should share proportionately in the loss. In that case, the policy of each insurer provided, in the event of other insurance, theirs should be treated as excess insurance and liability thereunder came into existence only after the limits of the other had been exhausted.

[The court then discussed a number of cases that followed the 9th Circuit analysis and result.]

We are of the opinion that in these later cases the courts have placed this problem in its true perspective by recognizing the absurdity of attempting to assume that where conflicting "other insurance" provisions exist by reason of overlapping coverages of the same occurrence the provisions of one policy must yield to the provisions of the other.

It may be contended with some slight basis, in reason, since the Oregon clause provides for prorating in proportion to the amount of valid insurance then in effect, its liability should be limited in that proportion. Thus, it would pay its prorata share upon that basis as "other valid and collectible insurance" and St. Paul would pay the balance under its excess clause. In this manner some effect is given to the "other insurance" clause of each policy.

Such a contention leads, however, to a return to the circular reasoning necessary to establish primary and secondary liability, for to sustain this contention such proration can only be given effect by determining the company carrying such "other insurance" clause is a primary insurer with limited liability. . . .

The "other insurance" clauses of all policies are but methods used by insurers to limit their liability, whether using language that relieves them from all liability (usually referred to as an "escape clause") or that used by St. Paul (usually referred to as an "excess clause") or that used by Oregon (usually referred to as a "prorata clause"). In our opinion, whether one policy uses one clause or another, when any come in conflict with the "other insurance" clause of another insurer, regardless of the nature of the clause, they are in fact repugnant and each should be rejected in toto. . . .

The trial court having erred in its conclusion of law that defendant as a primary insurer was, under its policy, liable for the full amount of the loss, the case is remanded with instructions to modify its finding to conform with the law as set forth in this opinion and to enter judgment for the plaintiffs and against the defendant for only one-half of the loss liability, together with plaintiffs' costs and disbursements.

The decree of the circuit court is affirmed as modified.

Notes and Questions

1. Subsequently the court modified the judgment in *Lamb-Weston* to allocate in proportion to the limits of the policies, in order to conform to industry practice. See Lamb-Weston, Inc. v. Oregon Auto. Ins. Co., 219 Or. 110, 346 P.2d 643 (1959).

This second *Lamb-Weston* case hints at a third way to allocate: in proportion to premiums. Would that method be sensible?

2. Is there a plausible way to reconcile a pro rata clause with either of the other two types, in order to give effect to both clauses?

3. To avoid application of the *Lamb-Weston* rule, a group of insurers agreed that where the two policies involved were a policy covering the involved car and a permissive driver's policy on his or her own car which was not involved in the accident, the policy covering the involved car would be primary and the drive-other-car coverage secondary. See Mutual of Enumclaw Ins. Co. v. Hambleton, 84 Or. App. 343, 733 P.2d 948, 950, n.1 (1987). Would that agreement have any effect against an insurer not party to it? Could such a party take advantage of the agreement?

4. For an early treatment of the general subject, see Comment, Concurrent Coverage in Automobile Liability Insurance, 65 Colum. L. Rev. 319 (1965), and Kahn, The "Other Insurance" Clause, 19 Forum 591 (1984).

5. St. Paul Mercury Ins. Co. v. Pennsylvania Casualty Co., 642 F. Supp. 180 (D. Wyo. 1986), applying Wyoming law, rejected *Lamb-Weston* and as to indemnity gave effect to the excess clause over the pro rata clause. As to defense costs, however, the insurers were required to share pro rata. Applying Pennsylvania law, the court in Contrans, Inc. v. Ryder Truck Rental, Inc., 648 F. Supp. 1461 (W.D. Pa. 1986), *aff'd,* 836 F.2d 163 (1987), faced with a conflict between an "escape" clause and an "excess" clause, overrode the first and made the contract containing it the primary insurance. Accord, State Farm Mut. Auto. Ins. Co. v. Bogart, 149 Ariz. 145, 717 P.2d 449 (1986). Can

you justify that result? It may be altered by relevant statutes, of course. State Farm Mut. Auto. Ins. Co. v. Fireman's Fund Ins. Co., 149 Ariz. 179, 717 P.2d 858 (1986). See also Gamble Skogmo, Inc. v. Aetna Casualty & Surety Co., 390 N.W.2d 343 (Minn. App. 1986).

6. The higher layers of coverage are less costly for the same amount of coverage than the lower layers. Is that a reason not to allocate in proportion to limits? Aviles v. Burgos, 783 F.2d 270, 281 (1st Cir. 1986) dealt with that problem in an auto insurance context. Crown Center Redevelopment Corp. v. Occidental Fire & Casualty Co., 716 S.W.2d 348 (Mo. App. 1986), dealt with the problem in far more complicated circumstances: the allocation of liability among primary and excess carriers in the Kansas City Hyatt Hotel case, where 25 insurers were involved in the settlement of losses aggregating an amount in nine figures.

2. The Boundary Problem

No matter how carefully language is chosen for coverage clauses and exclusions to separate the various liability coverages into mutually exclusive compartments, problems will arise along the boundary lines unless both areas are insured by the same insurance company without relevant differences in limits, deductibles, and other conditions (so that it doesn't matter in which compartment the coverage falls).

When concurrent coverage is clear and the problem is merely one of allocating the coverage between the policies, that is the problem of other insurance. When the problem is one of determining which policy, if any, provides the coverage, that is the *boundary* problem. Sometimes the boundaries overlap and both policies provide coverage. The most common setting for the problem is where one policy is a CGL policy and the other is an automobile policy.

PENNSYLVANIA GEN. INS. CO. v. CEGLA

381 N.W.2d 901 (Minn. App. 1986)

WOZNIAK, Judge.

This is an appeal from a finding of coverage under respondent's homeowner's insurance policy. We affirm.

Facts

In September 1983, Ernest Cegla loaded a roll of wire mesh into his truck. The roll was not tied down. Howard Cummings was driving his motorcycle behind Cegla when the wire fell onto the highway, causing Cummings to lose control of the motorcycle. Charles Habiger, who was following Cummings in a pickup truck, struck and killed Cummings.

Cegla admitted claims to both his vehicle insurance company, Allstate Insurance Company, and his homeowner's insurance company, Pennsylvania General Insurance Company. Allstate did not deny coverage. Pennsylvania General, however, denied coverage and commenced a declaratory judgment action. All parties move for summary judgment. The trial court found coverage under the Pennsylvania General homeowner's policy.

Issue

Does Cegla's homeowner's liability insurance policy provide coverage?

Analysis

The Pennsylvania General policy excludes bodily injury or property damage "arising out of the ownership, maintenance, use, loading or unloading of . . . a motor vehicle owned or operated by, or rented or loaned to any insured. . . ." Pennsylvania General claims this clause excuses it from liability for any claim arising out of this accident.

Cegla's failure to tie down the wire roll was, however, a nonvehicle-related act, triggering coverage under the homeowner's policy. It was a separate and independent act which concurred with the vehicle-related act of driving to cause Cummings' death.

This case is analogous to Waseca Mutual Insurance Co. v. Noska, 331 N.W.2d 917 (Minn. 1983), where the nonvehicle-related act of placing live embers in open barrels triggered coverage under a homeowner's policy when it concurred with the vehicle-related act of driving to cause a nine-day forest fire. See also Jorgensen v. Auto-Owners Insurance Co., 360 N.W.2d 397 (Minn. Ct. App. 1985), *pet. for rev. denied* (Minn. April 12, 1985) (motorist's effort to prevent further damage by removing gasoline can from trunk of burning car was not sufficient to break causal link between injury and use of automobile); North Star Mutual Insurance Co. v. Johnson, 352 N.W.2d 791 (Minn. Ct. App. 1984), *pet. for rev. denied* (Minn. Jan. 9, 1985) (alleged negligence in securing arms of farm sprayer attached to pickup truck was an independent act not related to operation or use of truck for purposes of farm policy exclusion).

Decision

The trial court is affirmed.

Notes and Questions

1. A child was injured in an automobile accident when a day care center car was used to transport children to a dance class. The center had both CGL and automobile policies, with different limits. Should both policies provide coverage? In United States Fidelity & Guar. Co. v. State Farm Mut. Auto. Ins. Co., 152 Ill. App. 3d 46, 504 N.E.2d 123, 105 Ill. Dec. 254 (1987), the court held they should because the automobile policies covered negligence in the operation of the car and the CGL policy covered the failure to provide sufficient and adequate supervision of the children. The existence of multiple proximate causes is the key to the result.

2. Duplicate insurance coverage appears frequently in building construction cases. In St. Paul Mercury Ins. Co. v. Huitt, 336 F.2d 37 (6th Cir. 1964), an accident occurred in the course of pouring concrete into the foundation of a building under construction. The person injured sued the owner of a crane used to move the bucket containing the concrete, who called on the liability insurer of the truck to defend, claiming there was coverage under the "loading and unloading" provision of that policy. The auto insurer declined to defend. The crane owner had general liability insurance, and that insurer then instituted a declaratory judgment suit to determine rights and duties under the policies. Applying Michigan law, the court held that both insurers must defend the crane owner.

> The obligation to defend is separate and distinct from the duty to provide coverage and to pay. . . . This is a contractual right of the insured irrespective of other insurance and irrespective of primary or excess coverage. . . . With regard to the providing of a defense, Huitt has double insurance and may call upon either or both carriers to fulfil their policy obligations in this respect. [Id. at 44.]

The court left open the question of contribution between the insurers.

3. Far beyond the construction setting of the previous case, the loading and unloading of commercial vehicles is a common place for the boundary problem to appear. The task is usually to draw the line between general liability and automobile insurance.

STATE CAPITAL INS. CO. v. NATIONWIDE MUT. INS. CO.

318 N.C. 534, 350 S.E.2d 66 (1986)

FRYE, Justice.

The issue in this case is whether liability for personal injuries suffered by a third party when a rifle accidently discharged while being removed by insured from a motor vehicle is covered by insured's automobile liability insurance policy or his homeowners liability insurance policy, or both. Under the facts presented in the instant case, we hold that coverage is provided by both policies.[1] We thus affirm the decision of the Court of Appeals.

On 13 November 1982, defendant Howard E. Anderson and defendant Milton Louis McKinnon traveled in Anderson's pickup truck to a tract of land in Warren County. . . . Anderson brought the truck to a stop on the left side of a logging road near a ravine. Both he and McKinnon left the truck, presumably to talk with some other hunting companions whom they had followed in order to survey the property. At some point McKinnon returned to the truck. After several minutes, Anderson spotted a deer and returned to the truck in order to retrieve his rifle. Anderson opened the driver's door, moved the back of the seat forward and reached in the area where the rifle lay. At the same time McKinnon began to exit the truck. When Anderson's hand came in contact with the rifle it discharged, causing a bullet to strike McKinnon in the leg. At the time of this accident, defendants Howard E. Anderson and Paula C. Anderson were covered under both an automobile liability insurance policy issued by defendant Nationwide Mutual Insurance Company ("Nationwide") and a policy of homeowners liability insurance issued by plaintiff State Capital Insurance Company ("State Capital").

Nationwide's automobile liability insurance policy provided in pertinent part as follows:

Part B
Liability Coverage
Insuring Agreement

We will pay damages for bodily injury or property damage for which any covered person becomes legally responsible because of an auto accident. . . .

---

1. This holding is of course subject to the general rule that claimants are not entitled to a double recovery.

Financial Responsibility Required

When this policy is certified as future proof of financial responsibility, this policy shall comply with the law to the extent required.

State Capital's homeowners liability insurance policy contained the following provision:

Section II — Exclusions

1. Coverage E — Personal Liability and Coverage F — Medical Payments to Others do not apply to bodily injury or property damage:
    e. arising out of the ownership, maintenance, use, loading or unloading of:
        (2) a motor vehicle owned or operated by, or rented or loaned to any insured. . . .

Plaintiff State Capital brought a declaratory judgment action seeking a determination of its rights and liabilities and those of defendant Nationwide with respect to the injuries suffered by defendant McKinnon. All parties waived jury trial; the trial judge instead made findings of fact, the essence of which are recounted above, and concluded that neither policy provided coverage for damages in this case. Defendants Anderson appealed. A unanimous panel of the Court of Appeals reversed the judgment of the trial court and held that both Nationwide's automobile liability policy and State Capital's homeowner's liability policy provided coverage. We affirm this decision for the reasons stated below.

The crucial issue in this case turns on a determination of the meaning given to the "arising out of" language in the compulsory motor vehicle liability statute, N.C.G.S. §20-279.21(b)(2), and the State Capital homeowners policy exclusion. It is particularly important in the instant case to recognize that different rules of construction govern the interpretation of policy provisions which *extend* coverage as opposed to policy provisions which *exclude* coverage. In construing the coverage provision of the Nationwide automobile policy, we follow the rule that provisions of insurance policies and compulsory insurance statutes which extend coverage must be construed liberally so as to provide coverage, whenever possible by reasonable construction. See Moore v. Hartford Fire Insurance Co., 270 N.C. 532, 155 S.E.2d 128 (1967); Jamestown Mutual Insurance Co. v. Nationwide Mutual Insurance Co., 266 N.C. 430, 146 S.E.2d 410 (1966). On the other hand, when construing the exclusion provision of the State Capital homeowners policy we are guided by the rule that provisions which exclude liability of insurance companies are not favored and therefore all ambiguous provisions will be construed against the insurer and in favor of the insured. Wachovia Bank & Trust Co. v. Westchester Fire Insurance Co., 276 N.C. 348, 172 S.E.2d 518 (1970).

I

We first consider whether the Nationwide automobile liability policy provides coverage for injuries resulting from the accidental shooting of McKinnon. The policy language states that Nationwide will insure Anderson against liability for which he "becomes legally responsible because of an auto accident." The compulsory motor vehicle liability statute provides that any motor vehicle policy certified as proof of financial responsibility shall insure the named insured against loss from the liability imposed by law "for damages arising out of the ownership, maintenance or use of such motor vehicle. . . ." N.C.G.S. §20-279.21(b)(2) (1985). It is well established in North Carolina that as a matter of law the provisions of the Financial Responsibility Act are written into every automobile liability policy. Nationwide Mutual Insurance Co. v. Chantos, 293 N.C. 431, 238 S.E.2d 597 (1977). Thus, the Nationwide automobile liability policy, when properly construed, provides coverage for damages "arising out of the ownership, maintenance or use" of the automobile. . . .

> The parties do not, however, contemplate a general liability insurance contract. There must be a causal connection between the use and the injury. This causal connection may be shown to be an injury which is the natural and reasonable incident or consequence of the use, though not foreseen or expected, but the injury cannot be said to arise out of the use of an automobile if it was directly caused by some independent act or intervening cause wholly disassociated from, independent of, and remote from the use of the automobile. (Citation omitted.)

Fidelity & Casualty Co. of N.Y. v. N.C. Farm Bureau Mutual Insurance Co., 16 N.C. App. 194, 198-99, 192 S.E.2d 113, 118, *cert. denied,* 282 N.C. 425, 192 S.E.2d 840 (1972).

In short, the test for determining whether an automobile liability policy provides coverage for an accident is not whether the automobile was a proximate cause of the accident. Instead, the test is whether there is a causal connection between the use of the automobile and the accident.

We find that such causal connection exists between the use of the automobile in this case, a pickup truck, and injuries to McKinnon. The transportation of firearms is an ordinary and customary use of a motor vehicle, especially pickup trucks. In addition, use of an automobile includes its loading and unloading. In the case *sub judice,* Anderson transported his .30-30 rifle in his pickup truck; as he attempted to unload the rifle from the truck, it discharged, causing injury to McKinnon. Since the transportation and unloading of firearms are ordinary and customary uses of a motor vehicle, and the injury-causing accident here resulted from the unloading of the transported rifle, such injuries were a natural and reasonable incident or consequence of the use of the motor vehicle. . . .

II

Next, we consider whether the exclusion in State Capital's homeowners policy excludes coverage for the injuries resulting from the accidental shooting of McKinnon. The State Capital policy insured Anderson against liability for damages for which he was liable because of bodily injury or property damage, but excluded coverage for such damages "arising out of the ownership, maintenance, use, loading, and unloading" of a motor vehicle. We first note that the determination that the injury "arose out of the use of an automobile" so as to provide coverage under the automobile liability policy does not necessarily mean that the homeowners policy does not provide coverage merely because it excludes from its policy accidents "arising out of the use" of a motor vehicle. We agree with the Court of Appeals that such a conclusion would ignore the established rule of construction that "[t]he two policies are not construed in light of each other; each policy is a separate contract of insurance between the company issuing it and the insured, and requires a separate and independent analysis in light of that relationship. Allstate Insurance Co. v. Shelby Mutual Insurance Co., 269 N.C. 341, 152 S.E.2d 436 (1967)." State Capital Insurance Co. v. Nationwide Mutual Insurance Co., 78 N.C. App. 542, 549, 337 S.E.2d 866, 870.

Keeping in mind the rules of construction, that all ambiguities in exclusion provisions are construed against the insurer and in favor of coverage, we find that under the facts in this case State Capital's homeowners policy provides coverage to Anderson for damages resulting from the injuries to McKinnon notwithstanding the exclusionary language. Although there are no North Carolina cases on point, a growing number of courts in other jurisdictions have held that similar provisions in homeowners and automobile policies provide concurrent coverage for the same accidents.

The seminal case finding concurrent coverage by a homeowners insurance policy and an automobile insurance policy for a shooting incident is State Farm v. Partridge, 10 Cal. 3d 94, 109 Cal. Rptr. 811, 514 P.2d 123. In that case, the insured (Partridge) and two friends were hunting jack rabbits by shooting out of the windows of Partridge's four-wheel drive Ford Bronco as he drove through the countryside. Partridge was shooting a .357 magnum pistol which he had modified by filing the triggering mechanism to give it a "hair trigger." Partridge spotted a jack rabbit running across the road and left the road to keep the rabbit in the car's headlights. During the chase the car hit a bump, the pistol discharged, and the bullet hit the middle passenger in the spine, paralyzing her. Partridge was insured under an automobile policy and a homeowners policy, both issued by State Farm, which contained language similar to the Anderson policies. The automobile policy afforded coverage for bodily injuries "caused by accident arising out of the ownership, maintenance or use including loading or unloading of the owned motor vehicle. . . ." The homeowners policy on the other hand excluded coverage for "bodily injury . . . arising out of the [o]wnership, [m]aintenance, [o]peration, [u]se, [l]oading or [u]nloading of . . . any [m]otor [v]ehicle." State Farm argued that the exclusionary language in the homeowners policy was the same as the coverage language in the automobile policy so that they were mutually exclusive and could not provide overlapping coverage. The Supreme Court of California rejected this argument.

First, the court stated that even when language in two insurance policies is similar, the rules of construction applied to an *exclusionary clause* are substantially different from the rules of construction applied to a *coverage clause*. Exclusionary clauses are interpreted narrowly while coverage clauses are interpreted broadly to provide the greatest possible protection to the insured. Since the terms of the policy must be construed against the insurance company, the same language in two different policies can have different meanings. . . .

The *Partridge* court, however, declined to predicate its decision on the ambiguity of the exclusionary clause. Instead it based its decision on a second rationale that the injury in that case had two joint causes: one arising from the negligent operation of the automobile and the other arising from the negligent tampering with the firing mechanism of the pistol. The court held that the homeowners policy covered the risk related to the pistol, while the automobile policy covered the risk related to the automobile.

Although there may be some question whether either of the two causes in the instant case can be properly characterized as *the* "prime," "moving," or "efficient" cause of the accident we believe that coverage under a liability insurance policy is equally available to an insured whenever an insured risk constitutes simply *a* concurrent proximate cause of the injuries. [Citations omitted.] That multiple causes may have effectuated the loss does not negate any single cause; that multiple acts concurred in the infliction of injury does not nullify any single contributory act.

State Farm v. Partridge, 10 Cal. 3d 94, 104, 109 Cal. Rptr. 811, 818, 514 P.2d 123, 130-31. . . .

In summary, the cases discussed above establish two principles with respect to determining the coverage of homeowners policies: (1) ambiguous terms and standards of causation in exclusion provisions of homeowners policies must be strictly construed against the insurer, and (2) homeowners policies provide coverage for injuries so long as a non-excluded cause is either the sole or concurrent cause of the injury giving rise to liability. Stating the second principle in reverse, the sources of liability which are excluded from homeowners policy coverage must be the sole cause of the injury in order to exclude coverage under the policy. . . .

III

For the reasons stated herein, we hold that both Nationwide and State Capital provide coverage under their respective policies. We note in addition that the reasoning in support of overlapping coverage is persuasive. Each insurance policy is a separate contract which must be interpreted in accordance with its own terms under the applicable rules of construction — not *in pari materia* with other policies which the insured may or may not own. See Allstate Insurance Co. v. Shelby Mutual Insurance Co., 269 N.C. 341, 152 S.E.2d 436. Furthermore, when the properly construed terms of more than one policy provide coverage for a single accident, this result is not burdensome to the insurance companies nor against public policy — the companies have been paid premiums to cover certain risks, and when the event insured against occurs, those companies should be required to provide coverage.

We, therefore, affirm the decision of the Court of Appeals.

Affirmed.

MITCHELL, Justice, dissenting.

Mindful as I am of the rules of construction which require in sum that insurance policies be construed against the companies issuing them, I nevertheless feel compelled by law and the clear terms of the insurance policies involved in this case to conclude that neither policy provided coverage under these facts. Accordingly, I must respectfully dissent.

The motor vehicle liability insurance policy issued by Nationwide Mutual Insurance Company in the present case included as a matter of law language insuring the named insured against loss from liability "for damages arising out of the ownership, maintenance or use of such motor vehicle. . . ." N.C.G.S. §20-279.21(b)(2) (1985). The majority states that the test for determining whether the motor vehicle liability policy provides coverage "is whether there is a causal connection between the use of the automobile and the accident." The majority then "finds" such a causal connection to exist in the present case. I do not agree. . . .

The simple fact of the matter is that in this case the accident arose out of the ownership and use of the rifle and was in no way causally connected to the use of the truck. I do not believe that the cases relied upon by the majority support its determination that a causal connection existed between the use of the truck in the present case and the injuries to McKinnon. Most of those cases involved situations in which the vehicle was in motion or being placed in motion by the driver at the time of the accident. . . . In each of those cases the actual driving or operation of the motor vehicle properly could have been found to be at least concurring negligence and one proximate cause of the resulting injury. The result should be different, however, when as in the present case the accident and resulting injury arose solely from the removal of a gun from a motor vehicle which was parked and not itself being driven or otherwise "used" at the time of the accident. Raines v. Insurance Co., 9 N.C. App. 27, 175 S.E.2d 299 (1970) (no coverage for accidental discharge of gun killing other occupant in parked automobile).

The majority next holds that the injury resulting from the accidental shooting of McKinnon was covered by the homeowner's policy issued by State Capital Insurance Company. That policy specifically excluded coverage, inter alia, for damages arising out of the "unloading" of a motor vehicle. In removing the rifle from the truck, Anderson clearly was "unloading" a motor vehicle. See Black's Law Dictionary 1378 (rev. 5th ed. 1979). The accident and resulting injury in this case arose from the unloading. In my view, the term "unloading" as used in the exclusionary section of the homeowner's policy clearly and unambiguously excludes coverage for the accident in the present case. Contra Travelers Insurance Co. v. Aetna Casualty & Sur. Co., 491 S.W.2d 363 (Tenn. 1973).

Although my heart might go to the insured in a case such as this, I simply can find no way in good conscience that my mind can follow. I dissent.

MEYER, J., joins in this dissenting opinion.

BILLINGS, Chief Justice, dissenting in part.

If the motor vehicle liability policy provides coverage in this case because the accident arose out of the use of the insured's motor vehicle, then I fail to understand how a homeowner's policy that specifically excludes from coverage bodily injury arising out of the use of a motor vehicle owned by the insured can be construed to provide coverage. To me, this is not a matter of "liberal" versus "strict" construction of insurance policies; we are merely asked to apply common sense to words chosen to prevent exactly what the majority determines is the result in the case sub judice. The exclusion in the homeowner's policy unmistakably notifies the insured that coverage is not provided if the liability arises out of the use of a motor vehicle owned by an insured. While there may be some ambiguity about whether under the circumstances the insured's liability arose out of the use of the insured's vehicle, once it is established either that the liability did nor did not arise out of that use, the terms and therefore the reach of neither policy are ambiguous.

I agree with Justice Mitchell's analysis of the coverage provided by the Nationwide Mutual Insurance Company's motor vehicle liability policy and therefore would hold that coverage is not provided by that policy. I disagree with Justice Mitchell in his conclusion that the State Capital Insurance Company's homeowner's policy does not provide coverage. As indicated above, since the accident did not arise out of the use of the motor vehicle, the exclusion contained in the other policy excluding coverage for liability arising out of the use of the motor vehicle does not apply. The only remaining question is whether the exclusion for liability arising out of the "loading or unloading" of a motor vehicle owned by an insured excludes the liability in the case sub judice.

The correct resolution of the question of coverage under the homeowner's policy is the construction of the word "unloading." If "unloading" is construed to mean the removal of any item from the vehicle, then the exclusion applies and coverage is not provided. If, however, the word is construed to mean the removal from the vehicle of cargo, defined as "the lading or freight of a ship, airplane, or vehicle," the transportation of which is the primary purpose for which the vehicle was being used, then the exclusion does not apply to the removal of the rifle from the vehicle in the case sub judice. Giving to the words "loading and unloading" the more restrictive construction, I would hold that the accident did not arise out of the insured's "unloading" of the vehicle and that the exclusion in the homeowner's policy does not apply. I would hold that the State Capital Insurance Company's policy alone provides coverage.

Notes and Questions

1. Many accidents have occurred while loaded guns were being taken out of or put into automobiles, usually on hunting trips. For recent answers to the question whether such accidents should be covered by the liability portions of the automobile policy or of the home-

owners policy, see Union Mut. Fire Ins. Co. v. Commercial Union Ins. Co., 521 A.2d 308 (Me. 1987), Criterion Ins. Co. v. Velthouse, 732 P.2d 180 (Alaska 1986), and Kohl v. Union Ins. Co., 731 P.2d 134 (Colo. 1986). The *Partridge* case, discussed in *State Capital*, is the leading case. Review the causation cases in Chapter 3; *Partridge* came in for vigorous criticism in *Garvey*.

2. In *State Capital,* the court held it is not necessary that the cause be proximate, only that there be "a" causal connection. Is this view sound? Does that mean that it is sufficient that it be a cause in fact?

3. The *State Capital* court declined to treat the homeowners policy "in pari materia with other policies which the insured may or may not own." Is there justification for treating the policy in pari materia with other policies the same insurer sells and is willing to issue or that are readily available on the market from other insurers?

4. If the same incident had occurred when the insured lived in the country and the truck, though still insured, was on blocks and inoperable, would the majority of the court reach the same result? Justice Mitchell would not. See Hanson v. Grinnell Mut. Reins. Co., 422 N.W.2d 288 (Minn. App. 1988).

5. Does the opinion of Chief Justice Billings suggest that in his view the proper result with respect to the homeowners policy may depend on whether the insured also has automobile insurance?

Problem

Homeowners insurance combines property coverage and comprehensive personal liability coverage. The latter is comparable (except for the lesser exposures individuals have) to comprehensive general liability insurance for businesses.

The insured owned a close corporation which in turn owned a Volkswagen Bus. The insured's minor son worked for the company and drove the bus, both on business and for personal use. While on a date he negligently hit a young boy on a bicycle, inflicting brain damage that might lead to damages in excess of the aggregate of all potentially available insurance. Company A insured the bus to a limit of $100,000 per person injured, paid its limit, and is not involved in this litigation. Company B issued insurance on the family cars. Those cars were not involved in the accident and the claim against Company B was dismissed. The insured had a homeowners policy issued by Company P, which is suing for a judgment declaring its lack of liability. This policy had a liability limit of $400,000. Finally, there was a personal umbrella policy with Company C.

Complex negotiations led to a settlement, leaving only the question of whether the homeowners policy covered the liability of the insured and his wife under the following statute:

§577-3. Natural Guardian; Liability for Torts of Child

The father and mother of an unmarried minor child are jointly the natural guardians of the child's person and property. They shall have equal powers and duties with respect to the child and neither shall have any right superior to that of the other concerning the child's custody or control or any other matter affecting the child; provided that if either parent dies or abandons the family or is incapable for any reason to act as guardian, the guardianship devolves upon the other parent, and that when the parents live apart, the court may award the guardianship to either of them, having special regard to the interests of the child. The father and mother of unmarried minor children shall jointly and severally be liable in damages for tortious acts committed by their children, and shall be jointly and severally entitled to prosecute and defend all actions in which the children or their individual property may be concerned. . . .

The relevant contract provisions are as follows:

Homeowners Policy

Coverage E — Personal Liability

This Company agrees to pay on behalf of the insured all sums which the insured shall become legally obligated to pay as damages because of bodily injury or property damage, to which this insurance applies, caused by an occurrence.

Exclusions
This policy does not apply:

1. Under Coverage E — Personal Liability and Coverage F — Medical Payments to Others:

a. to bodily injury or property damage arising out of the ownership, maintenance, operation, use, loading or unloading of:

(1) any aircraft; or

(2) any motor vehicle owned or operated by, or rented or loaned to any insured, but this subdivision (2) does not apply to bodily injury or property damage occurring on the residence premises if the motor vehicle is not subject to motor vehicle registration because it is used exclusively on the residence premises or kept in dead storage on the residence premises; or

(3) any recreational motor vehicle owned by any insured, if the bodily injury or property damage occurs away from the residence premises; but this subdivision (3) does not apply to a golf cart while used for golfing purposes.

[Exclusion (a) continues and is then followed by exclusions (b) through (f).]

Personal Umbrella Policy

Coverage: The Company will indemnify the *insured* for *ultimate net loss* which the *insured* shall become legally obligated to pay, in excess of the applicable underlying (or retained) limit, because of *personal injury* or *property damage* occurring during the policy period. . . . [Ultimate Net Loss is defined as the sum of damages and expenses the insured has to pay, with certain minor qualifications. — Ed.]

The supreme court of the jurisdiction has recently decided (1) that coverage language of policies (including exclusions) shall be interpreted in favor of the insured if they are ambiguous, (2) that mere complexity is not ambiguity, and (3) that interpretation of ambiguous policy language shall be guided by the "objectively reasonable expectations" of the parties, particularly the insured. There is no supreme state court precedent on all fours, but lower courts have held that there is coverage in this fact situation. Authority in the other states is overwhelmingly against coverage. See, for example, Hurston v. Dufour, 292 So. 2d 733 (La. App. 1974), *cert. denied,* 295 So. 2d 178 (La. 1974) (Louisiana is a state with a parents' liability act similar to that of the jurisdiction in this problem. Few if any other states have such sweeping statutes). Contra, Shelby Mut. Ins. Co. v. United States Fire Ins. Co., 12 Mich. App. 145, 162 N.W.2d 676 (1968) (The Michigan statute was at that time limited to $500 and applied only to malicious and willful acts of minors under 18 years of age residing in the parental home. Presumably it was directed mainly to vandalism in schools). The Michigan case stands alone, *except for the lower court decisions in the problem jurisdiction, one of which provides a detailed memorandum supporting the result written by a judge now on the state supreme court.*

1. How should the case be decided?

2. How would you structure an argument for the insurance company? Against it?

3. Compare the coverage of the homeowners policy (so far as it appears from the quoted portions of the policy) with the comprehensive general liability policy.

4.   Negligent Entrustment and Supervision

The previous problem case was adapted from Fortune v. Wong, 68 Haw. 1, 702 P.2d 299 (1985). Possible alternative theories of liability in cases like *Fortune* are negligent entrustment and negligent supervision. The first would be based on the defendant negligently putting a dangerous instrumentality into the hands of someone incapable of using it safely. The second would be based on the failure of the defendant, having the duty to do so, to supervise properly someone needing supervision.

Notes and Questions

1. Assume the facts of a case like that of the Problem, changed in only one particular: the father negligently entrusted the car to the son, knowing the latter was an incompetent or negligent driver. Should the homeowners policy provide coverage? The underlying tort of negligent entrustment (or that of negligent supervision) requires not only negligence in entrustment of the instrumentality (or in supervision) but also negligence (or merely incompetence?) on the part of the person to whom the instrumentality was entrusted. See Barnstable County Mut. Ins. Co. v. Lally, 374 Mass. 602, 373 N.E.2d 966 (1978); Potosky v. Fejes, 23 Ohio Misc. 2d 45, 492 N.E.2d 494 (Ohio C.P. 1986); Rubins Contractors, Inc. v. Lumbermens Mut. Ins. Co., 821 F.2d 671 (D.C. Cir. 1987). Would you expect the cases to be unanimous on this question of coverage? They are not. Compare Standard Mut. Ins. Co. v. Bailey, 868 F.2d 893 (7th Cir. 1989), applying Indiana law (homeowners policy unambiguously excludes coverage for negligent entrustment of a car), with Cone v. Nationwide Mut. Fire Ins. Co., 75 N.Y.2d 747, 551 N.E.2d 92, 551 N.Y.S.2d 891 (1989) (homeowners policy covers negligent entrustment of a car). In *Cone* there was a vigorous three judge dissent. Which is the preferable result?

2. Should the homeowners policy provide coverage if the instrumentality that was entrusted was a handgun, for which there is no specific exclusion in the policy?

3. In a 1986 case, parents were sued for negligent *supervision* of their son in allowing him to drink at a party in their home and then to drive. While driving he killed a third person. The son was under the age for legal consumption of alcoholic beverages. The policy also contained a "Severability of Insurance" clause, stating that "This insurance applies separately to each insured. This condition shall not increase our limit of liability for any one occurrence." How should the court decide the case? See Worcester Mut. Ins. Co. v. Marnell, 398 Mass. 240, 496 N.E.2d 158 (1986).

4. In Louis Marsch, Inc. v. Pekin Ins. Co., 140 Ill. App. 3d 1079, 491 N.E.2d 432, 96 Ill. Dec. 386 (Ill. App. 1985), the automobile exclusion clause of a comprehensive general liability policy successfully excluded coverage when the claim was based on a theory of negligent hiring of an employee. Is this the same in principle as a negligent entrustment theory?

5. In *Fortune,* the court made it clear that it did not intend to deal with the negligent entrustment problem, but in Hawaiian Ins. & Guaranty Co. v. Chief Clerk of First Circuit Court, 68 Haw. 336, 713 P.2d 427 (Hawaii 1986), the court directly faced it. How should the court decide the case, the personnel on the court being the same as those who decided *Fortune?*

H.   Particular Liability Coverages

1.   Environmental Impairment Liability Insurance

In a remarkably short period of time, the political atmosphere in the western world has undergone a sea change with respect to the spoliation of the environment in which we live. (It is too early to say much about the Eastern European countries, where the damage from past activity is much worse.) Having "fouled our nest," a large percentage of the population has become greatly concerned with minimizing or avoiding further damage to the environment and also with its restoration, undoing some of the damage done in the past.

Insufficient attention has been given to the difference. Whatever the costs and the difficulties, it is plausible to think of requiring users of products that would cause future harm to pay the cost of either preventing harm in the first place or repairing it after it has been caused. The naive assumption has frequently been made, not least by Congress, that the same approach can be followed with respect to harm done in the past. But the problems are different, especially with regard to the part insurance, and especially private insurance, can play. Even with respect to future damage, the role private insurance can play may be quite limited. For a theoretical look at the problem, see Abraham, Environmental Liability and the Limits of Insurance, 88 Colum. L. Rev. 942 (1988). Gordon & Westendorf, Liability Coverage for Toxic Tort, Hazardous Waste Disposal and Other Pollution Exposures, 25 Idaho L. Rev. 567 (1988), provides a practitioner's perspective.

a.   The Accident Policy

The problem arose first under the old "accident" policy. Under that policy (see *Beryllium*, Section B), would liability for pollution of wells by seepage from a waste dump have been covered? See Lancaster Area Refuse Auth. v. Transamerica Ins. Co., 437 Pa. 493, 263 A.2d 368 (1970), *rev'g* 214 Pa. Super. 80, 251 A.2d 739 (1969). The Pennsylvania Supreme Court, adopting the reasoning of the dissenting opinion in the court below, remanded the case with instructions to direct judgment for the insured.

The cases were not all in accord on the accident policy. Though a majority seem to have held that there was coverage, some held that the pollution damage was forseeable and not unexpected by the insured, and therefore not covered. See Soderstrom, The Role of Insurance in Environmental Litigation, 11 Forum 762, 765 n.11 (1976).

b. The Pollution Exclusion

As soon as decisions began to appear holding that insurers were on the risk for nonsudden pollution, whether under the accident policy or the occurrence policy, insurers began to add express pollution exclusion endorsements. The 1973 revision of the CGL policy sought to render the law certain with Exclusion (f).

The problem resurfaced even when the policies contained the pollution exclusion. The most frequent cases were those involving toxic seepage into aquifers from waste dumps or from industrial operations. In the following case, the source of the toxic substance was still more pedestrian — leaking underground storage tanks (L.U.S.T.) at gasoline stations. The first generations of such tanks were made from steel, which eventually corrodes and leaks, in addition to the leaks that would result sooner from other causes.

More recently such tanks have been made from noncorrodible material, but the problem of faulty connections and damage from earth tremors will always remain. The number of corrodible steel tanks still in the ground is immense. The tort exposure, and the *potential* insurance exposure, are almost beyond belief.

CLAUSSEN v. AETNA CASUALTY & SURETY CO.

259 Ga. 333, 380 S.E.2d 686 (1989)

CLARKE, Presiding Justice.

In this case we are called upon to interpret the meaning of the "pollution exclusion" clause of a comprehensive general liability insurance policy. For the reasons stated below, we hold that the insurance policy at issue does not preclude coverage for liability for environmental contamination caused by the discharge of pollutants over an extended period of time.

Briefly stated, the history of the case is as follows.[1] Since 1966, Henry Claussen has owned, either individually or through corporate entities, fifty-two acres of land known as Picketville. In 1968, the City of Jacksonville, Florida contracted to use the site as a landfill. Beginning in 1971, the City dumped industrial and chemical waste there almost exclusively. The City closed the site in 1977, and returned it to Claussen completely filled, graded and seeded. Claussen claims he had no knowledge that the site was used for dumping hazardous wastes.

---

1. A more complete version of the relevant facts may be found in Claussen v. Aetna Casualty & Surety Co., 865 F.2d 1217 (11th Cir. 1989); and Claussen v. Aetna Casualty & Surety Co., 676 F. Supp. 1571 (S.D. Ga. 1987).

In 1985, Environmental Protection Agency determined that the groundwater beneath the site had been contaminated by the release of hazardous substances. In a list ranking the 115 worst hazardous waste sites in the nation, Love Canal was ranked twenty-fourth, and Picketville was ranked twenty-sixth. The agency informed Claussen, the City and others that they were responsible for taking corrective action.

Henry Claussen then filed an action against Aetna Casualty & Surety Company and others seeking a declaratory judgment that the insurance company is obligated under a "comprehensive general liability" policy for the costs to be incurred in connection with the EPA's demand that the hazardous site be studied and cleaned up. Aetna denied coverage citing exclusion (f), commonly referred to as the "pollution exclusion" which states that coverage is excluded for:

> bodily injury or property damage arising out of the discharge, dispersal, or release or escape of smoke, vapors, soot, fumes, acids, alkalis, toxic chemicals, liquids or gases, waste materials or other irritants, contaminants or pollutants into or upon land, the atmosphere or any water course or body of water; but this exclusion does not apply if such discharge, dispersal, release or escape is sudden and accidental.

The federal district court granted Aetna's motion for summary judgment, holding that the exclusion clause precludes coverage for Claussen's environmental liabilities. The court found the clause to be clear and unambiguous and decided that dumping of toxic wastes occurring over several years was not "sudden" within the policy language. Claussen appealed to the Eleventh Circuit Court of Appeals which certified the following question to this court:

> Whether, as a matter of law, the pollution exclusion clause contained in the comprehensive general liability insurance policy precludes coverage to its insured for liability for costs for liability for the environmental contamination caused by the discharge of pollutants at the site over an extended period of time?
>
> To put it another way, does the insurance policy in this case require the insurance company to provide a defense and coverage to the insured for liability for the discharge of pollutants that occurred over an extended period of time?

1. "The construction of a contract is a matter of law for the court." OCGA §13-2-1. Extrinsic evidence to explain ambiguity in a contract becomes admissible only when a contract remains ambiguous after the pertinent rules of construction have been applied. Holcomb v. Ward, 239 Ga. 847, 238 S.E.2d 915 (1977). Under Georgia rules of contract interpretation, words in a contract generally bear their usual and common meaning. OCGA §13-3-2(2). However, "if the construc-

tion is doubtful, that which goes most strongly against the party executing the instrument or undertaking the obligation is generally to be preferred." OCGA §13-2-2(5). . . .

What is the meaning of the word "sudden" as it is used in the insurance policy? Claussen argues that it means "unexpected;" Aetna asserts that the only possible meaning is "abrupt." This seemingly simple question has spawned a profusion of litigation. The majority of courts considering the issue have adopted the meaning asserted by Claussen. See Developments — Toxic Waste Litigation, 99 Harv. Law. Rev. 1458, 1582 (1986). See also cases cited in Claussen v. Aetna Casualty & Surety Co., 865 F.2d 1217, 1218 (11th Cir. 1989). Other courts have decided that "sudden" cannot be defined without its temporal connotation. See, e.g., Claussen v. Aetna Casualty & Surety Co., 676 F. Supp. 1571 (S.D. Ga. 1987), and cases cited therein.

The primary dictionary definition of the word is "happening without previous notice or with very brief notice; coming or occurring unexpectedly; not foreseen or prepared for." Webster's Third New International Dictionary, at 2284 (1986). See also, Funk and Wagnalls Standard Dictionary, at 808 (1980); Black's Law Dictionary, at 1284 (1979). The definition of the word "sudden" as "abrupt" is also recognized in several dictionaries and is common in the vernacular. . . . [2] Thus, it appears that "sudden" has more than one reasonable meaning. And, under the pertinent rule of construction the meaning favoring the insured must be applied, that is, "unexpected."

2. Aetna next argues that construing "sudden" to mean "unexpected" violates another pertinent rule of construction, which requires that the contract be read so as to give all parts meaning. The policy states:

> The company will pay on behalf of the insured all sums which the insured shall become legally obligated to pay as damages because of property damage to which this policy applies, caused by an occurrence.

The policy goes on to define "occurrence" as "property damage neither expected nor intended from the standpoint of the insured." Aetna contends that if "sudden" is interpreted as "unexpected," it simply restates the definition of "occurrence." We do not agree. The pollution exclusion clause focuses on whether the *"discharge, dispersal or release"* of the pollutants is unexpected and unintended; the definition of occurrence focuses on whether the *property damage* is unexpected and unintended. The pollution exclusion clause therefore has the

---

2. "Abrupt" does not appear in the Webster's Third New International Dictionary as a definition of "sudden."

effect of eliminating coverage for damage resulting from the intentional discharge of pollutants.

3. Aetna also argues that the construction proposed by Claussen violates the cardinal rule of contract interpretation because it is inconsistent with the intention of the parties. They assert that pollution liability is an enormous risk that was not assessed in the process of underwriting this policy.

Sixteen years ago when the policy at issue here went into effect, it is unlikely that either party anticipated the extent of potential liability for pollution damage.[4] "The past two decades have seen an explosion of litigation seeking compensation for damage to the environment and injuries arising from environmental pollution." Note, The Pollution Exclusion Clause Through the Looking Glass, 74 Geo. L.J. 1237 (1986). Moreover, the Federal Superfund Act,[5] passed in 1980, imposed "retroactive strict liability" for the costs of cleaning up hazardous waste storage sites on the generators and transporters of hazardous wastes and on the owners and operators of the sites. Abraham, Environmental Liability and the Limits of Insurance, 88 Colum. L.R. 942, 957 (1988). Referring to the decade before CERCLA passed, one commentator noted:

> In the past, insurance was available at prices that did not reflect the full environmental risks of each insured firm. Insurers had little incentive to tailor premiums closely to an individual firm's risk profile, because such tailoring requires the expense of monitoring each firm and because insurers did not expect courts to impose significant waste-related liabilities. [Developments — Toxic Waste Litigation, 99 Harv. L. Rev. 1458, 1575 (1986).]

If Aetna had been aware of the yawning extent of potential liability, it almost certainly would have drafted its policy differently. However, the fact that it did not, cannot be construed to the detriment of the insured who purchased a "comprehensive general liability" policy. Under Georgia law, the risk of any lack of clarity or ambiguity in an insurance contract must be borne by the insurer. Ranger Ins. Co. v.

---

4. Documents in the record indicate that in 1970 Aetna considered environmental pollution to be a major societal problem. Drafting the pollution exclusion was certainly part of an effort to control the company's exposure to loss arising out of pollution. At that time, however, the company could not have anticipated the imposition of no-fault environmental liability. The company's emphasis was "to avoid writing any accounts . . . where there is wanton pollution with complete disregard for the public. . . ." See Appendix C-12 to Appellant's brief.

5. See, Comprehensive Environmental Response, Compensation and Liability Act of 1980 ("CERCLA"), Pub. L. No. 96-510, 94 Stat. 2767 (codified as amended in scattered sections of 26 U.S.C., 32 U.S.C., 42 U.S.C. and 49 U.S.C.)

Culberson, 454 F.2d 857 (5th Cir. 1971), *cert. denied,* 407 U.S. 916, 92 S. Ct. 2440, 32 L. Ed. 2d 691 (1972).

Further, the interpretation of the policy advanced by Claussen is not contrary to the interpretation Aetna gave the clause when it was adopted. Documents presented by the Insurance Rating Board (which represents the industry and on which Aetna participated) to the Insurance Commissioner when the "pollution exclusion" was first adopted suggest that the clause was intended to exclude only intentional polluters. The Insurance Rating Board represented "the impact of the [pollution exclusion clause] on the vast majority of risks would be no change." See *Claussen,* 676 F. Supp. at 1573.

4. Finally, Aetna argues that Claussen's proposed interpretation of the policy language contravenes public policy because it encourages the land owner to keep his head in the sand — to remain oblivious to ongoing polluting activities on his land. This argument would be somewhat persuasive, but for the many events that have taken place between the date of this policy and the present lawsuit. "Environmental liability insurance has recently undergone a shift from apparent under-deterrence to apparent over-deterrence of environmental damages." *Developments,* 99 Harv. L. Rev. 1458, 1574 (1986). Federal and state laws now require waste treatment facilities to carry insurance for both short and long term environmental risks or to meet a financial test alternative. See, Georgia Department of Natural Resources, Environmental Protection Division v. Union Timber Corporation, 258 Ga. 873, 375 S.E.2d 856 (1989). Insurance companies have become wary of insuring against environmental risks and have either dropped out of the field or are charging higher premiums. Id. In short, the situation has changed so that our decision is not likely to have any serious impact on prospective behavior.

In sum, we conclude that the pollution exclusion clause is capable of more than one reasonable interpretation. The clause must therefore be construed in favor of the insured to mean "unexpected and unintended."

Question answered.

All the Justices concur, except MARSHALL, C.J. and BELL and HUNT, J.J., who dissent.

HUNT, Justice, dissenting.

I respectfully dissent because in my view the Federal District Court was correct in finding the "pollution exclusion" clear and unambiguous. While "sudden" may have a number of meanings, and, over the years, may have been used in a number of contexts, in *this* context it clearly means abrupt and unexpected. Certainly, its use within this context does not encompass the gradual dumping of toxic wastes over a period of several years.

I am authorized to state that Chief Justice MARSHALL and Justice BELL join in this dissent.

Notes and Questions

1. Claussen v. Aetna Casualty & Surety Co., 754 F. Supp. 1576 (S.D. Ga. 1990), is a later example in the same litigation.

2. After cases like *Claussen,* what would you expect the market for coverage of liability of gasoline service stations to be like? Would the development of noncorrodible tanks improve the market? After a number of years of a greatly constricted market, the availability of coverage has increased considerably. See Shalowitz, EIL Market Flush with Tank Cover But Little Demand, Bus. Ins., Oct. 8, 1990, at 3. That is fortunate, because the Environmental Protection Agency's insurance coverage requirements are applying to more and more tank owners; for example, marketers with fewer than 13 underground tanks at multiple sites must comply with the EPA rules about insurance coverage by October 26, 1991. Id.

3. The cases have not all been in accord on the sweep of the pollution exclusion. In Transamerica Ins. Co. v. Sunnes, 77 Or. App. 136, 711 P.2d 212 (1985), the insured was the local Culligan water conditioning company, which periodically discharged pollutants into the city sewage system. The discharge was intended; the damage was not. The policy was held not to protect the insured, because of Exclusion (f). Accord, United States Fidelity and Guar. Co. v. Star Fire Coals, Inc., 856 F.2d 31 (6th Cir. 1988), applying Kentucky law and saying that "the phrase 'sudden and accidental' is not a synonym for 'unexpected and unintended.' " (The contention of insureds usually is that the terms are synonymous.) Fireman's Fund Ins. Cos. v. Ex-Cell-O Corp., 702 F. Supp. 1317, 1326 (E.D. Mich. 1988), applying Michigan law, held the same way: "Increasingly, the courts . . . are holding that 'sudden' includes a temporal aspect." Accord, Ray Indus., Inc. v. Liberty Mut. Ins. Co., 728 F. Supp. 1310 (E.D. Mich. 1989).

4. As the culmination of bitterly fought litigation involving the pollution of an aquifer by salt, rending the water unfit for irrigation, American Motorists Ins. Co. v. General Host Corp., 667 F. Supp. 1423 (D. Kan. 1987) held there was no coverage under the CGL policy.

5. In Waste Mgmt. of Carolinas, Inc. v. Peerless Ins. Co., 315 N.C. 688, 340 S.E.2d 374 (1986), the plaintiff sought a declaratory judgment against its insurers to compel defense and indemnification. The plaintiff operated a waste collection and transportation service. The United States sought an injunction and reimbursement of costs from the owner of the landfill, which in turn sought contribution from Waste Management. The latter tendered defense to its insurers, which

declined, relying on the pollution exclusion. The intermediate appellate court found that

> the word "sudden" is reasonably susceptible of differing constructions and we construe it not to mean just "instantaneous" but also "unforeseen" or "unexpected." This construction renders the pollution exclusion consistent with the definition of "occurrence" in the coverage provisions. [Id., 72 N.C. App. 80, 88, 323 S.E.2d 726, 732.]

The Supreme Court, however, thought the policy language was unambiguous. The conduct of the insured could not be regarded as "sudden." There was no coverage.

6. The treatment of "sudden and accidental" by a number of courts has led some insurers to broaden the pollution exclusion to exclude *all* pollution coverage, even "sudden and accidental" pollution. Even then they may not be home free, as Reliance Ins. Co. v. Kent. Corp. Inc., 896 F.2d 501 (11th Cir. 1990) shows. In a suit for damages to firemen fighting a dumpster fire, the United States District Court for the Northern District of Alabama granted the insurer's motion for summary judgment when the firemen alleged harm from hazardous gases. On appeal the court of appeals reversed and remanded saying that the judgment was premature — it remained to be proved whether the injuries were caused by a pollution incident or by an accidental fire. The plaintiffs could amend their complaint so that the injuries fell within policy coverage, that is, were not caused by pollution. The opinion was vacated after the parties settled. Id., 909 F.2d 424 (1990).

7. For a good summary of the subject as of its date, see Pfennigstorf, Insurance of Environmental Risks: Recent Developments, 1982 A.B.A. Envtl. L. Symp. 57, Research Contribution of the American Bar Foundation (1982), No. 1. A more summary treatment is Hourihan, Insurance Coverage for Environmental Damages Claims, 15 Forum 551 (1980). A case guessing at Delaware law, but especially interesting because it recounts at length the history of the defendant's efforts to prevent pollution from its landfill using the inadequate knowledge and technology of the late 1960s, is New Castle County v. Continental Casualty Co., 725 F. Supp. 800 (1989).

UNITED STATES AVIEX CO. v. TRAVELERS INS. CO.

125 Mich. App. 579, 336 N.W.2d 838 (1983)

[When a fire destroyed the plaintiff's chemical manufacturing facility, the water used in putting out the fire seeped into the groundwater percolating under the plaintiff's land at a rate of about 500 feet per year. The state Department of Natural Resources compelled the plaintiff to conduct testing, which cost $80,000, and also pressed it to clean up the contamination, estimated to cost in excess of $1 million. The state DNR threatened "escalated enforcement action . . . including a lawsuit for damages to the waters of the state." Defendant insurer conceded liability for "proximate" damage to neighbors' property, if any, but contended the damage to the water was excluded because it was to "property owned by the insured." The plaintiff sought declaratory relief. The trial court held that the defendant must defend and indemnify, including paying for the study and testing as well as any required action to correct the chemical contamination of the percolating ground water. The defendant appealed.]

BROWN, Judge.

In this case, plaintiff was faced with threats of legal action by the DNR. Although, as defendant argues, the DNR could seek legal redress in the form of an order for abatement of water pollution (M.C.L. §323.6; M.S.A. §3.526), a criminal complaint (M.C.L. §323.9; M.S.A. §3.529), or injunctive relief (M.C.L. §323.10; M.S.A. §3.529[1]), and so possibly never seek a remedy covered by the insurance policy, plaintiff nevertheless needed to know whether defendant would be required to defend against a covered remedy should such a remedy be sought. Only with this knowledge could plaintiff choose between voluntarily complying with the DNR's very real and repeated demands and opposing the DNR's actions.

Defendant next argues that its due process rights were violated by the trial court's order requiring defendant to pay for the expenses of the studies done prior to entry of the declaratory judgment. Defendant argues that a full hearing is required by the water resources act, M.C.L. §323.1 et seq.; M.S.A. §3.521 et seq., before an order to abate pollution may be enforced. In this case, plaintiff and the DNR agreed that the plaintiff should move immediately to prevent further off-site contamination, investigate the extent of the contamination, and implement a plan for preventing further contamination, and so plaintiff proceeded without a hearing. Defendant argues that this agreement denied defendant the opportunity to appear at a hearing to contest the necessity and reasonableness of the DNR's demands. . . .

Defendant was . . . entitled to a hearing before the Water Resources Commission upon request. Defendant, however, decided not to request a hearing, relying instead upon its denial of any obligation to plaintiff under the insurance contract. Plaintiff informed defendant throughout the proceedings of the DNR's demands and repeatedly requested defendant's intercession under the insurance contract. Under such circumstances, we can only conclude that defendant waived its right to request a hearing and cannot now complain that plaintiff reached an agreement with the DNR. Glover v. Kalamazoo, 98 Mich. App. 465, 469, 296 N.W.2d 280 (1980), *lv. den.*, 411 Mich. 951 (1981).

Defendant also questions the trial court's ruling that defendant is "obligated to defend any claim or action, and to pay for any costs of [plaintiff], for correcting chemical contamination, imposed by or resulting from a determination by a tribunal of competent jurisdiction". Defendant argues that this ruling incorrectly construes the insurance agreement to cover sums of money expended by plaintiff in response to equitable or injunctive orders, instead of covering only money paid or ordered to be paid as *compensation* for injury or loss. The issue has since been sharpened by the Attorney General's having filed a lawsuit against plaintiff seeking an injunction to compel plaintiff to immediately begin purging and cleansing of the contaminated groundwater, civil penalties of up to $10,000 per day, "all costs of this action, including enforcement costs, laboratory expenses, and attorney fees", and "any other relief [the] court deems proper and just".

The contract between defendant and plaintiff obligates defendant to "defend any suit against [plaintiff] seeking damages" and to pay "all sums which [plaintiff] shall become obligated to pay by reason of liability imposed by law upon [plaintiff] as damages because of . . . property damage". Thus, both the obligation to defend and the obligation to pay depend on the definition of "damages". As stated earlier, defendant interprets "damages" as compensation for injury or loss, and argues that costs incurred by plaintiff in complying with equitable or injunctive orders are noncompensatory. Plaintiff and intervenor interpret "damages" as sums which the insured is obligated to pay by reason of liability imposed upon him by law (in this case, M.C.L. §323.6; M.S.A. §3.526 and M.C.L. §323.10; M.S.A. §3.529[1]).

Defendant's argument is persuasive and supported by decisions from several other jurisdictions: Aetna Casualty & Surety Co. v. Hanna, 224 F.2d 499 (CA 5, 1955); Ladd Construction Co. v. Ins. Co. of North America, 73 Ill. App. 3d 43, 29 Ill. Dec. 305, 391 N.E.2d 568 (1979); Desrochers v. New York Casualty Co., 99 N.H. 129, 106 A.2d 196 (1954). In all three cases, the insurance provisions were similar, if not identical, to the insurance provision at issue here. The reasoning underlying the three opinions is aptly expressed in the following cite from *Aetna Casualty Co.*, supra, p. 503, where the court discusses whether the costs of complying with an injunction to remove fill dirt from a neighbor's property constitutes damages:

> Insofar as coverage is concerned, the obligation is solely "to pay," not to remove fill dirt, rocks and boulders, under Court order or otherwise. It is equally unreasonable to view the obligation as providing reimbursement to the Insured, for the undertaking is to pay *"on behalf of"* the Insured whatever he "shall become obligated to pay by reason of

the liability imposed upon him by law . . . *for damages* because of injury
or destruction of property. . . ."

Clearly, the policy covers only payments to third persons when
those persons have a legal claim for damages against the Insured on
account of injury to or destruction of property. (Emphasis in original.)

In our opinion, this reasoning interprets "damages" too narrowly.
Under M.C.L. §323.10; M.S.A. §3.529(1), the Attorney General is
empowered to file a suit "to recover the full value of the injuries done
to the natural resources of the state. . . ." This language clearly indicates the state's interest in its natural resources. Defendant agrees that
the contamination of subterranean and percolating water as a result of
the fire is "physical injury to tangible property" within the terms of the
insurance policy. If the state were to sue in court to recover in traditional "damages", including the state's costs incurred in cleaning up
the contamination, for the injury to the groundwater, defendant's obligation to defend against the lawsuit and to pay damages would be
clear. It is merely fortuitous from the standpoint of either plaintiff or
defendant that the state has chosen to have plaintiff remedy the contamination problem, rather than choosing to incur the costs of cleanup itself and then suing plaintiff to recover those costs. The damage to
the natural resources is simply measured in the cost to restore the
water to its original state. Chemical Applications Co., Inc. v. The
Home Indemnity Co., 425 F. Supp. 777, 778 (D. Mass., 1977); Lansco,
Inc. v. Dep't of Environmental Protection, 138 N.J. Super. 275, 284,
350 A.2d 520, 525 (1975), *aff'd,* 145 N.J. Super. 433, 368 A.2d 363
(1976), *cert. denied,* 73 N.J. 57, 372 A.2d 322 (1977). We therefore
affirm the trial court. Defendant must defend and indemnify plaintiff
against such claims and costs under the insurance policy. . . .

Affirmed.

Notes and Questions

1. Continental Ins. Cos. v. Northeastern Pharm. & Chem. Co.,
811 F.2d 1180 (8th Cir. 1987), dealt with the well-known incident at
Times Beach in Missouri. An oily waste containing dioxin was spread
on the streets of Times Beach to suppress dust. When the problem
surfaced, the federal government bought the city and relocated its
citizens. This case involved an incident that was obviously sudden. A
three judge panel of the 8th Circuit held that the injury to governmental "quasi-sovereign" interests was "property damage" within the
meaning of the policy. The opinion cited as authority the famous case
of Georgia v. Tennessee Copper Co., 206 U.S. 230 (1907), in which the
state of Georgia was held to have enough interest in property within its
boundaries to get an injunction against the discharge of sulfur dioxide

from a copper smelting plant in Tennessee that was denuding land in Georgia. The 1987 opinion in *Northeastern Pharmaceutical* went on to say that once there is property damage, cleanup costs are compensatory damages resulting therefrom. The panel was reversed on that point by the court en banc, which held by a 5-3 decision that "damages" do not include cleanup costs. 842 F.2d 977 (8th Cir. 1988).

2. The United States District Court for the District of New Jersey, following New Jersey law, held (inconsistently with *Northeastern Pharmaceutical*) that the costs of cleanup and closure of a landfill were covered under a CGL policy. The insured claimed even more: fines and penalties assessed against the township by the New Jersey Department of Environmental Protection were also covered. The court in Township of Gloucester v. Maryland Casualty Co., 668 F. Supp. 394 (D.N.J. 1987), said they were not.

3. Mraz v. Canadian Universal Ins. Co., 804 F.2d 1325 (4th Cir. 1986) held that cleanup costs were not damages. In Waste Mgmt. of Carolinas, Inc. v. Peerless Ins., 72 N.C. App. 80, 93, 323 S.E.2d 726, 735 (1984), *rev'd on other grounds,* 315 N.C. 688, 340 S.E.2d 374 (1986), the court decided that cleanup costs, though called "equitable relief," were "essentially compensatory damages for injury to . . . property" and as such were covered by the general liability policies. The North Carolina Supreme Court did not address this issue. Id. at 701, 340 S.E.2d at 383. Accord, Minnesota Mining and Mfg. Co. v. Travelers Indem. Co., 457 N.W.2d 175 (Minn. 1990). C.D. Spangler Constr. Co. v. Industrial Crankshaft and Engg. Co., 326 N.C. 133, 388 S.E.2d 557 (1990), agreed with *Waste Management* and went on to hold that compliance orders requiring certain remedial action were "suits" giving rise to a duty to defend. City of Johnstown v. Bankers Standard Ins. Co., 877 F.2d 1146 (2d Cir. 1989), held the insurer had a duty to defend against an action by the state for cleanup costs without discussing whether cleanup costs were damages. The case focused on the "expected or intended" clause and the "known risk" clause. Travelers Ins. Co. v. Ross Electric of Washington, Inc., 685 F. Supp. 742 (W.D. Wash. 1988), purporting to apply Washington law, held that cleanup costs were not covered on the ground that an action for their recovery would be equitable in nature, not legal. But in Boeing Co. v. Aetna Casualty & Surety Co., 113 Wash. 2d 869, 784 P.2d 507 (1990), the Supreme Court of Washington, en banc, answered "Yes" to the following question certified by the same federal court:

> Whether, under Washington law, the environmental response costs paid or to be paid by the insureds, as the result of action taken by the United States and the State of Washington under CERCLA, 42 U.S.C. §9601 et seq., constitute "damages" within the meaning of the comprehensive general liability policies issued by the insurers.

4. One exclusion intended to deal with the above problem reads, "It is further agreed that no coverage is provided for any cleanup of any watercourse, body of water, bog, marsh or wetland." Time Oil Co. v. Cigna Property & Casualty Ins. Co., 743 F. Supp. 1400 (W.D. Wash. 1990), applied that provision to exclude cleanup of an aquifer.

5. The United States brought action to obtain injunctive relief and get reimbursement for costs of investigation and enforcement activities in connection with a waste dump. The defendant had comprehensive general liability insurance that would cover damages for pollution. Maryland Casualty Co. v. Armco, Inc., 822 F.2d 1348 (4th Cir. 1987), distinguished damages and other forms of relief and held for the insurer. Cincinnati Ins. Co. v. Milliken and Co., 857 F.2d 979 (4th Cir. 1988), followed *Armco.* Purporting to apply Illinois law, Verlan, Ltd. v. John L. Armitage & Co., 695 F. Supp. 950 (N.D. Ill. 1988) held that damages did not include cleanup costs. Avondale Indus., Inc. v. Travelers Indem. Co., 697 F. Supp. 1314 (S.D.N.Y. 1988), *aff'd,* 887 F.2d 1200 (2d Cir. 1989), purporting to apply New York law, held that damages did include cleanup costs. It also held an administrative proceeding to be a "suit," requiring the company to defend. The first case in which a state's highest court decided the question was Boeing Co. v. Aetna Casualty & Surety Co., 113 Wash. 2d 869, 784 P.2d 507 (1990). It held that cleanup costs are damages within the meaning of the policy, but "safety measures or other preventive costs taken in advance of any damage to property" are not. Two justices dissented. The Supreme Judicial Court of Maine unanimously decided that cleanup costs were not damages. Patrons Oxford Mut. Ins. Co. v. Marois, 573 A.2d 16 (Me. 1990). A student note supporting the latter view is McCarthy, CERCLA Cleanup Costs Under Comprehensive General Liability Insurance Policies: Property Damage or Economic Damage?, 56 Fordham L. Rev. 1169 (1988). Another, McGrath, The Superfund Insurance Dilemma: Defining the Super Risks and Rights of Comprehensive General Liability Policies, 21 Ind. L. Rev. 735 (1988). There are other student notes on the subject.

6. The Environmental Protection Agency issues a "Potentially Responsible Party" (PRP) letter to possible defendants in enforcement proceedings. Ray Indus., Inc. v. Liberty Mut. Ins. Co., 728 F. Supp. 1310 (E.D. Mich. 1989) held that an insurer must defend against this letter as a "suit," following intermediate Michigan appellate court opinions involving similar Michigan Department of Natural Resources letters.

7. For a more extensive treatment of the subject of hazardous waste site liability from the perspective of insureds seeking coverage and their lawyers, see Chesler, Rodburg & Smith, Patterns of Judicial Interpretation of Insurance Coverage for Hazardous Waste Site Liabil-

ity, 18 Rutgers L.J. 9 (1986). See also Johnson, Construction and Application of Pollution Exclusion Clause in Liability Insurance Policy, 39 A.L.R.4th 1047 (1985). A view from the insurance company side is Ashley, Representation of the Insurer's Interests in an Environmental Damage Claim, 54 Def. Coun. J. 11 (1987).

8. The question of the kinds of suits against which an insurer must defend is not restricted to pollution cases. In Nationwide Ins. Co. v. King, 673 F. Supp. 384 (S.D. Cal. 1987), the insurance was a homeowners policy on a condominium. The association's rules forbade window air conditioners in front windows. The association sought to enjoin the condominium owner from violation of "covenants, conditions and restrictions." Must the insurer defend? The question whether the insurer must defend against an injunction long antedated pollution coverage questions. See Aetna Casualty & Surety Co. v. Hanna, 224 F.2d 499 (5th Cir. 1955); Annot., 53 A.L.R.2d 1132 (1957).

Should the insurer's duty to defend include an obligation to appeal a judgment adverse to the insured? See Annot., 69 A.L.R.2d 690 (1960).

c. The Development of EIL Insurance

Whether non-sudden (or perhaps even sudden) pollution coverage belongs in the class of risks that is excluded because it is uninsurable or in the class that is excluded for separate underwriting evaluation is not yet altogether certain. It depends to a considerable extent on the evolution of tort law on pollution over the next few years.

Partly to respond to the new federal environmental protection laws, which require certain polluters to prove financial responsibility, the insurance industry developed pollution liability (environmental impairment liability, or EIL) insurance as a separate line. Financial responsibility is most easily established by appropriate insurance. The crucial language of the coverage clause of the policy drafted by the Insurance Services Office in 1981 is as follows:

> The company will pay on behalf of the *insured* all sums which the *insured* shall become legally obligated to pay as compensatory damages because of *bodily injury* or *property damage* to which this insurance applies, provided that:
>> (1) such *bodily injury* or *property damage* is caused by a *pollution incident* which commences subsequent to the retroactive date shown in the declarations of this policy; and
>> (2) the claim for such damages is first made against the *insured* during the policy period and reported to the company during the policy period or within fifteen days after its termination. [Defined terms in italics.]

The definition of "pollution incident" in the policy is as follows:

"pollution incident" means emission, discharge, release, or escape of any solid, liquid, gaseous, or thermal contaminants, irritants, or pollutants directly from the *insured site* into or upon land, the atmosphere, or any watercourse or body of water, provided that such emission, discharge, release, or escape results in *environmental damage*. The entirety of any sudden or gradual emission, discharge, release, or escape from an *insured site* will be deemed to be one "pollution incident". [Defined terms in italics.]

Compare the "unifying directive" in *Michigan Chemical,* supra.

At the peak of its development in 1983, the EIL market wrote from $30 to $60 million annually in premiums. Ten insurance organizations, one a pool with 49 members, were in the market. There was also some accommodation business. Slightly in excess of a thousand policies were written. Even at its largest, therefore, the EIL market was inconsequential for a large country wracked by pollution problems and with immense potential claims visible to the naked eye. The inadequacy of insurance usage in comparison with the enormity of the problem can be seen by the estimates of potential retroactive liability for cleanup of Superfund sites, which range from the lower tens of billions of dollars to $100 billion or more. After the peak of the EIL market, four of the ten participants dropped out; the others reduced the limits they would cover and increased the self-insured retentions they required. By 1985 little was left of the flourishing though still tiny market that had existed in 1983. The demand for the coverage was never substantial, at least at the prices insurers felt they had to charge.

The improving market for underground storage tanks notwithstanding, the market for broader pollution coverage continues to be limited. Shalowitz, Insurers Offer Niche Pollution Products, Bus. Ins., Oct. 8, 1990, at 15, describes that limited market.

A summary of the unsuccessful attempt to "use" insurance as a regulatory device is to be found in Kunzman, The Insurer as Surrogate Regulator of the Hazardous Waste Industry: Solution or Perversion?, 20 Tort & Ins. L.J. 469 (1985) and references therein. Freeman, Tort Law Reform: Superfund/RCRA Liability as a Major Cause of the Insurance Crisis, 21 Tort & Ins. L.J. 517 (1986) is harshly critical of the retroactive effect of some of the recent federal legislation in the field of environmental legislation.

2. Directors and Officers Liability Insurance

As recently as 1965, the 1,265-page Property and Liability Insurance

Handbook, a standard and much-used work, did not mention directors and officers (D & O) liability insurance, at least in its index or table of contents. Some recent textbooks on insurance do not mention it. One that does has only the following to say:

> *Directors and Officers Liability.* An increasing number of officers and directors of business firms have been sued in recent years. The lawsuits are often initiated by angry stockholders who claim that mismanagement by officers and directors has resulted in financial losses to the stockholders. This exposure of directors and officers to liability lawsuits can be covered by a *directors and officers liability insurance policy.* (Emphasis in original). [Rejda, Principles of Insurance 276 (1982).]

In the third edition of his Liability of Corporate Officers and Directors, dated December 1978, William E. Knepper said that "liability insurance for corporate officers and directors has come into its own in the past ten years." §20.01. His use of the word "liability" itself suggests its newness, for one of the issues that quickly surfaced and may not yet be completely settled is whether the insurance is liability or indemnity insurance. See *Okada,* infra. In Chapter 20 of the 1985 Supplement to the Knepper book is an extensive discussion of the law relating to D & O Insurance, including a good deal of information about the state of the market at that date. See also, for more recent commentary, Johnston, Corporate Indemnification and Liability Insurance for Directors and Officers, 33 Bus. Law. 1993 (1978); Hinsey, The New Lloyd's Policy Form for Directors and Officers Liability Insurance — An Analysis, 33 Bus. Law. 1961 (1978).

In the late 1960s there was much writing in the academic journals about the new trend to authorize D & O insurance. New York's statute authorizing such insurance was enacted as N.Y. Laws 1969, Ch. 1007, and most other states also acted in the late 1960s. The coverage was initially developed at Lloyd's, and at first was copied virtually verbatim by American insurers when they took up that line of business. Bishop, New Cure for an Old Ailment: Insurance Against Directors' and Officers' Liability, 22 Bus. Law. 92 (1966) expressed serious reservations about the merits of such coverage and caustically criticized the drafting of the then-current policy as inept, and especially as showing abysmal ignorance of relevant corporation law. The current policy is not greatly different.

For the limited purposes of this section, it will be reasonable to take the following provisions from the general corporation law of Illinois as typical:

ILLINOIS REVISED STATUTES CH. 32, §8.75

Ill. Rev. Stat. ch. 32, §8.75 (1987)

§8.75. *Indemnification of officers, directors, employees and agents; insurance.*

(a) A corporation may indemnify any person who was or is a party, or is threatened to be made a party to any threatened, pending or completed action, suit or proceeding, whether civil, criminal, administrative or investigative (other than an action by or in the right of the corporation) by reason of the fact that he or she is or was a director, officer, employee or agent of the corporation, or who is or was serving at the request of the corporation as a director, officer, employee or agent of another corporation, partnership, joint venture, trust or other enterprise, against expenses (including attorneys' fees), judgments, fines and amounts paid in settlement actually and reasonably incurred by such person in connection with such action, suit or proceeding, if such person acted in good faith and in a manner he or she reasonably believed to be in, or not opposed to the best interests of the corporation, and, with respect to any criminal action or proceeding, had no reasonable cause to believe his or her conduct was unlawful. The termination of any action, suit or proceeding by judgment, order, settlement, conviction, or upon a plea of nolo contendere or its equivalent, shall not, of itself, create a presumption that the person did not act in good faith and in a manner which he or she reasonably believed to be in or not opposed to the best interests of the corporation or, with respect to any criminal action or proceeding, that the person had reasonable cause to believe that his or her conduct was unlawful.

(b) A corporation may indemnify any person who was or is a party, or is threatened to be made a party to any threatened, pending or completed action or suit by or in the right of the corporation to procure a judgment in its favor by reason of the fact that such person is or was a director, officer, employee or agent of the corporation, or is or was serving at the request of the corporation as a director, officer, employee or agent of another corporation, partnership, joint venture, trust or other enterprise, against expenses (including attorneys' fees) actually and reasonably incurred by such person in connection with the defense or settlement of such action or suit, if such person acted in good faith and in a manner he or she reasonably believed to be in, or not opposed to the best interests of the corporation, provided that no indemnification shall be made in respect of any claim, issue or matter as to which such person shall have been adjudged to be liable for negligence or misconduct in the performance of his or her duty to the corporation, unless, and only to the extent that the court in which such action or suit was brought shall determine upon application that, despite the adjudication of liability, but in view of all the circumstances of the case, such person is fairly and reasonably entitled to indemnity for such expenses as the court shall deem proper.

(c) To the extent that a director, officer, employee or agent of a corporation has been successful, on the merits or otherwise, in the defense of any action, suit or proceeding referred to in subsections (a) and (b), or in defense of any claim, issue or matter therein, such person shall be indemnified against expenses (including attorneys' fees) actually and reasonably incurred by such person in connection therewith.

(d) Any indemnification under subsections (a) and (b) (unless ordered by a court) shall be made by the corporation only as authorized in the specific case, upon a determination that indemnification of the director, officer, employee or agent is proper in the circumstances because he or she has met the applicable standard of conduct set forth in subsections (a) or (b). Such determination shall be made (1) by the board of directors by a majority vote of a quorum consisting of directors who were not parties to such action, suit or proceeding, or (2) if such a quorum is not obtainable, or, even if obtainable, if a quorum of disinterested directors so directs, by independent legal counsel in a written opinion, or (3) by the shareholders.

(e) Expenses incurred in defending a civil or criminal action, suit or proceeding may be paid by the corporation in advance of the final disposition of such action, suit or proceeding, as authorized by the board of directors in the specific case, upon receipt of an undertaking by or on behalf of the director, officer, employee or agent to repay such amount, unless it shall ultimately be determined that he or she is entitled to be indemnified by the corporation as authorized in this Section.

(f) The indemnification provided by this Section shall not be deemed exclusive of any other rights to which those seeking indemnification may be entitled under any by-law, agreement, vote of shareholders or disinterested directors, or otherwise, both as to action in his or her official capacity and as to action in another capacity while holding such office, and shall continue as to a person who has ceased to be a director, officer, employee or agent, and shall inure to the benefit of the heirs, executors and administrators of such a person.

(g) A corporation may purchase and maintain insurance on behalf of any person who is or was a director, officer, employee or agent of the corporation, or who is or was serving at the request of the corporation as a director, officer, employee or agent of another corporation, partnership, joint venture, trust or other enterprise, against any liability asserted against such person and incurred by such person in any such capacity, or arising out of his or her status as such, whether or not the corporation would have the power to indemnify such person against such liability under the provisions of this Section. . . .

———————

The history of D & O insurance has been stormy. Partly because of opinions like those that follow, it is likely to become stormier yet. After a period in the 1980s in which the market for the coverage tightened almost to the point of disappearing, the market softened in the late 1980s and the coverage became generally available. For the recent situation, see Hofmann, D & O Rates Rising, But Not Sharply, Bus. Ins., Oct. 8, 1990, at 75.

Below are the most important provisions of the directors and officers liability insurance policy in force in the next case *(Okada)*. To those actually quoted in the opinion several are added from other sources, probably from the identical policy. The extra provisions should help in the understanding of the *Okada* case itself, and also of the use and functioning of directors and officers liability insurance.

DIRECTORS AND OFFICERS LIABILITY INSURANCE POLICY*

[T]he Insurer Agrees:

(a) With the Directors and Officers of the Association that if, during the policy period, any claim or claims are made against the Directors and Officers, individually or collectively, for a Wrongful Act, the Insurer will pay, in accordance with the terms of this policy, on behalf of the Directors and Officers or any of them, their heirs, legal representatives or assigns all Loss which the Directors and Officers or any of them shall become legally obligated to pay.

(b) With the Association that if, during the policy period, any claim or claims are made against the Directors and Officers, individually or collectively, for a Wrongful Act, the insurer will pay, in accordance with the terms of this policy, on behalf of the Association, all Loss for which the Association is required to indemnify or for which the Association has, to the extent permitted by law, indemnified the Directors and Officers.

———————

*The following portions of this D & O policy are in common use; there is no standard policy, though all in use are similar.

1. Definitions

(d) The term "Loss" shall mean any amount which the Directors and Officers are legally obligated to pay or for which the Association is required to indemnify the Directors or Officers, or for which the Association has, to the extent permitted by law, indemnified the Directors and Officers for a claim or claims made against the Directors and Officers, for Wrongful Acts and shall include but not be limited to damages, judgments, settlements, costs (exclusive of salaries of officers or employees), and defense of legal actions, claims or proceedings and appeals therefrom and cost of attachment or similar bonds; provided however, such Loss shall not include fines or penalties imposed by law or matters which may be deemed uninsurable under the law pursuant to which this policy shall be construed.

(e) The term "Wrongful Act" shall mean any actual or alleged error, misstatement, misleading statement, act or omission, or neglect or breach of duty by the Directors or Officers in the discharge of their duties solely in their capacity as Directors of the Association, individually or collectively, or any matter claimed against them solely by reason of their being Directors or Officers of the Association.

3. Exclusions

(a) Except for Loss for which the Association is required to indemnify the Directors or Officers, or for which the Association has, to the extent permitted by law, indemnified the Directors or Officers, the Insurer shall not be liable to make any payment for Loss in connection with any claim made against the Directors or Officers:

(5) brought about or contributed to by the dishonesty of the Directors or Officers. However, notwithstanding the foregoing, the Directors or Officers shall be protected under the terms of this policy as to any claims upon which suit may be brought against them, by reason of any alleged dishonesty on the part of the Directors or Officers, unless a judgment or other final adjudication thereof adverse to the Directors or Officers shall establish that acts of active and deliberate dishonesty committed by the Directors or Officers with actual dishonest purpose and intent were material to the cause of action so adjudicated.

4. Limits of Liability

(b) The Insurer's maximum liability in each policy year for each Director and Officer insured hereunder shall be the limit of liability (including costs, charges and expenses as referred to in Clause 5) shown under Item 3 of the Declarations. For purposes of this Clause 4(b), a claim shall be deemed to be made at the date that notice is given to the Insurer pursuant to Clause 6(a) or 6(b), or at the date the claim is made against the Directors and Officers, whichever shall occur first.

(c) Notwithstanding Clause 4(b) above, the Insurer's maximum liability for a single Loss shall be the limit of liability (including costs, charges and expenses as referred to in Clause 5) shown under Item 3 of the Declarations.

(d) Claims based on or arising out of the same act, interrelated acts, or one or more series of similar acts, of one or more of the Directors or Officers shall be considered a single Loss and the Insurer's liability shall be limited to the limit of liability stated in Clause 4(b) and 4(c). In the event that more than one Director or Officer is included in the same Loss, it shall be expressly understood that the total amount of such Loss, for the purpose of determining the aggregate limit for each such involved Director or Officer, shall be apportioned pro rata among each such involved Director or Officer unless otherwise mutually agreed upon by the Director or Officer and the Insurer.

5. Costs, Charges and Expenses

(a) No costs, charges and expenses shall be incurred or settlements made without the Insurer's consent which consent shall not be unreasonably withheld; however, in the event such consent is given, the Insurer shall pay, subject to the provisions of Clause 4, such costs, settlements, charges and expenses.

(b) The Directors and Officers shall not be required to contest any legal proceedings unless counsel (to be mutually agreed upon by the Directors or Officers and the Insurer) shall advise that such claim should be contested by the Directors or Officers.

(c) The Insurer may at its option and upon request, advance on behalf of the Directors or Officers, or any of them, expenses which they have incurred in connection with claims made against them, prior to disposition of such claims, provided always that in the event it is finally established the Insurer has no liability hereunder, such Directors and Officers agree to repay to the Insurer, upon demand, all monies advanced by virtue of this provision.

Dishonesty is not covered because it is properly the subject of a fidelity bond (see Chapter 4). Dishonesty of directors who are not also officers (that is, employees) is not covered in the standard bond forms. See the Bankers Blanket Bond, under Insuring Agreements: Fidelity, and under Conditions and Limitations: Exclusions, §2(a), in Chapter 4. But under the guise of coverage against liability, claims are often made that might properly fall under the coverage of a fidelity bond.

The new definition of infidelity in the fidelity bond creates a potential gap in coverage between the bond and the D & O policy. Infidelity requires "manifest intent to cause the insured to sustain [the] loss, and to obtain financial benefit for the Employee or for any other person." Bankers Blanket Bond, Chapter 4, Insuring Agreement A. The D & O policy excludes loss "brought about or contributed to by the dishonesty of the Directors or Officers." Supra, Exclusion (5). It is possible that there may be no coverage under the policy because there was dishonesty and none under the bond because there was not enough dishonesty. In some instances coverage may overlap, creating subrogation problems between the surety on the bond and the insurer on the policy. For a discussion of the problem, see Schroeder, Handling the Complex Fidelity or Financial Institution Bond Claim: The Liability of the Insured's Officers and Directors and Their D & O Carrier, 21 Tort & Ins. L.J. 269 (1986), and other materials cited therein.

Much of the recent litigation over D & O insurance has been initiated on behalf of FDIC or FSLIC (or the Resolution Trust Corporation as successor to the FSLIC) as subrogees of the banks they have bailed out or sold to other banks. Another interesting group of cases has been brought by the liquidators of insolvent insurance companies against the officers and directors of those corporations, hoping for recovery against the D & O insurers of the insolvent insurers. It is hardly surprising, therefore, that the following exclusion, often called the *regulatory exclusion,* has recently been added to those previously standard in the policy:

It is understood and agreed that the Insurer shall not be liable to make any payment for loss in connection with any claim made against the Directors or Officers based upon or attributable to any action or proceeding brought by or on behalf of the Federal Deposit Insurance Corporation, the Federal Savings & Loan Insurance Corporation, any other depository insurance organization, the Comptroller of the Currency, the Federal Home Loan Bank Board, or any other national or state regulatory agency (all of said organizations and agencies hereinafter referred to as "Agencies"), including any type of legal action which such Agencies have the legal right to bring as receiver, conservator, liquidator, or otherwise; whether such action or proceeding is brought in the name of such Agencies or by or on behalf of such Agencies in the name of any other entity or solely in the name of any Third Party.

In American Casualty Co. v. FSLIC, 683 F. Supp. 1183 (S.D. Ohio 1988), the FSLIC argued that the exclusion is void because it conflicts with public policy. The same question was faced in Federal Savings and Loan Ins. Corp. v. Oldenburg, 671 F. Supp. 720 (D. Utah 1987). The two courts do not completely agree. How would you resolve the question? Why? The question was faced squarely by a state court, apparently for the first time, in Finci v. American Casualty Co., 82 Md. App. 471, 572 A.2d 1092 (1990), *cert. granted,* 320 Md. 636, 579 A.2d 281 (1990). The regulatory agency was the Maryland Deposit Insurance Fund (MDIC). The intermediate appellate court held the exclusion to be a violation of public policy, interfering with the proper implementation of MDIC's function.

Another new and related exclusion is called the *insured v. insured* exclusion. It precludes insurance against liability by one insured to another. The language is clear that the Institution is an insured, except for a shareholder's derivative action. *Finci* held this exclusion also to be void and unenforceable.

See also American Casualty Co. v. FDIC, 677 F. Supp. 600 (N.D. Iowa 1987), for discussion of both exclusions.

OKADA v. MGIC INDEM. CORP.

823 F.2d 276 (9th Cir. 1987)

FERGUSON, Circuit Judge:

Defendant MGIC Indemnity Corporation ("MGIC") appeals the district court's grant of summary judgment in favor of plaintiffs Glenn K. Okada, William E. Takabayashi, and Richard A. Cooke, Jr. ("insureds"), who were insured under a Directors and Officers Errors and Omissions policy issued by MGIC. The district court ruled that MGIC had a duty to pay the defense costs of insureds as those costs came due in lawsuits alleging losses caused by the insureds as directors of a savings and loan association ("the underlying lawsuits"); that more than one potentially covered "loss" was involved; and that MGIC acted in bad faith by refusing to pay, without condition, the insureds' defense costs in the underlying lawsuits, refusing to affirm or deny coverage of claims in the underlying lawsuits, and refusing to enter settlement negotiations in the underlying lawsuits. Okada v. MGIC Indem. Corp., 608 F. Supp. 383 (D. Hawaii 1985).

We affirm the rulings finding a duty to pay defense costs as they come due and more than one potentially covered "loss," but reverse the ruling that MGIC acted in bad faith.

I

Plaintiff insureds were three of the eight directors of First Savings & Loan Association of Hawaii ("First Savings"). MGIC issued a Directors and Officers Errors and Omissions insurance policy. . . . The policy covered each loss for up to $1 million each year for each director, with an aggregate annual limit for each director.

In 1980, First Savings became insolvent and the Federal Savings and Loan Insurance Corp. ("FSLIC") took control of the institution. In 1982, First Hawaiian Bank and FSLIC, as assignees of various shareholders' direct and derivative claims, filed the underlying lawsuits in federal district court against all eight directors of First Savings. See FSLIC v. Alexander, 590 F. Supp. 834 (D. Hawaii 1984). Each director hired defense counsel in the underlying lawsuits and sought payment from MGIC for the fees incurred. MGIC agreed to pay the costs as they came due, but reserved its right to contest coverage and to demand reimbursement if the policy did not cover the claims involved.

All eight directors accepted payments with MGIC's reservation of rights for nearly two years. After that time three of them, the insureds here, refused to accept payment with the attached reservation of rights. MGIC therefore stopped paying the defense costs of the three directors, who then filed this action in federal district court seeking a declaratory judgment that MGIC had a duty to pay, without condition, defense costs in the underlying litigation as those costs were incurred. The defense costs in the underlying lawsuits exceeded $1 million at the time of the district court decision.

The district court granted the insureds' motion for summary judgment. It ruled, first, that the policy was ambiguous because clause 5(c) conflicted with clause 1(d) and that the policy should be read against MGIC as the drafter of the adhesion contract. The court concluded that MGIC had a duty to pay the insureds' defense costs in the underlying action as they came due.

Second, the district court ruled that the underlying lawsuits involved separate alleged acts, each of which was a potential "loss" and could have given rise to a distinct claim. Therefore, even though the acts culminated in one result, First Savings' financial collapse, multiple potentially covered "losses" were involved. Because of the policy limits, MGIC could be liable for "multiple millions" in the underlying lawsuits.

Finally, the district court found that MGIC acted in bad faith because it "has refused to affirm or deny coverage, tender defense costs when due, or enter into settlement negotiations." MGIC timely appeals. . . .

III

Section 1(d) of the MGIC policy explains the limits of coverage. The policy covers "Loss," which is defined as "the amount which the Directors and Officers are legally obligated to pay . . . for a claim or claims made against the Directors and Officers for Wrongful Acts." This language establishes the policy as a liability, rather than indemnity, policy. This interpretation is confirmed by the captions to the policy's declarations, which clearly denominate the policy as "liability insurance."

MGIC does at times cryptically refer to its policy as an "indemnity-type policy." Insureds assert that MGIC argued earlier that the policy was an indemnity policy in an effort to avoid contemporaneous liability for defense costs. Whatever the case may be, the policy here is a liability policy. As the Fifth Circuit explained in Continental Oil Co. v. Bonanza Corp., 677 F.2d 455 (5th Cir. 1982):

> In a liability contract, the insurer agrees to cover *liability* for damages. If the insured is liable, the insurance company must pay the damages. In an indemnity contract, by contrast, the insurer agrees to reimburse expenses to the insured that the insurer is liable to pay and has paid. [Id. at 459.]

The policy here, based on loss as incurred and not as loss paid out by insureds, is a liability policy.

Since the policy is for liability rather than indemnity, payment by MGIC for loss is not conditioned upon the payment of damages by the directors. Whenever "loss" occurs (i.e., whenever the directors are "legally obligated to pay" on a covered claim), MGIC must pay that amount. The policyholders thus are assured that they need not expend their own funds in order to receive protection for liability.

The costs of the "defense of legal actions" are included in the definition of "Loss" in section 1(d). Thus, in the absence of other provisions, the policy demands that MGIC pay those costs when the directors become legally obligated to pay them. The issue in this case is whether MGIC effectively excluded such contemporaneous payment of costs by modifying the general rule encompassed in section 1(d).

MGIC claims that the provisions of section 5 of the policy (governing "costs, charges and expenses") exclude legal costs from the general rule of contemporaneous recovery. Section 5(a) qualifies the contemporaneous duty to pay costs, charges, and expenses by giving MGIC the right of approval over such expenditures. MGIC's discretion in reviewing costs, charges, and expenses, however, is not unlimited, for approval may not be "unreasonably withheld." MGIC argues that the "defense of legal actions" referred to in section 1(d) is included in the "costs, charges and expenses."

MGIC argues that section 5(c) further limits payment. Section 5(c) allows the payment of "expenses" prior to the disposition of claims. The payment of expenses, however, is within the complete discretion of MGIC. Nowhere does the policy define expenses, or explain how those expenses differ from the broader language of section 5(a), which covers "costs, charges and expenses." We therefore know that the defense of legal actions is covered by the policy, that costs, charges and expenses must be approved by MGIC, but that expenses are excluded from the general duty of contemporaneous payment.

We must interpret the policy to determine whether "expenses," excluded from contemporaneous payment under section 5(c), contain the "defense of legal actions," covered under section 1(d). It is a commonplace that a contract is interpreted to conform to the expectations of the parties at the time of the contracting. See E. Farnsworth, Contracts §77.7, at 478 (1982) ("The language of a contract is directed, not at describing experience, but at controlling human behavior. . . . The concern of the court is not the truth of this language but with the expectations that it aroused in those parties."). In contracts of insurance, however, Hawaii law applies a strict form of the rule of construction against the drafter of a contract. See Hurtig v. Terminix Wood Treating & Contracting Co., 692 P.2d 1153, 1154 (Hawaii 1984) ("[I]nsurance policies must be construed liberally in favor of coverage because they are contracts of adhesion."). Thus in examining the entire contract to ascertain and fulfill the reasonable expectations of the parties, see Sturla, Inc., v. Fireman's Fund Ins. Co., 67 Hawaii 203, 209, 684 P.2d 960, 964 (1984), conflicts will be resolved in favor of the insured since MGIC controlled the language of the agreement.*

With this background, the contract cannot be read to exclude defense costs from the effect of the general rule of a liability policy. Given the prosecution of this suit, MGIC clearly intended to exclude attorneys fees from immediate payment. At the time critical to our inquiry, however, the time of contracting, it could not have been clear to insureds that they would not be protected from the costs of fees. Section 1(d) provides the coverage in clear language; section 5(c) (we *now* know) attempts to postpone that coverage pending determination of liability on the underlying claims. The language of section 5(c) simply is unclear in its attempt. Nowhere are "expenses" defined; nor is it explained how they differ from the broader category of "costs, charges and expenses" of section 5(a). . . .

Our decision need not create havoc in the already disturbed field of D & O liability insurance. Reports discussing policies similar to the one at hand demonstrate a wide variety of policy language. The leading policy in this field, Lloyd's of London's "Lydando No. 1," upon which the MGIC policy appears to be based, contains references to costs, charges, and expenses in general. When the policy means to refer to

---

*There is reason to think the Court may have misunderstood the Hawaiian law. See Fortune v. Wong, 702 P.2d 299 (Hawaii 1988), a more recent case than any cited by the court. — ED.

defense costs, however, it expressly does so, avoiding the confusion that is MGIC's downfall here. See Lloyd's Lydando No. 1 Policy Form §6(C), reprinted in Hinsey, The New Lloyd's Policy Form for Directors' and Officers' Liability Insurance — An Analysis, 33 Bus. Law. 1961 (1978).

This result works no particular hardship on MGIC. MGIC's liability is limited to losses incurred with covered claims. . . .

The one exclusion from coverage that may be difficult to determine from the pleadings, section 3(a)(5), employs a mechanism to meet this problem. Section 3(a)(5) excludes loss brought about by the "active and deliberate dishonesty" of the directors. The exclusion is subject to a special provision that mandates payment unless a final judgment has been rendered confirming the directors' dishonesty. Section 3(a)(5) thus broadens coverage for the one case where coverage cannot be determined until judgment is reached. . . .

This suit was instituted at the behest of directors who refused to accept MGIC's reservation of rights regarding the costs advanced. MGIC may, of course, in payment of costs on covered claims as those costs come due, reserve its rights pursuant to the contract should the claims ultimately prove uncovered. For example, MGIC, while advancing costs, may reserve its rights under section 3(a)(5) should the directors' acts ultimately prove intentional rather than negligent. The directors have a right to the contemporary payment of costs. They have no right, however, to the unconditional payment of costs, when those conditions were clearly and unequivocally expressed.

We conclude that the district court correctly ruled that MGIC must make contemporaneous payments for legal defense on claims covered by the policy. MGIC may reserve its rights under the agreement, however, for the return of advances should the claims ultimately prove to be uncovered.

IV

MGIC argues that the district court finding of more than one potentially covered "loss" was premature, and that the evidence does not support the court's finding of more than one potential loss. The finding was not premature, however, because MGIC had paid more than $1 million. Because the policy limits are $1 million for each "loss," the court had to consider whether MGIC needed to pay any more defense costs. If more than one loss was involved, MGIC would continue to be responsible for the defense costs. The facts on which the district court based its finding are undisputed and, if true, establish that the district court was correct.

MGIC concedes that more than $1 million has been expended for defense costs in the underlying lawsuits, but argues that this amount is irrelevant because these defense costs are not a "loss" under clause 1(d), but rather an optional payment under clause 5(c). Therefore, MGIC argues, no "loss" has been paid; the first $1 million has not been expended, and it is unnecessary at this stage to determine whether another $1 million or more is available.[5] MGIC's argument rests primarily on its related argument that it had no duty to defend the underlying lawsuits. MGIC concedes that if it had a duty to defend then the defense costs would come out of the $1 million increments. However, its prematurity argument collapses because we find that it must make contemporaneous payments for legal defense on claims covered by the policy.

The district court found that the underlying lawsuits alleged several distinct acts potentially covered by the MGIC policy.[6] The district court reasoned that more than one "loss" can culminate in one overall result, First Savings & Loan's failure, but one result does not require finding only one "loss." Finally, the court reasoned that the parties contemplated more than one loss because the directors chose a $1 million "per loss" policy rather than one with a $1 million ceiling.[7] Thus, the district court finding was timely and correct. . . .

VI

We affirm the grant of summary judgment in favor of the insureds on the first two rulings: that the policy created a contemporaneous duty to pay costs and that the underlying lawsuits involved more than one potentially covered "loss." MGIC may reserve its rights under the contract for return of the advances should the losses ultimately prove uncovered. Because disputes of material fact remain, and because it is unclear whether Hawaii recognizes the duty of good faith and fair

5. The district court and both parties apparently agree that MGIC's duty to pay defense costs, if one exists, will end when the costs exceed the policy limits. It is unclear whether the agreement is based on the policy language that defense costs constitute a "loss" or on a general rule that the duty to defend lapses when the policy limits are exhausted.

6. For example, "(1) voting at separate times to authorize spot loans to home buyers; (2) authorizing five separate, unrelated large condominium project loans; [and] (3) ordering the move and renovation of corporate headquarters without having sufficient funds therefor."

7. The insureds chose the more expensive option for limits of liability, which provided for $1 million each loss, with an aggregate limit each policy year for each director and officer. The other option would have provided $1 million each year, regardless of the number of suits or the number of Directors and Officers insured.

dealing in insurance contracts, we reverse the summary judgment on the ruling that MGIC acted in bad faith.

Affirmed in part, reversed in part, and remanded.

Notes and Questions

1. Little v. MGIC Indem. Corp., 836 F.2d 789 (3d Cir. 1987), agrees with *Okada* on the defense cost issue. Not every court does. Id. at 796. Pepsico, Inc. v. Continental Casualty Co., 640 F. Supp. 656 (S.D.N.Y. 1986) also agrees with *Okada*.

2. What does the court mean when it calls the policy in *Okada* a liability rather than an indemnity policy? In a superseded version of the court's opinion, 795 F.2d 1450 (9th Cir. 1986), the court called the policy a "duty to defend" policy. With what was the court contrasting it? Is the dichotomy the same as the indemnity-liability one? In Quinlan v. Liberty Bank and Trust Co., 558 So. 2d 221 (La. 1990), the court said the D & O policy was a liability policy, not an indemnity policy. In Louisiana, the difference justified a direct action against the insurer.

3. Is the court right in saying that defense costs are included within the definition of "Loss"? In the same sense as in other kinds of liability policies?

4. If the insurer "consents to costs" under paragraph 5(a) above, must the insurer pay those costs if it turns out that there is no coverage? What relation does that provision have to paragraph 5(c), respecting the advancing of costs?

5. A heretofore unmentioned provision of the policy, in some form present in all liability policies, is the *no action clause*. It usually reads as follows:

> No action shall be taken against the Insurer unless, as a condition precedent thereto, there shall have been full compliance with all of the terms of this policy, nor until the amount of the Directors' and Officers' obligation to pay shall have been finally determined either by judgment against the Directors or Officers after actual trial or by written agreement of the Directors or Officers, the claimant and the Insurer.

Should the presence of that clause have any effect on the answers to the preceding questions?

6. Should MGIC's payment of more than $1 million for defense costs establish anything at all with respect to the existence of multiple losses?

7. For interpretation of the language from an industry perspective, see Oettle and Howard, D & O Insurance: Judicially Transforming a "Duty to Pay" Policy into a "Duty to Defend" Policy, 22 Tort & Ins. L.J. 337 (1987).

8. The D & O policy is really two policies in one, combining protection to the corporation and protection to the officers and directors. Only marketing considerations preclude the selling of the two coverages as distinct and separately rated policies.

9. The D & O policy has often been subjected to harsh criticism for its drafting defects. Originally developed at Lloyds, its drafting reflects the different way the insurance business is conducted in England, where precision of drafting takes second place to established business practice. When the D & O market was first opened up in this country, it was expected to provide a bonanza; as often happens, marketplace reality caught up with the insurers. The market became thin, with high deductibles and low limits, in the generally tight insurance market of the mid-1980s. As a result, many outside directors of corporations resigned because their corporations were unable to provide them satisfactory insurance protection. As of this writing the market has softened, and stories of the resignations of directors due to inadequate insurance are no longer seen in the press.

10. Polychron v. Crum & Forster Ins. Cos., 916 F.2d 461 (8th Cir. 1990), held that legal fees incurred during a grand jury investigation were within the policy coverage.

Problem

A small bank, X, discovered that one of its officers, A, had been speculating with bank funds for the bank's account in certain futures contracts and lost several million dollars.* Because a part of his conduct was criminal, after trial A temporarily resided in a penitentiary. Soon, the responsible regulatory agency (which might be FDIC, FSLIC, or in some states a state counterpart of those federal agencies) arranged a merger of X into another bank, Y, which succeeded to X's legal positions. In the course of the transaction, the relevant guarantee association agreed to indemnify Y for its losses in the merger, and by contract was itself subrogated to Y's and X's rights. At least 16 lawsuits resulted, including two by the guarantee association against various officers and directors for their failures to supervise and control the blameworthy A. Various counts were stated: failure of each board member and officer to exercise general supervision over A, failure of the board investment committee and certain officers to supervise or at least take notice of certain activities of A that should have triggered

*This problem is based, with some changes and with some oversimplification, on a recent case that was settled without trial. Prior to the settlement, there was a nonbinding opinion by a mediation panel created by order of the court. The precise facts and the identities of the parties cannot be disclosed because of a protective order of the court.

concern about his investment activity, failure to carry out certain board resolutions respecting disinvestment, cosigning applications for loans to deal with liquidity problems brought about in part by A's improper activity, providing an insurer false information in an application for a fidelity bond which resulted in the avoidance of the bond, and perhaps others. All of the acts were related through the fact that the ultimate harm was done by A's wrongful speculation in futures contracts.

Another action was brought by the officers and directors (excluding A, who would be disabled from coverage by the Wrongful Act language) against Y, seeking a declaratory judgment that Y must indemnify them for the damages they must pay the guarantee association, up to the policy limits. Y cross-claimed against the insurer, seeking a declaration that it must indemnify Y for what Y is required to indemnify the officers and directors. The insurance contract is in all important respects the same as the one quoted above.

1. In this complex aggregation of lawsuits, how would you decide in the declaratory judgment proceeding? The basic issue is: for how many "losses" (analogous to "occurrences" in other liability policies?) is the insurer liable? The pivotal language in the contract is that in §4(d).

2. How would you organize an argument that there was but one loss, rather than several?

3. How would you argue that there were as many losses as there were directors and officers?

4. Are there any tenable intermediate positions?

5. North River Ins. Co. v. Huff, 628 F. Supp. 1129 (D. Kan. 1985) also deals with the number of losses. The word used was "incident" rather than "occurrence." Should that make any difference in the result? See also National Union Fire Ins. Co. v. Ambassador Group, 691 F. Supp. 618 (E.D.N.Y. 1988) for a discussion of the number of losses under the clause at issue in the problem case. *Ambassador Group* represents the class of cases brought by liquidators of insurance companies against the insolvent companies' directors and officers, with the expectation of drawing on the D & O insurance.

6. A recent case deciding there was more than one loss is Eureka Federal Savings and Loan Association v. American Casualty Co., 873 F.2d 229 (9th Cir. 1989).

3. Products and Completed Operations

There is no need to go into great detail about these coverages: They have already appeared in many of the cases in this chapter, but certain points need emphasis.

Products and completed operations were initially treated as two branches of the same hazard. Drawing the line between them may sometimes be difficult. In those pre-1966 policies in which a definition appeared, completed operations was a subdivision of the "Products hazard." In the 1966 policy they were separated. See Henderson, Insurance Protection for Products Liability and Completed Operations — What Every Lawyer Should Know, 50 Neb. L. Rev. 415 (1971); Andersen, Current Problems in Products Liability Law and Products Liability Insurance, 31 Ins. Coun. J. 436 (1964); Annot., 58 A.L.R.3d 12 (1974).

The classic case of the completed operations hazard is that of building construction. (The architect is subject to a similar hazard but will cover it by a professional liability or malpractice policy.) Savannah Laundry & Mach. Co. v. Home Ins. Co., 189 Ga. App. 420, 376 S.E.2d 373 (1988), illustrates completed operations. The insured was sued by a person injured when a boiler door that had been repaired by the insured blew open. A completed operations exclusion precluded coverage.

One of the perennial uncertainties in completed operations coverage is when operations should be regarded as completed, for that divides this coverage from premises and operations liability, the first major category in comprehensive liability insurance. For an extensive contemporary treatment of completed operations, see Landis & Rahdert, The Completed Operations Hazard, 19 Forum 570 (1984).

In Friendship Homes, Inc. v. American States Ins. Cos., 450 N.W.2d 778 (N.D. 1990), a contractor negligently installed a fireplace. Two years after his "occurrence" policy had expired, there was a fire that did considerable property damage. The court held there was no liability because the fire did not take place within the policy period. Is the decision sound?

Laminated Wood Products Co. v. Pedersen, 76 Or. App. 662, 711 P.2d 165 (1985), illustrates the division between products and completed operations. An insured sued an insurance agent for failing to acquire completed operations coverage after the insured had been sued for alleged defects in prefabricated buildings produced by the insured. The court held for the defendant, inasmuch as completed operations coverage would not have provided coverage anyway: The hazard was a products hazard. The opinion cited a number of cases, as well as Henderson's article, supra.

Products liability covers liability for bodily injury and property damage to third persons as a result of defects in products. Even a casual look at the coverage clause makes it apparent that it provides no coverage for the expenses of recalling the product to preclude further liability. For discussion of recall insurance see Section F on the sister-ship exclusion.

4. Automobile Liability

By far the most common liability insurance coverage is in the automobile policy. There is still a plethora of litigation about it although most of the principal issues were settled long ago. Yet with many tens of millions of policies in effect, and an immense number of claims every year, it is inevitable that a good number will end up in court and quite a few in appellate opinions.

a. Policy Limits

Policy limits pervade all of liability insurance. They are especially important in the law and practice of automobile insurance. The available limits of insurance coverage in a case tend to determine the numbers around which negotiation occurs, and also tend to be crucial in determining when there are bad faith claims against insurers, as the materials in Chapter 8 will show. Automobile policy limits are most often written in the *form* $100/300/25,000. This means that the company has agreed to pay covered losses for bodily injury up to $100,000 per injured person and $300,000 per accident, and for property damage up to $25,000 per accident. The following case illustrates one recent problem in interpreting the limits.

McGOVERN v. WILLIAMS

741 S.W.2d 373 (Tex. 1987)

Robert McGovern, a City of Dallas employee, sustained personal injuries in an automobile accident. The City of Dallas, as subrogee, initiated suit against Linda Kay Williams for Mr. McGovern's personal injuries. Mr. and Mrs. McGovern later brought a separate action against Ms. Williams and others for Mr. McGovern's personal injuries and for Mrs. McGovern's loss of consortium. The two causes of action were consolidated and State Farm intervened in the suit. Ms. Williams' insurance policy with State Farm insured Ms. Williams to the extent of $10,000 per person and $20,000 per occurrence for bodily injury claims. State Farm tendered $10,000 pursuant to the "per person" policy limit. Mrs. McGovern disputed the amount of the tender, contending that she and Mr. McGovern were each entitled to $10,000 in insurance proceeds and that State Farm's obligation was $20,000. The trial court held State Farm was not obligated to pay the damages sustained by Mr. and Mrs. McGovern in excess of the $10,000 limit. The trial court accordingly accepted State Farm's tender of $10,000 and released State Farm from any further liability. The trial court also rendered judgment against Ms. Williams in favor of Mrs. McGovern for $10,000.

At issue in this case is whether loss of consortium is a separate "bodily injury" to a spouse for purposes of applying the minimum insurance policy limits contained in Ms. Williams' policy and required by the Texas Safety Responsibility Law, Tex. Rev. Civ. Stat. Ann. art. 6701h, §21 (Vernon 1977). Mrs. McGovern contends that her claim for loss of consortium constitutes a "bodily injury" as that term is used in Article 6701h, §21 and that she is entitled to independently recover from State Farm under the $10,000 "per person" liability limit. The provisions of Article 6701h, §21 require all motor vehicle liability policies to contain the following minimum limits:

> Ten Thousand dollars ($10,000) *because of bodily injury to or death of one person in any one accident* and, subject to said limit for one person, Twenty Thousand Dollars ($20,000) *because of bodily injury to or death of two (2) or more persons in any one accident. . . .* (emphasis added).

Mrs. McGovern argues the legislature intended Article 6701h to encompass loss of consortium as a separate "bodily injury" because the legislature's general intent in enacting the statute was to protect persons from loss caused by negligent motorists. She contends that bodily injury is not limited to actual physical contact but is to be liberally construed to include mental anguish and emotional trauma. Mrs. McGovern relies on Whittlesey v. Miller, 572 S.W.2d 665 (Tex. 1978) in which this court recognized loss of consortium as a separate and independent cause of action that arises as a result of negligent injury to one's spouse. Id. at 668. Mrs. McGovern thus contends that she is entitled to an independent recovery of $10,000 under the policy as a person who sustained "bodily injury."

The language of Article 6701h — "bodily injury to or death of one person in any one accident" — clearly refers to the person who is actually involved and physically or emotionally injured in the accident. The language of Article 6701h refers to liability limits due to bodily injury or death to any one or more persons *in* any one accident. It is undisputed that only Mr. McGovern was involved *in* the accident giving rise to his personal injuries. Thus, because only one person was involved in that accident, the limit of State Farm's liability is $10,000.

The term "bodily injury" cannot be reasonably construed to incorporate loss of consortium. While it is true that loss of consortium is a separate and independent cause of action, that action is a derivative claim that arises only as a consequence of injuries to one's spouse. *Whittlesey,* 572 S.W.2d at 667; Reed Tool Co. v. Copelin, 610 S.W.2d 736, 738 (Tex. 1981). The fact that Mrs. McGovern has a separate cause of action for loss of consortium does not mean, as Mrs. McGovern asserts, that loss of consortium constitutes a "bodily injury." . . .

We hold that when only one person is actually involved in an automobile accident and sustains bodily injury in that accident, Article 6701h limits recovery for any and all claims to the "per person" $10,000 limit. We further hold that the term "bodily injury" as used in Article 6701h does not encompass loss of consortium.

Our holding is based on sound public policy. To hold that loss of consortium is a "bodily injury" within the scope of Article 6701h would place loss of consortium claims on an equal footing with the bodily injury claims of those actually involved in motor vehicle accidents. Permitting a separate "per person" recovery for loss of consortium would give those suffering serious injuries from accidents no greater right to a share of the total available insurance proceeds from the occurrence than those asserting a derivative claim for loss of consortium. Subjecting loss of consortium to the "per person" limit will not deprive the spouse of his or her claim but will merely make a consortium claim and the bodily injury claim subject to the "per person" liability limit provided in the insurance policy. . . .

Notes and Questions

1. Accord, Tomlinson v. Skolnik, 44 Ohio St. 3d 11, 540 N.E.2d 716 (1989). The Massachusetts Supreme Judicial Court decided differently, concluding that the company was "obligated to make additional payments within the 'per accident' limit for loss of consortium claims by the victim's spouse or children." Bilodeau v. Lumbermens Mut. Casualty Co., 392 Mass. 537, 467 N.E.2d 137 (1984). The language of the policy was standard. The court did not suggest there was bodily injury, but the claimants had suffered damages as a result of bodily injury to the injured person.

2. In Wolfe v. State Farm Ins. Co., 224 N.J. Super. 348, 540 A.2d 871 (1988), *cert. denied*, 111 N.J. 654, 546 A.2d 562 (1988), plaintiffs' daughter died from carbon monoxide poisoning while in a third person's car. The court held that the action of the parents for emotional distress was a separate action, not a derivative claim, and that it was "bodily injury" within the meaning of that term in the automobile insurance policy. Each of them was therefore entitled to recover separately for emotional distress up to the per injury limit for each and up to the per accident limit for all injuries combined.

3. How would you interpret the coverage language of the automobile policy in *McGovern*, after seeing what the Massachusetts and New Jersey courts could achieve?

4. In Cincinnati Ins. Co. v. Phillips, 52 Ohio St. 3d 162, 556 N.E.2d 1150 (1990), the husband was injured in an automobile accident that was the fault of the other driver; he later died. The wife was injured. The court allowed recovery of three separate per person limits, one for the wife's personal injuries, one for the husband's claim for personal injuries, which survived his death, and one for the wrongful death claim of the wife for the death of the husband. Is the result sound?

b. Omnibus Coverage

This coverage is achieved in the contemporary plain language policy by defining the word *insured* to include "any person using your 'covered auto.' " That unqualified language would include a thief or other person driving without permission. Consequently, the policy says further that "[w]e do not provide Liability Coverage for any person . . . [U]sing a vehicle without a reasonable belief that that person is entitled to do so." The older policies defined the insured to include "any other person using such automobile, provided the actual use thereof is with the permission of the named insured." In some jurisdictions, the change of the qualification from a definition (and therefore from the coverage provisions) to the exclusions might itself change the result by shifting the burden of proof. See Chapter 1. But apart from that technical change, the coverage has been enlarged, for permission has ceased to be necessary.

Notes and Questions

1. In Canadian Indem. Co. v. Heflin, 151 Ariz. 257, 727 P.2d 35 (Ariz. App. 1986), the underage, unlicensed driver was at first a passenger with an older young woman who was intoxicated. Because of concern for his own safety, he required her to stop and let him drive. He drove too fast and lost control of the car. The court held it was a question of fact, to be determined at trial, whether he reasonably believed himself entitled to drive. Was the result sound?

2. Although historically airplane hull insurance was rather like marine insurance, in contemporary practice there is much reason to expect an aircraft policy, at least on a noncommercial plane, to mimic an automobile policy. For example, one much used aircraft policy defines the insured to include, with respect to liability coverages, "any person while using the *aircraft* with the permission of the *Named Insured* provided the actual use is within the scope of such permis-

sion." The policy in Bonner v. U.S. Fire Ins. Co., 494 So. 2d 1311 (La. App. 1986), *cert. denied,* 497 So. 2d 1017 (La. 1986) qualified a similar definition of the insured by saying the provision did not apply "[t]o any person operating the aircraft under the terms of any rental agreement . . . which provides any remuneration to the named insured for the use of the aircraft." One presumes the insured could buy back the excluded coverage for an additional premium.

c. Family Exclusion Provision

Insurers have always been concerned about "moral hazard" — the tendency of insureds to bring about an insured loss deliberately, or at least to be less diligent in trying to prevent it, because there is insurance. Another form of moral hazard is the temptation to collude with a person who claims to be injured, or to be injured more seriously than is actually the case. Many exclusions in various insurance policies can be explained by concern for moral hazard. One means of dealing with the problem is the "cooperation clause" which, in the plain language policy, requires a person seeking coverage to "[c]ooperate with us in the investigation, settlement or defense of any claim or suit."

In automobile liability insurance, insurers have been especially fearful of collusion between insured drivers and their family members. That has led in many policies to a "family exclusion provision," which may say, "[t]his policy does not apply . . . to bodily injury to the insured or any member of the family of the insured residing in the same household as the insured." By the weight of authority such provisions are valid and effective, in the absence of a statute mandating a contrary result: some courts however, will be alert to seek statutory warrant for finding such clauses void in violation of public policy. See Mutual of Enumclaw Ins. Co. v. Wiscomb, 97 Wash. 2d 203, 643 P.2d 441 (1982), *aff'g on reh'g* 95 Wash. 2d 373, 622 P.2d 1234 (1980), where the statutes involved were the financial responsibility statute, the uninsured motorist statute, and the underinsured motorist statute. The public policy they contained "overrides any 'freedom of contract' analysis — at least when the parties to the insurance contract have not truly bargained for such an exclusion." Id., 97 Wash. 2d at 213, 643 P.2d at 446. In the later case of Progressive Casualty Ins. Co. v. Jester, 102 Wash. 2d 78, 683 P.2d 180 (1984), a freedom of contract analysis prevailed in a 5-4 decision of the Washington Supreme Court when a motorcyclist deliberately chose not to purchase coverage for liability to a passenger. In Southeastern Fidelity Ins. Co. v. Chaney, 259 Ga. 474, 381 S.E.2d 747 (1989), the court said, "Because the exclusion in this case is broader than immunity under our tort system, it is against public policy and cannot be enforced."

d.   Insurance Fraud

Fraud against insurance companies is a serious problem in a complex industrial society. Its most common forms are arson in fire insurance (see Chapter 3) and fraud on automobile insurance companies (not including automobile theft, which is only an indirect crime against insurers). Groups of people often conspire to defraud insurers by faking automobile accidents, or by faking the extent of the injuries in real accidents. One state defines insurance fraud as follows:

§176.05.   Insurance Fraud; Defined

A fraudulent insurance act is committed by any person who, knowingly and with intent to defraud presents, causes to be presented, or prepares with knowledge or belief that it will be presented to or by an insurer or purported insurer, or any agent thereof, any written statement as part of, or in support of, an application for the issuance of, or the rating of an insurance policy for commercial insurance, or a claim for payment or other benefit pursuant to an insurance policy for commercial or personal insurance which he knows to: (i) contain materially false information concerning any fact material thereto; or (ii) conceal, for the purpose of misleading, information concerning any fact material thereto. [N.Y. Penal Law §176.05 (McKinney, 1988).]

Other sections provide definitions and a number of degrees of insurance fraud.

e.   The Modern Role of Automobile Insurance*

Automobile insurance began as a contract of pure indemnity with no purpose more expansive than protecting the assets of the insured on an entirely voluntary basis. A crucial clause of the early policy read:

No action shall lie against the corporation to recover for any loss under this policy, unless it shall be brought by the assured for loss actually sustained and paid by him in money in satisfaction of a judgment after the trial of the issue.

Under that provision the insurer would escape liability if the insured were insolvent and could not pay. A later stage was the following statute:

*A compact sketch of the following developments in automobile insurance up to the development of uninsured and underinsured motorist coverage, with particular reference to what happened in Wisconsin, is found in S. Kimball, Insurance and Public Policy 23-30 (1960).

> No policy of automobile insurance . . . shall be issued . . . unless there
> shall be contained within such policy a provision that the insolvency or
> bankruptcy of the person insured shall not release the insurance carrier.
> [1925 Wis. Laws ch. 372, §2.]

The statute further provided that action could in that case be brought
against the insurer. By this provision, the indemnity policy became a
liability policy.

In a few states, a direct action statute was enacted, permitting the
automobile insurer to be joined by the injured third party in the initial
action against the insured. Quite recently some states have permitted
direct action against the insurer by judicial decision.

Legislatures later passed laws requiring proof of financial responsibility after an adverse judgment as a condition of further permission
to drive. The law deprived a motorist of driving privileges when he or
she was unable to satisfy a judgment. The weakness of this law is
obvious: who would bother to sue to judgment an uninsured,
judgment-proof defendant just to perform the useful public service of
getting the financially irresponsible (and possibly bad) driver off the
road?

A somewhat more stringent variant, sometimes called the Safety
Responsibility Law, came later and usually replaced the earlier version.
It would deprive the financially irresponsible motorist of driving privileges if he or she was involved in an accident of defined severity,
without the necessity for judgment or even suit. If enforced, it was
reasonably effective in inducing drivers to acquire insurance.

Beginning before 1920, continuing efforts were made to compel
motorists to acquire liability insurance, albeit with low limits of coverage. Massachusetts passed a compulsory insurance law in 1926, but it
stood alone for thirty years largely because of insurance company
opposition based partly on the likelihood that compulsory insurance
might deprive insurers of part of their underwriting freedom, and
partly on the extreme difficulty of enforcing the law effectively. Why
would it be difficult to enforce?

In 1956, New York followed Massachusetts. Even that did not
break the logjam, though much of New York's insurance legislation
has been widely imitated. Compulsory insurance finally came to many
other states in the 1960s in connection with the no-fault automobile
insurance movement. Those states have required automobile liability
insurance as a condition to licensing of the car.

In connection with the New York debate over compulsory insurance in the 1950s, insurers developed uninsured motorist coverage as
their answer to the problem of the financially irresponsible motorist.
Persons insuring their own vehicles can buy first-party coverage in

which *their own* insurers compensate them if they are injured by uninsured (or by underinsured) motorists. It is at least plausible that this is the only practical approach to solution of the problem, though arguably compulsory insurance, which seems sound in principle, should be part of the solution, too. Clearly there are no panaceas.

In compulsory insurance states, it is estimated that at least five percent of drivers are uninsured and that this class includes the drivers most likely to have accidents. In noncompulsory states uninsured drivers may number from perhaps ten percent on up, depending on a variety of factors. Many think these estimates are much too low.

Laws respecting uninsured motorist coverage have become essentially universal in this country, though they vary greatly in detail. Some are mandatory. Others require insurance companies to offer such coverage, and sometimes only affirmative rejection by policyholders will eliminate the coverage. The statutes vary so much that it is not worthwhile to consider the subject in detail in an introductory course on insurance law. The complexity is illustrated by the enormous number of reported cases. The preface to a looseleaf service by Professor Alan Widiss of Iowa, Uninsured and Underinsured Motorist Insurance (2d ed. 1985), states that the book contains references to over 4,000 reported decisions.

The result of all these developments is that automobile indemnity insurance (now transformed into liability insurance so that the insurer is obligated to discharge the insured's liability whether or not the insured is able to pay in the absence of the insurance) has come in major part to serve social purposes, not merely to protect the assets of the insured.

Notes and Questions

1. In Safeco Ins. Co. v. Diaz, 385 N.W.2d 845 (Minn. App. 1986) the named insured was driving his brother's car. He would ordinarily be covered by his own insurance policy under the "Drive Other Cars" coverage. But that policy had an exclusion saying "[w]e do not provide Liability Coverage for any person . . . [u]sing *a* vehicle without a reasonable belief that that person is entitled to do so." (Emphasis added.) Id. at 846. He had no permission and it was doubtful that he had a reasonable belief that he did, but the court held such an exclusionary clause void because it was against the public policy established by the Minnesota No-Fault Act, which was enacted to "relieve the severe economic distress of uncompensated victims of automobile accidents. . . ." Id. at 849. Would the logic of *Diaz* lead the same court to

hold that the insurance provides protection to a third person, even if the car is driven by someone who has stolen it? (For no-fault insurance, see the next subsection).

2. In Rural Mut. Ins. Co. v. Peterson, 134 Wis. 2d 165, 395 N.W.2d 776 (1986), the insurer paid an injured third party pursuant to the financial responsibility law, even though the vehicle was not listed on an automobile fleet policy, and then successfully sought reimbursement from the insured under a clause that read:

> When this policy is certified as proof of financial responsibility . . . under the provisions of the motor vehicle financial responsibility law of any state or province, such insurance as is afforded by this policy . . . shall comply with the provisions of such law. . . . *The insured agrees to reimburse the company for any payment made by the company which it would not have been obligated to make under the terms of this policy except for the agreement contained in this paragraph.* [(Emphasis added by court). Id. at 169, 395 N.W.2d at 777.]

The social purpose of the financial responsibility law was satisfied by the protection of the third party, but no public policy consideration precluded the insurer from recovering from its own insured, under the circumstances of this case.

3. Would the mandatory character of insurance under the financial responsibility law override the "intended or expected" limitation or exclusion? In South Carolina Farm Bureau Mut. Ins. Co. v. Mumford, 299 S.C. 14, 382 S.E.2d 11 (S.C. App. 1989), the court said it did. The insured deliberately crashed her car into the plaintiff's truck in an attempt to commit suicide.

f. No-Fault Automobile Insurance

This subject is tangential to the main problems of the insurance law field, and really belongs in large part to tort law. Unfortunately, however, few torts teachers get to the subject in class, even when the casebooks they use contain substantial sections on it. Likewise, even if it were included in some detail in an insurance law casebook, it would almost surely be passed over by the insurance law teacher concerned with matters more central to the insurance institution.

The tort aspect of no fault automobile insurance is easily stated. By statute, bodily injury claims (though usually not property damage claims) suffered in an automobile accident, if they amount to less than a certain threshold amount (usually stated in dollars but sometimes stated by a verbal description) no longer will be the basis for a tort action. Instead the amount will be paid on a "first-party" basis by the injured person's own insurer. Beyond the threshold, tort law continues to apply.

On the insurance side, the policy is converted into what amounts to health and accident insurance (see Chapter 7) up to the threshold but remains traditional liability insurance beyond that amount.

This summary statement is not nearly as much as every lawyer should know about the subject (even just as an informed citizen) but it is all the purposes of this book will permit. More detailed but still brief treatment may be found in Keeton & Widiss, Insurance Law: Student Edition 410-425 (1988). The little space given to the subject in a book of over 1,300 pages, is an indication of the relative importance they give it in the context of *insurance* law (even though Judge Keeton was one of the dominant figures in the development of no-fault insurance). Their treatment will suffice to provide access to some of the most important of the voluminous literature on the subject. Many torts casebooks will do the same, viewing the subject from the torts perspective. The usual way of describing it in the torts books is as one of many "compensation systems."

Blume, State and Federal No-Fault Automobile Insurance Developments, 12 Forum 586 (1977) provides a brief summary of the status of the movement at that date as seen from an insurance trade association perspective.

It is worth noting that imaginative suggestions have been made for using no-fault insurance in other areas as well, notably in medical malpractice insurance. One such suggestion was made by Pollack, Medical Maloccurrence Insurance (MMI): A First-Party, No-Fault Insurance Proposal for Resolving the Medical Malpractice Controversy, 23 Tort & Ins. L.J. 552 (1988). It is no accident that such proposals come most frequently in areas in which there has been a "crisis" in the liability insurance market. Pollack discusses some prior proposals in the same area, associated with the names A. Ehrenzweig (late Professor of Law at California-Berkeley), C. Havighurst (Professor of Law at Duke), and J. O'Connell (Professor of Law at Virginia, for many years at Illinois). O'Connell was co-author with Keeton of the seminal book on no fault automobile insurance and has been the most innovative academic producer of no-fault proposals, both compulsory and voluntary, some of which might work if adopted. For one of his most recent proposals, see O'Connell, A Draft Bill to Allow Choice Between No-Fault and Fault-Based Auto Insurance, 27 Harv. J. on Leg. 143 (1990). It develops a bill earlier suggested in O'Connell & Joost, Giving Motorists a Choice Between Fault and No-Fault Insurance, 72 Va. L. Rev. 61 (1986). See also, for a comparative example, Brown, Deterrence in Tort and No-Fault: The New Zealand Experience, 73 Cal. L. Rev. 976 (1985). For an economist's input, see Danzon, Medical Malpractice (1985).

5.   The Current Frontier

One of the features that can be added to the basic coverage of the CGL policy is contained in the Broad Form CGL Endorsement, adding coverage for advertising injury, defined as "injury arising out of an offense committed during the policy period occurring in the course of the named insured's advertising activities, if such injury arises out of libel, slander, defamation, violation of right of privacy, piracy, unfair competition, or infringement of copyright, title or slogan."

As yet there are only a handful of decisions, most of them still on appeal. But many more cases are in process. Some seek to include fraud, patent infringement, and antitrust claims within advertising injury, even though their connection with advertising activities may be tenuous. How far the development will go is far from clear, but the possibilities are intriguing, for the amount of money potentially at stake in this commercially oriented litigation is enormous.

Not surprisingly, the leading edge of the development seems to be occurring in California. Equally unsurprising, a recent Illinois decision, International Ins. Co. v. Florists' Mut. Ins. Co., 559 N.E.2d 7 (Ill. App. 1990), declined to extend advertising injury to a particular antitrust lawsuit.

The nature of this commercial litigation, involving litigation expertise, elaborate discovery, and long trials, suggests that this area might become an important one in the legal practice in the near future. See NAC Re Corporation, Liability Bulletin, Jan. 15, 1991, at 1.

CHAPTER 6

Life Insurance and Annuities

A. Introduction

1. The Risks Guarded Against by Life Insurance

Life insurance provides a partial solution to a fundamental risk of the human condition. It mitigates the adverse financial consequences of a person's premature death while others are still dependent on that person to provide income or other services of economic value. Until that part of the life cycle has passed, life insurance is imperative unless the insured has considerable wealth, a family network that will provide the requisite support, or a willingness to let dependents become wards of the state. After that, life insurance is no longer needed for that purpose, though it may still be needed to pay off a mortgage, to provide liquid assets to pay estate taxes, to fund buy-sell agreements of interests in partnerships or close corporations, and for other special purposes.

A risk parallel to premature death is disability, which may reduce or eliminate the capacity to earn income temporarily or permanently. Total and permanent disability has even more serious financial consequences than premature death, for to the inability of the disabled person to provide support is added the continuing living costs of the disabled person, including expensive long-term health or custodial care. Disability income insurance and insurance against health care costs are part of the "health insurance" line (see Chapter 7) but an endorsement providing for the waiver of future life insurance premiums in the event of disability is commonly attached to a life insurance policy. That waiver provision neither provides income nor pays health care bills.

Premature death is not the only risk arising from the uncertainties about the duration of human life. A person may live too long and exhaust savings, becoming a financial burden to family members or the community or being reduced to abject poverty. Social security in the public sphere and annuities and pensions in the private sphere address that risk. Pensions and annuities are heavily regulated and raise difficult federal tax questions, among other complex problems. They will receive no more than passing mention in this chapter, for they are complicated and important enough to justify a separate course.

2.   Term Life Insurance

When life insurance is perceived as serving only the narrow protective function described above, the most suitable form of the coverage, at least in theory, is natural premium life, in which the premiums increase regularly with the mortality curve. Such insurance, while not unknown, is not a mainstay of the insurance market.

The most frequently marketed individual policy is guaranteed renewable term, that is, term insurance renewable periodically at the option of the insured. The insured can keep the insurance alive as long as the contract permits by periodic renewals (sometimes in five year increments or increments of some other length), with premiums increasing at each renewal approximately in parallel with the mortality curve. In this respect term life insurance is rather like property or liability insurance, except for the guarantee that renewal will be allowed. That guarantee is, in effect, insurance of insurability. At some point, it would no longer be cost-beneficial for the insured to continue the insurance. That would ordinarily occur at or near retirement, though it might be earlier. When that time comes the term insurance (or natural premium life) could simply be dropped, if it has not previously become non-renewable by its terms.

Individual term insurance leaves one important risk uncovered. Temporary financial difficulty may make it impossible to continue to pay premiums for a period of time. Because there is ordinarily no cash value in term life insurance, the insurance will lapse at once when premiums are not paid within the "grace period." Health problems, even relatively minor ones, may make it difficult or impossible to reinstate the insurance on reasonable terms once the financial squeeze has passed. This inadequacy of term insurance is one of the arguments used by sellers of insurance to induce buyers to apply for ordinary or whole life insurance, the savings element of which provides protection against just that risk.

3. Group Life Insurance

Term life insurance has grown enormously in recent decades, usually through employment-related group contracts. A group life policy through an employer is usually the most cost-efficient way to purchase term life insurance. Group life insurance makes it possible to avoid most of the ordinarily heavy front-end load of individual life insurance, a major portion of which is the commission to the producing agent. Substantial additional costs are found in the underwriting function and can be minimized in group insurance.

Group life insurance is often subsidized by the employer. Physical examinations are seldom required and underwriting tends to be minimal. It is common in group life insurance to eliminate or greatly simplify the age-grading that is crucial to soundly underwritten individual life insurance, thus providing cross-subsidies across cohorts and other classifications of the insured population. Both the age and health cross-subsidies tend to be affordable due to the cost and tax savings resulting from the context of the group insurance policy, so that everyone benefits, including society at large. Unless everyone benefits, there is an incentive for those that are disadvantaged by the scheme to decline to participate, reducing the aggregate benefit and initiating a spiral that may destroy the viability of the program. One of the reasons employers subsidize such programs is to ensure their viability by making sure all participants will do better within the group than by buying individual policies. One item of personal financial advice that can safely be given by one who is not a financial advisor is that an employed person should take maximum advantage of available and sound group term life insurance offered through the employer unless first satisfied that there are good personal reasons, or reasons peculiar to the particular group program, for rejecting it. So successful and so important has this development been since World War II that it alone has greatly reduced the relative role of ordinary life (or whole life) insurance in our society. Group life insurance in force in the United States, after making a slow start in the 1920s and 1930s, exceeded $3.2 trillion in 1988, which was 40 percent of the total life insurance in force.

Other group contracts have some but not all of the advantages of employee group policies. Various association group policies, such as those sold through professional associations, are also available. They also are worth consideration in one's personal financial planning, though they are often devised in part to provide revenue for the association, a goal in conflict with (and to be weighed against) the goal of minimizing life insurance cost. If a gift to the association is an objective of the insured, the portion of the premium going to the association may be tax deductible as a gift, if the association and the plan qualify.

There should be no facile assumption of deductibility, however, without making inquiry. See United States v. American Bar Endowment, 761 F.2d 1573 (Fed. Cir. 1985), *rev'd*, 477 U.S. 105 (1986).

4. Ordinary Life Insurance and Endowment Policies

Ordinary or whole life insurance differs from term insurance in two ways: It is structured to cover the whole of life and it is written on a "level premium" basis. The latter means that premiums are constant throughout the life of the policy. Because of the shape of the mortality curve the premiums are, in the early years, considerably in excess of the amount needed to provide pure insurance. As a result the insurance company has on its books a liability account called the *legal reserve,* roughly equivalent to the assets (and assumed interest thereon) accumulated from the premiums in early years that are in excess of the pure insurance cost (plus expenses). In later years, when claims exceed premiums, the company will make up the deficiencies out of that reserve. The actuarial theory underlying life insurance premiums, sometimes even written in terms comprehensible to the lay person, can be found in adequate detail in a standard life insurance text that has gone through multiple editions (beginning in 1915), Huebner, later Huebner & Black, and now Black & Skipper, Life Insurance (11th ed., 1987).

The simple principle underlying all life insurance actuarial science is that the legal reserve is defined by the following equation:

$$R = \Sigma \ B_{pv} - \Sigma \ P_{pv}$$

In the equation, R is the legal reserve, B represents benefits of any nature, and P represents premiums of any amount. The legal reserve measures the life insurance company's current notional obligations under its contracts if the company were liquidated at that point. The equation tells us that at any given time the required amount of that reserve is the amount by which the sum of the present value of all future benefits exceeds the sum of the present value of all future premiums.

Any deficiency in overall premiums must be made up out of surplus; any excess of premiums flows to surplus. In insurance terminology the reserve is a liability account, not an asset. In combination with all other liability and capital accounts, it must be matched by assets. The legal reserve constitutes, with some adjustments, the *cash value* of the policy, which is available to the insured (1) in cash on surrender of the policy, (2) to purchase a paid up policy in an amount less than the face amount of the existing policy, or (3) to purchase an *extended term* coverage in the face amount of the existing policy. These *surrender values* have been required and regulated by statute since the middle of the nineteenth century.

The above formula for the legal reserve is completely general. Premium payments need not be level but may vary, approximating the natural premium in early years while later increasing substantially. They may also be for a limited term, such as payment limited to twenty years (called *20 pay life* in insurance argot). Benefits, too, range widely, including the actuarial value of death benefits, the actuarial value of the waiver of premium for disability benefit, the present value of an endowment payable at a set time in the future, the actuarial value of double indemnity on accidental death, or anything else.

To determine the present value of the death benefits (the principle item in the benefits term of the equation), the benefit for each year is found with the formula $p_n B_{pv}$: the probability of a death payment (or other benefit) in year n times the present value of that benefit if it is paid in year n. The probability of death in any given year comes from the mortality table as the answer to the question, "What is the probability that a person alive at the date of the calculation will die in year n?" That information is empirical and is gathered separately for various uses. For calculation of ordinary life insurance reserves the mortality tables currently in use are the Commissioners 1980 Standard Ordinary Tables. Other tables are used for other policies, such as group, fraternal and annuities.

There are three types of life insurance: (1) term insurance, which is protection for a specified period only (just like fire insurance or automobile insurance), (2) whole life insurance, which provides protection for the entire duration of life, and (3) endowment insurance, which is a promise to pay a designated amount on death or, if the insured survives to a specified date, then on that date. Endowment insurance is often used to fund an educational program. These three basic forms of life insurance can be combined in an almost infinite number of ways to form products that meet varied needs.

Ordinary life insurance is said by its sellers to produce an "instant estate." Combining savings (to be invested by the insurer) with pure insurance, it has traditionally been promoted as a savings vehicle and historically served as the most important savings device for many people. Its role as a savings vehicle has been greatly reduced in recent decades by several factors. The most important has been the explosive growth of private pensions since World War II in that segment of the society that would otherwise make use of ordinary life insurance to provide "savings" for retirement. Tax deferred savings vehicles — IRAs, Keoghs, SEPs, and SRAs — further reduce the comparative advantages of life insurance. The development of mutual funds has also provided alternative ways to save with lesser administrative and selling costs. Mutual funds do not, when used outside of the tax deferred programs mentioned above, have the tax advantages of life insurance, nor do they provide for insurance against premature death (an instant estate).

5. Life Insurance as a Savings Medium

In recent years it has been fashionable to denigrate life insurance as a savings medium. The criticism is partly sound but often greatly overstated. To the extent that the criticism is based on very high front-end loading, it is justified, but some other savings vehicles also have heavy front-end loads without the offsetting advantages possessed by life insurance. That disadvantage is minimized in some special situations, such as a well-designed group insurance program.

To the extent that the criticism is based on a comparison of rates of earnings on the invested "savings," it is often the result of an erroneous assumption that insurance companies only pay about three or four percent — the rate of interest assumed for discounting to compute the reserve — on the invested funds. That notion is based on fundamental misunderstandings of actuarial science and life insurance accounting conventions, particularly the latter. The guaranteed rates of interest are *not* directly related either to premium rates or to actual earnings credited to the policies. The following statements should suffice to show the complexity of the matter:

1. The interest rates used in calculating the reserves are required by law to be very conservative, as are the mortality tables with which they are combined for that calculation, because the insurer must absolutely guarantee fixed dollar payouts that may occur many decades in the future. Satisfaction of these reserve requirements is a prerequisite for continued operation as an insurer under state regulation.

2. Different assumptions as to both mortality and interest earnings may be used to calculate actual premium rates. Those assumptions may be less conservative and tend to reflect the company's own experience and financial position.

3. The conservatism required in the reserve and the somewhat lesser conservatism reflected in the actual premium rates means that the company is likely to have "earnings" considerably in excess of those anticipated from statutory assumptions or even the assumptions made for setting premiums. The excess derives from (a) better mortality experience than assumed, (b) lower costs than those assumed, and most importantly, (c) investment earnings in excess (and in recent years greatly in excess) of those guaranteed in calculating the reserve or assumed in the premium rates.

4. The excess over the amount needed to satisfy the guarantee can, in a stock company, go to shareholders as dividends or increases

in surplus. That has accounted in part for the rapid growth and very large profits of the more successful stock life companies. In a mutual company, too, the excess can be used to build up surplus, sometimes rendered obscure in various special reserves. The excess can also, in either a stock or mutual company, go to policyholders under a participating policy as a credit against a premium payment or as an increase in the face value of the policy. If there is approximately *full* participation in a mutual company, there is no inherent reason the risk-adjusted earnings of an insurance company should be much different from those of other savings vehicles. Indeed, some insurers have been effective investors: They have had lots of practice. The whole matter is too complex for further discussion here, but it may be useful to know that the amounts actually credited as earnings by some fully participating life insurance companies were, at their peak, well into double digits. Because life insurance investments tend to be long term, earnings tend to lag behind changes in interest rates. During the upward movement of interest rates, life insurance companies look less successful as investors than they really are; during a period of decline in interest rates they look much better for they have locked in higher rates for a substantial part of their asset portfolios.

Thus one should neither assume that ordinary life insurance is altogether outmoded for investment purposes because of new financial instruments, nor on the other hand be too ready to accept the puffing assertions of life insurance agents. Relevant tax rules seem to be constantly in flux, but some life insurance products have been among the savings vehicles best able to provide tax shelters.

Even apart from tax considerations, individual whole life insurance still has a legitimate use, though group term, private pensions, and the development in recent times of a multitude of other investment vehicles available to persons of modest means have greatly reduced the relative importance of traditional forms of life insurance as a pure savings medium. The total obligations and surplus of American life insurers amounted to $1.167 trillion in 1988; the total of savings through the medium of life insurance (including annuities) was not much less than $1 trillion. American Council of Life Insurance, 1989 Life Insurance Fact Book Update 41.

The life insurance business has been busy during this period in developing its own new savings-oriented vehicles, too, of which *universal life* is the best known and most widely touted. Universal life is one version of so-called "flexible premium" plans. Within wide limits, the insured pays whatever premium he or she wishes in a given year. From that premium is subtracted expense charges and mortality costs for the year. The remainder, increasing at the insurer's current interest rates, flows into the cash value of the policy, which is simultaneously savings and the policy's reserve. The generalized actuarial formula above is still the basic vehicle for the necessary calculations, though the actual computations are very complex and would not have been possible before the advent of high speed computers.

Universal life is based on concepts that are a century old, and it was suggested as a possible product for the market as early as the middle of this century. The first serious proposals were made only in the early 1970s, however, and the first successful product was marketed by Life of California (later E.F. Hutton Life), beginning in 1979. It has been a great success story, for by 1982 it accounted for about 9 percent of the market (measured by premiums) of all individual life insurance sold and by 1985 it accounted for an estimated 38 percent. Black & Skipper, Life Insurance 85 (11th ed. 1987). Its sensitivity to changes in the financial environment were apparent, however, when it had dropped back noticeably in both relative and absolute terms in 1987 and 1988. American Council of Life Insurance, Life Insurance Fact Book Update 6 (1989).

In thinking about personal investment vehicles, one can not ignore taxes. Traditionally there have been built-in tax advantages to a life insurance policy and to an insurance operation, though for pure savings purposes these cannot match the tax advantages of IRAs and Keoghs, which can also avoid the heavy front-end load that is the bane of traditional life insurance. But unlike all other vehicles, insurance combines the tax advantage with protection against premature death.

Traditional life insurance law problems are numerous; they will be sampled, but only lightly, in this chapter.

B.   Formation of the Contract

A life insurance policy, and any other insurance policy for that matter, is basically a contract. In general, ordinary contract law governs its formation. A few peculiarities in the application of contract law to life insurance are, however, worth noting even in an elementary treatment.

1.   Offer and Acceptance

In life insurance law, a peculiarity in the rules of offer and acceptance results from the fact that life insurance policies tend to be written after a "hard sell." The life insurance *agent* (usually only a solicitor and not a true agent) aggressively pursues the prospect until the latter gives in and signs an application for insurance. Contrary to what one might expect, usually the application is only an offer requiring subsequent acceptance by the insurer. That is not always the case: In Andrew Jackson Life Ins. Co. v. Williams, 566 So. 2d 1172 (1990), the agent's proposal was considered the offer.

The insurer needs that usual contract formation sequence so it can "underwrite" or evaluate the risk at a qualified office before committing itself to issue the policy. Acceptance usually takes place at the home office (or a regional office) of the company. In ordinary cases the processing of the application is finished within two or three weeks and the application (offer) is either accepted or rejected, unless the insurer asks for more information, or a further physical examination, in which case the process will take longer. On occasion, however, there is unreasonable delay in processing the application, and sometimes the applicant dies during the period of waiting.

Under ordinary contract law there would be no acceptance, no contract, and no obligation to pay. In insurance law there is liability if the processing delay is unreasonable. On some occasions the result has been explained on a contract theory, with the delay plus retention of the prepaid premium constituting acceptance. That distorts traditional contract doctrine. The following leading case provides another approach to the problem.

DUFFIE v. BANKERS LIFE ASSN.

160 Iowa 19, 139 N.W. 1087 (1913)

LADD, J. The plaintiff is the widow of Joseph M. Duffie, who departed this life July 9, 1911. He had applied to the defendant association on June 8th preceding for a certificate of membership therein, stipulating the payment of an indemnity of $2,000 upon his death; but the association had failed to accept or reject the application, and, in this action, recovery of that amount as damages is sought by plaintiff, who was named as proposed beneficiary in the application, on the ground "that defendant negligently failed to take any action upon said application before the death of said Joseph M. Duffie and negligently failed either to issue to him a certificate of insurance as provided for therein or to reject said application and give him notice thereof in sufficient time to enable him to procure other insurance," and, in consequence of such negligence, she was deprived of the benefit of the insurance. The widow, as a duly appointed and qualified administratrix, filed a petition of intervention, wherein she prayed judgment for damages to the estate of deceased on the grounds: "That defendant's said agent carelessly and negligently failed to send the application of said decedent to the home office of the defendant association after he had been examined by defendant's examining physician at Tama, Iowa; that, in consequence of such negligence on the part of said agent, no policy or certificate of life insurance was issued to said applicant by the defendant association; that, if said application had been forwarded by said agent to the home office of the defendant association as soon as said applicant was examined by defendant's examining physician at Tama, Iowa, the defendant association would have issued and delivered a policy or certificate of life insurance for $2,000 to said applicant before he died, and such insurance would have been in force at the time of his death." At the conclusion of plaintiff's evidence, the court directed a verdict for the defendant, and this is the only ruling of which complaint is made.

The facts admitted or proven on the trial first should be stated. The defendant is a mutual assessment insurance association. T. P. Rogers, at the time in question, was its general agent, and had authority from the association to take the application and receive the notes hereinafter mentioned. Duffie's application for membership in the association closed in words following: "I agree to accept the certificate of membership issued hereon and that the same shall not take effect until said certificate (signed by the secretary or assistant secretary) is issued and received by me during my continuance in good health. This application and the certificate issued thereon, together with the articles of incorporation and by-laws (not reducing the insurance provided) which may be hereafter adopted, shall constitute the agreement or contract between me and the said association. I certify that I have carefully read the foregoing application. [Signature of the applicant in his own handwriting] Joseph M. Duffie." This was at the date mentioned, and at the same time the applicant executed to Rogers his promissory note for $17 as membership fee required to be paid when making such application, and delivered to Rogers a guarantee deposit note for $34 required by the articles of corporation and by-laws of defendant. For these Rogers gave Duffie a receipt in the words following: "The Bankers' Life Association of Des Moines, Iowa. I have this day taken the application of Mr. J. M. Duffie of Tama, Iowa, for $2,000 insurance in the Bankers' Life Association, upon which he has given his guarantee note for $34.00 and paid in cash January 9, 1912, $17.00, all of which is to be returned promptly if the application is declined. The first quarterly payment on the insurance applied for will be due January 31, 1912. T. P. Rogers, Solicitor. Dated at _____, June 8, 1911." On the back of this receipt, this appears: "Agents should not promise that certificate will be issued in less time than is reasonably assigned to do the work, as disappointment may result, especially as frequently occurs, an extra amount of business comes in a bunch. The home office does all it can to expedite the issue and the agent can add material help if he will see that all applications are properly completed and full information given. If delay is unusual write for cause."

Rogers informed Duffie at the time that he could go to the office of Dr. Thompson within a day or two for examination, and the application would then be sent to the association and explained to him; that the notes would be returned if the applications were rejected. To his inquiry as to how soon the insurance would be in force, Rogers responded, "Upon the passage of the physical examination required by their physician." Rogers left the application with Dr. Thompson on the same day, and two days later Duffie called and was examined by that physician, who informed the applicant that he had passed a satisfactory examination and that he (the doctor) had recommended him for membership of the association.

As required by defendant's rules, the physician mailed to Dr. Will, medical director of defendant, on the same day, a slip of paper signed by him showing that he had made the medical examination of Duffie, and this reached defendant's office June 12, 1911. Rogers had been in the habit of calling at Thompson's office for the application with the examination, and the doctor left these on the desk for him, where it remained until he learned that Duffie had drowned, whereupon the physician mailed them to defendant. The medical examination disclosed that Duffie, who was 32 years of age, was in fine physical condition. He is conceded to have been a man of good habits, good financial ability, and of good moral character. He had done all that was required of him to obtain the insurance. The defendant was actively engaged through its agents in soliciting members of the association to whom certificates of insurance might be issued, and on an application of one Herman, procured by Rogers, June 5, 1911, defendant issued a certificate June 24th following. The defendant paid the $17 note out of its funds and caused it to be canceled July 28, 1911, after the association had been advised of the claim now made against it in this action, and it tendered the surrender of the guaranteed deposit note.

It is to be observed that the petition does not proceed on the theory that from the retention of the application and unreasonable time without acting thereon acceptance of the application is to be presumed, nor on the theory that defendant is estopped from denying such acceptance because of having misled the applicant in some way. See Winchell v. Iowa State Ins. Co., 103 Iowa, 189, 72 N.W. 503. The action is not based on contract either express or implied, but solely on tort; the theory of the plaintiff being that, having solicited and received the application for insurance, it owed the applicant the affirmative duty either of rejecting the application or of accepting it within a reasonable time, and upon breach of such duty it is liable for all damages suffered in consequence of such breach. Let us first ascertain whether the evidence was sufficient to carry the issues involved in such a claim to the jury.

I. Might defendant have been found to have been negligent? The association was responsible for the conduct of Rogers when acting within the scope of his agency, and it is admitted that he allowed the application to lie on the physician's desk a month lacking a day, though it was his duty to forward it promptly to the association. But he was not alone at fault, for the association was aware as early as June 12, 1911, that the application had been taken, and yet did nothing in the matter during the 27 days intervening his death. In the case of another application taken at about the same time and in the same vicinity there was a delay of but 19 days in issuing the certificate. We think whether defendant in the exercise of ordinary diligence should have passed on the application prior to Duffie's death was fairly put in issue. The association was bound by the acts of its agents and chargeable with any consequences that resulted from the failure of Rogers to promptly forward the application and physician's report. In other words, if the association was under a duty to promptly act on the application and notify Duffie, as we think it was, it cannot shield itself from the responsibility by the fact that the application and medical report had not been received by it and therefore it could not act. . . .

II. But it is argued that it was as much the duty of the applicant to inquire as it was that of the insurer to give the information, and this or similar expressions will be found in several decisions holding that mere silence on the part of the insurer is not as strong evidence of acceptance as of rejection. Whether this were so or not, as bearing on whether an acceptance should have been inferred, it cannot be said that the duties of the parties were reciprocal. The applicant had done all he could or was required to do in the matter. He had the right to assume that the application would be forwarded immediately after the medical examination and was so assured. This, with the suggestion that the certificate would be in effect after passing the physical examination, was well calculated to lull him into supposed security. Moreover, about all he could have done was to withdraw his application and apply to another insurer for a policy, and this, one who has applied to a company of his choice would quite naturally hesitate to do. Under the circumstances, it cannot be said, as a matter of law, that the deceased was at fault in not stirring defendant to action by inquiry as to the cause of delay or in not withdrawing his application. At the most, this also was an issue appropriate for the determination of the jury.

III. Assuming then that the defendant was negligent and Duffie without fault as the jury might have concluded, can it be said that but for such negligence a certificate of insurance would have been issued?

We think the jury might have found that, in all reasonable probability, had the association passed upon the application, it would have been accepted. Duffie was a young man of 32 years, his medical examination was satisfactory, and the physician had recommended him; his employment as a farmer was not hazardous, and his character all that could be desired. The association was actively soliciting members, and it seems to us that the record leaves little if any doubt but that, had the association ever passed on the risk, it would have been accepted and the certificate issued. . . .

But it is said that a certificate or policy of insurance is simply a contract like any other, as between individuals, and that there is no such thing as negligence of a party in the matter of delay in entering into a contract. This view overlooks the fact that the defendant holds and is acting under a franchise from the state. The legislative policy, in granting this, proceeds on the theory that chartering such association is in the interest of the public to the end that indemnity on specific contingencies shall be provided those who are eligible and desire it, and for their protection the state regulates, inspects, and supervises their business. Having solicited applications for insurance, and having so obtained them and received payment of the fees or premiums exacted, they are bound either to furnish the indemnity the state has authorized them to furnish or decline so to do within such reasonable time as will enable them to act intelligently and advisedly thereon or suffer the consequences flowing from their neglect so to do. Otherwise the applicant is unduly delayed in obtaining the insurance he desires, and for which the law has afforded the opportunity, and which the insurer impliedly has promised, if conditions are satisfactory. Moreover, policies or certificates of insurance ordinarily are dated as of the day the application is signed, and, aside from other considerations, the insurer should not be permitted to unduly prolong the period for which it is exacting the payment of premium without incurring risk. . . .

IV. The application named plaintiff as his beneficiary, and, had the certificate issued, likely she would have been named therein as such. But there was no contract, and the negligence, if any, was that of failing to discharge a duty owing the deceased. Had the certificate issued, whether plaintiff or some one else were beneficiary would have been optional with the insured, and as the injury, if any, was to him, his representative alone can maintain the action for resulting damages. See Schmidt v. Association, 112 Iowa, 41, 83 N.W. 800, 51 L.R.A. 141, 84 Am. St. Rep. 323.

As to plaintiff the judgment is affirmed. Because of the error in not submitting the issues to the jury, the judgment against the intervener is reversed.

PRESTON, J., takes no part.

Notes and Questions

1. Is this tort soundly conceived? What is the duty and to whom is it owed? Who has a claim against the insurer? If there is a conceptual difficulty, should it preclude recovery despite the manifest injustice? Or would denial of recovery be unjust?

2. Consistent with tort law generally, the claimant must show harm proximately caused by the delay. Huff v. Standard Life Ins. Co., 897 F.2d 1072 (11th Cir. 1990). How could such harm be shown?

3. Should it make a difference, under either a tort or a contract theory, whether the insured paid the initial premium at the time of making the application?

4. What statute of limitations should apply? See Ray v. Mid South Underwriters, Inc., 526 So. 2d 1297 (La. App. 1988), where the problem arose in automobile insurance.

5. Many, but far from all, courts have followed the *Duffie* approach. In a recent case, Life & Casualty Ins. Co. v. Central Steel Products, Inc., 709 S.W.2d 830, 832 (Ky. App. 1985) (discretionary review denied and opinion ordered published by Supreme Court, June 3, 1986), the court said:

> We think that *Jenkins* and *Neafus* merely establish that under certain circumstances, an insurance company will be held liable on its contract when it had unreasonably delayed or arbitrarily rejected an application for insurance. These cases do not create a duty to accept or reject an application in a reasonable time, the breach of which creates negligence *per se* for the insurance company. Thus the trial court erred by instructing the jury that Central Steel could recover on that ground.

6. Is it appropriate to use waiver or estoppel as a device for finding liability? Some courts have done so.

7. See Annot., 1 A.L.R.4th 1202 (1980), for a collection of the cases on the subject.

2. Payment of the Premium

The payment of the initial premium is governed by general contract law. A promise to pay it, or payment by a premium note, or any other arrangement, is perfectly valid if the terms of the agreement so provide. The more interesting problems arise with respect to payment of subsequent premiums.

Notes and Questions

1. An applicant was uncertain which of two policies to acquire, one for $525,000 or one for $300,000. The company sent both, with the understanding that the applicant would decide which to buy and would return the other. The policies were delivered in January. In April the applicant was diagnosed as having terminal cancer. In May, he sent the premium for the larger policy. In August he died. The application said, in relevant part:

Part I, ¶2:

Payment of the 1st premium (if after the date below) will mean I represent that such statements and answers would be the same if made at the time of such payment.

Part I, ¶3:

[T]he policy will take effect on the date it is delivered, provided its delivery and payment of any required cost are made while each person to be insured is living.

The insurer resisted payment on the ground that under the terms of the application the applicant had misrepresented that he did not have cancer. How would you decide the case? See Kleckner v. Mutual Life Ins. Co., 822 F.2d 1316 (3d Cir. 1987).

2. Each premium is fully earned as paid, and the insured is not entitled to the return of any part of the life insurance premium when death occurs early in the period for which the premium is paid. James R. Soda, Inc. v. United Liberty Life Ins. Co., 24 Ohio St. 3d 188, 494 N.E.2d 1099 (1986). Should the same doctrine apply to all kinds of insurance, if there is no contrary provision of the contract or of a statute?

3. Premiums on a life insurance policy were paid monthly by preauthorized check. There was also a 31-day grace period provision. A premium due April 22 was not paid because the check was dishonored. The premium due May 22 was duly paid. The insured died on June 25. If the May payment were applied to the April premium the grace period would have expired and the policy would have lapsed, but if nonpayment of the April premium was waived by accepting the May premium, the policy had not lapsed. The May premium check stated, "This check when paid is a receipt for amounts due on the policies listed. The date of this check indicates the premium due month." Should the beneficiary recover? For one

answer, see Bohannon v. Guardsman Life Ins. Co., 224 Neb. 701, 400 N.W.2d 856 (1987).

4. In an earlier posture of the federal income tax law, it was advantageous for some persons to acquire life insurance in large sums and each year borrow to the maximum against the cash value to pay most of the annual premiums, because of the high tax rates and the deductibility of the interest on the policy loan. In Roberts v. Metropolitan Life Ins. Co., 808 F.2d 1387 (10th Cir. 1987), the insured made payments of premiums on a $250,000 policy in that way, paying quarterly and using the cash value to pay as much of the premium as it would cover, paying the remainder in cash. He fell into the practice of paying the remainder after he was informed of its amount by the company. The cash payments were made after the grace period. For the next to last quarter's payment before death, the cash payment was one hundred days late; for the last quarter it was six days late. At that point the company required an application for reinstatement and then refused reinstatement because Roberts was no longer insurable, tendering refunds for the last two payments. Roberts then died. Should the company be required to pay on the policy because of its practice?

3. Binding Receipts

The old-fashioned way of issuing life insurance contracts was for the person interested in buying insurance to fill out and sign an application (the offer), undergo a medical examination, and be insured only when the company delivered the policy in exchange for the premium (the delivery constituting the acceptance). From the insurance company's perspective, this process created the special problem that it gave the applicant an opportunity for second thoughts and a chance to back out prior to acceptance, or even after acceptance but before there was any practicable way to collect the premium.

This was not merely an occasional problem. Because life insurance characteristically involved a "hard sell," applicants frequently changed their minds between application and payment. To improve their practical position by getting money in hand, insurers developed the "conditional" or "binding" receipt. In return for payment of premium *at the time of the application,* the receipt purported to give immediate coverage, subject to various conditions that sometimes would make the immediate coverage illusory, if read literally. For a compact discussion of binding receipts, see Keeton & Widiss, Insurance Law: Student Edition 52-70 (1988).

GAUNT v. JOHN HANCOCK MUT. LIFE INS. CO.

160 F.2d 599 (2d Cir.), *cert. denied,* 331 U.S. 849 (1947)

[The text of this opinion is found in Chapter 1, Section C.]

Notes and Questions

1. While many cases follow the *Gaunt* approach, others do not. See Ford v. Lamar Life Ins. Co., 513 So. 2d 880 (Miss. 1987), where the court gave effect to the literal meaning of the terms of the conditional (or binding) receipt.

2. A few companies deal with the problem in quite another way. Their binding receipts give unconditional *temporary* insurance. Pending insurer action on the application, the applicant is covered. If the application is accepted, the temporary insurance is merged into the permanent policy; if the application is rejected, the coverage terminates. It is possible that the cost of providing such temporary insurance (which will be free only if the application is rejected) may be less than the cost of fighting (and in many states losing) the claims made and suits thereon litigated by indignant beneficiaries. Are there good reasons an insurer might not wish to provide such temporary insurance?

3. Should a court find that a binding receipt creates unconditional temporary insurance, notwithstanding the company's contrary language and intention? Duggan v. Massachusetts Mut. Life Ins. Co., 736 F. Supp. 1072 (D. Kansas 1990) did so, relying on Service v. Pyramid Life Ins. Co., 201 Kan. 196, 440 P.2d 944 (1968) and Tripp v. Reliable Life Ins. Co., 210 Kan. 33, 499 P.2d 1155 (1972).

4. There are various classes of binding receipt. In some, the coverage is retroactively effective if the insurer actually *approves* the application at the home office, in others is effective at the issuance of the receipt if the applicant is *insurable* under the insurer's rules in effect at the time (an objective standard), and in some others only if the insurer is *satisfied* that the applicant is insurable (a subjective standard). Other possible formulations combine the foregoing. Should the results in cases claiming coverage depend in any degree on the formulation of the receipt?

5. A survey linking the binding receipt problem with the delayed acceptance problem treated earlier is Brenner, Controversy Over Temporary Personal Insurance After 112 Years, No Signs Yet of an Early Peace, 22 Tort & Ins. L.J. 388 (1987).

6. The life insurance binding receipt problem (or a reasonable

facsimile thereof) can also arise in insurance other than life. See McCollum v. Continental Casualty Co., 151 Ariz. 492, 728 P.2d 1242 (Ariz. App. 1986). A recent survey of the binding receipt problem is Widiss, Life Insurance Applications and Interim Coverage Disputes: Revisiting Controversies About Conditional Binding Receipts, 75 Iowa L. Rev. 1097 (1990).

C. Ownership Interests in Life Insurance

The law of third party beneficiaries developed, at least in part, in life insurance cases. Under that law, if a person took out a life insurance policy on his or her own life and designated another as a donee beneficiary, the latter acquired a vested interest upon formation of the contract. Because that result was not consistent with the intentions of most persons who buy life insurance, it thereupon became customary to reserve in the insurance contract itself a right to change the beneficiary, thereby making the "gift" ambulatory. If there is such a reservation, the person who contracts for the policy becomes its "owner" and may change the beneficiary, assign the policy either absolutely or as security, or terminate it and receive its cash value.

Legal problems abound, nevertheless. Every policy has a clause that requires certain formalities for a change in beneficiary, such as a requirement that a change designation is effective only when a request for a change (accompanied by the policy) is filed at the home office of the company in a form satisfactory to the company. If the insured were to die while seeking to make a change but before the change is perfected under the terms of the policy, should the old or the new beneficiary prevail? Again, if the policy is assigned for security (or absolutely) without a change of beneficiary, who should prevail, the assignee or the designated beneficiary?

The only legitimate interest the insurer has is not to have to pay twice. The law should provide that protection unless the insurer has fair notice of the attempted change of beneficiary or assignment; if it does have adequate notice, the insurer can protect itself by interpleading if it has good reason to be in doubt. After the insurer interpleads, the resolution of the rights among the other parties could then be settled on the basis of public policy considerations having nothing to do with the structure or operation of the insurance business, though a part of "insurance law" nonetheless. The existence of such problems telegraphs itself and the applicable law can then be looked up. Extensive attention to the problem is not necessary here; the following cases will suffice to give the flavor of the matter.

CAPITOL LIFE INS. CO. v. PORTER

719 S.W.2d 908 (Mo. App. 1986)

CRANDALL, Judge.

James A. Porter (insured) was issued a life insurance policy by the Capitol Life Insurance Company (insurer). The insurer's records listed Lynn G. Porter, insured's wife, as beneficiary under the policy. After the insured's death, a change of beneficiary form was found among his personal belongings. The form designated Theresa Porter, his mother, as the new beneficiary. Theresa Porter and Lynn S. Porter both claimed that they were entitled to the proceeds of the insurance policy. Insurer interpled the proceeds to the court and was discharged. Lynn Porter (wife) appeals from the judgment of the trial court, in a court-tried case, awarding the proceeds to Theresa Porter (mother). We affirm.

The record reveals that the insured was thirty-three years of age when he died [of cancer.] Prior to his death, he worked as a custodian for a school district in St. Louis County and also served in the United States Naval Reserve. He was issued a life insurance policy in the amount of $10,000 on which his wife was named as beneficiary. She and insured separated in December, 1982, after she brought an action for dissolution of their marriage. On December 20, 1982, insured executed a change of beneficiary form on which he designated his mother as the new beneficiary under the policy. The application was signed by the insured and witnessed by a family friend. The insured told his mother and the witness that he was changing the beneficiary on his policy because of the pending dissolution action. He also said that he was going to mail the form to the insurer.

At that time, the insured had been experiencing chronic pain and weakness in the upper left side of his body and, to a lesser extent, in his right arm. In fact, the insured had directed his mother to print her name on the beneficiary form because it was too painful for him to write.

From that time on, the insured was confined to a wheelchair. Five days a week, his father drove him 60 miles, one-way, to the hospital for radiation therapy. His muscle strength and physical condition were deteriorating rapidly. He needed assistance in performing all the basic bodily functions. He was fed and carried about by his parents. Characterized as a "slow learner" prior to his illness, he became even more "vague" as his physical condition got worse. In May, his parents and some friends drove the insured to Connecticut, a trip he wanted to make before he died. The insured died on June 2, 1983.

Throughout his illness his wife did not help care for him. She was not with him when he died and did not attend his funeral.

After his death, his parents found the completed change of beneficiary form among the insured's personal effects which he had stored in their basement during his illness. His mother forwarded the form to the insurer and filed a claim for the proceeds of the policy. Wife also filed a claim. Faced with conflicting claims, the insurer brought this interpleader action.

The trial judge awarded the proceeds of the insurance policy to the insured's mother. The court found that the insured had "substantially complied with the conditions imposed by the policy" and that the "circumstances concerning his illness [had] prevented him from forwarding the form to the insurance company." . . .

Wife contends that, since the insured never mailed the form, he did not do all within his power to exercise his right to change the beneficiary. She relies on several cases to support this argument. In [Persons v. Prudential Ins. Co. of America, 233 S.W.2d 729 (Mo. 1950)], the insured mailed the change of beneficiary form, but died while the form was in transit. In [Woodman Accident and Life Co. v. Puricelli, 669 S.W.2d 64 (Mo. App. 1984)], the executed forms were delivered to the insured's agent who did not forward them to the insurer until after the insured's death. The unique facts of the present case make it distinguishable from either case cited by the wife.

It is axiomatic that what constitutes substantial compliance will vary with the circumstances of each case. Here, the insured did not comply with the strict terms of the policy. He did, however, take a number of positive steps to effect the change of beneficiary. He obtained the correct change of beneficiary form, executed the form properly and in the presence of a witness, explained to his mother and the witness why the change was being made, and expressed his intent to forward the form to the insurer. See, e.g., Connecticut General Life Ins. Co. v. Gulley, 668 F.2d 325, 327 (7th Cir. 1982), *cert. denied,* 456 U.S. 974, 102 S. Ct. 2237, 72 L. Ed. 2d 848 (1982). The only further step needed to complete the change of beneficiary would have been for the insured to mail the executed form to the insurer. . . .

In the present case, the evidence and all the reasonable inferences therefrom indicate that there were unusual circumstances which prevented the insured from mailing the change of beneficiary form to the insurer and which distinguishes this case from either *Woodman* or *Persons.* The insured was a "slow learner" who became progressively vague as his health deteriorated. He was subjected to a debilitating operation which resulted in the amputation of his left arm and entire shoulder. He underwent radiation treatments on a daily basis for approximately one month. His illness and the prescribed treatments left him physically and mentally spent and totally dependent upon his parents. His condition steadily declined until his eventual death. The judgment of the trial court is affirmed.

Notes and Questions

1. The insured, before his death, provided to the insurer's general agent a form intended to change the beneficiary from his wife to his sons. The form actually used was called a "Designation of Beneficiary," rather than a "Change of Beneficiary." The wife argued that the incorrect form was a fatal "defect" in the procedure followed? On interpleader, which beneficiary should win? See Provident Life and Accident Ins. Co. v. Buerge, 703 S.W.2d 590 (Mo. App. 1986).

2. The insured filled out a form to change the beneficiary from his wife, who had filed for divorce, to his mother. He left the form with the local office of the insurer, went home and within the hour committed suicide. The policy said that a change would be effective "when a written request for such change satisfactory to the company is received at its home office." Is the change of beneficiary effective? See Quinn v. Quinn, 498 N.E.2d 1312 (Ind. App. 1986).

3. Under some circumstances, an oral request to change the beneficiary has been held to be substantial compliance. See Bell v. Parker, 563 So. 2d 594 (Miss. 1990).

4. The cases thus far considered deal with the "substantial compliance" doctrine. Is there any less reason to require literal compliance than in the execution of a will?

5. New medical technology and new views about the time of death have created interesting change-of-beneficiary problems. In Crobons v. Wisconsin Natl. Life Ins. Co., 790 F.2d 475 (6th Cir. 1986), two partners made an oral agreement to insure each other's lives. One partner, Wyant, purchased a policy on the life of his partner, Crobons, naming Crobons wife as beneficiary. While Crobons was comatose in the hospital (indeed, his "spontaneous brain functions had irreversibly ceased," which is the time of death under the Michigan Death Act), Wyant quickly sought to change the beneficiary to himself. Death was indicated on the death certificate as occurring at a still later date, after the execution of the change of beneficiary. There might have been questions about the power to change the beneficiary and whether enough had been done to effect a change, but they did not need to be addressed, for the court applied the Michigan Death Act and found that the evidence that death occurred on the earlier date was sufficient to rebut the presumption that death came when indicated on the death certificate. Thus the purported change came too late and the wife was the proper recipient of the proceeds.

6. New financial devices, too, affect the change-of-beneficiary problem. The person whose life is insured is usually but not always the owner of the policy. Only the owner can change the beneficiary. The insured in Fidelity Bankers Life Ins. Co. v. Dortch, 318 N.C. 378, 348 S.E.2d 794 (1986), transferred the ownership of his policy to a bank as

trustee of his Keogh plan. Thereafter only the bank, not the insured, could change the beneficiary; the insured's attempt to do so was ineffective. See also Hunnicutt v. Southern Farm Bureau Life Ins. Co., 256 Ga. 611, 351 S.E.2d 638 (1987).

7. If the parties live (or have lived) in a community property state and community property has been used to pay some or all of the premiums, complicated problems can arise. See Comment, Handling Community Property Claims Against Life Insurance in California: The Modified Risk Payment Theory, 18 Pac. L.J. 969, 977-1001 (1987), which describes various approaches and their problems. A case that illustrates the complications that community property law introduces into that aspect of the insurance law is Estate of Alarcon, 149 Ariz. 336, 718 P.2d 989 (1986). In *Alarcon,* the personal representatives of husband and wife contested entitlement to the proceeds of a life insurance policy on the husband's life. After the husband announced that he would seek a divorce, the wife shot him; she then shot herself and died before he did. Two principles were in conflict in the case. One was the principle that a beneficiary who feloniously kills the insured may not take under the policy; the other was the principle that the wife was half owner of the policy, the premiums having been paid from community funds. The intermediate appellate court, reversing the trial court, held that the wife's property interest in the policy survived her death and entitled her estate to a half interest in the policy proceeds, as her community property interest and not as beneficiary of the policy. Id., 149 Ariz. 340, 718 P.2d 993. The Arizona Supreme Court vacated the opinion of the intermediate appellate court and reinstated that of the trial court, noting that the policy, being a term policy, had no value at the moment of her death which could survive to her estate. Upon her death the community was dissolved, and then upon his death the proceeds went to the alternate beneficiary, his estate.

8. In Porter v. Porter, 107 Wash. 2d 43, 726 P.2d 459 (1986), the Supreme Court of Washington did not have to face the complications introduced by homicide. For cash value policies, the court allocated entitlement to the proceeds in proportion to the separate and community funds used to pay the premiums. For term policies, the court adopted a "risk payment" doctrine, under which the funds used to pay the most recent premiums determined whether the proceeds were separate or community. Among other sources, the court referred to Cross, The Community Property Law in Washington (Revised 1985), 61 Wash. L. Rev. 13, 43 (1986). See Aetna Life Ins. Co. v. Bunt, 110 Wash. 2d 368, 754 P.2d 993 (1988), which is in agreement on the effect of community property on proceeds of a term policy.

9. An unusual "ownership" interest usually exists in "burial"

insurance, which is life insurance with a small face amount, found most often in areas of relative poverty. Such policies are usually issued by burial associations tied to particular funeral homes. Several generations ago they were far more common than now, but Gregg Burial Assn. v. Emerson, 289 Ark. 47, 709 S.W.2d 401 (1986), shows that burial insurance does still exist. The policy provided that the secretary-treasurer of the burial association had "exclusive right to furnish services and supplies . . . of a value equal to the face amount of the Membership Certificate." Id. at 49, 709 S.W.2d at 403. Perhaps one should not be surprised that the court, following a previous case dealing with identical language, found the language ambiguous and permitted another funeral home to recover on the basis of assignments of the policy proceeds.

10. Section 632.41(2) of the Wisconsin Insurance Code deals with the problem underlying *Gregg Burial,* stating, "No contract in which the insurer agrees to pay for any of the incidents of burial may provide that the benefits are payable to an undertaker or any other person doing business related to burials." What rationale explains enactment of such a statute? Is it a sound provision?

11. By divorce decree, a father was required to maintain a certain policy on his life with his children designated as the beneficiaries of the policy. After the divorce he remarried and changed the beneficiary to his new wife. Upon his death, who is entitled to the proceeds of the policy? Suppose that without knowledge of the divorce decree the insurer pays the proceeds to the new beneficiary, and the court finds that the children are entitled. Should it have to pay again? See Dossett v. Dossett, 712 S.W.2d 96 (Tenn. 1986).

WISCONSIN INSURANCE CODE §632.48(1)(b)

Wis. Stat. §632.48(1)(b) (1989)

(1) [N]o life insurance policy . . . may restrict the right of a policyholder or certificate holder:

(b) If the designation of beneficiary is not explicitly irrevocable, to change the beneficiary without the consent of the previously designated beneficiary. . . . [A]s between the beneficiaries, any act that unequivocally indicates an intention to make the change is sufficient to effect it.

[The official comment to this explicit statutory departure from the "substantial compliance" doctrine states that the section was "not intended to declare Wisconsin common law but to state a new point of departure for case law."]

Notes and Questions

1. An insured instructed his attorney to take any steps necessary to change the beneficiary, previously a business associate, so that the proceeds would "go for the benefit of [his] family." Was that sufficient in Wisconsin to effect a beneficiary change? See Empire Gen. Life Ins. Co. v. Silverman, 135 Wis. 2d 143, 399 N.W.2d 910 (1987).

2. An employee designated beneficiaries under a group policy which provided for change of beneficiary by filing written notice with the employer. It also provided that after receipt by the employer, the change related back to the date the notice was signed even if the employee was not then living. The employee executed a will which purported to change the beneficiary. After death the insurer interpleaded, removing from the case any interest the insurer might have in having the employee comply with the formalities provided for in the policy. Under the Wisconsin law, to whom should the proceeds be paid? In the absence of such a statute as Wisconsin's? For the latter situation, see Burkett v. Mott, 152 Ariz. 476, 733 P.2d 673 (Ariz. App. 1986).

3. What effect would the Wisconsin statute have, if any, on the cases where divorce decrees settled the property rights of the parties to the divorce?

PRUDENTIAL INS. CO. v. PARKER

840 F.2d 6 (7th Cir. 1988)

POSNER, Circuit Judge.

The issue in this interpleader action is whether James A. Parker is entitled to all or only one half of the proceeds of a $35,000 serviceman's group insurance policy on his son Bryan, who was killed in an accident while on active duty with the Navy. The issue turns on whether James Parker was "the beneficiary" that his son "designated by a writing received prior to death . . . in the uniformed services." 38 U.S.C. §770(a). If not (and the district court thought not), the statute provides for the proceeds to go to the serviceman's parents. Implicitly this means half to each one, which often is of little significance but here is of great significance because Bryan's parents are divorced.

Bryan had signed and mailed to his father both a card designating James Parker as his beneficiary and a similar form with the same designation; both were witnessed by "Denise Ferguson 653" (or, more likely perhaps, "GS3"). These are official forms and presumably Miss Ferguson is a Navy personnel clerk, but either it has proved impossible to track her down or Mr. Parker's lawyer simply has failed to search for her; and a search of Navy records revealed no receipt of a beneficiary-designation form from Bryan Parker. There is little doubt that he wanted to designate his father as beneficiary; although it is always possible that he merely wanted his father to think he was his beneficiary, this conjecture implies a degree both of calculation and of knowledge of military-insurance law that seems implausible to impute to Bryan Parker. But it is not possible on this record to determine whether Bryan ever submitted the designation-of-beneficiary form to the Navy and therefore whether the Navy ever received it, as section 770 requires for the designation to be valid. See Prudential Ins. Co. v. Smith, 762 F.2d 476, 481-82 (5th Cir. 1985).

The background of the statute (which has never been construed by this court) is discussed fully in Stribling v. United States, 419 F.2d 1350, 1353-55 (8th Cir. 1969). The language concerning the receipt of a written designation of beneficiary comes from an earlier statute designed to overrule a case in which a beneficiary named in the deceased's holographic will had been allowed to recover the insurance proceeds even though the insured had neither designated the beneficiary to, nor filed the will with, his employer. It is so difficult to reconstruct a person's donative intentions after his death that rules relating to bequests have often been strictly construed, and apparently section 770 is in this tradition. See Metropolitan Life Ins. Co. v. Manning, 568 F.2d 922, 926 (2d Cir. 1977); Prudential Ins. Co. v. Warner, 328 F. Supp. 1128, 1130 (W.D. Va. 1971).

Coomer v. United States, 471 F.2d 1 (5th Cir. 1973), cannot carry the day for James Parker. The witness to the designation of beneficiary, corresponding to Miss Ferguson in this case, was the person designated by the Navy to receive such designations, and he did receive it, but then it was lost in the Navy's files. The statute, however, just requires receipt. (To like effect as *Coomer* is Shores v. Nelson, 248 Ark. 155, 450 S.W.2d 543, 544 (1970).) If we knew who Miss Ferguson was, it might turn out that this case was just like *Coomer*. But we do not know who she is or whether she received a designation of beneficiary form or merely witnessed the documents that Bryan mailed to his father.

We are left with a residual doubt because of the treatment of the issue in cases involving private contracts of life insurance. Even though such contracts invariably require that a written designation of beneficiary be received by the insurance company to be effective, courts often relax this requirement considerably in the name of substantial compliance. See Annot., 78 A.L.R.3d 466, 494-506 (1977). A striking example is our own decision in Connecticut General Life Ins. Co. v. Gulley, 668 F.2d 325 (7th Cir. 1982). The insured had died after executing, but before mailing, the change of beneficiary form (the newly designated beneficiary mailed it after the insured died). We held that this was substantial compliance with the contract, even though the contract stated (more emphatically than section 770): "No change of Beneficiary will take effect until received by the Insurance Company. . . ." Yet the legislative history of section 770 suggests that Congress was (for reasons not revealed by that history) dissatisfied with the application of the substantial-compliance doctrine in cases involving government life insurance. Although that dissatisfaction is not clearly embodied in the text of the statute, the legislative thrust is apparent and we are therefore bound. We confess to having no idea why federal employees' life insurance should be treated differently in this regard from other people's life insurance, and point out that the government has no financial stake in these cases: not only is the sole dispute over who shall collect the proceeds, but the insurance program is administered by private carriers.

Affirmed.

Notes and Questions

1. Judge Posner did not see why government life insurance should be treated differently from life insurance contracts in the private sector. Can you see any public policy considerations justifying this difference from ordinary private commercial insurance?

2. Change of beneficiary under a Federal Employees' Group Life Insurance (FEGLI) policy must satisfy more stringent requirements than under state law. See O'Neal v. Gonzalez, 653 F. Supp. 719 (S.D. Fla. 1987), *aff'd*, 839 F.2d 1437 (1988).

ROUNTREE v. FRAZEE

282 Ala. 142, 209 So. 2d 424 (1968)

PER CURIAM.

This appeal is to review a final decree of the Circuit Court of Dallas County, in Equity, which gave appellee relief on her complaint to recoup a sum of money on a life insurance policy which was assigned to a mortgage creditor and upon death of the insured, the amount of the policy was paid to the creditor.

We now advert to the undisputed facts leading up to the litigation. Appellee and the insured, William Josiah Rountree, were man and wife when the Equitable Life Assurance Society of the United States on April 6, 1956, issued a life insurance policy in the sum of $15,000 on the life of the husband, naming appellee as beneficiary.

The policy was issued to the insured at his instance. He paid or caused to be paid all the premiums.

Following negotiations suggested by the local agents of Equitable, Mrs. Margaret Miller Childers, one of the appellants, loaned the insured $15,000, secured by a mortgage on some real estate owned by the insured. The insured, on May 18, 1956, assigned the policy to Mrs. Childers as collateral security for the loan. The loan was consummated on the date the policy was assigned; the policy was also delivered on the same date. The assignment was made on a form furnished by the insurance company. The form was filed with the company. The policy provided that the assignment could be made without the consent of the beneficiary, and it also permitted a change of beneficiary without the consent of the named beneficiary. The wife joined in the mortgage, but not the assignment.

Appellee and her husband, William Josiah Rountree, the insured, were divorced in Dallas County in 1958. There were no children born to their union. The parties entered into a separation agreement with respect to certain property rights. This agreement was approved by the trial court rendering the decree of divorce, and was incorporated into and made a part of the final decree.

We quote paragraphs 3 and 6 of the agreement, which appellants contend are relevant to the issues involved in the instant suit: . . .

> 6. Except as herein otherwise provided each party may dispose of his or her property in any way, and each party hereby waives and relinquishes any and all right, he or she may now have or hereafter acquire, under the present or future laws of any jurisdiction, to share in the property or in the estate of the other as a result of the marital relationship, including without limitation, dower, thirds, curtesy, statutory allowance, widow's allowance, homestead rights, right to take in intestacy, right to take against the will of the other, and right to act as administrator or executor of the others estate, and each party will at the request of the other execute, acknowledge, and deliver any and all instruments which will be necessary and advisable to carry into effect this mutual waiver and relinquishing of all such interest rights and claims.

The insured died on September 13, 1962, unmarried, and without making application for a change of beneficiary. The proceeds of the insurance policy, namely, $15,000, were paid to the assignee, Mrs. Childers, which sum was credited on December 11, 1962, to the mortgage indebtedness, leaving a balance unpaid of $4,945.15. Neither the credit nor the balance is disputed or challenged. Appellee was not responsible for the debt.

The trial court, pursuant to the pleading, entered a declaratory final decree which favored the named beneficiary, who is the appellee. The decree, meeting the aspects of the declaratory petition and the prayer for relief, held that the estate of decedent, the insured, was indebted to appellee (complainant below) in the sum of $15,110 with interest at the rate of 6% from December 11, 1962. . . .

The court also decreed that the complainant (appellee) was subrogated to the right of Mrs. Childers under the mortgage of Mr. Rountree to Mrs. Childers to the extent of $15,110 with interest at 6% per annum from December 11, 1962. . . .

As we view the assignments of error and the contentions of the parties as here presented and argued, the issues are encompassed as follows:

(1) Did the divorce extinguish appellee's rights as an eligible beneficiary?

(2) Did the assignment of the policy amount to a change of beneficiary?

(3) Did the divorce agreement preclude appellee from asserting any claim against the estate of the insured or to the insurance money or its equivalent?

(4) Was appellee entitled to be subrogated to the mortgage? . . .

Appellants contend that the assignment of the policy to the mortgagee had the effect of changing the beneficiary thereby divesting appellee of any interest in the policy. The case of Merchants' Bank v. Garrard, 158 Ga. 867, 124 S.E. 715, is cited in support of this contention. We have examined this case and will not undertake to differentiate the facts, if such could be done, from those in the instant case. We are not in accord with the holding that the assignment constituted a change of beneficiary. We do note that the appellate court ordered the balance of the insurance money, after the debt to the assignee had been satisfied, to be paid to the original beneficiary. The court must have construed that the assignment was only a *pro tanto* change of beneficiary.

We are impressed with the opinion of the Supreme Court of Louisiana in the case of Douglass v. Equitable Life Assurance Society, et al., 150 La. 519, 90 So. 834, which held that the beneficiary could be changed only in the manner specified in the policy. The policy there under consideration authorized, as in the instant policy, a change of beneficiary without the consent of the named beneficiary. By coincidence the appellee insurance company is the same company which issued the policy in the instant case. . . .

Nowhere in the assignment or in the transaction between the insured and the mortgagee do we find any agreement that the insurance money was to be the primary security for the payment of the mortgage debt. The mortgage creditor had the option at her election to resort to the insurance money or the real property for the payment of the debt. If the mortgagee had resorted to the real property described in the mortgage, then certainly in the event the debt was paid from the exhaustion of the real property or a sale thereof, appellee would have been entitled to the insurance as the named beneficiary in the policy.

But the mortgagee elected to collect and apply the insurance money in *pro tanto* extinguishment of the mortgage debt. The debt was that of the insured, and not that of appellee. The husband lawfully pledged appellee's insurance money for the payment of this debt. But, as we have pointed out, he did not make this fund a primary pledge to secure the debt. Should appellee be deprived of this fund at the whim of the mortgagee and free the other security, i.e., the real estate of decedent's estate, from any obligation to pay the debt? We do not decide the point, but we have serious doubts that the mortgagee could have been restrained from exercising her option. However, we think that equity has the power to make an adjustment that will protect the beneficiary, namely, appellee, from having to pay the debt which was not hers. . . .

In the instant case, the insured could have defeated the right of the beneficiary by: (1) He could have exercised the power of appointment and named another beneficiary; (2) he could have designated the assignee as beneficiary *pro tanto*; (3) he could have made the proceeds of the policy a primary fund from which his debt was to be discharged; (4) he could have provided in the assignment that the beneficiary was to have no rights of subrogation or reimbursement. As stated by appellee, the insured did none of these, but merely assigned the policy as collateral security with the result that the insurance policy was not primarily liable for the debt.

We conclude that the adjudication of the trial court is free from the assigned and argued errors, and the decree should be and the same is affirmed.

Notes and Questions

1. The *Rountree* doctrine was recently applied in Winstead v. Peoples Bank, 144 Ill. App. 3d 502, 493 N.E.2d 1183, 98 Ill. Dec. 162 (1986). Winstead made a collateral assignment of a life insurance policy to a bank (ANB) as security for farm operating loans. His wife, Marilyn, was beneficiary of the policy. Under the insured's will, however, she was only a partial beneficiary. The proceeds of the policy were paid to ANB to reduce a debt which would have been a legitimate claim against the estate, and for which ANB also held a security interest on other assets. (Collection of life insurance proceeds is an easier way to collect all or part of a debt than proceeding against either

the estate or other property on which the creditor holds security interests.) Marilyn requested that

> the assets of Winstead's estate be marshalled in order to replace the proceeds of the life insurance policy, or alternatively that she be subrogated to the claim which but for the life insurance proceeds, ANB would have had against both Winstead's estate and the estate assets in which the bank held a security interest. [Id. at 504, 493 N.E.2d at 1185, 98 Ill. Dec. at 164.]

Winstead provided no instructions as to the order in which assets were to be used to pay the debt. The court decided that Marilyn was entitled to subrogation, and therefore found it unnecessary to decide on the alternative relief requested, "whether this is a proper case for marshalling the insurance proceeds with the estate assets which secured the decedent's debts." Id. at 164. Would that have been an equivalent or a less satisfactory form of relief for Marilyn?

D.   Coverage Problems

The life insurance policy is nearly an all-risk policy. There are coverage problems nonetheless.

1.   Who *Is* the Insured?

LIGHTNER v. CENTENNIAL LIFE INS. CO.
242 Kan. 29, 744 P.2d 840 (1987)

HERD, Justice:

This is a declaratory judgment action. Gerald Lightner, special administrator of the estate of Jessie Lightner, appeals a judgment in favor of Centennial Life Insurance Company; Kansas Department of Revenue; and Lloyd and Vivian Lightner, co-administrators of the estate of Dale Lightner. Gerald brought suit to determine the proper payee of proceeds from six life insurance policies owned by Jessie Lightner. The district court held Centennial properly paid the proceeds to the estate of Jessie's husband, Dale Lightner.

This dispute arose from the following facts. Dale and Jessie Lightner, husband and wife, were killed simultaneously in an automobile accident in 1980. It is undisputed that at the time of the accident,

Jessie was both owner and sole beneficiary of six insurance policies on the life of her husband. The policies had been issued by Life of America, Inc., and assumed by Centennial in 1972.

The Lightners died intestate, leaving eight children to share equally in both estates. Gerald claims that by wrongfully paying the proceeds of the policies, totaling $329,075.92, to the larger estate of Dale rather than the smaller estate of Jessie, Dale's estate is exposed to substantially greater federal estate tax liability.

The sole issue is whether the policies are ambiguous and require this court to construe their terms to determine the proper beneficiary under the facts of this case. The district court, in granting summary judgment in favor of Centennial, read the beneficiary provisions of the insurance contracts in light of K.S.A. 58-704. K.S.A. 58-704 provides that in cases of simultaneous death, policy proceeds are payable "as if the insured had survived the beneficiary." Thus, Dale, as *insured* in this instance, is deemed to have survived Jessie. The court then looked to the insurance policies to see where the proceeds were to go when the sole beneficiary dies before the insured. The beneficiary clause in five of the policies provides:

> Unless otherwise provided herein, if any beneficiary dies before the Insured, the interest of such beneficiary shall vest in the surviving beneficiary or beneficiaries, if any; otherwise in the executors, administrators or assigns of the Insured.

The sixth policy is similar. . . .

Applying the clear language of these provisions, the district court held Dale was the *insured*. Thus, Centennial paid the proceeds to Dale's estate. . . .

The confusion in this case results from the different meanings of the word *insured*. In life insurance, *insured* usually refers to the person whose death obligates the insurer to pay. 2A Couch on Insurance §23:1 (2d ed. rev. 1984). However, the word may also refer to the applicant, the owner, or a person who is both the beneficiary and premium payor. 44 C.J.S., Insurance §49; Black's Law Dictionary 726 (5th ed. 1979). Jessie was all of these: applicant, owner, beneficiary, and premium payor. Both she and Dale could properly be termed the *insured*.

There is usually no difficulty with the term because in the typical situation the owner of the policy insures his own life for the benefit of another. In such a typical case, Dale would have applied for, paid for, and owned the policies on his life, with the proceeds upon his death going to Jessie as beneficiary.

Appellant contends the policies in question were drafted with only this typical scenario in mind. The printed provisions make no distinction between the insured and the owner; between the person whose life is insured, Dale, and the person who owns the policy, Jessie. He argues the drafter used the word *insured* in provisions where *owner* was actually meant.

Appellant agrees the first use of *insured* in the beneficiary clauses refers to Dale, as the person whose life is insured, but argues the second use of *insured* refers to the owner of the policy, Jessie. He contends the drafter intended payment to go to the owner of the policy if no beneficiary survived, not to the estate of the person whose life was insured.

Centennial says the second use of *insured* in the beneficiary clause indicates it has the same meaning as its first use in the clause; i.e. referring to the person whose death will make the proceeds payable. It argues it would be nonsense to assume the second use of insured means *owner* when the first clearly does not. . . .

Appellant argues the district court's analysis was improper in that it ignored provisions in the contract which show Centennial did not use the term *insured* consistently. He calls attention to six provisions in the contract which use the word *insured* to mean *owner*. They are:

1. The beneficiary clause in the first five policies states if the beneficiary dies before the insured, the proceeds are to go to the "executors, administrators or *assigns* of the Insured." Emphasis added. Appellant argues this provision makes sense only when it is understood *insured* sometimes denotes *owner* in the policy. Only Jessie, as owner, had the right to assign the policies.

Centennial counters with the argument that *assigns* is simply a legal phrase which was used mechanically. It also argues that while Dale admittedly did not have the right to assign the policy as such, he might have assigned his estate's contingent right to take the proceeds. The term *assigns* is broad, and can encompass those who take remotely. Black's Law Dictionary 109 (5th ed. 1979); Hoffeld v. United States, 186 U.S. 273, 22 S. Ct. 927, 46 L. Ed. 1160 (1902) (*assignees*).

2. The parties repeat their arguments over the assignment clause in the policies: "Any assignment of this Policy by the Insured shall operate so long as such Assignment remains in force, and to the extent thereof, to transfer the interest of any revocable beneficiary."

3. The loan provision of the policy states: "At any time while this policy shall be in force, . . . the Company, on the sole security of this policy and on receipt thereof, . . . will loan to the Insured any sum which shall not exceed the cash value of the policy. . . ."

Appellant points out Dale had no right to obtain loans against the policy. It was Jessie who had the right, and it was Jessie only who exercised that right.

Finding the insurance policies are ambiguous, we are constrained to construe the policies as a whole, rather than limiting our scrutiny to the beneficiary clause. See Kennedy v. Classic Designs, Inc., 239 Kan.

540, 543-44, 722 P.2d 504 (1986). We should also take into consideration the intent of the parties in making the contract. Crestview Bowl, Inc. v. Womer Constr. Co., 225 Kan. at 340, 592 P.2d 74. . . .

The policies, read in their entirety, use the term *insured* to refer to both the one whose life is insured and the owner of the policy. The term is thus ambiguous where these entities are two different people. We hold Jessie Lightner purchased the policies of insurance on the life of her husband, Dale Lightner, for the specific purpose of preventing the proceeds of the policies from becoming a part of Dale Lightner's estate. We therefore hold the Estate of Jessie Lightner is entitled to the proceeds from the policies of insurance on Dale Lightner's life. . . .

Notes and Questions

1. Are you persuaded that a word can have two different meanings in the same sentence?

2. In an omitted passage, the opinion quotes a later policy in which "Insured" and "Owner" — two different words — were used in that same provision, to make the intent clearer. Should that affect the interpretation of the policy in litigation here?

3. The use of the term "Owner" in life insurance policies is a helpful refinement of rather recent vintage.

2. Double Indemnity

Double indemnity provisions provide for double payment on death under certain circumstances, most often as a consequence of an accident.* Unlike the basic coverage, they do not ordinarily provide all-risk coverage and tend to have many more limitations than the basic coverage. You will not be surprised to learn that the word "accident," or comparable words, have produced the same problems in the double indemnity context that they have with other kinds of insurance.

Notes and Questions

1. One way double indemnity differs from the primary death benefit is the usual provision that death must occur within a given period after the accident and not merely as a proximate consequence of it. In Burne v. Franklin Life Ins. Co., 451 Pa. 218, 301 A.2d 799

---

*There is no reason in principle not to have triple or other multiple provisions. Multiple indemnity other than double indemnity is uncommon, however.

(1973), the double indemnity coverage was limited to cases where death resulted within 90 days of the accident. The limitation was challenged as contrary to public policy. Is it? Many cases have dealt with the problem. Comment, The Validity of Time Limitations in Accidental Multiple Indemnity Death Provisions of Life Insurance Policies, 28 Vill. L. Rev. 378 (1982-1983) reviews cases and policy considerations, and discusses *Burne*.

2. A double indemnity provision applied if death was caused solely by "external, violent and accidental means." Fryman was killed in a motorcycle accident. At the time he had a blood alcohol level of .20 and was driving at an excessive rate of speed. Was there coverage within the policy language? See Fryman v. Pilot Life Ins. Co., 704 S.W. 2d 205 (Ky. 1986).

3. In Harrington v. New England Mut. Life Ins. Co., 873 F.2d 166 (7th Cir. 1989), *aff'g* 684 F. Supp. 174 (N.D. Ill. 1988), the insured was a suspected felon who was killed accidentally as a result of a high speed police chase. He seems in fact to have been guilty of a brutal crime and was attempting to escape the scene of the crime with his victim. Should his guilt matter in deciding this civil case? To the extent of the double indemnity, the life insurance policy is, in effect, an accident policy. The same problem also exists in health (accident and sickness) policies. See Chapter 7.

3. Premium Waiver on Disability

A premium waiver in the event of disability is a supplemental benefit often contained in life insurance policies. A small actuarially calculated supplementary premium is charged for it. The policy also contains specific provisions for giving notice and making proof of disability in order to keep the policy in effect. American Gen. Life Ins. Co. v. First American Natl. Bank, 19 Ark. App. 13, 716 S.W.2d 205 (1986), held that the existence of disability, not proof thereof, fixed liability under the provision, and that failure to give notice and make proof within the prescribed time operated as a condition subsequent. What would be the significance of that characterization?

4. The Grace Period

Life insurance policies incorporate a "grace period" of 30 (sometimes 31) days after a premium due date during which the premium may be paid before the policy is forfeited. The provision is often required by statute.

One of the options ordinarily available to the owner of a cash value life insurance policy is having premiums automatically paid out of the cash value, if they are not otherwise paid within the grace period. Payment in that manner operates as a loan to the insured. In the event of death, the loan together with contractually specified interest will be deducted from the death benefit. The insured may also repay the loan and the accrued interest.

The cash value of the policy is also a source of borrowing that is completely at the option of the insured, which makes it a valuable resource under certain circumstances. Further, the interest rate on the loan is prescribed by statute or contract, and may be considerably lower than the market rate for loans from other sources. The latter fact can sometimes cause serious cash flow problems for life insurance companies when prevailing market interest rates are significantly higher than the policy loan interest rate. Why?

E. Exclusions

Life insurance is now essentially all-risk coverage, but in the mid-nineteenth century some policies written in northern States had provisions somewhat like the following, which made the policy "null, void and of no effect" if the insured

> shall die upon the seas or shall pass beyond the settled limits of the United States (excepting into the settled limits of the British Provinces of the two Canadas, Nova Scotia, or New Brunswick,) or shall visit those parts of the United States which lie south of the thirty-sixth degree of North Latitude, between the first of June and the first of November, or shall pass to or west of the Rocky Mountains, or shall enter into any military or naval service whatsoever, (the militia not in actual service excepted), or shall be personally employed as an Engineer or Fireman in charge of a steam engine, or as Conductor or Brakeman upon a railroad, or as an officer, hand, or servant of any steam vessel, or in the manufacture or transportation of gunpowder, or induce delirium tremens, or shall die by his own hand, or in a duel, or in consequence thereof, or by the hands of justice, or in the known violation of any law of the States, or of the United States, or of any government where he may be. [Adapted from a policy in Works, Coverage Clauses and Incontestable Statutes: The Regulation of Post-Claim Underwriting, 1979 U. of Ill. L. Forum 809, 814, n.14.]

Many of the early prohibitions were qualified by language like "without the consent of this Company, previously obtained and endorsed upon this policy." How extensively consent was given would be difficult to learn.

1. Suicide

The only explicit exclusion that is now nearly universal is of suicide during one or two years after the date of issue of the policy. In the event of such suicide, the insurer promises only to refund premiums paid, subject to any indebtedness on the policy. In the United States, at least, coverage of suicide is generally not excluded coverage after that initial period, except in "double indemnity" coverage. A characteristic provision of a life insurance policy would state, "If the insured shall commit suicide while sane or insane within two years from the date of issue hereof, the liability of the Company under this Policy will be limited to the premiums that have been paid hereon less any indebtedness."

Notes and Questions

1. Various problems can arise under suicide clauses. Suppose the suicide occurs within the excluded period, but the insured is insane. In the absence of the words "while sane or insane," would the suicide be covered? The very presence of those words may suggest how some courts answered the question before the words were added.

2. Might there even yet be forms of self-destruction that would be covered despite the "sane or insane" language? In Searle v. Allstate Life Ins. Co., 38 Cal. 3d 425, 696 P.2d 1308, 212 Cal. Rptr. 466 (1985), the California Supreme Court held there was, though it recognized that its view was a minority position. The insured, depressed by health problems and in the course of a family disturbance, killed himself by pointing a gun at his head and pulling the trigger. The court did not think the language ambiguous, and thought (contrary to the opinion of the intermediate appellate court) that an insane person could commit suicide, but said the exclusion only applies if the insured, whether sane or insane, "committed the act of self-destruction with suicidal intent." Id. at 437, 696 P.2d at 1315, 212 Cal. Rptr. at 473. The insurer has the burden of proving not only the act of self-destruction but "that the act was committed with suicidal intent, i.e. the purposeful or intentional causing of death." Id. Irresistible impulse would not negate such intent, however. Justice Bird disagreed with the majority on the ambiguity question. She thought "suicide, whether sane or insane" was inherently ambiguous and that the contrary view was outmoded nineteenth-century law. Justice Mosk's dissenting opinion is useful because he assiduously collected both statutory and case law relevant to the question.

3. Is it possible to exclude coverage for self-destruction more clearly than by the words "while sane or insane?" If so, how?

4. One effective way to exclude coverage for *certain acts* of self-destruction is illustrated in Capital Bank & Trust Co. v. Equitable Life Assurance Socy., 542 So. 2d 494 (La. 1989). An exclusion for death resulting from "any drug, poison, gas or fumes, voluntarily or involuntarily taken, administered, absorbed or inhaled, except for an occupational accident resulting from a hazard incidental to the Insured's occupation." Id. at 495, n.2. If the intent is only to exclude suicide, does the language sweep too broadly? Does that suggest that the intent was something else? If so, what? Despite the express exclusion, the court held that there was coverage. The cause of death was smoke inhalation, and the court held, 3-2, that "gas or fumes" did not include smoke. Was the decision sound?

5. The fact of suicide is not always clear; juries are prone to find that death was caused by something else. See, for example, Mustard v. St. Paul Fire & Marine Ins. Co., 183 Neb. 15, 157 N.W.2d 865 (1968) (While standing or walking in middle of railway track crossing, insured was killed by an unscheduled train). There is also a strong presumption against suicide. See Broun v. Equitable Life Assurance Socy., 69 N.Y.2d 675, 504 N.E.2d 379, 512 N.Y.S.2d 12 (1986) (In case where deceased was found floating in bathtub with high level of toxicity in body, decision was for the jury.) See also Cline, Defense of a Suicide Case, 16 Forum 726 (1981); Ring, Obtaining Insurance Proceeds Over a Suicide Defense, 16 Forum 743 (1981).

6. In Evans v. National Life and Accident Ins. Co., 22 Ohio St. 3d 87, 488 N.E.2d 1247 (1986) (insured an apparent suicide from self-inflicted gunshot wounds), the court affirmed a finding that there was competent, credible evidence to overcome the presumption against suicide. It held that the presumption was not evidence but a rule of procedure that, once rebutted, was extinguished, and further held that the burden of proof is different on the basic coverage and the double indemnity provision. The court noted that while the insurer must prove suicide for the basic coverage, the claimant must establish accidental death for the double indemnity. The beneficiary did not sustain the burden of proving accidental death for purposes of the double indemnity provision.

7. Should Russian roulette fall within the suicide exclusion? This is occasionally still a problem. See C.M. Life Ins. Co. v. Ortega, 562 So. 2d 702 (Fla. App. 1990).

2. War Risk Exclusions

Policies issued during time of war or impending war have usually had a war clause. Such clauses are often removed by endorsement at the end of hostilities. Because most servicemen have been young and lightly insured except by such government programs as World War II's National Service Life Insurance, which of course did not exclude the war risk, the war clause has turned out to be much less important than insurers thought it would be. Nevertheless there has been a substantial amount of litigation, much of it turning on the precise language of the clause in question.

In New York Life Ins. Co. v. Bennion, 158 F.2d 260 (1946), *cert. denied,* 331 U.S. 811 (1947), where the insured was killed in the Japanese attack on Pearl Harbor, the court held that the insured died as the result of "war or any act incident thereto." In some other Pearl Harbor cases, however, the insurer won, for the insured was not in the military service of any country "at war," though Congress declared war retroactively the next day.

What should be the result of litigation when the death took place in an undeclared but very real war such as Vietnam? Would it matter whether the death took place during the time we merely provided "advisers" to South Vietnam or while we were engaged in full-scale hostilities using American troops? What would be the result in the case of minor hostilities that never evolved into real war, such as an attack on an American ship followed by a single act of retaliation?

Arguably the insurer should succeed in excluding coverage for cases like Korea, Vietnam, and Iraq. But should deaths in Lebanon, in and around Nicaragua or El Salvador or in the Persian Gulf during the Iraq-Iran War be covered? Should the death of a tourist or a journalist as a result of Middle Eastern terrorism? In the latter case, does it matter whether sponsorship by a particular government can be proved?

War clauses sometimes contain definitions of war. See, Fehring v. Universal Fidelity Life Ins. Co., 721 P.2d 796 (Okl. 1986), in which the policy provided, "War as used herein means declared or undeclared war or any conflict between the armed forces of countries or governments, or of any coalition of countries or governments through an international organization or otherwise." Id. at 797.

Much litigation took place over the difference between *status* clauses ("while the insured is in military service") and *result* clauses ("death resulting from war or any act incident thereto"). The difference in the effect of the two exclusions should be apparent. The language is not ambiguous, yet many cases were litigated to a final appeal, perhaps hoping for a favorable application of the reasonable expectations doctrine.

3.   The Aviation Exclusion

An aviation exclusion in some form was common in the early days of flying and a limited exclusion may sometimes be found even now, although now special risks from flying are more likely to be taken into account in the underwriting process than in the coverage of the policy. The exclusion is still found often in double indemnity provisions. In its usual form it excluded coverage for death in an airplane accident except when the insured was a fare-paying passenger on a regularly scheduled plane.

At the underwriting level, pilots of private aircraft may find insurance expensive if they can obtain it at all; the point is that even after exclusions disappear their purposes may be at least partially achieved by underwriting practice.

4. Other Exclusions

Because of the long period during which a life insurance policy may remain in force without any reason to bring it into conformity with contemporary practice, cases may continue to surface in which exclusions of almost any vintage may be before the courts.

Notes and Questions

1. In Fehring v. Universal Fidelity Life Ins. Co., 721 P.2d 796 (Okl. 1986), a double indemnity provision excluded death by "homicide, intentional or unintentional." The insured was found lying beside his tractor, dead from a gunshot wound in the head. No weapon was found. The court found the evidence equally consistent with an accident, and awarded judgment to the beneficiary, holding that the clause "bears with it the connotative requirement that the act, whether intentional or unintentional . . . be culpable and thus unlawful in nature." The insurer had the burden of showing that the death fell within the exclusion. Is this a sound result?

2. Occasionally there may be an express exclusion of death resulting from a crime. In Richardson v. Colonial Life & Accident Ins. Co., 723 S.W.2d 912 (Mo. App. 1987), the court gave effect to a provision that the policy did not cover "any loss caused or contributed to by, or occurring as follows: 'Crime — Committing or Attempting to Commit any Crime.' " In *Richardson,* the death actually took place *after* a robbery, when the insured was shot by his partner while they were quarrelling over the division of the proceeds. How would you decide that case?

3. In Prater v. J.C. Penney Life Ins. Co., 155 Ill. App. 3d 696, 508 N.E.2d 305, 108 Ill. Dec. 144 (1987), an express exclusion of death as a result of "the commission or attempted commission of an assault or felony by such Insured" was given effect.

5.   Implied Exceptions in Life Insurance

It is just as reasonable for implied exceptions to exist in life insurance as in fire and ocean marine insurance. For this purpose, life insurance resembles ocean marine more than it does fire insurance because it is essentially an all-risk policy rather than one covering specified perils.

Notes and Questions

1. For the same reasons that arson by the insured is not a covered risk in fire insurance, suicide by the person who insures his or her own life was originally held to be impliedly excepted from coverage as a matter of public policy. See, for example, Ritter v. Mutual Life Ins. Co., 169 U.S. 139 (1898), where the first Justice Harlan said that public policy precluded recovery under the contract. He used fire insurance and arson as an analogy.

2. The implied exception has been replaced in the United States by the limited exclusion for one or two years, established by insurance contract evolution. Should *all* suicide still be excluded from coverage, as a matter of public policy?

3. Suicide is not the only possible implied exception to coverage. If an insured person is shot and killed by his intended victim while he is engaged in the crime of armed robbery, would the insurance company have to pay? Molloy v. John Hancock Mut. Life Ins. Co., 327 Mass. 181, 97 N.E.2d 422 (1951), held that the beneficiary could not recover. Should it make any difference whether the beneficiary was the estate of the criminal or an innocent third party? In Davis v. Boston Mut. Life Ins. Co., 370 Mass. 602, 351 N.E.2d 207 (1976), the Supreme Judicial Court of Massachusetts overruled *Molloy* without suggesting any such distinction. The high speed police chase in *Harrington,* supra Section D(2), also raises a question of implied exception.

4. A problem no longer prevalent but still interesting is whether the insurance company must pay on the death of a person executed for crime. The cases are split and many of those denying recovery discuss such ancient notions as corruption of blood, attainders, and forfeiture for crime.

5. It would be hard to doubt the propriety of the universal rule that a murderer who is a beneficiary may not receive the proceeds of the policy, but note the problem introduced by community property as discussed in *Estate of Alarcon,* supra Section B. If the insurer interpleads the primary and secondary beneficiaries after the primary beneficiary has been convicted of murdering the insured but while the conviction is on appeal, should the distribution be postponed pending the result of the appeal? Over a dissent State Farm Life Ins. Co. v.

Davidson, 144 Ill. App. 3d 1049, 495 N.E.2d 520, 90 Ill. Dec. 139 (1986), said it should not. Would you agree? In Doe v. American Gen. Life Ins. Co., 139 Misc. 2d 80, 526 N.Y.S.2d 904 (Sup. Ct., Bronx County 1988), the beneficiary was suspected of homicide, but after three years she had not yet even been arrested. The court held she was entitled to the proceeds but not to punitive damages for the delay in payment.

6. Should a murderer who is insane within the standards of the criminal law be able to recover as the beneficiary of a life insurance policy? Over a dissent, Ford v. Ford, 307 Md. 105, 512 A.2d 389 (1986), held recovery was possible. With which opinion would you agree?

7. Implied exceptions are treated at some length by Keeton & Widiss, Insurance Law: Student Edition §5.3(b) (1988).

CHAPTER 7

Health Insurance

A. Introduction

From being a penniless orphan, health insurance (often called health and accident insurance, or accident and sickness insurance) has expanded rapidly in recent decades to become perhaps the most important line of insurance, at least when measured by premium volume. The combined annual premium volume for commercial insurance companies and for Blue Cross/Blue Shield plans now considerably exceeds $100 billion.

Various types of policy fall under the heading of health insurance: hospital expense insurance, surgical expense insurance, regular medical expense insurance, major medical insurance, and disability income insurance. Each may be written for both sickness and accidents, or for accidents only, though in general the latter variation should be discouraged as too limited. Within each type there is an almost infinite variety of specifications for the coverage.

Despite the enormous premium volume in health insurance, some types of coverage are among the most troubled types of insurance. The escalating costs of health care, now over 12 percent of GNP and rising, may not be controllable except by measures so drastic as to threaten severe damage to our health care establishment. A basic change to some form of national health insurance is one of the alternatives now under consideration, though there is also powerful opposition to such a change.

The magnitude of the expenditure on health care and the nature of the health care markets has led to consideration of the concentration of market power in the field. For a sketch of some problems raised, see 51 Law & Contemp. Prob. No. 2 (Spring 1988).

The legal problems of health care, or even of the less comprehensive subject of health insurance, would in complexity and difficulty justify a full separate course. In this book the subject must be introduced with no hope of exhibiting its full range and complexity. A few topics will be treated in reasonable depth; many others, of perhaps equal or greater importance, cannot even be sketched.

For example, various cost containment measures, particularly in connection with medicare and medicaid, were once expected to stem the rising tide of costs but have not done so. While cost containment is certainly the most important issue in health insurance, its treatment would also be too complex for an introductory book on insurance law. Efforts at cost containment have brought with them a number of new organizational structures, such as health maintenance organizations (HMOs) and preferred provider organizations (PPOs). In an important sense they are insurers but they are far different from the traditional commercial insurers. Blue Cross and Blue Shield, now several decades old, together constitute the dominant health insurance market in many parts of the country. They, too, are somewhat different from commercial insurers. Exploration of the complexities and peculiarities of HMOs, PPOs, and "The Blues" is beyond the scope of this book.

This chapter deals primarily with commercial health insurers. Most of them are also in either the life insurance or the property-liability insurance markets, but some are only health insurers.

B. Formation of the Contract

There are few peculiarities in the formation of health insurance contracts. Perhaps the most significant is the frequent use of the conditional receipt, which has already been treated in the chapter on life insurance. There are no important differences of principle in its use in health insurance.

In Wernle v. Country Life Ins. Co., 142 Ill. App. 3d 145, 491 N.E.2d 449, 96 Ill. Dec. 403 (1986), a widow of an applicant sued the insurer, alleging coverage. After explaining the various types of conditional receipts, the court decided that the receipt in the case could be interpreted as either an insurability or an approval receipt. Over a dissent, it reversed the order of dismissal and remanded the case for further proceedings.

Notes and Questions

1. An agent for the defendant company took an application for medical insurance and an initial premium from the plaintiff, and gave a conditional receipt which provided coverage from the date of the application or the date of the last required medical examination, whichever was later. The agent allegedly represented that the plaintiff would be covered immediately, but should have known that she was not insurable. As a consequence of the representation the plaintiff cancelled other insurance that would have covered her for the accident that soon occurred. On conflicting evidence the court held that the jury could properly find that the agent had sufficient authority to make the insurer liable for the representations, and held that the insurer and the agent were liable for actual and for punitive damages. Washington Natl. Ins. Co. v. Strickland, 491 So. 2d 872 (Ala. 1985). The opinion discusses the agency problem at length, though the discussion is unclear. On the above facts, would you reach the same result? *How* would you reach that result?

2. *Strickland* also discussed various kinds of agency relationships in insurance. As between the agent and the company, who should pay?

C. Coverage

1. Preexisting Conditions

One hazard against which health insurers generally wish to protect themselves is the existence of a preexisting physical condition that signals a high probability of subsequent loss. In general, a provision excluding coverage for preexisting conditions is unobjectionable from a public policy viewpoint and therefore is enforceable. One particular preexisting condition exclusion almost universally contained in health insurance policies is of coverage for childbirth within a specified period after inception of the policy. For group insurance coverage the period is usually nine months; for individual coverage it is often considerably longer.

The next case deals with the converse problem.

PROVIDENCE HOSPITAL v. MORRELL

160 Mich. App. 697, 408 N.W.2d 521 (1987)

Per Curiam.

Third-party defendant United Fidelity Insurance Company insured third-party plaintiff Russell Morrell and his wife under a group medical insurance policy issued to Morrell Builders, of which Russell Morrell was both owner and an employee. In May of 1982, United Fidelity notified Morrell Builders that the group policy coverage would terminate as of July 1, 1982. This termination was in accordance with the thirty-day notice requirement contained in the policy.

At the time of their termination, Morrell's wife, Norah, was pregnant. In September of 1982, she delivered her baby at Providence Hospital. The cost of delivery and related expenses totalled over $2,000. United Fidelity declined coverage based upon the termination and Russell Morrell failed to pay the bill. As a result, the hospital sued Morrell, who thereafter instituted the instant third-party action against United Fidelity.

The district court entered judgment in favor of Morrell in the amount of $2,329.05 plus interest. United Fidelity appealed and the Wayne Circuit Court, Helene N. White, J., affirmed without opinion. United Fidelity now appeals by leave granted and we affirm.

The insurance policy at issue in this appeal clearly provides that a "covered expense" is incurred on the date that the service is provided. The policy further provides that either party may terminate the policy on any premium due date provided there is thirty days written notice. It is undisputed that United Fidelity properly complied with the termination provision of the policy. Thus, by the provisions of the policy, Norah Morrell's medical expenses related to the pregnancy which were incurred after July 1, 1982, are not covered by the explicit terms of the terminated policy. Therefore, the question before us is whether public policy will permit enforcement of this insurance policy to relieve United Fidelity of liability for Norah Morrell's pregnancy-related medical expenses. We conclude that public policy will not permit this result.

Although both parties cite cases from foreign jurisdictions in support of their positions, there is little Michigan case law available for our analysis. Auto-Owners Ins. Co. v. Blue Cross & Blue Shield of Michigan, 132 Mich. App. 800, 349 N.W.2d 238 (1984), considered a similar issue in the context of the respective liabilities of two different insurance carriers. In *Auto Owners,* a woman was seriously injured in an automobile accident and was unable to return to work. Auto Owners provided her no-fault automobile insurance coverage and Blue Cross covered her medical expenses through a group health policy through the insured's employer. Blue Cross commenced paying the medical expenses and continued until the injured woman was dropped from the employer's health plan when she was unable to return to work. Although there was a conversion provision in the Blue Cross policy, the injured woman did not exercise that option. Thereafter, Auto Owners began the payment of medical expenses under the no-fault policy and commenced an action against Blue Cross to recover those benefits. This Court concluded that Blue Cross properly terminated coverage and that, by the terms of the Blue Cross policy, Blue Cross was not liable for expenses incurred after termination, even though those expenses arose from an injury received prior to termination. Although the *Auto Owners* case supports defendant's position in the case at bar, we note that the *Auto Owners* Court explicitly noted in several places that that case involved a suit between two insurance carriers and not between an insured and insurer. Indeed, the Court specifically stated that "we doubt that Auto-Owners is entitled to the presumptions which could be applied to the subscribing member." Id. at 818, 349 N.W.2d 238.

Also of some relevance to the case at bar is Murphy v. Seed-Roberts Agency, Inc., 79 Mich. App. 1, 261 N.W.2d 198 (1977). In *Murphy*, the plaintiffs were physicians covered under a master medical malpractice policy issued by the California Union Insurance Company through the defendant. After the policy became effective, the insurance company notified plaintiffs that it was cancelling the policy pursuant to a cancellation clause contained in the policy. The cancellation notice offered to renew the policy for one year at a much higher premium. The trial court granted summary judgment in favor of the defendant, which this Court reversed concluding that there existed genuine issues of material fact which needed to be resolved before the court could conclude whether the cancellation was enforceable. Specifically, the Court noted that "public policy considerations may void an attempted cancellation of an insurance policy, even under an unrestricted contractual right to cancellation." Id. at 14, 261 N.W.2d 198.

While the *Murphy* case supports the Morrells' position that public policy should prevent termination, we note that the insurer's conduct in *Murphy* was more egregious than in the case at bar. In *Murphy*, the insurance policy which was issued was for a three-year term with a single premium paid in advance. The insurer attempted to cancel the policy in mid-term in order to obtain a higher premium. In the case at bar, the policy was terminated as of a premium due date and there is no indication that United Fidelity terminated the group policy for the purpose of avoiding Norah Morrell's claim or that United Fidelity otherwise terminated in bad faith. . . .

Although the termination provisions of the policy at issue, as well as the provision that only those expenses incurred during the life of the policy are covered, have a clear meaning and definition in the policy, we do not believe that the public policy of this state will permit the enforcement of such a termination or cancellation clause where the effect is to render a now uninsurable person without insurance coverage for those conditions which exist at the time of termination. In the case at bar, Norah Morrell was pregnant at the time of the termination of the United Fidelity policy. An insurance company cannot assume a risk when a person is apparently healthy and, thereafter, disavow the risk when the person has developed an illness or other coverable condition.

Therefore, we hold that where, as here, an insured develops a condition during the life of a health insurance policy and that policy is subsequently cancelled or terminated by the carrier, the carrier remains liable for those expenses which arise from that condition where those expenses would be covered by the policy had it not been terminated. We specifically note, however, that we do not hold today that the carrier, if it cancels, remains liable for expenses which may thereafter arise from conditions which did not exist at the time of termination. Moreover, we today conclude only that a liability exists between an insurance company and its insured which continues to exist in a limited manner following cancellation or termination of a policy; we are not considering a claim, as in *Auto Owners,* supra, where the question is the respective liability of two separate insurance carriers. That is, were we considering a case in which a second insurance company provided coverage to Norah Morrell following the termination of the United Fidelity policy and chose to cover Norah Morrell's pregnancy expenses, we would not necessarily conclude that that second insurance company could thereafter recover against United Fidelity. . . .

Affirmed. Costs to appellee.

Notes and Questions

1. Can *Morrell* and *Auto-Owners* be reconciled? By affirming the result in the above opinion while disapproving some of its language, the Michigan Supreme Court suggests a way. *Morrell,* 431 Mich. 194, 427 N.W.2d 531 (1988).

2. The court thought *Murphy* more egregious than *Morrell.* Do you agree? If so, is it sufficiently so as to justify an award of punitive damages in a jurisdiction where that would be allowed in a proper case?

2. Coordination of Benefit (COB) Clauses

"Other insurance" clauses, examined in both property and liability insurance contexts, had the objectives of precluding duplicate recovery by the policyholder so far as possible, and of establishing priorities among concurrent coverages. Duplicate recovery would increase the moral hazard and add to the expense of the pure indemnification that is the principal purpose of those lines of insurance, and would create antisocial incentives. In most circumstances, "other insurance" clauses should deter knowledgable policyholders from duplicating coverages and from overinsuring. For those who lack the requisite knowledge, at least they prevent the insureds from reaping the windfall benefit of their uneconomic dual protection.

In health insurance the problem is not exactly the same. Like life insurance, health insurance deals in some part with intangible and unquantifiable values. If a policyholder is compensated for the hospital and medical expenses of a sickness, and even for loss of income, has the policyholder then been made whole if he or she is still ill, suffering perhaps from a permanent and total disability? A *fortiori,* life insurance can only remedy (part of) the economic loss from a death, not the intangible losses that loom much larger for some closely related persons. While the same phenomenon exists to a limited extent in property and liability insurance, in all ordinary cases the woes brought about by insurable events in those fields can be substantially repaired by appropriate quantities of coin of the realm.

Duplicate coverage creates a moral hazard problem for health insurers as well. That problem is sometimes dealt with by subrogation clauses. Often, too, it can be dealt with by the use of coordination of benefits (COB) clauses. The results of the three devices — other insurance clauses, subrogation, and COB clauses — are similar.

In the absence of any of the three types of coordinating clauses, whenever two health insurance coverages overlap, whether intentionally or otherwise, each insurer must pay to the full extent of its coverage. This results from the fact that health insurance contracts are not treated as contracts of indemnity, and that subrogation is not generally available in "personal" insurance. Duplicate coverage occurs frequently, especially with the medical benefits provision in automobile insurance, which is an accident coverage. A person injured in an automobile accident may sometimes be able to recover medical benefits under each of two or even more automobile policies, and also from sundry other sources such as health insurance policies (one or more), tort recovery, workers compensation, employers' wage continuation plans, and others. For an example, see Strzelczyk v. State Farm Mut. Auto. Ins. Co., 113 Ill. 2d 327, 497 N.E.2d 1170, 100 Ill. Dec. 808 (1986), in which the duplication was of recovery from the medical payments coverage of two separate automobile insurance policies.

Another common situation in which multiple coverage is possible is in group health insurance provided in connection with employment. Often two or more wage-earners in the family each have coverage through their employers. Each policy may cover other family members. Though a single coverage may be inadequate, multiple coverages may be more than necessary to make the ill person financially whole.

Duplication can be prevented by insurers through COB clauses which provide that the insurer whose policy contains the clause is obligated to pay only that part of the loss not covered elsewhere. When the alternative benefits come from insurance, the COB clause is merely an excess "other insurance" clause under a different name. If both insurers have COB clauses, the problem is analogous to the one when two property or liability insurers each have "excess" or "escape" other insurance clauses, but COB clauses, unlike other insurance clauses, also apply where there is only a single insurance policy.

One intriguing problem arises from the manner in which two-earner group health insurance coverages have been coordinated. Consistent with the historical perception that the husband was the primary earner for the family, his policy has often been made primary by policies and by courts. Not unexpectedly this has resulted in some feminist opposition. This difficulty is not easy to resolve. It is conceded — indeed, alleged — that the husband's coverage will often prove to be the more adequate: Should that bear on which should be primary?

One other resolution has been to use age as the test, and make the older partner's coverage primary. Perhaps that is as satisfactory as any other rule that does not potentially require litigation between companies to settle the question. Yet another solution is to make the policy which has the best coverage for the particular situation the primary one.

Public policy issues may be raised by the existence of COB clauses, as the following case suggests.

CODY v. CONNECTICUT GEN. LIFE INS. CO.

387 Mass. 142, 439 N.E.2d 234 (1982)

ABRAMS, Justice.

We granted the parties' applications for direct appellate review to determine whether the public policy of this Commonwealth permits coordination-of-benefits clauses in insurance contracts.[1] We conclude that coordination-of-benefits clauses do not violate the public policy of this Commonwealth unless the company engaged in misleading marketing practices, or the insurance contract as a whole is without substantial economic value.

We summarize the facts. The defendant Connecticut General Life Insurance Co. entered into a group contract of insurance with Sun Oil Company (Sun Oil), effective January 1, 1970. Under the contract, the defendant agreed to pay eligible Sun Oil employees, who become

---

1. Coordination-of-benefits clauses allow a company to deduct benefits from other sources from the benefits otherwise provided by the insurance contract.

totally disabled, fifty per cent of their base monthly earnings[2] up to $5,000 a month. The contract also contained two coordination-of-benefits clauses. The first clause provided that the benefits under the contract would be reduced by certain other income benefits, including workers' compensation, and fifty per cent of the amount of the employee's primary Social Security benefits.[3] The second clause stated that if the sum of the employee's benefits under the contract, other income benefits,[4] and benefits from Social Security,[5] exceed seventy-five per cent of the employee's base monthly earnings, the benefits under the contract would be reduced until the sum of all benefits equals seventy-five per cent of the employee's base monthly earnings.

The plaintiff William F. Cody, an employee of Sun Oil, elected to purchase the coverage provided by this group contract. Through payroll deductions, the plaintiff paid a portion of the monthly premium for this coverage. The plaintiff never saw a copy of the insurance contract. The defendant did not distribute copies of the insurance contract to the employee-beneficiaries. Instead, the defendant sent a copy of the contract to Sun Oil. Sun Oil then distributed to its employees a booklet describing the benefits provided under the contract. The plaintiff testified that after reading the booklet, he believed that he would receive seventy-five per cent of his base pay in the event of a long term disability.[6]

As an employee, the plaintiff trained new tractor-trailer drivers for Sun Oil. On March 1, 1971, a driver trainee hit an obstruction on Route 95 in Groveland and lost control of the truck he was driving. The plaintiff, a passenger in that truck, was severely injured as a result

2. The term base monthly earnings means (a) with respect to each hourly employee, his hourly rate of pay multiplied by 174 hours; and (b) with respect to each salaried employee, his gross monthly salary excluding overtime, bonuses, commissions, and other remuneration.

3. Before a disabled employee can receive any benefits under the contract, he must wait twenty-six weeks. Since the accident in this case occurred on March 1, 1971, the plaintiff was not eligible to receive any benefits before September 1, 1971.

4. Other income benefits include any periodic cash payments on account of the employee's disability under (a) any employee sponsored group insurance coverage, toward which Sun Oil makes contributions, except benefits paid under scheduled injuries or permanent partial awards; (b) any State or Federal government disability or retirement plan; (c) any State or Federal workers' compensation or similar law, except benefits paid under scheduled injuries or permanent partial awards; (d) the maintenance provisions of the Jones Act, as applicable to seamen employed by Sun Oil.

5. These Social Security benefits include benefits payable to the employee's dependents on account of the employee's disability.

6. The plaintiff may have based this belief on the coordination-of-benefits clause that provided that if benefits from all sources exceed seventy-five per cent of the employee's base monthly earnings, the benefits under the contract will be reduced until benefits from all sources equal seventy-five per cent of the employee's base monthly earnings.

of this accident. From the date of the accident until April 15, 1981, the date of the trial, the plaintiff has not worked. The plaintiff received no benefits under the contract.

In February, 1977, the plaintiff sued the defendant in the Superior Court. The plaintiff alleged a breach of the insurance contract by the defendant's failure to pay him any benefits. At trial, the parties stipulated that the insurance contract controlled this action. The parties also stipulated that if the judge interpreted the contract to allow the defendant an offset for fifty per cent of the plaintiff's primary Social Security benefits, plus the full amount of workers' compensation payments received between September 1, 1971, and April 15, 1981, the plaintiff would not be entitled to any payments under the contract; if the judge interpreted the contract to allow the defendant to offset only fifty per cent of the plaintiff's primary Social Security benefits, the plaintiff would be entitled to $27,168.05 under the contract; if the judge interpreted the policy to allow no offsets at all, the plaintiff would be entitled to $52,402.70 under the contract. . . .

Over the plaintiff's objection, the judge determined the amount of damages himself. The judge found that under the insurance contract the plaintiff was entitled to recover fifty per cent of his base monthly earnings reduced by his Massachusetts workers' compensation benefits and by fifty per cent of his primary Social Security benefits. Since these offsets reduced the plaintiff's benefits under the insurance contract to nothing, the judge entered judgment for the defendant. We affirm the judgment.

The plaintiff appeals, claiming that the judge erred: (1) in failing to submit the issue of damages to the jury, and in entering judgment for the defendant; and (2) in enforcing the coordination-of-benefits clauses. We conclude that the judge correctly determined the question of damages himself. We also believe that the judge did not err in enforcing the coordination-of-benefits clauses contained in the contract. We add, however, that coordination-of-benefits clauses will no longer be enforced if they are misleading or if they render the insurance contract as a whole without substantial economic value. . . .

2. *Coordination-of-benefits clauses.* Relying on Kates v. St. Paul Fire & Marine Ins. Co., 509 F. Supp. 477 (D. Mass. 1981), the plaintiff claims that the judge erred in enforcing the coordination-of-benefits clauses, because they violate public policy. We agree with the plaintiff that *Kates,* supra at 491, correctly states the public policy of this Commonwealth, that insurance contracts may not be misleading, and that coverages may not be "unrealistically limited" or so limited in scope as to be of no "substantial economic value." However, in this case, the insurance contract took effect, and the plaintiff's injury occurred, before the Legislature enacted the statutes that are the source of this public policy. We therefore believe that it would be unfair to apply this public policy in this case.

In the *Kates* case, supra, the judge correctly found one source of this public policy in G.L. c. 175, §110E.[11] Pursuant to G.L. c. 175, §110E, inserted by St. 1973, c. 1081, the Commissioner of Insurance may issue rules and regulations "to establish minimum standards of full and fair disclosure, for the form and content of policies of accident and sickness insurance which provide medical, surgical, or hospital expense benefits. . . ." Among the purposes of these rules and regulations are the "elimination of provisions which may be misleading . . ."; and the "elimination of coverages which are so limited in scope as to be of no substantial economic value." G.L. c. 175, §110E(*b*), (*e*). Although G.L. c. 175, §110E, expressly does not cover "general" or "blanket" disability insurance contracts like that at issue in this case, the *Kates* decision properly determined that the policies set out in that statute apply to such contracts. Cf. Mailhot v. Travelers Ins. Co., 375 Mass. 342, 348 & n.7, 377 N.E.2d 681 (1978); Gaudette v. Webb, 362 Mass. 60, 70, 284 N.E.2d 222 (1972). Since G.L. c. 175, §110E, was enacted after the effective date of the insurance contract at issue in this case, and after the injury giving rise to this claim, we believe it would be unfair to apply the public policy set out in that statute.

However, we think it is appropriate to elaborate on this policy for future cases. In the *Kates* case, the insurance contract clearly provided that payments on account of workers' compensation and Social Security would be deducted from the benefits provided by the policy. Nevertheless, the judge concluded that the contract was misleading. "In view of the marketing of this coverage through the workplace, employees electing to participate could reasonably expect to receive lifetime benefits if totally disabled from an injury sustained in their employment. Even though one who has all the relevant information about social security and worker compensation benefits could ascertain by close analysis of the coordination-of-benefits provisions that . . . [under the policy he would receive few benefits for on-the-job injuries], it would not be reasonable to expect that this fact would be discovered by a person who was considering whether to apply for participation." Id. at 491-492. Thus, the *Kates* case demonstrates that a company's marketing techniques may make even a totally unambiguous insurance contract misleading. Since misleading insurance contracts violate the public policy of this Commonwealth, we believe that courts must limit the enforcement of these contracts to avoid unconscionable results. Cf. Zapatha v. Dairy Mart, Inc., 381 Mass. 284, 408 N.E.2d 1370 (1980); Commonwealth v. DeCotis, 366 Mass. 234, 242,

11. There are other statutory sources for this policy. For example, G.L. c. 93A, §2, inserted by St. 1967, c. 813, §1, prohibits "unfair or deceptive acts or practices in the conduct of any trade or commerce," including insurance. See Dodd v. Commercial Union Ins. Co., 373 Mass. 72, 75-76, 365 N.E.2d 802 (1977). In addition, the Commissioner of Insurance must make sure that insurance policies are readable. See G.L. c. 175, §2B, inserted by St. 1977, c. 801. §1.

316 N.E.2d 748 (1974); Lechmere Tire & Sales Co. v. Burwick, 360 Mass. 718, 720-721, 277 N.E.2d 503 (1972).

If the insurance contract is not misleading, we think that the court must go on to decide whether the contract as a whole is without substantial economic value. The determination whether the contract is without substantial economic value is similar to an examination of the substantive unconscionability of a contract. A court must determine whether the contract terms are unreasonably favorable to one party. See Zapatha v. Dairy Mart, Inc., 381 Mass. 284, n.13, 408 N.E.2d 1370 (1980). Hence, a court should find that an insurance contract like that at issue in this case has substantial economic value as long as the premiums reflect the anticipated effect of any coordination-of-benefits clause.

Finally, we note that coordination-of-benefits clauses serve the public purpose of avoiding duplicate recoveries for the same injuries. Mailhot v. Travelers Ins. Co., 375 Mass. 342, 347-348, 377 N.E.2d 681 (1978). These clauses enable insurance companies to charge lower premiums. See Lamb v. Connecticut Gen. Life Ins. Co., 643 F.2d 108, 109 n.1 (3d Cir. 1981); Connecticut Gen. Life Ins. Co. v. Craton, 405 F.2d 41, 47 (5th Cir. 1968). We therefore conclude that unless the company engaged in misleading marketing practices, or the insurance contract as a whole is without substantial economic value, coordination-of-benefits clauses do not violate the public policy of this Commonwealth.

Judgment affirmed.

Notes and Questions

1. Why should the statute not have been regarded as declaratory of the common law, thus permitting the court to hold for the insured, a result the court appears to have thought desirable? Note that the court relies in part on a statute enacted prior to the effective date of the policy. See footnote 11 for the statute prohibiting unfair or deceptive acts or practices.

2. Weiss v. CNA, 468 F. Supp. 1291 (W.D. Pa. 1979), applied Pennsylvania law to find that COB clauses were not contrary to public policy. This is a particularly persuasive case about the appropriateness of COB clauses, for at that date Pennsylvania law was thought to include a principle based on Hionis v. Northern Mut. Ins. Co., 230 Pa. Super. 511, 327 A.2d 363 (1974), requiring explicit explanation to the insured of exclusions from coverage. Though the *Hionis* principle itself no longer has validity in Pennsylvania, *Hionis* was perhaps accurately indicative of an insured-friendly public policy of the state.

3. An insurer issuing only cancer insurance complained that another insurer was engaged in prohibited restraints of trade by issuing

broad coverage health insurance with COB clauses. What should be the result of a case raising that issue? American Family Life Assurance Co. v. Blue Cross of Florida, Inc., 486 F.2d 225 (5th Cir. 1973), *cert. denied*, 416 U.S. 905 (1974), held that the competition was lawful, however difficult it might be to meet it. The issuer of the narrower policy could have inserted a COB clause of its own but would then probably be squeezed out of the market, for the narrow coverage would have little purpose. Does it anyway? The principal advantage of such narrow coverage to the policyholder is either to make double recovery possible or to fill gaps in a program of insurance. Sometimes, indeed, narrow policies (and especially "dread disease" policies that often cover only cancer) are marketed with the express objective of providing "something extra" in situations many people find particularly distressful to contemplate. That helps make them marketable. Some insurance commissioners have tried to suppress their sale. Should legislatures suppress them as a matter of public policy? Or should legislatures give the commissioners the requisite power to do so, whenever the policies are either inherently misleading or are without substantial economic value? Might such policies still serve a useful purpose, even granting their limited economic utility? Does that depend on the existence of COB clauses?

4. In Metcalf v. American Family Mut. Ins. Co., 381 N.W.2d 37 (Minn. App. 1986), the plaintiff was covered by an employer group health plan, Medicare, and an individual family health care policy purchased from defendant. Insured had end stage renal disease, covered by Medicare under 42 U.S.C. §426.1(b)(1). The Medicare policy was "secondary to benefits payable under employer group health plans." Id. at 38. The family policy excluded "costs of care, services or supplies to the extent that any such charge is covered under any national, state or other government plan." Id. The group policy paid over $38,000, then Medicare paid $581.60. At issue was how much the family policy should pay. The family policy did not contain a COB clause. Plaintiff claimed that defendant should pay those costs not actually *paid* by Medicare, which would amount to the difference between the total amount and $581.60. Defendant family insurer contended it should not have to pay any costs already paid for by either the group carrier or by Medicare. The court held for the insurer. Would you?

5. In another case involving integration with Medicare benefits, the private insurance policy provided that

M. Integration with Medicare

1. Any benefits payable under the medical expense insurance provisions of this policy will be reduced by the amount of any benefits or compensation to which the insured individual is entitled under Medicare. The reduction will apply whether or

    not the individual has received, or made application for, such
    other benefits.
2. An insured is deemed "entitled" to all Medicare benefits for
    which he or she is or has been eligible.

The clause had been approved by the Illinois Department of Insurance.
The insured did not receive the Medicare benefits to which he was
entitled because of failure to satisfy certain technical requirements of
the Medicare entitlement process. Should the insured recover from the
private insurer the amount he might have received from Medicare by
timely compliance with the Social Security Administration's procedures? See Jeczala v. Lincoln Natl. Life Ins. Co., 146 Ill. App. 3d 1043,
497 N.E.2d 514, 100 Ill. Dec. 536 (1986).

3. Subrogation

One form of accident and sickness insurance is designed to pay the
medical and hospital costs of an injured or sick person, and another
form is intended to replace all or part of lost wages. In both cases the
insured is "indemnified." Yet accident and sickness insurance early
became identified with life insurance as a contract (sometimes misde-
scribed as an "investment" contract) to which legal (or equitable) subrogation (that is, subrogation effective as a matter of law and not of
contract) did not apply, rather than as a contract of indemnity like
property insurance to which subrogation did apply even without a
contractual provision for it. In property insurance, which was in most
cases a contract to indemnify the insured against loss, the insurer that
paid the property loss in full was then subrogated to the insured's
claims, if any, against a tortfeasor who caused the loss. Ironically,
while subrogation would permit an automobile insurer to recoup from
a third party tortfeasor its payment for damage to the car, it would not
apply to permit the insurer to recover for its payments to the same
insured for out-of-pocket medical expenses under the medical benefits
provisions of the same policy.
    In periods when insurance company financial performance is
unsatisfactory, it can sometimes marginally help the bottom line to be
able to claim subrogation rights under accident and sickness coverages,
whether in automobile insurance or in other kinds of insurance. By
about 1950, it began to be common to insert a provision for subrogation to the insured's claims for bodily injury against third party
tortfeasors in automobile insurance contracts, in Blue Cross/Blue
Shield contracts, and in some other insurance contracts. This so-called
"conventional" subrogation was generally given effect. In Michigan
Hosp. Serv. [Blue Cross] v. Sharpe, 339 Mich. 357, 63 N.W.2d 638

(1954), there was no subrogation clause and the court held there was no right to subrogation. Accord, American Pioneer Life Ins. Co. v. Rogers, 296 Ark. 254, 753 S.W.2d 530 (1988). With facts otherwise almost identical to those in the above *Sharpe* case, the companion case of Michigan Medical Serv. [Blue Shield] v. Sharpe, 339 Mich. 574, 64 N.W.2d 713 (1954), there *was* a subrogation clause and as a result the court held there was a right to subrogation. But see Maxwell v. Allstate Ins. Cos., 728 P.2d 812 (Nev. 1986), holding such a subrogation clause to be contrary to public policy:

> [W]e conclude that it violates public policy to allow an insurer to collect a premium and then allow the insurer to subrogate its interest and deny the insured his benefits. Precluding the subrogation of the insurer does not result in a double recovery for the insured because the insured is merely receiving the benefits for which he has already paid.

Which position is preferable? Would not the public policy announced in *Maxwell* be equally applicable to property insurance, where subrogation is allowed even without a subrogation clause in the contract? More recently, Waye v. Bankers Multiple Line Ins. Co., 796 S.W.2d 660 (Mo. App. 1990), took a position consistent with *Maxwell.*

The following case will illustrate the matter and show that the subrogation clause does not solve all problems for the insurer.

LUDWIG v. FARM BUREAU MUT. INS. CO.

393 N.W.2d 143 (Iowa 1986)

Larson, Justice.

The plaintiff, Jeannette Ludwig, was insured under an automobile policy with Farm Bureau Mutual Insurance Company (hereinafter Farm Bureau) which provided coverage for medical expenses incurred by occupants of the insured vehicle. The policy also provided for subrogation for any medical payments made by it. In 1980, while the plaintiff was traveling in Kansas with her husband and mother-in-law, her car was involved in a collision with a truck. All three were injured, and Farm Bureau paid their medical expenses. The three occupants of the car then sued the truckline. Farm Bureau served notice of its subrogation rights on the trucker's insurance company.

The suit against the truckline was settled. A summary of the settlement showed a total amount of $45,000.00 received, with $13,223.26 allocated for subrogation claims for the three victims ($9380.97 for Farm Bureau and the balance for Blue Cross and Blue Shield, whose claim is not involved here). The balance of $31,776.72 was distributed to Jeannette Ludwig and the other two plaintiffs.

Farm Bureau was not involved in the settlement proceedings, however its subrogation interests were protected by the trucker's insurance company which issued a separate check for medical expenses, made payable jointly to Farm Bureau and Jeannette Ludwig. When a disagreement arose over who was entitled to this check, Ludwig filed suit with Ludwig as plaintiff "on behalf of all similarly situated Iowa policyholders and insureds of Farm Bureau Mutual Insurance Company."

The district court, Charles Barlow, J., refused to certify the suit as a class action, and the case proceeded to trial with Jeannette Ludwig as the sole plaintiff. (She raises the court's refusal to grant class-action status as an issue on cross appeal.)

The district court, James L. McDonald, J., ruled that Farm Bureau was entitled to be reimbursed for its payments of medical expenses only if Ludwig had been "made whole" by the settlement with the truckline. The court concluded she had not been made whole and denied reimbursement. Farm Bureau appealed. We reverse and remand on the appeal and affirm on the cross appeal.

The subrogation section of the policy provided:

> Upon payment under part II of this policy [the "medical protection" provision] the Company shall be subrogated to the extent of such payment to the proceeds of any settlement or judgment that may result from the exercise of any rights of recovery which the injured person or anyone receiving such payment may have against any person or organization and such person shall execute and deliver instruments and papers and do whatever else is necessary to secure such rights. Such person shall do nothing after loss to prejudice such rights.

Farm Bureau concedes that it cannot recover under this subrogation provision unless its insured has been "made whole" for her loss. . . .

On the question of whether she had been made whole by her settlement with the trucker, the plaintiff proceeds from the premise that all settlements are by their nature compromises and necessarily result in less than full compensation. She testified that she had settled the case and accepted less than her actual losses because of the delay and mental stress inherent in a trial, not because her case was worth less than what she had demanded. She believed she would have received more if she had gone to trial. Under these circumstances, she argues, a presumption of inadequacy should be recognized.

Farm Bureau, on the other hand, argues that, when a settlement is made without the involvement of the subrogee, the insured is presumed to be "made whole." It argues that such rule is especially necessary where, as in this case, the insurance company's rights to proceed directly against the third party are effectively destroyed by the insured's general release of the third party. It also points to the language in the subrogation agreement which prohibits the insured from doing anything to prejudice its subrogation rights. . . .

The district court did not adopt either of these presumptions, proceeding instead to make a determination from the evidence as to whether Ludwig had been fully compensated. It found that Ludwig's medical expenses, lost wages, expense of hired help, and car damage were established and attributed specific dollar amounts to those items. It noted that the plaintiff's medical expenses had been paid by Farm Bureau and that she had also been paid for them through the third-party settlement. It concluded, however, that she still had not been "made whole," because her claims for pain and suffering and disability had not been fully paid.

We believe this was error. An insured need not be paid in full for pain and suffering and disability before subrogation for medical expenses is allowed. Here the medical expenses advanced by Farm Bureau were made a specific item of settlement, and Jeannette Ludwig testified she knew at the time of the settlement that Farm Bureau and Blue Cross were to receive the amounts of their medical payments and that she was to get $20,000 for her other damages.

The plaintiff relies on the Wisconsin case of Rimes v. State Farm Mutual Automobile Insurance Co., 106 Wis. 2d 263, 316 N.W.2d 348 (1982), which involved a similar fact situation. An insurance company, which had paid out under the medical-pay provisions of its automobile policy, attempted to recover a portion of the settlement proceeds from its insured. The district court there found, in a "mini-trial" on the subrogation claim, that the total damages to the insured parties was $300,433.54 and the settlement amount of $125,000.00 was therefore inadequate to make them whole. The Wisconsin Supreme Court, in a split decision, affirmed. The majority stated this to be the rule:

> Under Wisconsin law the test of wholeness depends upon whether the insured has been completely compensated for *all* the elements of damages, *not merely those damages for which the insurer has indemnified the insured*. Thus the mere fact that the settlement figure of $125,000 exceeded the insurer's claim for subrogation is immaterial. The injured or aggrieved party is not made whole unless *all* his damages arising out of a tort have been fully compensated. [Id. at 275, 316 N.W.2d at 355 (emphasis added).]

In *Rimes*, there was no effort to isolate the settlement proceeds attributable to medical expenses because, under the court's approach, it would make no difference; if a third-party settlement left unsatisfied *any* elements of the claim, the insurer could not recover its medical payments. This ruling appears to stem from the Wisconsin court's view that the amounts of recovery for various elements of the third-party action cannot be separately identified. The court said that "the cause of action against a tort-feasor is indivisible. Accordingly, it is only where there has been full compensation for all the damage elements of the entire cause of action that the insured is made whole." Id. . . .

We disagree with the holding of the *Rimes* case. The amounts recovered against a third party for separate elements of a claim can be identified and credited toward subrogation claims, even though other elements of the third-party claim may not be fully satisfied. Allocation of the separate amounts could be done in the settlement documents, as in this case.[2] In the case of trial it could be done by special interrogatories, *Westendorf,* 330 N.W.2d at 702; Dockendorf v. Lakie, 240 Minn. 441, 448, 61 N.W.2d 752, 756-57 (1953), or by separate findings by the court in a nonjury case. See Iowa R. Civ. P. 179(a).

The purpose of subrogation is to prevent unjust enrichment of one party at the expense of another. See Restatement of Restitution §162, at 653 (1937); 73 Am. Jur. 2d Subrogation §4, at 601 (1974). When the total of the insured's recovery from a third party, and the insurance company's payments under the policy, still are less than the loss sustained, the insured has not been made whole, and the insurer may not recover against him. 6A Appleman, supra, §4094, at 265. This principle is a salutary one; if any loss remains after reimbursement by the third party, it should be borne by the insurer who has been paid to assume such losses. Holding otherwise could result in a windfall to the insurer.

In this case, Farm Bureau's policy did not agree to indemnify Ludwig for pain and suffering or disability. Yet, denial of its claim for medical expenses because Ludwig had not also recovered for other elements of damage would have the effect of making Farm Bureau an insurer against those losses as well. This would be a windfall to an insured who has not paid for such protection. . . .

We hold it was error to deny Farm Bureau's subrogation claim to the excess of Ludwig's recovery over and above her medical expenses. We remand for entry of judgment accordingly. On remand, the court shall consider whether Ludwig should be given credit for a portion of

---

2. In the present case, the settlement amounts attributed to medical expenses were made clear by the settlement documents. In many cases, however, identification of specific amounts will be more difficult. A lump sum settlement might be made. Or the insured and the third party, perhaps being less than solicitous about the interests of a subrogee, might attempt to establish by agreement that the settlement included little or no reimbursement for medical expenses, thus increasing the insured's net recovery. See Westendorf v. Stasson, 330 N.W.2d 699, 702 (Minn. 1983). When the amount attributed to the subrogated claim cannot be determined by other means, a mini-trial, such as that used in *Rimes,* might be required.

the attorney fees incurred in the collection of this amount from the third party. See generally Skauge v. Mountain States Telephone Co., 172 Mont. 521, 565 P.2d 628 (1977); United Pacific Insurance Co. v. Boyd, 34 Wash. App. 372, 661 P.2d 987 (1983); State Farm Mutual Auto Insurance Co. v. Geline, 48 Wis. 2d 290, 179 N.W.2d 815 (1970); 6A Appleman, supra, §4096, at 287-88; 44 Am. Jur. 2d Insurance §1820, at 808. We express no view as to whether such allowance should be made.

Reversed and remanded on appeal; affirmed on cross appeal.

Notes and Questions

1. Should complete indemnification of the insured be a prerequisite to subrogation of an insurer? Always? Does the policy at issue in *Ludwig* so provide?

If the answers to the first two of the questions are yes, in general, but not always, what circumstances besides complete indemnification would justify subrogation? In a fidelity insurance case, the New York Court of Appeals held that the insurer was not barred by equitable considerations from subrogation *pro tanto* against the insured's accounting firm that (allegedly) negligently failed to detect an embezzler. To hold otherwise would, in effect, give the accounting firm liability insurance coverage for which it had not paid. Federal Ins. Co. v. Arthur Andersen & Co., 75 N.Y.2d 366, 552 N.E.2d 870, 553 N.Y.S.2d 291 (1990).

2. An Arkansas statute gives to an insurer paying certain medical payment and income disability benefits a statutory lien on tort recoveries for the injury. See Daves v. Hartford Accident & Indem. Co., 302 Ark. 242, 788 S.W.2d 733 (1990) (applying Ark. Stat. Ann. §23-89-207 (1989), which refers to §§23-89-202(1) and (2), cited erroneously in the case as §201(1) and (2)).

3. For treatment of the nature and problems of insurance subrogation, see Kimball & Davis, The Extension of Insurance Subrogation, 60 Mich. L. Rev. 841 (1962).

4. Mandated Coverages

In recent years the market in health insurance, already greatly constrained by regulation and by intra-industry collaboration in the development of policy forms, has been further confined by a succession of statutes in the various states that can be characterized as "mandated coverage." One possible explanation for the origin of such provisions is that in years when state budgets were tight but the liberal agenda of humanitarian and welfare projects relating to health was still incomplete, members of the health and human services establishment sought to use the health insurance companies as an involuntary vehicle for cross-subsidization of medical costs that in some earlier periods might have been supported by general state revenues. The effect of the provisions is to shift the cost of the specified health care from persons afflicted to insureds as a class. Is this compulsory shifting of costs justified? If there is to be redistribution, should it be done through tax-supported schemes rather than through cross subsidization that is internal to the private insurance industry? Are the tax benefits available for group health insurance a justification for the compulsory cost shifting in such insurance? The following excerpt illustrates mandated coverages.

WISCONSIN STATUTES CH. 632: DISABILITY INSURANCE

Wis. Stat. §§632.78-632.91 (1989)

§632.78   Required Provisions for Disability Insurance Policies

(2) KIDNEY DISEASE TREATMENT. Every disability insurance policy which provides hospital treatment coverage on an expense incurred basis shall contain a clause providing for coverage for hospital inpatient and outpatient kidney disease treatment, which may be limited to dialysis, transplantation and donor-related services, in an amount not less than $30,000 annually, as defined by the department of health and social services under s. 632.89 (6). No insurer is required to duplicate coverage available under the federal medicare program, nor duplicate any other insurance coverage the insured may have. Coverage under this subsection may not be subject to exclusions or limitations, including deductibles and coinsurance factors, which are not generally applicable to other conditions covered under the policy.

(3) HOME CARE

(a) Every disability insurance policy which provides coverage of expenses incurred for in-patient hospital care shall provide coverage for the usual and customary fees for home care. . . .

§632.88   Policy Extension for Handicapped Children

(1) TERMINATION OF COVERAGE. Every hospital or medical expense insurance policy or contract that provides that coverage of a dependent child of a person insured under the policy shall terminate upon

attainment of a limiting age for dependent children specified in the policy shall also provide that the age limitation may not operate to terminate the coverage of a dependent child while the child is and continues to be both:

(a) Incapable of self-sustaining employment because of mental retardation or physical handicap; and

(b) Chiefly dependent upon the person insured under the policy for support and maintenance.

(2) Proof of Incapacity. . . .

§632.89 Required Coverage of Alcoholism and Other Diseases

(1) Definitions. . . .

(2) Required Coverage for all Insurers under Chapter 611 and 613.

(a) *Scope.* Each group disability policy, joint contract or contract providing hospital treatment coverage shall include coverage for:

1. Inpatient hospital treatment of mental and nervous disorders, alcoholism and drug abuse.

(b) *Exclusions in coverage.* Except as provided in par. (c), coverages under pars. (a) and (d) may not be subject to exclusions or limitations which are not generally applicable to other conditions covered under the policy or contract.

(c) *Minimum confinement.* Coverages under par. (a) 1 may not provide less than 30 days' confinement in any calendar year.

(d) *Outpatient treatment.* Every contract or joint contract issued by an insurer subject to this section providing coverage for outpatient treatment shall provide coverage for outpatient services for mental and nervous disorders, alcoholism and drug abuse including but not limited to partial hospitalization services, prescribed drugs and collateral interviews with patients' families, relating to diagnosed alcoholism, drug abuse, or mental and nervous disorders of the patient, in an amount not less than the first $500 in any calendar year for any alcoholism or drug abuse services, or for outpatient services provided by or under contract for a board established under s. 51.42, and $500 for any other outpatient services for mental and nervous disorders. No contract or joint contract written in combination with major medical coverage shall be required to provide coverage under this paragraph for more than $500 for any combination of disabilities required to be covered under this paragraph. The department of health and social services may by rule promulgated under ch. 227 adjust this amount at 2-year intervals to reflect changes in the cost of medical care.

(3) Additional Required Coverage for Corporations Subject to Ch. 613. Any corporation subject to ch. 613 is subject to sub. (2) and

in addition its group disability policies, joint contracts or contracts which provide for hospital treatment or outpatient treatment shall provide:

(a) Outpatient hospital treatment of alcoholism;

(b) Outpatient and home dialysis treatment for kidney disease and kidney transplantation expenses; and

(c) Protection for both recipient and donor of any transplant organs, as provided in s. 49.48 (3)(b).

(4) AMOUNT OF PROTECTION FOR ORGANIZATIONS SUBJECT TO SUB. (3). Coverage under sub. (3)(b) and (c), combined with coverage under s. 632.78 (2), shall not be less than $30,000 annually.

(5) MEDICARE EXCLUSION. No insurer or other organization subject to this section is required to duplicate coverage available under the federal medicare program.

(6) RULES. The department of health and social services may by rule impose reasonable standards for the treatment of kidney diseases required to be covered under this section and s. 632.78 (2), which shall not be inconsistent with or less stringent than applicable federal standards.

§632.90   Tuberculosis Coverage

(1) No policy of disability insurance, whether under subch. II of ch. 40 or otherwise, may include hospital or medical expense coverage unless it contains a provision for a minimum 90 days' continuous coverage of costs for tuberculosis charges, fees or maintenance under ch. 50, including both inpatient care and outpatient dispensary charges or fees. This section applies to all such policies issued, delivered or renewed after August 5, 1973.

(2) The following health or sickness or casualty insurance policies shall not be subject to this section:

(a) Any policy which does not provide hospital expense reimbursement or medical expense reimbursement coverage.

(b) Any policy which only provides benefits for accidental bodily injury, whether or not such policy provides medical services in conjunction with such injury.

(c) Any policy which only provides specific benefits for specific diseases.

§632.91   Coverage of Newborn Infants

(1) No policy of disability insurance whether under subch. II of ch. 40, or otherwise, which provides coverage for a member of the

insured's family may be issued unless it provides that benefits applicable for children shall be payable with respect to a newly born child of the insured from the moment of birth.

(2) Coverage for newly born children required under this section shall consider congenital defects and birth abnormalities as an injury or sickness under the policy and shall cover functional repair or restoration of any body part when necessary to achieve normal body functioning, but shall not cover cosmetic surgery performed only to improve appearance. . . .

Notes and Questions

1. The Wisconsin mandated coverages by no means exhaust the possibilities. An interesting example, provided by Minnesota, is "coverage for hair prostheses worn for hair loss suffered as a result of alopecia areata." Minn. Stat. §62A.28(subd. 2) (1989).

2. Would alcoholism and drug abuse be included within the meaning of "sickness" in the absence of a statute mandating coverage for them? See Hayden v. Guardian Life Ins. Co., 500 So. 2d 831 (La. App. 1986).

3. A problem akin to mandated coverages exists in connection with proposed prohibition of certain kinds of medical testing in the underwriting process, such as a prohibition of testing for HIV antibodies (popularly known as the AIDS test). For two contrasting views on the subject, see Schatz, The AIDS Insurance Crisis: Underwriting or Overreaching, 100 Harv. L. Rev. 1782 (1987), and Clifford & Iuculano, AIDS and Insurance: The Rationale for AIDS-related Testing, 100 Harv. L. Rev. 1806 (1987). An interesting discussion of the two articles (and the problem, too) is Stone, The Rhetoric of Insurance Law: The Debate over AIDS Testing, 15 Law & Social Inquiry 385 (1990). See also Stone, AIDS and the Moral Economy of Insurance, The American Prospect 62 (Spring 1990).

5. Coverage for "Accident" and "Sickness"

Accident and sickness insurance are closely related, and are often covered in combination under the title "disability" insurance, "accident and health" insurance, or "accident and sickness insurance." But accident and sickness are not synonymous, but complementary, and policies customarily treat them somewhat differently. Distinguishing between the two is not always simple, and much may turn on the result.

WEST v. COMMERCIAL INS. CO.

528 A.2d 339 (R.I. 1987)

FAY, Chief Justice.

The plaintiff brought this civil action in Superior Court to enforce disability payments under an insurance policy issued by the defendant, Commercial Insurance Company of Newark, New Jersey (insurer). At trial, at the close of the plaintiff's case, the defendant moved for a directed verdict on three grounds, only one of which was granted and which therefore forms the basis of this appeal.

The essential facts leading up to the granting of defendant's motion for directed verdict and subsequent judgment entered thereon are as follows.

The plaintiff, Bon C. West (West), in January 1978 was shoveling snow from his walkway. "As he was shoveling the snow he took a little bit of snow on the shovel and . . . as he turned slightly he felt something pop or snap in his back. He was immediately . . . physically disabled." The pain was such that West had to crawl to his house. He went to bed and two days later saw Dr. Henry S. Urbaniak. The doctor prescribed bed rest and the wearing of a back support. Throughout the period between 1978 and 1980 West, when pain would arise, would take bed rest and wear his back support. Around April 1, 1980, however, the pain became unbearable, and he again sought out Dr. Urbaniak. The doctor prescribed two successive periods of total bed rest. When this did not ease the back pain, more intensive diagnostic tests were performed. Those tests showed disc damage and a laminectomy was performed in May of 1980.[1]

Because of West's disability the insurer paid West benefits under a policy insuring against "loss or disability resulting directly from accidental bodily injury . . . or . . . loss or disability . . . resulting from sickness."

Under that policy, payments would be made under the "accident" provision for 260 weeks whereas payments under the "sickness" provision would be limited to 52 weeks.

West received payment up to and including the 52nd week when payment stopped. West, believing that he was insured for this injury under the accident provision, instituted suit in Superior Court in order to collect for the full 260-week period.

At a jury trial West presented evidence of the injury and its occurrence, as well as medical testimony concerning the injury. At the close of plaintiff's case, defendant moved for a directed verdict on three

---

1. "Laminectomy — removal of that part of a vertebra which covers the spinal cord posteriorly."

grounds. The trial justice denied defendant's motions concerning whether adequate notice of claim under the terms of the policy had been given and whether plaintiff had offered sufficient evidence of having been totally disabled from performing the duties covered under the policy. The trial justice did grant defendant's motion for directed verdict on the grounds that Kimball v. Massachusetts Accident Co., 44 R.I. 264, 117 A. 228 (1922), was dispositive of the case at bar. Essentially defendant argued, and the court agreed, that there was no evidence that the occurrence of this injury was brought about by "accidental means" as that term is understood and construed in *Kimball*. Therefore, the injury was not an "accidental bodily injury," which would be covered under this policy. The trial justice granted defendant's motion for directed verdict and entered judgment thereon.

The plaintiff appeals from the directed verdict and judgment on the ground that *Kimball* and the "accidental means" cases are inapplicable to the case at bar. The plaintiff argues that the evidence as presented establishes an "accidental bodily injury" as a matter of law or at least presents sufficient evidence on that question to require submission to the jury. The plaintiff also argues that the accidental means/result distinction adopted in *Kimball* should be overruled and instead a rule should be adopted that would recognize the common understanding of the term "accident," which would therefore meet the reasonable understanding and expectations of policy holders.

We are in complete agreement with plaintiff that the holding in *Kimball* is inapplicable to the case at bar. The insurance policy in *Kimball* insured against "loss or disability as herein defined, resulting directly, independently and exclusively of any and all other causes from bodily injury effected solely through accidental means." 44 R.I. at 265, 117 A. at 228. The court, in construing that terminology, stated: "In determining that an injury occurred by 'accidental means' it should appear that the cause or means governed the result and not the result the cause; and that, however unexpected the result might be, no recovery could be allowed *under such a provision* unless there was something unexpected in the cause or means which produced the result." (Emphasis added.) Id. at 269, 117 A. at 230. Further, this court in *Kimball* quoted Lehman v. Great Western Acc. Asso., 155 Iowa 737, 133 N.W. 752, 42 L.R.A. (N.S.) 562, in which the Iowa court construed the phrase "accidental means," stating: "It is not sufficient that there be an accidental, that is, an unusual and unanticipated result. The 'means' must be accidental, that is, involuntary and unintended." 44 R.I. at 270, 117 A. at 230.

In the case at bar, no such limiting language appears anywhere in the policy that would invoke the means/result distinction as delineated in *Kimball*. The policy in question here uses the terminology in the insuring clause, "This policy insures against: (1) loss or disability resulting directly from accidental bodily injury . . . or (2) loss or disability . . . resulting from sickness." There are no definitions of "accidental bodily injury" or "sickness" in the policy. Further, in part 10 of the policy entitled "Exceptions and Reductions," the only limitations appearing thereunder exclude or limit coverage for death or disability or other loss occurring during wartime or as a result of suicide, air travel, or pregnancy, except as expressly provided for in other provisions in the policy.

Thus we are left with a policy that provides for insurance coverage for disability "resulting directly from accidental bodily injury." "In interpreting the contested terms of the insurance policy, we are bound by the rules established for the construction of contracts generally. . . . The language used in the policy must be given its plain, ordinary, and usual meaning." Malo v. Aetna Casualty and Surety Co., 459 A.2d 954, 956 (R.I. 1983). Unquestionably, the plain, ordinary, and usual understanding of "accidental" does not give rise to a meaning limited to the characterization of the causation of the injury exclusive of the characterization of the injury itself. Indeed, Webster's Third New International Dictionary 11 (1976) defines both "accidental injury" and "accidental means." "Accidental injury" is defined as "injury occurring as the unforeseen and chance result of a voluntary act" whereas "accidental means" is defined as "an act or event preceding harm or damage to an insured that is sudden, unexpected, and not intended or designed by any person."[2] Here no contention is made that West, in shoveling his walkway, intended to injure his back while turning his body while shoveling snow. Nor is such an injury to be expected or foreseen as being the natural and probable consequence of turning one's body while shoveling snow.

2. Although there exists a technical distinction between accidental-"means" and accidental-"results" language, that distinction may never occur to the average policy purchaser reading the language of a policy that uses such technical terminology. Indeed, considerable authority exists for the view that such technical terms should be rendered legally synonymous and the policy then be interpreted based upon what the average policy purchaser would understand as its coverage. See 10 Couch on Insurance 2d §41:31 (Rev. ed. 1982).

The insurance company, as drafter of the policy, has the opportunity to choose the language used therein. Therefore, it should choose language that clearly delineates the policy's coverage to the average policy purchaser without resort to terminology that is understood by the average person as meaning one thing and by the insurance company and insurance industry as meaning yet quite another thing.

The recognition that this opportunity exists in the insurer has given rise to rules of statutory construction such that " 'when the language employed by an insurer is ambiguous or susceptible to one or more reasonable interpretations, it will be strictly construed against the insurer.' . . . The test to be applied is not what the insurer may have intended, but what the ordinary insured, unskilled in the parlance of the industry, would reasonably have understood." Gleason v. Merchants Mutual Insurance Co., 589 F. Supp. 1474, 1480 (D.R.I. 1984). . . .

We think the term "accidental bodily injury," giving the terminology its plain, ordinary, and usual meaning, would describe an injury to the body that was unexpected and/or unintended by the insured without regard to any distinction between the resultant injury and the "means" or causation of that injury. The fact that the insured was injured while doing an act that he fully intended to do, shoveling snow, does not take the occurrence of this injury out of the bounds of an "accidental bodily injury" since it was not expected that this activity would result in injury. Accordingly, based upon the record of the case that we had before us, we find that it was error for the trial justice to have granted defendant's motion for directed verdict. The unintended and unforeseen back injury that resulted from West's snow-shoveling activities in January 1978 was, under the terms of this policy, an "accidental bodily injury" as a matter of law.

Consequently, the plaintiff's appeal is sustained, the judgment appealed from is reversed, and the case is remanded to the Superior Court for further proceedings.

Notes and Questions

1. An insured had a life insurance policy with double indemnity payable if death was the "result of external, violent and accidental bodily injuries, directly and independently of all other causes." The double indemnity provision of the life insurance policy is, in effect, an accident policy. The police discovered the insured sitting in a car with a woman he had abducted and raped. In the high-speed chase that followed, the insured was killed. The beneficiary of the policy was insured's mother, innocent of insured's crime. Harrington v. New England Life Ins. Co., 684 F. Supp. 174 (N.D. Ill. 1988), *aff'd,* 873 F.2d 166 (7th Cir. 1989), held the insurer must pay the double indemnity. Is the result sound?

2. A painter developed toluene diisocyanate asthma from exposure to a paint and sealer while spray painting the interiors of railroad cars. He claimed monthly accident benefits for life under a clause of the insurance contract promising such payment for periods of disability resulting from "bodily injury . . . effected through accidental cause." Monthly benefits for sickness would continue for only 12 months. Should he recover for a year or for life? See Ball v. Benefit Trust Life Ins. Co., 704 S.W.2d 677 (Mo. App. 1986).

3. An insured successfully underwent triple coronary bypass surgery. Soon afterward he suffered several grand mal seizures and became totally disabled as a result of brain damage. He claimed monthly income benefits of $1,500 under the policy. The payments were to continue for only five years if the disability resulted from

"sickness" but for life if it resulted from an "injury," which was defined as "bodily injuries which result independently of all other causes from an accident. . . ." He was in his early forties, so the difference might be very substantial. Glassman v. Transamerica Occidental Life Ins. Co., 642 F. Supp. 1 (N.D. Ill. 1986). The trial court gave partial summary judgment for the insured, saying the disability was accidental, but this was reversed and remanded without published opinion in 834 F.2d 173 (7th Cir. 1987). Would a provision that disability resulting from medical or surgical treatment would be illness rather than injury have any effect on the result?

4. The economic consequences of loss of income from total and permanent disability (or disability for a lesser time) do not change depending on whether the disability results from sickness or from accident. Why should insurers wish to treat sickness less generously than accident? As a judge, would you feel justified in eliminating the disparity by interpretive devices? If so, how could you rationalize the result? Given that statutes have already interfered greatly with the freedom of health insurers to provide such insurance coverage as they may wish, would you as a legislator eliminate the disparity between accident and sickness exhibited in the foregoing cases?

5. A couple insured by a group policy covering "illness" was unsuccessful in their efforts to conceive another child. The wife did not ovulate on a regular basis because of a pathological condition, and the husband had a low sperm count. An inexpensive insemination procedure was unsuccessful, and a more complex and expensive procedure was then tried. Though the earlier treatments were paid for by the group insurer, it declined to pay for the more expensive attempts. In Witcraft v. Sundstrand Health and Disability Group Benefit Plan, 420 N.W.2d 785 (Iowa 1988), the court held that the insurer must pay. Do you agree with the result? The issue is now being debated extensively at the legislative level.

6. An insurer provided benefits for the loss of extremities "directly and solely as a result of accidental bodily injuries." Loss contributed to or caused by "disease or bodily or mental infirmity, or medical or surgical treatment thereof" was excluded. An arteriogram was performed to determine whether kidney disease caused the plaintiff's hypertension. The procedure dislodged cholesterol plaques in the plaintiff's aorta; the loosened plaques created embolisms in the feet, resulting in gangrene and, ultimately, amputation. Was this loss, which was caused by a diagnostic procedure, covered by the policy? See Simmons v. Provident Mut. Life Ins. Co., 496 So. 2d 243 (Fla. App. 1986).

7. The deceased was a hemophiliac who received a transfusion from which he acquired AIDS. The immediate cause of his death was pneumonia. His surviving spouse sought to recover under an accidental

death policy that excluded any loss resulting from "sickness or disease or medical or surgical treatment therefore except pyogenic infection which shall occur through an accidental cut or wound." Should she recover? In Cheney v. Bell Natl. Life Ins. Co., 70 Md. App. 163, 520 A.2d 402 (1987), *aff'd,* 315 Md. 761, 556 A.2d 1135 (1989), the court said "no." If the transfusion had been the consequence of blood loss in an automobile accident, would you reach a different result? If so, why?

8. Whatever your view about the result of the preceding case, should a legislature add AIDS and its resulting diseases to the list of statutorily mandated coverages?

6. Miscellaneous Coverage Problems

A wide range of problems appears in the litigation about health insurance coverage. Malingering is a serious moral hazard for the insurer, which tries to confine it by the insertion of various phrases in the policy; each raises its interpretive questions. Much health insurance is marketed to groups. In group marketing, communication between insurer and individual certificate holders, or insureds, leaves much to be desired, with resulting uncertainty about coverage because of the doctrines of waiver and estoppel. Then, too, the relevant facts in health insurance cases are even more numerous than in other lines of insurance, making it especially difficult to draft contracts that satisfactorily anticipate all possible problems.

Notes and Questions

1. Some policies restrict disability benefits for sickness to a "confining sickness." One policy specified confinement "to his residential premises or yard, except for necessary visits to a hospital or doctor's office for treatment." After suffering a severe myocardial infarction, plaintiff became disabled. In stretches of three or four blocks at a time, however, he walked for therapeutic purposes, sometimes as much as two miles a day. Should the plaintiff recover benefits under the policy? See Crowell v. Federal Life & Casualty Co., 397 Mich. 614, 247 N.W.2d 503 (1976).

2. For a case in which an insurer's unduly strict application of the "confining sickness" clause led to liability under a bad faith claim, see Wetherbee v. United Ins. Co., 265 Cal. App. 2d 921, 71 Cal. Rptr. 764 (1968), summarized in Chapter 8.

3. A frequently litigated dispute is over the meaning of the words "total disability." The problem is akin to the "confining sickness"

problem. In one case, the term was characteristically defined as "the complete inability of the insured to engage in his regular occupation, [but after 24 months] of continuous disability, the term 'total disability' shall mean the complete inability of the Insured to engage in any gainful occupation." Rowe v. Home Security Life Ins. Co., 289 S.C. 236, 345 S.E.2d 758 (S.C. App. 1986). In its charge to the jury, the court remarked that the jury could have found that plaintiff "was able to perform work for which he was 'reasonably fitted' and which will provide him '*a* standard of living.' " Id. at 239, 345 S.E.2d at 760. The appellate court found that insufficient to preclude recovery. Why not?

4. Malingering is an omnipresent moral hazard in disability coverage. Can you suggest ways to deal with it that are not inexcusably harsh?

5. A special problem of contract interpretation arises in group accident and sickness insurance with respect to coverage. The insurer frequently supplies the employer with literature to be passed out to the employees who are covered by the group policy. Sometimes that literature, prepared for understanding by ordinary lay persons, is inconsistent with the more technical language of the policy itself. The policy terms are more likely to state what the insurer intended. In case of disagreement, which language should govern? Romano v. New England Mut. Life Ins. Co., 362 S.E.2d 334 (W. Va. 1987) opts for the literature passed out to the employees. Should it matter what the reasonable expectations of the insured may have been, whether objectively established or subjectively determined by the court?

6. Fittro v. Lincoln Natl. Life Ins. Co., 111 Wash. 2d 46, 757 P.2d 1374 (1988), holds that, with respect to a group health and disability policy, if a statute requires the company to issue a certificate, the terms of the certificate will prevail over those of the master policy.

7. The plaintiff's right common iliac artery in his right leg was accidentally severed by surgeons. Before the error was discovered, he also suffered irreversible nerve damage. As a result his right foot was rendered useless. He sought reimbursement under his accidental death and disablement policy pursuant to coverage for "actual severance." Should he recover? See DeWitt v. A State Farm Insurance Companies Retirement Plan for United States Employees, 905 F.2d 798 (4th Cir. 1990).

D.   Credit Life and Disability Insurance

Credit life and credit accident and sickness insurance are written to protect both borrower and lender in credit transactions. For the borrower, they ensure that a debt will not overhang the borrower's estate or the borrower in the event of death or disability before the debt is paid. The person principally benefited by such insurance, however, is the creditor, who receives payment for the debt without the necessity of locating assets and exercising available creditor's remedies against them.

Credit life and credit disability insurance present all the problems of their parent insurance lines, and more besides. For example, they present special regulatory problems. Those problems result mostly from the frequent *de facto* tie-in arrangements that exist with credit institutions despite the best efforts of the law to untie them. An outgrowth of those tie-in arrangements is a pernicious tendency to a kind of "reverse competition" which makes those insurers most successful that charge the highest premium rates.

The following case provides the flavor of credit accident and sickness insurance.

MILTON v. PILGRIM LIFE INS. CO.

500 So. 2d 434 (La. App. 1986)

WATKINS, Judge.

Plaintiff, the insured under a credit disability policy, sued the insurer after it discontinued disability benefits. The lender, the primary irrevocable beneficiary of the policy, was not a party to the lawsuit. Because the lender is an indispensable party, we vacate the trial court judgment in favor of the plaintiff and remand.

Statement of Facts

In connection with the purchase of a pick-up truck, plaintiff, Robert Milton, purchased credit life insurance and credit disability insurance[1] policies from the defendant, Pilgrim Life Insurance Company of America ("Pilgrim"). The irrevocable primary beneficiary of the policies was the lender, G.M.A.C.

Milton became disabled nearly eight months later, and filed disability claims with Pilgrim. Pilgrim paid disability benefits until October of 1980, when the benefits were discontinued. Milton filed suit, alleging that his disability continued beyond October, and seeking

---

1. Credit insurance protects both the borrower and lender against losses due to the death, disability, or insolvency of the borrower. The policy generally covers the balance of the loan due with the proceeds payable to the lender. See Black's Law Dictionary 722 (5th ed. 1979). See generally, 1 J. Appleman & J. Appleman, Insurance Law and Practice §§59-65.

damages, penalties, and attorney's fees from Pilgrim. G.M.A.C. was not made a party to the lawsuit.

Pilgrim filed exceptions of no right of action and nonjoinder of an indispensable party, G.M.A.C. These exceptions were dismissed by the trial court, and a bench trial on the merits was held on November 11, 1982. By judgment rendered on August 27, 1985, the trial court awarded Milton the balance due on the credit disability policy, plus penalties and damages for injury to Milton's credit record.

Pilgrim appealed and now presents four assignments of error. Because our treatment of the first assignment results in a remand to the trial court, we will not address the remaining assignments of error, which challenge the trial court's finding as to the length of Milton's disability, granting of a new trial, and award of general damages.

Statement of Law

Pilgrim contends that the trial court erred in dismissing its exceptions of no right of action and nonjoinder of an indispensable party.

No Right of Action

Pilgrim argues that Milton assigned the credit disability policy to G.M.A.C., and therefore, on the authority of LSA-C.C.P. art. 698 and *Lafleur v. National Health & Life Insurance Co.*, 185 So. 2d 838 (La. App. 3d Cir. 1966), G.M.A.C. has the sole right of action. There is, however, no evidence that the policy was assigned; Milton remained the insured on the policy and merely selected G.M.A.C. as the beneficiary. As there was no assignment of the policy, article 698 and *Lafleur* are not applicable.

A policy of credit disability insurance, like a policy of credit life insurance, is for the benefit of both the creditor and the debtor. The creditor is protected, in the event of the debtor's disability or death, by the proceeds. So, too, is the debtor and his family. See, e.g., 1 J. Appleman & J. Appleman, Insurance Law & Practice, §60 (1981) [hereinafter *Appleman*]. The creditor is not the sole person with an interest in performance of the insurance contract, because the debtor and those claiming through him are damaged when the insurer fails to perform. *Appleman* at §62.35. Credit disability insurance is designed to protect the debtor from liability should he become disabled. As long as the note to G.M.A.C. remained unpaid, the debtor, Milton, was liable on the note absent any agreement by G.M.A.C. that he would be released. Therefore, Milton had an insurable interest in maintaining the credit disability policy because of his liability on the note. See

Succession of Spinks v. Smothers, 341 So. 2d 1201, 1202-03 (La. App. 1st Cir. 1976), *writ refused,* 343 So. 2d 200 (La. 1977) (credit life insurance). Milton therefore had a right of action against Pilgrim when the payments were not made. See LSA-C.C.P. arts. 681, 927(5).

We hold that the insured debtor on a credit disability insurance policy has a right of action to enforce the policy, even though the creditor is made the irrevocable beneficiary.

Nonjoinder of an Indispensable Party

Pilgrim next argues that G.M.A.C. is an indispensable party to the lawsuit, on the authority of LSA-C.C.P. art. 641 and State, Dep't of Highways v. Lamar Advertising Co. of La., 279 So. 2d 671 (La. 1973).

Civil Procedure article 641 states that an action may not be adjudicated unless all indispensable parties are joined. Indispensable parties are defined as "those whose interests in the subject matter are so interrelated, and would be so directly affected by the judgment, that a complete and equitable adjudication of the controversy cannot be made unless they are joined in the action." It has been stated by our Supreme Court that "parties should be deemed indispensable only when that result is absolutely necessary to protect substantial rights." *Lamar,* 279 So. 2d at 677.

As the irrevocable beneficiary of the credit disability policy, G.M.A.C. has a direct interest in the outcome of the litigation and could be directly affected by the judgment. In addition, the failure to join G.M.A.C. could conceivably subject Pilgrim to additional litigation. As such, we hold that the irrevocable creditor beneficiary of a credit disability insurance policy is an indispensable party to an action to enforce the policy.

Accordingly, we vacate the judgment of the trial court, and remand for joinder of G.M.A.C. as a party to the lawsuit.

Reversed and remanded.

PART III

Institutional Problems of Insurance

CHAPTER 8

Litigation Problems, Especially in Liability Insurance

A. Introduction

The usual liability insurance policy imposes on the insurer the duty to defend the insured at the insurer's expense and the duty to indemnify. The duty to defend may appear in at least two forms: (1) under an independent heading, separate from the agreements to indemnify, called something like "Defense, Settlement, Supplementary Payments," or (2) as an integral part of the main insuring paragraph stating the insurer's duties as being (a) to indemnify and (b) to defend. The first form was the more common in early policies; the second seems more common now. The change may express the current perception that, in nearly all circumstances, the duty to defend is of great importance and sometimes even overshadows the duty to indemnify. To regard the duty to defend as purely ancillary to the duty to indemnify is a significant error, as *Gray v. Zurich,* Chapter 1, teaches. The duty to defend is sometimes even the raison d'être for the particular insurance policy.

As *Gray* also shows, while the two duties are related they have different ranges. Even when the duty to defend derives from the duty to indemnify, its scope is likely to be much broader. See Annot., 50 A.L.R.2d 458 (1956). One common doctrinal formulation is that if the third party's complaint can possibly encompass any event for which there may be an obligation to indemnify, there is a duty to defend. There are few qualifications to that doctrine.

Traditionally, perhaps because of the perception of the duty to defend as *supplementary,* the cost of defense is additional to the policy limits, but that is not inevitable. Modern developments in torts have made the cost of defense a major factor in the economics of insurance. Insureds are sometimes more interested in establishing a right to defense than to indemnity. This is especially true in "long tail" business, when they are relying on very old policies which usually had low limits but did not expressly qualify the duty to defend by a provision that the duty ceased when the policy limits were exhausted by payment of judgments or settlements. See Chapter 5.

In more recent policies, the possible interpretation that there was no limit on defense costs was remedied and the duty to defend expressly terminated upon exhaustion of the limits by judgment or settlement. Even that restriction has not always satisfied insurers in the tight markets of the mid-1980s, and in many future policies the duty to defend may cease to be supplementary in any sense, with defense costs being expressly included within policy limits. That is usually the case now with excess policies (see Chapter 9), and it has already occurred even in some primary policies. One must be especially alert for this wrinkle in a nonstandard policy.

The duty to defend is also a *right* to defend, to investigate, and to settle. In a few cases, notably in medical malpractice insurance, it is common for the insurer's right to settle at its own discretion to be circumscribed or even altogether eliminated. Sometimes disagreement between insurer and insured on settling may be arbitrable, by contract.

Partly because the insurer usually has a nearly unlimited right to settle, it has a correlative obligation to perform its duties and exercise its privileges fairly. Failure to do so may lead to liability for bad faith.

B.   Bad Faith

1.   The General Nature of the Problem

As an alternative to contract damages for breach of the duties to defend and indemnify the insured, most states now recognize a separate cause of action in tort based upon breach of an independent, judicially imposed duty to fulfill contractual obligations in good faith.

To handle an insured's defense in good faith, the insurer must do several things: it must determine whether the complaint against the insured states facts that could potentially lead to liability falling within the policy coverage and, if so, proceed with the defense; it must not withdraw from the insured's defense in bad faith; it must handle the mechanical aspects of the insured's defense (investigation, depositions, settlement negotiations, conduct at trial, etc.) in good faith. Then, if liability and coverage are established, the insurer must pay without inappropriate resistance or delay.

A strong policy reason for recognizing the tort of bad faith for breach of the duty to defend or to indemnify lies in the frequent inadequacy of the contract measure of damages. An insurer subject only to contract damages would often have little to lose from refusing to defend or to indemnify, other than harm to its customer relations. If a court later determines that the insurer should have defended the insured, the insurer must then pay the insured's attorney's fees and incidental expenses of the evaded lawsuit and (if the risk is also held to be covered) the amount of the judgment up to the policy limits. The total is just what it would have cost to perform, plus the cost of defending the insured's suit to establish the duty as well as any adverse consequences of differences in the skill and cost of defense of the underlying tort suit.

Often the insured would choose not to assert his rights through legal proceedings; then the insurer would have a clear gain. Even if the insured does assert his rights, the court may conclude that there is no duty to indemnify or even to defend. At a crassly opportunistic level, the balance of incentives would seem to lead insurers to deny defense (or indemnity) unless the duty to defend (or indemnify) is clear *and* the insured seems likely to assert his or her rights by a lawsuit.

On the other hand, if the tort of bad faith is recognized, the insurer is at risk of more generous damages, including the duty to pay a judgment above the policy limits — often called extra-contractual damages — as well as the insured's attorney's fees and expenses. In appropriate cases, the insurer may also be liable for mental distress and even punitive damages. Once these more extensive damage categories are available, the incentives for the insurer to decline a tender of defense or to refuse to indemnify are substantially lessened. The real question now, especially with punitive damages as a possibility, is whether the balance of incentives may have shifted too far. The insurer may decide to defend and even indemnify in cases where the probability is that there is no duty to do so. Recognizing that the underlying conflict of interests is in some sense between the class of premium payers and individual claimants, might there be public policy concern about shifting the balance of incentives so far? If so, what remedy that is not excessive might there be for insurer bad faith?

If the judgment was within the policy limits, the insured has limited concern for how the insurer conducted the defense, at least if the case proves to be within the duty to indemnify. But bad faith or even negligent refusal to defend, or defense conducted badly, can culminate in a judgment beyond the policy limits, giving the insured reason to be seriously concerned about the handling of the defense.

If the insurer believes it is under no duty to provide a defense for the insured, how can it avoid defending without subjecting itself to the risk of excess liability? Would a suit for declaratory judgment suffice? Can the insurer ever recover the costs of defense from the insured if a defense is assumed when it need not have been? Can the insurer be subrogated to a claim for the recovery of defense costs against the filer of a frivolous lawsuit?

If a conflict of interest exists between the insurer and the insured, there may be a duty *not* to defend because of the conflict. But in that case, the insurer will have a duty to *pay for* the defense, which would ordinarily resolve the conflict satisfactorily.

The standard auto and homeowners liability policies declare that the insurer "may make any investigation and settle any claim or suit that we [the insurer] decide is appropriate." Compare this with the clause that declares that the insurer "will . . . provide a defense at our [the insurer's] expense by counsel of our choice." There is no explicit contractual *duty* to settle in the liability insurance contract, but the combination of the *duty* to defend (using counsel of the *insurer's* choice) and the *authority* to settle together give the insurer effective control of the case. Does this imply a further duty of the insurer to settle a claim within the policy limits when the tort plaintiff offers to do so? Is such a duty imposed by law?

2. The Development of Bad Faith Doctrine in Third-Party Cases

One can trace quite far back in time the efforts of policyholders to impose on the insurer the risk of a judgment in excess of the policy limits if the insurer declines an offer to settle within those limits, despite the absence of a stated contractual duty to settle. Such an attempt was made in Attleboro Mfg. Co. v. Frankfort Marine Accident & Plate Glass Ins. Co., 171 F. 495 (Cir. Ct., D. Mass. 1909).

Wisconsin Zinc Co. v. Fidelity & Deposit Co., 162 Wis. 39, 155 N.W. 1081 (1916), involved a complaint by an insured for the insurer's refusal to settle before trial. The complaint had counts in contract, tort for negligence, and tort for fraud (deceit). On a demurrer, the Wisconsin Supreme Court found no duty in contract or in negligence but ruled for the insured on the fraud count.

The bad faith action emerged fully developed in Hilker v. Western Auto. Ins. Co., 204 Wis. 12, 235 N.W. 413 (1931), *aff'd on reh'g*, 204 Wis. 1, 231 N.W. 257 (1931). The court placed considerable emphasis on the control over the litigation by the insurer, considering that on that account

a duty on the part of the insurer to the insured arises. It arises because the insured has bartered to the insurance company all of the rights possessed by him to enable him to discover the extent of the injury and to protect himself as best he can from the consequences of the injury. He has contracted with the insurer that it shall have the exclusive right to settle or compromise the claim, to conduct the defense, and that he will not interfere except at his own cost and expense. . . .

It is the right of the insurer to exercise its own judgment upon the question of whether the claim should be settled or contested. But because it has taken over this duty, and because the contract prohibits the insured from settling, or negotiating for a settlement, or interfering in any manner except upon the request of the insurer . . . its exercise of this right should be accompanied by considerations of good faith. [Id. at 14, 235 N.W. at 414.]

Notes and Questions

1. *Wisconsin Zinc* upheld a complaint for fraud. *Hilker* merely speaks of "bad faith." Does the bad faith cause of action sound in tort or does it establish some new damage rules in contract? Does it matter? Compare Home Indem. Co. v. Snowden, 223 Ark. 64, 264 S.W.2d 642 (1954) with Southern Farm Bureau Casualty Co. v. Parker, 232 Ark. 841, 341 S.W.2d 36 (1940) and Southern Farm Bureau Casualty Co. v. Hardin, 233 Ark. 1011, 351 S.W.2d 153 (1961).

2. *Hilker* used strongly plaintiff-oriented language for such an early case. Yet the contemporaneous movement of American case law in many other states was in the same direction. Annot., 40 A.L.R.2d 162, 178-180 (1955), lists a substantial number of cases in the country that by then had found a duty of good faith in settlement of third-party claims under liability insurance contracts. Some of them seem to consider negligence in settlement a sufficient basis for liability for judgments in excess of policy limits. It said that a great majority of the courts that had considered the issue had so decided. Id. at 178. The outstanding academic authority of that generation on insurance litigation addressed the question at a theoretical level in Keeton, Liability Insurance and Responsibility for Settlement, 67 Harv. L. Rev. 1136 (1954). An insightful contemporary analysis is Syberud, The Duty to Settle, 76 Va. L. Rev. 1113 (1990).

3. It was not until a whole generation after *Hilker* that the Supreme Court of California at last reached the question. One might think that a bit tardy for such an activist court, though the adventitious way issues get to final appellate courts may be responsible. The court placed some reliance on *Hilker* in reaching the liability-for-bad-faith result in *Comunale* (which follows) and was foreshadowed in California by decisions of lower courts. See Brown v. Guarantee Ins. Co., 155 Cal. App. 2d 679, 319 P.2d 69 (1957).

COMUNALE v. TRADERS & GENERAL INS. CO.

50 Cal. 2d 654, 328 P.2d 198 (1958)

GIBSON, Chief Justice.

Mr. and Mrs. Comunale were struck in a marked pedestrian crosswalk by a truck driven by Percy Sloan. Mr. Comunale was seriously injured, and his wife suffered minor injuries. Sloan was insured by defendant Traders & General Insurance Company under a policy that contained limits of liability in the sum of $10,000 for each person injured and $20,000 for each accident. He notified Traders of the accident and was told that the policy did not provide coverage because he was driving a truck that did not belong to him. When the Comunales filed suit against Sloan, Traders refused to defend the action, and Sloan employed competent counsel to represent him. On the second day of the trial Sloan informed Traders that the Comunales would compromise the case for $4,000, that he did not have enough money to effect the settlement, and that it was highly probable the jury would return a verdict in excess of the policy limits. Traders was obligated to defend any personal injury suit covered by the policy, but it was given the right to make such settlement as it might deem expedient. Sloan demanded that Traders assume the defense and settlement of the case. Traders refused, and the trial proceeded to judgment in favor of Mr. Comunale for $25,000 and Mrs. Comunale for $1,250.

Sloan did not pay the judgment, and the Comunales sued Traders under a provision in the policy that permitted an injured party to maintain an action after obtaining judgment against the insured. See Ins. Code, §11580, subd. (b)(2). In that suit judgment was rendered in favor of Mr. Comunale for $10,000 and in favor of Mrs. Comunale for $1,250. This judgment was satisfied by Traders after it was affirmed in Comunale v. Traders & General Ins. Co., 116 Cal. App. 2d 198, 253 P.2d 495.

Comunale obtained an assignment of all of Sloan's rights against Traders and then commenced the present action to recover from Traders the portion of his judgment against Sloan which was in excess of the policy limits. The jury returned a verdict in Comunale's favor, but the trial court entered a judgment for Traders notwithstanding the verdict.

The following questions are presented on Comunale's appeal from the judgment: (1) Did Sloan have a cause of action against Traders for the amount of the judgment in excess of the policy limits? (2) Was Sloan's cause of action against Traders assignable? (3) Was the cause of action barred by the statute of limitations?

Liability in Excess of the Policy Limits

In determining whether Traders is liable for the portion of the judgment against Sloan in excess of the policy limits, we must take into consideration the fact that Traders not only wrongfully refused to defend the action against Sloan but also refused to accept an offer of settlement within the policy limits. It is not claimed the settlement offer was unreasonable in view of the extent of the injuries and the probability that Sloan would be found liable, and Traders' only reason for refusing to settle was its claim that the accident was not covered by the policy. Because of its wrongful denial of coverage, Traders failed to consider Sloan's interest in having the suit against him compromised by a settlement within the policy limits.

There is an implied covenant of good faith and fair dealing in every contract that neither party will do anything which will injure the right of the other to receive the benefits of the agreement. Brown v. Superior Court, 34 Cal. 2d 559, 564, 212 P.2d 878. This principle is applicable to policies of insurance. Hilker v. Western Automobile Ins. Co., 204 Wis. 1, 231 N.W. 257, 258 (affirmed on rehearing, 235 N.W. 413). In the Hilker case it is pointed out that the rights of the insured "go deeper than the mere surface of the contract written for him by the defendant" and that implied obligations are imposed "based upon those principles of fair dealing which enter into every contract." 231 N.W. at page 258. It is common knowledge that a large percentage of the claims covered by insurance are settled without litigation and that this is one of the usual methods by which the insured receives protection. See Douglas v. United States Fidelity & Guaranty Co., 81 N.H. 371, 127 A. 708, 712, 37 A.L.R. 1477; Hilker v. Western Automobile Ins. Co., supra. Under these circumstances the implied obligation of good faith and fair dealing requires the insurer to settle in an appropriate case although the express terms of the policy do not impose such a duty.

The insurer, in deciding whether a claim should be compromised, must take into account the interest of the insured and give it at least as much consideration as it does to its own interest. See Ivy v. Pacific Automobile Ins. Co., 156 Cal. App. 2d 652, 320 P.2d 140. When there is great risk of a recovery beyond the policy limits so that the most reasonable manner of disposing of the claim is a settlement which can be made within those limits, a consideration in good faith of the insured's interest requires the insurer to settle the claim. Its unwarranted refusal to do so constitutes a breach of the implied covenant of good faith and fair dealing.

There is an important difference between the liability of an insurer who performs its obligations and that of an insurer who breaches its contract. The policy limits restrict only the amount the insurer may have to pay in the performance of the contract as compensation to a third person for personal injuries caused by the insured; they do not restrict the damages recoverable by the insured for a breach of contract by the insurer.

The decisive factor in fixing the extent of Traders' liability is not the refusal to defend; it is the refusal to accept an offer of settlement within the policy limits. Where there is no opportunity to compromise the claim and the only wrongful act of the insurer is the refusal to defend, the liability of the insurer is ordinarily limited to the amount of the policy plus attorneys' fees and costs. Mannheimer Bros. v. Kansas Casualty & Surety Co., 149 Minn. 482, 184 N.W. 189, 191. In such a case it is reasoned that, if the insured has employed competent counsel to represent him, there is no ground for concluding that the judgment would have been for a lesser sum had the defense been conducted by insurer's counsel, and therefore it cannot be said that the detriment suffered by the insured as the result of a judgment in excess of the policy limits was proximately caused by the insurer's refusal to defend. Cf. Lane v. Storke, 10 Cal. App. 347, 350, 101 P. 937. This reasoning, however, does not apply where the insurer wrongfully refuses to accept a reasonable settlement within the policy limits.

Most of the cases dealing with the insurer's failure to settle involve an insurer who had assumed the defense of the action against the insured. It is generally held that since the insurer has reserved control over the litigation and settlement it is liable for the entire amount of a judgment against the insured, including any portion in excess of the policy limits, if in the exercise of such control it is guilty of bad faith in refusing a settlement. Brown v. Guarantee Ins. Co., 155 Cal. App. 2d 679, 682, 319 P.2d 69; Ivy v. Pacific Automobile Ins. Co., 156 Cal. App. 2d 652, 320 P.2d 140; see Annotation, Duty of Liability Insurer to Settle or Compromise, 40 A.L.R.2d 168, 178; Roos, A Note on the Excess Problem, 26 Cal. State Bar J. 355, 356. Those cases are, of course, factually distinguishable from the present one since Traders never assumed control over the defense. However, the reason Traders was not in control of the litigation is that it wrongfully refused to defend Sloan, and the breach of its express obligation to defend did not release it from its implied duty to consider Sloan's interest in the settlement.

We do not agree with the cases that hold there is no liability in excess of the policy limits where the insurer, believing there is no coverage, wrongfully refuses to defend and without justification refuses to settle the claim. See State Farm Mut. Auto. Ins. Co. v. Skaggs, 10 Cir., 251 F.2d 356, 359, and Fidelity & Casualty Co. of New York v. Gault, 5 Cir., 196 F.2d 329, 330. An insurer who denies coverage does so at its own risk, and, although its position may not have been entirely groundless, if the denial is found to be wrongful it is liable for the full amount which will compensate the insured for all the detriment caused by the insurer's breach of the express and implied obligations of the contract. Certainly an insurer who not only rejected a reasonable offer of settlement but also wrongfully refused to defend should be in no better position than if it had assumed the defense and then declined to settle. The insurer should not be permitted to profit by its own wrong. . . .

. . . Section 3358 provides that a person cannot recover a greater amount in damages for the breach of an obligation than he could have gained by full performance. The question is what would Sloan have gained from the full performance of the policy contract with Traders. Cf. Henderson v. Oakes-Waterman, Builders, 44 Cal. App. 2d 615, 618, 112 P.2d 662. If Traders had performed its contract, it would have settled the action against Sloan, thereby protecting him from all liability. The allowance of a recovery in excess of the policy limits will not give the insured any additional advantage but merely place him in the same position as if the contract had been performed.

It follows from what we have said that an insurer, who wrongfully declines to defend and who refuses to accept a reasonable settlement within the policy limits in violation of its duty to consider in good faith the interest of the insured in the settlement, is liable for the entire judgment against the insured even if it exceeds the policy limits. . . .

The judgment is reversed with directions to the superior court to enter judgment on the verdict.

Notes and Questions

1. In an omitted part of the opinion, the court discussed the assignability of the insured's cause of action to the third-party claimant, and held it could be assigned. At that time it was the doctrine in California that a cause of action for personal injury could not be assigned. Fifield Manor v. Finston, 54 Cal. 2d 632, 354 P.2d 1073, 7 Cal. Rptr. 377 (1960). How could the court in *Comunale* get around that rule?

2. The action was brought within the statute of limitations period for breaches of contract but was beyond the period for torts. The court held that where a case sounds both in tort and in contract, the plaintiff could elect between the two. If contract is elected for statute of limitations purposes, should the plaintiff therefore be limited to the contract measure of damages? Could the court find that the trial court's award of damages in excess of limits was consistent with a contract theory of recovery?

3. The potential scope of the relief available from this new tort

cause of action became clearer in 1967 in Crisci v. Security Ins. Co., 66 Cal. 2d 425, 426 P.2d 173, 58 Cal. Rptr. 13 (1967). Crisci, the insured, won a judgment of $91,000 against the insurer for bad faith, including $25,000 for mental suffering. The insurer had rejected a $9,000 settlement offer by the third-party claimants (who had originally sued for $400,000) at a time when she had offered to pay $2,500 of the settlement. Her policy had a $10,000 limit and the subsequent verdict against her was for $101,000. The court noted that after arranging a settlement with the plaintiffs under which she lost her property, "Mrs. Crisci, an immigrant widow of 70, became indigent. She worked as a babysitter, and her grandchildren paid her rent. The change in her financial condition was accompanied by a decline in physical health, hysteria, and suicide attempts." Id. at 433, 426 P.2d at 176, 58 Cal. Rptr. at 16. The court stated that the general rule of damages in tort is that the injured party may recover for all detriment incurred whether it could have been anticipated or not. This includes the right to recover for mental suffering as an "aggravation of damages". The court believed that although there was no claim for physical injuries there was little risk of a fictitious claim because the actual property loss was substantial. The court matter-of-factly concluded that Crisci could recover for mental distress resulting from interference with a property right and that this was consistent with prior decisions. As a matter of fact, this award for mental distress without an invasion of physical integrity was itself a landmark decision. See Allen, Insurance Bad Faith Law, 13 Pac. L.J. 833 (Apr. 1982).

4. It was one thing to enable the insured to recover against the insurer for judgments in excess of limits when the third party had offered to settle within limits and the insurer had declined; it was a major step beyond that when the courts allowed punitive damages. In Cain v. State Farm Mut. Auto Ins. Co., 47 Cal. App. 3d 783, 121 Cal. Rptr. 200 (1975), the court held that punitive damages were recoverable from the insurer in bad faith actions, as in every tort action where the defendant has acted "with the intent to vex, injure or annoy, or with a conscious disregard of the plaintiff's rights," and upheld an award of $33,000 for compensatory damages (the portion of the underlying judgment in excess of the policy limits) and $115,000 punitive damages for the insurer's conscious disregard of the insured's interests. Id. at 239, 121 Cal. Rptr. at 207. How often do you suppose an insurer, however stingy it may be in its claims policy and practice, actually has an intent "to vex, injure or annoy?" Having a "conscious disregard of the insured's interests" may occur with considerably greater frequency.

5. Making a claim for punitive damages in bad faith cases now seems to be standard practice in actions by insureds against insurers. First Insurance Co., for example, in the action against Wong, Chapter

5, was motivated to make an all-out defense by the insured's claim for $2.5 million compensatory and $3.5 million punitive damages.

6. What conduct constitutes bad faith is difficult to ascertain and varies among jurisdictions. The traditional view was that bad faith was the virtual equivalent of fraud, requiring proof of actual intent and conscious wrongdoing. For example, see Johnson v. Hardware Mut. Casualty Co., 108 Vt. 269, 187 A. 788 (1936); *Wisconsin Zinc,* supra; Annot., 20 A.L.R.4th 23 (1983). A few courts have broadened the liability to include a *negligent* refusal to defend. See Murphy v. Clancy, 83 Ill. App. 3d 779, 404 N.E.2d 287, 38 Ill. Dec. 863 (1980), *aff'd in part and rev'd in part on other grounds, sub nom.* Murphy v. Urso, 88 Ill. 2d 444, 430 N.E.2d 1079, 58 Ill. Dec. 828 (1981); Dumas v. Hartford Accident & Indem. Co., 94 N.H. 484, 56 A.2d 57 (1947). That may be a less substantial change than at first it appears to be. The court in *Hilker,* supra p. 488, recognized that "[n]egligence has been used by some courts to mean the same thing that other courts have designated as bad faith," 204 Wis. at 13, 235 N.W.2d at 414. See also Ranger County Mut. Ins. Co. v. Guin, 723 S.W.2d 656 (Tex. 1987); Parich v. State Farm Mut. Auto. Ins. Co., 919 F.2d 906 (5th Cir. 1990) (applying Louisiana law) for bad faith claims based on negligence.

7. Some cases seem to have gone the ultimate distance, making the duty to settle one which results in de facto strict liability if an excess judgment is awarded. While no state seems to have adopted a strict liability rule expressly, in Johansen v. California State Auto. Assn. Inter-Insurance Bureau, 15 Cal. 3d 9, 538 P.2d 744, 123 Cal. Rptr. 288 (1975), California seems to have adopted one implicitly. Justice Tobriner, speaking for a unanimous court, said:

> An insurer who denies coverage *does so at its own risk, and, although its position may not have been entirely groundless,* if the denial is found to be wrongful it is liable for the full amount which will compensate the insured for all the detriment caused by the insurer's breach of the express and implied obligations of the contract. (quoting *Comunale,* 50 Cal. 2d at 660). Accordingly, contrary to the defendant's suggestion, an insurer's "good faith," though erroneous, belief in noncoverage affords no defense to liability flowing from the insurer's refusal to accept a reasonable settlement offer. [(Emphasis in original) (Id. at 15, 538 P.2d at 748, 123 Cal. Rptr. at 292.)]

The Supreme Court of New Jersey also seems in dictum to have accepted a strict liability standard in Rova Farms Resort v. Investors Ins. Co., 65 N.J. 474, 323 A.2d 495 (1974). Strict liability is advocated, together with a complex proposal for solving all related problems, in Note, Insurer's Liability for Refusal to Settle: Beyond Strict Liability, 50 So. Cal. L. Rev. 751 (1977).

8. An insurer can be held liable in tort for conducting the defense of the insured at less than an appropriate standard of performance. Again jurisdictions are in conflict as to whether it suffices for the insurer to conduct the insured's defense in good faith, or whether a negligence standard will be imposed. In Kooyman v. Farm Bureau Mut. Ins. Co., 267 N.W.2d 403 (Iowa 1978), the plaintiff alleged that in preparing for trial, the insurance company was negligent in investigating the claims against the insured and the defenses available, in evaluating the potential for an adverse verdict, and in failing to negotiate a settlement. The trial court dismissed the case. On appeal the Iowa Supreme Court affirmed as to the count sounding in negligence, saying it had previously adopted the "bad faith" rule and would admit evidence only of those acts of negligence that tended to show true bad faith. The court reversed and remanded. On a second appeal the court held that there was sufficient evidence for the case to have gone to the jury on the true bad faith issue. Again it reversed and remanded. 315 N.W.2d 30 (Iowa 1982). But in Continental Ins. Co. v. Bayless & Roberts, 608 P.2d 281 (Alaska 1980), the court held it was enough that the attorney hired by the insurer negligently conducted the insured's defense. For cases illustrating the various ways in which insurers handle defenses negligently, see Annot., 34 A.L.R.3d 533 (1970).

9. "Actual intent and conscious wrongdoing" would seem to permit the insurer to consider its own interests first, so long as it did not weigh too lightly those of the insured. Some jurisdictions have now moved farther, defining good faith by requiring the insurer to give *equal* consideration to the interests of its insured and its own interests. See, for example, General Accident Fire & Life Assurance Corp. v. Little, 103 Ariz. 435, 443 P.2d 690 (1968); Cain v. State Farm Mut. Auto. Ins. Co., 47 Cal. App. 3d 783, 121 Cal. Rptr. 200 (1975). Some jurisdictions even insist that when the two interests conflict, the company must give paramount consideration to the interests of its insured to the disadvantage of its own. See Zumwalt v. Utilities Ins. Co., 360 Mo. 362, 228 S.W.2d 750 (1950). There are courts that state that the insurer can best demonstrate its good faith in negotiations for settlement by acting as if there were no policy limits applicable to the claim so that the risk of loss would be entirely its own. See Bollinger v. Nuss, 202 Kan. 326, 449 P.2d 502 (1969) ("The fairest method of balancing the interests is for the insurer to treat the claim as if it alone were liable for the entire amount.") The test used in *Crisci* was "whether a prudent insurer without policy limits would have accepted the settlement offer," citing earlier intermediate courts of appeals in California. Is that the same test? Another developing view is that an insurance company must take an active role, and "that, in some circumstances at least it has an affirmative duty to seize whatever reasonable opportunity may present itself to protect its insured from excess liability," such as

by initiating settlement negotiations and bargaining towards settlement. Alt v. American Family Mut. Ins. Co., 71 Wis. 2d 340, 347, 237 N.W.2d 706, 713 (1976).

10. The bad faith tort is now almost universally accepted in third party cases. One indication of this is the readiness of the 8th Circuit to uphold a bad faith claim under South Dakota law without being able to cite any South Dakota authority. See Stoner v. State Farm Mut. Auto. Ins. Co., 780 F.2d 1414 (8th Cir. 1986), *subsequent appeal,* 856 F.2d 1195 (8th Cir. 1988). But see Glenn v. Fleming, 799 P.2d 79 (Kan. 1990), where the Kansas Supreme Court, while recognizing a bad faith claim, regards it as a contract claim.

11. Suppose the insured does not have assets to pay a judgment in excess of the policy limits and is satisfied with the handling of the case by the insurer, despite the awarding at trial of a judgment greatly in excess of the limits and despite its being upheld on appeal. May the third-party claimant sue the insurer without first getting an assignment from the insured? The court in Murray v. Allstate Ins. Co., 209 N.J. Super. 163, 507 A.2d 247 (1986), said "no" over a strong dissent. Which is the better view?

Problem

A 19-year-old boy suffered severe injuries when a car in which he was a passenger ran into a bridge abutment. He sued the driver. Defense was tendered to the purported insurer of the driver, which declined to defend on the ground that there was no coverage. (The Supreme Court of Wisconsin thought the question of coverage was "fairly debatable.") Under Wisconsin procedure, Wis. Stats. §803.04(2)(b), the insurer sought and obtained a bifurcated trial and the issue of coverage was tried first, resulting in a judgment establishing that there was coverage. Two days later the insurer offered its policy limits; nine months later it agreed to defend. After negotiations, the parties entered into a stipulation of judgment under which the insurer was to be held liable for its limits ($16,000), the insured was to be held liable for $175,000, and the injured person was to be assigned all the causes of action the insured had against the insurer in satisfaction of the stipulated judgment against the insured. Thus the insured was home free, except for the unreimbursed costs of the coverage case.

The court below was said by the majority opinion to be "indignant that an insurer would delay settlement negotiations until the coverage issue has been judicially determined, particularly when liability and excess damages are undisputed." In an action on the assigned claim, the case came to the Wisconsin Supreme Court on certification from a lower court which had held that the insurer had both "breached its contract with its insured and committed the tort of bad faith in refusing to negotiate a settlement within policy limits when [the insurer] had sought a separate trial on the issue of coverage."

How would you decide the case? Compare your analysis with those of the Wisconsin Supreme Court in Mowry v. Badger State Mut. Casualty Co., 129 Wis. 2d 496, 385 N.W.2d 171 (1986), where both the majority (whose opinion may be sound on the facts as stated, though the insurer was guilty of some delays) and the dissenters seem to ignore what may be the most important fact in the case: that the insured came out of the whole confused matter financially unharmed and actually with more protection than it had bargained for. The author of a student note at 70 Marq. L. Rev. 725 (1987) also missed that point. It is true that technical doctrine would evaluate the rights of the parties *before* rather than after the assignment of a claim. But both the dissent and the author of the note did not put the result on technical doctrine, but on policy grounds — on notions like the insurer's superior ability to bear the loss, and generalized and fuzzy public policy notions about fairness and justice. When the decision is based on such general grounds, it seems at least plausible that post-assignment facts are relevant. Do you think they are?

3. Bad Faith in First-Party Cases

The doctrinal problems in developing a right of action for bad faith in first-party cases are difficult. *Hadley v. Baxendale* is still alive, setting limits for the recovery of contract damages in the absence of special circumstances communicated to the promisor. The special circumstances that most often appear in the cases involve serious emotional trauma. The possibility of emotional trauma in the settlement process would *never* be communicated to the insurer in advance of the contract, for it would not have been foreseen as a possibility.

Nevertheless, beginning with some of the more outrageous displays of insensitivity by insurance adjusters, the courts could easily have moved in the direction of expanding damages in contract to include the loss of peace of mind. Peace of mind is, after all, much of what an insured is buying when purchasing insurance, and the insurer knows it. Insurers trade upon peace of mind in promoting their wares, with slogans like "good hands people," "like a good neighbor, State Farm is there" and "a piece of the Rock!"

Instead of expanding the doctrine of contract damages, however, the courts followed the third-party cases and extended the tort of bad faith into the first-party area. Perhaps it helped that refusal to pay or delay in paying was sometimes denominated "vexatious refusal to pay," suggesting the "intentional infliction of emotional distress," another recently developed tort.

Establishing liability in tort leads to the possibility of punitive damages and sometimes to judgments for insureds that are themselves outrageous. Expectation damages, on the contrary, with peace of mind being one of the insured's usual expectations when purchasing insurance, would not have been any more difficult to recognize and might have been easier to contain within tolerable limits. See Comment, The Expectation of Peace of Mind: A Basis for Recovery of Damages for Mental Suffering Resulting from the Breach of First Party Insurance Contracts, 56 S. Cal. L. Rev. 1345 (1983).

The California courts led in establishing rights of action for the bad faith of insurers in settling first-party claims, though (perhaps) unfortunately they did so through tort doctrines rather than by expanding expectation damages in contracts. The incentive to develop such a remedy may arise in any first-party insurance contract, but the early cases seem to have been in disability (health) insurance. The problem seems still to make its most frequent appearance there, perhaps because the injustice to the insured seems particularly egregious in cases involving serious illness or accident.

An early case in the series developing the doctrine was Wetherbee v. United Ins. Co., 265 Cal. App. 2d 921, 71 Cal. Rptr. 764 (1968). Plaintiff had a disability policy that provided there was no obligation to pay unless there was a "confining sickness." She sought to terminate it but was induced not to do so by representations known by the defendant to be false (the court said). She was totally and permanently disabled by a stroke. The defendant began to pay but discontinued payment when her doctor answered with an unqualified "no" to a question whether she was "continuously" confined within the house. The crucial fact was that she went to the doctor's office monthly "with the aid of a crutch, a foot brace and the assistance of another person." Id. at 932, 71 Cal. Rptr. at 770. At trial, the plaintiff recovered $1,050 in contract damages (the amount of the benefits due) and $500,000 in punitive damages. On appeal, the insurer relied on the traditional rule that punitive damages may not be awarded for breach of contract. The appellate court found the punitive damages excessive, but upheld an award of some amount of such damages based on the tort of fraudulently inducing the plaintiff to continue the contract, not because of misrepresentations about the terms of the contract but because of misrepresentations of its intention to live up to those terms. Was it sound to make a tort case out of this straightforward breach of contract?

Fletcher v. Western Natl. Life Ins. Co., 10 Cal. App. 3d 376, 89 Cal. Rptr. 78 (1970), was decided subsequently by an intermediate appellate court. The trial court awarded the plaintiff $60,000 in compensatory damages and $180,000 in punitive damages, the latter being the amount to which the trial court reduced $640,000 on a conditional order for a new trial. The plaintiff accepted the reduced award. The case had gone to the jury on a theory of intentional infliction of emotional distress. The facts as stated in the opinion do suggest outrageous conduct by the insurer. The policy provided for a maximum of two years payment for sickness, and thirty years payment for accidental injury. The plaintiff suffered injuries at work from lifting a 361-pound bale of rubber. He had a hernia operation, and during his convalescence defendant paid under the sickness coverage. Thereafter, however, he had difficulties with his back, also resulting from the "accident." Payments to plaintiff were resumed, apparently this time under the injury provision. On what seems a thin pretext, defendant sought both to terminate payments and recover payments already made (or reach a compromise settlement on the latter) on the theory that the back problem was congenital and that plaintiff had failed to report that in the application, thus making the coverage voidable for "concealment." He apparently knew nothing of a congenital back problem, even if one did exist. This conduct by the insurer would be shocking enough under any circumstances, but when coupled with the facts that plaintiff had eight children, seven of them in school, and that the family had been living on his wages of approximately $289 per week, the economic and emotional distress suffered by the plaintiff becomes quite apparent.

When sued, defendants conceded that their conduct was outrageous, but contended

> that their conduct was privileged in that it constituted settlement negotiations; that there is no evidence that plaintiff suffered emotional distress of sufficient severity to establish the tort; and that if plaintiff's emotional distress was of sufficient severity, there was no evidence that such was caused by defendant's conduct. [Id. at 394, 89 Cal. Rptr. at 88.]

The court was not persuaded and held that the facts supported an action for intentional infliction of emotional distress. But the court went on:

> . . . We further hold that, independent of the tort of intentional infliction of emotional distress, such conduct on the part of a disability insurer constitutes a tortious interference with a protected property interest of its insured for which damages may be recovered to compensate for all detriment proximately resulting therefrom, including economic loss as well as emotional distress resulting from the conduct or from the economic losses caused by the conduct, and, in a proper case, punitive damages.

Although it might be possible to rest our decision solely upon the first holding, we make the latter holding because we believe that it squares with the economic, social and legal realities of the problem presented. . . . The tort of intentional infliction of emotional distress is designed to redress primarily invasions of the personal interest in emotional tranquility, not economic losses. . . . A rule placing the emphasis where it belongs and permitting recovery of all proximately caused detriment in a single cause of action is more likely to engender public respect for and confidence in the judicial process than a rule which would require attorneys, litigants and judges to force square pegs into round holes. [Id. at 401, 89 Cal. Rptr. at 93.]

The court affirmed the judgment.

Then came Gruenberg v. Aetna Ins. Co., 9 Cal. 3d 566, 510 P.2d 1032, 108 Cal. Rptr. 480 (1973), where the Supreme Court of California at last had an opportunity to deal with a first-party bad faith problem, arising in the settlement of a fire insurance claim. *Gruenberg* is summarized within the opinion in the *Anderson* case, which follows:

ANDERSON v. CONTINENTAL INS. CO.

85 Wis. 2d 675, 271 N.W.2d 368 (1978)

HEFFERNAN, J. We conclude that, upon the pleading of appropriate facts, an insured may assert a cause of action in tort against an insurer for the bad faith refusal to honor a claim of the insured.

The appeal is from an order of the circuit court, which dismissed the plaintiffs' complaint on defendants' motion grounded on the assertion that, in Wisconsin, no cause of action arises on behalf of a named insured, even where, under the pleadings, it is conceded that the insurer acted in bad faith in its refusal to honor the claim of the insured. The plaintiffs are Jacob R. Anderson and his wife, owners of a home in the City of Milwaukee. Effective October 1, 1973, they obtained a home owner's insurance policy from the Continental Insurance Company, which, among other things, provided coverage for loss occasioned by fire, lightning, explosion, or smoke. While the policy was in effect, the plaintiffs, Anderson and wife, returned to their home on November 30, 1975, to discover that the walls, carpeting, furniture, draperies, and clothing in the house were covered with an oil and smoke residue, which allegedly was the result of a fire or an explosion in the furnace. On the following day, Continental Insurance Company was given notice of the damage.

It is alleged by the plaintiffs that the Underwriters Adjusting Company was delegated by Continental Insurance Company to handle the claim on behalf of Continental. Underwriters called in cleaners, who attempted to renovate and clean the premises and its contents. It nevertheless was necessary, according to the complaint, for the plaintiffs to repaint, clean, and restore the premises, and to replace carpets which shrank due to excessive cleaning ordered by Underwriters Adjusting Company. A pecuniary loss of $4,611.77 was alleged by the plaintiffs.

The Andersons attempted to negotiate with Underwriters as the agent for Continental Insurance Company, but all said negotiations were "to no avail."

It is alleged that Continental Insurance Company, Underwriters Adjusting Company, and Underwriters' manager in the area, Bernard A. Anderson, refused to negotiate in good faith concerning the amount of payment, and that each of them has submitted offers in settlement which were completely unrealistic and which had no relation to the damage incurred by the plaintiffs.

The plaintiff homeowners further recite that, when it became apparent that negotiations were not forthcoming or were to no avail, they retained an attorney to represent them in their claim against the insurance company. The complaint recites that counsel immediately filed a sworn proof of loss, which set forth in detail the inventory, the cost and the value, and the amount claimed in respect to the damages sustained. The proof of loss was filed within the time limit prescribed by the policy. On January 16, 1976, the proof of loss was transmitted to Underwriters Adjusting Company at Wauwatosa to the attention of B. A. Anderson. On January 23, 1976, the proof of loss was returned to plaintiffs' counsel by Underwriters' agent, B. A. Anderson, on behalf of Continental and Underwriters Adjusting Company. On January 28, 1976, the proof of loss was sent to Continental's home office in New York City. On February 3, 1976, plaintiffs' counsel was informed by Continental that the proof of loss had been referred to a Continental Vice President in charge of the Western Department of Continental. On February 19, 1976, plaintiffs' counsel made inquiry in respect to the disposition of the proof of loss; and on March 3, 1976, Roger S. Olson, Senior Vice President of Continental, informed plaintiffs' counsel that the matter had been turned over to Underwriters Adjusting Company and that B. A. Anderson, to whom counsel had sent the proof of loss on January 16, was authorized to handle any claims under the policy. After these peregrinations of the document, Continental again returned the proof of loss to plaintiffs' counsel.

The plaintiffs have alleged that the consistent refusal of Continental Insurance Company, Underwriters Adjusting Company, and B. A. Anderson to accept the sworn proof of loss and the refusal to negotiate in good faith were done with the knowledge and design of avoiding the obligations under the insurance contract. It is alleged that the conduct of each of the defendants was wilful, fraudulent, intentional, and in bad faith and for the purpose of discouraging, avoiding, or reducing the payment due under the terms of the policy. It is further alleged that each of the defendants acted maliciously and oppressively, with the design and intent to harass the plaintiffs maliciously and in an outrageous manner. Compensatory damages in the sum of $15,000 and punitive damages in the sum of $100,000 are demanded. . . .

The plaintiffs' complaint gives adequate notice of the circumstances of the claim and the nature of the claim asserted. From a pleading viewpoint, the complaint is sufficient. It alleges a tort by an insurer, because it is alleged the insurer and the other defendants acted in bad faith intentionally and maliciously for the purpose of harassing the plaintiffs to discourage them from asserting their rightful claim and to prevent them from collecting the amounts due under the insurance policy. This claim was entirely separate and apart from the claim for the breach of the insurance contract, which is not questioned at this stage of the proceedings.

The plaintiffs have therefore stated a claim upon which relief could be granted in some jurisdictions of the United States. It is conceded by the defendants that, under the tort rules adopted by the Supreme Court of California, particularly in Gruenberg v. Aetna Ins. Co., 9 Cal. 3d 566. 108 Cal. Rptr. 480, 510 P.2d 1032 (1973), a cause of action or a claim for relief would be stated. It is asserted by the defendants on this appeal that such cause of action does not exist, however, in Wisconsin. . . .

When it is recognized that recovery is sought for the tort and not for the breach of contract, the cliches which are relied upon by the defendants — e.g., "Punitive damages are not allowed for a mere breach of contract" — become irrelevant. The question whether punitive damages are permissible thus is not to be disposed of on grounds that what the plaintiffs assert is a breach-of-contract action, but rather must be considered under a discussion of whether the facts surrounding the tort of bad faith evidence such conduct that punitive or exemplary damages are permissible. This question will be discussed later in the opinion.

We emphasize at this juncture only that the tort of bad faith is not a tortious breach of contract. It is a separate intentional wrong, which results from a breach of duty imposed as a consequence of the relationship established by contract. This rationale had its origin in an opinion of this court. Hilker v. Western Automobile Ins. Co., 204 Wis. 1, 231 N.W. 257, 235 N.W. 413 (1930, 1931). . . .

The rationale which recognizes an ancillary duty on an insurance company to exercise good faith in the settlement of third-party claims is equally applicable and of equal importance when the insured seeks payment of legitimate damages from his own insurance company. That such a duty arises out of the relationship between the contracting parties themselves cannot be doubted. As black letter law, Restatement, Law of Contracts 2d, sec. 231 (Tentative Drafts Nos. 1-7. Rev. and Edited, 1973), provides: "Every contract imposes upon each party a duty of good faith and fair dealing in its performance and its enforcement."

Where, as in *Hilker* or in the later case of Alt v. American Family Mut. Ins. Co., 71 Wis. 2d 340, 237 N.W.2d 706 (1976), the insurance company which is charged with settling a claim of a third party against its insured acts in bad faith, its breach of a "fiduciary duty" is rather clear. Yet a similar responsibility of fair dealing toward the named insured is equally required when a claim is that of the insured. As the California court in *Gruenberg,* supra at 575, stated:

> It is manifest that a common legal principle underlies all of the foregoing decisions; namely, that in every insurance contract there is an implied covenant of good faith and fair dealing. The duty to so act is imminent (*sic*) in the contract whether the company is attending to the claims of third persons against the insured or the claims of the insured itself. Accordingly, when the insurer unreasonably and in bad faith withholds payment of the claim of its insured, it is subject to liability in tort.

The leading case which recognizes a cause of action in tort against an insurer for the breach of its duty of good faith in dealing with its insured is *Gruenberg,* supra. That case reached the California Supreme Court on appeal from an order dismissing the plaintiff's complaint following defendant's assertion on demurrer that such cause of action did not exist. In procedural aspects, therefore, *Gruenberg* is similar to the appeal before this court. Gruenberg lost his restaurant in a fire. He alleged that a claims adjuster for his insurer falsely told a state arson investigator that Gruenberg was over-insured. Felony arson charges were then filed against Gruenberg. Because the criminal charges were pending, Gruenberg, on the advice of his counsel, refused to make a statement to the insurer concerning the fire. Because of this refusal, the insurance company refused coverage and refused to accept a later offered statement of Gruenberg submitted after the arson charges were dismissed.

While the facts in *Gruenberg* are more aggravated than those alleged in the instant case, they are similar in that each evinces purposeful conduct by the insurance company designed to evade payment of the claim. *Gruenberg* is of special significance to the law of this jurisdiction, because its theory of a tort of bad faith is traceable to the Wisconsin case of Hilker v. Western Automobile Ins. Co. It was upon the rationale of *Hilker* that the California court concluded that insurers owe their own insureds a duty of good faith in the settlement of first-party claims. We accept the *Gruenberg* rationale to be applicable to first-party claims which may be asserted in Wisconsin against insurance companies.* . . .

The law which obliges the insurance company to pay proved and itemized fire and smoke damages to the Andersons is unquestioned. Under no view of the applicable law is that obligation "fairly debatable."

Whether a claim is "fairly debatable" also implicates the question whether the facts necessary to evaluate the claim are properly investigated and developed or recklessly ignored and disregarded.

To show a claim for bad faith, a plaintiff must show the absence of a reasonable basis for denying benefits of the policy and the defendant's knowledge or reckless disregard of the lack of a reasonable basis for denying the claim. It is apparent, then, that the tort of bad faith is an intentional one. "Bad faith" by definition cannot be unintentional. "Bad faith" is defined as "Deceit; duplicity; insincerity." American Heritage Dictionary of the English Language (1969), p. 471. The same dictionary defines "deceit" as a "stratagem; trick; wile" (p. 342), and duplicity as "Deliberate deceptiveness in behavior or speech." (p. 405). . . .

It is appropriate, in applying the test, to determine whether a claim was properly investigated and whether the results of the investigation were subjected to a reasonable evaluation and review. In the instant case, insofar as the complaint alleges, the insurer and the other defendants refused even to consider the nature and extent of the plaintiffs' damages, and specifically rejected and spurned the opportunity to evaluate and consider the submitted proof of loss. The pleading of the plaintiffs was sufficient in this respect. . . .

Under these tests of the torts of bad faith, an insurance company, however, may challenge claims which are fairly debatable and will be found liable only where it has intentionally denied (or failed to process or pay) a claim without a reasonable basis.

We are satisfied that the application of the test formulated above, which recognizes the intentional nature of the tort of bad faith and puts the test upon an objective basis, will minimize the fears expressed by the defendant insurance company that to permit claims for bad faith will result in extortionate lawsuits. Such result cannot follow when an insurance company in the exercise of ordinary care makes an investigation of the facts and law and concludes on a reasonable basis that the claim is at least debatable. . . .

It is apparent, however, that another aspect of the *in terrorem* nature of an action for bad faith arises because it is an intentional tort. Intentional torts may in some circumstances result in not only compensatory damages, but also punitive damages and damages for emotional injury. . . .

Gruenberg does not explicitly mention *Hilker* and does not seem to be traceable to it, unless possibly through *Crisci* and *Comunale*. — ED.]

In the absence of pleading and proof of the intentional infliction of emotional distress, however, the tort of bad faith falls within the second category described above, where substantial other damages in addition to the emotional distress are required if there is to be recovery for damages resulting from the infliction of emotional distress. In the bad faith cause of action against an insurance company, we therefore conclude that to recover for emotional distress in the absence of pleading and proof that there was an intentional infliction of emotional distress, the plaintiff must plead and prove substantial damages aside and apart from the emotional distress itself and the damages occasioned by the simple breach of contract. . . .

We do not conclude, however, that the proof of a bad faith cause of action necessarily make punitive damages appropriate. Punitive damages are awarded to punish a wrongdoer and to serve as a deterrent. Mid-Continent Refrigerator Co. v. Straka, 47 Wis. 2d 746, 178 739, N.W.2d 28 (1970). . . . For punitive damages to be awarded, a defendant must not only intentionally have breached his duty of good faith, but in addition must have been guilty of oppression, fraud, or malice in the special sense defined by *Mid-Continent v. Straka.* See also, Silberg v. California Life Ins. Co., supra, at 462.

By the Court. — Order reversed and cause remanded for trial.

Notes and Questions

1. California has been the leading state in the development of first-party bad faith claims. Currently an issue in California law is whether, and if so, how far to extend the bad faith tort doctrine, including punitive damages, to noninsurance commercial contracts. For a recent case extending the doctrine into the commercial banking area, see Commercial Cotton Co. v. United California Bank, 163 Cal. App. 3d 511, 209 Cal. Rptr. 551 (1985). See Comment, Commercial Cotton Co. v. United California Bank: Newest Extension of Bad Faith Litigation into Commercial Law, 16 Sw. U.L. Rev. 645 (1986). The same problem has appeared in other states, too.

There seems to be some judicial hesitation to extend the doctrine, even in California. One reason for the special treatment of insurance contracts has been said to be the unequal bargaining position of the parties to insurance contracts, yet in what sense can that be asserted when the insured is a Fortune 500 company and the insurer is much smaller? If disparity in size, insurance sophistication, or bargaining power should be dispositive, should there then be separate rules for insurance contracts when the insured is a Fortune 500 corporation and when it is an independent corner drugstore? Or should the result be fact-specific? Does it make any difference whether the insured has a professional risk or insurance manager, or relies on a major broker? Or whether the insured is in a business requiring negotiated (or "manuscript") policies? Whether the insured is itself in the financial business, as a large (or medium-sized or small) bank or stockbroker? Whether the insurance bought is central to its business, rather than peripheral, such as products liability for a manufacturer? Review McNeilab, Inc. v. North River Ins. Co., 645 F. Supp. 525 (D.N.J. 1986), *aff'd without opinion,* 831 F.2d 287 (1987) (the Tylenol case) in Chapter 1.

2. A recent case confirmed California's posture that the insurer is in bad faith when it fails to investigate further after being informed of new witnesses. Frommoethelydo v. Fire Ins. Exch., 42 Cal. 2d 208, 721 P.2d 41, 228 Cal. Rptr. 160 (1986).

3. Alabama has joined the ranks of states that recognize a first-party bad faith cause of action. See Aetna Life Ins. Co. v. Lavoie, 470 So. 2d 1060 (Ala. 1984). *Lavoie* has its own interesting history. A judgment for the plaintiff in the amount of $1,650 on the contract claim and $3.5 million in punitive damages was affirmed by the Alabama Supreme Court, then vacated and remanded by the United States Supreme Court for failure of one of the Alabama Supreme Court justices to recuse himself. Id, 475 U.S. 813 (1986). On remand, the Alabama Supreme Court ordered remittitur of $3 million and affirmed the court below conditionally. Id, 505 So. 2d 1050 (Ala. 1987). A number of separate opinions indicate some uncertainty about the exact state of the law in Alabama.

4. Is the claim for bad faith damages an asset that can be garnished? Stevenson v. Samkow, 142 Ill. App. 3d 293, 491 N.E.2d 1318, 96 Ill. Dec. 850 (1986) said the insurer held no assets the plaintiff could reach in a garnishment proceeding. Would the same reason apply to an assignment of the insured's right against the insurer?

5. In discussing Arkansas cases, one clear distinction between third party and first party cases was isolated, at least for that state. Casey, Bad Faith in First Party Insurance Contracts — What's Next?, 8 U. Ark. Little Rock L.J. 237, 245-246 (1985-1986). Professor Casey points out that for third party actions negligence is enough, but that for first party cases there must be *affirmative* misconduct. Is that a distinction you would be willing to make if no precedent binds you?

LAWTON v. GREAT SOUTHWEST FIRE INS. CO.

118 N.H. 607, 392 A.2d 576 (1978)

BROCK, Justice.

In this action the plaintiff seeks damages against his insurance company for its alleged failure to make payment of a fire loss pursuant to a fire insurance policy between the plaintiff and the defendant. After hearing, the trial court granted the defendant's motion to dismiss counts 1 and 2 of the plaintiff's declaration, which alleged an intentional failure and a negligent failure to make payment pursuant to the policy, and portions of count 3, which sought consequential damages in excess of the policy limits. Plaintiff's exceptions to these rulings were reserved and transferred by Flynn, J.

The plaintiff is the owner of a commercial building, located in Manchester, that was substantially damaged by fire on July 31, 1975. At the time, a portion of the premises was insured against fire by the defendant. The policy provided coverage up to $250,000 and also contained a loss of rentals endorsement with a limit of $55,000. Over the course of three-and-a-half months following the fire, the plaintiff and the defendant engaged in various negotiations in an effort to determine and settle the loss, which need not be further detailed here other than to note that no agreement concerning the extent of loss was ever reached and that the plaintiff's claim was never settled.

On November 19, 1975, the plaintiff brought the current action against the insurance company. In count 1 of this declaration, plaintiff alleges that the defendant "willfully, intentionally or recklessly and wantonly" failed to make payment to him pursuant to the policy "in an effort to compel and coerce [him] to compromise a claim against the defendant for an amount far less than for value, and to accept far less than full performance of defendant's contractual obligations. . . ." Count 2 alleges negligent failure to make payment pursuant to the policy. Count 3 is a plea in assumpsit alleging that the defendant failed to perform its obligation under the policy "to make fair, prompt and equitable payment. . . ." In all three counts plaintiff seeks recovery for damages which he alleges resulted from the defendant's failure to effectuate a prompt and equitable settlement, "including but not limited to, irreparable damage to the plaintiff's business and credit reputation, pain, suffering and mental anguish, and severe emotional distress; loss of use of his property, loss of business opportunity, additional damage to the property occasioned by the defendant's delay, and other financial damages. . . ." all in the amount of $500,000. The trial court granted the defendant's motion to dismiss counts 1 and 2, on the ground that there is no recovery "*ex delicto* for the wrongful or wilful or negligent refusal of an insurer to settle a first party insurance claim. . . .", and dismissed count 3 to the extent that it sought damages in excess of the insurance policy limits, on the ground that the damages available to the insured are limited to the contractual amount. For the reasons hereinafter stated, we affirm the court's ruling dismissing counts 1 and 2 of the plaintiff's declaration, and reverse its ruling relating to count 3. . . .

We first consider count 3 of the plaintiff's declaration, which alleges a breach of contract. The defendant advances three arguments in support of the court's ruling limiting the damages recoverable by the plaintiff to the policy limits: First, an insurance contract is merely an agreement to pay money, and that for breach of such an agreement the damages are limited to the money due, with interest; second, the contract itself restricts the insurer's liability to the policy limits; and third, the consequential damages plaintiff alleges to have suffered in his declaration could not have been foreseen at the time the parties executed the policy, and that therefore the defendant is not chargeable therewith.

It is true that generally the damages available for breach of a contractual obligation to pay money are the amount due, with interest. Smith v. Wetherell, 89 N.H. 106, 108, 193 A. 216, 218 (1937), *aff'd on rehearing*, 89 N.H. 106, 194 A. 129 (1937); Richards v. Whittle, 16 N.H. 259, 260 (1844). This rule has been applied to restrict damages for breach of an insurance contract to the contract amount, plus interest. 16 J. Appleman, Insurance Law and Practice §8881, at 634 (1968) (and cases cited). The rule rests on the theory that money is always available in the market at the lawful rate of interest, and on the desirability of having a measure of damages of easy and certain application. 11 S. Williston, Contracts §1410, at 606 (3d ed. 1968). We find these reasons unconvincing, however. First, money is not always available in the market at the lawful rate of interest. "Aside from the fact that the commercial rate of interest might be double the legal rate, it is highly unlikely that a claimant who has recently suffered economic disaster would be able to obtain a loan at all." Note, The Availability of Excess Damages for Wrongful Refusal to Honor First Party Insurance Claims — An Emerging Trend, 45 Fordham L. Rev. 164, 169 (1976) (footnotes omitted). Second, the desirability of simplicity in determining the extent of damages is insufficient to justify the denial of damages that are capable of proof and otherwise compensable. See Note, id.; Reichert v. Gen. Ins. Co. of America, Cal., 59 Cal. Rptr. 724, 730, 428 P.2d 860, 866 (1967), *vacated on other grounds,* 68 Cal. 2d 822, 69 Cal. Rptr. 321, 442 P.2d 377 (1968).

Defendant's argument that the insurance contract itself restricts the damages that are recoverable for breach of the contract to the policy limits is also unpersuasive. The policy limits restrict the amount the insurer may have to pay in the performance of the contract, not the damages that are recoverable for its breach. See, e.g., Home Indem. Co. v. Bush, 20 Ariz. App. 355, 513 P.2d 145 (1973); Asher v. Reliance Ins. Co., 308 F. Supp. 847, 851-52 (D.C. Cal. 1970); Reichert v. Gen. Ins. Co. of America, supra 59 Cal. Rptr. at 729, 428 P.2d at 865. The subject insurance contract limits the insurer's liability to $250,000 for damages that result from the casualties insured against, not its liability for damages resulting from its own breach of contract.

Defendant's third argument correctly proceeds on the theory that the damages recoverable for breach of a contract are limited to the damages that "the defendant had reason to foresee as a probable result of its breach when the contract was made." Emery v. Caledonia Sand & Gravel Co., 117 N.H. 441, 446, 374 A.2d 929, 932 (1977). However, we do not think that the financial injuries that the plaintiff alleges he suffered as a result of the defendant's failure or delay in payment are never foreseeable as a matter of law. Insurance is often obtained because the insured is not in a position to personally bear the financial loss occasioned by a casualty, and serious financial injuries may often result from an insurer's refusal or delay in payment.

> Where the owner of a heavily mortgaged motel or other business property suffers a substantial fire loss, the owner may be placed in financial distress, may be unable to meet his mortgage payments and may be in jeopardy of losing his property and becoming bankrupt. A major, if not the main, reason why a businessman purchases fire insurance is to guard against such eventualities if his property is damaged by fire. [Reichert v. Gen. Ins. Co. of America, Cal., 59 Cal. Rptr. 724, 428 P.2d 860, 864 (1967), *vacated on other grounds*, 68 Cal. 2d 822, 69 Cal. Rptr. 321, 442 P.2d 377 (1968); see Eckenrode v. Life of America Ins. Co., 470 F.2d 1, 5 (7th Cir. 1972).]

To limit the insurer's liability to the policy limits plus interest as a matter of law would unnecessarily encourage insurers to delay settlement in an attempt to coerce a financially pressured claimant into accepting an unfair settlement, because its only liability would be to pay its original obligation and interest. See Note, The Availability of Excess Damages For Wrongful Refusal to Honor First Party Insurance Claims — An Emerging Trend, 45 Fordham L. Rev. 164 (1976); 16 J. Appleman, Insurance Law and Practice §8881 at 633 (1968); Lambert, Commercial Litigation, 35 Am. Trial Lawyers Assn. L.J. 164, 225-26 (1974). In a given case the defendant may in fact have reason to know that its failure or delay in payment will cause the insured severe financial injuries. Whether the defendant had knowledge of the facts and reason to foresee the injury will normally be a question of fact for the jury. See Emery v. Caledonia Sand & Gravel, supra at 406, 374 A.2d at 932; Johnson v. Waisman Bros., 93 N.H. 133, 135, 36 A.2d 634, 636 (1944); 5 A. Corbin, Contracts §1011 (1964).

The insured must, of course, prove that the insurer's failure or delay in payment was a breach of contract. Not every delay or refusal to settle or pay a claim under the policy will constitute a breach of the contract. . . .

Where the defendant's failure to make prompt payment under the policy is to coerce the insured into accepting less than full performance of the insurer's contractual obligations, as is alleged here, there is a breach of this covenant. Whether the defendant's delay was in fact in bad faith, whether the damages alleged to have resulted from the delay were in fact foreseeable, and whether these damages could have been avoided with reasonable efforts by the insured are questions for the jury. We hold that the trial court erred in ruling as a matter of law that the damages available to the insured for a breach of the insurance contract are limited to the policy amounts.

We next consider the plaintiff's counts sounding in tort.

Counts 1 and 2 seek to plead a tort claim for what is essentially a breach of contract. We are not unmindful of an emerging trend in other jurisdictions to hold insurers liable in tort for the wrongful refusal or delay to make payments due under an insurance contract. See 16 J. Appleman, Insurance Law and Practice §8881 (Supp. 1977) (and cases cited therein.) However, we are not persuaded by the reasoning of these cases. . . .

The cases from other jurisdictions holding an insurer liable in tort in these circumstances proceed on the theory that the insurer has a special relationship to the insured which warrants the imposition of an independent legal duty to deal fairly with the insured. See Mustachio v. Ohio Farmers Ins. Co., 44 Cal. App. 3d 358, 118 Cal. Rptr. 581 (1975); Fletcher v. Western Natl. Life Ins. Co., 10 Cal. App. 3d 376, 89 Cal. Rptr. 78 (1970). They find precedent for such a duty in the cases holding an insurer to a duty of reasonable care in the settlement of third-party liability claims and plaintiff would have us adopt their reasoning by pointing to the cases from our own jurisdiction recognizing that the insurer has a duty of reasonable care in the settlement of a third-party liability claim. Dumas v. State Farm Mut. Auto Ins. Co., 111 N.H. 43, 274 A.2d 781 (1971); Dumas v. Hartford Accident and Indem. Co., 92 N.H. 140, 26 A.2d 361 (1942); Foster v. Calderwood, 118 N.H. 508, 389 A.2d 1388 (1978). However, the policies that warranted recognition of such a duty to the insured in the third-party liability claim are inapplicable in the case of the first-party claim. "The dilemma presented by the absolute control of trial and settlement vested in the insurer by the insurance contract and the conflicting interests of the insurer and insured" in the third-party claim requires that the insurer recognize the conflict and give due regard to the interests of the insured. Dumas v. State Mut. Auto Ins. Co., supra 111 N.H. at 46, 274 A.2d at 783. This dilemma is lacking in the first-party claim. The insurer is not in a position to expose the insured to a judgment in excess of the policy limits through its unreasonable refusal to settle a case, nor is it in a position to otherwise injure the insured by virtue of its exclusive control over the defense of the case. We therefore find no basis for extending the duty recognized in those cases to the first-party claim. See Baxter v. Royal Indem. Co., 285 So. 2d 652 (Fla. App. 1973), *cert. denied,* 317 So. 2d 725 (Fla. 1975). We hold that allegations of an insurer's wrongful refusal or delay to settle a first-party claim do not state a cause of action in tort. . . .

In so holding we take cognizance of the fact that the legislature has established mechanisms designed to deal with insurer malfeasance in this area, which, in our opinion, vitiates the need for recognition of a new cause of action in tort. RSA 407:22 requires that every fire insurance policy issued in this State include a provision entitling each party, upon written demand, to select disinterested appraisers to appraise the loss, whose determinations shall be binding. See Salganik v. U.S. Fire Ins. Co., 80 N.H. 450, 118 A. 815, (1922). The availability of this procedure "reduc[es] the hazards of the claim materializing into one for extra-contract damages." Kornblum, The Defense of the First Party Extra-Contract Case: Strategy in Negotiations and Discovery, 12 Forum 721, 730 (1977). In addition, RSA 417:4 XII declare it to be an unfair trade practice, if committed without just cause and performed with such frequency as to indicate a general practice, of refusing to attempt to effectuate prompt and equitable settlements where liability has become reasonably clear, or of unreasonably compelling claimants to institute litigation to recover amounts due under insurance policies. See also N.H. Official Regulations and Bulletins — Insurance Department, Reg. No. 10. Penalties are prescribed to protect the consumer from these practices. RSA 417:10, :13, :19 (Supp. 1977). In addition, the insured has his remedies in equity for a settlement procured through fraud or as a result of mutual mistake, see Maltais v. Natl. Grange Mut. Ins. Co., 118 N.H. 318, 386 A.2d 1264 (1978); 6 J. Appleman, supra §3980 (1972); or may be entitled to attorney fees if the insurer acted in bad faith in promoting unnecessary litigation. Jeannont v. N.H. Pers. Commn., 118 N.H. (decided this day); Harkeem v. Adams, 117 N.H. 687, 377 A.2d 617 (1977). The availability of these remedies, while insufficient in our opinion to restrict plaintiff's recovery for breach of the insurance contract to the policy limits as a matter of law, militates against recognition at this time of an independent action in tort for an insurer's wrongful refusal or delay to settle a first-party insurance claim. See RSA 417:5-a (Supp. 1971). We therefore hold that the trial court on the pleadings before it did not err in dismissing counts 1 and 2 of the plaintiff's declaration. . . .

Exceptions sustained in part and overruled in part; remanded.

Notes and Questions

1. Iowa seems not to have adopted the tort of bad faith for first-party claims yet. See Northwestern Natl. Ins. Co. v. Pope, 791 F.2d 649 (8th Cir. 1986), applying Iowa law and discussing Iowa cases, in particular Pirkl v. Northwestern Mut. Ins. Assn., 348 N.W.2d 633 (Iowa 1984). *Pirkl* does not categorically reject the bad faith tort in

first-party cases for all circumstances, but by suggesting that punitive damages are possible in some breach of contract cases may have made it unnecessary to create the tort to give the same relief.

2. The Court of Special Appeals of Maryland rejected a first-party bad faith claim in Johnson v. Federal Kemper Ins. Co., 74 Md. App. 243, 536 A.2d 1211 (1988). Mississippi applies the doctrine in a life insurance context. Mutual Life Ins. Co. v. Estate of Wesson, 517 So. 2d 521 (Miss. 1987).

3. In Federal Kemper Ins. Co. v. Hornback, 711 S.W.2d 844 (1986), the Supreme Court of Kentucky declined to consider an insurer a fiduciary to its insured and overruled an earlier intermediate appellate court that created a first-party bad faith tort in a different case. Comment, First-Party Bad Faith in Kentucky: What Remains After Federal Kemper Insurance Co. v. Hornback?, 75 Ky. L.J. 939 (1986), criticizes *Hornback*. In December 1989, the Kentucky Supreme Court reconsidered the matter and, over a dissent urging the need for stability in the law, held that there could be first party recovery for bad faith, including consequential and punitive damages. Curry v. Fireman's Fund Ins. Co., 784 S.W.2d 176 (Ky. 1989). A dissenting judge in *Hornback* had expressed the view that Kentucky stood alone in its announced position. Clearly it did not: New Hampshire (*Lawton*), Maryland (*Johnson*), and Iowa (*Pirkl*) seem not to have the doctrine. Many other states have not weighed in as yet; some (perhaps many) of those may opt against the first-party bad faith doctrine.

4. Thornton, Extracontractual and Punitive Damage Liability of Insurers, Primary and Reinsurance Coverages, 13 Forum 754 (1978) surveys the development of bad faith claims as of that date.

4. The Creation of a Cause of Action by Statute

The existence of a statutory remedy for unfair claims settlement practices was one of the reasons New Hampshire (in *Lawton*) felt it unnecessary to create a tort in first-party insurance cases. One of the cited New Hampshire statutes developed in the following way.

In 1947 the National Association of Insurance Commissioners (NAIC) developed a Model Act Relating to Unfair Methods of Competition and Unfair and Deceptive Acts and Practices in the Business of Insurance, to comply with the McCarran Act requirement that there be state regulation of insurance to escape federal antitrust laws. 15 U.S.C. §1012(b) (1945). See discussion in Chapter 10. The Model Act was based, in part, on the Federal Trade Commission Act and has been adopted (with some changes) by substantially all states.

No section in the original Model Act dealt with claims settlement practices, but one was added in the 1970s as an outgrowth of the consumerist movement. Most of the statute is directed to the protection of insureds, but a few sections have been read with generous poetic license as intended also to protect third-party claimants. The administrative enforcement of the statute has so far been erratic but has been directed at *patterns* of claims practices, not individual instances. That was the intention of the drafters. Nevertheless, the statute was a convenient peg on which to hang an argument for a new private cause of action. California was the first to exercise the necessary poetic license in reading the statute. The case in which it did so, *Royal Globe,* has been both lauded and excoriated, has been followed elsewhere by a few cases, but has subsequently been overruled in California.

The theory that prevailed in *Royal Globe* had already been unsuccessfully tried out in other jurisdictions. See Farris v. United States Fidelity & Guar. Co., 284 Or. 453, 587 P.2d 1015 (1978). Yet *Farris* is notable as a case where the legendary "smoking gun" was actually found. In internal correspondence, the insurer's claims manager wrote at the time of rejecting the claim (despite being aware that there *was* coverage), "[Let's] bluff it out we can always buy out at a later date." *Farris* is a good case for reviewing the theories and posture of the law on the eve of *Royal Globe.*

ROYAL GLOBE INS. CO. v. SUPERIOR CT. OF BUTTE COUNTY

23 Cal. 3d 880, 592 P.2d 329, 153 Cal. Rptr. 842 (1979)

Subdivision (h) of section 790.03 of the Insurance Code, a provision of the Unfair Practices Act (Ins. Code. §790 et seq., hereinafter called the act) provides that insurers are prohibited from engaging in certain unfair claims settlement practices set forth in the section.[1] The sole issue in this proceeding is whether an individual who is injured by

1. All references will be to the Insurance Code, unless otherwise stated.

Section 790.03 provides in part: "The following are hereby defined as unfair methods of competition and unfair and deceptive acts or practices in the business of insurance. . . .

(h) Knowingly committing or performing with such frequency as to indicate a general business practice any of the following unfair claims settlement practices:

(1) Misrepresenting to claimants pertinent facts of insurance policy provisions relating to any coverages at issue.

(2) Failing to acknowledge and act reasonably promptly upon communications with respect to claims arising under insurance policies.

(3) Failing to adopt and implement reasonable standards for the prompt investigation and processing of claims arising under insurance policies.

the alleged negligence of an insured may sue the negligent party's insurer for violation of the subdivision.

Ruth M. Keoppel (plaintiff) filed an action for personal injuries incurred as a result of a fall when she slipped at a food market. She joined as defendants Royal Globe Insurance Company (defendant), which had issued a policy of liability insurance to the market, and Robert E. Hunt Company (Hunt), an independent adjusting company which provided adjustment services to Royal Globe and was alleged to be its agent. According to the complaint, defendant violated subdivision (h)(5) of the act in that it had refused "to attempt in good faith to effectuate a prompt, fair, and equitable settlement" of plaintiff's claim although "liability [had] become reasonably clear," and Hunt had advised plaintiff not to obtain the services of an attorney, in violation of subdivision (h)(14). Plaintiff sought damages for physical and emotional distress, as well as punitive damages.

------

(4) Failing to affirm or deny coverage of claims within a reasonable time after proof of loss requirements have been completed and submitted by the insured.

(5) Not attempting in good faith to effectuate prompt, fair, and equitable settlements of claims in which liability has become reasonably clear.

(6) Compelling insureds to institute litigation to recover amounts due under an insurance policy by offering substantially less than the amounts ultimately recovered in actions brought by such insureds, when such insureds have made claims for amounts reasonably similar to the amounts ultimately recovered.

(7) Attempting to settle a claim by an insured for less than the amount to which a reasonable man would have believed he was entitled by reference to written or printed advertising material accompanying or made part of an application.

(8) Attempting to settle claims on the basis of an application which was altered without notice to or knowledge or consent of, the insured, his representative, agent, or broker.

(9) Failing, after payment of a claim, to inform insureds or beneficiaries, upon request by them, of the coverage under which payment has been made.

(10) Making known to insureds or claimants a practice of the insurer of appealing from arbitration awards in favor of insureds or claimants for the purpose of compelling them to accept settlements or compromises less than the amount awarded in arbitration.

(11) Delaying the investigation or payment of claims by requiring an insured, claimant, or the physician of either, to submit a preliminary claim report, and then requiring the subsequent submission of formal proof of loss forms, both of which submissions contain substantially the same information.

(12) Failing to settle claims promptly, where liability has become apparent, under one portion of the insurance policy coverage in order to influence settlements under other portions of the insurance policy coverage.

(13) Failing to provide promptly a reasonable explanation of the basis relied on in the insurance policy, in relation to the facts or applicable law, for the denial of a claim or for the offer of a compromise settlement.

(14) Directly advising a claimant not to obtain the services of an attorney.

(15) Misleading a claimant as to the applicable statute of limitations.

Defendant demurred to the complaint and filed a motion for judgment on the pleadings on the grounds that the California Insurance Commissioner (commissioner) has the exclusive power to enforce subdivision (h), that a third party claimant has no standing to bring an action under the subdivision because it was intended by the Legislature only to protect the interests of the insured, and that plaintiff may not sue both the insured and the insurer in the same lawsuit. The trial court overruled the demurrer and denied the motion. Defendant seeks a writ of mandate, directing the trial court to vacate its orders.

We hold that a third party claimant may sue an insurer for violating subdivisions (h)(5) and (h)(14), but that the third party's suit may not be brought until the action between the injured party and the insured is concluded.

The purpose of the act is "to regulate trade practices in the business of insurance . . . by defining . . . such practices in this State which constitute unfair methods of competition or unfair or deceptive acts or practices and by prohibiting the trade practices so defined or determined." (§790.) Section 790.02 prohibits any person from engaging in any trade practice defined in section 790.03 as "an unfair or deceptive act or practice in the business of insurance." The commissioner is empowered to investigate the affairs of insurers (§790.04), and if he has reason to believe that an insurer is engaged in an unfair or deceptive act or practice defined in section 790.03, he shall, after notice and hearing, issue a cease and desist order. (§790.05.) A penalty of $50 may be imposed for violation of such an order, or $500 for a wilful violation, and subsequent violations may result in suspension or revocation of an insurer's license. (§790.07.)

The act was adopted in 1959, and was patterned after the National Association of Insurance Commissioners' model legislation. In 1959, neither the model bill nor the California act contained a provision prohibiting unfair claims settlement practices, but in 1972, after the model legislation was amended to include such prohibitions, California enacted Assembly Bill No. 459, adding subdivision (h), patterned after the model act. There were, however, some differences between the California act and the model legislation, to which we will refer infra.

In considering the issues before us, we determine, first, whether a private litigant may bring an action to impose civil liability for violation of section 790.03 or whether the commissioner has the sole authority to enforce the terms of the section by the issuance of cease and desist orders to prevent future misconduct.

In making this determination, we turn to the language of the act. Section 790.09 provides that a cease and desist order issued by the commissioner under the provisions of the act shall not absolve an insurer from "*civil liability* or criminal penalty *under the laws of this*

State arising out of the methods, acts or practices found unfair or deceptive." (Italics added.) This provision appears to afford to private litigants a cause of action against insurers which commit the unfair acts or practices defined in subdivision (h). . . .

Defendant insists that section 790.09 does not provide affirmative authority for the filing of a civil suit based on alleged violations of the act, and contends that the section was merely intended to allow a party to bring a civil action on the basis of authority derived from other provisions of law. It should be noted in this connection that, while the model act states that a person shall not be absolved of liability under any "other" state laws, the California act in section 790.09 eliminates the word "other" and provides that an insurer shall not be absolved from "civil liability . . . under the laws of this State" arising out of the insurer's unfair acts. . . .

[Defendants argued, *inter alia* (1) that the legislative history of the act showed no intention to create a private cause of action, putting in evidence to that effect a letter from the insurance commissioner who sponsored the legislation, (2) that the act was analogous to the Federal Trade Commission Act, which created no private cause of action, and (3) that the insurer's duty runs only to the insured and therefore that a third party claimant has no standing even if there is a private right of action.]

In the present case, plaintiff does not seek to rely upon the violation of the insurer's duty to its insured to settle plaintiff's claim. Rather, she relies upon the insurer's duty owed to her as a claimant under subdivisions (h)(5) and (h)(14) of section 790.03, a duty created by those statutory provisions and owed directly to plaintiff as a claimant.

Another contention of defendant is that a third party claimant may not base an action against an insurer upon a single instance of unfair conduct specified by subdivision (h), but that improper conduct is actionable only if it is committed with such frequency as to indicate a general business practice.

The language of the subdivision is ambiguous in this respect. It prohibits "Knowingly committing or performing with such frequency as to indicate a general business practice" any of the unfair claims settlement practices set forth. It is unclear whether the words "with such frequency as to indicate a general business practice" were intended to modify both the terms "Knowingly committing" and "performing."[9] Amicus curiae, the California Trial Lawyers Association, suggest that the language quoted provides for two alternative methods by which the prohibited acts may be shown, i.e., a violation of the subdivision occurs if the prohibited acts are knowingly committed on

9. The model does not contain the word "knowingly."

one occasion or, if knowledge cannot be established, then it will suffice if the acts were performed with such frequency as to indicate a general business practice. This interpretation of the meaning of the section has been adopted by a commentator in reviewing certain amendments to subdivision (h) in 1975. (Review of Selected 1975 California Legislation (1976) 7 Pacific L.J. 484.) Amicus curiae representing State Farm Mutual Automobile Insurance Company claims, on the other hand, that the reference to unfair "practices" in the phrase in question implies repeated misconduct, and that, if the provision had been intended to render actionable a single unfair act, correct punctuation would call for placing commas around the phrase, "or performing with such frequency as to indicate a general business practice."

The ambiguity in the introductory language is not dispelled by the listing of the matters which constituted unfair conduct, for some of these are referred to in the singular and others in the plural. For example, subdivision (h)(1) prohibits misrepresenting to claimants "insurance policy provisions relating to . . . coverages," while subdivision (h)(15) proscribes misleading "a claimant as to the applicable statute of limitations."

It seems clear to us that this issue is not independent of the matters we have discussed above. If, as we conclude, the act affords a private party, including a third party claimant, a right to sue an insurer for violating subdivision (h), it is inconceivable that the Legislature intended that such a litigant would be required to show that the insurer committed the acts prohibited by that provision "with such frequency as to indicate a general business practice." There would be no rational reason why an insured or a third party claimant injured by an insurer's unfair conduct, knowingly performed, should be required to demonstrate that the insurer had frequently been guilty of the same type of misconduct involving other victims in the past. The department's policy is to require repeated misconduct as the basis for the enforcement of subdivision (h); while repetition of prohibited acts is relevant to the duty of the insurance commissioner to issue a cease and desist order, to an aggrieved private litigant who can demonstrate that the insurer acted deliberately, the frequency of the insurer's misconduct and its application to others is irrelevant. Although the language of the statute is not clear, if the premise is accepted that a private party may bring an action for an insurer's violation of subdivision (h) under the rationale of *Greenberg* and *Shernoff,* then a single violation knowingly committed is a sufficient basis for such an action.

Finally, we agree with defendant that plaintiff may not sue both the insurer and the insured in the same lawsuit. Section 1155 of the Evidence Code provides that evidence of insurance is inadmissible to prove negligence or wrongdoing. The obvious purpose of the provision is to prevent the prejudicial use of evidence of liability insurance in an action against an insured. (See, e.g., Citti v. Bava (1928) 204 Cal. 136, 139 [266 P. 954]; Rising v. Veatch (1931) 117 Cal. App. 404, 406 [3 P.2d 1023].) A joint trial against the insured for negligence and against the insurer for violating its duties under subdivision (h) would obviously violate both the letter and spirit of the section.

Moreover, unless the trial against the insurer is postponed until the liability of the insured is first determined, the defense of the insured may be seriously hampered by discovery initiated by the injured claimant against the insurer. In addition, damages suffered by the injured party as a result of the insurer's violation of subdivisions (h)(5) and (h)(14) may best be determined after the conclusion of the action by the third party claimant against the insured. Thus, plaintiff's claim against defendant was brought prematurely and the trial court should have sustained defendant's demurrer and granted the motion for judgment on the pleadings on that ground.

Let a writ of mandate issue to direct the trial court to vacate its orders and to enter judgment for defendant.

Bird, C. J., Tobriner, J., and Newman, J., concurred.

[Richardson, J., did not think the statute created a new private remedy for insurer misconduct. For quite different reasons, therefore, he concurred in entering judgment for the defendant.]

Notes and Questions

1. Does the plaintiff in *Royal Globe* meet the threshold conditions stated in paragraph 1(h): "Knowingly committing or performing [the objectionable practice] with such frequency as to indicate a general business practice?" What interpretations will that language bear? Which is preferable?

2. What should be made of California's addition of "knowingly" to its version of the Model Act?

3. Should the omission of the word "other" in the clause saving existing causes of action make the difference the court says it does?

4. Some of the proscribed practices relate to insureds and some to claimants. Does that support the court's result?

5. How important is the limitation the court placed on the direct action (that it must await the conclusion of the underlying tort action)? Why should there be such a limitation if the cause of action against the insurer is based on the fact that the claim is one "in which liability has become reasonably clear?"

6. The court in Klaudt v. Flink, 202 Mont. 247, 658 P.2d 1065

(1983), not only agreed with *Royal Globe* that the third party had a cause of action, it went even farther, thinking it appropriate that the third party's action be joined with the action against the insured. But Fode v. Farmers Ins. Exch., 221 Mont. 282, 719 P.2d 414 (1986), modified *Klaudt* to require the underlying tort case to be determined first, as in *Royal Globe*. K-W Industries, Division of Associated Technologies, Ltd. v. National Surety Corp., 231 Mont. 461, 754 P.2d 502 (1988), applied *Klaudt* to suretyship, but did not need to address the procedural point made in *Fode*.

7. Kentucky created a third-party cause of action under its Unfair Claims Settlement Practices Act. State Farm Mut. Auto. Ins. Co. v. Reeder, 763 S.W.2d 116 (Ky. 1988). Jenkins v. J.C. Penney Casualty Ins. Co., 280 S.E.2d 252 (W. Va. 1981), did the same, employing the following four point test derived from Cort v. Ash, 422 U.S. 66 (1975), to determine whether a private cause of action exists based on a statute violation:

(1) the plaintiff must be a member of the class for whose benefit the statute was enacted;
(2) consideration must be given to legislative intent, express or implied, to determine whether a private cause of action was intended;
(3) an analysis must be made of whether a private cause of action is consistent with the underlying purposes of the legislative scheme; and
(4) the private cause of action must not intrude into an area delegated exclusively to the federal government.

8. In Moradi-Shalal v. Fireman's Fund Ins. Cos., 46 Cal. 3d 287, 758 P.2d 58, 250 Cal. Rptr. 116 (1988), the Supreme Court of California reconsidered and overruled *Royal Globe*. The case is particularly interesting for the court's careful consideration of the problems of overruling an established case. Several factors entered into the decision: (1) of 19 courts considering the question under comparable statutes, 17 declined to follow the California lead (a remarkable rejection rate), (2) overwhelming scholarly condemnation of the case (see the listed articles and notes, id. at 64), (3) a subsequent report on the subject by the National Association of Insurance Commissioners (NAIC), (4) subsequent legislative history, (5) adverse consequences of the decision on the world of litigation, and (6) analytical difficulties in defining the scope of *Royal Globe*. A single judge (Mosk, the author of the majority opinion in *Royal Globe*) dissented vigorously, almost indignantly. Comment, The Overruling of *Royal Globe*: A "Royal

Bonanza" for Insurance Companies, But What Happens Now?, 3 Pepperdine L. Rev. 763 (1969), criticizes *Moradi-Shalal.*

9. Among the cases holding that a statute corresponding to the one in *Royal Globe* does not create a third-party cause of action, see Julian v. New Hampshire Ins. Co., 694 F. Supp. 1530 (D. Wyo. 1988); Tank v. State Farm Fire & Casualty Co., 105 Wash. 2d 381, 715 P.2d 1133 (1986). But some cases have held that the statute does create a cause of action on behalf of the insured. See Crystal Bay General Improvement Dist. v. Aetna Casualty & Surety Co., 713 F. Supp. 1371 (D. Nev. 1989).

10. Fowler, Statutory Third-Party Unfair Practice Suits Following Settlement: The Impact of *Royal Globe*'s Conclusion Requirement, 22 Tort & Ins. L.J. 640 (1987), discusses some of the aftermath of *Royal Globe*; Theisen, Recent Developments in Private Rights of Action Under the Unfair Claims Settlement Practices Act, 23 Tort & Ins. L.J. 19 (1987), summarizes the developments prior to the California reversal of *Royal Globe.*

FLORIDA STATUTES §624.155

Fla. Stat. §624.155 (1986)

(1) Any person may bring a civil action against an insurer when such person is damaged:

(b) By the commission of any of the following acts by the insurer:

1. Not attempting in good faith to settle claims when, under all the circumstances, it could and should have done so, had it acted fairly and honestly toward its insured and with due regard for his interests. . . . Notwithstanding the provisions of the above to the contrary, a person pursuing a remedy under this section need not prove that such act was committed or performed with such frequency as to indicate a general business practice.

Question

1. This part of the Florida Insurance Code is repealed as of October 1, 1991 under Laws 1982, c. 82-243, §809(1), subject to review under §11.61, the so-called Regulatory Sunset Act. Would you agree that so long as it survives, it creates explicitly and clearly the right of action the *Royal Globe* court found by convoluted reasoning?

ILLINOIS INSURANCE LAW §155

Ill. Rev. Stat. ch. 73, §767 (1989)

§155. Attorney Fees. (1) In any action by or against a company wherein there is in issue the liability of a company on a policy or policies of insurance or the amount of the loss payable thereunder, or for an unreasonable delay in settling a claim, and it appears to the court that such action or delay is vexatious and unreasonable, the court may allow as part of the taxable costs in the action reasonable attorney fees, other costs, plus an amount not to exceed any one of the following amounts:

(a) 25% of the amount which the court or jury finds such party is entitled to recover against the company, exclusive of all costs;

(b) $25,000 [$5000 before an amendment effective January 1, 1986.];

(c) the excess of the amount which the court or jury finds such party is entitled to recover, exclusive of costs, over the amount, if any, which the company offered to pay in settlement of the claim prior to the action.

(2) [Modifies the above for multiple policies and suits on the same loss].

Notes and Questions

1. The Illinois statute was originally enacted in 1975, but later amended and somewhat strengthened. Does this provision apply to what would be, in other states, first-party bad faith claims? Is it a satisfactory solution to the first party bad faith problem?

2. Scroggins v. Allstate Ins. Co., 74 Ill. App. 3d 1027, 393 N.E.2d 718, 30 Ill. Dec. 682 (1979), declined to give judgment to a third-party claimant based on the statute. The plaintiff urged the example of *Royal Globe* on the court, which referred the plaintiff to the legislature for such relief. Combs v. Insurance Co. of Illinois, 146 Ill. App. 3d 957, 497 N.E.2d 503, 100 Ill. Dec. 525 (1986), holds that §155 preempts a first-party claim for bad faith. Zakarian v. Prudential Ins. Co. of America, 626 F. Supp. 420 (N.D. Ill. 1984), agrees but notes an apparent split of authority both among the state intermediate appellate courts and among federal district judges interpreting Illinois law. See also National Union Fire Ins. Co. v. Continental Illinois Corp., 652 F. Supp. 858 (N.D. Ill. 1986).

3. Tennessee Code §56-7-105 (1987 Supplement) and Louisiana Revised Statutes §22:658 also provide statutory remedies similar to those treated above.

5. Punitive Damages

So long as the action by the insured against the insurer is clearly one in contract, the courts are reluctant to award punitive damages because that is inconsistent with contract damages theory. As the bad faith cause of action becomes one in tort, however, the barriers against punitive damages begin to fall.

The appellate courts of California have upheld larger and larger awards of punitive damages in bad faith cases. In Moore v. American United Life Ins. Co., 250 Cal. App. 3d 610, 197 Cal. Rptr. 878 (1984), one court of appeals upheld a $2.5 million punitive damage award for the insurer's bad faith denial of disability benefits; the compensatory award was $30,000. Soon thereafter, another court of appeals upheld a $3 million punitive damage award in Betts v. Allstate Ins. Co., 154 Cal. App. 3d 688, 201 Cal. Rptr. 529 (1984); the compensatory award was $500,000. To determine whether the $3 million punitive damage award was excessive, the court examined three factors: the reprehensibility of the insurer's conduct, the wealth of the defendant insurance company, and whether there was a reasonable relationship between the punitive and compensatory damages. The court found Allstate's conduct in handling the defense of the insured and its refusal to settle within the policy limits when liability in excess of those limits was reasonably clear sufficiently reprehensible to allow the jury to award such a large amount of punitive damages. Second, the court found that $3 million was less than one-half week's earnings for Allstate, and thus was well within the guideline apparently established in Wetherbee v. United Ins. Co., 18 Cal. App. 3d 266, 270-271, 95 Cal. Rptr. 678 (1971), of one week's earnings as a reasonable amount for a punitive damage award. The $2.5 million award upheld in *Moore* was 3.4 weeks of the defendant's 1980 net income. The *Moore* court said such an award was not excessive as a matter of law. The third criterion, relation to compensatory damages, was also found to have been met in *Betts*. The court thought no single ratio appropriate, and further, that

> courts do not evaluate this particular relationship by a rigid formula but rather by the fluid process of adding and subtracting different considerations: if the defendant's conduct is sufficiently reprehensible, the ratio between compensatory and punitive damages is less important; however, where the ratio of compensatory to punitive damages is extremely high and the conduct is somewhat less reprehensible, this ratio carries more weight. [Id. at 713, 201 Cal. Rptr. at 542.]

The ratio in *Betts* was only 6:1 ($3 million punitive to $500,000 compensatory) but the ratio upheld in *Moore* was 83:1 ($2.5 million punitive to $30,000 compensatory).

California is not alone in allowing multimillion dollar punitive damage awards. The Arizona Supreme Court affirmed punitive damages of $3 million in Sparks v. Republic Natl. Ins. Co., 132 Ariz. 520, 647 P.2d 1127 (1982), *cert. denied,* 459 U.S. 1070 (1982). Compensatory damages were $1.5 million. Yet in Linthicum v. Nationwide Life Ins. Co., 150 Ariz. 326, 723 P.2d 675 (1986), the same court pointed out that more is required to justify punitive damages than the mere establishment of the tort. The defendant's conduct must be " 'aggravated, outrageous, malicious or fraudulent' combined with an evil mind." Id. at 332, 723 P.2d 681. Further, the proof must be clear and convincing. The court held that punitive damages were not appropriate.

Hawkins v. Allstate Ins. Co., 733 P.2d 1073 (Ariz. 1987), *cert. denied,* 484 U.S. 874 (1987), returned to the questions discussed in *Sparks* and *Linthicum.* The trial court admitted the testimony of former Allstate adjusters to the effect that there was an established company policy to "chisel" on automobile collision settlements. In total loss cases, the market value of the destroyed car would be calculated with such deductions as $35 for cleaning (however clean the car might be), $5 for tire wear (whatever the condition of the tires), and so forth. The Supreme Court held the evidence admissible on the issue of bad faith. The court followed *Linthicum* on the burden of proof question, but would apply it only prospectively, and therefore not in the case at issue. The court declined to consider certain constitutional issues on the ground that they had not been properly preserved, and upheld an award of $15,000 compensatory and $3.5 million punitive, in a case where the "chiseling" at maximum was $1,500.

In Independent Life & Accident Ins. Co. v. Peavy, 528 So. 2d 1112 (Miss. 1988), the court upheld an award of $250,000 punitive damages in a disability claim when the actual damages were only $412.20. The court noted that the award was less than two tenths of one percent of the company's net worth.

Notes and Questions

1. The preceding cases were selected not because they are typical but because they are extreme. Perhaps they show there can be abuse in the awarding of punitive damages in bad faith cases. Arguably, for that reason they raise questions about what limits, if any, should be placed on punitive damages awards, assuming the desirability of awarding punitive damages at all. Perhaps they raise also the question whether punitive damages should be awarded in bad faith cases.

2. The merits of punitive damage awards in insurance bad faith cases has been variously assessed by commentators. Levine, Demon-

strating and Preserving the Deterrent Effect of Punitive Damages in Insurance Bad Faith Actions, 13 U.S.F. L. Rev. 613 (1979), waxes positively enthusiastic about punitive damages as having a "desirable, reformative impact." Beckman, Constitutional Issues in Insurance Claim Litigation, 22 Tort & Ins. L.J. 244 (1987), talks of the "in terrorem and extortionate nature of these actions" and urges that the courts deny them all. With which, if either, do you agree and why? If with neither, how would you deal with the matter?

3. A prominent defense attorney surveyed the situation in Kornblum, Extracontract Actions Against Insurers: What's Ahead in the Eighties?, 19 Forum 58 (1983).

4. Shimola v. Nationwide Ins. Co., 25 Ohio St. 3d 84, 495 N.E.2d 391 (1986), held that punitive damages for bad faith (in a first-party case) could not be awarded without proof of actual damages. Over a dissent the court held there was no such proof in the case. Should bad faith punitive damages be awarded "in the air"?

5. Is the three-pronged test of *Betts* useful to determine whether the jury has awarded punitive damages capriciously? Should evidence regarding the insurer's financial status be admitted? Should the jury be instructed that it can award one week's net income? How would your answer be affected for third-party cases by the fact that there are few things in this uncertain world as difficult to measure in the short run as the net income or profit of a liability insurance company because of the uncertainty inherent in reserves for reported but not-yet-liquidated losses and for incurred but not-yet-reported losses. Under modern tort law doctrine, claims such as those based on exposure to asbestos may not be made for decades, in some cases.

6. The only ways to establish financial results with finality in liability insurance are (1) to "sell" the reserves to another solvent insurer by payment of a fixed sum of money, thus transferring the uncertainty to that other company, and (2) to reinsure the particular year's results into a succeeding year, thus transferring the uncertainty to a later reporting period.

The first method has been used to some extent in recent years. Under the title "runoff reinsurance" it has been provided by some Lloyds syndicates, with catastrophic results to some of them. Because of the peculiarities of statutory insurance accounting, under which loss reserves are not discounted to present value, the transferor establishes an immediate one-time increase in earnings and the transferee a corresponding decrease. This suggests that sometimes the primary motivation for such transfers may be tax-related or regulation-related.

The second method is the standard accounting procedure of syndicates at Lloyds, London, making possible the closure of the books on a given year at the end of three operating years, by reinsuring open claims into the next succeeding year for a fixed consideration. Of course, the uncertainty remains, leaving only the questions of who bears it or what year's business bears it. For Lloyds, it is in part a transfer from some persons to other persons and in part a transfer from one year to the following year for the same persons: Changes in the membership of the Lloyds syndicate or changes in members' percentages of participation may be made at the end of each year. In recent years the uncertainty of some years' results has been too great. It has not been possible to close the books on some bad years by reinsuring into future years; the difficult years have had to be left open for considerable periods.

7. What is the proper measure of punitive damages if the insurer is operating at a loss? Should the propriety of punitive damages be measured against underwriting profit (which is negative much of the time, even for successful companies), or against profit from operations, which is only occasionally negative? Would the income test eliminate, for insurers that currently operate at a loss, all incentive to act in good faith? Aren't the insurers that are operating at a loss the very ones most likely to act in bad faith in an effort to improve their position?

8. Is aggregate wealth (or size) ever an appropriate measuring rod? Is not a large insurer exposed to more such claims because of its size than is a smaller insurer engaged in equally reprehensible conduct?

9. The amended Illinois Insurance Code §155, as interpreted, and other similar statutes establish standards and limits for appropriate punitive damages in insurance cases. See Section c(4).

6. Insurability of Punitive Damages

The previous section dealt with punitive damages against insurance companies which have acted in bad faith in the settlement of claims. Another quite different punitive damages issue is a coverage question: Whether insurance against punitive damages is consistent with public policy. If the answer to the public policy question is that insurers may assume the risk of punitive damages if they wish, it leads to the question of whether they have actually done so in a given insurance policy.

FIRST BANK (N.A.)-BILLINGS v. TRANSAMERICA INS. CO.

290 Mont. 93, 679 P.2d 1217 (1984)

GULBRANDSON, J.

The United States District Court for the District of Montana has certified two questions to this Court for instructions concerning Montana law.

First Bank Billings has been named a defendant in three wrongful repossession cases, two of which have been filed in the District Court of the Thirteenth Judicial District, Yellowstone County, and one in the United States District Court for the District of Montana. Transamerica has undertaken the defense of First Bank, but has reserved its rights under its insurance contract with the bank and has denied any coverage for punitive damages under this contract. Transamerica argues that the public policy of Montana forbids such coverage. On motion of First Bank, the United States District Court has certified the following questions to this Court:

(1) Does the public policy of Montana permit insurance coverage of punitive damages? . . .

For the reasons stated below, we conclude in response to the first question that insurance coverage of punitive damages is not a violation of public policy. . . .

Counsel for First Bank have presented ten considerations in support of permitting insurance coverage of punitive damages. Transamerica has mounted a strong challenge to all of these considerations. We recognize that there is considerable authority supporting the positions of both parties. See generally Annot., 16 ALR4th 11 (1982) (comparing and contrasting different views on liability insurance coverage as extending to liability for punitive or exemplary damages). We note, however, that most of the important decisions, as well as the major arguments of the parties, emphasize three primary considerations as ultimately dispositive of the questions before us. These are (1) public policy as expressed in constitutions and statutes; (2) the purpose of punitive damages; and (3) the circumstances under which punitive damages become available to aggrieved plaintiffs. Although we address these matters separately in this opinion, we recognize that they are interrelated to a high degree, and we therefore are careful not to sever the important ties that bind them together.

Public Policy as Expressed in the Constitution and Statutes

We find nothing in the Montana Constitution declaring a public policy on the question before us. We therefore turn to relevant statutes and case law construing the same. . . .

In summary, we find no express policy by the legislature on the subject of insurance coverage for punitive damages. Although reasoned arguments can be made for reading some kind of prohibition into the language of the punitive damages statute, we decline to do so without first examining judicial construction of that statute and then considering the practical consequences of awarding punitive damages.

Public Policy in Light of Judicial Decisions

As noted above, a major aim of awarding punitive damages is punishment of the defendant for oppressive, fraudulent or malicious conduct. We have also recognized that an award of punitive damages can serve as a deterrent to like conduct by other individuals. First Security Bank v. Goddard (1979), 181 Mont. 407, 423, 593 P.2d 1040, 1049; Butcher v. Petranek (1979), 181 Mont. 358, 363, 593 P.2d 743, 745. Whether both goals will be served adequately by permitting insurance coverage of punitive damages has been the principal concern of courts that have already addressed the coverage question.

Several courts have followed the lead of the Court of Appeals of the Fifth Circuit and have concluded that the mutual goals of punishment and deterrence are defeated if coverage is permitted. In Northwestern Natl. Cas. Co. v. McNulty (5th Cir. 1962). 307 F.2d 432, Circuit Judge John Minor Wisdom made this oft-quoted observation:

> Where a person is able to insure himself against punishment he gains a freedom of misconduct inconsistent with the establishment of sanctions against such misconduct. It is not disputed that insurance against criminal fines or penalties would be void as violative of public policy. The same public policy should invalidate any contract of insurance against the civil punishment that punitive damages represent.
>
> The policy considerations in a state where . . . punitive damages are awarded for punishment and deterrence, would seem to require that the damages rest ultimately as well as nominally on the party actually responsible for the wrong. If that person were permitted to shift the burden to an insurance company, punitive damages would serve no useful purpose. Such damages do not compensate the plaintiff for his injury, since compensatory damages already have made the plaintiff whole. And there is no point in punishing the insurance company; it has done no wrong. In actual fact, of course, and considering the extent to which the public is insured, the burden would ultimately come to rest not on the insurance companies but on the public, since the added liability to the insurance companies would be passed along to the premium payers. Society would then be punishing itself for the wrong committed by the insured. [307 F.2d at 440-441.]

Upon reflection, we grant the intellectual appeal of Judge Wisdom's reasoning, and recognize that it has been both praised and followed in other jurisdictions. Nevertheless, we find that this reasoning does not address the substance of punitive damages law as applied in Montana. To determine public policy concerning insurance coverage of punitive damages solely on deductive conclusions like those articulated by Judge Wisdom "is to lean upon a slender reed." Missouri v. Holland (1920), 252 U.S. 416, 434, 40 S.Ct. 382, 384, 64 L. Ed. 641, 648.

Oregon Supreme Court Justice Hans Linde correctly observed in his concurring opinion in *Harrell,* supra, that "[a] court-made public policy against otherwise lawful liability insurance can be defended, not *because* the purpose of punitive damages is always deterrence and *because* insurance will always destroy their deterrent effect, but only *when* these considerations apply." (emphasis his). 279 Or. 199, 567 P.2d at 1029. Empirical observation informs us that many kinds of willful and wanton conduct are never successfully deterred by punitive damage awards. This is especially true in automobile accident cases. See, e.g., the discussion in Lazenby v. Universal Underwriters Ins. Co. (1964), 214 Tenn. 639, 383 S.W.2d 1, concerning the failure of civil and criminal sanctions to deter wrongful conduct on the highways. We have few doubts that the deterrent impact is minimal in cases involving other types of tortious conduct. This leaves punishment as perhaps the only effectively realizable goal of awarding punitive damages. However, as will be pointed out in the discussion infra, punishment in the context of punitive damages may come as a wholly unanticipated aspect of one's conduct, thus weakening the case against permitting insurance coverage of all punitive damage awards.

In the instant dispute, First Bank fears that its insurance contract with Transamerica will become virtually worthless if it is exposed to punitive damage awards without the possibility of coverage. The Bank also claims that such a fine line exists between conduct justifying imposition of punitive damages and conduct not justifying such damages that permitting coverage is not in violation of public policy. Both arguments warrant serious attention.

The contract issued by Transamerica to First Bank is not unlike many insurance agreements. It includes coverage for false arrest, detention, or imprisonment, malicious prosecution, wrongful entry or eviction, libel and slander, racial or religious discrimination, and wrongful repossession. All of these torts give rise to claims for punitive damages; on this there is no dispute. In many cases involving these torts, actual damages may be minimal, but the punitive damages extremely high. Indeed, many claims for relief are not made financially worthwhile without the prospect of recovering punitive damages. See *Harrel,* supra, 279 Or. 199, 567 P.2d at 1029 (Linde, J., concurring). Assuming that coverage was deemed contrary to public policy, and in the event of minimal, if any compensatory damages, an insured facing a significant award of punitives would receive little solace from what would amount to a worthless insurance policy. . . .

We have recently attempted to come to grips with the problem of uncertainty in the area of punitive damages. In Owens v. Parker Drilling Co., (Mont. 1984), 676 P.2d 162, 41 St. Rep. 66, this Court acknowledged the expanded availability of punitive damage awards based on concepts like gross negligence, recklessness and unjustifiability. With respect to presumed malice as a ground specified in Section 27-1-221, MCA, for imposing exemplary or punitive damages, this Court adopted the following standard:

> When a person knows or has reason to know of facts which create a high degree of risk of harm to the substantial interests of another, and either deliberately proceeds to act in conscious disregard of or indifference to that risk, or recklessly proceeds in unreasonable disregard of or indifference to that risk, his conduct meets the standard of willful, wanton, and/or reckless to which the law of this State will allow imposition of punitive damages on the basis of presumed malice. [*Owens,* supra, 676 P.2d 162, 41 St. Rep. at 69.]

Although we have described this standard as "more definitive and perhaps more stringent than those of the past," *Owens,* supra, 676 P.2d 162, 41 St. Rep. at 69, we acknowledge that fact-finders may still wrestle with concepts like recklessness and reasonableness, such that defendants may not know that their conduct constituted presumed malice until after trial, and that a defendant in one case may never know the sting of punitive damages while another defendant in a similar case may be faced with financing a sizeable award. Similarly, we have yet to work out a definitive standard for "oppression" within the meaning of Section 27-1-221.

Even though we are further down the road to refining the concept of punitive damages than are many other state courts, the law is still in such a state of flux as to warrant caution on the issue of whether public policy prohibits coverage of punitive damages in all cases. We therefore decline the opportunity to define limits for insurance coverage of punitive damages. Insurance companies are more than capable of evaluating risks and deciding whether they will offer policies to indemnify all or some conduct determined by judges or juries to be malicious, fraudulent or oppressive. A likely response to this opinion by some carriers may be the drafting of specific exclusions of coverage of punitive damages. However, the fact that some individuals may be willing to pay higher premiums for such coverage may convince carriers to extend coverage in some situations. It is conceivable that a combination of different approaches by insurance companies may result in a delineation of the limits of coverage better than anything this Court could establish.

Conclusion

We find that providing insurance coverage of punitive damages is not contrary to public policy. Transamerica admittedly has set forth a strong argument in support of an opposite holding, but we find the consequences of adopting that position unacceptable. The problems posed by insurance coverage of punitive damages are unquestionably like those inherent in the Gordian Knot. Unlike Alexander the Great, however, we cannot make a clean slice through our version of the Knot, in order to unravel all the aspects of the question before us, without working an injustice to many policy holders. Alexander dealt only with an inanimate object; we deal with people. Use of the judicial sword therefore is inappropriate in this case. Here, we must "untie" the knot, painstaking as the process may be. Until such time that the law of punitive damages is more certain and predictable, or until the legislature alters the law of punitive damages or expressly declares a policy against coverage in all cases, we leave the decision of whether coverage will be permitted to the insurance carriers and their customers.

Notes and Questions

1. As the court in *First Bank* recognizes, many jurisdictions have decided that insurance against punitive damages for one's own oppressive behavior or malicious wrongdoing is contrary to public policy, following Northwestern Natl. Casualty Co. v. McNulty, 307 F.2d 432 (5th Cir. 1962). Many of those jurisdictions, however, allow individuals to insure themselves against vicariously assessed punitive damages, such as against an employer because of the malicious wrongdoing of his employees. The proffered justification for such an exception is that the function of punitive damages as a deterrent to future conduct by others is no longer present if the liability is vicarious. Should that apply equally to corporations, which can only act through individuals? Does it matter whether the corporation operates through a large bureaucracy or is an individual's alter ego? If the answer is different for the two, where is the line to be drawn along the continuum between the two? Again, might it matter whether the large corporation is structured with tight central control or is greatly decentralized in operation?

2. Numerous cases discuss the deterrence rationale in considering whether to allow insurance against the award of punitive damages. See Beaver v. Country Mut. Ins. Co., 95 Ill. App. 3d 1122, 420 N.E.2d 1058, 51 Ill. Dec. 500 (1981); Skyline Harvestore Systems, Inc. v. Cen-

tennial Ins. Co., 331 N.W.2d 106 (Iowa 1983). See also Comment, Punitive Damages: An Appeal for Deterrence, 61 Neb. L. Rev. 651 (1982).

3. Is the *First Bank* court sound in recommending that the insurance market determine whether punitive damages may be covered? The court suggests doubt about the deterrent effect of punitive damages. Would the extra premium that would have to be paid to receive punitive damage protection and the risk of losing coverage or having premiums increased serve as an adequate deterrent?

4. Are punitive damage awards effective in deterring bad faith settlement practices by insurance companies? Might they overdeter? Is there any reason insurance companies should not be able, in turn, to purchase insurance against having to pay damages, whether compensatory or punitive, in bad faith cases? Such insurance might be called "insurance against extra-contractual claims." See Ott v. All-Star Ins. Corp., Chapter 9.

5. The court in *First Bank* does not address the issue of whether the standard liability insurance policy is to be interpreted to cover punitive damages, and discusses only the public policy aspect of the problem. The policy generally reads, "The Company will pay on behalf of the insured all sums which the insured shall become legally obligated to pay as damages because of bodily injury or property damage to which this insurance applies." Are punitive damages "damages because of bodily injury or property damage to which this insurance applies" or are they damages because of the malicious conduct of the insured? Compare Schnuck Markets, Inc. v. Transamerica Ins. Co., 652 S.W.2d 206 (Mo. App. 1983) (representing the latter) with Skyline Harvestore v. Centennial Ins. Co., 331 N.W.2d 106 (Iowa 1983) (representing the former). Only *Skyline* needed to address the public policy issue. Does the intentional act exclusion negate coverage for most punitive damage situations? For all those situations, perhaps, where public policy demands there be no coverage?

6. A public policy (if there is one) against allowing malicious actors to buy insurance protection against punitive damages must be balanced against the countervailing public policies of providing a source of funds for injured third parties (if that is a policy rather than merely a judicial tendency) and against interference with contracts. The Supreme Court of Wyoming recently said, "We will not invalidate a contract entered into freely by competent parties on the basis of public policy unless that policy is well settled, unambiguous and not in conflict with another public policy equally or more compelling." Sinclair Oil Corp. v. Columbia Casualty Co., 682 P.2d 975, 979 (Wyo. 1984). It decided that because there was no clear public policy against insuring against punitive damages, the court would follow the public policy favoring freedom of contract and uphold the contract as writ-

ten. See also Valley Forge Ins. Co. v. Jefferson, 628 F. Supp. 502 (D. Del. 1986), where the court, applying Delaware law, found both that an automobile policy covered punitive damages and that there was no public policy against such coverage. It discussed explicitly the question of whether punitive damages in an automobile case were damages "for bodily injury or property damage." Are they?

C. Conflict of Interest in Insurance Litigation

There is no inevitable conflict of interest between insurers and insureds as classes. Indeed, the broader the protection insurers can intentionally supply to insureds, the more they can justifiably charge in premiums and the greater the potential for profit. Insurers are conduits between premium payers and claimants; in first-party insurance, the one class is a sub-class of the other. It is between the classes of premium payers and claimants that there is inherent tension.

Except in the short run, and in particular fact situations, the insurer has good reason to be neutral between premium payers and claimants. Given reasonable stability (and hence predictability) over the long run it should make little difference to insurers how particular questions are decided.

In the settlement of individual claims, however, the insured and the insurer may easily come into conflict. At the margin of policy coverage, the conflict is apparent in all kinds of insurance. In most first-party insurance, such conflict is straightforward, and if it cannot be settled by negotiation, its natural outcome is either arbitration or a lawsuit.

In third-party liability insurance, where as a matter of course there is conflict with third-party claimants, insurers and insureds are basically on the same side in individual cases. It is usually in the interest of both insurers and insureds to minimize particular claims. Given reasonable stability and predictability, however, the insurer in third-party insurance has no more reason in liability than in first-party insurance to wish recoveries *generally* limited, unless they mount to a level where they destroy the utility of the insurance mechanism for the policyholders' industries or even make those industries unviable. Rapid or unpredictable increases in the frequency or severity of liability, however, can play havoc with the insurance business.

In liability insurance, the conflict may become especially complex in the discharge of the insurer's duty to defend. The attorney appointed by the insurer to defend the insured may also be in a conflicted position, for he or she must consider potential legal liability and, in many cases, ethical violations for failure to represent the insured properly.

There have already been many cases in this book involving a conflict of interest in liability insurance between an individual insurer and an insured, each having an interest in limiting its own financial burden. Every instance in which a third party claimant against an insured includes in the complaint a count for an intentional assault is such a case. For the insured, this means having attorneys paid for by the insurance company settle the matter quickly within the policy limits, obtain complete exoneration by trial or dismissal with prejudice, or in cases bound to exceed the policy limits, keep the judgment to a minimum. (In *Steele,* the next case, that interest of the insured was clearly recognized in the negotiations, especially in the concern for the difference between a covenant not to sue and a general release).

On the other hand, the insurer would sometimes be just as well off with a determination that the insured is liable but on grounds that would take the case outside of the policy coverage as it would be by complete exoneration of the insured. The insurer's best chance to optimize its own interests in the individual case might then be to sacrifice the insured rather than to defend vigorously and wholeheartedly. When interests conflict in that stark way, the ethical and legal duties of the attorney appointed by the insurer to represent the insured may be clear; there may also be a temptation to any attorney with questionable standards to act improperly, simply because the insurer is the long term provider of legal business, while the insured is usually a stranger. In some cases the ethical obligations may not be so clear, creating true dilemmas for even the most principled attorney.

The following materials explore some aspects of the litigation problems in insurance resulting from conflicts of interest, especially those involved in lawyers' representation of clients. Dondanville, Defense Counsel Beware: The Perils of Conflicts of Interest, 18 Forum 62 (1982) introduces the problem and discusses a number of cases including three presented in this book. A more recent article, Holmes, A Conflicts-of-Interest Roadmap for Insurance Defense Counsel: Walking an Ethical Tightrope Without a Net, 26 Willamette L. Rev. 1 (1989), discusses in great detail the various problems defense counsel may face. The article includes an exhaustive bibliography, and is organized around the several different lawyering operations in litigation.

The lawyer's ethical obligations constitute an important aspect of the conflict problems discussed herein. A proposal to deal with some of the problems can be found in Comment, The Representation of Conflicting Interests by Insurance Defense Counsel: A Proposal for Ohio, 15 Ohio N.U.L. Rev. 563 (1988).

1.   The Sensitively Handled Case

The bad faith case in liability insurance is closely related to conflict of interest problems. If an insurer or the attorney appointed by it to defend the insured improperly handles a matter where a conflict exists, that handling is likely to be a sufficient basis for a bad faith judgment. In the following case, the attorney appointed by the insurer to represent the insured, together with the insurer, handled a subtle problem in a way that was not only proper but to all appearances was thought through with some care. With the advantage of 20/20 hindsight, however, perhaps one can see ways in which the insurer and the lawyer might have performed even better.

STEELE v. HARTFORD FIRE INS. CO.

788 F.2d 441 (7th Cir. 1986)

POSNER, Circuit Judge.

The common law of Illinois makes it a civil wrong for a liability insurer to refuse, in bad faith, to settle litigation against the insured, thereby exposing the insured to a judgment in excess of the policy limits. We must consider the meaning of "bad faith" in the factual setting of this case.

The story begins with a lawnmower accident in 1974 to Charles E. Steele, Jr., who was five years old at the time. His grandfather, Hershel Bauman, was using a mower manufactured by Artic Enterprises Inc. to cut the grass at the home of Harry Tjardes, a neighbor, who paid Bauman for this service. Charles was riding on the back of the mower. He fell off, and Bauman accidentally backed the mower over Charles's foot; the resulting injury was so serious that the foot had to be amputated. Bauman and his wife had a homeowners' policy, issued by the Hartford Fire Insurance Company, which provided liability coverage of $25,000 for bodily injury. The policy provided, "This Company shall not be obligated to pay any claim or judgment or to defend any suit after the applicable limit of this Company's liability has been exhausted by payment of judgments or settlements."

The Hartford offered Charles's father $25,000, the full policy limits, in exchange for a general release of liability. The settlement had to be approved by an Illinois court, which appointed James Walker as the boy's guardian ad litem and then on Walker's recommendation rejected the settlement. By giving a general release, Walker would have given up the right to sue on Charles's behalf both Harry Tjardes — the owner of the property on which the accident had occurred and therefore arguably the employer pro tem. of Bauman and if so liable for

Bauman's negligence under the principle of respondeat superior — and Artic Enterprises, which would be liable on the ground of products liability if the lawnmower had been defective or unreasonably dangerous.

The settlement having fallen through, the Hartford hired a local lawyer, Guy Fraker, to defend against Charles's claim. Walker wrote Fraker offering to settle with the Hartford for $25,000 plus a covenant not to sue Bauman, explaining, "The nature of the injury makes it clear that [if the claim were prosecuted to a jury verdict] the verdict would exceed the policy coverage of $25,000 and thus create a judgment against Mr. Bauman in excess of the insurance coverage. However, it is not the desire of the guardian to invade the personal assets of Mr. Bauman if the claim can be promptly settled for the amount of insurance coverage. . . ." Upon receipt of this letter Fraker wrote the Baumans to explain the situation, and in particular that if they settled for just a covenant not to sue rather than a general release, "There is a real possibility that either of these parties [Tjardes and Artic] would turn around and sue you, seeking indemnity." He added, "This is a fairly complex problem and one which I would strongly urge you to discuss with your own personal attorney of your choice."

The Baumans replied that they had no personal attorney and wanted to discuss the matter with Fraker. They met at Fraker's office for more than an hour and he explained to them with the aid of a diagram the difference between a general release and a covenant not to sue. Fraker testified that at the end of the conference the Baumans told him "that this thing had been a real tragedy for them. They wanted the injured party to have the money, but they also wanted this to be at an end, and they did not wish to have continued exposure on their own part to a lawsuit." Fraker wrote a confirmatory letter to the Baumans, summarizing the conference in some detail. Again he explained that if Walker refused to give a general release, "This would leave them [i.e., the Steeles and Walker] in a position where they could make claim against either the manufacturer of the lawn mower or the owner of the property. There is a distinct possibility then that either of these parties would sue you and seek indemnity from you. If the Hartford pays the $25,000.00 and does not obtain a Release, your personal assets would then be exposed out over by either of these parties. . . . You indicated to me that as far as you were concerned you did not want the Hartford to settle the case and pay the policy limits unless they could obtain a Release, fully clearing you of further potential liability."

Walker remained adamant in his refusal to settle the case with the Hartford in exchange for a general release and in 1976 he brought a suit in state court on Charles's behalf against Bauman, Tjardes, and Artic. The Hartford retained Fraker to defend the claim against Bauman. Tjardes moved unsuccessfully to obtain summary judgment on

Walker's claim against him, but then agreed with Fraker to waive any right to seek indemnity from Bauman in the event that Walker obtained a judgment against Tjardes, provided that Fraker settled Walker's claim against Bauman. Apparently Tjardes's lawyer thought that a settlement of Walker's claim against Bauman would operate as a release of Walker's claim against Tjardes as well. Armed with this agreement, and knowing that under Illinois law as it then stood a manufacturer sued for products liability could not get indemnity from a joint tortfeasor (though the law was in flux, and the risk of such an action could not be entirely discounted), Fraker now offered to settle the suit against Bauman for the policy limits plus a covenant not to sue. Before Walker responded to this offer the Illinois Supreme Court changed its mind about indemnity, see Skinner v. Reed-Prentice Division Package Machinery Co., 70 Ill. 2d 1, 15 Ill. Dec. 829, 374 N.E.2d 437 (1977), and Artic promptly filed a third-party claim against Bauman for indemnity of any damages that it might be ordered to pay in Walker's suit. Fraker thereupon withdrew the offer to Walker, and this removed the premise of the deal with Tjardes. A few weeks later the Illinois Supreme Court decided not to apply its new rule on indemnity to pending cases. See id. at 16-17, 15 Ill. Dec. at 836, 374 N.E.2d at 444 (1978).

Settlement efforts having failed, Walker's case against the three defendants proceeded to trial. At the start of the trial Walker offered to settle with Tjardes for $25,000 plus an agreement not to seek indemnity against Bauman. This offer was consistent with Walker's earlier assurance to Fraker that he would not seek to collect a judgment out of Bauman's personal assets. The record contains no evidence of what those assets might be; the district judge's statement that Bauman was "impecunious" has no basis in the record.

Tjardes now counteroffered $10,000 (and the covenant), but Walker refused. Walker settled with Artic for $25,000. Fraker then offered to pay the full policy limits in exchange for just a covenant not to sue Bauman, but Walker refused; the offer, he said, had come too late. The case came on for trial against Tjardes and Bauman. The trial judge granted a directed verdict for Tjardes. The jury brought in a verdict against Bauman of $135,000 for Charles and $30,000 for his father. The Hartford paid $25,000, the policy limits, in partial satisfaction of the judgment.

Walker brought a supplementary proceeding against Bauman to collect the unpaid balance of the judgment. That proceeding was settled by Bauman's assigning to the Steeles his right to sue the Hartford for bad faith. The Steeles then brought this suit against the Hartford, which removed the case to federal district court. [Judge Posner carefully discussed the propriety of removal under the federal rules].

After a three-day bench trial, the district judge awarded judgment for the Steeles in the amount of the excess judgment against Bauman, and the Hartford has appealed.

We may assume without having to decide that whether the insurance company acted in bad faith in not advising the Baumans to settle Walker's claim for the policy limits plus a covenant not to sue is a question of fact within the meaning of Rule 52(a) of the Federal Rules of Civil Procedure. The cases assume this without discussion. See, e.g., Bailey v. Prudence Mutual Casualty Co., supra, 429 F.2d at 1390. The issue of bad faith is similar in character to that of negligence, especially since, as we are about to see, negligence may be deemed bad faith in a refusal-to-settle case such as this. These "mixed questions of law and fact" as they are sometimes called — it would be more informative to describe them as questions of the application of law to fact — sometimes are reviewed under the clearly-erroneous standard applicable to questions classified as factual, sometimes receive plenary appellate review like pure issues of law, and sometimes are reviewed under an intermediate standard. See Piper Aircraft Corp. v. Wag-Aero, Inc., 741 F.2d 925, 937 (7th Cir. 1984) (concurring opinion). The standard most favorable to the appellees would of course be the clearly-erroneous standard, and as the appellant doesn't challenge it we shall apply it.

But this does not carry the day for the appellees. We think the district court's determination that Fraker and the Hartford were guilty of bad faith was clearly erroneous, for our review of the record leaves us with a strong conviction that the insurance company acted throughout in perfectly good faith. The company incurred significant expenses (Fraker's fees) in an effort to protect its insured from an excess judgment, and it kept the insured fully advised of its strategy all the way.

The company, acting as it was required to do as the perfectly loyal and reasonably intelligent agent of its insured, had to balance two risks. The first was that if it held out for a general release Walker would refuse to settle, would go on to victory in the courtroom, would obtain a judgment in excess of the policy limits, and would then levy on Bauman's personal assets. This risk was not great. Because the Baumans were Mrs. Steele's parents and Charles's grandparents, the Steeles did not want to levy on Mr. Bauman's personal assets; and although Charles's suit was not in the control of the Steeles, the guardian ad litem, Walker, had assured Fraker that he would not levy against the Baumans. There is no suggestion that Bauman is a man of wealth (the low policy limits suggest he is not); and it is hardly likely that Mrs. Steele, imitating King Lear's bad daughters, would turn Charles's grandparents out of their home in order to satisfy a judgment in excess of the policy limits. Fraker could therefore reasonably believe that Walker would not press the matter to a trial against Bauman. A somewhat greater danger was that Walker would obtain damages against Tjardes and Artic, one or both of whom would turn around and seek indemnity against Bauman; no family relationship would inhibit either of them from trying to collect a judgment out of Bauman's personal assets. This risk may have been rather slight also. Bauman might not have sufficient liquid assets to be worth suing, and anyway Walker's claim against Tjardes was tenuous, depending as it did on successfully characterizing Bauman as an employee rather than independent contractor of Tjardes. Since, as it turned out, Bauman had supplied the mower and Tjardes had not supervised Bauman's mowing, the latter characterization was by far the more plausible. See, e.g., Cable v. Perkins, 121 Ill. App. 3d 127, 76 Ill. Dec. 638, 459 N.E.2d 275 (1984); Kuberski v. Noonan, 23 Ill. App. 3d 237, 318 N.E.2d 677 (1974). Finally, Artic, except for a brief interval during the settlement negotiations, seemed not to have a legal right to indemnity.

The weakness of Walker's claim against Tjardes is a two-edged sword. It reduced the threat of a third-party claim against Bauman but increased the likelihood that Walker would in the end agree to give Bauman a general release. An additional reason why Walker might ultimately yield on the issue of the release would be the Steeles' desire not to collect a judgment out of Bauman's personal assets. They would be doing this indirectly if they got judgments against Tjardes and Artic, either of whom turned around and got a judgment for indemnity against Bauman; and Fraker could reasonably believe that an awareness of this possibility might influence Walker in negotiating the issue of the general release, though in the end it did not. Moreover, weak as it appears to have been, Walker's claim against Tjardes was strong enough to induce Tjardes (actually his insurance company) to offer $10,000 to settle it. If the offer had been accepted Tjardes could have turned around and sued Bauman for indemnity, which is conventionally available where an employer is held liable for his employee's tort under the doctrine of respondeat superior (the ground for the action against Tjardes). See Stawasz v. Aetna Ins. Co., 99 Ill. App. 2d 131, 240 N.E.2d 702 (1968); Embree v. Gormley, 49 Ill. App. 2d 85, 199 N.E.2d 250 (1964); Prosser and Keeton on the Law of Torts §51, at p. 341 and n.6 (5th ed. 1984). Though not wealthy, Bauman might be good for $10,000, or a sufficient fraction of that amount to make suit worthwhile. Evidently Artic, which did sue Bauman, thought so. To prevent the risk of an indemnity action from materializing, Fraker wanted to hold out for a general release from Walker; but the problem was that by giving it to him Walker would be giving up a chance to get some additional damages, from Tjardes or Artic or both.

Fraker's best strategy might have been to work out a three-cornered arrangement among himself, Walker, and Tjardes, whereby both Walker and Tjardes would agree not to sue Bauman; and to take his chances with Artic. But in fact he tried this approach. By November 1977 the elements of such a deal were in hand, but it fell apart the next month when the risk materialized. Later, when Fraker tried to resurrect the deal, Tjardes balked at the amount demanded by Walker; and by the time Artic had fallen out of the picture again, Walker was no longer willing to settle the case on his original terms.

The fact that Fraker let the reins slip from his hands would not establish bad faith in any common meaning of the term. Nevertheless there is authority in Illinois for extending the term to include a negligent failure to settle within the policy limits; see in particular Browning v. Heritage Ins. Co., 33 Ill. App. 3d 943, 947, 338 N.E.2d 912, 916 (1975). The idea behind this extension (an idea nowhere expressed, and just a guess on our part) may be that the insurance policy implicitly commits the insurer to use due care to protect the insured from an excess judgment. Why an insurer should be thought voluntarily to assume a duty whose faithful fulfillment can only encourage people to underinsure is not clear to us. Generally it has been thought that more than simple negligence is required. See, e.g., Voccio v. Reliance Insurance Cos., 703 F.2d 1, 2 (1st Cir.1983). In the absence of any holding by the Illinois Supreme Court, and any explanation in the decisions of the lower courts of Illinois, we are entitled to doubt that simple negligence is enough under Illinois law — though that court assumed it was enough in Smiley v. Manchester Insurance & Indemnity Co., 71 Ill. 2d 306, 313-15, 16 Ill. Dec. 487, 490-91, 375 N.E.2d 118, 121-22 (1978). But we need not resolve our doubts; we can assume without having to decide that negligence is enough; for we do not think that a reasonable factfinder could deem Fraker's representation even negligent, let alone in bad faith in some stronger sense. Mistake is not negligence; the duty of good faith does not make the insurance company an insurer against the uncertainties inherent in the settlement process. Indeed, "mistake" may be the wrong word. The proper perspective for judging Fraker is ex ante (before the fact) rather than ex post. If Fraker chose the correct course on the basis of what he knew, he should not be called mistaken because of unavoidable uncertainty about whether the course would succeed.

Fraker demonstrated good faith in the ordinary sense of these words by protecting the insured's interests at the expense of the insurance company's. If he had gotten Bauman to settle on the terms originally offered by Walker, the insurance company would have been off the hook; the policy allowed it to walk away as soon as it settled for the full policy limits. Instead it hung around (in the person of its agent, Fraker), vainly trying to defend Bauman against an excess judgment — vainly trying to obtain a release from Tjardes — and incurred legal expenses in these endeavors. We do not suggest that this was altruism, for we know what would have happened if the company had settled on Walker's original terms. If and when Tjardes and Artic filed claims for indemnity against Bauman (Artic actually did file such a claim, as we said), Bauman would have accused the insurance company of having settled prematurely with Walker in order to avoid the expense of defending the third-party claims. It seems, then, that whatever Fraker did he would be exposing the Hartford to a claim of bad faith. It cannot be the law that every excess judgment must be paid by the insurance company, so that in effect liability insurance policies have no limits. Such a strange result would not even help policyholders in the long run; insurance companies would have to charge much higher prices, especially for policies with low limits.

The principal evidence of bad faith on which the district court relied was, first, the Baumans' deposition testimony that they didn't understand the complex legal fix they were in, and, second, a letter Fraker wrote the Hartford early on explaining what he conceived to be a potential conflict of interest between the Baumans and the Hartford. The first piece of evidence is of very slight relevance. The duty to represent the insured in good faith includes a duty to explain clearly and simply the legal choices facing the insured; it is not an absolute duty to enlighten where enlightenment may be impossible because of the insured's refusal to listen or his incapacity to understand the most patient and lucid explanation. Uncontradicted evidence consisting of Fraker's letters and diagram shows that he explained the legal situation to the Baumans with great care. If they didn't understand, it was not his fault. He advised them to consult their own lawyer, and they refused. He couldn't make them, and is not chargeable with their misunderstanding. His letters to them are in fact models of how to explain law to laymen. Although he can be criticized for having exaggerated the danger of a suit for indemnity by Artic as Illinois law then stood, in fact he was prophetic, for Illinois law changed in the course of the litigation. Only the fact that the Illinois Supreme Court decided to make the change prospective spared the Baumans the acute danger of being forced to indemnify Artic (unless Walker gave Bauman a general release) as Fraker feared.

Fraker's letter to the insurance company is the "smoking gun." But it is smoke without fire. The letter said:

> The question is, of course, do we have to take less than a full release in order to remain in good faith to our insured. There are two reasons we would want to obtain a full release. One is consistent with the interest of our insured, one is not. There is the obvious possibility here of third party action. In the event there is an action against other potential defendants, this would expose the personal assets of the insured to such an action. Here, our interests are consistent. The other is that it would expose the Hartford to costs of defense which The Hartford should be concerned about, but the insured should not be and accordingly, the conflict. To refuse this settlement for the latter reason would be bad faith.

If the policy had required the Hartford to bear all legal expenses arising out of an insured event, the dilemma identified by Fraker would have been a real one. But the policy states in language that could not be clearer that once the Hartford paid the full policy limits in settlement of a claim against the insured it would have no further obligation to defend him. The Steeles argue that maybe the term "settlement" as used in the insurance policy excludes a covenant not to sue, but that is nonsense. A covenant not to sue is a common form of settlement, and is certainly within the contemplation as well as literal terms of the policy. It is apparent that Fraker was not familiar with the policy; more surprising is why no one at the Hartford straightened him out.

Even if there was no actual conflict of interest between the Baumans and the Hartford — no way in which the Hartford could have been made worse off by settling with Walker in exchange for a covenant not to sue Bauman rather than a general release — if Fraker, mistakenly thinking there was a conflict, had tried to push the Baumans to hold out for a general release, he and therefore his principal would have been guilty of bad faith. But there is no evidence of that either. He advised them to get their own lawyer. He told the Baumans as accurately as he could what he perceived the tradeoffs to be between the alternative courses of action. True, he did not tell them that the median jury verdict for the loss of a foot was $175,000, but this was not a material omission. The Baumans knew they faced the risk of an excess judgment and faced it either way — in a suit by the Steeles and in an indemnity action by Tjardes and (less probably) Artic. If the Steeles got a $175,000 judgment against Bauman he would be personally liable for $150,000 (the difference between the judgment and the policy limits). If they got a judgment for $150,000 against Tjardes ($175,000 minus the amount that they would have received from his joint tortfeasor, Bauman, by virtue of the insurance policy), Tjardes would have a claim for $150,000 against Bauman. Although the Steeles were likelier to win a judgment against Bauman than against Tjardes because Tjardes's liability was more doubtful than Bauman's, Tjardes was likelier actually to levy on Bauman's assets than the Steeles were, so that the choice of which risk the Baumans should run was a close one. These risks came from the fact that the Baumans had bought a policy with such low limits. Maybe they could afford no more; but it was not the Hartford's fault that they faced an inescapable dilemma. Fraker laid out the relevant considerations to the Baumans as clearly as it was possible to do and they made their choice. The Steeles say that Fraker should have advised the Baumans of his imagined conflict of interest. But if he had told them, erroneously, that the insurance company would be better off holding out for a general release, this would not, so far as appears, have altered their decision — a decision motivated by their perception of their own self-interest.

Fraker's mistake, even if negligent in some sense — even if a breach of ethical duty to the Baumans, whose lawyer he was as well as the Hartford's — cannot impose liability on the Hartford, because the mistake did not cause him to subordinate the Baumans' interests to that of the Hartford. The only relevant bad faith is that which causes the insurance company to act otherwise than it would do if acting in perfect good faith. Without proof of causation, there can be no recovery of damages. Voccio v. Reliance Ins. Cos., supra, 703 F.2d at 3-4. Fraker only had to give the Baumans' interests equal weight; for whatever reason he gave these interests paramount weight. To press for a general release could only help the Baumans, since (unlike the otherwise somewhat similar case of Stoner v. State Farm Mutual Automobile Ins. Co., 780 F.2d 1414, 1418-19 (8th Cir. 1986)) the Hartford would have been off the hook by settling for the full policy limits in exchange merely for a covenant not to sue. . . . The law does not punish one for doing the right thing for the wrong reason.

Granted, Fraker did not inquire into the strength of the Steeles' case against Tjardes, which was material to the menace of a suit by Tjardes against Bauman for indemnity. But this omission was not the basis of the district court's decision, and does not by itself create liability. For there is (once again) no suggestion that the investigation would have altered Fraker's advice. We know the claim against Tjardes had some colorable merit because Tjardes offered $10,000 in settlement and the Steeles refused, evidently thinking they could do better at trial, though in the event they did worse. Had they accepted the settlement or won at trial Tjardes would probably have sought indemnity from Bauman. Fraker was not unreasonable to think this a greater threat than the threat (which never materialized) of the Steeles' collecting a judgment against Bauman after assuring him (via Walker's letter) that they would not do so.

We note finally the anomaly of the district court's awarding the Steeles more than $100,000 when there is no evidence that they would or could have collected any of this money from Bauman. The potential harm to the Baumans from the alleged bad faith of the insurance company came from exposing Mr. Bauman to a judgment in excess of the policy limits. But that could hurt the Baumans only to the extent that the excess was collected out of his assets. Suppose he had no assets, present or prospective (the significance of this qualification will become apparent in a moment). Then the Baumans were not damaged at all and the damage claim they assigned to the Steeles should have been worth nothing. Or suppose they had assets, but, consistently with Walker's assurance, the Steeles would not have tried to levy on them (apparently all the Steeles wanted from the Baumans was the assignment of this cause of action); again it would be impossible to see how the Baumans had lost $140,000 ($135,000 + $30,000 − $25,000) because of the excess judgment. It is true that Illinois is usually classed with those states which hold that an insured can recover an excess judgment caused by the insurer's failure to settle the litigation in good faith even without proof that the insured would or could have paid the judgment. See Annot., 63 A.L.R.3d 627, 641 (1975), citing Wolfberg v. Prudence Mutual Casualty Co., 98 Ill. App. 2d 190, 240 N.E.2d 176 (1968). Actually the picture is more complicated. *Wolfberg* holds only that the fact of having a judgment entered against you causes harm, even if the judgment is not collected. The court in *Wolfberg* may have been concerned that the judgment might make it harder for the insured to borrow money, though the court didn't say so. A later case adds that it is always possible that the insured might acquire some assets, or be discovered to have had them all the time, before the statute of limitations governing suits on judgments ran out — in which even he would have to pony up. Smiley v. Manchester Ins. & Indemnity Co., 13 Ill. App. 3d 809, 814, 301 N.E.2d 19, 22 (1973). A case distinguished in *Wolfberg*, however, Childress v. State Farm Mutual Automobile Ins. Co., 97 Ill. App. 2d 112, 119-20, 239 N.E.2d 492, 496 (1968), had held that an insured who was contractually protected against execution of the excess judgment could not obtain damages, and zero assets could be as good a protection as a contract. The Illinois Supreme Court has not spoken to the issue.

The path of reconciling *Wolfberg* to *Childress* lies in recasting the issue as one of amount of damages. The fact that an excess judgment cannot be fully executed does not excuse the insurer from liability or show that the insured has incurred no damages at all, because even an unexecuted judgment can cause an injury, present or future, that can be monetized. But the damages need not be exactly equal to the amount of the excess judgment; they could be more or less. Cf. Elas v. State Farm Mutual Automobile Ins. Co., 39 Ill. App. 3d 944, 949, 352 N.E.2d 60, 64 (1976). Here it seems plain that they were less — maybe zero (which if true is further evidence that Fraker had the Baumans' best interests at heart). Since the insurance company has not argued the point we do not rely on it but merely note it for future reference. We rest our decision entirely on the absence of evidence that the insurance company represented Bauman in bad faith.

The judgment is reversed with directions to dismiss the complaint.

Reversed.

Notes and Questions

1. The lawyer's dilemma is how to balance two conflicting loyalties. While formally the attorney represents the insured, a one-time

client, it is natural for even the most ethical lawyer subconsciously to give considerable weight to the interests of the insurer that pays the bills and has the option to give or deny more cases to the attorney.

The nature and direction of the duties are not always as clear as everyone would wish. Is the insurer the true client, and the insured only a nominal one? Some courts have thought so. Is there dual representation of the insured and the insurer. Most courts have thought so. Or is there an exclusive obligation to protect the insured's interests, even at the sacrifice of the insurer's? Increasingly that view prevails. These varying views exist in a context where the temptations are obvious and nearly always favor the interests of the insurer. If the majority view prevails, how does one weight the interests of the two clients when they conflict? Rather than solving the ethical problem, the majority view exacerbates it: It *creates* conflict.

2. In a thoughtful article, Morris, Conflicts of Interest in Defending Under Liability Insurance Policies: A Proposed Solution, 1981 Utah L. Rev. 457, Prof. Morris describes the various conflicts and proposes as a solution that the proper posture of the attorney is "undivided loyalty to the insured." He thinks the standard is already "ethically mandated as well as contractually required by the insurance policy." As you read the following materials, consider whether his view is correct as to present law and whether it is normatively sound.

3. Suppose an insurer properly defends its insured in a case in which both battery and negligence are alleged, and the jury finds there was negligence but not battery. Is the insurer, which is not a party to the tort action, collaterally estopped to prove in a subsequent action that the conduct was intentional and therefore that there was no coverage? In Allstate Ins. Co. v. Atwood, 71 Md. 107, 523 A.2d 1066 (Md. App. 1987), the court held that it was, and it could have intervened in the case as a separate party. Is that a sound result? It is obvious that the insurer is not permitted to manage the underlying tort case so as to swing the finding toward intentional tort. Is there any reason it should not afterward be permitted to protect its interests by arguing that the underlying tort case was wrongly decided?

2. Defense Under Reservation of Rights

If an insurer defends the insured without expressing any reservations, only to find later that there is no coverage under the policy, the insurer is likely to have waived the "no-coverage" defense and will have to indemnify as if there were coverage, at least if the insured was prejudiced. It is therefore customary for the insurer with any doubt about coverage to defend under a reservation of rights. Usually the insurer will seek to obtain a "nonwaiver agreement" from the insured, who usually has no option: refusal to agree to or at least to acquiesce in the reservation of rights will justify the insurer in declining to defend, after which the insured's only options are to defend himself and sue on the insurance contract or to seek a declaratory judgment to determine in advance of the underlying suit whether there is coverage under the policy or at least a duty to defend. Because of the necessary outlay of money, neither may be a practical alternative for any except well-financed corporate insureds. (Among them, it happens frequently.) Besides, the insurer is usually in a better position to arrange with qualified attorneys for the defense.

Would it not be a natural practice for the insurer always to issue a reservation of rights letter, just in case the facts turn out to warrant a finding of no coverage? If you think this bad social policy, how would you provide a disincentive?

MARYLAND CASUALTY CO. v. PEPPERS

64 Ill. 2d 187, 355 N.E.2d 24 (1976)

RYAN, Justice:

Plaintiff, Maryland Casualty Company (Maryland), filed a suit for declaratory judgment against Robert and Tincy Peppers and James Mims for a declaration of whether under a policy of liability insurance there was a duty to defend its insured Peppers in a personal injury action filed by Mims, who had been shot by Robert Peppers, and for a declaration of whether there was coverage under the policy for this occurrence. Peppers later filed a counterclaim for declaratory judgment against St. Paul Fire & Marine Insurance Company (St. Paul) seeking a declaration that the occurrence was covered and that St. Paul was required to defend the personal injury action under a homeowner's insurance policy it had issued on Peppers' residence. The policies issued by Maryland and by St. Paul both specifically excluded coverage for injuries intentionally inflicted.

After a bench trial the circuit court of St. Clair County found that Peppers had intentionally caused the injury and therefore the occurrence was not covered by the Maryland policy and also found that the property on which the occurrence happened was not the property insured by the general liability policy issued by that company. As to St. Paul, the court found that the act was an intentional act and that this alone is sufficient to hold that there was no coverage. The court went on to state that the question was not one of coverage but whether or not St. Paul is now estopped from asserting that there is no coverage under its policy because it undertook the defense of Peppers.

The court found that there was no coverage under the policy. However, it also found that St. Paul is obligated to defend Peppers. The appellate court affirmed the holding as to Maryland but modified the judgment as to St. Paul, holding that in addition to defending Peppers in the personal injury action St. Paul must also provide policy coverage for the occurrence. It was the opinion of the appellate court that because St. Paul had engaged attorneys to defend Peppers it was estopped from denying coverage under its policy. 29 Ill. App. 3d 26, 329 N.E.2d 788.

Robert and Tincy Peppers owned a tract of land facing Collinsville Road in East St. Louis. On January 18, 1971, three buildings, all owned by Peppers, were located on this land. A Pizza Hut was located at 8408½ Collinsville Road. There was no policy of insurance on this property covering liability for personal injuries. Next to the Pizza Hut at 8412 was a building which was insured by Maryland under a general liability policy. Adjacent to that building was Peppers' home at 8414, which was insured by St. Paul under a homeowner's policy of insurance. This policy also provided liability coverage in certain situations for personal injuries incurred off the property insured. Because the Pizza Hut had been burglarized on numerous occasions Peppers had been staying in that building at night. On January 18, 1971, Peppers was awakened by a noise at the door which he determined was caused by someone trying to break in. When he went to the door he saw a person fleeing. He shouted for him to stop and then fired his shotgun, wounding the fleeing person, James Mims. . . .

The controlling question as to Maryland's coverage and duty to defend involves the location of the occurrence. The policy that company issued to Peppers and his wife was an "Owner's, Landlord's and Tenant's Liability Policy" and was limited by its terms to pay on behalf of the insured all sums which the insured shall become legally obligated to pay for bodily injury or property damage caused by an occurrence and arising out of the ownership, maintenance, or use of the *insured premises*. The insured premises is described in the policy as 8412 Collinsville Road, East St. Louis, Illinois. The trial court found that this policy did not cover the occurrence in question, which arose out of the ownership, maintenance and use of the Pizza Hut located at 8408½ Collinsville Road. This finding is fully supported by the evidence. Also there is no evidence which in any way establishes that Maryland is estopped from denying coverage for this occurrence. There are also no allegations in Mims' complaint which, under the principles discussed later, would impose an obligation on Maryland to assume the defense of Peppers.

As to St. Paul, the trial court properly held that this company was obligated under its policy to defend Peppers in the Mims case. The complaint was in three counts. Count I alleged that Peppers had assaulted Mims with his shotgun. Count II alleged that Peppers had negligently and carelessly fired the shotgun at Mims, and count III alleged that Peppers had willfully and wantonly fired the shotgun at Mims. Thus, count I alleges only intentional injuries not covered by the policy, whereas the allegations of count II would not encompass an intentional injury, and the allegations of count III may or may not encompass intentional injuries. It appears from the complaint that Peppers is charged with both conduct for which the policy affords coverage and conduct for which it does not.

In determining whether the insurer owes a duty to the insured to defend an action brought against him, it is the general rule that the allegations of the complaint determine the duty. If the complaint alleges facts within the coverage of the policy or potentially within the coverage of the policy the duty to defend has been established. This duty to defend extends to cases where the complaint alleges several causes of action or theories of recovery against an insured, one of which is within the coverage of a policy while the others may not be. The trial court properly held that St. Paul was obligated to defend Peppers.

The appellate court held that St. Paul, by undertaking the defense of Peppers in the Mims case, is estopped to deny coverage under the policy. In considering the question of estoppel, it is helpful to again look at the chronology of events. The injury was inflicted on January 18, 1971, and Maryland was immediately notified by Peppers. That company made an investigation and informed Peppers on March 26, 1971, that there was no coverage under its policy of liability insurance. On April 14, 1971, Mims filed his personal injury suit against Peppers, who, through his personal attorney, Massa, filed a motion to dismiss the complaint on May 13, 1971. Thus, Peppers was represented by his own counsel, who, so far as the record discloses, has never withdrawn his appearance. It was not until July 21, 1971, more than 3 months after the complaint was filed and more than 2 months after Peppers' attorney had entered his appearance and filed his motion to dismiss, that Peppers decided to look to St. Paul for a defense and for coverage under the homeowner's policy. At that time a copy of the complaint was sent to the insurance agent with the request that it be forwarded to St. Paul. The next action involving St. Paul as disclosed by the record is a letter from a firm of attorneys to Peppers on February 11, 1972, informing him that they had been employed by St. Paul to represent him and on the same day the filing of an answer in the Mims case by those attorneys. On March 6, 1972, 24 days later, these attorneys, with leave of court, withdrew the answer and their appearance for Peppers.

[On May 15, 1972, Peppers filed a counterclaim against St. Paul in the declaratory judgment action, seeking a declaration of rights and liabilities under the St. Paul homeowners policy issued to him on Peppers' home at 8414 Collinsville Road.]

It is generally held that an insurer may be estopped from asserting a defense of noncoverage when the insurer undertakes the defense of an action against the insured. However, it is also the general rule that the undertaking must result in some prejudice to the insured. (See Annot., 38 A.L.R.2d 1148, 1157 (1954).) In Gibraltar Insurance Co. v. Varkalis, 46 Ill. 2d 481, 263 N.E.2d 823, the insurer caused an answer and an appearance to be filed on behalf of its insured in a wrongful death action. Fourteen months later, during which time the insurer had continued the exclusive representation of the insured, the insurer advised the insured that it was representing him under a reservation of rights. Significantly, the court concluded that "[d]uring the interim [the insurer] acted on behalf of [the insured] as though no questions of policy coverage were involved, thus clearly causing him to wholly rely for his defense on the efforts of [the insurer]." (46 Ill. 2d 481, 488, 263 N.E.2d 823, 827.) Interpreting this language the court in Northwestern National Insurance Co. v. Corley (7th Cir. 1974), 503 F.2d 224, decided that the quoted language implicitly requires a showing of prejudice to the insured before estoppel is established. The appellate court of this State similarly construed *Gibraltar* in Greater Chicago Auction, Inc. v. Abram, 25 Ill. App. 3d 667, 323 N.E.2d 818.

Whether an insured is prejudiced by an insurer's conduct in entering an appearance and assuming the defense of an action is a question of fact. Prejudice will not be conclusively presumed from the mere entry of appearance and assumption of the defense. If, however, by the insurer's assumption of the defense the insured has been induced to surrender his right to control his own defense, he has suffered a prejudice which will support a finding that the insurer is estopped to deny policy coverage.

There is nothing in the record to establish that Peppers was not at all times represented by his own attorney, Massa, or that in reliance on the attorneys hired by St. Paul he was induced to surrender the right to conduct his own defense. The finding of the trial court that St. Paul was not estopped to deny coverage is not contrary to the manifest weight of the evidence.

As stated earlier, the trial court, in the declaratory judgment action, found that Peppers had intentionally caused the injury to Mims. By virtue of the interrelation of the various issues involved in the litigation between Mims and Peppers and between Peppers and St. Paul we must conclude that this finding by the trial court constituted an abuse of the discretion vested in it by section 57.1 of the Civil Practice Act (Ill. Rev. Stat. 1971, ch. 110, par. 57.1).

Mims' complaint against Peppers had been filed more than 4 months before Maryland filed the original complaint for declaratory judgment and 13 months before Peppers, by way of counterclaim, sought a declaration of his rights under his policy of insurance with St. Paul. The Mims complaint was in three counts. Under the principle of collateral estoppel the finding in the declaratory judgment action that the injury was intentionally inflicted could possibly establish the allegations of the assault count in the complaint and might preclude Mims' right to recover under the other theories alleged. (See Farmers Oil and Supply Co. v. Illinois Central R.R. Co., 6 Ill. App. 3d 965, 286 N.E.2d 68; 22 Am. Jur. 2d Declaratory Judgments, sec. 102 (1965).) In a case quite similar to ours the appellate court held that the ruling and judgment of the trial court in a declaratory judgment action under such circumstances were "premature" and should be reversed. (Allstate Insurance Co. v. Gleason, 50 Ill. App. 2d 207, 200 N.E.2d 383.) We agree with that holding. The finding of the trial court in our case that the injury was intentional was not proper in this declaratory judgment action. This issue was one of the ultimate facts upon which recovery is predicated in the Mims personal injury action against Peppers, which had been filed considerably before the declaratory judgment action had been instituted.

The holding that St. Paul is obligated to defend Peppers and that it was not proper in the declaratory judgment action to determine that the injury was intentional creates a situation in which there is an unresolved conflict between the interests of the insured and of the insurer. In the personal injury action if Peppers is held responsible, it would be to his interest to be found negligent, which, under the policy of insurance, would place the financial loss on St. Paul. On the other hand it would be to St. Paul's interest to have a determination that Peppers intentionally injured Mims, which, by the terms of the policy, would relieve St. Paul of the obligation to pay the judgment. The existence of conflicts of this nature has been widely recognized by the courts and writers, with little accord as to the resolution of the problem. Because of this conflict of interests, serious ethical questions prohibit an attorney from representing both the interests of St. Paul and of Peppers. (See Illinois Code of Professional Responsibility, E.C. 5-14, 5-15, 5-17 (1970), adopted by the Board of Governors of the Illinois State Bar Association and the Board of Managers of the Chicago Bar Association.) If Peppers is willing to accept the defense furnished by the attorney engaged by St. Paul after full disclosure to him by the attorney of the conflicting interests, the requirement of the Code of Professional Responsibility will be satisfied. Also, if St. Paul waives its defense of noncoverage by the policy of an intentional injury and defends without asserting a reservation of rights or nonwaiver agreement as to such an injury the conflict of interests will be removed.

Absent the acceptance of the defense by Peppers or the waiver by

St. Paul, Peppers has the right to be defended in the personal injury case by an attorney of his own choice who shall have the right to control the conduct of the case. By reason of St. Paul's contractual obligation to furnish Peppers a defense it must reimburse him for the reasonable cost of defending the action. Also, St. Paul is entitled to have an attorney of its choosing participate in all phases of this litigation subject to the control of the case by Peppers' attorney, and St. Paul is not barred from subsequently raising the defense of noncoverage in a suit on the policy.

The judgment of the appellate court affirming the circuit court as to Maryland Casualty Company is affirmed. The judgment of the appellate court holding that St. Paul Fire & Marine Insurance Company is estopped to deny coverage under its policy is reversed. The judgment of the circuit court of St. Clair County is affirmed, but its finding that the injury was not within the coverage of either policy because it was intentionally inflicted is vacated. . . .

Notes and Questions

1. If an insurer begins the defense of the insured, then withdraws in midstream, without either sending the insured a reservation of rights letter or bringing a declaratory judgment proceeding, may it subsequently contend that it has no duty under the contract? Is this a proper situation in which to apply the notions of waiver, estoppel, or election? See Beckwith Mach. Co. v. Travelers Indem. Co., 638 F. Supp. 1179 (W.D. Pa. 1986). If the result is based on estoppel, how promptly must the insurer seek to reserve its rights? See Northwestern Natl. Ins. Co. v. R. S. Armstrong & Bros. Co., 627 F. Supp. 951 (D.S.C. 1985).

2. Does an insurer that defends under a reservation of rights have standing in the underlying tort suit, for the defense of which it is paying, to request a determination of its duty to indemnify? In First State Ins. Co. v. J & S United Amusement Corp., 67 N.Y.2d 1044, 495 N.E.2d 351, 504 N.Y.S.2d 88 (1986), the court held there was no standing. Then how does it determine whether it has that duty?

3. State Security Ins. Co. v. Globe Auto Recycling Corp., 141 Ill. App. 3d 133, 490 N.E.2d 12, 95 Ill. Dec. 539 (1986), held that when both intention and negligence were alleged, the insurer had a duty to defend but that because of the conflict of interests, the duty could be discharged by reimbursing the insured for the costs of defense. Would you go farther and say it *must* be discharged in that way?

4. Pepper Constr. Co. v. Casualty Ins. Co., 145 Ill. App. 3d 516, 495 N.E. 2d 1183, 99 Ill. Dec. 448 (1986), held that the insurer may *not* defend when there is a conflict of interest but instead *must* reimburse the insured for defense costs.

Negation of coverage alone is not a sufficient conflict of interest to preclude an insurer from defending its insured. A conflict of interest has been found, however, where an underlying complaint asserts claims that are covered by the insurance policy and other causes which the insurer is required to defend, but which it asserts are not covered by the policy. [Id. at 518, 495 N.E.2d at 1184, 99 Ill. Dec. at 449.]

Why would the court make that distinction?

5. Golotrade Shipping and Chartering, Inc. v. Travelers Indem. Co., 706 F. Supp. 214 (S.D.N.Y. 1989), applying New York law, required the insurer to pay for counsel selected by the insured in a case where there was a potential conflict.

6. A California case seems to have changed insurer practice. San Diego Navy Federal Credit Union v. Cumis Ins. Socy., Inc., 162 Cal. App. 3d 358, 208 Cal. Rptr. 494 (1984), held that defense under a reservation of rights *creates* a conflict of interest and that the insurer must pay for the independent counsel of the insured. One of the counsel for the plaintiff has said that it stopped

the knee-jerk reaction of many insurers who in the past issued reservation of rights letters or nonwaiver agreements to their insureds on any pretext whatever. The incentive for the insurer to stop this practice is to avoid having to pay for the insured's independent counsel and avoid losing the right to control the defense of the lawsuit. Immediately following the *Cumis* decision, many carriers began withdrawing their previously issued reservation of rights letters. [Saxon, Conflicts of Interest: Insurers' Expanding Duty to Defend and the Impact of "Cumis" Counsel, 23 Idaho L. Rev. 351, 360 (1986-87).]

A critical comment is The *Cumis* Decision — What Has It Done to Insurance Policies?, 23 Cal. W. L. Rev. 125 (1986). It is not surprising that California lawyers now speak of *Cumis* counsel. The California Legislature enacted Civil Code §2860, effective January 1, 1988, as a result of a battle between trial lawyers and tort reform advocates. Rather than clarify the law, it may have muddied it. See Brown & Romaker, *Cumis,* Conflicts and the Civil Code: Section 2860 Changes Little, 25 Cal. W.L. Rev. 45 (1988).

7. Alabama has addressed the issue differently:

The mere fact that the insurer chooses to defend its insured under a reservation of rights does not *ipso facto* constitute such a conflict of interest that the insured is entitled at the outset to engage defense counsel of its choice at the expense of the insurer. [L & S Roofing Supply Co. v. St. Paul Fire & Marine Ins. Co., 521 So. 2d 1298, 1304 (Ala. 1987).]

The court imposes "an enhanced obligation of good faith," to be measured by criteria set forth in the case. When those criteria have not been met, the insured may engage defense counsel at the expense of the insurer.

8. If the insurer loses a declaratory judgment action against its insured that seeks to establish that it has no obligation to defend, can the insured recover attorney fees for its defense of that action? If the insured counterclaims for damages for failure to defend, can the costs of the counterclaim be recovered? See Commercial Union Ins. Co. v. International Flavors & Fragrances, Inc., 639 F. Supp. 1401 (S.D.N.Y. 1986).

PARSONS v. CONTINENTAL NATL. AM. GROUP

113 Ariz. 223, 550 P.2d 94 (1976)

GORDON, Justice:

Appellants Ruth, Dawn and Gail Parsons obtained a judgment against appellant Michael Smithey, and then had issued and served a writ of garnishment on appellee, Continental National American Group (hereinafter referred to as CNA). The Superior Court of Pima County entered judgment in favor of the garnishee, CNA and from this judgment appellants appealed. The Court of Appeals, Division Two, reversed the judgment of the Superior Court, 23 Ariz. App. 597, 535 P.2d 17 (1975). Opinion of the Court of Appeals vacated and judgment of the Superior Court of Pima County reversed, and it is ordered that the judgment be entered in favor of appellants in the sum of $50,000.

We accepted this petition for review because of the importance of the question presented. We are asked to determine whether an insurance carrier in a garnishment action is estopped from denying coverage under its policy when its defense in that action is based upon confidential information obtained by the carrier's attorney from an insured as a result of representing him in the original tort action.

Appellant, Michael Smithey, age 14, brutally assaulted his neighbors, appellants Ruth, Dawn and Gail Parsons, on the night of March 26, 1967.

During April, 1967 Frank Candelaria, CNA claims representative, began an investigation of the incident. On June 6, 1967 he wrote to Howard Watt the private counsel retained by the Smitheys advising him that CNA was "now in the final stages of our investigation," and to contact the Parsons' attorney to ascertain what type of settlement they would accept. Watt did contact the Parsons' attorney and requested that a formal demand settlement be tendered and the medical bills be forwarded to Candelaria. On August 11, 1967 Candelaria wrote a detailed letter to his company on his investigation of Michael's background in regards to his school experiences. He concluded the letter with the following:

In view of this information gathered and in discussion with the boy's father's attorney, Mr. Howard Watts, and with the boy's parents, I am reasonably convinced that the boy was not in control of his senses at the time of this incident.

It is, therefore, my suggestion that, and unless instructed otherwise, I will proceed to commence settlement negotiations with the claimant's attorney so that this matter may be disposed of as soon as possible."

Prior to the following dates: August 15, 1967, August 28, 1967, and October 23, 1967, Candelaria tried to settle with the Parsons for the medical expenses and was unsuccessful.

On October 13, 1967 the Parsons filed a complaint alleging that Michael Smithey assaulted the Parsons and that Michael's parents were negligent in their failure to restrain Michael and obtain the necessary medical and psychological attention for him. At the time that the Parsons filed suit they tendered a demand settlement offer of $22,500 which was refused by CNA as "completely unrealistic."

CNA's retained counsel undertook the Smithey's defense and also continued to communicate with CNA and advised him on November 10, 1967:

> I have secured a rather complete and confidential file on the minor insured who is now in the Paso Robles School for Boys, a maximum-security institution with facilities for psychiatric treatment, and he will be kept there indefinitely and certainly for at least six months. . . .
>
> The above referred-to confidential file shows that the boy is fully aware of his acts and that he knew what he was doing was wrong. It follows, therefore, that the assault he committed on claimants can only be a deliberate act on his part.

After CNA had been so advised they sent a reservation of rights letter to the Smitheys stating that the insurance company, as a courtesy to the insureds, would investigate and defend the Parsons' claim, but would do so without waiving any of the rights under the policy. The letter further stated that it was possible the act involved might be found to be an intentional act, and that the policy specifically excludes liability for bodily injury caused by an intentional act. This letter was addressed only to the parents and not to Michael.

In preparing for trial the CNA attorney retained to undertake the defense of the Smitheys interviewed Michael and received a narrative statement from him in regards to the events of March 26, 1967, and then wrote to CNA: "His own story makes it obvious that his acts were willful and criminal."

CNA also requested an evaluation of the tort case and the same attorney advised CNA: "Assuming liability and coverage, the injury is worth the full amount of the policy or $25,000.00."

On the issue of liability the trial court directed a verdict for Michael's parents on the grounds that there was no evidence of the parents being negligent. This Court affirmed, Parsons v. Smithey, 109 Ariz. 49, 504 P.2d 1272 (1973). On the question of Michael's liability the trial court granted plaintiff's motion for a directed verdict after the defense presented no evidence and there was no opposition to the motion. Judgment was entered against Michael in the amount of $50,000.

The Parsons then garnished CNA, and moved for a guardian ad litem to be appointed for Michael which was granted by the trial court. On November 23, 1970 appellee Parsons offered to settle with CNA in the amount of its policy limits, $25,000. This offer was not accepted.

CNA successfully defended the garnishment action by claiming that the intentional act exclusion applied. The same law firm and attorney that had previously represented Michael represented the carrier in the garnishment action.

Appellants contend that CNA should be estopped to deny coverage and have waived the intentional act exclusion because the company took advantage of the fiduciary relationship between its agent (the attorney) and Michael Smithey. We agree.

The attorneys, retained by CNA, represented Michael Smithey at the personal liability trial, and, as a result, obtained privileged and confidential information from Michael's confidential file at the Paso Robles School for Boys, during the discovery process and, more importantly, from the attorney-client relationship. Both the A.B.A. Committee on Ethics and Professional Responsibility and the State Bar of Arizona, Committee on Rules of Professional Conduct have held that an attorney that represented the insured at the request of the insurer owes undivided fidelity to the insured, and, therefore, may not reveal any information or conclusions derived therefrom to the insurer that may be detrimental to the insured in any subsequent action. The A.B.A. Committee on Ethics and Professional Responsibility in Informal Opinion Number 949 stated:

> If the firm does represent the insured in the personal injury action, to subsequently reveal to the insurer any information received from the insured for possible use by the insurer in defense of a garnishment proceeding by the injured person, would be a clear violation of both Canon 6 and Canon 37 regarding confidences of a client. A successful defense of the garnishment proceeding by the insurer would be contrary to the interests of the insured, because if the insurer is not obligated to pay the judgment, execution against the insured can be expected. The result would not be different in practical effect from a suit directly against the insured to escape liability under the policy.

If the firm does not defend the insured in the personal injury action, the firm cannot reasonably expect the attorney who does represent the insured to furnish either to the firm or to the insurer, for use in a garnishment action by the injured person against the insurer, information that attorney learns during the course of defending the insured, since that attorney should not be expected to breach his professional obligations by furnishing information Canons 6 and 37 prohibit him from furnishing. (August 8, 1966.)

[Arizona Ethics Opinion No. 261, adopted November 15, 1968, is similar, and Arizona Ethics Opinion No. 282, adopted May 21, 1969, states:]

No better statement of the basis for our position on this question occurs to us than the following quotation from the Blakslee article cited above (55 A.B.A. Jour. at p. 263):

Although the opinions of the Committee state that the lawyer represents both the insurer and insured, *it is clear that his highest duty is to the insured and that the lawyer cannot be used as an agent of the company to supply information detrimental to the insured. . . . But counsel should not be expected to communicate information received in confidence or to betray confidences lodged in them by trusting clients.* To do so would not only destroy public confidence in the legal profession, but also would make defense attorneys investigators for carriers.

The attorney in the instant case should have notified CNA that he could no longer represent them when he obtained any information (as a result of his attorney-client relationship with Michael) that could possibly be detrimental to Michael's interests under the coverage of the policy.

The attorney representing Michael Smithey in the personal injury suit instituted by the Parsons had to be sure at all times that the fact he was compensated by the insurance company did not "adversely affect his judgment on behalf of or dilute his loyalty to [his] client, [Michael Smithey]". Ethical consideration 5-14. Where an attorney is representing the insured in a personal injury suit, and, at the same time advising the insurer on the question of liability under the policy it is difficult to see how that attorney could give individual loyalty to the insured-client. "The standards of the legal profession require undeviating fidelity of the lawyer to his client. No exceptions can be tolerated." Van Dyke v. White, 55 Wash. 2d 601, 349 P.2d 430 (1960). This standard is in accord with Ethical Consideration 5-1.

EC 5-1. The professional judgment of a lawyer should be exercised, within the bounds of the law, solely for the benefit of his client and free of compromising influences and loyalties. Neither his personal interests, the interests of other clients, nor the desires of third persons should be permitted to dilute his loyalty to his client.

The attorney in the present case continued to act as Michael's attorney while he was actively working against Michael's interests. When an attorney who is an insurance company's agent uses the confidential relationship between an attorney and a client to gather information so as to deny the insured coverage under the policy in the garnishment proceeding we hold that such conduct constitutes a waiver of any policy defense, and is so contrary to public policy that the insurance company is estopped as a matter of law from disclaiming liability under an exclusionary clause in the policy. . . . The evidence further shows that CNA could have settled the Parsons' claim against Michael Smithey well within the policy limits and refused to do so on the basis that the settlement was "completely unrealistic." It is clear from the record that the carrier failed to enter into good faith settlement negotiations. Farmers Insurance Exchange v. Henderson, 82 Ariz. 335, 313 P.2d 404 (1957). In the instant case the further fact that the carrier believed there was no coverage under the policy and so refused to give any consideration to the proposed settlements did not absolve them from liability for the entire judgment entered against the insured. State Farm Auto Ins. Co. v. Civil Service Emp. Ins. Co., 19 Ariz. App. 594, 509 P.2d 725 (1973). Opinion of the Court of Appeals vacated; judgment of the trial court reversed and judgment entered in favor of appellants Parsons in the sum of $50,000.

Notes and Questions

1. In Lieberman v. Employers Ins. of Wausau, 84 N.J. 325, 419 A.2d 417 (1980), a physician-insured gave written consent to the settlement of a malpractice claim against him. Soon thereafter and before a settlement had been reached, he received information indicating fraud or malingering on the part of the patient. He sought to withdraw his consent to settlement but the insurer refused. The attorney who was retained by the insurer but who should have been representing the insured physician did not keep the latter properly informed of the instructions received from the insurer. The attorney settled the case. As a result the physician's premiums increased by 150 percent under a surcharge program because there were multiple payouts in excess of a certain amount. The physician sued the insurer for breach of contract and the attorney for breach of duties arising out of the attorney-client relationship. The court held the consent could be revoked.

If the case had gone to trial and had been adjudicated or perhaps settled, it would have been possible that the surcharge would not have been levied, or might not have been so large. The plaintiff had to show damages and the case was remanded for trial on that issue, but the roles would be reversed: the physician would be plaintiff in this case, though he would have been defendant in the suit for malpractice. Is an effective "suit within a suit" possible when the roles of plaintiff and defendant are reversed?

2. The *Lieberman* court gave discretion to the trial court as to the "manner in which the plaintiff may proceed to prove his claim for damages and that the appropriate proceedings should, if not otherwise agreed upon between the parties, be settled through pretrial proceedings." Id. at 343, 419 A.2d at 427. How would you handle that problem, if you were the trial judge?

3. A conflict of interest between insurer and insured frequently arises when the insurer is on the property risk for one insured and the liability risk for another. This occurs most often in automobile insurance, where insurers like State Farm, Allstate, and Nationwide control significant portions of the total national market. Some other insurers have similar concentrations in more localized areas, such as in Rawlings v. Apodaca, 151 Ariz. 149, 726 P.2d 565 (1986), where plaintiff Rawlings was insured for an inadequate amount against fire on his dairy farm with Farmers Insurance Co. of Arizona, which also carried Apodaca's liability insurance. Rawlings sued Apodaca for negligently causing the fire by burning trash in violation of Arizona law. The insurer failed to provide Rawlings with its investigative report on the fire, which was prepared in connection with Rawlings's fire insurance claim. The insurer was held to have breached its obligation of fair dealing and was liable in tort for bad faith.

3.   Dual Representation

Some cases allow an attorney to "wear two hats" if certain conditions are met. For example, in Coscia v. Cunningham, 250 Ga. 521, 299 S.E.2d 880 (1983), the insurer arranged for the insured under a liability policy to be represented by an in-house lawyer. The third party moved to disqualify the employed lawyer on the ground that the employer had an indirect financial interest in the case, and also by reason of asserted violation of the law forbidding the practice of law by a corporation. The insured had been advised of the possibility of excess liability and that he might wish to have independent counsel as well. The court held, over a dissent, that the use of in-house counsel was permissible. Full disclosure and consent of both parties is another basis for dual representation.

The insurer involved in *Coscia* was the Travelers which, by common report, has moved a long way toward the handling of much of its litigation through the use of in-house counsel. Some other companies have as well, believing the costs of litigating can be considerably lessened if more is done by salaried counsel and if much more of the companies' legal business is controlled from their home offices. This phenomenon is not limited to the insurance business.

4. The Reciprocal Duty

The marine warranty and misrepresentation cases said that insurance is a contract *uberrimae fidei*, putting an obligation "of the utmost good faith" on the insured. The bad faith cases place a similar duty of the utmost good faith on the insurer. Might that suggest that in claims settlement the insured has a similar reciprocal duty? In dictum, California Casualty Gen. Ins. Co. v. Superior Court, 173 Cal. App. 3d 274, 218 Cal. Rptr. 817 (1985) suggests as much. In Fleming v. Safeco Ins. Co., 160 Cal. App. 3d 31, 206 Cal. Rptr. 313 (1984), the trial court reduced plaintiff's recovery on the basis of comparative bad faith. The point was not appealed. See Houser et al., Comparative Bad Faith: The Two-Way Street Opens for Travel, 23 Idaho L. Rev. 367 (1986); Shipstead and Thomas, Comparative and Reverse Bad Faith: Insured's Breach of Implied Covenant of Good Faith and Fair Dealing as Affirmative Defense or Counterclaim, 23 Tort & Ins. L.J. 215 (1987).

5. Res Judicata and Collateral Estoppel

These doctrines, though primarily dealt with in other courses, have especially important implications for insurance litigation, where difficulties tend to develop in cases where there are patent conflicts of interest between insurer and insured.

Notes and Questions

1. Suppose, for example, that an insurer must defend an insured under a liability policy when the complaint alleges both an intentional tort (excluded from coverage) and negligence. There is always the possibility of collusion or, more commonly, an inclination for the plaintiff's counsel to press more vigorously for a judgment based on negligence rather than on intentional tort, for the insurance may be the only promising source of assets from which to recover. Should the

insurer be allowed to raise the issue of intention versus negligence by a declaratory judgment proceeding before trial of the underlying lawsuit? Or by intervening in its own capacity in that lawsuit? Or by a subsequent declaratory judgment proceeding? Or by a refusal to pay and a subsequent trial on the same issue? Are the determinative issues in the two suits the same, whichever of these methods is chosen? The court in Allstate Ins. Co. v. Atwood, 319 Md. 247, 572 A.2d 154 (1990), thought so. It dealt with the problem in some detail. The resolution chosen was to allow the insurer to initiate a declaratory judgment proceeding after the tort trial, where such a conflict of interest exists:

> . . . The trial judge in that declaratory judgment action would first determine, as a legal matter, whether the issue, which was resolved in the tort trial and which determines insurance coverage, was fairly litigated in the tort trial. If the declaratory judgment judge decides that the issue was fairly litigated in the tort trial, there should be no relitigation of that issue in the declaratory judgment action. Instead, a final judgment would be entered in the declaratory judgment action declaring that the issue was fairly litigated in the tort trial and that the insurer is bound by the outcome of the tort case against its insured. On the other hand, if the judge in the declaratory judgment action determines that the issue was not fairly litigated in the tort trial, then the insurer should be permitted to relitigate the matter in the declaratory judgment action. [Id. at 261.]

Is this resolution fair to both the insurer and insured? Can you devise (or choose) a better solution to the problem? See also State Farm Fire & Casualty Co. v. Finney, 244 Kan. 545, 770 P.2d 460 (1989).

2. In Spears v. State Farm Fire & Casualty Ins., 291 Ark. 465, 725 S.W.2d 835 (1987), a disc jockey was struck by a baseball bat. The insurer defended its insured(s), the perpetrator(s), with a reservation of rights based on the "expected or intended" language of the homeowners policy. The insurer told counsel to consider only the insured's best interest and not to direct the trial so that the jury would find an intentional tort. The jury found insureds guilty of both negligence and wanton and willful disregard of the rights of others. After the tort suit, the insurer filed a declaratory judgment suit against its insured(s) to determine liability, contending the conduct had been an intentional tort. The insureds moved for summary judgment claiming res judicata based on the results of the underlying tort suit. Should it be granted? Is this case different in principle from *Atwood*? See also Wear v. Farmers Ins. Co., 49 Wash. App. 655, 745 P.2d 526 (1987).

3. Murphy v. Urso, 88 Ill. 2d 444, 430 N.E.2d 1079, 58 Ill. Dec. 828 (1981), dealt with a case where the issues would have been different. A passenger in a van owned by Urso but driven by Urso's

employee, Clancey, sued Clancey for negligence and Urso for negligent entrustment. The coverage issue depended on whether Clancey had permission to drive the bus; the underlying tort suits depended in the one case on whether there was negligence and in the other on whether there was also negligent entrustment. The issue of coverage remained to be determined even after the tort issues were decided.

4. One issue in collateral estoppel is whether one who is not a party to the first case may use it in a subsequent case. Manzanita Park, Inc. v. Insurance Co. of North America, 857 F.2d 549 (9th Cir. 1988), allowed it to be used defensively.

CHAPTER 9

Complex and Unusual Insurance Arrangements

So far this book has focused on legal problems that can, in principle at least, arise in straightforward contracts between one insured and one insurer, in what an Illinois appellate judge called the "rather primitive method of having an insurance company agent or salesman sell a policy to a customer on an individual basis." American College of Surgeons v. Lumbermens Mut. Casualty Co., 142 Ill. App. 3d 680, 683, 491 N.E.2d 1179, 1182, 96 Ill. Dec. 719, 722 (1986). It is true that in many of the cases already treated the arrangement was much more complex than that. Furthermore, a few of the problems already dealt with could have appeared only in complex arrangements involving, for example, primary and excess carriers with conflicting positions.

This chapter explores in greater detail a few of the more complex arrangements. It also deals with arrangements that are not especially complicated but that are outside the mainstream of the insurance business, and treats in varying degrees of detail surplus lines insurance, excess coverage, reinsurance, captive companies, pools or syndicates, risk retention and purchasing groups, and group insurance.

A. Surplus Lines

Each state licenses "surplus lines" agents or brokers to place business with insurers not admitted to the state when the business cannot be placed with admitted companies. Such agents or brokers are occasionally called *excess lines* agents or brokers because much of the nonadmitted business is at excess layers of coverage. New York, for example, provides that

> The superintendent may issue an excess line broker's license to any person . . . licensed as a broker . . . to procure, subject to the restrictions herein provided, policies of insurance from insurers which are not authorized to transact business in this state of the kind or kinds of insurance specified [below.] [N.Y. Ins. Law §2105 (McKinney 1985).]

The exact provisions of the surplus lines statutes vary greatly. They establish special rules for taxing such insurance and make some attempt to protect domestic policyholders from unreliable surplus lines insurers.

It is important that it be possible to place business on a surplus or excess lines basis, for even in the largest states, or in some cases even in whole countries, it is not always possible to obtain the needed coverage from admitted insurers, sometimes not at all and sometimes not to the level of coverage needed or desired. The following case describes the use and regulation of surplus lines insurers and agents (or brokers).

FARMERS & MERCHANTS STATE BANK v. BOSSHART

400 N.W.2d 739 (Minn. 1987)

KELLEY, Justice.

The owners of a supper club which had been destroyed by fire brought this action against respondent insurance agents who had sold them a fire insurance policy written by a surplus lines insurer. The owners claim the liability of the agents arises from the Minnesota agents liability law which imposes personal liability on a person who participates in the sale of insurance on behalf of any insurance company which is required to be, but is not, authorized to engage in the business of writing insurance in this state. Minn. Stat. §60A.17, subd. 12 (1986). That statute exempts liability for agents who sell surplus lines insurance "pursuant to Minn. Stat. §60A.20," the Surplus Lines Insurance Law. In denying the owner's motion for summary judgment, the trial court ruled that Minn. Stat. §60A.17, subd. 12 is not applicable to Minn. Stat. §§60A.195-.209 (1986). The trial court "certified . . . that this finding is important and doubtful." The question raised by the certification is whether an insurance agent who participates in the sale of a fire insurance policy by a "surplus lines" insurer, in violation of the Surplus Lines Insurance Act (Minn. Stat. §§60A.195-.209) (1986), is entitled to be exempted from the agent's liability created by Minn. Stat. §60A.17, subd. 12 (1986). The trial court by "finding," in effect, that Minn. Stat. §60A.17, subd. 12 (1986) was "not applicable" answered the question in the affirmative. We disagree.

In March of 1983, appellants Charles and Stanley Walker (the Walkers) purchased from Kenneth Vopatek on a contract for deed an establishment known as Shadybrook Supper Club. Additionally, improvements to the premises were financed by a mortgage to Farmers & Merchants State Bank of Pierz (Bank). The Walkers were required by the contract to maintain casualty insurance policies naming the Bank and Vopatek as additional insureds. To comply with that requirement, the Walkers obtained appropriate insurance from the Yosemite Insurance Company, a licensed insurer holding a Certificate of Authority to market property and casualty insurance in the State of Minnesota.

Minnesota's statutory scheme regulating the marketing of insurance contemplates that the insurance company shall ordinarily be licensed. Minn. Stat. §60A.07, subd. 4 (1986). When a company is properly licensed, the state issues to it a "Certificate of Authority." Minn. Stat. §60A.051 (1986). The objective of the licensure requirements is ultimately to ensure solvency of the companies to pay losses which might be incurred by Minnesota residents. That objective is furthered by compelling licensed insurers to participate in the Minnesota Insurance Guaranty Association. The Association assesses all licensed companies to create a fund to pay any claims made against any insolvent Guaranty Association members. Additionally, the licensed members of the Association participate in an organized program designed to aid in the detection and notification of the possible insolvency of a member. See generally Minn. Stat. §§60C.01-.20 (1986).

However, certain insurance coverages desired by insureds are not always available from regularly authorized and licensed insurers. To meet this demand, Minnesota has created an exception to the general rule that only licensed and authorized insurers may market policies in the state by enactment of the Surplus Lines Insurance Act. 1963 Minn. Laws, ch. 385, originally codified at Minn. Stat. §§60.931-.947, and then at §60A.20, now Minn. Stat. §§60A.195-.209 (1986). The Surplus Lines Insurance Act permits certain licensees, who are specially regulated agents and brokers, to place insurance with out-of-state insurers not licensed and who do not have a Certificate of Authority to write insurance in Minnesota.

The Yosemite policy provided fire insurance coverage to the Walkers through September 1985. However, in November 1983, a representative of the defendant agency, Central Minnesota Casualty, Inc. (herein referred to as Bosshart) recommended to the Walkers a switch from Yosemite to coverage by the Union Indemnity Company, a surplus lines insurer unauthorized to write insurance in Minnesota unless it, and persons licensed to place insurance with it, comply with the Surplus Lines Insurance Act.

Respondent Bosshart was aware of two disclosure requirements contained in the Surplus Lines Insurance Act. One required the policy to contain a conspicuous disclosure notice on the face of the policy in red ink informing the insured that the policy was a surplus lines policy, and that should the named insurer become insolvent, loss payment was not guaranteed. The other provision mandates a similar disclosure by the surplus lines agent or broker who is called a licensee — in this case, respondent Bosshart. The Union Indemnity Company policy issued to the Walkers omitted the disclosure stamp required by Minn. Stat. §60A.207 (1986). Bosshart, likewise, failed to disclose the risk to the Walkers as required by Minn. Stat. §60A.198, subd. 5 (1986). Moreover, during the course of the transaction, Bosshart purported to act as "broker." In fact, it lacked a license to serve as a surplus lines insurance agent or broker in Minnesota. It did so even though Minn. Stat. §60A.198, subd. 1 prohibited it from placing coverage with a surplus lines insurer without licensure as provided by the Surplus Lines Insurance Act.

During the policy period, in June 1985 the Shadybrook Supper Club was destroyed by fire. Shortly thereafter, the Union Indemnity Company was placed in receivership under the laws of the State of New York. The Walkers' claim remains unpaid.

The answer to the question certified is governed by the interpretation of the statute permitting the assessment of personal liability against any person who participates in the placement of insurance with an unauthorized and unlicensed insurer. . . .

[The court then parsed the statutory language, consulted various textbooks on grammar, and concluded by discussing some public policy considerations.]

That the public policy of the state does not favor the issuance of policies written by unlicensed and unauthorized insurance carriers is evidenced by the prohibition against placement of insurance with a surplus lines carrier if coverage is available from a licensed and authorized insurer. Minn. Stat. §60A.201 (1986). The statute further demonstrates this policy by providing that surplus lines insurance may be offered only by an agent or broker licensed under the statute to do so. Minn. Stat. §60A.198, subd. 1 (1986). The act additionally requires strict compliance with the detailed and comprehensive requirements and regulations before an insurance agent or broker can become a licensee. Minn. Stat. §§60A.198, subd. 3, 60A.199, 60A.201-.203, 60A.204, subd. 2, 60A.205 (1986). . . .

To hold the agent's personal liability law (Minn. Stat. §60A.17, subd. 12 (1986)) to be inapplicable in circumstances similar to those existing here would plainly frustrate the legislative intent to afford notice and protection to the insurance consumer, leaving the consumer without any remedy for subsequent loss flowing from a clear violation of statutorily imposed duties. . . .

We conclude not only that appellant's grammatical analysis of the statute is correct, but also that a consideration of the public policy issues involved in the two statutes manifests a legislative intent that an agent who participates in violation of the Surplus Lines Insurance Act (Minn. Stat. §§60A.196-.209 (1986)) is not entitled to be exempted from agent's liability under Minn. Stat. §60A.17, subd. 12 (1986).

Accordingly, we answer the certified question in the negative and remand to the trial court for further proceedings.

Notes and Questions

1. Wisconsin Statutes §618.44, in a subchapter of the insurance code dealing with "Permissible Business by Unauthorized Insurers," provides:

> An insurance contract entered into in violation of this chapter is unenforceable by, but enforceable against, the insurer. The terms of the contract are governed by this code and rules promulgated thereunder. If the insurer does not pay a claim or loss payable under the contract, any person who assisted in the procurement of the contract is liable to the insured for the full amount of the claim or loss, if he knew or should have known the contract was illegal.

2. In an omitted passage, the *Bosshart* opinion mentions the Minnesota Insurance Guaranty Association, created by statute. On the insolvency of a member, the association will pay the insolvent member insurer's losses and sometimes its unearned premiums. (The detailed rules for operation of the Association are complex and while, with one or two exceptions, all states follow the same general pattern, they differ in detail from state to state.) Licensed insurers are compelled to be members; surplus lines insurers are not. The Association is a fairly recent creation, to protect policyholders and third-party claimants against most loss from the insolvency of admitted and regulated insurers. In the 1980s, however, it became apparent that serious losses could be suffered from the insolvency of surplus lines insurers even by sophisticated resident policyholders despite their placing of business with surplus lines insurers outside the state through experienced and sophisticated surplus lines brokers. A number of surplus lines insurers have become insolvent. Although providing similar guaranty schemes for surplus lines business has been much discussed, the creation and management of such a Guaranty Fund at the individual state level would present enormous difficulties. At the time of this writing only New Jersey has established a Surplus Lines Guaranty Fund.

B.   Excess Insurance

Historically, the most frequent instances of difficulty in placing insurance locally occurred when very large limits of coverage were needed. For that reason, many authorizing statutes speak of excess *and* surplus lines companies. Often excess layers of insurance are written on a nonadmitted or surplus lines basis after the primary coverage is placed in admitted companies. But excess insurance cannot properly be defined in terms of the admission of insurers to the jurisdiction because excess insurance is very often placed with admitted companies, making it unnecessary to place it through surplus lines agents or brokers. Cf. New York Insurance Law §2105, supra. On the other hand, *surplus* lines are, by definition, not available in the jurisdiction.

Many of the cases appearing in previous chapters of this book have involved excess layers of insurance. This section focuses in more detail on the use of such insurance.

Like reinsurance, the subject of the next section, excess insurance provides coverage for an amount of risk beyond what the primary insurer is willing to shoulder; unlike reinsurance, it is placed directly by the insured or its broker through explicit arrangements in which one insurer (the primary insurer) provides an initial layer of coverage while other insurers (the excess insurers) supply higher layers. The relationships between the insured and the insurers of the higher layers are direct. In the usual case there is no direct relationship between primary and excess insurers, though they are likely to be aware of each other.

If the primary insurance is $1 million and the first excess policy is $9 million, the latter is described as $9 million excess of $1 million ($9 million XC $1 million), bringing the total coverage to $10 million. There may be any number of excess layers. The next might be, for example, $25 million excess of $10 million ($25 million XC $10 million), bringing the coverage to $35 million, and so on as long as the insured wants more coverage and can find it in the market.

The cost of coverage differs by layer. In the lower layers, called the "working layers" because they are frequently involved with loss claims, the cost will be markedly higher than in the "catastrophe" layers, which are expected to be tapped only rarely. Thus the latter have small premium volume in relation to potential (but not expected) losses. To give some sense of the numbers, one recent policy provided coverage of $25 million XC $10 million for a premium of about $250,000. If the excess layer for one year were fully used, as is presumably always *possible* (else the insurance would not be written), the cost to the insurer would be the equivalent of 100 years of premiums on the risk, without considering expenses of operating the business. Apparently, the insurer does not anticipate that its layer will often be penetrated at all; it is even more unlikely that it will be hit for amounts approaching the maximum coverage. But consider the 1988 Piper Alpha oil platform loss, estimated at $1.4 billion, or the 1989 chemical plant explosion in Texas with probable loss well over $1 billion. In those cases excess layers were certainly tapped and, for many of them, exhausted.

The relatively low cost of excess layers creates hard problems. The excess insurers, receiving comparatively little premium income for their low-probability risk, are nevertheless at risk for enormous sums. The theory of insurance economics involves the application of the "law of large numbers" to the assumption of risks to lessen the relative probability of a catastrophe to the insurer that is out of all proportion to its premium income. To ensure that application, any layer of coverage is likely to be divided among multiple insurers, and the risk undertaken by any excess insurer is nearly certain to be partially or even almost wholly reinsured. In the excess layers, failure to reinsure and simultaneously to guess wrong is a formula for quick insolvency, as some underwriters learn from time to time. Some lawsuits and arbitrations are currently in process involving enormous stakes, based on that kind of overweening confidence that the low probability risk would not materialize.

Sometimes the higher layers are placed in pools or syndicates, involving wide initial distribution of the risk among participants in the pools. Illustrations of the various ways of providing excess coverage have already appeared in this book, especially in Chapter 5.

Excess insurance may be written by insurers that write little if any primary insurance; it is not uncommon for them also to write reinsurance extensively. They often operate with a minimum of personnel. When writing reinsurance they tend to rely heavily on the underwriting and other services of the primary carriers, to which they pay "ceding commissions." When writing excess insurance, they often use one or more managing general agents to handle the home office functions so they can operate with a skeleton staff. Even if they operate with a full staff, they often deal exclusively through wholesale brokers who, in turn, deal with retail brokers or agents. See the Appendix. Sometimes there is interlocking ownership and control between such an insurer and its managing general agents.

Excess coverage may also come about through the interpretation of "other insurance" clauses if one policy is interpreted so that coverage attaches only after another or others are exhausted. In previous chapters, various cases have already illustrated the messy problems "other insurance" clauses can produce.

1. The "Jumbo" Risk

A generation ago, a building like McCormick Place in Chicago, which burned with insured losses amounting to about $100 million, would have been counted a jumbo risk that would have been hard to place. In the early days of air travel, the first wide-bodied jets, with hull values that exceeded $15 million, were also counted as jumbo risks: there was some doubt that the big planes would ever fly, not because of any mechanical difficulty but because of the problems in obtaining adequate property and liability insurance. The world was scoured for insuring capacity and devices were finally developed to provide the insurance. Today the needed insurance amounts to more than $100 million for the hulls and perhaps up to half a billion dollars for liability. Still, the worldwide aviation market now satisfies the need. Even the several costly crashes of recent years have not, as of this writing, disturbed the aviation market nor resulted in dramatic premium rate increases.

Today there are more dramatic examples of jumbo risks than big aircraft. Ken Carter, Chief Executive of Lloyd Thompson (a brokerage firm in London), in an unpublished address to the American Bar Association in July 1985 entitled "Marketing a Jumbo Risk at Lloyd's and Managing it Thereafter," furnished the following one.

An offshore oil production platform with several dozen wells produces in the aggregate upwards of 200,000 barrels of oil per day and has a population of three hundred people. In the northern section of the North Sea there are over a dozen such platforms. Replacement values range up to nearly $2 billion dollars each. Suppose one of those platforms were destroyed by a blowout: In addition to the replacement cost there would be costs for the removal of debris, cleanup costs, and the cost of controlling the well or wells that had blown out. (Workers compensation or equivalent coverage and potential liability for bodily injury is ignored here.) The total potential property risk has been estimated as in the range of $2.5 billion, plus or minus a few hundred million dollars. The number of such risks is too limited to provide an adequate spread of risk. For that reason, the total insuring capacity of the whole world may not be enough to cover such a risk in full, even if brokers mobilize all the capacity that can be found, including insuring capacity in the communist world. Much of the coverage would be in excess layers, and at each layer there would be extensive subdivision and reinsurance.

Despite the potentially enormous losses that may result from one event and be covered by one insurance program, when the previous paragraph was first written no single loss had yet approached that amount. The largest single insured property loss to that time had been about $350 million, caused by an explosion in a chemical plant in Texas. It was insured by a pool in Bermuda, of which the insured chemical company was a shareholder-member. That pool purchased reinsurance from more than 200 reinsurers. McIntyre, World's Reinsurers Respond to $350 Million Hopewell Loss, Bus. Ins., Sept. 19, 1988, at 70. (For further discussion of pools see infra, this chapter.)

However, since the first writing of the previous paragraph the North Sea Piper Alpha oil platform loss of 1988 amounted to an estimated $1.4 billion of insured coverage for the single incident, and another chemical plant explosion in Texas occurred in 1989 with a probable insured loss of over $1 billion.

The foregoing are all property losses. One of the largest *liability* losses from a single event to date is certainly that of Union Carbide, stemming from the Bhopal disaster. Though that game is not completely played out, the score at the beginning of the ninth seems to be somewhat in excess of $450 million liability for Carbide, of which the insurance coverage seems to be about $250 million. When the Bhopal incident occurred, street gossip immediately appeared in the trade press to the effect that Union Carbide had $200 million of coverage, and had rejected an opportunity to acquire another $100 million layer for a premium in five figures. If the latter were accurate, Carbide's decision not to increase its coverage must be accounted one of the more expensive insurance mistakes of modern times. Or was it a mistake? How do you ever know how much insurance is enough for such an operation? In early 1989 the Bhopal litigation was settled for a figure approaching a half billion dollars. Apparently Union Carbide had coverage for about $200 million; the rest was a charge on earnings that was lower than expected such that its stock (which seems to have been over-discounted for the expected loss) jumped over two points in the next session of the market. The civil case seems finally to have been put to rest in 1991 by a decision of the Supreme Court of India. India's Supreme Court Upholds Award for Bhopal Gas Victims, The Reuter Bus. Report, Oct. 3, 1991.

To ensure close correspondence of the primary and excess coverages, the excess carrier may use a "following form." This means that the excess policy will, in effect, adopt the language of the primary policy so that the two will provide the same coverage except for amount, and the excess will pick up the coverage in the same terms and at the precise point the primary leaves off. Sometimes upper levels of excess coverage may follow in some respects but not in all, creating the possible need for litigation to determine the degree to which the policies fit together.

2. The Umbrella Cover

The most common example of explicit excess coverage is the umbrella liability policy, which may be written to cover individuals (Personal Umbrella Policy) or business enterprises (Commercial Umbrella Policy). For very large risks there may be a primary umbrella policy with excess umbrella policies layered above it.

The umbrella policy is more than excess coverage. As the name itself suggests, it is intended to cover the insured relatively comprehensively, though it too has exclusions. An umbrella policy requires specific underlying primary coverage. If the underlying coverage is missing, the insured will find it has retained that risk for its own account as a self-insurer, *including the obligation to defend.*

Whenever there are gaps in the underlying coverage, however, the umbrella insurer is a primary insurer and is treated as such, including having the obligation to defend. Aetna Casualty and Surety Co. v. Centennial Ins. Co., 838 F.2d 346 (9th Cir. 1988) (applying California law). The obligation to indemnify, however, will be subject to a "retained limit," which serves the same purpose as is served by a deductible in property insurance.

When a primary policy underlies the umbrella coverage so that the umbrella insurer is an excess carrier, the latter does not have the duty to defend. This is the duty of the underlying or primary carrier, or of the insured if the primary layer is retained rather than insured.

Allocation between carriers of the duty to defend when there is overlapping primary coverage has been exhaustively treated in German & Gallagher, Allocation of the Duties of Defense Between Carriers Providing Coverage to the Same Insured, 47 Ins. Couns. J. 224 (1980). The article covers both cases where the primary-excess relationship is planned and those where it is a result of coincidence. For an updated discussion, see Comment, Excess Insurer's Duty to Defend After Primary Insurer Settles Within Policy Limits: Wisconsin After *Loy* and *Teigen,* 70 Marq. L. Rev. 285 (1987).

For cases where there is underlying coverage, whether through a purchased policy or self-insurance, the umbrella policy pays the *ultimate net loss* in excess of the underlying limit and up to the limits of the umbrella policy. Ultimate net loss is typically defined in the commercial umbrella policy as

> the total of the following sums arising out of one occurrence to which this policy applies:
>
> (a) all sums which the insured or any organization as his insurer, or both, become legally obligated to pay as damages, whether by reason of adjudication or settlement, because of personal injury, property damage or advertising liability; and
>
> (b) all expenses incurred by the insured or any organization as his insurer, or both, in the investigation, negotiation, settlement and defense of any claim or suit seeking such damages, excluding only (1) the salaries of the insured's or insurer's regular employees, (2) office expenses of the insured or any insurer, and (3) all expense included in other valid and collectible insurance. [Alliance of American Insurers, 1986 Policy Kit for Students of Insurance 274 (1986).]

Ultimate net loss excludes *unallocated* loss adjustment expenses, that is, expenses not properly attributable to the defense of particular claims. This is true whether the policyholder carries primary insurance or is self-insured; the obligation of the umbrella carrier is the same whether the policyholder chooses to be insured or to self-insure. It follows that the policyholder is treated as if it were a primary insurer. If there is self-insurance, the limit of the self-insured layer is called the *Self-Insured Retention,* or SIR. The SIR is similar to a deductible, but because it includes allocated loss adjustment expenses, it is not the same as a deductible or as the retained limit.

Any of the above can be changed by using different wording in the policy; in particular the personal umbrella policy may be different in important respects from the commercial umbrella. Only careful parsing of the language will reveal the extent of the differences, for with umbrella insurance and other excess insurance we have left the realm of standard language: though the language is similar, we are no longer dealing with mass-produced consumer products but with policies designed to deal with catastrophic losses.

Typically, the personal umbrella policy will require underlying automobile liability insurance with limits of perhaps $100/250/25,000 and personal liability insurance (usually through a homeowners policy) with liability limits of perhaps $100,000. The excess layer of the personal umbrella would most often increase the coverage to $1,000,000, though the limit can be much more. None of these numbers are sacrosanct; they may vary among companies, may vary as to formulation, theoretically may be subject to negotiation, and may increase over time. An umbrella policy was involved in Fortune v. Wong, Chapter 5.

In commercial situations where there are multiple layers of insurance, the bottom layer may be administered by an insurance company under an "exhibit" policy that contains an endorsement on the policy (or is accompanied by a collateral agreement) providing for full reimbursement of the insurer by the insured. In that case the insurance company is at risk only if the policyholder becomes insolvent. Why might that arrangement be preferred to in-house handling of the SIR, perhaps modified by contracting out claims adjustment services in whole or in part to professional claims adjusters? Why would the underlying policy be called an "exhibit" policy?

Problem

An insured is faced with a large number of similar claims, as in some products liability situations. Explain how the following expenses would be dealt with under the definition of ultimate net loss set forth above: (1) a special legal defense team put together, partly from existing staff from the insured's legal department and partly from new lawyers hired from outside, and devoted to general defense work though not the handling of particular claims or lawsuits; (2) a scientific research team, partly from inside and partly brought in from outside, to do research in-house relevant to the claims that were surfacing and to develop expert witnesses for the torts cases; (3) legal expenses of the insured's regular outside counsel hired to supervise (not to try) all the cases being defended; (4) research grants made without strings to academic institutions to do research on the causation of the harm being claimed against the insured.

Problem

A commercial umbrella policy usually includes a schedule listing the underlying insurance policies. In recent years, the schedule for large policyholders has tended to list a SIR as the underlying coverage for products liability. The self-insured policyholder would be liable for punitive damages if awarded in the underlying tort case.

A certain umbrella policy contains an exclusion that reads, "Except insofar as coverage is available to the Insured under the underlying insurances, set out in the attached schedule, this policy shall not apply . . . [t]o punitive or exemplary damages awarded against any insured." A punitive damages award is entered in an underlying products liability case that is large enough to penetrate the excess coverage if applicable. The products liability coverage is listed in the schedule as a SIR. Does the punitive damages portion of the award count toward the exhaustion of the SIR? Is the umbrella carrier liable for punitive damages after the SIR is exhausted? Ford Motor Co. v. Northbrook Ins. Co., 838 F.2d 829 (6th Cir. 1988), treating the SIR as if it were underlying insurance, gave one answer.

———————————

The foregoing problem could arise with various ramifications. Suppose a SIR of $1 million and one claim in which there is an award of $1 million compensatory damages and $1 million punitive damages. Compare this with the same SIR and two claims in succession (but with some time interval between), each of which results in $500,000 in compensatory damages and $500,000 in punitive damages: Should these two situations be treated alike or differently? What should be the result in each situation?

If the underlying insurer is no longer obligated to defend for any reason consistent with the requirement of having underlying insurance, the umbrella insurer must pick up the defense. Some umbrella policies are drafted to "contribute to the costs incurred by the Insured in the ratio that its proportion of the ultimate net loss, as finally adjusted, bears to the whole amount of such ultimate net loss." Such a provision was interpreted and applied in American Excess Ins. Co. v. MGM Grand Hotels, Inc., 102 Nev. 601, 729 P.2d 1352 (1986), apportioning expense costs in the defense of the claims (more than 3,000 of them) arising out of the 1980 MGM Hotel fire in Las Vegas.

The MGM fire is interesting for other reasons as well. The hotel had only $30 million of liability insurance in advance of the fire, but for a premium modest in relation to the potential maximum liability, it was able to purchase retroactive insurance for an additional coverage of all claims. The retroactive policy proved to be a loser for the insurance companies: It was issued at a time of very high interest rates, presumably on the assumption that disposition of the liability claims would be very slow. In fact they were disposed of unexpectedly quickly while interest rates rapidly declined, so that anticipated investment earnings were far less than was counted on by the insurers.

Notes and Questions

1. Insureds had a policy providing property, liability, and umbrella insurance. The three coverages were separate and distinct in the policy. The first two scheduled various specified locations where the insured did business, while the umbrella coverage had no such schedule but covered the insureds more generally. It specified underlying limits of $500,000 and a retained limit of $10,000. The insured acquired another location, which was not endorsed on the scheduled policies. A third person was injured at the newly acquired location and the question arose whether the umbrella coverage applied as a primary coverage. The claimant argued that one of the umbrella's purposes is to provide primary insurance where the primary policy does not. The court in Coates v. Northlake Oil Co., 499 So. 2d 252 (La. App. 1986), *cert. denied,* 503 So. 2d 476 (1987), decided for the insurer and held the insured was covered only after the $500,000 underlying limit was reached. Was it correct?

3. Duties of Primary Insurer to Excess Insurer

In situations in which an insurer would have a duty to an insured to settle a claim against the insured, would the insurer owe a similar duty to an excess insurer? If so, on what theory would you base the result? United States Fire Ins. Co. v. Nationwide Mut. Ins. Co., 735 F. Supp.

1320, 1324 (E.D.N.C. 1990), puts it on the ground of "equitable subrogation," quoting as authority a passage from Continental Casualty Co. v. Reserve Ins. Co., 307 Minn. 5, 8, 238 N.W.2d 862, 864 (1976), and citing other cases. Accord, Fireman's Fund Ins. Co. v. Continental Ins. Co., 308 Md. 315, 519 A.2d 202 (1987); American Centennial Ins. Co. v. American Home Assurance Co., 729 F. Supp. 1228 (N.D. Ill. 1990).

Suppose further that the insured has a substantial self-insured retention, as in most current products liability insurance policies. Does the insured as "insurer" of the first layer of risk owe a duty to the insurer of the next layer (and subsequent layers) of coverage to settle within the self-insured retention under the same conditions as would a primary insurer of that first layer?

Finally, in the gaps (if any) in the underlying coverage, the insured will be subject to a "retained limit," which is closely analogous to a deductible. Should there be a difference in result between self-insured retention and retained limit? If the retained limit were actually termed a deductible? Should it matter whether the insured with a self-insured retention is a true self-insurer or simply is not insured for the first layer of risk?

GENERAL ACCIDENT FIRE & LIFE ASSURANCE CORP. v. AMERICAN CASUALTY CO.

390 So. 2d 761 (Fla. App. 1980)

Baskin, Judge.

John Brown, Jr., was sued when a neighbor's young child drowned in his pool. Following an adverse jury verdict resulting in a settlement of $690,000, the pool owner's excess insurance carrier, American Casualty Company of Reading, Pennsylvania, sued the primary insurance carrier, General Accident Fire and Life Assurance Corporation, Ltd., for General Accident's bad faith refusal to negotiate and settle the parents' claims. General Accident appeals an adverse final judgment of $100,000 entered pursuant to a jury verdict as well as awards of attorneys' fees and pre-judgment interest. . . .

On December 12, 1971, the MacDiarmids' twenty-three month old daughter wandered into a neighbor's unprotected pool and drowned. John Brown, Jr., the pool owner, was insured by General Accident's liability insurance coverage up to $300,000 and by an American Casualty excess liability insurance policy of $1,000,000. The MacDiarmids sued Brown and his two liability insurers. General Accident, the primary carrier, defended the action in accordance with its contractual obligation to its insured. American Casualty, the excess carrier, did not take an active role in the litigation; instead, it followed the usual insurance industry custom of notifying the primary carrier and asking to be kept informed. Discovery proceedings disclosed that defendants were potentially exposed to a large adverse judgment. On November 13, 1973, counsel for General Accident and its local adjuster were convinced that the MacDiarmids would probably win and that the verdict would be substantial. Counsel for General Accident wrote his client on November 28, 1973, stating that "[T]his case is taking overtones of a very serious exposure and I suggest that you carry the matter at your full reserve of $300,000." . . .

The MacDiarmids' counsel also wrote to counsel for General Accident demanding that the case be settled for $1,000,000. The demand was later reduced to $900,000. The adjuster was asked to contact American Casualty to see if it would contribute toward a settlement if General Accident "threw in" its policy. The adjuster did not contact the excess carrier. Instead, General Accident, at the direction of the home office, took the position that the MacDiarmids' opening demands were outrageous and refused to negotiate with them unless they made a more reasonable settlement offer.

Shortly before the action went to trial, American Casualty wrote to General Accident demanding that General Accident make an effort to settle the case. General Accident did not respond to the letter. General Accident never offered its policy limits to the MacDiarmids as requested by American Casualty. In fact, General Accident made no offer of any kind to the MacDiarmids until the trial started. At that time, General Accident offered $25,000 to settle the case. The offer was refused.

The jury returned a verdict of $700,000, and judgment was entered against Brown and his two carriers. The matter was eventually settled for $690,000, with General Accident paying its $300,000 limits and American Casualty paying the remaining $390,000. American Casualty then filed suit against General Accident alleging that it had been damaged by General Accident's "bad faith" refusal to negotiate with the MacDiarmids and to settle their claim for a reasonable amount. The action proceeded to trial. Testimony revealed the claim probably could have been settled for $400,000. . . .

When the issue presented itself in Beck v. Kelly, 323 So. 2d 667 (Fla. 3d DCA 1975), the court . . . stated:

> In cases where recovery of such excess [judgment] is based upon the ground that the insurer's conduct in failing to effect a settlement within the policy limits amounts to bad faith, *there can be no liability on the part of the insurer in the absence of an offer by the person claiming against the insured to settle within the policy limits.* (Emphasis added). [Id. at 668.]

In *Beck,* however, the *insurer* tendered the offer to settle within policy limits and the existence of an offer by the claimant was not germane to the resolution of the case. The *Beck* rule was followed in Chastain v. Federal Insurance Co., 338 So. 2d 214 (Fla. 3d DCA 1976).

Other courts, however, have held different views. In Thomas v. Western World Insurance Co., 343 So. 2d 1298 (Fla. 2d DCA 1977), the court refused to accept the requirement of an offer to settle before imposing liability as a rule of law. The court held that an insurer might be liable for bad faith in circumstances where no offer of settlement was made. The court in *Thomas* dealt with an insurer's failure to defend. . . .

The excess carrier, to the extent of its limit of liability, stands in the shoes of the insured and assumes the rights as well as the responsibilities that the insured would normally have against the primary carrier. See generally Ranger Insurance Co. v. Travelers Indemnity Co., 389 So. 2d 272 (Fla. 1st DCA 1980). Equitable subrogation principles permit the excess carrier to proceed against the primary carrier when the primary carrier's bad faith refusal to negotiate a settlement has caused the excess carrier to become liable for an excess judgment.

Requiring an offer to settle within policy limits may be a sound rule in those situations involving only a judgment proof insured and one insurer and in which bad faith can be proved only by the refusal to accept a settlement within policy limits. When an insured is not judgment proof or when an excess insurer exists, absence of an offer to settle within policy limits is not dispositive of the question of bad faith on the part of the primary insurer.

The primary insurer assumes the duty of negotiating to settle in good faith by virtue of its control of its insured's defense. See generally Boston Old Colony Insurance Co. v. Gutierrez, 386 So. 2d 783 (Fla. 1980). The excess insurer has no control. Blind adherence to the *Beck* rule would force an excess insurer to enter the litigation to defend itself against the primary insurer's bad faith, in contravention of customary insurance practices.

In summary, an offer to settle within policy limits may be a factor to consider in determining an insurer's good faith in the handling of an insured's defense, but it should not be a prerequisite to the imposition of liability for a primary insurer's bad faith refusal to settle. The rule requiring an offer to settle within policy limits, designed to protect an insured from an insurer, does not apply to situations in which an excess insurance policy is at issue or in which an insured is financially able to pay an excess judgment. See Peter v. Travelers Insurance Co., 375 F. Supp. 1347 (C.D. Cal. 1974). In these situations, the settlement offer is only one factor to be considered in arriving at a determination of bad faith.

To the extent our decision conflicts with Beck v. Kelly, supra, we recede from Beck v. Kelly. Under the *Beck* rule, the primary carrier's bad faith failure to negotiate would be without remedy. The court cannot countenance so great a disservice to other interested parties. We therefore hold that an offer to settle within the primary carrier's policy limits is not a prerequisite to its liability to the excess carrier. The trial court correctly denied General Accident's motions for directed verdict. . . .

For the foregoing reasons, the decision of the trial court is affirmed.

Notes and Questions

1. It is not clear from the opinion why General Accident was liable only for $100,000.

2. In *General Accident,* the primary insurer's bad faith conduct did not harm the insured because of the high limits of the excess coverage. Only the excess carrier was hurt. Would you reach the same result? Other cases that did are Commercial Union Ins. Co. v. Medical Protective Co., 426 Mich. 109, 393 N.W.2d 479 (1986) and Transit Casualty Co. v. Spink Corp., 94 Cal. App. 3d 124, 156 Cal. Rptr. 360 (1979). The latter case was overruled by *Safeway Stores,* which follows.

3. In Insurance Co. of North America v. Home Ins. Co., 644 F. Supp. 359 (E.D. La. 1986), a merely negligent primary insurer was held liable for 25 percent of the excess insurer's loss resulting from settlement in excess of primary policy limits under Louisiana's comparative negligence rules. The excess insurer was also negligent in failing to monitor the very large exposure.

4. Should the rights of the excess insurer against the primary insurer precisely parallel those an insured would have if there were no excess coverage? The tripartite relationship is intriguingly similar to the relationships among an equity owner of real property and first and second mortgagees. Should the excess insurer come in between the primary insurer and insured and have the rights of the insured vis-à-vis the primary insurer, just as the second mortgagee for some purposes comes between the first mortgagee and the equity owner and has the rights the latter would have if there were no second mortgage? Suppose the insured *is* the primary insurer, by virtue of a SIR. What should be the result?

COMMERCIAL UNION ASSURANCE COS. v. SAFEWAY STORES, INC.

26 Cal. 3d 912, 610 P.2d 1038, 164 Cal. Rptr. 709 (1980)

BY THE COURT:

We granted a hearing herein in order to resolve a conflict between Court of Appeal opinions in this case and the earlier case of Transit

Casualty Co. v. Spink Corp. (1979) 94 Cal. App. 3d 124, 156 Cal. Rptr. 360. After an independent study of the issue, we have concluded that the thoughtful opinion of Justice Sabraw (assigned) for the Court of Appeal, First Appellate District, 158 Cal. Rptr. 97, in this case correctly treats the issues, and that we should adopt it as our own opinion. That opinion, with appropriate deletions and additions,* is as follows:

This case presents the question of whether an insured owes a duty [ ] to its excess liability insurance carrier which would require it to accept a settlement offer below the threshold figure of the excess carrier's exposure where there is a substantial probability of liability in excess of that figure.

Facts:

At all times relevant herein Safeway Stores, Incorporated (hereafter Safeway) had liability insurance coverage as follows:

(a) Travelers Insurance Company and Travelers Indemnity Company (hereafter Travelers) insured Safeway for the first $50,000 of liability.

(b) Safeway insured itself for liability between the sums of $50,000 and $100,000.

(c) Commercial Union Assurance Companies and Mission Insurance Company (hereafter conjunctively referred to as Commercial) provided insurance coverage for Safeway's liability in excess of $100,000 to $20 million.

One Hazel Callies brought an action against Safeway in San Francisco Superior Court and recovered judgment for the sum of $125,000. Thereafter, Commercial was required to pay $25,000 of said judgment in order to discharge its liability under the excess insurance policy.

Commercial, as excess liability carrier, brought the instant action against its insured Safeway and Safeway's primary insurance carrier, Travelers, to recover the $25,000 which it had expended. Commercial alleged that Safeway and Travelers had an opportunity to settle the case for $60,000, or possibly even $50,000, and knew or should have known that there was a possible and probable liability in excess of $100,000. It was further alleged that said defendants had a duty to settle the claim for a sum less than $100,000 when they had an opportunity to do so. Commercial's complaint attempts to state two causes

---

*Brackets together, in this manner [ ], are used to indicate deletions from the opinion of the Court of Appeal; brackets enclosing material (other than the editor's parallel citations) are, unless otherwise indicated, used to denote insertions or additions by this court. (Estate of McDill (1975) 14 Cal. 3d 831, 834, 122 Cal. Rptr. 754, 537 P.2d 874.)

of action against Safeway and Travelers, one in negligence and another for breach of the duty of good faith and fair dealing.

Safeway demurred to the complaint on the grounds of failure to state a cause of action. The court sustained the demurrer with 20 days' leave to amend. When Commercial failed to amend its complaint, the complaint was dismissed as to Safeway. Commercial now appeals from the judgment of dismissal.[ ]

The present case is unusual in that the policyholder, Safeway, was self-insured for liability in an amount below Commercial's initial exposure. While this status may explain Safeway's reluctance to settle, it remains to be determined if the insured owes an independent duty to his excess carrier to accept a reasonable settlement offer so as to avoid exposing the latter to pecuniary harm. [Both of Commercial's theories of recovery, negligence and breach of good faith, depend upon the existence of such a duty.]

It is now well established that an insurer may be held liable for a judgment against the insured in excess of its policy limits where it has breached its implied covenant of good faith and fair dealing by unreasonably refusing to accept a settlement offer within the policy limits (Crisci v. Security Ins. Co., 66 Cal. 2d 425, 429 [58 Cal. Rptr. 13, 426 P.2d 173]; Comunale v. Traders & General Ins. Co. (1958) 50 Cal. 2d 654, 661 [328 P.2d 198, 68 A.L.R.2d 883]). The insurer's duty of good faith requires it to "settle within policy limits when there is substantial likelihood of recovery in excess of those limits." (Murphy v. Allstate Ins. Co. (1976) 17 Cal. 3d 937, 941 [, 132 Cal. Rptr. 424, 426, 553 P.2d 584, 586].)

Although an insurance policy normally only carries an express statement of a duty to defend, an insurer's duty to settle is derived from the implied covenant of good faith and fair dealing which is part of any contract (see 4 Witkin, Summary of Cal. Law (8th ed., 1974) §754, p. 3050, and cases collected therein). This duty was first recognized in Comunale v. Traders & General Ins. Co., supra, 50 Cal. 2d 654, 328 P.2d 198. The rationale for the *"Comunale* duty" was articulated by [ ] [us] at page 659, 328 P.2d at page 201: "It is common knowledge that a large percentage of the claims covered by insurance are settled without litigation and that this is one of the usual methods by which the insured receives protection. (See Douglas v. United States Fidelity & Guaranty Co., 81 N.H. 371 [127 A. 708, 712]; Hilker v. Western Automobile Ins. Co. [204 Wis. 1, 231 N.W.2d 257] supra.) . . .

> The insurer, in deciding whether a claim should be compromised, must take into account the interest of the insured and give it at least as much consideration as it does to its own interest. (See Ivy v. Pacific Automobile Ins. Co., 156 Cal. App. 2d 652, 659 [320 P. 2d 140].) When

there is great risk of a recovery beyond the policy limits so that the most reasonable manner of disposing of the claim is a settlement which can be made within those limits, a consideration in good faith of the insured's interest requires the insurer to settle the claim. Its unwarranted refusal to do so constitutes a breach of the implied covenant of good faith and fair dealing.

It has been held in California and other jurisdictions that the excess carrier may maintain an action against the primary carrier for [ ] [wrongful] refusal to settle within the latter's policy limits (Northwestern Mut. Ins. Co. v. Farmer's Ins. Group (1978) 76 Cal. App. 3d 1031 [143 Cal. Rptr. 415]; Valentine v. Aetna Ins. Co., 564 F.2d 292; Estate of Penn v. Amalgamated General Agencies (1977) 148 N.J. Super. 419 [372 A.2d 1124]). This rule, however, is based on the theory of equitable subrogation: Since the insured would have been able to recover from the primary carrier for a judgment in excess of policy limits caused by the carrier's wrongful refusal to settle, the excess carrier, who discharged the insured's liability as a result of this tort, stands in the shoes of the insured and should be permitted to assert all claims against the primary carrier which the insured himself could have asserted (see Northwestern Mut. Ins. Co. v. Farmers' Ins. Group, supra, 76 Cal. App. 3d at pp. 1040, 1049-1050, 143 Cal. Rptr. 415). Hence, the rule does not rest upon the finding of any separate duty owed to an excess insurance carrier.

Commercial argues that the implied covenant of good faith and fair dealing is reciprocal, binding the policyholder as well as the carrier (see Liberty Mut. Ins. Co. v. Altfillisch Constr. Co. (1977) 70 Cal. App. 3d 789, 797 [139 Cal. Rptr. 91]). It is further contended, in effect, that turnabout is fair play: that the implied covenant of good faith and fair dealing applies to the insured as well as the insurer, and thus the policyholder owes a duty to his excess carrier not to unreasonably refuse an offer of settlement below the amount of excess coverage where a judgment of liability above that amount is substantially likely to occur.

This theory, while possessing superficial plausibility and exquisite simplicity, cannot withstand closer analysis. We have no quarrel with the proposition that a duty of good faith and fair dealing in an insurance policy is a two-way street, running from the insured to his insurer as well as vice versa (Liberty Mut. Ins. Co. v. Altfillisch Constr. Co., supra, 70 Cal. App. 3d at p. 797, 139 Cal. Rptr. 91; Crisci v. Security Ins. Co., supra, 66 Cal. 2d at p. 429, 58 Cal. Rptr. 13, 426 P.2d 173). However, what that duty embraces is dependent upon the nature of the bargain struck between the insurer and the insured and the legitimate expectations of the parties which arise from the contract.

The essence of the implied covenant of good faith in insurance policies is that " 'neither party will do anything which injures the right of the other to receive the benefits of the agreement' " (Murphy v. Allstate Ins. Co., supra, 17 Cal. 3d at p. 940, 132 Cal. Rptr. at p. 426, 553 P.2d at p. 586, quoting from Brown v. Superior Court (1949) 34 Cal. 2d 559, 564 [212 P.2d 878]). One of the most important benefits of a maximum limit insurance policy is the assurance that the company will provide the insured with defense and indemnification for the purpose of protecting him from liability. Accordingly, the insured has the legitimate right to expect that the method of settlement within policy limits will be employed in order to give him such protection.

No such expectations can be said to reasonably flow from an excess insurer to its insured. The object of the excess insurance policy is to provide additional resources should the insured's liability surpass a specified sum. The insured owes no duty to defend or indemnify the excess carrier; hence, the carrier can possess no reasonable expectation that the insured will accept a settlement offer as a means of "protecting" the carrier from exposure. The protection of the insurer's pecuniary interests is simply not the object of the bargain. . . .

In the instant case, whether Commercial could harbor any legitimate expectation that its insured would settle a claim for less than the threshold amount of the policy coverage must be determined in the light of what the parties bargained for. The complaint makes no reference to any language in the policy which would give rise to such expectation. We must therefore ask the question: Did Safeway, when it purchased excess coverage, impliedly promise that it would take all reasonable steps to settle a claim below the limits of Commercial's coverage so as to protect Commercial from possible exposure? Further, did Commercial extend excess coverage with the understanding and expectation that it would receive such favorable treatment from Safeway under the policy? We think not. . . .

We acknowledge that equity requires fair dealing between the parties to an insurance contract. We view the *Kaiser* and *Liberty* cases as pointing up a recognition in the law that the insured status as such is not a license for the insured to engage in unconscionable acts which would subvert the legitimate rights and expectations of the excess insurance carrier.

However, we are unable to derive from this sound principle, the precipitous conclusion that the covenant of good faith and fair dealing should be extended to include a *"Comunale* duty" — that is, a duty which would require an insured contemplating settlement to put the excess carrier's financial interests on at least an equal footing with his own. Such a duty cannot reasonably be found from the mere existence of the contractual relationship between insured and excess carrier in the absence of express language in the contract so providing.

We observe that an apparently contrary conclusion has been

reached by the Third District in the recent case of Transit Casualty Co. v. Spink Corp. [ ] [supra] 94 Cal. App. 3d 124, 156 Cal. Rptr. 360. [ ] [We disapprove that case] insofar as it holds that an insured's duty of good faith and fair dealing to his excess carrier compels him to accept a settlement offer or proceed at his peril where there is a substantial likelihood that an adverse judgment will bring excess insurance coverage into play.

In conclusion, we hold that a policy providing for excess insurance coverage imposes no implied duty upon the insured to accept a settlement offer which would avoid exposing the insurer to liability. Moreover such a duty cannot be predicated upon an insured's implied covenant of good faith and fair dealing. If an excess carrier wishes to insulate itself from liability for an insured's failure to accept what it deems to be a reasonable settlement offer, it may do so by appropriate language in the policy. We hesitate, however, to read into the policy obligations which are neither sought after nor contemplated by the parties. (End of Court of Appeal opinion.)

The judgment is affirmed.

Notes and Questions

1. Puritan Ins. Co. v. Canadian Universal Ins. Co., Ltd., 775 F.2d 76 (3d Cir. 1985), *rev'g* 586 F. Supp. 84 (E.D. Pa. 1984), reaches the same result as *Safeway Stores*.

2. Why would the insurance arrangements have Safeway insuring itself for the second layer, rather than the first where the smaller claims would be? Would it make more sense for the insurer to insist on a deductible or retained limit for each claim to eliminate from the insurance (and from the claims adjustment costs) most of the frequent slip and fall claims (usually small) in Safeway stores?

3. Moelmann, Deductibles Under Financial Institution Bonds: Conflicts and Obligations, 16 Forum 942 (1981), discusses *Spink* and *Safeway Stores*.

4. We have thus far seen the obligation to deal with third party claims in good faith as it appears in three contexts: the simple insurer-insured situation (see Chapter 8); the tripartite situation in which there is an insured, a primary insurer, and an excess insurer; and the situation in which the insured is in effect a self-insurer for an intermediate layer. Other problems may exist. Thus, the attorney chosen by the primary insurer may have duties to the excess insurer as well as to the insured and the primary insurer. See Bergadano & Seymour, Duty of Defense Counsel to the Excess Insurance Carrier, 20 Forum 489 (1985). See also the excellent discussion in Sybrude, The Duty to Settle, 76 Va. L. Rev. 1113, 1201 (1990).

5. Under whatever title, the self-insured first layer has increased in importance in recent years; the amount involved there, or in whatever intermediate layers the insured's broker is unable to place, may be substantial enough to make the problems discussed here loom large, but its use often results in advantages to both sides. Small claims can be dealt with by the insured, concomitantly reducing the premium (often substantially), though the arrangement may add considerably to the insured's internal administrative costs. One clear saving is of the state premium tax, which is most often three percent of the premium. From the insurer's point of view, the insured can be counted on to be more concerned with loss prevention and with the efficient handling of claims. These latter considerations have become especially important in products liability insurance.

But many problems still exist. If the deductible is stated as "per claim," the insured may no longer have significant protection when claims are many but relatively small. For example, bodily injury asbestos claims tend individually to be relatively small, with an occasional outsized one, but come in immense numbers. If the deductible (or self-insured retention) is "per occurrence," the problems of identifying the occurrence can be serious. See Chapter 5. If there are few but large occurrences, the SIR or deductible will not be a serious problem to the insured, but a "per occurrence" *limit* may be. Conversely, if the occurrences are many but small, the deductible or SIR becomes a serious problem to the insured. (Policies are commonly written with a high limit per occurrence that is the same as the aggregate limit. Why?)

6. For a discussion of the "triangular" set of relationships and duties urged by the excess insurer in *Safeway Stores,* see Ingram, Triangular Reciprocity in the Duty to Settle Insurance Claims, 13 Pac. L.J. 859 (1982), approving a tripartite duty. Several cases have explored the duty of an insured to the insurer. In addition to those already discussed, see Offshore Logistics Services v. Arkwright Boston Mfrs. Mut. Ins. Co., 469 F. Supp. 1099 (E.D. La. 1979), *aff'd,* 639 F.2d 1142 (5th Cir. 1981). Like *Spink,* this case supports the existence of an insured's duty to settle within the retained limits. Note, Insurance Settlements: An Insured's Bad Faith, 31 Drake L. Rev. 877 (1981-1982) traces the history of the bad faith action and argues for holding the insured to good faith dealing when there is a self-insured retention. Shipstead & Thomas, Comparative and Reverse Bad Faith: Insured's Breach of Implied Covenant of Good Faith and Fair Dealing as Affirmative Defense or Counterclaim, 23 Tort & Ins. L.J. 215 (1987), provides a recent discussion of the problem. The best discussion is Sybrude, supra note 4.

7. Could the uncertainties created by cases like *Safeway Stores* be dealt with effectively through contract provisions? If so, what kind of provision would you add to the contract?

4. The Drop-Down Problem

If a primary insurer becomes insolvent, it is an important question whether the first excess insurer *drops down* to provide primary insurance. The following case deals with the problem.

GULEZIAN v. LINCOLN INS. CO.

399 Mass. 606, 506 N.E.2d 123 (1987)

WILKINS, Justice.

This is the second of two cases we decide today dealing with the question whether excess liability insurance coverage drops down to replace primary coverage if a primary insurer becomes insolvent. See Massachusetts Insurers Insolvency Fund v. Continental Casualty Co., 399 Mass. 598, 506 N.E.2d 118 (1987).

In March, 1980, a fire in a Haverhill apartment building owned by the plaintiff caused injury and death to occupants of the building. Actions were commenced against the plaintiff, who was insured for general liability as to the apartment house to the amount of $500,000 by the Ambassador Insurance Company (Ambassador) as primary insurer and by the defendant Lincoln Insurance Company (Lincoln) to an additional amount of $1,000,000 as an excess insurer under an umbrella liability policy. Ambassador undertook the defense of the actions against the plaintiff, but, in September, 1984, Ambassador was declared insolvent and went into receivership in Vermont.[1] Lincoln declined to afford coverage within the limits of the underlying coverage or to provide a defense. In August and December, 1984, the plaintiff sent Lincoln letters purporting to be demands pursuant to G.L. c. 93A (1984 ed.). The plaintiff commenced this action in February, 1985, seeking (1) a declaration that Lincoln's umbrella policy provides both defense coverage and indemnity coverage "over and above sums collectible by the plaintiff pursuant to underlying coverage," and (2) relief pursuant to G.L. c. 93A.

Lincoln moved for summary judgment, and the plaintiff in turn sought a partial summary judgment declaring Lincoln's obligation to provide the coverage prayed for in the plaintiff's complaint. The motion judge allowed Lincoln's motion. An amended summary judgment was entered declaring that Lincoln was not obliged to defend the

---

1. We understand that Ambassador was a nonadmitted insurance company in Massachusetts. Consequently, under G.L. c. 175D, §1(4) (1984 ed.), Ambassador was not an "insolvent insurer," and the Massachusetts Insurers Insolvency Fund would not stand in for Ambassador (G.L. c. 175D, §5(1)(a) (1984 ed.)) if the Lincoln coverage does not drop down.

plaintiff in the underlying lawsuits; that Lincoln was only obliged to indemnify the plaintiff over and above $500,000, subject to policy limits; and that Lincoln's refusal to provide primary indemnity and defense coverage was not a violation of G.L. c. 93A. The plaintiff appealed. We granted Lincoln's application for direct appellate review.

Although we agree with the motion judge's reasoning in certain respects, we conclude that Lincoln's policy should be read to drop down to provide indemnity coverage to the extent that Ambassador's insolvent estate does not.

1. The line of contention between Lincoln and the plaintiff is clearly defined. Both parties agree that, if the Lincoln policy provides that it will drop down if the relevant primary insurance is uncollectible, Ambassador's insolvency will cause the Lincoln coverage to drop down. See Massachusetts Insurers Insolvency Fund v. Continental Casualty Co., supra at 599-600 n.2, 506 N.E.2d 118, and cases cited. The issue then is whether Lincoln's excess policy provides that the lower limit of its indemnity coverage will be reduced to offset the consequences of the insolvency of a primary insurer.

The Lincoln umbrella policy is not a model of precise draftmanship. In the section defining its indemnity coverage, the policy states that it will cover "Ultimate Net Loss" (a term defined as damages for covered losses and certain related litigation expenses) in excess of "the retained limit." The retained limit is a deductible of $10,000. No mention is made in the coverage section of the consequences of any underlying insurance. That subject comes up for the first time two sections later where the policy states that Lincoln is liable only for the "Ultimate Net Loss" in excess of the greater of (a) the retained limit if no underlying insurance is applicable to the occurrence or (b) "the total of the *applicable* limits of liability of the Underlying Insurance as stated in the Schedule of Underlying Insurance and the applicable limits of any other Underlying Insurance collectible by the Insured" (emphasis supplied).[2]

The plaintiff makes much of the words "applicable limits,"

___

2. Section III in its entirety reads as follows: "UNDERLYING LIMIT — RETAINED LIMIT: The Company shall be liable only for Ultimate Net Loss resulting from any one occurrence in excess of either (a) the total of the applicable limits of liability of the Underlying Insurance as stated in the Schedule of Underlying Insurance and the applicable limits of any other Underlying Insurance collectible by the Insured, less the amount, if any, by which any aggregate limit of such insurance has been reduced by payment of loss during the period of this Policy, hereinafter called the Underlying Limit, or (b) if the insurance afforded by such Underlying Insurance is inapplicable to the occurrence, the amount stated in the Declarations as the Retained Limit, whichever is greater. The limits of liability of any Underlying Insurance Policy shall be deemed applicable irrespective of any defense which the underlying insurer may assert because of the insured's failure to comply with any condition of the Policy subsequent to an occurrence."

arguing that they must mean recoverable limits, and that, because the limits of the underlying Ambassador policy are not recoverable, the Lincoln coverage must drop down. If we consider solely the words quoted above, the word "applicable" refers to that underlying coverage, if any, listed in the schedule, that provides indemnity for damage claims arising out of an occurrence (i.e., accident). See Whitney v. American Fidelity Co., 350 Mass. 542, 543-544, 215 N.E.2d 767 (1966) (no insurance was "applicable" when policy did not provide coverage for particular loss). The policy refers to the limits of the primary insurance coverage which the insured agrees to maintain. This is the view expressed by the motion judge. It is supported by case authority. See Continental Marble & Granite v. Canal Ins. Co., 785 F.2d 1258, 1259 (5th Cir. 1986); Molina, United States Fire Ins. Co., 574 F.2d 1176, 1178 (4th Cir. 1978). We agree with the conclusion that the words "applicable limits" are not ambiguous, viewing those words in isolation in the first sentence of section I of the policy. We shall return to the question whether, in the context of the entire policy, the words "applicable limits" have another meaning.

The plaintiff relies further on the provision in section III that makes the Lincoln policy excess of the limits of applicable coverage stated in the schedule of underlying insurance and "the applicable limits of *any other* Underlying *Insurance collectible* by the Insured" (emphasis supplied). Here the plaintiff's claim is that, if "other" applicable insurance must be "collectible," the scheduled primary insurance also must be "collectible." The insurance company's purpose in inserting this language concerning other insurance collectible by the insured was, no doubt, to make its coverage excess of any first dollar insurance not listed in the schedule which becomes available in the circumstances of any accident causing a covered loss. If the Lincoln policy had said "any other collectible insurance," the argument that the underlying scheduled coverage must also be "collectible" would be stronger. Even as written, however, courts have read substantially similar language to mean that the underlying scheduled insurance as well as any other insurance must be collectible. Although the conclusion that in context the word "collectible" applies to the underlying scheduled insurance is debatable (see Poirrier v. Cajun Insulation, Inc., 501 So. 2d 800, 809 (La. Ct. App. 1986) (Byrnes, J., dissenting in part)), we need not decide the point. Other language in the policy creates an ambiguity as to whether the excess coverage drops down when the underlying insurance is not collectible. That ambiguity should be resolved in favor of the insured.

Earlier in this opinion we indicated that the reference in a portion of the policy to the "applicable limits" of the underlying coverage referred to any underlying policy that was relevant in relation to the particular kind of damage claim asserted (automobile, general liability, etc.). The policy uses the word "applicable" in the same section in another sense, one that tends to equate "applicable" with "collectible." The last sentence of section III, quoted in note 2 above, provides that, if the benefit of underlying insurance is unavailable because of the insured's failure to comply with a post-occurrence policy condition (such as cooperation with its insurer), the underlying insurance policy "shall be deemed applicable" and the excess coverage will not drop down. If the word "applicable" had only the precise, restricted meaning we attributed to it earlier in this opinion, this sentence would be unnecessary. This sentence opens up the thought that applicability can be determined by postoccurrence events, including the uncollectibility of the primary insurance. The insured is told that, if the primary insurance is not collectible because of his fault, the excess insurance will not drop down. The insured is not told, however, that the policy will not drop down if the primary insurance is not collectible through no fault of the insured, such as the postoccurrence insolvency of the primary insurer.

The seeming uncertainty whether the policy drops down if the underlying insurance is uncollectible through no fault of the insured is augmented by paragraph nine of the Conditions. "The insurance afforded by this Policy shall be excess insurance over any other valid and *collectible* insurance available to the Insured *whether or not described in the Schedule of Underlying Insurance* . . . and applicable to any part of Ultimate Net Loss. . . ." (emphasis supplied). The implication is that Lincoln's coverage is excess only of collectible insurance, including the primary insurance listed in the schedule of underlying insurance. If to this point an eyebrow is not raised to the level which marks a discernible policy ambiguity, the language of paragraph seven of the conditions provides the necessary impetus. That section says that "[t]he company's liability . . . shall not attach until the amount of the *applicable* Underlying Limit has been paid by or on behalf of the Insured. . . ." (emphasis supplied). If "applicable Underlying Limit" in this section does not mean "recoverable" or "collectible" limits, an insured would obtain no benefit from his excess coverage upon the insolvency of his primary insurer if he could not himself provide the funds necessary to pay claims equal to the primary insurer's deficiency. If, however, "the applicable Underlying Limit" means the recoverable or collectible underlying limit, the suggested unconscionable policy interpretation is avoided.

It seems likely that Lincoln did not contemplate the insolvency of a scheduled underlying insurer in drafting its policy. The phenomenon of the insolvency of an insurer is not, however, so rare as to excuse that omission of attention to detail. The result is that Lincoln issued a policy in which it generated uncertainty as to what should happen on the insolvency of a primary insurer. On traditional analysis (see Cody v.

Connecticut Gen. Life Ins. Co., 387 Mass. 142, 146, 439 N.E.2d 234 (1982)), the ambiguity must be construed against Lincoln. The Lincoln indemnity coverage drops down to cover the consequences of Ambassador's insolvency.

2. The excess policy is clear that Lincoln is not required to assume the defense of the underlying tort actions. Section II provides, as the plaintiff concedes, that Lincoln need not defend suits if the occurrence is covered by an underlying policy listed in the schedule of underlying insurance. An underlying policy covered the occurrence in this case. . . .

4. The judgment is vacated. A new partial summary judgment shall be entered declaring that (1) the Lincoln Insurance Company umbrella policy provides indemnity coverage with respect to all losses covered by that policy over and above sums collectible by the plaintiff pursuant to the underlying coverage, and (2) unless the parties now agree otherwise, Lincoln Insurance Company is not obliged to assume the defense of the underlying tort claims against the insured.

So ordered.

Notes and Questions

1. A companion case to *Gulezian*, Massachusetts Insurers Insolvency Fund v. Continental Casualty Co., 399 Mass. 598, 506 N.E.2d 118 (1987), reached the same result, but the case differed in one important respect: The primary insurer was an admitted company and therefore within the coverage of the state guaranty fund. The excess policy issued by Continental Casualty Company provided that "if the applicable limit of liability of the underlying insurance is less than as stated in the schedule of underlying insurance because the aggregate limit of liability of the underlying insurance has been reduced this policy becomes excess of such reduced limit of liability." Id. at 600, n.3., 506 N.E.2d at 120. Is it easier or harder in this case to reach a result favorable to the insured than it is in *Gulezian*?

2. There was a strong dissent in *Gulezian*. Are you persuaded by the majority opinion? What line of analysis might the dissent follow? The same judge dissented in *Massachusetts Insurers Insolvency Fund*, and on the same ground.

3. If you are persuaded by the *Gulezian* opinion, can you redraft the policy to avoid a drop down? Or if you are not persuaded, how would you redraft it to avoid the need for litigation to establish the "pro-insurer" position? The excess insurers in Central Waste Systems, Inc. v. Granite State Ins. Co., 231 Neb. 640, 437 N.W.2d 496 (1989), and Harville v. Twin City Fire Ins. Co., 885 F.2d 276 (5th Cir. 1989), successfully drafted their policies to avoid a drop down on the primary

insurer's insolvency. Other cases holding that there was no drop down are Mission Natl. Ins. Co. v. Duke Transp. Co., 792 F.2d 550 (5th Cir. 1986) and Zurich Ins. Co. v. Heil Co., 815 F.2d 1122 (7th Cir. 1987).

4. Werner Indust., Inc. v. First State Ins. Co., 217 N.J. Super. 436, 526 A.2d 236 (1987), used "reasonable expectations" language and what it considered to be an ambiguity to hold that the excess policy should drop down. The court carefully confined its decision, saying that the parties were free to allocate risks as they choose. On appeal, the New Jersey Supreme Court reversed. It adhered to the analysis of the court below, but found no ambiguity. Id., 112 N.J. 30, 548 A.2d 188 (1988). Accord, Highlands Ins. Co. v. Gerber Products Co., 702 F. Supp. 109 (D. Md. 1988).

5. If the excess policy does drop down, on whatever theory, for how much is the excess insurer liable: for its own limits or for the combination of the primary insurer's limits and its own? For one answer, see Northmeadow Tennis Club, Inc. v. Northeastern Fire Ins. Co., 26 Mass. App. Ct. 329, 526 N.E.2d 1333 (1988).

6. It is common for the excess policy to have a clause to the effect that "it is a condition of this Certificate that the Underlying Policies be maintained in full effect during the period of this Certificate except for the reduction of any aggregate limits contained therein solely by payment of claims." Would that have an effect on the result?

7. In Continental Marble & Granite v. Canal Ins. Co., 785 F.2d 1258 (5th Cir. 1986), the insured sought a declaration that an excess liability policy dropped down to become primary if the primary insurer became insolvent. The court recognized that the greatly reduced risk assumed by the excess insurer "is reflected in the cost of the policy." Id. at 1259. Is it appropriate for a court to take account of the premium level in deciding whether an excess policy should drop down? In TXO Production Corp. v. Twin City Fire Ins. Co., 685 F. Supp. 156 (E.D. Tex. 1988), the court said that

> Faced with the growing problem of primary insurer insolvency, the courts, including the Fifth Circuit, have repeatedly refused to "transmogrify" umbrella and excess insurance policies by saddling those insurers with the risk of a primary insurer's insolvency — a peril contemplated by neither the insured nor the excess carrier at the time the policy was issued. [Id. at 158.]

But if the court does not inquire into the reasonable expectations of the insured, how does it know that neither the insured nor the excess carrier intended a drop down?

8. In the usual excess-type "other insurance" clause in policies covering the same risk, the policy is said to be "excess over any other collectible insurance." Is that a drop-down problem? With that lan-

guage what should be the result if the other insurer becomes insolvent? For an example, see Gladstone v. D. W. Ritter Co., 183 Misc. 2d 922, 508 N.Y.S.2d 880 (Sup. Ct. 1986).

C.   Reinsurance

1.   The Nature of Reinsurance

A reinsurance contract is a contract between insurers: One insurer (the assuming company) insures the other (the ceding company). Except in unusual situations there is no legal relationship between the reinsurer and the original insured. This has been firmly established by case law. Bank, The Role of Reinsurance, Bus. Ins., Apr. 16, 1984, at 39, briefly reviews the cases from the perspective of the reinsurer.

Reinsurance is less standardized than direct insurance in both policy terms and insurance practices. There are numerous forms of reinsurance, some of them described briefly in the next subsection.

In 1963 there were about 180 professional reinsurers with aggregate net premium volume of approximately nine billion Swiss francs. Two thirds of that volume was accounted for by the 25 largest reinsurers. The largest was the Swiss Re Group, second was the Munich Re, the third and fourth were American companies, the fifth German, and the sixth the state-operated French company. Five additional countries were represented among the top 25 companies. Perhaps it is surprising that so soon after World War II eight of the top 25 companies were German. European domination of reinsurance at that time is surprising too in view of the fact that about two-thirds of the world insurance premium volume and 70 percent of world insurance assets in 1963 were American. Aggregate world insurance assets in 1963 approximated $250 billion. Not surprisingly the American percentages have declined steadily since then, despite rapid growth in absolute terms. The American share of world premium volume had dropped to less than half in the 1980s, even before the decline in the value of the dollar. The 1963 figures come from North American Reinsurance Corp., Experiodica, Vol. 2, Nos. 1, 10 and 12 (1964).

The volatile character of the recent insurance market has resulted in ebbs and flows in the cadre of reinsurance practitioners. Because little except a modest amount of capital and presumed expertise is needed to get into the reinsurance business, which is essentially unregulated, entry into the business is easy whenever conditions look favorable to hungry entrepreneurs. Companies come in and go out of reinsurance ranks with great rapidity. Stories in the trade press in the same period, sometimes even in the same journal issue, bear titles such as "Reinsurers Attract New Capital" and "Several Reinsurers Withdraw from Market." See Bus. Ins., Nov. 11, 1985, at 3 and 10 respectively.

The variability of the reinsurance market is regularly displayed in the annual Rendez-Vous de Septembre in Monte Carlo, where the registration list is called "The Bible" of reinsurance. Registrants sometimes fail to appear because in the interim they have dropped out of the business. Any trade press story on a particular Rendez-Vous tells of the reinsurers that have dropped out of particular classes of business and those that have decided to take a flyer in new classes. For example, see McIntyre & Shapiro, Rendez-Vous Shows Who's Still in Business, Bus. Ins., Sept. 23, 1985. A massive amount of reinsurance business is done at those annual events.

Relative to direct insurance, reinsurance has grown explosively in recent decades. The worldwide 1988 premium volume of reinsurance reached $92 billion. With that growth the character of the business has changed. The rate of growth of the business is suggested by the statement of Walter Diehl, Chairman of the Board of the Swiss Reinsurance Company, that the membership of a key reinsurance trade association had increased from 11 to 360 in the previous 12 years. Diehl, Professionalism in Reinsurance, Sigma 2 (Mar. 1981).*

Diehl went on to describe the reinsurer's function as it had been told to him 28 years before, when he joined the company:

> Reinsurance is totally different from direct insurance. Knowledge of direct insurance is not undesirable but is not absolutely essential. Experience is everything in reinsurance and this can only be acquired on the job. The reinsurer carefully selects his clients, but then trusts them absolutely, whether it be in risk assessment, rating, claims settlement, accounting, etc. There is no other business which depends so much on confidence. "Uberrimae fides" reigns in this branch of the economy. The reinsurer has to be open, sociable, cultivated; he has to make friends easily, know the world, not ask too many questions and stick to his customers through thick and thin. Series of good reinsurance years are occasionally interrupted by loss years. The reinsurer knows that, as a result of natural fluctuations, bad years are again followed by good years. There is such a thing as a result cycle, which is repeatedly shown here. In addition to this balancing of results over time, the international reinsurer achieves a balance of a geographical nature. If business is bad in Germany, France will most certainly show better results, etc. [Id. at 2.]

---

*Sigma is a company periodical published by the North American Reinsurance Corporation.

He then commented on the professional requirements for a reinsurer in 1981: Gone was the notion that the reinsurer would always "follow the fortunes" of the insurer. Trust and loyalty had become less important on both sides. The reinsurer now needed an immense fund of knowledge, of both the direct business and the people and companies engaged in it, as well as of those factors especially relevant to a reinsurer's worldwide activity. Id. at 3.

The following statement made by a London lawyer at the Rendez-Vous in 1985 is revealing:

> In rough terms, the gentlemanly way the market conducted itself 15 years ago has broken down. So rather than go to arbitration or come to some kind of agreement, reinsurers and insurers are going to court. [Shapiro, Lawyers Take Their Case to Annual Rendez-Vous, Bus. Ins., Sept. 23, 1985, at 51.]

The dramatic change in the reinsurance business also led to fraudulent conduct on the part of some of the new and unknown players, causing heavy losses to direct insurers, particularly to "small, financially desperate" ones that needed reinsurance at any cost. For an illustrative if extreme case, see Lancaster, Small Insurer's Collapse Unveils Broad Troubles in Reinsurance Field, Wall St. J., Dec. 8, 1982, at 1. The fraud was run-of-the-mill in character and made possible by the changing climate of reinsurance. Since there is little regulation of reinsurance all over the world, such frauds are easy to perpetrate when the market is tight.

Large numbers of insolvencies in both direct insurance and reinsurance have occurred during the 1980s, and dozens of insurers and reinsurers have gone down the tube. In one lawsuit in progress in 1988, the plaintiff complained that the defendant (a managing general agent) had placed reinsurance for the plaintiff (an insurance company) with about 175 companies, 32 of which were either in liquidation or on the verge of it. Immense amounts of reinsurance claims appeared to be uncollectible. In another proceeding for the rehabilitation of a large insurance company, it was alleged that the insurer had written off more than $50 million in bad debt because of reinsurer insolvencies. Indeed, where once reinsurance was regarded as a stabilizing factor for direct insurers, it is now regarded as a threat to the solvency of many direct insurers.

The systemic importance of reinsurance has always been great: Now that many reinsurers are going under, it has become important to understand reinsurance where once it was enough to know it was there.

Inflation is a far greater threat to reinsurers than to direct insurers. This is especially true in liability insurance, particularly the long tail lines, where losses do not "run off" the books for years. Inflation tends to increase the losses of the reinsurer by a far larger percentage than it does those of the direct insurer. Assume, for example, that the net retention on a single risk (the amount the direct insurer is willing to carry at its own risk) is $100,000, and that it reinsures the rest. Assume further that many losses approach and a few exceed $100,000. As losses increase with inflation, the direct insurer's losses on single risks still never exceed $100,000. The reinsurer bears most of the risk of inflated claims payments in that context. Of course, inflation is only one factor governing the size of losses.

More and more efforts of casualty actuaries are devoted to the solution of the problem. One method is the development of new agreements that neutralize the effect of inflation as far as possible. Another more difficult method is to create better theory and better techniques for pricing the reinsurance in the first place. For a brief and technical discussion of the second method, see Benktander & Fowler, Calculated Lag Factors — How Reliable Are Current Methods in a Trend Situation?, Best's Review 16 (April 1981).

In a similar way, the trend toward larger and larger verdicts in some fields such as some kinds of medical malpractice (in real rather than merely in nominal terms) falls most heavily on reinsurers.

The following case illustrates the nature of reinsurance and its differences from direct insurance. It states most of the legitimate reasons for using reinsurance.

OTT v. ALL-STAR INSURANCE CORP.

99 Wis. 2d 635, 299 N.W.2d 839 (1981)

HEFFERNAN, J. . . .

This case arises out of litigation which came before this court in Gould v. All-Star Insurance Co., 59 Wis. 2d 355, 208 N.W.2d 388 (1973). The facts recited in that opinion show that Douglas Gould was injured while diving on the premises of DeNoon Beach, Inc. Those injuries left him a quadriplegic. Gould sued DeNoon and its liability insurer, All-Star Insurance Corporation (the company). The company has agreed to pay on behalf of DeNoon all sums up to $100,000 which DeNoon would become legally obligated to pay as damages because of bodily injury resulting out of the ownership, maintenance, or use of the insured premises. Gould obtained a judgment against DeNoon and the company for a sum in excess of $500,000. This court affirmed the judgment. After judgment, All-Star paid the policy limits of $100,000 plus costs to Gould. North Star Reinsurance Corporation, which had entered into a reinsurance agreement with All-Star in 1968, pursuant to that agreement paid 85 percent of that amount to All-Star. Subsequently, DeNoon Beach, Inc., became insolvent.

The present action was commenced against North Star and All-Star by Robert Ott, the receiver of DeNoon. He alleged that All-Star committed the tort of bad faith in its handling of the Gould claim and alleged that North Star was the liability insurer of All-Star in respect to its tortious failure to settle within policy limits.

The original agreement between North Star Reinsurance Corporation of New York (reinsurer) and the All-Star Insurance Corporation (company) became effective on May 15, 1968. This agreement set forth conditions under which the reinsurer would pay the company for its losses on insurance policies written by the company for its own insureds.

Article III of the original agreement in parts relevant to this controversy provided:

> *Article III*
> *LIABILITY REINSURED:*
> The actual payment by the Company of any loss (except in the event of insolvency of the Company) shall be a condition precedent to any recovery under this Agreement, and subject to such condition, the liability of the Reinsurer shall follow that of the Company and shall be subject within the applicable policy limits in all respects to all the general and special stipulations, clauses, waivers and modifications of the Company's policy, binder, or other undertaking, and any endorsements thereon. . . .

As a part of the original agreement, Exhibit A, attached thereto, provided, inter alia, the following with respect to losses paid by All-Star arising out of third party bodily injury claims against its insureds:

> *Exhibit A*
> Attached to and made a part of AGREEMENT No. NS-1142
> EXCESS REINSURANCE OF
> Third Party Bodily Injury (including Medical Payments). . . .
> *Section 1*
> . . . [North Star] shall indemnify and reimburse the Company for all losses paid in cash by the Company in excess of [the first $15,000] as respects each accident, subject to a maximum liability of Nine Hundred Seventy Thousand Dollars ($970,000) to the Reinsurer. . . . The foregoing reinsurance shall apply only to those claims resulting from any one accident which are covered within the actual limits of liability attaching under policy or policies of the Company provided, however, said limits of liability shall not exceed the following: . . .
> Third Party Bodily Injury Business $100,000 each person

The agreement, however, was later altered by a number of addenda. One of these, Addendum 5 (effective January 11, 1971) added the following paragraph to immediately follow the above-quoted language of Article III:

> ADDENDUM NO. 5
> Attached to and made a part of AGREEMENT No. NS-1142
> 1. The following wording shall be added to the first paragraph of Article III *LIABILITY REINSURED*:
> Notwithstanding the foregoing it is also agreed that should the Company become legally obligated to pay a loss in excess of its policy limits the Reinsurer agrees to assume seventy-five percent (75%) of that part of such loss (plus proportionate loss expense) which is in excess of the policy limit. However, in the event the applicable policy limit is less than the Company's retention at the time of the loss, the amount hereby assumed by the Reinsurer shall be limited to seventy-five percent (75%) of that part of the loss (plus proportionate loss expense) which is in excess of said retention. In no event, however, shall the liability of the Reinsurer, respecting such loss, exceed the maximum amounts of liability set forth in the Exhibits attached hereto.

Addendum 5, quoted above, controls the disposition of the present controversy. Although not added to the original agreement until January 1, 1971, it was in effect at the time of Gould's injury. The record does not disclose whether a separate premium schedule existed for the coverage provided by Addendum 5; but at oral argument, it was acknowledged by counsel for North Star that Addendum 5 provided coverage not included in the original reinsurance treaty. That Addendum, plaintiff Ott claims, interjected into an otherwise standard reinsurance agreement, constitutes a liability insurance contract insuring the company against the tort of bad faith.

The trial court dismissed the plaintiff's complaint on the ground that the contract between the company and the reinsurer was a reinsurance agreement and not a liability policy. It concluded, therefore, that the direct action provision of sec. 632.24, Stats.,[1] was not applicable — that personal jurisdiction could not be obtained therefor under sec. 801.05(10) and 803.04(2)(b). It is also pointed out that DeNoon Beach had no common law right of action against the reinsurer, because DeNoon was not privy to the contract between the company and the reinsurer.

The Court of Appeals without discussion or analysis summarily affirmed the trial court's order of dismissal. The Court of Appeals took the same position as the trial court. It assumed that North Star

---

1. "632.24 *Direct action against insurer.* Any bond or policy of insurance covering liability to others for negligence makes the insurer liable, up to the amounts stated in the bond or policy, to the persons entitled to recover against the insured for the death of any person or for injury to persons or property, irrespective of whether the liability is presently established or is contingent and to become fixed or certain by final judgment against the insured."

was simply the reinsurer of All-Star and relied on the accepted rule that an insured cannot sue its insurer's reinsurance company.

The plaintiff Ott does not disagree with the proposition of law relied upon by the trial court and Court of Appeals. Rather, he asserts that the analysis of both courts begs the question. Both the trial court and the Court of Appeals, plaintiff contends, assume that, because the document in its totality is entitled, "Reinsurance Agreement," the law in respect to reinsurers is applicable. Those courts, plaintiff asserts, assumed the very point in issue. Ott contends that Addendum 5, added to the treaty in 1971, cannot appropriately be construed as a reinsurance agreement, but only as an independent insuring clause by which North Star agreed to become the liability insurer of the company for the company's tortious conduct which exposed its insureds to liability in excess of the policy limits.

If the agreement, Addendum 5, constituted no more than a reinsurance agreement, it is clear that the trial court and the Court of Appeals were correct. If those courts incorrectly failed to perceive that Addendum 5 in fact constituted a separate insurance agreement insuring a risk resulting from the company's own conduct, they were clearly wrong in their conclusions. If Addendum 5, by which the reinsurer agreed to "assume" 75 percent of the losses "in excess of [All-Star's] policy limit" which All-Star may "become legally obligated to pay" was not indemnity reinsurance, but instead was a contract which made North Star a direct liability insurer of All-Star with respect to any actions against All-Star for its negligence, direct action may be brought by the injured party against the tortfeasor's insurer. . . .

. . . This court, however in Franklin Mutual Insurance Co. v. Meeme Town Mutual Fire Ins. Co., 68 Wis. 2d 179, 181, 228 N.W.2d 165 (1975), adopted the definition of the term used in 13 Appleman, Insurance Law and Practice:

> Reinsurance is a contract whereby one insurer for a consideration contracts with another to indemnify it against loss or liability by reason of a risk which the latter has assumed under a separate and distinct contract as the insurer of a third person. P. 460, sec. 7693.

Primary insurers, such as All-Star, may purchase reinsurance for a variety of purposes:

> 1. To reduce their exposure to liability on particular risks and to obtain a greater spread of risk;
> 2. To protect against accumulations of losses arising out of catastrophes;
> 3. To reduce total liabilities to a level appropriate to their premium volume and capital;

4. To provide greater capacity to accept new risks and write policies involving larger amounts than could otherwise be written;

5. To help stabilize operating results; and

6. To obtain assistance with new concepts and lines of insurance. [Nutter, Insurer Insolvencies, Guaranty Funds, and Reinsurance Proceeds, 29 Fed. Ins. Counsel Q. 373, 374 (1979).]

Reinsurance is written in two basic types: "Pro rata" and "excess." In "pro rata" insurance, the reinsurer and the primary insurer share in an agreed fixed proportion of the premiums paid by the primary insured and in any losses which occur. In an "excess" (or excess of loss) reinsurance agreement, the reinsurer becomes liable on a loss only when the loss exceeds an agreed dollar amount. This amount, for which the insurer alone is responsible, is known as the insurer's "retention." See generally, Nutter, Insurer Insolvencies, Guaranty Funds, and Reinsurance Proceeds, supra, 374; Dowd, Punitive or Extra-Contractual Awards Against Insurers: The Reinsurer's Role, 28 Fed. Ins. Counsel Q. 281, 282 (1978); Evans, The Many Dimensions of "Follow the Fortunes," 40 Ins. Counsel J. 318, 323 (1973); K. Thompson, Reinsurance 111-13, 132-38 (3rd ed. 1951).

The terms of the original agreement between the company and the reinsurer prior to the amendment of Article III by Addendum 5 clearly constituted a reinsurance treaty of the "excess" type. Not only did Exhibit A so denominate it, but the effect of the agreement accorded with the criteria approved by this court in *Franklin Mutual*. . . .

At oral argument, counsel for both litigants agreed that, in intent and in operation, the agreement as originally drawn was one of "reinsurance" and did not constitute in any sense a policy of insurance intended to protect the company against liability for its own torts. Ott argues, however, that what was originally clearly a contract of reinsurance only was partially converted into a liability insurance agreement by Addendum 5, which became effective on January 1, 1971. Unlike the prior provisions of the agreement, which in all cases limited the reinsurer's liability only *up to the company's policy limits,* Addendum 5 imposed responsibility on the reinsurance company for losses *in excess of policy limits.* For such excess amounts, North Star agreed to pay 75 percent of All-Star's losses. . . .

North Star does not dispute that liability for such excess may be incurred. The reinsurer, however, characterizes its responsibility under Addendum 5 as simply additional "reinsurance" and not as a separate insurance agreement added to the reinsurance treaty. As stated before, if it is merely additional reinsurance, no direct action can be brought by a party not privy to the contract. If, however, North Star has insured All-Star for All-Star's own torts, it is a liability insurer and may be sued directly. . . .

When an insurance claim by an injured third party is litigated rather than settled, it may result in judgment against the insured party that is in excess of policy limits. This occurred in the instant case when trial resulted in a judgment of over $500,000-$400,000 in excess of coverage. Under these circumstances the insured, DeNoon, became liable to Gould for the balance of the judgment that remained unpaid by All-Star. DeNoon in this action is attempting to recover its own exposure to liability from All-Star by proving that All-Star's negligent or bad faith failure to settle the claim within the applicable policy limits caused DeNoon's exposure. . . .

In the wake of *Employers Reinsurance,** many insurers saw the need for express contractual coverage of their own exposure to such tort actions to protect themselves against judgments *in excess of policy limits* for which they might become liable. Thus, according to one commentator, were born "Excess of Policy Limits Clauses" such as Addendum 5 in the present agreement. These clauses were inserted into insurers' treaties with their reinsurers. Dowd explains their origin:

> The Judgment in Excess of Policy Limits Clause was designed to deal with the loss in excess of policy limits situation. This clause, the specific provisions of which vary from reinsurer to reinsurer, generally provides if and under what conditions the reinsurer will participate in the awards arising from excess judgments. . . .
> The Judgment in Excess of Policy Limits Clause is relatively widely used and provides the reinsurer will participate in such excess verdicts but not to exceed the reinsurance contract limits. The degree of participation by the reinsurer varies, sometimes fixed at a percentage amount, sometimes a proportion of the excess award. This clause and its participation element is the subject of negotiation between the parties. [Dowd, Punitive or Extra-Contractual Awards Against Insurers: The Reinsurer's Role, supra, at 284-286.]

In light of the language of the clause in the present case, the inherently limited scope of the nature of reinsurance, the historical background of the development of "excess of policy limits" clauses, implications drawn from scholarly and insurance industry commentary, and the relative bargaining positions of insurance companies between themselves, Addendum 5 in the present case must be held to constitute direct liability insurance running from North Star to All-Star against the latter's liability to its own insured for tortious failure to settle. Consequently, North Star is subject to direct action by Ott, the receiver of DeNoon Beach. . . .

Counsel for North Star stated at oral argument that North Star, a

---

*Employers Reinsurance Corp. v. American Fidelity and Casualty Co., 196 F. Supp. 553 (1959), held a reinsurer not liable to the reinsured company for the latter's liability to its insured for tortious failure to settle, that is, for bad faith. — ED.

New York corporation, apparently does not, by its charter, write underlying liability policies, nor did he believe it had the authority to do so in Wisconsin. Be that as it may — the record provides no evidence one way or the other — it does not, under Wisconsin law, immunize North Star, as All-Star's contractual liability insurer, from Ott's direct action. This is because, although insurers in Wisconsin may not transact business without a valid certificate of authority (sec. 601.04(2), Stats.), nor beyond the terms of their certificate (sec. 610.11(1)), and although insurers domiciled in other states may not engage in practices forbidden in their home state (sec. 610.21(2)), out-of-state insurers who act contrary to their authority may have their contract enforced *against* them (sec. 618.44; sec. 631.15(1)). If, as we indeed conclude, Addendum 5 created a liability insurance contract, it will be enforced in Wisconsin.

Counsel also pointed out that the 1971 revised insurance code expressly exempts reinsurance from its regulatory scope. . . .

Because Addendum 5 is insurance, not reinsurance, the exemption of the statute is inapplicable. Moreover, the underlying policy which exempts from regulation interinsurer agreements is based on the sophistication of insurance companies and their ability to deal with one another on terms of equal bargaining and knowledge as to the meaning of the contractual arrangements. This means that it is the position of the state that insurance companies, dealing at arm's length, will be held to their contractual obligations. No state insurance law is available to exonerate North Star from its contractual obligations.

No argument based on public policy has been advanced why a liability insurer seeking protection against claims by its own insured for tortious failure to settle cannot, and should not, execute such an agreement with another insurer. Obviously, however, principles of good draftsmanship would compel the formulation of an agreement in a manner which identifies it clearly as being what it is in fact — a liability policy as to which the company assuming the risk is subject to direct action by the insured. Unfortunately, in this case it was placed in the reinsurance agreement with the result, whether intentional or inadvertent, that it created initial uncertainty as to the true nature of the agreement, the scope of its coverage, and the parties who may and may not invoke its provisions in a legal action.

We conclude that, because Addendum 5 constitutes liability insurance rather than reinsurance indemnity, the direct action statute (sec. 632.24, Stats.) is applicable, and Ott's direct action against North Star should not have been dismissed. . . .

Decision reversed, and cause remanded to the trial court for further proceedings.

Notes and Questions

1. What is the purpose of the parenthetical phrase in the first sentence of Article III of the reinsurance agreement? Do you suppose its insertion by the reinsurer was voluntary?

2. The court says that reinsurance may be either pro rata or excess. Alternative terminology is *proportional* and *nonproportional*. Either treaty or facultative reinsurance may be proportional or non-proportional. See Section C(2) for a classification of reinsurance.

3. The opinion notes that the reinsurer's liability was capped at $970,000 "*in toto.*" How would the primary insurer protect itself against a large number of claims that aggregated far more than it wished to pay and far more than the aggregate sum against which this contract would protect it?

4. What does the "follow the fortunes" clause suggest about the role of reinsurance in the insurance industry?

5. The legitimate purposes of reinsurance are fairly fully stated in the case. One use, which is sometimes legitimate and sometimes not, results from some peculiarities of insurance accounting. When a policy is written, the entire premium received (initially an asset) is offset on the liability side by an unearned premium reserve account (a liability). The heavy expenses of putting the policy on the books must be expensed rather than capitalized and amortized, resulting in a heavy charge against surplus for new business. One desirable result of this technical accounting rule is to restrain the rate of expansion of the insurer's business, which in principle is good. But it is difficult in practice for an insurer simply to say "no" to potential business, for it would lose the goodwill of agents or brokers as well as the chance to expand rapidly. It therefore prefers to write the insurance anyway and then reinsure it on a quota share basis. See Section C(2). The insurer will receive a reinsurance commission (also called a *ceding* commission) that repays the marketing expenses and may also provide a margin for profit. It also preserves the possibility of keeping the business in the future when the insurer's financial situation permits it to keep more of the risk. On the balance sheet, the quota share of the unearned premium reserve is transferred to the reinsurer, thus strengthening the financial position of the insurer. Used properly this is a perfectly legitimate practice, but it can also be used fraudulently. The insurer must make its annual report to the insurance regulator as of midnight Dec. 31, and the regulator judges the soundness of the insurer in part on that report. One blatantly fraudulent device is for the insurer to reinsure a substantial portion of its business on December 31 and then reverse the transaction on January 1. In its most obvious form this practice can no longer be indulged in, but some illicit variations would be hard to detect. Contemporary regulatory techniques are probably adequate to deal with this particular practice.

2. The Forms of Reinsurance

In *Ott* the court began but did not continue very far to state a typology of reinsurance contracts. This section seeks to describe the main types of reinsurance and their uses.

There are two kinds of reinsurance. *Facultative* reinsurance is specially arranged for a particular risk. It enables the reinsurer to make its own underwriting decisions on each policy. *Treaty* reinsurance exists if there is a master agreement that governs in advance the instances in which there will be reinsurance. The treaty often relates only indirectly to particular underlying insurance contracts.

The direct insurer and reinsurer can choose to arrange their coverages in a variety of ways. In *proportional* reinsurance, they share the coverage on a percentage basis. The simplest such arrangement is for a *quota share* to be *ceded* on each risk written by the direct insurer. If the sharing is only for risks above a certain size, the reinsurance is likely to be called *surplus share*. In proportional reinsurance, the cedent and the reinsurer share losses in the agreed upon percentages.

The ceding insurer has incurred expense in writing the underlying insurance. In quota share reinsurance, the primary insurer will receive a *reinsurance commission* to cover those expenses and (the cedent hopes) to provide a margin for profit. The amount or rate of the ceding commission is a matter for negotiation.

In *nonproportional* insurance, the reinsurer may insure the direct insurer against having single losses in excess of an agreed amount, aggregate losses of a specified class within a determined period in excess of an agreed amount, or losses in excess of predetermined amounts out of a single event. These are all *excess of loss* coverages, and they don't exhaust the possible variations. There may also be an excess of loss *ratio* coverage, in which the reinsurer will pay if the direct insurer's loss ratio exceeds a specified figure in a set period of time. For obvious reasons no such insurance is available that will guarantee a direct insurer a profit, but such coverage may be available to protect the direct insurer from excessive loss on the business.

In long-tailed lines of insurance, an insurer may wish to cap its future losses on an existing "book" of business and find a reinsurer that will write "runoff reinsurance" to provide that protection. This permits the reinsured company to close out that book with a predictable maximum loss, subject to the continuing risk that the reinsurer will become insolvent. Such business can either make or consume a fortune for the reinsurer, for its essence is assuming unpredictable, potentially catastrophic, risks. Some Lloyds syndicates have recently had disastrous experience from writing runoff reinsurance for insurance companies or for other Lloyds syndicates on American liability insurance.

STONEWALL INS. CO. v. FORTRESS REINSURERS MANAGERS, INC.

83 N.C. App. 263, 350 S.E.2d 131 (1986)

In September 1973, North River Insurance Company (hereinafter "North River") issued its policy of liability insurance to the Florida Eastcoast Railroad (hereinafter "Railroad"), effective from 9 September 1973 through 9 September 1974. Under the terms of the coverage, the Railroad was responsible for defending and paying each claim which fell within the initial $300,000 of liability, and any loss in excess of $300,000 was insured by the North River policy up to $2,000,000.

Prior to the inception of the policy period, North River purchased from Stonewall Insurance Company (hereinafter "Stonewall") a policy of reinsurance on the Railroad risk. Stonewall's reinsurance policy insured, on a pro-rata basis, $1,225,000 of North River's liability under its policy with the Railroad.

On 7 September 1973, Fortress Reinsurers Managers, Inc., (the corporate defendant's name was subsequently changed to Penn Re, Inc., hereinafter referred to as "Penn Re") agreed to reinsure $500,000 of the exposure Stonewall had on the North River-Railroad policy. Penn Re's Certificate of Facultative Reinsurance contained a retention provision which is the subject of the present appeal. The retention provision reads:

> The Company [Stonewall] warrants to retain for its own account the amount of liability specified in Item 3 unless otherwise provided herein, and the liability of the Reinsurer specified in Item 4 shall follow that of the Company, except as otherwise specifically provided herein, and shall be subject in all respects to all the terms and conditions of the Company's policy.

The amount of company retention shown in Item 3 of the Reinsurance Certificate issued to Stonewall was $500,000.

Stonewall, at the time it contracted for reinsurance of the North River-Railroad policy, had in existence a reinsurance treaty with a third company, the American Mutual Reinsurance Company (hereinafter "AMRECO"). The terms of that treaty excluded from automatic coverage a railroad risk such as that covered by North River's policy with the Railroad. Pursuant to the terms of the treaty, Stonewall submitted its reinsurance of the North River policy on the Railroad for consideration as a special cession. Prior to 9 September 1973, AMRECO waived the exclusions in the treaty and issued its Special Cession Certificate wherein Stonewall would remain liable on the first $50,000 of loss and AMRECO would be liable on the remaining $450,000.

On 11 December 1973, an accident occurred involving Jack Russell and the Railroad. Thereafter, North River made payment under its policy with the Railroad for that accident. Stonewall made payment to North River under its policy of reinsurance with North River in the amount of $1,263,775.75 on this claim. Subsequently, Stonewall made demand upon Penn Re in an amount totalling $500,563, such sum representing Penn Re's share of losses and expenses paid by Stonewall for the Russell claim.

Further, an accident occurred on 16 March 1974 involving the Railroad and R.J. Bernard. North River, under its policy insuring the Railroad, made payment to Bernard in the amount of $400,000. North River made demand upon Stonewall for payment in the amount of $246,163.75, representing Stonewall's portion of losses and expenses incurred on the Bernard claim. Stonewall made payment to North River in the amount of $246,163.75 under its policy reinsuring North River and, in turn, made demand upon Penn Re for payment in the amount of $100,475, said sum representing Penn Re's share of paid losses and expenses by Stonewall on the Bernard claim.

Penn Re denied liability on both claims by contending that the $500,000 shown by Stonewall as the amount of company retention in Item 3 of the Reinsurance Certificate was not retained by Stonewall "for its own account" as required by the company retention provisions. The $500,000 designated as company retention was made up of $50,000 retained "net" by Stonewall and $450,000 reinsured under its treaty with AMRECO through the Special Cession Certificate issued by AMRECO to Stonewall.

On 16 September 1981, Stonewall filed this civil action and sought (i) $601,038.39 in damages based on alleged breach of the certificate of reinsurance, (ii) $10,000,000 in punitive damages, and (iii) treble damages for unfair trade practices in violation of G.S. 75-1.1. Penn Re answered and asserted, among other defenses, that although Stonewall warranted to defendants that it was retaining $500,000 of the risk reinsured by the certificate, Stonewall breached that provision of the certificate by reinsuring $450,000 (90%) of that amount without informing defendants, thereby relieving defendants of any liability under the certificate of reinsurance.

On 10 November 1982, Judge Robert L. Farmer entered summary judgment for Penn Re on Stonewall's claims for punitive and treble damages. Stonewall's remaining contract claim was tried before Judge Bailey, sitting without a jury. Judge Bailey concluded that compliance with the warranty of retention was a condition precedent to Penn Re's obligation to reimburse Stonewall for any losses pursuant to the certificate and that Stonewall had materially breached the warranty of retention. From judgment in favor of defendants, plaintiff appealed. From the trial court's denial of its motion to amend its answer and counterclaim, defendants cross-appealed.

PARKER, Judge.

Plaintiff first contends that the trial court erred in failing to conclude as a matter of law that amounts Stonewall reinsured through treaty insurance are held by plaintiff "for its own account," or, alternatively, that Penn Re's company retention language is ambiguous and that such ambiguity must be construed in favor of Stonewall. The question is what do the words "for its own account" mean. Plaintiff contends that "for its own account" means net retention plus treaty reinsurance; defendant contends "for its own account" means only net retention. Net retention is that amount which the reinsured insurance carrier will pay on an insured claim. Treaty reinsurance is that portion of an insured claim which has been ceded to another insurance company, and which will be paid by that insurance carrier.

Plaintiff argues that because premiums charged for treaty reinsurance are calculated to cover the losses incurred such that the reinsured will ultimately pay in full any losses, the amount of company retention reinsured through treaty reinsurance is in fact an amount held for its own account. In other words, since plaintiff will ultimately be required to pay the amount ceded to AMRECO, plaintiff has not reduced its risk and has retained for its own account the full $500,000.

In interpreting the language of a contract, "words of a contract referring to a particular trade will be interpreted by the courts according to their widely accepted trade meaning." Peaseley v. Coke Co., 282 N.C. 585, 597, 194 S.E.2d 133, 142 (1973). The instant case concerns a specialized area of insurance law; therefore, parol evidence as to the meaning of the term "for its own account" was necessary to determine the usual and ordinary meaning of that term in the reinsurance industry. After hearing substantial evidence from both parties as to the meaning of the term in the reinsurance industry, the trial judge found "that the phrase 'for its own account' is not ambiguous and did not permit Stonewall to reinsure any portion of the warranted retention in any fashion without the express approval of the defendants." . . .

. . . We hold that the trial court did not err in finding the term "for its own account" unambiguous and in ruling as a matter of law that the term did not include both net retention and treaty reinsurance. . . .

The rule has long been established in this jurisdiction that one party's failure to comply with a condition precedent to a contract relieves the other party of its duty to perform under the contract irrespective of the party's good faith or the prejudicial effect. See, e.g., Parrish Tire Co. v. Morefield, 35 N.C. App. 385, 241 S.E.2d 353 (1978). Representatives of Fortress who testified explained that having the ceding company actually liable on the risk was significant to Fortress in terms of management and handling of claims. We hold that plaintiff's compliance could reasonably be expected to influence the decision of the insurance company and that the trial court did not err in concluding that plaintiff's breach of the condition precedent was material. Bryant v. Nationwide Mutual Insurance Co., 313 N.C. 362, 329 S.E.2d 333 (1985). . . .

Plaintiff next argues that the trial court erred in reciting that the reinsurance between Stonewall and AMRECO was facultative reinsurance. The court did not find that the special cession was facultative reinsurance, but rather that it was "not treaty reinsurance" and had the "essential characteristics" of facultative reinsurance. As the trial judge noted, the other findings and conclusions made it unnecessary to decide what kind of reinsurance the special cession was. Plaintiff has nowhere contended that the term "for its own account" included facultative reinsurance. Plaintiff's position is that the term includes net retention plus treaty reinsurance. For this reason, this error, if any, was not prejudicial to plaintiff's claim. Further, there was evidence to support the trial court's finding that the insurance was not treaty insurance. Penn Re's expert testified as follows:

> The objective of both treaty and facultative is primarily the same thing. It's a mechanism through which liability is transferred from one company, the reinsured company, to a second company, the reinsuring company. The facultative transfer of that liability is done on an individual risk basis, which gives both the ceding company and the assuming company the opportunity to thoroughly consider that individual risk and that individual piece of business and to consider the liability which is being transferred one to the other.
>
> Treaty business does exactly the same thing, except the transfer is on a book of business, rather than on a single piece of business. Both forms of reinsurance are done under contract and the provisions of those contracts are negotiable between the two parties.

Another reinsurance expert testified as to characteristics of facultative reinsurance such as (i) reinsurance of an individual risk, (ii) an individually derived premium for the risk, (iii) specific underwriting information on the risk and (iv) the reinsurer's right to accept or reject a particular risk. Plaintiff's witnesses testified in accord with this testimony by defendants' experts. This Court is bound by the trial judge's findings when there is competent evidence to support those findings. This assignment of error is overruled. . . .

The judgment of the trial court is
Affirmed.

Notes and Questions

1. Relative to some judgments in torts, the amounts involved in *Stonewall* are not great. Further, and perhaps more crucial, North

River had $194 million capital and surplus at year-end 1986 while
Stonewall had over $65 million at the same time. Why would first
North River and then Stonewall wish to "lay off" such large percentages of the risk they assumed? What insight does their practice provide
into the way the insurance business operates? Into the purposes of
reinsurance?

2. Why would it be significant to Fortress how extensively Stonewall remained on the risk? Can't Fortress take care of its own interests
when it also is in the business of writing insurance?

3. Why might it make a difference whether the reinsurance with
AMRECO was facultative or treaty reinsurance?

3. Characteristic Reinsurance Policy Terms

a. *The Insolvency Clause*

Originally the reinsurance contract, like most other early liability
insurance, was a contract of indemnity; that is, it was formulated in
such a way as to require the reinsurer to pay only "upon proof of
payment by the Reinsured" or language to the same effect. In Fidelity
& Deposit Co. v. Pink, 302 U.S. 224 (1937), the Supreme Court gave
effect to the language and held that the Reinsurer need not pay on
insolvency of the Reinsured if the Reinsured had not paid. This means
that the reinsurer would gain an advantage from the insolvency of the
ceding company, for it would not have to pay at all. Prior cases had
held otherwise on different contract language. As a result of *Fidelity &
Deposit,* the New York Superintendent of Insurance obtained passage
of a statute requiring an insolvency clause in the reinsurance contract.
See N.Y. Ins. Law §1308(a)(2)(A)(i) (McKinney 1985). The crucial part
of this clause might read, "In the event of the insolvency of the Company, this reinsurance shall be payable directly to the liquidator or
other receiver of the Company without diminution because of the
insolvency of the Company." Most states have a similar statute. The
purpose of the clause is self-evident: It prevents the Reinsurer from
taking advantage of the insolvency to reduce its obligations and makes
the full amount promised by the Reinsurer available for the liquidation
proceeding.

Many reinsurance transactions are with non-American companies, over which an American court may not have personal jurisdiction. If the contracts are executed elsewhere, under some choice of law
results the foreign law may govern them. The mechanism for enforcing
the insolvency clause requirement and other regulatory provisions
against such insurers is indirect but ingenious and, properly used, very

powerful. It will be discussed in Chapter 10. The result is that most reinsurance contracts have the above insolvency clause or one much like it.

b. The Cut-Through Endorsement

An original insured will have been provided coverage by the ceding company, which then reinsures the risk. A crucial question that arises most often when the ceding company becomes insolvent is whether the original insured has any direct rights under the reinsurance contract. The vast majority of courts answer that question by saying that the original insured is not an intended third party beneficiary and has no enforceable rights under the contract. See, for example, Leff v. NAC Agency, 639 F. Supp. 1426 (E.D. Mich. 1986). Note, Reinsurance and Reinsurer Insolvency: The Problem of Direct Recovery by the Original Insured or Injured Claimant, 29 UCLA L Rev. 872, 878 (1982) said that only a single case disagreed with that general rule. The note tries, somewhat naively, to justify a rule that would permit direct recovery from the reinsurer in the event of insolvency of the direct insurer. The weakness in the analysis is that it would prefer the individual claimant over others injured by the insolvency. Under the prevailing doctrine, the reinsurer is required to pay in full, and the liquidator will then distribute the available assets in accordance with the statutorily determined priority system.

Although the insured rarely has direct rights against the assuming insurer under a reinsurance contract, it sometimes becomes important for a particular purchaser of insurance to have (or even appear to have) that additional protection. This is sometimes provided by a *cut-through endorsement*, so named because it cuts through the usual route of claims payment from reinsurer to insurer to insured and provides for direct payment to the insured.

In a recent liquidation, it appeared that a reinsurer of the insolvent insurer had issued thousands of cut-through endorsements. Upon insolvency the insureds with the endorsements brought suit to recover under them. Should they recover or should their potential recoveries be regarded as unlawful preferences under the state's insolvency laws? If they cannot be enforced on insolvency of the direct insurer, of what use are they? See Bank, Cut-Through Endorsements, Bus. Ins., Oct. 10, 1983, at 51.

c. The Arbitration Clause

Characteristically a reinsurance contract contains a binding arbitration clause, with the object of resolving in an informal way inherently complex questions in disputes between ceding and assuming companies. Typically the arbitration is conducted before a three-person panel, two arbitrators chosen by the parties and an impartial umpire chosen in some neutral way. Occasionally a single impartial umpire is used as the sole arbiter. Parallel to the increasing use of discovery and dilatory motions in litigation, there is increasing elaboration of arbitration, which was once considered informal, expeditious and inexpensive. In addition to the desire for efficiency and expedition, insurance companies desire confidentiality. This is very difficult in a lawsuit, though courts do sometimes issue protective orders keeping proprietary information gathered in discovery confidential except as used in the trial. In arbitration, there is no reporting of decisions and no precedential value to a decision even if it becomes known. Extensive use of binding arbitration results in the comparative absence of reinsurance from the reported case law. The parties and the arbitrators often act under an agreement of confidentiality. Some information about arbitrations does leak, however, and tends to show up in the trade press. Its accuracy is always uncertain.

But arbitration as an alternative to suit does not inevitably produce the results hoped for. In McLeod, Reinsurance Arbitration Not Meeting Goal, Bus. Ins., Nov. 10, 1986, a reporter for the journal says that "[p]art of the problem stems from the increasingly contentious nature of arbitrations and the failure of arbitration panels to control tactics that some describe as 'abuses' of the arbitration process." See also Nonna & Strassberg, Reinsurance Arbitration: Boom or Bust?, 22 Tort & Ins. L.J. 586 (1987). If you as an arbitrator wished to achieve the objectives of the arbitration clause as stated previously, would you control the use of discovery, depositions, and numerous expert witnesses? To what extent? What would you do about procedural rules? About the use of outside counsel instead of salaried personnel?

d. Notice and Proof of Loss

The need for notice to a reinsurer is different than to a direct insurer. A typical notice clause in a reinsurance contract reads:

> In the event of an accident, disaster, casualty or occurrence which either results in or appears to be of such a serious nature that it will probably result in a loss involving this Agreement, the Company shall give notice as soon as reasonably practicable to the Reinsurers, and the Company shall keep the Reinsurers advised of all subsequent developments in connection therewith.
>
> The Reinsurers agree to consider the loss settlements of the Company to be satisfactory proofs of loss, and amounts falling to the share

of the Reinsurers shall be immediately payable by the Reinsurers to the Company upon reasonable evidence of the amount paid or to be paid by the Company.

Now consider the following case.

LIBERTY MUT. INS. CO. v. GIBBS

773 F.2d 15 (1st. Cir. 1985)

LEVIN H. CAMPBELL, Chief Judge.

In this diversity action applying Massachusetts law, plaintiff-appellant Liberty Mutual Insurance Co. ("Liberty") appeals from a judgment entered on a jury verdict in the District Court of Massachusetts, holding defendants-appellees Carol A. Gibbs and a consortium of insurance underwriters (collectively, Lloyd's of London, here "Lloyd's") not liable to Liberty on a claim arising under a reinsurance contract. We affirm.

In the policy of reinsurance, Lloyd's agreed to indemnify Liberty for 80% of all payments Liberty became obligated to make in excess of $250,000 under a general liability policy that Liberty had issued to Boston Edison Co. The reinsurance contract provided in relevant part:

> It is a condition precedent to any liability under this policy that
> a. [Liberty] shall upon knowledge of any loss or losses which may give rise to a claim under this policy advise [Lloyd's] thereof as soon as reasonably possible.

Liberty's principal arguments on appeal are that the district court misconstrued the meaning of the claims cooperation clause, and erred in ruling that lack of prejudice is no defense to a denial of coverage for late notice.

On May 24, 1972, after colliding with another car, an automobile drove up on a sidewalk and struck a Boston Edison utility pole in Lexington, Massachusetts, causing the pole to fall and injure two pedestrians, one of whom was Arthur Bernier. Both victims initially sued the drivers of the two cars in state court, but in May of 1974, they made Boston Edison a party defendant. The ad damnum for Bernier's claim was $750,000. Liberty, whose attorney handled Boston Edison's defense, did not notify Lloyd's of Bernier's claim during the pre-trial and trial phases of the litigation. On December 22, 1977, the jury returned a verdict for Bernier against Boston Edison in the amount of $465,000 plus interest. By letter dated January 19, 1978, Liberty notified Lloyd's of the judgment, and requested indemnification under the reinsurance policy. On October 27, 1978, Lloyd's denied liability on the ground that Liberty's failure to provide prompt notice of the Bernier claim violated the terms of the claims cooperation clause. Liberty commenced this action in April of 1979.

I

The claims cooperation clause required Liberty, as a condition precedent to Lloyd's liability, to seasonably inform Lloyd's of "any loss or losses which may give rise to a claim" under the reinsurance policy. In its rulings and jury instructions, the district court construed this language as referring to any losses that presented a "reasonable possibility" of resulting in a claim under the reinsurance policy.

Liberty contends that that construction was erroneous. Instead, it believes the court should have defined the clause as referring only to any losses that presented a "reasonable likelihood" of resulting in a claim under the reinsurance policy. Liberty argues that notice is less critical to a reinsurer than to a primary insurer, because the primary insurer normally bears the burden of promptly investigating the facts relating to the claim. See, e.g., Security Mutual Casualty Co. v. Century Casualty Co., 531 F.2d 974, 978 (10th Cir.), *cert. denied,* 429 U.S. 860, 97 S. Ct. 161, 50 L. Ed. 2d 137 (1976). Because the reinsurance contract did not expressly afford Lloyd's any right to investigate or defend primary claims, Liberty believes the claims cooperation clause was met by Lloyd's being told only of those losses that were reasonably *likely* to result in awards greater than $250,000, so that Lloyd's could adjust its reserves accordingly.

We sustain the district court's construction. We find the language of the claims cooperation clause to be unambiguous. The district court's construction comports literally with it. Losses which "may" give rise to a claim denote, we think, losses which present "a reasonable possibility," not merely a reasonable likelihood. Under Massachusetts law, "[w]here the wording of the contract is unambiguous, the contract must be enforced according to its terms." Edmonds v. United States, 642 F.2d 877, 881 (1st Cir. 1981). We see no basis for rewriting the contract whether or not, as an original proposition, it could have been better written as Liberty now proposes. . . .

II

Liberty contends that the district court erred in ruling that lack of prejudice to Lloyd's would be no defense to Lloyd's denial of coverage for late notice. Liberty argues that it was entitled to try to establish lack of prejudice under Mass. Gen. Laws Ann. ch. 175, §112 (West Supp. 1984-85), which provides in relevant part:

> An insurance company shall not deny insurance coverage to an insured because of failure of an insured to seasonably notify an insurance company of an occurrence, incident, claim or of a suit founded upon an occurrence, incident or claim, which may give rise to liability insured against unless the insurance company has been prejudiced thereby.

As an initial matter, it is doubtful whether section 112 was intended to apply to reinsurance contracts. Although the Massachusetts courts have yet to address the question, the Massachusetts Insurance Laws expressly provide that "the hazards under [reinsurance] contracts shall be deemed distinct in nature from the hazard insured." Mass. Gen. Laws Ann. ch. 175, §2A (West 1972). Strictly speaking, the reinsurance contract between Liberty and Lloyd's can be considered a contract of indemnity, not a contract "insuring against liability . . . on account of bodily injury or death" within the meaning of section 112. See Friend Brothers, Inc. v. Seaboard Surety Co., 316 Mass. 639, 642, 56 N.E.2d 6, 8 (1944). This construction comports with the apparent purpose behind section 112, which is to protect lay policyholders from the hypertechnical application of notice requirements inserted in forms drafted by primary insurance carriers. See Johnson Controls, Inc. v. Bowes, 381 Mass. 278, 280-82, 409 N.E.2d 185, 187 (1980). That rationale would not extend to a situation like the present, involving two experienced insurance underwriters who bargained at arm's length. Id. . . .

Affirmed.

Notes and Questions

1. Does *Gibbs* suggest any change in the climate of the reinsurance business in the last 30 years?

2. Would you reach the same result the court did?

3. In an omitted part of the opinion, the court said that §112 did not apply because it had been enacted after the events on which this case was based. Liberty Mutual went on to argue, unsuccessfully, that §112 only declared the common law.

4. Is there any good reason to treat reinsurance differently from direct insurance, as the court seems to have done in this case?

4. Reinsurance of Punitive Damages

OTT v. ALL-STAR INS. CORP.

99 Wis. 2d 635, 299 N.W.2d 840 (1941)

[The text of this opinion is found in Section C(1).]

A liability insurance carrier may sometimes be at risk because its policy has insured against punitive damages imposed upon its policyholders. That coverage may be intentional but more often will result from the adverse decision of a court about the scope of policy coverage. Whether or not the coverage was intended the insurer will have limited its exposure in accordance with its usual practices by policy limits and reinsurance.

An insurer may also be at risk for punitive damages assessed directly against it for bad faith settlement of claims. The problem can exist for first party insurers as well as third party insurers to the extent that the particular jurisdiction has allowed punitive (or extra-contractual) damages in such cases. The insurer cannot confine that exposure by policy limits but can only protect itself from primary liability by its settlement practices and by buying insurance protection against its own liability. Do the ordinary reinsurance treaties into which it has entered protect it against such exposure to bad faith judgments? If not, it can sometimes buy liability insurance against the extra-contractual damages assessed in bad faith cases, as in *Ott*. Should the same public policy considerations apply as with respect to insurance against punitive damages imposed on original insureds?

5. Fronting and Captives

Fronting takes place in a variety of contexts, including the occasional use as an unethical (and perhaps even illegal) way to evade regulatory controls. Even when legitimate, it may be used as a device to avoid (as distinguished from "evade", precisely as in tax law) regulation or taxation or both. Perhaps a sound public policy would stop some uses of fronting that are now legal; others may be perfectly appropriate from any perspective.

Tight insurance markets tend to induce individual insureds, or groups of insureds, to desire better control over their own destinies. That can sometimes best be achieved through creation of a *captive* insurer they can own or at least control. Although to meet their long-term needs it must be operated wisely, so that it remains solvent and viable, it may be operated to provide a more dependable market at prices they can set though not truly control.

Captives are sometimes created when agents who produce large blocks of profitable business for companies (especially large agents or brokers dealing with commercial accounts) feel they can obtain profits at two stages of the transaction if they also own the insurer. They may suffer from some illusions about the way pricing is done in the insurance market, but if they bring additional capital to the market and provide additional competition, who is to complain, at least if they are operated soundly?

The mechanism is to create a captive insurer offshore, which can be done with a minimum of regulatory red tape and until fairly recently with some hope of escaping immediate federal taxation. Frequent places for offshore organization of captives have been Bermuda, various Caribbean islands, and the Channel Islands, among others. As a nonadmitted company, the captive cannot issue direct insurance except on a surplus lines or excess basis; instead, an admitted company that satisfies all the regulatory criteria of the crucial states is used as a *fronting* company. The front then reinsures the entire risk with the captive, in some arrangements retaining a small percentage of the risk on a quota share basis. The fronting company may also take higher layers of the risk as a retrocessionaire, or retrocession may be arranged with other reinsurers. In addition, the fronting company may provide various other services for the reinsured, such as underwriting, claims adjustment, and the like, on whatever basis may be agreed upon. The fronting company charges a fee for whatever services it renders, including one for serving as the fronting company.

Fronting can be lucrative. Some large insurers have become fronting companies as a significant part of their activity. The word has invidious connotations from other uses in our society, but it should be remembered that fronting in insurance is not inherently bad, though it can be used to achieve undesirable objectives.

Captives become more useful in periods of tight markets; the very tight market of the middle 1980s produced many captives, including some (though a few of those prefer not to be called captives) sponsored by very large American industrial corporations. Those particular "captives," usually stock companies that are heavily capitalized, deal primarily in excess layers of insurance to very high levels.

The softening of the market in the late 1980s has resulted in a slowdown in the formation of captives. As an art form, the captive is here to stay.

D. Pools and Syndicates

In tight markets, whether because risks are new, because of bad experience, or simply because the need for insurance is great and there are not large numbers of risk units, it is often necessary to provide insurance by pooling the resources of many insurers. Sometimes a pool is formed, or participated in, or financed in part, or reinsured, by governmental agencies.

Perhaps the best known of the pools are those formed to provide insurance for nuclear risks. The Price-Anderson Act of 1957 capped liability for nuclear accidents at $560 million and required licensees to insure up to the amount of liability insurance available, then $60 million, to which the Nuclear Regulatory Commission added indemnity protection of $500 million. The following articles describe the first twenty years of the program from different perspectives: Lowenstein, The Price-Anderson Act: An Imaginative Approach to Public Liability Concerns, 12 Forum 594 (1977); Marrone, The Price-Anderson Act: The Insurance Industry's View, 12 Forum 605 (1977); Wilson, Nuclear Liability and the Price-Anderson Act, 12 Forum 612 (1977).

The exclusion of nuclear risks is now standard in all kinds of insurance policies. Two insurance pools, the American Nuclear Insurers (stock companies) and the Mutual Atomic Energy Reinsurance Pool, together have a combined capacity of $160 million, representing the maximum amount of commercially available liability insurance against nuclear risks. On top of that is the federal guarantee under the Price-Anderson Act. A fairly recent, very compact, and partisan treatment of the subject will be found in American Enterprise Institute for Public Policy Research, Renewal of the Price-Anderson Act (1985).

On the property insurance side, the risks are mostly those of owners of nuclear-powered electricity generating plants. They have developed offshore controlled companies to provide themselves with coverage beyond that available in the regular commercial market.

E.   Risk Retention Groups and Purchasing Groups

The commercial property-liability business is subject to wide cyclical swings, largely because of the impossibility of getting reliable information in advance about the cost of the product. Especially in long tail lines of liability business, the cost of the insurance product sold for a fixed price may not be known even approximately for a decade or more after the sale. In some instances (such as products liability insurance covering manufacturers of products containing asbestos), it may not be fully known for several decades. Long after the books have been closed on a year's business, late groups of claims may emerge; all losses paid at that point go straight to the bottom line, constituting a charge on surplus.

The information dilemma alone is not enough to account for the cyclical nature of the insurance business, but other causal factors are difficult to discern. Economists tend to look for pure economic forces to drive a cycle and for single forces if possible. See Priest, The Current Insurance Crisis and Modern Tort Law, 96 Yale L.J. 1521 (1987), for one attempted explanation. But psychology may play a substantial role. An approach by an economist to explaining the insurance cycle, with recognition of the interplay between economics and psychology, is Stewart, Profit Cycles in Property-Liability Insurance, Monograph 5 in Long & Randall, ed., 1 Issues in Insurance 273 (3rd ed. 1984).

The unusually tight insurance market in the mid-1970s came as one in the regular series of insurance business cycles. It was explicable in part by the eruption of whole classes of tort claims. Medical malpractice claims were probably the most prominent,* though products liability tort doctrine also expanded explosively since the mid-1960s, epitomized by the adoption throughout the country of the doctrines capsulized in §402A of the Restatement of Torts. The most devastating class of tort claims, asbestos claims, had begun to emerge at the time of the crisis of the 1970s but did not yet dominate the thinking of insurance companies.†

In 1981, after several years of study of the problem, Congress passed legislation to authorize creation of risk retention groups and purchasing groups in the effort to create a market. It was reacting belatedly to the crisis of the 1970s, and in doing so, preempted a part of the state regulatory scheme. The 1981 Act applied only to products liability insurance and its counterpart, completed operations insurance. Little happened under the 1981 Act, for by then the hard market had been replaced by an unprecedentedly soft one. This cyclical turn was exacerbated this time by extraordinarily high interest rates that led insurance companies to compete mindlessly for premiums to invest. Products liability insurance turned out to be relatively easy to obtain and there was little incentive to go outside the existing commercial market for coverage. For a lengthy discussion of the 1981 Act and a Risk Retention Group created under it, see Home Warranty Corp. v. Caldwell, 777 F.2d 1455 (11th Cir. 1985).

---

*The insurance crisis of the mid-1970s was often called the crisis in medical malpractice insurance.

†Asbestos claims were only beginning to surface. The first successful case was Borel v. Fiberboard Paper Products Corp., 493 F.2d 1076 (5th Cir. 1973), *cert. denied*, 419 U.S. 869 (1974). As of the date of this writing, asbestos claims have caused at least four major industrial companies to seek protection under Chapter 11 of the Federal Bankruptcy Code, and there is no certainty that we have seen the end. The largest of those, Manville Corporation, has gone through and emerged from the Chapter 11 proceedings, having made arrangements for major payments of its resources, present and future, to asbestos claimants. The insurance litigation on asbestos claims is still in full swing. See cases in Chapter 5.

A more serious "insurance crisis" erupted in the mid-1980s caused by a truly tight market that succeeded the quite unusual insurance company losses in the preceding soft market of the early 1980s. That led to another Congressional enactment in 1986 that broadened the authorization of risk retention groups and purchasing groups to all liability insurance, again preempting the state regulatory scheme. There has been more activity under the 1986 Act, for many policyholders have felt the same need for assurance of a market that in other contexts led to the formation of many captive insurers.

A risk retention group is essentially a mutual insurance company of the kind that has often appeared in tight markets through much of American history. Ultimately those mutuals either disappear or else grow to become part of the commercial market. Once there, they are subject to the same forces, whatever they may be, that produce cycles. Risk retention groups were insulated from most state regulation of insurance by provisions to preempt the state law.

One of the misconceived but prevalent state laws in the regulatory statutes forbids the creation of "fictitious groups" to purchase insurance, with the savings mass marketing makes possible. The fictitious group statutes mainly protect the interests of agents, and in the process prevent some important savings in the marketing of insurance: Marketing through groups can sometimes reduce the acquisition cost of insurance by a substantial amount. For an extensive discussion of the subject, see Kimball & Denenberg, Mass Marketing of Property and Liability Insurance (1970), one of the monographs in the U.S. Department of Transportation Automobile Insurance and Compensation Study.

The federal legislation authorizing the purchasing groups likewise preempted certain state regulatory legislation. Unlike the language dealing with risk retention groups, however, only certain state regulatory statutes were preempted as they applied to purchasing groups. Insurance Co. of Pa. v. Corcoran, 850 F.2d 88 (2d Cir. 1988), for example, held purchasing groups to be subject to rate and form regulation.

F.   Group Insurance

1.   Employment Groups

Especially in life and health insurance, insurance coverage has in recent decades increasingly been part of the employment benefit package, both under collective bargaining agreements and for workers not under such agreements. Group life insurance through employers was discussed briefly in Chapter 6.

The Employee Retirement Income Security Act of 1974 (ERISA) deals broadly with employee benefit plans. One provision preempted state law with a savings provision exempting insurance regulation from the preemption. The preemption section, an effort to compromise significant controversies, was badly drafted and its meaning is not very clear. See Employee Legal Service Plans: Conflicts Between Federal and State Regulation, ch. 3, in Legal Service Plans: Approaches to Regulation 189 (Pfennigstorf & Kimball, eds. 1977), which offers a close textual analysis of the preemption provision of ERISA, specifically directed to legal expense insurance but applicable more generally. It will be a long time before there are enough authoritative decisions to determine what the section really means.

Graves v. Blue Cross of Cal., 688 F. Supp. 1405 (N.D. Cal. 1988), held that the savings clause in the ERISA preemption provision preserved state regulation of claims settlement practices.

2. Association Groups

A somewhat looser relationship than coemployment is often the basis for group insurance. Membership in associations is one such relationship: Group insurance taking advantage of such a relationship is a species of mass marketing that offers the possibility of substantial savings in marketing costs. One case that illustrates the way in which association group insurance works in the medical field is American College of Surgeons v. Lumbermens Mut. Casualty Co., 142 Ill. App. 3d 680, 491 N.E.2d 1179, 96 Ill. Dec. 719 (1986).

Group insurance, like large commercial policies, often involves the "unbundling" of insurance services. In the traditional insurance contractual relationship the insurer bore the risk and also performed all of the administrative tasks associated with the insurance. The use of a deductible (or retained risk) would leave some of the risk with the insured and, in the process, might often leave some of the administrative work there, especially that connected with small claims within the deductible amount. On the other hand, some contracts leave most of the risk (usually excepting the risk of catastrophic losses) with the insured but transfer much or even all of the administrative work to an Administrator, which in its primary activity is often an insurer. There are also Third Party Administrators (TPAs) who bear no risk and merely administer self-insurance programs for others.

3. Terms of Group Policies

Group insurance policies in health insurance are almost infinitely various. A large group may resemble a self-insurance scheme with the insurer serving mainly an administrative function. For somewhat smaller groups, there may also be a risk transfer element in the coverage of catastrophic levels of risk by the insurer. Retrospective or experience rating schemes make the group insurer look functionally equivalent to an excess of loss reinsurer.

CHAPTER 10

Regulation of Insurance

Insurance is one of the most heavily regulated of all businesses. The primary regulation by the insurance commissioners of the various states is both intensive and intrusive. In addition, various aspects of the business are regulated in some degree by federal agencies, including but not limited to the Department of Justice, the Federal Trade Commission, the Internal Revenue Service, the Department of Labor, and the Securities and Exchange Commission. Various committees of the Congress also engage in indirect regulation through an interminable series of investigations and hearings that in the aggregate put considerable pressure on the insurance industry and on the state regulators. Chief, and most persistent, among them has been the Antitrust and Monopoly Subcommittee of the Judiciary Committee of the U.S. Senate.

What follows in this chapter is but a sampling of the very complex field of insurance regulation.

Article I, Section 8 of the U.S. Constitution states, "The Congress shall have power . . . [t]o regulate commerce with foreign nations, and among the several states, and with the Indian tribes."

Paul v. Virginia, 75 U.S. (8 Wall.) 168 (1868), held (1) that insurance is not commerce, and (2) that an insurance contract was a local transaction and thus (even if commerce) was not the kind with which the commerce clause is concerned. It followed, the court held, that Congress had no power over insurance under the commerce clause. Under authority of *Paul*, a comprehensive state insurance regulatory system developed.

In United States v. South-Eastern Underwriters Assn., 322 U.S. 533 (1944), the district court, ruling on a demurrer to an indictment returned against insurance companies and their executives for violation of the Sherman Antitrust Act, relied on *Paul* and quashed the indictment. The Supreme Court, however, overruled *Paul* and held that insurance *is* commerce and is, in proper cases, subject to the Sherman Act. Industry concern about the threatened shift of regulation from the states to the newly active and intrusive federal regulatory apparatus, and state concern about possible loss of tax revenues and regulatory power, led to the quick enactment of the McCarran-Ferguson Act, which follows. The objectives of the act are set forth in §1.

McCARRAN-FERGUSON ACT

15 U.S.C. (1976 ed. §§1011-1015 (1945))

Section 1

Congress declares that the continued regulation and taxation by the several states of the business of insurance is in the public interest, and that silence on the part of the Congress shall not be construed to impose any barrier to the regulation or taxation of such business by the several States.

Section 2

(a) The business of insurance, and every person engaged therein, shall be subject to the laws of the several States which relate to the regulation or taxation of such business.

(b) No Act of Congress shall be construed to invalidate, impair, or supersede any law enacted by any State for the purpose of regulating the business of insurance, or which imposes a fee or tax upon such business, unless such Act specifically relates to the business of insurance: *Provided*, That after June 30, 1948, the Act of July 2, 1890, as amended, known as the Sherman Act, and the Act of October 15, 1914, as amended, known as the Clayton Act, and the Act of September 26, 1914, known as the Federal Trade Commission Act, as amended, shall be applicable to the business of insurance to the extent that such business is not regulated by State law.

Section 3

(a) Until June 30, 1948, the Act of July 2, 1890, as amended, known as the Sherman Act, and the Act of October 15, 1914, as amended, known as the Clayton Act, and the Act of September 26, 1914, known as the Federal Trade Commission Act, and the Act of June 19, 1936, known as the Robinson-Patman Anti-Discrimination Act, shall not apply to the business of insurance or to acts in the conduct thereof.

(b) Nothing contained in this chapter shall render the said Sherman Act inapplicable to any agreement to boycott, coerce, or intimidate, or act of boycott, coercion, or intimidation.

Section 4

Nothing contained in this chapter shall be construed to affect in any manner the application to the business of insurance of the Act of July 5, 1935, as amended, known as the National Labor Relations Act, or the Act of June 25, 1938, as amended, known as the Fair Labor Standards Act of 1938, or the Act of June 5, 1920, known as the Merchant Marine Act, 1920.

A.   What IS Insurance?

In the introduction to this book, I stated that I had not seen a good definition of insurance, and would make no attempt to provide one. Yet it is often necessary to decide whether a contract is one of insurance or whether an activity is the doing of an insurance business in order to determine whether the activity is subject to federal antitrust law or state insurance regulation, whether the contract is subject to state premium taxation, or whether a company is to be taxed by the IRS as an insurance company or another kind of company. The following materials raise a few of the current issues.

HERTZ CORP. v. CORCORAN
137 Misc. 2d 403, 520 N.Y.S.2d 700 (1987)

MARTIN B. STECHER, Justice:

This is an action for a declaratory judgment. As the only issue is one of statutory interpretation, and there is no question of fact or factual interpretation, summary judgment is therefore appropriate as only questions of law are involved.

The issue is whether the collision damage waiver (CDW) offered by plaintiff car rental agency to its customers in New York for a fee over and above that which they pay as rental for vehicles is "insurance" within the meaning of Insurance Law §1101(a)(1), thereby requiring plaintiff to be licensed by the New York State Department of Insurance.

Based upon this Court's construction of Insurance Law §1101(a)(1) as well as the application of the doctrine of stare decisis, I hold that this CDW does not constitute insurance.

Under Hertz' usual rental agreement, Hertz bears the risk of any loss of or damage to a rented vehicle due to causes other than collision or rollover (e.g., fire, vandalism, theft and storms), irrespective of the presence or absence of neglect by the renter. The renter, however, is liable to Hertz for any damage to the rental vehicle caused by collision or rollover, irrespective of fault. At the time the customer signs the rental agreement, he or she is given the option of electing or declining to obtain the renter's waiver of the right to look to the customer for collision damage by checking an appropriate box on the form. If the customer elects to accept the CDW, there is an additional charge. The effect of accepting CDW is to shift the risk of collision damage *eo instante* from the customer to Hertz.

Insurance Law §1101(a) defines the term "insurance contract" as including,

> . . . any agreement or other transaction whereby one party, the "insurer," is obligated *to confer benefit of pecuniary value upon another party,* the "insured" or "beneficiary," dependent upon the happening of a fortuitous event in which the insured or beneficiary has, or is expected to have at the time of such happening, a material interest which will be adversely affected by the happening of such event. [Emphasis added].

Insurance Law is founded upon the concept of indemnification whereby the insured is compensated for the actual property loss sustained by him as a result of the perils insured against [McAnarney v. Newark Fire Insurance Co., 247 N.Y. 176, 184, 159 N.E. 902 (1928); Naiman v. Niagara Fire Insurance Co., 285 A.D. 706, 708, 140 N.Y.S.2d 494; 29 N.Y. Jur., Insurance §5, at p. 28].

A waiver is "the voluntary abandonment or relinquishment of a known right" [Jef-paul Garage Corp. v. Presbyterian Hospital, 61 N.Y.2d 442, 446, 474 N.Y.S.2d 458, 462 N.E.2d 1176], here the lessor's right to look to the renter for indemnification for collision damage. At common law, a bailee-renter is liable to the bailor for all damage to the bailed property unless the damage was not caused by the bailee's own fault [Klar v. H & M Parcel Room, Inc., 270 A.D. 538, 541, 61 N.Y.S.2d 285, *aff'd* 296 N.Y. 1044, 73 N.E.2d 912]. Under the contract, absent the collision damage waiver, the renter, as set forth above, is responsible for such damage irrespective of fault. Thus, the effect of the renter's acceptance of the CDW is to shift the risk of any loss for damage to the rented vehicle due to a collision entirely to the lessor. To interpret the word "waiver" — a passive declination to enforce a right — to mean "indemnify," which, in this context means to stand between another claimant and the renter, as the defendant would have this Court do, is to misconstrue the plain meaning of language [see Atlantic National Insurance Co. v. Armstrong, 65 Cal. 2d 100, 112, 52 Cal. Rptr. 569, 416 P.2d 801] and ignore the ordinary and accepted meaning of words [McKinney's Cons. Laws of N.Y., Statutes, Book 1, §94].

Ordinarily, collision damage insurance is provided by a carrier to an insured to indemnify the insured against loss sustained by him, the insured. The insured must have an insurable interest in the property [Ins. L. 3401] which clearly the daily renter doesn't have. Of course, one without an insurable interest may contract to provide insurance for the benefit of one who does have an insurable interest, presumably what the Superintendent is arguing here. But such a concept applied to these facts is irrational for it requires us to say that Hertz, for a fee paid by the customer, is indemnifying Hertz from damage to Hertz' property. But one cannot indemnify himself — he merely accepts his own loss — and an agreement whereby Hertz accepts its own loss is not an agreement of indemnification and therefore is not a contract of insurance.

While it is conceivable that Hertz could procure collision damage insurance and resell it to its customers and thereby be involved in an activity subject to regulation by the Superintendent [Ollendorff Watch Co. v. Pink, 279 N.Y. 32, 36-37, 17 N.E.2d 676] no such allegation much less evidence is offered concerning the collision damage waiver.

Defendant's legal position is premised upon an opinion by the attorney general of the State of New York dated December 31, 1986, which was requested by and given to the Superintendent without any opportunity by any car rental company to be heard. In that opinion, the attorney general reversed his predecessor's 1977 opinion and concluded that the CDW clause found in automobile rental agreements is insurance for purposes of section 1101 of the Insurance Law. . . .

The decision by Mr. Justice Evans in the *Kramer** case was affirmed without opinion by the Appellate Division, First Department [100 A.D.2d 937, 474 N.Y.S.2d 160] and the Court of Appeals denied leave to appeal [63 N.Y.2d 605, 481 N.Y.S.2d 1023, 471 N.E.2d 462].

Defendant attempts to distinguish the *Kramer* case from this case based upon the fact that underlying *Kramer* were 1982 statistics where

---

*Kramer v. Avis Car Leasing, Inc., Index 23344/82 Sup. Ct. N.Y. County, had held a CDW not to be insurance — Ed.

the typical cost of the CWD was $5.50 per day, 9% of the average daily rental rate; whereas in 1983 (the year used by the attorney general in his 1986 opinion), these figures had risen to $8 and 13%, respectively. This is difference without legal distinction. It may be reason for the Legislature to consider regulating this activity, but it does not expand the authority of the Superintendent. . . .

Accordingly, the plaintiff's motion for summary judgment on its action for a declaratory judgment is granted and the judgment shall declare that plaintiff's collision damage waiver does not constitute a contract of insurance. . . .

Notes and Questions

1. As a matter of public policy, should the commissioner seek to regulate collision damage waivers sold by rental car companies? At $8 per day (the figure specified in the case for 1986), the rental agencies were charging $2,920 per year for the functional equivalent of collision insurance. (Since then, the price has risen substantially.) Does that fact alone justify regulating the waivers as insurance? Whether collision damage waivers should be regulated as insurance was an issue of some importance for a number of years in the 1980s, but has not been much in evidence recently. The issue was settled by statute in some states, while various credit card companies seized upon the issue as a marketing device and assumed the risk of collision damage if the credit card was used to pay for the rental.

2. State ex rel. Duffy v. Western Auto Supply Co., 134 Ohio St. 163, 16 N.E.2d 256 (1939), held road hazard warranties under which tires would be replaced when they failed for any cause to be insurance contracts. In State ex rel. Herbert v. Standard Oil Co., 138 Ohio St. 376, 35 N.E.2d 437 (1941), a less expansive warranty applicable only to tires damaged because of defects was held not to be insurance. In both instances the insurance commissioner had brought quo warranto proceedings on the ground that the warrantors were selling insurance without a license. Can both decisions be right? As a matter of sound public policy, should the insurance commissioner seek to regulate in either case? Griffin Systems, Inc. v. Ohio Dept. of Ins., 61 Ohio St. 3d 552, 575 N.E.2d 803 (1991), followed *Herbert* in a case involving a motor vehicle repair contract covering only defects in auto parts.

3. If a garage provides a "guaranteed maintenance contract" to maintain a truck in good repair, has it issued an insurance policy? Over a dissent, the court in Transportation Guar. Co. v. Jellins, 29 Cal. 2d 242, 174 P.2d 625 (1946), held "no."

4. Some large automobile manufacturers now sponsor Vehicle Service Agreements (VSAs) that are sold at the time a new car is pur-

chased for an extra consideration. The details vary, but VSAs generally provide for various services on the car; the dealer is then protected by contract against the costs of the service. These arrangements show up in regulatory contexts in various ways: in determining whether to regulate the original vehicle service agreements as insurance, in determining how to regard the backup contracts, and in some recent cases, in determining the status of the backup contracts upon insolvency of the company providing them. Cases on several of these problems are likely to appear soon in the reporters.

5. Similar contracts are sold for the more expensive television sets.

6. Is a contract to provide necessary legal services of defined kinds for a fixed annual fee a contract of insurance? If so, should it be regulated?

7. The answers to the previous questions may depend in some measure on the perceived purposes of insurance regulation. For a discussion providing background for the subject, see Kimball, The Purpose of Insurance Regulation: A Preliminary Inquiry in the Theory of Insurance Law, 45 Minn. L. Rev. 471 (1961).

B. Jurisdiction Over Insurers

Some insurers do business in single states, others in only a handful of states, and many (including most of the large and well-known insurers) do business in nearly all of the states. Even the latter, however, may do business in some states through wholly owned subsidiaries called *pup companies*. Some pup companies exist in order to avoid the application of those states' regulation to the parent company's entire operation.

For example, success in the traditional life insurance business depended heavily on agent quality, that is, salesmanship. Competition in such life insurance tended to be "reverse competition," focussing not on prices to the insurance buyer but on obtaining the most effective agents. This led to generous commission rates, driving up premiums. Of course that competition is also self-limiting: beyond some point increased commissions adversely affect sales because of increased premium rates. But the product is both immensely variable and generally quite opaque, giving considerable freedom for that reverse competition.

New York limited commissions with the following statute:

> No domestic life insurance company, and no foreign or alien life insurance company doing business in this state, shall make or incur in

any calendar year total field expenses [as defined in the statute] in excess of the total field expense limit, [also as defined]. [N.Y. Ins. Law §4228(a) (McKinney 1985).]

Like much New York regulation this statute had extraterritorial effect upon companies admitted to do business in New York. In order to pay more commissions in other states than New York's rule would allow, many companies did not enter New York in their own names, instead forming pup companies.

Most insurance companies, including many of the industry leaders, conformed to this New York rule (and many other New York rules) everywhere, for it has long been a considerable advantage in the insurance marketplace to be able to say one's company was regulated by New York's strict law and its historically effective insurance department. That advantage was a counterweight to the freedom to pay higher commissions. Weisbart, Extraterritorial Regulation of Life Insurance (1975), provides a thorough treatment of the subject.

The extent to which admitted insurers are subject to state legislative power is limited only by constitutional restrictions and practical politics.

An insurer admitted to do business in a state naturally consents to be subject to the jurisdiction of the state's courts. Usually a provision in the state insurance code makes the state insurance commissioner, or sometimes the attorney general, the insurer's agent for the service of process, in the absence of, or sometimes in addition to, the availability of another appropriate representative of the insurer. The jurisdictions of legislatures and courts do not rest on identical grounds.

The limits on the subjection of *nonadmitted* insurers to the jurisdiction of state courts, legislatures, and insurance commissioners of states with which they have some connection is a complex question.

IN RE ALL-STAR INS. CORP.

110 Wis. 2d 72, 327 N.W.2d. 648 (1983)

BEILFUSS, Chief Justice.

This is an appeal from judgments entered based upon orders granting summary judgment in favor of the plaintiff in two actions which were consolidated before the circuit court and for purposes of appeal.

These appeals arise out of the liquidation of the All-Star Insurance Corporation. All-Star, a Wisconsin corporation formerly engaged in the business of insurance, was ordered into liquidation on March 1, 1977, pursuant to ch. 645, Stats. 1977. The plaintiff, Roderick B.

NcNamee was appointed Special Deputy Commissioner of Insurance for the purposes of All-Star's liquidation. In this capacity, the plaintiff commenced these actions against the defendants, APS Insurance Agency, Inc. (APS) and Lee M. Scarborough & Company (Scarborough), to recover sums allegedly due under separate agencies contracts between the two defendants and All-Star.

Both defendants separately entered into agency agreements with All-Star and served as agents soliciting applications for insurance for All-Star pursuant to these agreements. APS is an Illinois corporation and entered into an agency contract with All-Star on June 1, 1973. APS's relationship with All-Star began at All-Star's initiation, when All-Star asked APS to serve as its agent. In October, 1975 APS stopped serving as All-Star's agent pursuant to an order from the Illinois Insurance Commissioner. Scarborough is a Louisiana corporation and entered into its agency contract with All-Star on April 18, 1973. It appears that the agency agreement was in effect until the time All-Star was ordered into liquidation, but the record is not entirely clear on this point.

The only contacts either defendant ever had with Wisconsin were their respective agency contracts with All-Star and their actions incident to those contracts. Neither defendant is licensed to do business in Wisconsin. The defendants have no place of business, office, property, mailing address, telephone listing, bank account nor any agents or employees in the state. Neither defendant has engaged in any business in the state, nor has authorized any agent or employee to transact business in Wisconsin. All the contacts between the defendants and All-Star pursuant to the agency contracts occurred outside of Wisconsin or by interstate mail or telephone.

In 1979 the plaintiff commenced these actions against the defendants to recover unpaid premium and unearned commissions allegedly owed to All-Star under the contracts. Both defendants moved to dismiss the complaints for lack of personal jurisdiction. The trial court consolidated the cases for the hearing on the merits of the motions.

The trial court denied the motions finding personal jurisdiction pursuant to sec. 645.04(5)(a), Stats. The court rejected the defendants' contention that the exercise of personal jurisdiction pursuant to this statute was unconstitutional. The court held that the Supreme Court's decision in McGee v. International Life Ins. Co., 355 U.S. 220, 78 S. Ct. 199, 2 L. Ed. 2d 223 (1957), allowed the exercise of personal jurisdiction pursuant to such a special jurisdictional statute primarily because of the regulated nature of the insurance industry.

The trial court subsequently entered summary judgment in favor of the plaintiff on the merits of the actions as to both defendants. APS appealed both the personal jurisdiction issue and the determination on the merits. Scarborough appealed only as to the issue of personal jurisdiction. We accepted the appeal on certification from the court of appeals.

The issue on appeal is whether a Wisconsin court may constitutionally exercise jurisdiction over the defendants pursuant to sec. 645.04(5)(a), Stats. We hold that the assertion of jurisdiction pursuant to this statute does not violate due process.

The determination of whether Wisconsin courts have jurisdiction over a non-resident defendant is a two-step process. First, it must be determined whether the defendants' contacts with Wisconsin subject them to jurisdiction under a Wisconsin long arm statute. If so, then the court must determine whether the exercise of jurisdiction under the statute comports with due process requirements. Hasley v. Black, Sivalls & Bryson, Inc., 70 Wis. 2d 562, 575, 235 N.W.2d 446 (1975); Zerbel v. H.L. Federman & Co., 48 Wis. 2d 54, 60, 179 N.W. 2d 872 (1970).

Because this case arises out of the liquidation of All-Star, jurisdiction over the defendants is asserted under sec. 645.04(5)(a), Stats., which provides:

> (5) PERSONAL JURISDICTION, GROUNDS FOR. In addition to other grounds for jurisdiction provided by the law of this state, a court of this state having jurisdiction of the subject matter has jurisdiction over a person served pursuant to s. 801.11 in an action brought by the receiver of a domestic insurer or an alien insurer domiciled in this state:
>
> (a) If the person served is obligated to the insurer in any way as an incident to any agency or brokerage arrangement that may exist or has existed between the insurer and the agent or broker, in any action on or incident to the obligation;

This statute is a special jurisdictional statute applicable in liquidation proceedings under ch. 645, Stats. The statute allows the exercise of jurisdiction over any person who is obligated to a Wisconsin insurer involved in a ch. 645 proceeding, incident to an agency or brokerage agreement: Both defendants concede that the language of sec. 645.04(5)(a) covers their situation. Thus, the only issue before this court is whether the exercise of jurisdiction pursuant to this statute is constitutional.

The fourteenth amendment limits the power of a state court to render a valid personal judgment against a nonresident defendant. World-Wide Volkswagen Corp. v. Woodson, 444 U.S. 286, 291, 100 S. Ct. 559, 564, 62 L. Ed. 2d 490 (1980). A state court may exercise jurisdiction over a nonresident if "minimum contacts" exist between the defendant and the forum such that the assertion of jurisdiction is consistent with " 'traditional notions of fair play and substantial justice.' " International Shoe Co. v. Washington, 326 U.S. 310, 316, 66

S. Ct. 154, 158, 90 L. Ed. 95 (1945), quoting Milliken v. Meyer, 311 U.S. 457, 463, 61 S. Ct. 339, 342, 85 L. Ed. 278 (1940). Physical presence is not required; the defendant need only act indirectly in the state. Wisconsin Electrical Manufacturing Co., Inc. v. Pennant Products, Inc., 619 F.2d 676, 678 n.6 (7th Cir. 1980). The relationship between the defendant and the forum must be such that it is reasonable and fair to require the defendant to defend the particular suit in the particular forum. *World-Wide Volkswagen,* 444 U.S. at 291, 100 S. Ct. at 564. Thus, the touchstone of the exercise of jurisdiction is reasonableness and fairness.

The defendants contend that the exercise of jurisdiction in these actions violates due process. They assert that the statute is unconstitutional on its face because it allows the exercise of jurisdiction without requiring even a single isolated contact with Wisconsin. They further contend that the statute, as applied, is unconstitutional because it allows the exercise of jurisdiction where the nonresident's only contact with the state is a contract with a Wisconsin plaintiff. We believe that under the decision in McGee v. International Life Ins. Co., 355 U.S. 220, 78 S. Ct. 199, 2 L. Ed. 2d 223 (1957) both these arguments fail.

McGee involved a suit instituted in California by the beneficiary of a life insurance policy against the Texas insurance company which denied coverage. The only contacts between the insurer and California were the mailing of a reinsurance certificate to the insured in California and the policyholder's payment of the premiums by mail. The court found that due process was not violated by the exercise of jurisdiction based on these minimal contacts finding that "[i]t is sufficient for purposes of due process that the suit was based on a contract which had substantial connection with that State." 355 U.S. at 223, 78 S. Ct. at 201. The court reasoned:

> The contract was delivered in California, the premiums were mailed from there and the insured was a resident of that State when he died. It cannot be denied that California has a manifest interest in providing effective means of redress for its residents when their insurers refuse to pay claims. These residents would be at a severe disadvantage if they were forced to follow the insurance company to a distant State in order to hold it legally accountable. When claims were small or moderate individual claimants frequently could not afford the cost of bringing an action in a foreign forum — thus in effect making the company judgment proof. Often the crucial witnesses — as here on the company's defense of suicide — will be found in the insured's locality. Of course, there may be inconvenience to the insurer if it is held amenable to suit in California where it had this contract but certainly nothing which amounts to a denial of due process. Cf. Travelers Health Assn. v. Virginia ex rel. State Corporation Comm'n, 339 U.S. 643 [70 S. Ct. 927,

94 L. Ed. 1154]. There is no contention that respondent did not have adequate notice of the suit or sufficient time to prepare its defenses and appear." 355 U.S. at 223-24, 78 S. Ct. at 201-02.

This court as well as the United States Supreme Court have both recognized that *McGee* is based on the principle that states have a strong interest in providing their citizens with a forum in insurance disputes. . . .

Thus, where the state's interest in "providing effective means of redress for its residents" is strong, as in the highly regulated area of insurance, the minimum contacts requirements of *International Shoe* can be met through a single isolated contract. *Zerbel*, 48 Wis. 2d at 69, 179 N.W.2d 872. . . .

We find that the *McGee* decision is applicable and controlling in this case. This case arises out of liquidation proceedings instituted pursuant to ch. 645, Stats. Ch. 645 was enacted in 1967 as the product of a comprehensive study and revision of the insurance laws and redesigned all aspects of insurance delinquency proceedings. It sets up a comprehensive framework for the complete, orderly and efficient liquidation of insolvent Wisconsin insurance companies in order to fairly distribute the unavoidable burden of delinquency. The purposes are more explicitly stated in sec. 645.01(4), which provides: . . .

As part of this chapter the legislature enacted sec. 645.04(5)(a), Stats., which allows Wisconsin courts to obtain jurisdiction over nonresident agents and brokers in order to efficiently and inexpensively gather up the outstanding assets of the insolvent insurer. As stated in the interpretative commentary accompanying sec. 645.04(5):

> Sub. (5): This subsection extends the jurisdiction of the Wisconsin court in order to strengthen the hand of the receiver. *In so doing, however, it still assures "fair play and substantial justice,"* (see International Shoe Co. v. Washington, 66 S. Ct. 154 [158] 326 U.S. 310, 316, 90 L. Ed. 95, 161 A.L.R. 1057 (1945)) *to any defendants affected by this new basis of jurisdiction. When a formal delinquency proceeding begins, agents' balances are likely to constitute a large share of the insurer's assets. Moreover, they are assets difficult to collect. To facilitate gathering the funds, the Wisconsin courts are given expanded personal jurisdiction, making it easier and more economical to reduce these claims to judgment.* Of course, actual collection will still require proceedings where the defendant's assets can be found, but the full faith and credit clause and the Uniform Enforcement of Foreign Judgments Act (s. 270.46) [U.L.A.] will make that part of the task easier.

Moreover, because these actions are just two of many instituted against agents of All-Star, it is clear that most of the witnesses and evidence is located in Wisconsin. The burden and inconvenience on the defendants in having to defend in Wisconsin rather than Louisiana or Illinois is not so unreasonable that it results in a denial of due process. . . .

In conclusion, we believe that it is fair and reasonable to exercise jurisdiction over the defendants. The litigation is connected to the forum because it involves the liquidation of a Wisconsin insurer. The defendants are linked to Wisconsin by virtue of their contracts with All-Star and their actions incident to the contracts. Wisconsin has a manifest interest in providing an efficient and inexpensive forum in which to liquidate domestic insurance companies in order to protect its citizens. Finally, the burden on the defendants to defend in Wisconsin is not unreasonable. Therefore we hold that the defendants are amenable to the jurisdiction of the Wisconsin courts in these actions based on their agency contracts with All-Star. . . .

Case No. 81-1349 is remanded to the court of appeals for further proceedings not inconsistent with this opinion.

Judgment affirmed in Case No. 81-1350.

Notes and Questions

1. Appeal to the United States Supreme Court in *All-Star* was dismissed for want of a substantial federal question. Id. 461 U.S. 951 (1983). The seminal cases here are *International Shoe* and *McGee*, discussed in *All-Star*.

2. *Unpaid premium* is self-explanatory, but *unearned commission* is not. An agent who places a policy and remits the premium to the company does so on a net basis, that is, the commission is first deducted from the premium. If the policy were cancelled within the policy period, a provision of the policy normally calls for the repayment of the "unearned premium" to the insured, calculated on a pro rata basis (at least if it is the company that cancels). The premium is considered, for that purpose, to be "earned" gradually over the policy period, not instantaneously at inception.* If the policy is terminated, as it is by law under most state statutes when there is an order for liquidation, a proportional part of both the premium and the commission is earned and the remainder is unearned. The agent is obligated to

---

*The original view on the question is that the premium is fully earned immediately upon attachment of the risk, subject to any contrary contractual or statutory provisions. Such contrary provisions are so common, however, that most persons, even when generally familiar with insurance practice, suppose erroneously that the underlying rule is otherwise. Problems requiring that the question be answered authoritatively seldom arise and as a result the cases are few. Nevertheless, the rule seems clear enough. See Vance on Insurance 347 (3rd ed. 1951); Clarke, The Law of Insurance Contracts 247, §13-12 (1989).

repay the unearned commission to the liquidator, not to the policy-holder. The policyholder may claim the unearned premium (including unearned commission) in the liquidation but in some states it has a lower priority than loss claims and is unlikely to be reached in distrib-uting the assets of the insolvent estate. A good deal of unearned com-mission proves to be uncollectible without suit, and sometimes even after suit. Why is this so?

3. In an effort to maximize the assets of insolvent insurance com-panies for purposes of distribution to claimants, the Insurers Supervi-sion, Rehabilitation and Liquidation Model Act of the National Association of Insurance Commissioners (NAIC) provides that

> A. (1) An agent, broker, premium finance company, or any other person, other than the insured, responsible for the payment of a premium shall be obligated to pay any unpaid premium for the full policy term due the insurer at the time of the declaration of insolvency, whether earned or unearned, as shown on the records of the insurer.. . . .
> (2) An insured shall be obligated to pay any unpaid earned premium due the insurer at the time of the declaration of insolvency, as shown on the records of the insurer. [NAIC, Model Laws, Regulations and Guidelines 555-30 (1987).]

Whether this provision is enforceable against agents in another state was recently decided at the trial court level. What result would you expect? See Hager as Liquidator of Iowa Natl. Mut. Ins. Co. v. Anderson-Hutchinson Ins. Agency, 1989 U.S. Dist. Lexis 13614. Why would a distinction with respect to unearned premium be made between the obligation of the insured and that of all other persons?

4. A Delaware corporation with headquarters in Connecticut, where it manufactured a product used in oil drilling, insured its prod-uct anywhere in the world (for property loss, not for liability) through a Connecticut broker which placed the business with Scandinavian companies. The premiums were paid from Connecticut. If losses occurred, payment was to be made through the Connecticut broker. The insurers also had (and exercised) the right to inspect the insured's books in Connecticut. When some of the property was lost, the insured sued in Connecticut. The insurers moved to dismiss for lack of jurisdiction and on the ground of forum non conveniens. In Teleco Oilfield Services, Inc. v. Skandia Ins. Co., 656 F. Supp. 753 (D. Conn. 1987), the court denied the motion to dismiss on either ground.

5. In 1987, Louisiana amended its general long-arm statute to permit judicial jurisdiction on any basis consistent with the Louisiana and United States Constitutions. That statute was applied to a case where the contacts of the transaction with Louisiana were similar to those in *Teleco* — perhaps even more tenuous — and held that there

was jurisdiction. First Guar. Bank v. Attorneys' Liab. Assurance Socy., 506 So. 2d 595 (La. App.), *rev'd,* 515 So. 2d 1080 (La. 1987).

6. A Tennessee company issued a policy to a Tennessee resident who subsequently moved to Florida. Prior to that move he was in an accident in Arizona. That was the only Arizona connection of either party. The company declined to pay and the insured sued in Arizona. The company "has no offices or agents in Arizona, is not licensed to do business in Arizona, and, aside from Batton's claim, has never investigated, adjusted, settled, or defended a claim in Arizona." Batton v. Tennessee Farmers Mut. Ins. Co., 153 Ariz. 267, 736 P.2d 1 (1986), *aff'd as mod.,* 153 Ariz. 268, 736 P.2d 2 (1987), held the contact did not meet the constitutional requirements.

C. What Is the "Business of Insurance"?

The McCarran Act speaks in terms of the "business of insurance." A natural interpretation would be that the business of insurance is the business that insurance companies engage in, or that they engage in when they are not acting completely outside their natural sphere, or that insurance companies ordinarily do. As so often in the interpretation of statutes, however, the natural assumption turns out to be wrong. For a treatment of the way in which the Supreme Court has (in the opinion of the author) misread the intentions of Congress on this question, see Kimball & Heaney, Emasculation of the McCarran-Ferguson Act: A Study in Judicial Activism, 1985 Utah L. Rev. 1. Yet by definition the Supreme Court is always right, at least until it changes its mind. For that reason the scope of the reverse preemption made possible by the McCarran Act, pursuant to prevailing Supreme Court analysis, is crucial. The following case is the culmination of the development with respect to the meaning of "business of insurance": It is not the most recent case but it is the most important.

GROUP LIFE & HEALTH INS. CO. v. ROYAL DRUG CO.

440 U.S. 205 (1979)

Mr. Justice STEWART delivered the opinion of the Court.

The respondents, 18 owners of independent pharmacies in San Antonio, Tex., brought an antitrust action in a Federal District Court against the petitioners, Group Life and Health Insurance Co., known as Blue Shield of Texas (Blue Shield), and three pharmacies also doing business in San Antonio. The complaint alleged that the petitioners had violated §1 of the Sherman Act, 15 U.S.C. §1, by entering agreements to fix the retail prices of drugs and pharmaceuticals, and that the activities of the petitioners had caused Blue Shield's policyholders not to deal with certain of the respondents, thereby constituting an unlawful group boycott. The trial court granted summary judgment to the petitioners on the ground that the challenged agreements are exempt from the antitrust laws under §2(b) of the McCarran-Ferguson Act, 59 Stat. 34, as amended, 61 Stat. 448, 15 U.S.C. §1012(b), because the agreements are the "business of insurance," are "regulated by [Texas] law," and are not "boycotts" within the meaning of §3(b) of the Act, 59 Stat. 34, 15 U.S.C. §1013(b). 415 F. Supp. 343 (WD Tex.). The Court of Appeals for the Fifth Circuit reversed the judgment. Holding that the agreements in question are not the "business of insurance" within the meaning of §2(b), the appellate court did not reach the other questions decided by the trial court. 556 F.2d 1375. We granted certiorari because of intercircuit conflicts as to the meaning of the phrase "business of insurance" in §2(b) of the Act: 435 U.S. 903.

I

Blue Shield offers insurance policies which entitle the policyholders to obtain prescription drugs. If the pharmacy selected by the insured has entered into a "Pharmacy Agreement" with Blue Shield, and is therefore a participating pharmacy, the insured is required to pay only $2 for every prescription drug. The remainder of the cost is paid directly by Blue Shield to the participating pharmacy. If, on the other hand, the insured selects a pharmacy which has not entered into a Pharmacy Agreement, and is therefore a nonparticipating pharmacy, he is required to pay the full price charged by the pharmacy. The insured may then obtain reimbursement from Blue Shield for 75% of the difference between that price and $2.

Blue Shield offered to enter into a Pharmacy Agreement with each licensed pharmacy in Texas. Under the Agreement, a participating pharmacy agrees to furnish prescription drugs to Blue Shield's policyholders at $2 for each prescription, and Blue Shield agrees to reimburse the pharmacy for the pharmacy's cost of acquiring the amount of the drug prescribed. Thus, only pharmacies that can afford to distribute prescription drugs for less than this $2 markup can profitably participate in the plan.

The only issue before us is whether the Court of Appeals was correct in concluding that these Pharmacy Agreements are not the "business of insurance" within the meaning of §2(b) of the McCarran-

Ferguson Act. If that conclusion is correct, then the Agreements are not exempt from examination under the antitrust laws. Whether the Agreements are *illegal* under the antitrust laws is an entirely separate question, not now before us.

II

A

As the Court stated last Term in St. Paul Fire & Marine Ins. Co. v. Barry, 438 U.S. 531, 541, the starting point in a case involving construction of the McCarran-Ferguson Act, like the starting point in any case involving the meaning of a statute, is the language of the statute itself. See also Blue Chip Stamps v. Manor Drug Stores, 421 U.S. 723, 756 (POWELL, J., concurring). It is important, therefore, to observe at the outset that the statutory language in question here does not exempt the business of insurance companies from the scope of the antitrust laws. The exemption is for the "business of insurance," not the "business of insurers":

> The statute did not purport to make the States supreme in regulating all the activities of insurance *companies*; its language refers not to the persons or companies who are subject to state regulation, but to laws "regulating the *business* of insurance." Insurance companies may do many things which are subject to paramount federal regulation; only when they are engaged in the "business of insurance" does the statute apply. SEC v. National Securities, Inc., 393 U.S. 453, 459-460. (Emphasis in original.)

Since the law does not define the "business of insurance," the question for decision is whether the Pharmacy Agreements fall within the ordinary understanding of that phrase, illumined by any light to be found in the structure of the Act and its legislative history. Cf. Ernst & Ernst v. Hochfelder, 425 U.S. 185, 199, and n.19.

B

The primary elements of an insurance contract are the spreading and underwriting of a policyholder's risk. . . .

The significance of underwriting or spreading of risk as an indispensable characteristic of insurance was recognized by this Court in SEC v. Variable Annuity Life Ins. Co., 359 U.S. 65. That case involved several corporations, representing themselves as "life insurance" companies, that offered variable annuity contracts for sale in interstate commerce. The companies were regulated by the insurance commissioners of several States. Purchasers of the contracts were not entitled to any fixed return, but only to a pro rata participation in the investment portfolios of the companies. Thus a policyholder could receive substantial sums if investment decisions were successful, but very little if they were not. One of the questions presented was whether these variable annuity contracts were the "business of insurance" under §2(b) of the McCarran-Ferguson Act. The Court held that the annuity contracts were not insurance, even though they were regulated as such under state law and involved actuarial prognostications of mortality. Central to the Court's holding was the premise that "the concept of 'insurance' involves some investment risk-taking on the part of the company." 359 U.S., at 71. Since the variable annuity contracts offered no guarantee of fixed income, they placed all the investment risk on the annuitant and none on the company. Ibid. The Court concluded, therefore, that the annuities involved "no true underwriting of risks, the one earmark of insurance as it has commonly been conceived of in popular understanding and usage." Id., at 73 (footnote omitted). Cf. German Alliance Ins. Co. v. Lewis, 233 U.S. 389, 412 ("The effect of insurance — indeed it has been said to be its fundamental object — is to distribute the loss over as wide an area as possible").

The petitioners do not really dispute that the underwriting or spreading of risk is a critical determinant in identifying insurance. Rather they argue that the Pharmacy Agreements do involve the underwriting of risks. As they state in their brief:

> In Securities and Exchange Commission v. Variable Annuity Life Insurance Co., 359 U.S. 65, 73 (1959), the "earmark" of insurance was described as the "underwriting of risks" in exchange for a premium. Here the risk insured against is the possibility that, during the term of the policy, the insured may suffer a financial loss arising from the purchase of prescription drugs, or that he may be financially unable to purchase such drugs. In consideration of the premium, Blue Shield assumes this risk by agreeing with its insureds to contract with Participating Pharmacies to furnish the needed drugs and to reimburse the Pharmacies for each prescription filled for the insured. In short, each of the fundamental elements of insurance is present here — the payment of a premium in exchange for a promise to indemnify the insured against losses upon the happening of a specified contingency.

The fallacy of the petitioners' position is that they confuse the obligations of Blue Shield under its insurance policies, which insure against the risk that policyholders will be unable to pay for prescription drugs during the period of coverage, and the agreements between Blue Shield and the participating pharmacies, which serve only to minimize the costs Blue Shield incurs in fulfilling its underwriting obligations. The benefit promised to Blue Shield policyholders is that their premiums will cover the cost of prescription drugs except for a $2 charge for each prescription. So long as that promise is kept, policyholders are basically unconcerned with arrangements made between Blue Shield and participating pharmacies. . . .

C

Another commonly understood aspect of the business of insurance relates to the contract between the insurer and the insured. In enacting the McCarran-Ferguson Act Congress was concerned with:

> The relationship between insurer and insured, the type of policy which could be issued, its reliability, interpretation, and enforcement — these were the core of the "business of insurance." Undoubtedly, other activities of insurance companies relate so closely to their status as reliable insurers that they too must be placed in the same class. But whatever the exact scope of the statutory term, it is clear where the focus was — it was on the relationship between the insurance company and the policyholder. SEC v. National Securities, Inc., supra, at 460.

The Pharmacy Agreements are not "between insurer and insured." They are separate contractual arrangements between Blue Shield and pharmacies engaged in the sale and distribution of goods and services other than insurance. . . .

III . . .

C

References to the meaning of the "business of insurance" in the legislative history of the McCarran-Ferguson Act strongly suggest that Congress understood the business of insurance to be the underwriting and spreading of risk. Thus, one of the early House Reports stated: "The theory of insurance is the distribution of risk according to hazard, experience, and the laws of averages. These factors are not within the control of insuring companies in the sense that the producer or manufacturer may control cost factors." H.R. Rep. No. 873, 78th Cong., 1st Sess., 8-9 (1943). See also S. Rep. No. 1112, 78th Cong., 2d Sess., 6 (1944); 90 Cong. Rec. 6526 (1944) (remarks of Rep. Hancock).

Because of the widespread view that it is very difficult to underwrite risks in an informed and responsible way without intra-industry cooperation, the primary concern of both representatives of the insurance industry and the Congress was that cooperative ratemaking efforts be exempt from the antitrust laws. . . .

IV

If agreements between an insurer and retail pharmacists are the "business of insurance" because they reduce the insurer's costs, then so are all other agreements insurers may make to keep their costs under control — whether with automobile body repair shops or landlords. Such agreements would be exempt from the antitrust laws if Congress had extended the coverage of the McCarran-Ferguson Act to the "business of insurance companies." But that is precisely what Congress did not do.

For all these reasons, the judgment of the Court of Appeals is affirmed.

Mr. Justice BRENNAN, with whom THE CHIEF JUSTICE, Mr. Justice MARSHALL, and Mr. Justice POWELL join, dissenting.

The McCarran-Ferguson Act, 59 Stat. 33, as amended, 15 U.S.C. §§1011-1015, renders the federal antitrust laws inapplicable to the "business of insurance" to the extent such business is regulated by state law and is not subject to the "boycott" exception stated in §1013(b). The single question presented by this case is whether the "business of insurance" includes direct contractual arrangements ("provider agreements") between petitioner Blue Shield and third parties to provide benefits owed to the insurer's policyholders. The Court today holds that it does not.

I disagree: Since (a) there is no challenge to the status of Blue Shield's drug-benefits *policy* as the "business of insurance," I conclude (b) that some provider agreements negotiated to carry out the policy obligations of the insurer to the insured should be considered part of such business, and (c) that the specific Pharmacy Agreements at issue in this case should be included in such part. Before considering this analysis, however, it is necessary to set forth the background of the enactment of the McCarran-Ferguson Act.

I

SEC v. National Securities, Inc., 393 U.S. 453, 459 (1969), recognized that the legislative history of the McCarran-Ferguson Act sheds little light on the meaning of the words "business of insurance." See

S. Rep. No. 20, 79th Cong., 1st Sess. (1945); H.R. Rep. No. 143, 79th Cong., 1st Sess. (1945). But while the legislative history is largely silent on the matter, it does indicate that Congress deliberately chose to phrase the exemption broadly. Congress had draft bills before it which would have limited the "business of insurance" to a narrow range of specified insurance company practices, but chose instead the more general language which ultimately became law. . . .

Since continuation of state regulation as it existed before *South-Eastern* was Congress' goal, evidence of what States might reasonably have considered to be and regulated as insurance at the time the McCarran-Ferguson Act was passed in 1945 is clearly relevant to our decision. This does not mean that a transaction not viewed as insurance in 1945 cannot be so viewed today.

> We realize that . . . insurance is an evolving institution. Common knowledge tells us that the forms have greatly changed even in a generation. And we would not undertake to freeze the concep[t] of "insurance" . . . into the mold [it] fitted when these Federal Acts were passed." SEC v. Variable Annuity Life Ins. Co., 359 U.S. 65, 71 (1959).

It is thus logical to suppose that if elements common to the ordinary understanding of "insurance" are present, new forms of the business should constitute the "business of insurance" for purposes of the McCarran-Ferguson Act. The determination of the scope of the Act, therefore, involves both an analysis of the proximity between the challenged transactions and those well recognized as elements of "insurance," and an examination of the historical setting of the Act. On both counts, Blue Shield's Pharmacy Agreements constitute the "business of insurance."

II

I start with common ground. Neither the Court, ante, at 230 n.37, nor the parties challenge the fact that the drug-benefits policy offered by Blue Shield to its policyholders — as distinguished from the contract between Blue Shield and the pharmacies — is the "business of insurance." Whatever the merits of scholastic argument over the technical definition of "insurance," the policy both transfers and distributes risk. The policyholder pays a sum certain — the premium — against the risk of the uncertain contingency of illness, and if the company has calculated correctly, the premiums of those who do not fall ill pay the costs of benefits above the premiums of those who do. See R. Mehr & E. Cammack, Principles of Insurance 31-32 (6th ed. 1976). An important difference between Blue Shield's policy and other forms of health insurance is that Blue Shield "pays" the policyholder in goods and services (drugs and their dispensation), rather than in cash. Since we will not "freeze the concep[t] of 'insurance' . . . into the mold it fitted" when McCarran-Ferguson was passed, this difference cannot be a reason for holding that the drug-benefits policy falls outside the "business of insurance" even if our inquiry into the understandings of what constituted "insurance" in the 1930's and 1940's were to suggest that a contrary view prevailed at that time.

Fortunately, logic and history yield the same result. It is true that the first health insurance policies provided only cash indemnities. However, although policies that specifically provided drug benefits were not available during the 1930's and 1940's, analogous policies providing hospital and medical services — rather than cash — were available.

[Justice Brennan then discussed the history of Blue Cross and Blue Shield. — Ed.]

III

The next question is whether at least some contracts with third parties to procure delivery of benefits to Blue Shield's insureds would also constitute the "business of insurance." Such contracts, like those between Blue Shield and the druggists in this case, are known as "provider agreements." The Court, adopting the view of the Solicitor General, today holds that no provider agreements can be considered part of the "business of insurance." It contends that the "underwriting or spreading of risk [is] an indispensable characteristic of insurance," ante, at 212, and that "[a]nother commonly understood aspect of the business of insurance relates to the contract between the insurer and the insured." Ante, at 215. Because provider agreements neither themselves spread risk, nor involve transactions between insurers and insureds, the Court excludes them from the "business of insurance."

The argument fails in light of this Court's prior decisions and the legislative history of the Act. The Court has held, for example, FTC v. National Casualty Co., 357 U.S. 560 (1958), that the advertising of insurance, a unilateral act which does not involve underwriting, is within the scope of the McCarran-Ferguson Act. And the legislative history makes it abundantly clear that numerous horizontal agreements between insurance companies which do not technically involve the underwriting of risk were regarded by Congress as within the scope of the Act's exemption for the "business of insurance." For example, rate agreements among insurers, a conspicuous congressional illustration, see, e.g., 91 Cong. Rec. 1481, 1484 (1945) (remarks of Sens. Pepper and Ferguson), and the subject of the South-Eastern Underwriters case, see SEC v. National Securities, Inc., 393 U.S., at 460, do not themselves spread risk. Indeed, the Court apparently concedes that arrangements among insurance companies respecting premiums and benefits would constitute the "business of insurance," despite their failure to fit within its formula. Ante, at 221 and 224-225, n.32. . . .

. . . *Some* kind of provider agreement becomes a necessity if a service-benefits insurer is to meet its obligations to the insureds. The policy before us in this case, for example, promises payment of benefits in drugs. Thus, some arrangement must be made to provide those drugs for subscribers. Such an arrangement obtains the very benefits promised in the policy; it does not simply relate to the general operation of the company. A provider contract in a service-benefit plan, therefore, is critical to "the type of policy which could be issued" as well as to its "reliability" and "enforcement." It thus comes within the terms of SEC v. National Securities, Inc., 393 U.S., at 460. That case explained that the "business of insurance" involves not only the "relationship between insurer and insured," but also "other activities of insurance companies [that] *relate so closely* to their status as reliable insurers that they too must be placed in the same class." Thus, "[s]tatutes aimed at protecting or regulating . . . [the insurer/insured] relationship, *directly or indirectly*, are laws regulating the 'business of insurance.' " Ibid. (emphasis added).

V

The process of deciding what is and is not the "business of insurance" is inherently a case-by-case problem. It is true that the conclusion advocated here carries with it line-drawing problems. That is necessarily so once the provider-agreement line is crossed by holding some to be within the "business." But that is a line which history and logic compel me to cross. I would hold that the *concept* of a provider agreement for benefits promised in the policy is within the "business of insurance" because some form of provider agreement is necessary to fulfill the obligations of a service-benefit policy. I would hold that *these* provider agreements, Blue Shield's Pharmacy Agreements, are protected because they (1) directly obtain the very benefits promised in the policy and therefore directly affect rates, cost, and insurer reliability, and (2) themselves constitute a critical element of risk "prediction." The conclusion that these kinds of agreements are the "business of insurance" is that reached by every Court of Appeals except the Court of Appeals in this case. . . .

Finally, the conclusion that Blue Shield's Pharmacy Agreements should be held within the "business of insurance" does not alone establish whether the agreements enjoy an exemption from the antitrust laws. To be entitled to an exemption, petitioners still would have to demonstrate that the transactions are in fact truly regulated by the State, 15 U.S.C. §1012(b), and that they do not fall within the "boycott" exception of 15 U.S.C. §1013(b). The District Court held for petitioners on both issues. Neither issue was reached by the Court of Appeals, however, in light of its holding that the contracts were not the "business of insurance." Accordingly, I would reverse the judgment of the Court of Appeals and remand the case for further proceedings.

Notes and Questions

1. On remand, the Court of Appeals affirmed the district court decision that there was no boycott. Id., 737 F.2d 1433 (1984), *cert. denied*, 469 U.S. 1160 (1985).

2. See Kennedy, The McCarran Act: A Limited "Business of Insurance" Antitrust Exemption Made Ever Narrower — Three Recent Decisions, 18 Forum 528 (1983). The title suggests an excessive emphasis on the antitrust aspects of McCarran. For a somewhat different emphasis, see Kimball & Heaney, Emasculation of the McCarran-Ferguson Act: A Study in Judicial Activism, 1985 Utah L. Rev. 1. There is an unfortunate tendency of commentators to think of McCarran solely in terms of rate setting and antitrust. See Shenefield, Insurance — The New Frontier of Deregulation, 16 Forum 679 (1981); Gregory, Public Regulation of the Insurance Industry after *Barry* and *Royal Drug*: McCarran-Ferguson at the End of the Decade, 16 Forum 371 (1981).

3. The Illinois Director of Insurance, as Rehabilitator of one insurance company, brought action against the New York Superintendent as Liquidator of another. The action was to compel arbitration under the Federal Arbitration Act, pursuant to an arbitration clause in a reinsurance contract between the two companies. The New York insurance liquidation act precluded arbitration; the Federal Arbitration Act commanded it. How should the court decide the case? See Washburn v. Corcoran, 643 F. Supp. 554 (S.D.N.Y. 1986). On a parallel question, see Gordon v. United States Dept. of the Treasury, 846 F.2d 272 (4th Cir. 1988), *cert. denied*, 488 U.S. 954 (1988).

4. Alleghany Corporation is basically a family holding company, but it is listed on the New York Stock Exchange. It engages in investment, and is usually an active rather than a passive investor. It sought to acquire up to 20 percent of the stock of the St. Paul Companies, the holding company of a sizeable stable of wholly-owned insurance companies, domiciled in nine states. The holding company and the principal insurers were domiciled in Minnesota. Under insurance holding

company acts in effect in 47 states, it was necessary for Alleghany to obtain permission of the insurance commissioners in each state where an insurance company subsidiary was domiciled to acquire more than ten percent of that company's stock. Minnesota and some other states gave permission; Wisconsin and a few other states (including North Dakota) denied it, in part because the controlling owners of Alleghany refused to comply fully with the disclosure requirements of the statute. In Alleghany Corp. v. Pomeroy, 700 F. Supp. 460 (D.N.D. 1988), the Court held North Dakota's statute unconstitutional as a violation of the commerce clause. The court held that *McCarran* did not protect it from challenge. The fight between Alleghany and St. Paul was bare-knuckled, and no doubt there would have had to be a similar case in each of the states denying permission, carried to the circuits and per-haps eventually to the Supreme Court, before the fight was over. At least two circuits were involved. The Wisconsin statute sufficiently differs from the others that the arguments in that case would need to be changed. But as often happens, the matter ended eventually without final determination of the applicable rule. How would you decide the case?

D. Regulation of Policy Terms

One way the states intervene in the business of insurance is by controlling the terms of insurance policies. The control is exercised at various levels. The standard fire insurance policy is the prime example of such regulation at the most basic level, for legislatures have man-dated the precise language of the entire policy.

Massachusetts was the first state to enact a standard fire insur-ance policy in 1873. Other states followed. New York's policy of 1886 ultimately became the model for most of the states. It was drafted by a committee of the National Board of Fire Underwriters. The 1886 pol-icy continued in use until replaced by another New York form in 1918, which in turn was used until a new policy was enacted in 1943. That policy was adopted by nearly all the states, and continues in effect to the present in most states. The standard policy was an obstacle to the development of multiperil policies such as homeowners, but compa-nies managed to get around the problem by using endorsements. Wis-consin sought to simplify the matter by repealing its standard fire insurance policy in 1975 and leaving the matter to the market, but other states have not followed that lead.

There is little basis for challenging the constitutionality of the legislative mandate, except for isolated provisions. One example is the provision the policy contains for mandatory appraisal and arbitration. That provision was challenged as unconstitutional deprivation of the right to jury trial in Molodyh v. Truck Ins. Exch., 304 Or. 290, 744 P.2d 992 (1987).

The provisions of mandated coverage statutes in the health insurance field are almost as extreme in control over contract terms as the standard fire policy. They require insurers that write health insurance to include in their coverage such expensive items as kidney dialysis, handicapped children, newborn infants, alcoholism, and tuberculosis. See, for example, Wis. Stats. §§632.78(2), 632.88, 632.89, 632.90 and 632.91 (discussed in Chapter 7). The next case deals with a challenge to such statutes.

Standard life insurance policies were enacted in a few states in the first decades of this century, but were later repealed. They were replaced, in many states, by a handful of required provisions and sometimes supplemented by a number of prohibited provisions. Required provisions deal, inter alia, with non-forfeiture options, providing for cash values, extended term insurance, or paid-up whole life insurance in a reduced amount.

Standard provisions exist in large numbers in the health insurance area, in addition to the mandated provisions mentioned above. Their usual characteristic is that they are mandated if a company chooses to deal with a specified subject, but not otherwise. They fill many pages of the typical insurance code.

Policies are substantially uniform in automobile insurance and in primary general liability insurance, though not in excess policies or policies written in the surplus lines market. Standard policies are not required by statute or administrative edict for these fields, but except for surplus lines they must be approved by insurance commissioners. They are usually developed by industry committees or by the Insurance Services Office, which was created by the insurance business for that purpose (among others).

EUBANKS v. NATIONAL FEDERATION STUDENT PROTECTION TRUST

290 Ark. 541, 721 S.W.2d 644 (1986)

GEORGE ROSE SMITH, Justice.

The principal appellee, National Federation Student Protection Trust, is an association whose membership includes local schools in Arkansas and throughout the United States. The Trust annually offers an accident insurance program to its member schools, with students and school employees being eligible for the insurance. On July 19,

1985, after some preceding correspondence, an attorney in the State Insurance Commissioner's office wrote a letter to the Kansas insurance agency which administers the insurance program, stating that the Trust's program would not be in compliance with the Arkansas Insurance Code until the group policy and certificates had been approved by the Insurance Department.

Upon receipt of that letter the Trust, without resorting to its administrative remedy before the Commissioner, filed this suit to enjoin the Commissioner from interfering with the Trust's sale of the insurance in Arkansas. The other plaintiffs are the Chicago insurance company that writes the master policy, the Kansas insurance agency, and the Nashville, Arkansas, insurance representative who travels the state selling the plan to school districts. The complaint was filed four days after the July 19 letter. It states a variety of grounds for injunctive relief, one being that the Commissioner's Bulletin 15-81, on which the attorney's letter was based, is arbitrary and capricious. On the day the complaint was filed the chancellor signed an ex parte temporary restraining order which, after the case had been tried, was made final by the decree entered on November 26, 1985. The Commissioner's appeal was filed in this court under Rule 29(1)(c).

The Commissioner makes two arguments for reversal, but we need discuss only his first point, that the chancellor erred in finding the Bulletin to be arbitrary and capricious. We emphasize at the outset that the plaintiffs, though having the burden of proof, offered no evidence to support their allegation of arbitrariness and capriciousness. No one from the Commissioner's office, for example, was called to explain the basis for the Bulletin. The defendants did not supply the deficiency. Consequently the trial court's ruling in effect declared that the Bulletin is invalid on its face. We cannot agree with that conclusion.

The Bulletin provides that if the parent pays the entire premium, a student accident plan cannot coordinate benefits with other insurance or declare itself to be "excess," that is, applicable only to the extent that a claim is not covered by other insurance. The Bulletin goes on to provide that if the school and the parent both pay part of the premium, the benefits can be coordinated. Finally, if the school pays the entire premium, "the plan can be anything," including being excess insurance. The chancellor's decree recites that the Commissioner's classification according to who pays the premium is capricious and arbitrary, because the insured has the same expectation of benefits regardless of who pays the premium.

The facts about the insurance plan are simple. The Trust annually obtains a basic policy and makes the coverage available to its member schools. The Trust itself pays nothing to the insurance company and receives no commission. The Arkansas representative sells the plan to school districts. He testified that in 1984 his gross premium income was between $500,000 and $600,000, on which he receives a commission. The insurance company or its agency provides the school districts with information about the coverage and furnishes printed handbills, often called flyers, which are distributed to the children with instructions to take the flyers home to their parents. The flyer used in this instance provided a parent with basic information about the insurance, including a statement that it was excess coverage.

On the facts before us it is evident that Bulletin 15-81 was issued as a consumer-protection measure. Our Insurance Code contains various provisions for the protection of purchasers of insurance. For instance, the Code prohibits misrepresentations made to obtain insurance business, Ark. Stat. Ann. §66-3015 (Repl. 1980), prohibits excessive premiums, §66-3023, and broadly authorizes the Commissioner to make reasonable rules and regulations to aid in putting the provisions of the Code into effect. §66-2111. One of the Commissioner's responsibilities has been to safeguard the interest of consumers who buy insurance.

We think it plain that the Commissioner was acting within his authority in seeking to protect the parents in the present situation. We do not imply that the coverage offered through the Trust in 1985 was not a good value, but the area is undeniably one in which scrutiny is proper. Whatever premiums the insurance company is to receive must be paid by the school district, by the parents, or by both. Our school districts perennially operate on tight budgets. When the school board, composed of elected citizens, decides to spend school funds for the insurance of school children, parents may reasonably assume that the outlay is prudent, whether the district pays all or only part of the premium. But the situation is vastly different when the parent pays all the premium himself without the school board's having committed its own funds. Here the parent sees only the flyer, which has a semblance of official sanction by reason of having come from the public school. Accident coverage for a student during school time is $12 a year, which might very well seem to be a bargain, and so it might have been. But the July 19 letter to the Trust, which was attached as an exhibit to the complaint, not only referred to the group policy and the certificates but went on to say: "In view of the Department's previous problems with the advertisement material used by representatives of the [Trust], the Department is requesting that all solicitation material be filed for approval."

The standard for judicial review of administrative action is that the action will be regarded as arbitrary and capricious only where it is not supportable on any rational basis. Partlow v. Ark. State Police Commn., 271 Ark. 351, 609 S.W.2d 23 (1980). In the field of equal protection, a classification is not arbitrary if it rests upon a difference having a fair and substantial relation to the purpose of the measure. Corbitt v. Mohawk Rubber Co., 256 Ark. 932, 511 S.W.2d 184 (1974). The burden of showing that a rule has no rational basis is on the party challenging the rule. Streight v. Ragland, 280 Ark. 206, 655 S.W.2d 459 (1983). The plaintiffs did not sustain that burden; they did not even attempt to. The Commissioner's Bulletin is not invalid on its face, which in the absence of proof concludes our inquiry.

Reversed.

Notes and Questions

1. A dissenter in *Eubanks* expressed the view that the commissioner was acting beyond his authority. The statute provided, "The Commissioner shall disapprove any form filed under Section 276, or withdraw any previous approval thereof, only if the form . . . [c]ontains . . . any inconsistent, ambiguous, or misleading clauses, or exceptions and conditions which deceptively affect the risk purported to be assumed in the general coverage of the contract." Does the quoted ground for disapproval justify the action of the Commissioner?

2. The subject of regulation of policy terms was exhaustively treated in Kimball & Pfennigstorf, Legislative and Judicial Control of the Terms of Insurance Contracts: A Comparative Study of American and European Practice, 39 Ind. L.J. 675 (1964), and Administrative Control of the Terms of Insurance Contracts: A Comparative Study, 40 Ind. L.J. 143 (1965). Although there has been much change in other parts of insurance regulation, as well as in the detail of this subject, its main outlines remain the same as in the 1960s.

E. Cancellation and Nonrenewal

Traditionally life insurance policies have been noncancellable by the insurer and, as was seen in Chapter 6, after a period of contestability, cannot be contested on any ground except nonpayment of premium.

Property and liability policies, on the other hand, were traditionally cancellable by either party: in the case of the insurer only after notice (often ten days) to give the insured some time to find other insurance. Of course they were also always contestable for adequate reasons.

In the 1960's legislatures began to restrict the right of insurers to cancel a policy during its term and in some cases even the right to decline to renew it at expiration except in conformity with statutory procedures and sometimes for statutorily authorized reasons. Most recently, some statutes (or voter initiatives) have even forbidden non-renewal for almost any reason. The fight thus precipitated is not over. The whole development began in automobile insurance, where there was a "crisis" in the 1960s; later it was extended to some other policies. The most recent expansion of the proscription is most often limited to automobile insurance.

In Glockel v. State Farm Mut. Auto. Ins. Co., 224 Neb. 598, 400 N.W.2d 250 (1987), the Nebraska Supreme Court answered a certified question from the U.S. District Court for Nebraska, "Whether the *exclusive* method of terminating an automobile liability insurance policy is controlled by [the Nebraska statute]." The court interpreted the statute to forbid termination of a valid contract in any way other than that prescribed by the statute, except that rescission ab initio for material misrepresentation was a common law right not precluded by the statute. It need hardly be pointed out that a differently formulated statute might also bar rescission, subject to constitutional limitations such as one based on the contract clause.

Notes and Questions

1. Among the grounds for cancellation under Revised Statutes of Nebraska §44-515, the statute at issue in *Glockel*, are: nonpayment of premium, fraud or material misrepresentation affecting the policy or in the presentation of a claim thereunder, violation of any of the terms or conditions of the policy, suspension or revocation of a driver's license, and conviction of larceny of an automobile. This is not as severe as some cancellation statutes.

2. The Nebraska statute was enacted in 1972, paralleling a Wisconsin statute enacted by 1969 Wis. Laws ch. 144. In explaining the reasons for the act, the official commentary to the Wisconsin act said:

> Recognizing that arbitrary cancellation of automobile liability insurance was a serious problem, the insurance industry in 1960 attempted to meet it on a voluntary basis. Most writers of automobile insurance adopted a new policy endorsement restricting the company's right to cancel, reduce or refuse to renew automobile liability coverages. This voluntary response by the industry did not, however, solve the problem completely. [1969 Wis. Laws 144, p. 36.]

Despite its origin in concern about what was thought to be arbitrary midterm cancellation of *automobile* policies, the Wisconsin statute extended the provision to *all* contracts subject to required approval or to subsequent disapproval by the insurance commissioner. Was that extension sound?

3. The Wisconsin statute distinguished between midterm cancellation and nonrenewal, strictly limiting the former to nonpayment of premium and reasons that were specified in the policy *and had been approved by the commissioner.* Anniversary cancellation (for multi-year contracts) and nonrenewal were permitted generally, under stringent conditions about advance notice, to give the policyholder a chance to shop for replacement coverage. The provision also required the same advance notice if there was to be renewal but on different terms. This also was intended to give the insured a chance to shop the market if premiums were to be increased or other changes unfavorable to the policyholder were to be made. Failure to give such notice would result in continuation of the policy on the original terms. Difficult problems are concealed within the word "different."

F. Regulation of Reinsurance

1. Introduction

With the increasing importance of reinsurance,* there has been renewed attention to the question how far it needs to be regulated. Traditionally, it was assumed that because reinsurance transactions were entered into between equally sophisticated and informed parties, they needed no regulation. But no careful observer of the insurance market can think that all direct insurers (or all reinsurers, for that matter) are staffed by astute and well-informed personnel.

More important, however, reinsurance has a potentially enormous impact on policyholders of the ceding company. When a primary insurer becomes insolvent, one of its principal assets is likely to be reinsurance recoverables. In that situation a good many reinsurers become "slow pay" debtors, particularly if the business they have written with the insolvent insurer has been unprofitable business or if they are themselves in difficulty. The reinsurers may often be able to make plausible rationalizations, for the information given by the primary insurer may have been potentially misleading and on the margin of being ground for rescission.† As an alternative to trying to rescind, reinsurers

---

*The use of reinsurance fluctuates; as of this writing it appears to have declined somewhat from a few years ago, but the long range trend is upward. A recent study by Swiss Re calculated the worldwide reinsurance premium in 1988 at $92 billion.

†In recent years there have been innumerable reinsurance arbitrations testing whether there was ground for rescission of the reinsurance contract. The results have

may try to negotiate a commutation of their debts for a reduced amount, sometimes a paltry one: Harried liquidators eager to get assets into the pipeline and get the liquidation over with may be easy marks for any reinsurer willing to play hardball and take maximum advantage of the liquidator's need. The case for increased regulation of reinsurers is strong, and rests on the needs of the ultimate policyholders, not the needs of the supposedly more sophisticated insurers.

With the vast increase in the demand for reinsurance and the consequent increase in the number of reinsurers in all corners of the world, it is no longer easy for even the truly astute insurance entrepreneur to evaluate reinsurers. When Lloyds, Swiss Re, Bavarian Re, and the like were the only names to consider, there was indeed little reason for concern about the soundness of reinsurers and their ability to pay.

The situation is now different. One industry spokesman recently estimated that there were over ten thousand reinsurers located all over the world, including a good number of government monopolies in developing countries. See Aldred, Rules Don't Address Reinsurer Worries: Expert, Bus. Ins., May 4, 1987, at 36. By the mid-1980s the traditional view that reinsurance was a safe haven was replaced by great concern in regulatory circles for adequate regulation of reinsurers. Many of the numerous reinsurance companies had become insolvent. "There are now some 130 reinsurance companies currently in liquidation in the U.S. alone." Id.

The potential for insolvency of reinsurers places many direct insurers at risk of losing money through uncollectible reinsurance, which earlier could be judged one of the minor and normal risks of engaging in business, but now offers more serious consequences than the mere loss of money. Such an insolvency (and particularly numerous such insolvencies) could have a domino effect and bring down direct insurers as well. That was the primary, and not implausible, fear. In the mid-1980s North American Reinsurance Corporation, one of the well-known American reinsurance companies, repeatedly inserted an advertisement in the trade press entitled, "Are You Getting the Reinsurance You're Paying For?" The lead sentence said that "[i]ndustry estimates suggest that much of the $50 billion in outstanding reinsurance recoverables may never be paid!" Whatever the uncollectible portion, the large amounts at risk are striking. While the figures chosen for this advertisement were certainly chosen for maximum impact, easily demonstrable losses are very large. One news story reporting that five direct insurers had written off $200 million because of uncollectible reinsurance is enough to show the

---

gone both ways and have often followed the Solomonic technique of dividing the baby: although available legal doctrine would have allowed for only an all-or-nothing result, arbitrators are free from the constraint of following rules.

seriousness of the problem. Hilder, Uncollectable Reinsurance Hurts Firms, Wall St. J., Apr. 1, 1986, at 6.

The primary purpose of insurance regulation, everywhere throughout the world, is to be sure that the insurer (or the reinsurer) can pay claims when called on to do so. If this requires substantial regulation of reinsurers, who can argue that such regulation should not be undertaken?

Because reinsurance is much more international than direct insurance, however, it is difficult for a jurisdiction, even a national state, to provide adequate direct regulation.

In the United States the traditional technique for regulating reinsurers that have chosen not to be admitted is at once indirect, subtle, and potentially effective. It works by operating on the direct insurer, over which each state in which it has been admitted has fairly effective power. In its annual reports, or at the time of examinations in situ, the direct insurer may take credit in its accounts for "reinsurance ceded" (that is, may be allowed to reduce its reserves for unearned premiums and for losses and loss expenses on its balance sheet to reflect its reinsurance contracts) only if the reinsurer satisfies the regulator. If it cannot, the primary insurer's accounts may not meet the financial requirements of the regulatory system unless its surplus is sufficient to satisfy the regulator that it will remain solid even if the reinsurer fails. To get the necessary relief on its balance sheet, the direct insurer relies on appropriate action by the reinsurer.

2. The Standby Letter of Credit (LOC)

Under the NAIC Model Law on Credit for Reinsurance, which is effective in a substantial number of states, the reinsurer may satisfy the regulator by being admitted to do business in the jurisdiction (on essentially the same basis as a direct insurer) or in another American jurisdiction with satisfactory standards, or by maintaining an adequate trusteed surplus in the United States. An additional method of satisfying the regulatory requirement is by providing security, which may be met by a deposit of cash or satisfactory securities, or by "clean, irrevocable, unconditional letters of credit, issued or confirmed by a qualified United States financial institution, as defined in Section 3A." NAIC Model Laws, Regulations and Guidelines, at 803-3 (1987).

Because the letter of credit (LOC) mechanism requires no transfer of cash or its equivalent, it is the method of providing security preferred by nonadmitted reinsurers. It became widely used after 1961, when the New York Insurance Department issued a ruling stating that New York would allow financial statement credit when unauthorized reinsurance was secured by an LOC. State regulations prescribe limitations on the use of LOCs.

Under the Model Law, the LOC must be clean, irrevocable, and unconditional. It must be payable on presentation of a sight draft signed only by an authorized signatory of the beneficiary, *without any accompanying documents*. Once established, it may not be modified or revoked without the consent of the beneficiary. It must contain an "evergreen clause," providing for automatic renewal unless there is specified notice of nonrenewal prior to expiration.

The letter of credit device has some drawbacks. It is issued by a bank but is an off-balance sheet contingent liability of the bank. If a bank that on the surface appeared sufficiently strong were to issue standby letters of credit in an excessive amount on behalf of reinsurers *and other customers* (a constant temptation because it does not affect the bank's balance sheet and does bring in considerable revenue) the letters might prove valueless in an economic downturn because too many of them might be called on at once. Thus, in practical effect, the banking industry, with problems enough of its own, is serving as the reinsuring vehicle of last resort for the insurance industry. This risk is not imaginary. The amount of off-balance sheet contingent liability issued by American banks is enormous.

Excessive use of LOCs has been criticized from the point of view of the banks as well. See Gabriel, Standby Letters of Credit: Does the Risk Outweigh the Benefits?, 1988 Colum. Bus. L. Rev. 705.

It is interesting that letters of credit have also been used to guarantee municipal bonds. The American Insurance Association challenged that use of LOCs as insurance. The District of Columbia Circuit expressed the view that it was within the power of the Comptroller of the Currency to allow a national bank subsidiary to offer such "insurance." American Ins. Assn. v. Clarke, 865 F.2d 278 (1988).

Brokers interested primarily in the use of LOCs to guarantee municipal bonds have described the weaknesses of LOCs:

> Aaa-rated bonds secured by a bank's letter of credit are becoming more common but also more controversial. An LOC is a bank's promise to pay any debt that the issuer is unable to cover. LOC's are only as strong as the guarantor bank. . . . And with the growing uneasiness about under-reported obligations of U.S. banks, LOC's are a source of concern since they are off-the-balance-sheet commitments. However, LOC's can only add safety to municipals. [Stoever Glass & Co's Newsletter of July 22, 1985, at 5.]

While LOCs do add safety to the obligations for which they stand as surety, the real question is how much safety they add compared to the perception of what they add.

Even if the banks are able to respond on their LOCs, however, there are some drawbacks to their use. A reinsurer may bring an action to enjoin drawdowns on its LOCs, so even if the court eventually denies the request for an injunction, there may be substantial delay in getting at the money. For an illustration, see Taravella, Litigation Casts Shadow on Letters of Credit, Bus. Ins., Nov. 12, 1984, at 29.

Despite contentions that the letter of credit, however clean and irrevocable it may be and however clear the so-called "evergreen clause" is, cannot be a satisfactory protective device for the insurance industry, up to this point reinsurers have successfully resisted some not-so-strenuous efforts to eliminate its use. The more the use of the LOC is hedged about with restrictions, the less attractive it becomes, for the reinsurer must pay the bank a fee to obtain its guarantee. See Tract & Henderson, Regulating Letters of Credit, Best's Review 40 (Feb. 1985). Yet the fee may be well worth paying.

Some figures may help put the matter in perspective. At the end of 1984, the nation's 15 largest banks are said to have had combined assets of $852.25 billion, and also to have been subject to $923.63 billion in contingent liabilities. See Schatz, Letter of Credit: An Old Financial Instrument Finds New Uses, Barron's, July 8, 1985, at 20. (Of course, not all the contingent liabilities were on LOCs, and not all the LOCs protect reinsurers.) The FDIC reported $169.6 billion in outstanding LOCs issued by U.S. commercial banks as of June 30, 1986. Those two numbers fail to agree by a considerable margin and the reasons for the difference are unclear. What *is* clear is that the amounts are very large. Proposed federal banking regulations would constrict the volume of LOCs by requiring them to be supported by capital. See Greenwald, Proposals Could Cut Availability of LOCs, Bus. Ins., Nov. 10, 1986, at 32.

3.   Regulation of Reinsurance Intermediaries

In 1976, Pritchard & Baird, a leading reinsurance intermediary firm, became insolvent, leading to a multi-million dollar loss and to the enactment of §122-a of the New York Insurance Law (now divided among several sections, from §2101 to §2120). Regulation 98 of the New York Insurance Department required reinsurance intermediaries to take steps to ascertain the financial condition of reinsurers. It focused on common law duties but emphasized them in a way that made such intermediaries uncomfortable. As a result, reinsurance intermediaries strenuously opposed the regulation. See Tarnoff, N.Y. Regulation 98 Will Hurt Industry, Intermediaries Say, Bus. Ins., Oct. 25, 1982, at 20.

The common law situation is explored in the following case.

MASTER PLUMBERS LTD. MUT. LIAB. CO.
v. CORMANY & BIRD

79 Wis. 2d 309, 255 N.W.2d 533 (1977)

DAY, Justice.

This is an appeal from a judgment in favor of the defendants-respondents entered at the close of plaintiff-appellant's case-in-chief on August 26, 1975. Plaintiff Master Plumbers Limited Mutual Insurance Company (Master Plumbers) is a Wisconsin corporation with offices in Milwaukee and licensed by the State of Wisconsin to write worker's compensation, liability and automobile insurance for plumbing and heating contractors and allied trades. Defendant Cormany & Bird, Inc., Milwaukee, is a Wisconsin corporation which obtains reinsurance for various clients including the plaintiff. Defendant Agency Managers Limited (Agency Managers), New York City, is a New York Corporation in the business of underwriting which also participated in contracts for reinsurance for the plaintiff.

This action alleges the defendants were negligent in obtaining reinsurance with a New York Company which ultimately became insolvent. As a result, plaintiff was liable for claims under policies which it had written and then reinsured with the insolvent company. The action commenced August 8, 1972. Trial was to a jury.

In 1953 Master Plumbers asked Cormany & Bird to obtain reinsurance for it. With reinsurance, Master Plumbers could write insurance policies with coverage in excess of its minimum capital and surplus retention required by law. Master Plumbers and the reinsurers would share both the premiums and the liabilities arising from claims in proportions fixed by the reinsurance contract or "treaty."

Cormany & Bird secured reinsurance through a New York reinsurance broker. The reinsurers were represented by Agency Managers which in effect acted as a reinsurance department for the various reinsurers who severally shared the risk. Agency Managers collected premiums and negotiated and settled claims on behalf of the reinsurers.

The reinsurance treaty was entitled "Contract No. 182." From 1960 to 1963, Agency Managers and Master Plumbers executed addenda to Contract No. 182, each effective on the anniversary date of the main contract. Their purpose was to name the participating reinsurers and to allocate their respective risks. From 1958 to 1963 Citizens Casualty Company of New York was one of several participating reinsurers.

In 1963 Citizens Casualty was made the sole reinsurer — assuming 100 per cent of the reinsurance risk. The record is silent as to any subsequent change in Contract No. 182 regarding allocation of risk until January 1, 1968, when Citizens Casualty no longer was on the risk. In the interim, Master Plumbers sustained liabilities on two insurance claims which were settled for sums in excess of its primary retention. Also in the interim, Citizens Casualty was declared insolvent by a court of the state of New York and finally liquidated.

The Supreme Court Appellate Division of New York found Citizens Casualty insolvent as of December 31, 1967. On June 17, 1971, after unsuccessful attempts to rehabilitate the company, the Supreme Court, Special Term, granted the petition of the New York Superintendent of Insurance for an order forcing liquidation of the company.

At trial, John D. Bird, one of the officers of Cormany & Bird, testified that during the period of 1963 to 1967 he did not inform Master Plumbers of any change in the financial condition of Citizens Casualty and said he did not know of any.

Mr. Bird testified he referred to Best's Insurance Guide in 1963 when Citizens Casualty assumed the entire reinsurance risk. On June 23, 1971, after Master Plumbers had been informed by Agency Managers of Citizens Casualty's problems, Mr. Bird wrote Master Plumbers a letter which in part said,

> In 1963, when the collateral was changed to Citizens, I checked Best's and found that their surplus met the requirements of the State of Wisconsin, and also that their combined loss ratio was a respectable 94.7%. . . . Subsequent to 1963, I did not check their financial position which, of course, is where I erred."

There was no evidence introduced at trial that Citizens Casualty was other than qualified or financially sound in 1963.

The trial court dismissed the action at the close of plaintiff's case-in-chief because the proof to that point showed that at the time the reinsurance was obtained Citizens Casualty was both authorized to do business and solvent. . . .

The general rule is that where an agent provides a policy in a company which is solvent or generally considered so, he is not personally liable for a loss which occurs when the company subsequently becomes insolvent. Beckman v. Edwards, 59 Wash. 411, 110 P. 6 (1910), citing Gettins v. Scudder, 71 Ill. 86 (1873); accord, Eastham v. Stumbo, 212 Ky. 685, 279 S.W. 1109, 1110 (1926).

> An insurance broker is bound to exercise reasonable skill and diligence in the transaction of the business entrusted to him and he will be responsible to his principal for any loss resulting from his failure to do so. . . . However, absent proof that the agent in some manner breached

his duty, he is not liable when the company in which the policy is procured later becomes insolvent. . . . [Kane Ford Sales, Inc. v. Cruz, 119 Ill. App. 2d 102, 255 N.E.2d 90, 91 (1970).]

The alleged negligence of the defendant must be considered in light of his knowledge at the time the policy was issued, and not at the time of the loss and failure to pay the claim. Williams-Berryman Ins. Co. v. Morphis, 249 Ark. 786, 461 S.W.2d 577, 578 (1971). Also see, 3 Couch on Insurance, 2d sec. 25.48, pp. 354-355; 16 Appleman Insurance Law and Practice, sec. 8833, p. 468 (revised volume); 43 Am. Jur. 2d Insurance sec. 178.[3]

In the case at bar there is no evidence by which it can be inferred the defendants knew or should have known of financial problems on the part of Citizens at the time it placed the insurance, nor that it had or should have had such knowledge until the New York court proceeding when Citizens was declared insolvent. By this time, the claims against Master Plumbers had already been incurred. Under the rules previously mentioned, therefore, defendants breached no duty to Master Plumbers. . . .

The only evidence admitted at trial from which this court could impute notice of Citizens' insolvency consists of the written opinions of the New York courts. The earliest finding of insolvency was as of December 31, 1967. The latest date in the record when defendants placed the risk with Citizens, however, was in 1963. As to that year there is no evidence by which to infer defendants knew or should have known Citizens faced insolvency.

Master Plumbers introduced and the court admitted pages from Best's Insurance Guide which digest financial data for various companies. While they indicate that Citizens sustained underwriting losses for five years between 1962 and 1967 these figures did not establish insolvency. . . .

In summary, no evidence was introduced at trial tending to show defendants knew or should have known Citizens had financial problems when, in 1963, it placed Citizens on the reinsurance risk. Nonsuit was properly granted.

Judgment affirmed.

---

3. In a case cited by Master Plumbers, a federal district court applying Texas law held that an insurance agent has a duty to inform his clients when the agent knew or should have known that the insurer had become insolvent, or to replace the insurance. Cateora v. British Atlantic Assurance. Ltd., of Nassau, 282 F. Supp. 167 (S.D. Texas 1968). While that case seems to extend the general rule by finding an on-going duty on the part of the agent to monitor the well-being of the insurer with which he has placed the insurance, the court explicitly found that the agent had undertaken to keep the plaintiff insured and that his knowledge of the insolvency was actual or imputed before the insured's loss occurred.

Notes and Questions

1. Would you consider that *Master Plumbers* states a rule applying to *all* intermediaries placing reinsurance for a principal? Suppose, for example, a managing general agent is empowered to receive applications and underwrite policies, to handle claims adjustment, to retain a specified maximum line for the insurer-principal, and then to reinsure the remainder of the risk. How would you describe the potential liability of the MGA if it placed reinsurance with reinsurers that subsequently became insolvent?

2. Years ago the C.E.O. of a leading British insurance company said to the author that in his opinion insurance regulation had gone in the wrong direction in the United States. He thought that instead of focusing on the solidity of insurers, the broker placing the business should be made the guarantor of the insurance placed. What is the merit of such an approach, at least with respect to reinsurance? Should a distinction be made between agents and brokers? What objections would you see to such a proposal?

3. Following some reinsurance scandals, the British Department of Trade (the insurance regulatory agency) required each insurer to provide additional information about its reinsurers in its annual reports. (The British regulatory system focuses on disclosure requirements, while the American system focuses on substantive controls.) See British Insurers Told to Report More Data on Reinsurance Firms, Wall St. J., Dec. 16, 1982, at 29.

G. Rate Regulation

There was a time when rate regulation dominated the regulatory activity of state insurance commissioners. The initial response of the states to the passage of the McCarran-Ferguson Act was to enact rate regulatory statutes, nearly all based on the so-called Commissioners-All Industry bill. It provided for a statutory standard, universally adopted by the states, that rates shall not be "excessive, inadequate or unfairly discriminatory." In almost all states, the system required prior approval, meaning that those rates subject to regulation had to be approved by the insurance commissioner before they could be used. In each such statute, however, a "deemer clause" provided that the rates were to be "deemed" approved unless the commissioner disapproved them or took other designated action within a specified time. The history of state insurance rate regulation is long and complicated. The litigated cases have been collected and well analyzed in Mintel, Insurance Rate Litigation (1983).

Although one of the statutorily declared purposes of rate regulation is to protect the "solidity" of companies by ensuring that the rates are "not inadequate," in practice that has (at least in recent decades) not been an important focus of regulatory activity. If it had been, the recent disastrous insurance crises might, at least in theory, have been avoided or at least mitigated.

Much more important in the operation of the rate regulatory process has been the restrictions regulators have put on rate increases. Often the restrictions have been politically motivated: Nearly always commissioners have resisted, and seldom have they demanded or even encouraged, rate increases. The predictable result was that insurers tended to ask for more than they really needed so there would be room for bargaining. Presumably most of the time insurers ultimately got most of what they really needed, or else the business would not have survived or at least would not have grown. Often they got the needed increases after undue delay. The rate regulatory process has thus been distorted, changing an approval process to a negotiating process.

Insurers have, on the whole, survived and managed to grow large. Whether rate regulation prevented them from getting the return on investment that the degree of risk in the insurance business justifies is a difficult question, defying a general answer. Yet one clue is presently emerging in connection with automobile rate regulation. Such limitations on automobile insurance rates as those resulting from California Proposition 103, its imitators elsewhere, and other legislative and regulatory resistance to rate increases seems to be resulting currently in the complete withdrawal of many leading insurance companies from the automobile insurance business throughout the United States. Within the several months previous to this writing a number of such major companies have announced their complete withdrawal from that market. The author's automobile insurance policy was one casualty of that development, requiring him to shop for a new carrier.

The following cases provide some sense of the contemporary operation of the rate regulatory process.

NATIONWIDE MUT. INS. CO. v. COMMONWEALTH INS. DEPT.

104 Pa. Commw. 301, 522 A.2d 1167 (1987)

CRUMLISH, JR. President Judge.

The Travelers Indemnity Company, Allstate Insurance Company, and Nationwide Mutual Insurance Company have filed petitions for review and applications for special relief and for stay and/or supersedeas of Acting Insurance Commissioner Constance B. Foster's orders dated February 11, 1987, suspending and postponing their collective insurance premium rate increases. The Insurance Department (Department) has filed amended complaints in equity and applications for preliminary injunctions seeking to enjoin Travelers and Allstate from violating those February 11, 1987 orders and directing them to refund any premiums which have been or may be collected in violation of those orders.

Following comprehensive review of the pleadings, briefs, exhibits and hearing thereon in each of these proceedings, this Chancellor finds that petitioners' actions are essentially appeals of administrative adjudications and therefore we will at this time consider petitioners' applications for stay and/or supersedeas.

In order for a petitioner to succeed in an application for stay pending appeal, one must (1) make a strong showing that he is likely to prevail on the merits, (2) demonstrate that without the requested relief, he will suffer irreparable injury, (3) demonstrate that other interested parties in the proceedings will not be substantially harmed if relief is granted, and (4) show that the public interest will not be adversely affected. Pennsylvania Public Utility Commission v. Process Gas Consumers Group, 502 Pa. 545, 467 A.2d 805 (1983).

With respect to the first prong of the *Process Gas* test, it is important to note that this matter involves only one issue. That narrow issue is whether petitioners' rate increases can be validly implemented pending the Acting Insurance Commissioner's resolution of the complaints challenging the rate increases. Hearings on those complaints are scheduled for March 3, 10 and 12, 1987. *In this proceeding,* it is not the function of the Chancellor to decide if the complaints are valid nor does the Chancellor have the authority to do so.

Pursuant to Section 17(a) of the Casualty and Surety Rate Regulatory Act, Acting Insurance Commissioner Constance B. Foster entered orders suspending petitioners' automobile insurance rate increases. Section 17(a) provides:

Hearing Procedure and Judicial Review

(a) Any insurer, rating organization or person aggrieved by any action of the Commissioner, except disapproval of a filing or a part thereof as provided for in section five hereof, or by any rule or regulation adopted and promulgated by the Commissioner, shall have the right to file complaint with the Commissioner and to have a hearing thereon before the Commissioner. Pending such hearing and the decision thereon the Commissioner may suspend or postpone the effective date of his previous action, rule or regulation.

Petitioners contend that Acting Commissioner Foster erroneously invoked Section 17(a) as authority for her February 11, 1987 orders because it is Section 5(b) of the Rate Act which exclusively controls a Commissioner's authority to enter orders on rate filings which are "in effect." Section 5(b) provides:

(b) Any person or organization aggrieved with respect to any filing which is in effect may make written application to the Commissioner for a hearing thereon: Provided, however, that the insurer or rating organization that made the filing shall not be authorized to proceed under this subsection. Such application shall specify the grounds to be relied upon by the applicant. If the Commissioner shall find that the application is made in good faith, that the applicant would be so aggrieved if his grounds are established, and that such grounds otherwise justify holding such a hearing, he shall, within (30) days after receipt of such application, hold a hearing upon not less than ten (10) days written notice to the applicant and to every insurer and rating organization which made such filing.

If, after such hearing, the Commissioner finds that the filing or a part thereof does not meet the requirements of this Act, he shall issue an order specifying in what respects he finds that such filing or a part thereof fails to meet the requirements of this Act, and stating when, within a reasonable period thereafter, such filing or a part thereof shall be deemed no longer effective. Copies of said orders shall be sent to the applicant and to every such insurer and rating organization. Said order shall not affect any contract or policy made or issued prior to the expiration of the period set forth in said order.

Section 5(b) thus requires a Commissioner acting upon complaint to hold a hearing *before* an order is entered prospectively cancelling a rate filing or a part thereof. These provisions have been examined, reviewed and resolved by our Supreme Court in Hartford Accident and Indemnity Co. v. Insurance Commissioner, 505 Pa. 571, 482 A.2d 542 (1984), and by this Court in Insurance Department v. Adrid, 24 Pa. Cmwlth. 270, 355 A.2d 597 (1976), and Pennsylvania Society of Oral & Maxillofacial Surgeons v. Insurance Commissioner, 98 Pa. Cmwlth. 439, 513 A.2d 1086 (1986). Collectively, these cases instruct us that Section 5(b) provides the exclusive remedy by which rate filings "in effect" are challenged, while Section 17(a) allows challenges to rate filings which are either unapproved or have been approved but are not yet effective.

The clear distinction between these provisions and the orderly review provided therein becomes confused when the facts evolving from the instant petitions are applied thereto.

Petitioners' rate increases became "effective" herein not by Commissioner approval but by force of law under Section 4(d) of the Rate Act, which "deems" a rate filing to become effective after it has been on file for a waiting period of thirty (30) days or for sixty (60) days if the Commissioner grants an extension thereof. . . .

The record as developed at a hearing before this Chancellor clearly establishes that the Commissioner's office did not, within the legislatively mandated thirty-day period, issue orders extending or disapproving these rate filings. Thus, by operation of Section 4(d), the rate filings were "deemed" in effect by petitioners at the end of each appropriate waiting period.

Acting Commissioner Foster, who entered office with these deadlines having elapsed, contends that the regular negotiation process following rate increase submissions, as evidenced by the amended filings, suspends the operation of the thirty-day waiting period. She also argues that she properly acted upon complaints by ordering hearings under Section 17(a) because the "deemer" provision constitutes an "approval," thus granting her authority to act *before* the insurer's proposed effective date.

Although the evidence at the hearing established that petitioners had never before resorted to the use of the deemer provision in rate filings with the Commissioner, all parties were aware of the possibility that a deemer was involved. . . .

Thus, since Section 4(d) is the vehicle which authorizes the rate increases, Acting Commissioner Foster is powerless to suspend or postpone petitioners' rate increase implementation dates because Section 17(a) requires a Commissioner to amend *his (her) previous action.* We can find no action by former Commissioner Grode disapproving the rate filings. Section 17(a) does not give a Commissioner the authority to revoke a Section 4(d) "deemer" increase until a hearing on the validity of a rate filing is held.

Following his careful review of the pleadings, briefs, argument and evidence, this Chancellor finds that petitioners have met their burden of demonstrating a strong likelihood of success on the merits. . . .

The administration of these procedures has been delegated to the Insurance Commissioner. This Chancellor is convinced that the procedural provisions of the Rate Act, if properly followed by the Commissioner, best serve the public interest. . . .

Conclusion

Travelers, Allstate and Nationwide submitted rate filings proposing premium increases of thirteen to over twenty-seven percent. These filings were submitted during the administration of former Governor Thornburgh and former Commissioner Grode. These premiums were reviewed and discussed and certain changes in the rate proposals were supported by Commissioner Grode's deputies. Tentative agreements on premium increases between ten and fifteen percent, as evidenced by amended rate filings, were reached.

The record discloses that while the rates were pending formal approval by Commissioner Grode, news stories and editorials in a Philadelphia newspaper appeared. The substance of these materials was that the rates were unreasonably excessive but were being approved by the Thornburgh administration. In short, no action was taken and the burden shifted to the incoming administration to evaluate the increased rates. Thus, the insurance companies, facing continuing economic losses, utilized the Rate Act to protect their interests. The Acting Insurance Commissioner, finding this situation thrust upon her, sought through letter correspondence to have the companies revoke their "deemers." Subsequently, Acting Commissioner Foster, through Deputy Commissioner Buzby, refused to meet and discuss a solution. This left petitioners with no alternative but to rely on the deemer provision. Beset with the urgency of critical decision, Acting Commissioner Foster attempted to circumvent the established Rate Act procedure and entered the February 11, 1987 orders. Thus, the petitioners had no other alternative but to resort to this Court for relief.

As reviewed earlier, this Chancellor finds that the Acting Commissioner is without authority to suspend or postpone a rate filing in effect as a result of the Section 4(d) deemer provision. This is not to say that, after hearing, the Acting Commissioner may not enter an appropriate order adjusting the rates. Indeed, this is the Commissioner's prerogative and duty.

This Chancellor grants stay of the February 11, 1987 Acting Insurance Commissioner's orders. If unreasonable delay is encountered, appropriate action will be taken.

Notes and Questions

1. What is the justification, if any, for the "deemer" clause in the rate regulation statute? For the difference in procedure between prior approval and subsequent disapproval?

2. The rate regulation statute in the preceding case is the Commissioners-All Industry Law worked out by cooperative regulator-industry effort, to provide the regulation required by §2(b) of the McCarran Act.

3. Would a policyholder be an "aggrieved party" under §17(a) of the statute? If so, can there ever be finality in the setting of rates?

4. The insurers' position here was that they were about to be denied needed increases in rates. That has not always been the problem faced by the companies. In the 1950s the so-called direct writers were filing rates lower than those of the "bureau companies." After such

cut-rates are filed, are competitors with higher rates "aggrieved parties" for purposes of the statute, thus giving them standing to contest approval of rates lower than they were charging?

5. In an omitted part of the opinion, the court said that though economic harm alone was not the irreparable harm necessary under *Process Gas* for the petitioners to get the relief sought, they presented "credible testimony of the chaos which will occur to their billing, collection and other clerical divisions if appropriate relief is not entered. Strict adherence to the Rate Act must be enforced to maintain a sound insurance industry." Because an insurance company has a very high volume of usually small transactions, numerous routines must be worked out, requiring a good deal of time and effort. Insurers who may be legally free to promulgate rates without advance approval but subject to subsequent disapproval (the rule in a number of states) often will not promulgate rates without at least informal approval by the insurance commissioner. Thus a "subsequent disapproval" or a "file and use" law may be forced into the "prior approval" mode by an aggressive insurance department.

> For forms of government let fools contest
> Whate'er is best administered is best.*

Is there merit, in this limited context, in Alexander Pope's well-known couplet?

6. The paragraphs toward the end of the opinion explain in muted form one of the perennial problems insurance companies face when they operate in an active rate regulatory environment. Political pressures operating on the governor and the commissioner tend to make them hostile to rate increases. More than one insurance commissioner has been fired (or eased out!) by the governor for granting increases the commissioner thought necessary but that were politically inconvenient. As a result, despite the fact that there are well-established techniques for calculating appropriate rate changes, obtaining rate increases has become a bargaining process, with the initial request being high enough to achieve a reasonable compromise position. The author has served on numerous occasions as a hearing officer on rate filings, and has usually felt it appropriate, based on the facts presented, to recommend a reduction of the requested rate increases. Sometimes the commissioner has followed his recommendations, but sometimes has further reduced the rates below them, perhaps because of political pressures invisible to the hearing officer. For recent years, at least, it is not plausible to contend that the regulators are captives of the regulated, at least so far as rate regulation is concerned.

---

*A. Pope, Essay on Man, Epistle III, line 303.

7. Toward the end of the 1960s a relaxation of the rate regulatory regime occurred. Many states no longer required prior approval, though subsequent disapproval remains possible in most states. The justification for the change was that insurance companies, unlike utilities, have no natural monopoly. Indeed, for most classes of business, the thousands of existing insurance companies generally engage in extensive, sometimes cutthroat, competition. The competition is especially vigorous in commercial insurance, where individual premiums are often very large. That competition, coupled with a regular cycle of optimism and pessimism that is not easy to explain, led to the insurance crises of the 1970s and 1980s (as well as comparable if less severe crises going back for generations). First, insurance is substantially underpriced, leading to serious underwriting losses (and even operating losses). Subsequent insolvencies follow, then a reaction leads to a drastic tightening of the market. That tightening leads to a profitable period, followed by competition leading to underpricing and a new cycle. Very tight markets at one point in the cycle may lead to a consumer reaction that would bring more stringent rate regulation: Its advocates (including such consumerists as Ralph Nader) suffer from the illusion that stringent rate regulation will necessarily *lower* rates, when it may lead instead to the destruction of markets.

8. Regulation of the rates of Blue Cross/Blue Shield is directed more toward the cash flow needs of the "Blues" than toward balance sheet solidity. Thus, the objective of the regulation is to maintain free assets (here called reserves, unlike in most insurance) at or near a standard set by the regulator. See, for example, Blue Cross & Blue Shield v. Caldarone, 520 A.2d 969 (R.I. 1987). Despite the difference in approach, which should enable the regulator and regulated together to preserve the soundness of the company, at least one Blue Cross/Blue Shield organization has recently been put into a liquidation procedure.

WAL-MART STORES, INC. v. CRIST

855 F.2d 1326 (8th Cir. 1988), *cert. denied,* 489 U.S. 1090 (1989)

BEAM, Circuit Judge.

Wal-Mart Stores, Inc. (Wal-Mart) appeals from a decision of the district court ordering it to pay $19,946,038.20 in premiums and interest to the receiver of an insolvent insurance carrier, Transit Casualty Company (Transit), which carrier issued policies of workers' compensation insurance covering Wal-Mart employees in the states in which Wal-Mart conducted business. Wal-Mart contends that the district court drew erroneous legal conclusions from certain undisputed facts presented over seven days of trial. We agree and reverse.

Background

The facts of this case are lengthy and complex. The district court issued an opinion which sets forth the numerous transactions giving rise to this litigation, see Wal-Mart Stores, Inc. v. Crist, 664 F. Supp. 1242 (W.D. Ark. 1987), and we will not attempt to restate each of the district court's findings here. We will, however, discuss those facts essential to an understanding of the issues presented on appeal and to our resolution of those issues.

Wal-Mart owns and operates a very successful chain of retail stores, with facilities in eighteen states at the times relevant to this appeal. In each of these states, as required by law, Wal-Mart provided workers' compensation insurance for its employees. Beginning in 1980, Wal-Mart became self-insured for its workers' compensation obligations and for its general liability risks in all states in which it conducted business except Texas and a few southern states in which it maintained only a limited number of employees. Wal-Mart remained self-insured through late 1982, at which time John Sooter, Wal-Mart's Director of Risk Management, sought proposals for renewal or replacement of the workers' compensation policy covering Wal-Mart's Texas employees. Offers were solicited through Wal-Mart's insurance consultant, Alexander & Alexander (A & A). One of the quotes which A & A presented to Wal-Mart was from Transit through its agent Carlos Miro.

Carlos Miro owned and operated Miro & Associates, an underwriting agency in Dallas, Texas. In May of 1982, Miro entered into a "Managing Agency Agreement" with Donald F. Muldoon & Co., Inc. (Muldoon), a Transit general agent who possessed authority to appoint sub-agents. This agreement authorized Miro to issue and place insurance coverage on Transit's behalf. Miro was provided with blank Transit policy forms for this purpose, and quickly became Transit's most productive agent.

The quote which Miro provided for Wal-Mart's Texas workers' compensation coverage, utilizing Transit policy forms, was quite favorable. Upon receipt of the Texas proposal, Wal-Mart asked Miro to provide a quote for workers' compensation coverage for all Wal-Mart employees to replace the self-insurance arrangement utilized by Wal-Mart in the other states. Miro gladly accepted Wal-Mart's invitation, obtained and reviewed Wal-Mart's payroll data and loss history for several prior years, and arranged a meeting in Dallas to present his proposal.

Miro offered to provide workers' compensation insurance coverage for all Wal-Mart employees for a flat and guaranteed premium of $3,500,000.00. The premium was to be unaffected by any factor other than an increase or decrease in Wal-Mart's estimated annual payroll, a change in which would increase or decrease the premium proportionately. The district court found, though Miro did consider Wal-Mart's loss history in reaching the $3.5 million figure, that Miro quoted the premium as a guaranteed flat rate, not to be adjusted or influenced by the amount of claims paid. This arrangement was very attractive to Wal-Mart, according to Sooter, not only because of the competitive price, but because Wal-Mart could budget in advance for a fixed maximum premium expense. Wal-Mart accepted Miro's bid, and received a cover note and binder from Miro which set forth the terms of the agreement.

Somewhere between thirty and sixty days after the coverage took effect, Miro sent A & A the Transit policy which purportedly embodied the agreement. A & A reviewed the policy, considered it satisfactory, and sent it to Wal-Mart who also reviewed its terms. The policy contained a provision for computation of premium in accordance with standard manual rates promulgated by the National Council of Compensation Insurers, which rates were on file with the appropriate state regulatory bodies. The various rates were multiplied by estimated payroll for each job classification to reach an aggregate premium. The policy was structured so that the premium obtained after multiplication of rates times payroll, less discounts, was exactly $3,500,000.00, as agreed upon. However, to reach this result, Wal-Mart's estimated payroll, reported by Transit to be $547,000,000.00, was reduced on the face of the policy to approximately $250,000,000.00. If the actual payroll estimate had been used, the total premium due would have been well in excess of the agreed upon figure. Wal-Mart and A & A were both aware that the estimated payroll had been depressed, but took no action and accepted the policies. In fact, A & A advised Wal-Mart that this was a common practice in the insurance industry and that it should be of no concern. Additionally, certain endorsements were attached to the policy which, if enforced, would have operated to raise the premium if losses proved greater than expected. Wal-Mart and A & A were also aware of these provisions, but apparently assumed they would not be enforced, since to do so would violate the premium portion of the agreement. A similar policy was issued for the following year, for the same $3.5 million maximum premium. Payroll figures utilized in the renewal policy were also substantially depressed.

Near the end of the second policy year, problems began to surface. Claims on the Wal-Mart policies turned out to be well beyond any of the parties expectations, and far in excess of premiums collected on the policies. Transit asserts that amounts paid to date on the two policies approximate $21,000,000.00. It is not surprising, therefore, that Transit soon learned that Miro's captive reinsurers, with whom the entire risk on the Wal-Mart policies had been reinsured, had stopped paying claims.[3] Shortly thereafter, Miro's agency with Transit was terminated, and Transit demanded additional premium payments from Wal-Mart in accordance with the rates set forth in the issued policies and Wal-Mart's actual payroll.

Upon receipt of Transit's demand for additional premium, Wal-Mart filed this suit for a declaratory judgment seeking enforcement of the agreement entered into with Miro. Transit answered, alleging that the agreement which Wal-Mart seeks to enforce is contrary to law and unenforceable. Transit also counterclaimed for nearly $20,000,000.00 in additional premiums it claims Wal-Mart owes pursuant to the terms of the two policies. Wal-Mart denied liability on the counterclaim, and filed a third-party claim against A & A, seeking recovery of any amounts which Wal-Mart is required to pay to Transit. After making thorough and detailed factual findings, the district court concluded (1) that Miro exceeded his authority, both actual and apparent, in entering into the agreement with Wal-Mart; (2) that the premium provisions of the agreement are illegal and unenforceable under state insurance law; and (3) that Wal-Mart is bound by the terms which were actually embodied in the Transit policies, though those terms differ substantially from the actual agreement which had been reached. The court ordered Wal-Mart to pay additional premiums to Transit, in accordance with the manual rates set forth in the policies and with Wal-Mart's actual payroll figures. Wal-Mart appeals each of these determinations.

Discussion

1. Miro's Authority

The district court first concluded that Miro's actual authority was limited by the terms of the agency agreement in force between Miro and Muldoon (acting in behalf of Transit), which agreement prohibited Miro from entering into agreements utilizing premium rates not on file with appropriate state regulatory authorities. The agreement authorized Miro to issue policies "subject to and in accordance with the insurance laws and regulations of each State, and in accordance with rates, filings, forms, policy limits, underwriting guidelines governing acceptance . . . as directed, filed, and promulgated by [Transit]." Wal-

3. The Wal-Mart policies had been 100% reinsured through offshore captive reinsurance companies under Miro's control. Transit had made a conscious effort to expand its involvement in such offshore captive reinsurance ventures, in which Transit served merely as the "fronting" company, permitting the use of its policy forms for a percentage fee. Assuming all risks were properly reinsured with solvent companies, Transit believed it was protected from exposure on the insured risks.

Mart argues that this language amounts merely to "instructions" to act lawfully, and that Miro was actually authorized to issue whatever policies he deemed prudent. [The Court agreed with the district court that Miro had no actual authority but found that he did have apparent authority. — ED.] If an agent acts within the scope of his apparent authority, his acts bind the principal, whether actually authorized or not, and even if contrary to express direction. See Landmark Savings Bank v. Weaver-Bailey Contractors, Inc., 22 Ark. App. 258, 739 S.W.2d 166, 169 (1987).

Transit does not dispute that the first portion of this test, conduct by the principal, is satisfied in this case through Transit's provision of blank policy forms to Miro. The more difficult issue is whether Wal-Mart acted reasonably in believing that Miro possessed sufficient authority to enter into the $3.5 million agreement. We believe it did.

In reaching its conclusion on this issue, the district court focused primarily upon two facts: Wal-Mart's sophistication as an insurance purchaser and the very low premium offered by Miro. The court concluded that the deal offered by Miro was "too good to be true," and that Wal-Mart, as an experienced and knowledgeable insurance buyer, should have known that no reasonable insurer would permit an agent to offer a policy on such terms. There are two flaws in this approach. First, such an analysis places great weight upon events which took place subsequent to the time the contract was agreed upon. The terms offered by Miro appear extraordinarily favorable only because of Wal-Mart's loss experience over the two years following the initiation of the policy. There was testimony that workers' compensation claims filed by Wal-Mart employees over several years preceding 1982 in the states in which Wal-Mart was self-insured averaged just over $2 million per year. Projected losses for the first policy year were estimated to be under $3 million. Thus, while a $3.5 million guaranteed premium was certainly a competitive offer, it was by no means unreasonably low in comparison to Wal-Mart's demonstrated loss history at the time. The reasonableness of Wal-Mart's actions and perceptions must be judged at the time the contract was entered into, under the facts and circumstances then existing. The district court erred in relying so heavily on Wal-Mart's disastrous loss experience, something about which all the parties were unaware at the relevant point in time.

Additionally, we believe that the district court's analysis improperly imposed upon Wal-Mart an unreasonable level of expertise in state workers' compensation insurance laws and practices. The court found, and we agree, that Wal-Mart was a sophisticated insurance consumer. However, the court also found that such sophistication should have been adequate for Wal-Mart to know without question, before receipt of the actual policy from Transit, that Miro's proposal, in any form, would not have been satisfactory to state insurance regulators. An insured whose principal business is retail sales cannot be reasonably expected to maintain such expertise in the intricacies of state workers' compensation regulatory requirements in each of the many states in which it does business. Under the district court's analysis, Wal-Mart would have been obligated to ascertain, for example, whether its insurer had utilized proper rating classifications in each state, whether those classifications had been properly applied to filed rates, and whether the insurer had properly applied filed rate deviations, if any, in each relevant state. Imputing such knowledge, and the investigatory obligations which follow, in an area as complex as workers' compensation regulatory requirements and filings to an insured even as sophisticated as Wal-Mart is not reasonable under the circumstances of this case.

Moreover, the standard applied by the district court imposes an obligation upon Wal-Mart to know when a quoted insurance premium is too low, and to reject it. Such an approach would require an insured to engage in an underwriting analysis of the risk involved to make an educated determination regarding the adequacy of the quoted premium. We believe that the duty to make this determination is better placed upon the insurer, who is undoubtedly in a better position to evaluate the relevant facts. While there may be a point at which a quoted premium is so small in light of previous loss experience that an insured should be charged with knowledge of its inadequacy, we do not believe that this case presents such a scenario.

We find, therefore, that the district court erred in its reliance upon Wal-Mart's purported knowledge of future losses, the requirements of state workers' compensation regulations, and the intricacies of premium underwriting in finding that Wal-Mart acted unreasonably in believing that Miro was within his authority in offering the $3.5 million agreement. Further, the court improperly failed to consider evidence of the circumstances which existed at the time the agreement was reached. The record reflects that at that time, the insurance industry was extremely competitive. Witnesses referred to the "soft market" for insurance products which was then in existence in which premiums were lowered to obtain preferred clients. Wal-Mart was aware that insurers were willing to reduce premiums to obtain its business. Wal-Mart also knew that there existed numerous mechanisms by which filed workers' compensation rates could be legitimately adjusted to achieve a quoted premium. Devices such as premium discounts, retrospective rating, policy dividends, rate deviations and scheduled rating were available to legally reduce premium charges below what would have to be paid pursuant to filed rates.[6] We believe, at the time Miro

6. For example, there was testimony that in 1984, Transit had filed and received approval in Arkansas for separate 15 and 50 percent deviations from filed rates. Accordingly, the actual premium charged by Transit in 1984 could have been up to 65

approached Wal-Mart with his bid, that Wal-Mart could have reasonably believed that the $3.5 million premium was potentially within the bounds of state requirements. Through hindsight, we now know that the Miro bid was unreasonably low. To require Wal-Mart to have made such a determination in 1982, given the nature of the insurance market at the time and the numerous ways in which an insurer might have achieved such a rate, is improper. Miro acted within his apparent authority when he offered Wal-Mart the $3.5 million guaranteed premium, and Transit is, therefore, bound by his actions.

2. Legality of the Agreement

We must next consider whether the district court correctly found that the premium agreement violates state law. The district court found that there was no need to examine the laws of each individual state in which Wal-Mart did business to make this determination because the agreement violated basic principles of workers' compensation law common to each state's regulatory system. The court found that an agreement to provide workers' compensation coverage for a fixed premium, not to be adjusted for any factor other than a change in payroll, and not tied in any way to rate filings in effect in any state violated the basic statutory concept of workers' compensation, that all employers must provide a specified level of coverage for injured workers at specified and approved rates. The court also found that the agreement was contrary to anti-rebate laws in effect in each relevant state. Wal-Mart argues that both of these conclusions are in error, and that the premium agreement is, or could have been, completely legal and fully enforceable in all states.

After reviewing the record and the workers' compensation laws of the states involved, we agree that the agreement is illegal and violates the law of each state, but for reasons different than those expressed by the district court. First, while it is true, as Wal-Mart contends, that there has been a marked trend away from strict regulation of the rates which workers' compensation insurers must charge, all states, including those in which insurers are free to charge whatever rates they desire (the so-called "open-rated" states), require that insurers file their rating schedules and policy forms for review by state authorities, who may reject rate proposals which would result in inadequate, excessive or discriminatory charges. In addition, each state prohibits any person or organization from knowingly submitting false or

---

percent less than the actual rates filed in Arkansas. The premium which the district court ordered Wal-Mart to pay is based upon filed rates with no discounts or deviations.

misleading information to the regulatory authorities responsible for such review. Regardless of the degree of control and supervision each state exercises over the specific rates workers' compensation insurers may charge, all require that these informational filings be made. We believe that the arrangement in effect in this case stands in clear violation of this statutory requirement.

There is no dispute that the manner in which the policies issued to Wal-Mart reached the agreed upon premium was by manipulation of payroll amounts. The payrolls for each state were depressed below what was actually anticipated in order to reach the $3.5 million total, with no intent by either party to adjust the payroll figures to reflect actual amounts at a later time. The district court found, and we agree, that all parties, at some time during the policy period, knew that the payroll figures had been depressed, should have taken action to resolve the misrepresentations, but did nothing. As written by Miro, the policies did not embody the parties' actual agreement, which was to provide coverage for the full employee payroll for $3.5 million. As written, therefore, the policies operated to deceive state regulatory authorities, because, in actuality, they embody a rating schedule which the parties never planned to file with any state. It would be impossible for state regulators to test the policies to ascertain whether the rates charged were inadequate, excessive or discriminatory, because the policies on their face did not reveal the true rates being charged. While the policies theoretically could have been structured to meet the $3.5 million bottom line through the use of legitimate discounting procedures, such legitimate procedures were not utilized here. The policies materially misrepresented information required by law to be reported truthfully in every state. They were deceptive as written, and thus violate the laws of each state involved. [The court held that to order Wal-Mart to pay normal premiums was not the proper way to deal with an illegal contract. — ED.]

We find that a more fitting resolution to this dispute is to apply the doctrine of in pari delicto, and leave the parties as they presently stand. Arkansas has recognized and applied the doctrine of in pari delicto when parties to an illegal contract are equally culpable. "The general rule with respect to illegal contracts is that neither courts of law nor of equity will interpose to grant relief to the parties, if they have been equally cognizant of the illegality." . . .

The level of culpability of the parties was best put, we think, by the district court when it said, "there is more than enough fault to go around in this case." *Wal-Mart*, 664 F. Supp. at 1269. The district court's opinion explains in detail the various activities of Transit, through its agent Miro, and of Wal-Mart, by which each was or became an active participant in carrying out the illegal portions of the insurance contract. Transit is charged with responsibility for the acts of its agent, Miro, who structured the deal from the start. Wal-Mart, as the district court found, became aware of the depressed premium figures, and did nothing. Though Wal-Mart acted reasonably in its belief at the outset that Miro could have lawfully structured the policies to reach the quoted premium, when the policies were later delivered and Wal-Mart became aware of the manner in which the quoted premium was actually achieved, the reduction of payroll, Wal-Mart should have taken corrective action. It is at this point, when Wal-Mart saw how Miro structured the policies, that Wal-Mart became chargeable with the illegality. We believe the district court correctly concluded that all parties were active and willing participants in a knowingly illegal venture.

Accordingly, we find that the district court should have found the parties in pari delicto and refused to grant relief of any sort. . . . The district court should have denied relief on both Wal-Mart's action for a declaratory judgment and Transit's counterclaim for payment of premiums.

One further comment on the practical effect of such a resolution of this case is necessary. As noted, while Transit has paid somewhere between $16 and $21 million in claims on the two workers' compensation policies, the parties expect that a significant amount of claims are yet to be filed and paid. The ultimate responsibility for payment of these claims, in the absence of valid workers' compensation insurance coverage, rests with Wal-Mart as the employer. . . .

Conclusion

The district court placed the primary responsibility for compliance with state workers' compensation laws upon the insured, Wal-Mart. Given all the circumstances of this case, we believe this obligation more appropriately rests with the insurer, Transit. We reverse the decision of the district court with respect to Transit's counterclaim, and remand with directions to dismiss the case without relief to any party.

Notes and Questions

1. The history of this insurance relationship tells us much about the causes and course of the recent insurance crisis in commercial liability insurance. For its sins, Transit became insolvent; Wal-Mart, of course, did not.

2. Applying the in pari delicto doctrine in this case seems plausible. Focusing on the interests of other policyholders in the continued soundness of Transit, can a case be made that it is not in fact sound?

3. Commercial liability insurance is essentially free of the kind of rate regulatory constraints that appeared in Wal-Mart, but workers compensation stands on a different footing. It is still governed almost everywhere by prior approval rate regulation, even for commercial insurance. Is there good reason for the difference?

4. The universal standard for insurance premium rates subject to regulation is that they must not be "excessive, inadequate, or unfairly discriminatory." In the statutes of many states, including Oklahoma, some guidelines are provided for determining whether those standards are met. In Oklahoma ex rel. Turpen v. Oklahoma State Board for Property and Casualty Rates, 731 P.2d 394 (Okla. 1986), the Board had approved a 25.9 percent increase in rates when the National Council of Compensation Insurers had requested a 41.9 percent increase. The Supreme Court of Oklahoma vacated the order and remanded the proceedings, saying that if "the evidence fails to support a preliminary determination that existing rates are inadequate, the Board cannot validly approve any rate increase." Id. at 405. Would you consider the decision correct based on the approach to the problem adumbrated in that statement? There was a dissent. What would its reasoning be?

H. Rehabilitation and Liquidation

The ultimate regulatory acts of the insurance commissioner are to petition the court to put an insurer into rehabilitation or liquidation, and then to proceed with the complicated process either petition initiates. If the petition is for rehabilitation, the commissioner often finds it necessary subsequently to petition the court to convert the rehabilitation into a liquidation.

Rehabilitation is occasionally successful but usually it is not. Insurance, like banking, is a financial institution that depends in part for its success on the confidence of its customers. Once it is known that an insurer is in formal rehabilitation proceedings, its clientele is apt to melt away, at least if the market is not so tight that any insurance seems better than none. Still, there are circumstances under which rehabilitation seems worth a try; one is if interested parties are willing to inject more capital into the shaky enterprise. There are sometimes "going concern" values and marketing structures that make such an effort worthwhile. The acquirer of a successful operating insurance company will often pay substantially more than balance sheet net worth to make the acquisition. Further, the mere possession of licenses to do business in a substantial number of states is an asset that may be of considerable worth, for it may shorten greatly the time required to get a new business going. Indeed, there is an existing market for corporate shells and licenses in the insurance world. One recent transaction involved the purchase of the charter of an insolvent insurer, together with such help as that insurer's liquidator could provide in getting licenses renewed in various states.

Liquidation almost always, though sometimes unnecessarily, involves substantial losses to policyholders and other creditors and long delay in the payment of even the portion of claims that does get paid.

Insurance companies are exempted from application of the Federal Bankruptcy Code of 1978. 11 U.S.C. §109(b)(2). They are rehabilitated or liquidated under state law. Many current state statutes are based on the National Association of Insurance Commissioners Model Act, which is traceable to Wisconsin Laws of 1967, ch. 89. That statute, while borrowing eclectically from other states, also borrowed heavily from the Federal Bankruptcy Act of 1898, as amended to the 1960s. See Kimball, History and Development of the Law of State Insurer Insolvency Proceedings: An Overview, 1986 A.B.A. Natl. Inst. on Ins. Insolvency 10. A wide selection of relevant documents, including the Wisconsin Act with official comments, will be found in an accompanying volume, Reference Handbook on Insurance Company Insolvency.

1.   Interstate Relations in Insolvency Proceedings

Many insurance companies undergoing rehabilitation or liquidation proceedings operate in most or even all states. Insolvency proceedings are normally dominated by the domiciliary jurisdiction, but claims (and often assets) are also found in other states, leading to ancillary proceedings in addition to the primary proceeding. The state acts have elaborate and approximately uniform provisions for the interstate relations problems, but they do not always work well. An insurance commissioner managing an ancillary liquidation is apt to conduct it to the advantage of citizens of his/her own state, if it should happen that the assets located there are greater in proportion to claims in the jurisdiction than are those in the domicile in proportion to all claims. In that case the ancillary receiver may resist subordinating the ancillary proceeding to the domiciliary proceeding, as good practice would require. This problem, essentially one of marshalling assets for equitable payment of all unsecured claims, is a strong (though not necessarily a compelling) reason that is sometimes urged for preferring federal insolvency proceedings for insurance companies.

To secure the interests of local policyholders, insurance statutes often prescribe that deposits of securities must be left with the insurance commissioner. Sometimes under the statute the deposits are held in trust for a limited class of policyholders. Those deposits become assets in the ancillary jurisdiction. For a case dealing with the extent to which such deposits are available for payment of claims in the ancillary jurisdiction, see Oregon v. Early Am. Ins. Co., 84 Or. App. 252, 733 P.2d 919 (1987).

2. Priorities and Offsets

When an insurer must be liquidated, the extent to which it can perform its social role even in its death throes depends on the system of priorities. The list of priorities varies considerably among the states. All would put first the inevitable claims for administrative costs; nearly always the second priority is small wage claims. Then, as a result of 31 U.S.C. §3173 ("priority of government claims") come the claims of the United States for taxes and sometimes as a claimant under insurance policies. After that, some jurisdictions treat all claims alike; in the Model Act, however, the priority is: loss claimants, then claimants for unearned premiums, then general creditors. In the Model Act some small classes of claims are postponed to those of general creditors, and the list ends with various classes of ownership claims (which have no chance of ever being reached unless the liquidation is for some reason other than insolvency).

A unique and ultimately ineffective feature of modern state insurance liquidation statutes was the effort to postpone government claims, including especially claims for federal and state taxes, to a low priority. The Wisconsin code (where this feature was initiated) classified government claims with general creditors and the Model Act postponed them even behind general creditors. Two cases testing that subordination and finding it ineffective under the McCarran Act were Idaho ex rel. Soward v. United States I.R.S., 858 F.2d 445 (9th Cir. 1988), *rev'g* 662 F. Supp. 60 (D. Idaho 1987) and Gordon v. United States Dept. of the Treasury, 846 F.2d 272 (4th Cir. 1988), *aff'g* 668 F. Supp. 483 (D. Md. 1987), *cert. denied,* 488 U.S. 954 (1988). In the former case, the federal government was claiming for taxes; in the latter it was a claimant under an insurance policy. The result was based on the proposition that the liquidation of insurance companies is not the business of insurance, and purported to apply *Royal Drug,* supra Section C, and Union Labor Life Ins. Co. v. Pireno, 458 U.S. 119 (1982).

The analysis of the federal district court in the Idaho case postponing the federal tax claim is arguably obsolete after *Royal Drug* and *Pireno.* There remains a lingering hope in some quarters that the liquidator can avoid giving priority to federal and state claims, but that depends on the U.S. Supreme Court, which denied applications for certiorari in both the above cases.

The author drafted the first statute to subordinate the federal government in this way and sketched out the argument for supporting the statute in the commentary to 1967 Wis. Laws ch. 89, §645.68. The analysis in that comment contained the sketched out argument that, fully worked out, prevailed in the Idaho District Court. The argument became far less compelling after the Supreme Court's narrow interpretation of the business of insurance in *Royal Drug*. Perhaps it is still permissible to believe (1) that *Royal Drug* is unsound and (2) that even if it remains the law of the land, the determination of priorities in the liquidation of insurance companies will ultimately be found to be within the strict criteria spelled out in *Royal Drug* for delimiting the business of insurance.

When the previous paragraph was written, the probability of achieving that result seemed very small: Two circuits had decided adversely to the liquidators, and the Supreme Court had twice denied certiorari. Technically the denial of certiorari has no clear meaning, so the issue was therefore not definitively settled. In July, 1991, the Sixth Circuit reopened the issue, holding in Fabe v. United States Dept. of the Treasury, 939 F.2d 341 (6th Cir. 1991), that the priority statute was within the business of insurance and hence the state priority rule prevailed over the federal statute. With an intercircuit conflict, the chances of a definitive Supreme Court decision are somewhat increased.

The comments on the various subsections in §645.68 provide a fairly detailed rationale for the priority system created by the Wisconsin statute and followed by all state laws enacted since, though with some changes of detail.

Often an insurer in liquidation is also a reinsurer. At first glance it might seem that ceding companies reinsured by the insolvent are also insureds and should stand in a priority position with other policyholders. The cases are clear, however, that cedents rank as general creditors, not as policyholders. For a recent illustration, see In Re Liquidations of Reserve Ins. Co., 122 Ill. 2d 555, 524 N.E.2d 538, 120 Ill. Dec. 508 (1988).

When an insurer becomes insolvent, there will be instances in which the general law of setoff applies. It is less clear just what that law is. The most common situation where setoff is claimed is by reinsurers of the insolvent company. Reinsurers may claim to be entitled to set what the reinsured company owes them for premiums under the reinsurance contract off against the amount owed by the reinsurer for losses under the contract. That is not an implausible result.

Sometimes insurers have engaged in reciprocal or cross reinsurance, that is, each has reinsured the other, whether in the same contract or, more often, in separate contracts. Then the question of setoff may arise when the solvent company seeks to set loss claims owed to it under one reinsurance contract off against loss claims owed by it under another contract. Reciprocal or cross reinsurance of that kind is much more common than a few decades ago, and there is a serious and open question whether setoff goes so far.

The whole area of setoff is in flux; whatever the law is now — and that is not altogether clear — it may be changed. At this writing the question is under serious consideration in the National Association of Insurance Commissioners. While its recommendations do not ipso facto become law, they are likely at least to get a hearing in the various legislatures. There is at least a possibility that recommended changes will be enacted by some of the individual states.

In contemporary liquidations, the amounts at stake are enormous. Liquidations are currently in process in which the estimated deficiency in the accounts of the insolvent companies exceeds a billion dollars. The extent to which setoff is allowed between the insolvents and reinsurers may make a major difference in the assets available to the estates in at least the larger insolvencies. For that reason, litigation is under way in several of the larger insolvencies to settle the existing rules. Such litigation is not likely to arise often, however, because of the predilection of liquidators for commuting (or compromising) claims against debtors of the estate, including reinsurers.

I. Unfair Practices

The McCarran Act permitted "reverse" preemption of the Federal Trade Commission Act by the states. Although the states acted with somewhat less alacrity than they did to preempt the Sherman Act, to the extent McCarran permitted them to, they did also enact unfair marketing practices acts, precluding application of the Federal Trade Commission Act. Only regulatory procedures would be used for enforcement.

Considerably later, unfair claims adjustment practices came under vigorous attack, and the states added a section to their unfair marketing practices acts prohibiting unfair claims adjustment practices. See the discussion in Chapter 8 regarding the effort to find within the statute warrant for creating a private cause of action for such practices.

Insurance Market Organization: A Primer

The risks or hazards against which insurance provides protection may be classified in various ways. There is no advantage in attempting to create a rigorous conceptual classification, for insurance *policies* tend to be created and structured as a result of historical and market forces, not logic. Policies reflect regulatory limitations, insurers' views of how the market might best function to their advantage, and the demand for new coverages created by the flow of events.

The contemporary automobile policy, for example, covers many risks of disparate character: property insurance against a wide range of hazards, insurance against liability, medical expense insurance, and more. It is a multiline policy that exists in its present form because of the overwhelming importance of the automobile in our society; nearly half of the premiums in the property/liability sector* of the American insurance market goes into automobile insurance. A single insurer, State Farm Mutual, received over $15 billion in automobile insurance premiums in 1989. National Underwriter, Apr. 23, 1990, at 9.

The organizing principle of the automobile policy is the automobile, not the conceptual nature of the coverages. Homeowners and farmowners policies similarly are multiple peril policies that cut across kinds of insurance. Those policies have as their organizing principle the home and the farm.

Automobile insurance provides an apt illustration of the effect of

---

*The property/liability sector includes all major lines of insurance except life, annuities and accident and sickness insurance. Some minor lines, such as title, political risk, mortgage guaranty and other financial guaranty insurance may not be treated as property-liability insurance. A few of them, such as title and mortgage guaranty insurance, are usually required to be issued by monoline companies.

regulatory limitations. At an earlier date no insurance company was permitted to insure against both liability and physical damage risks. As a result it took two different insurance companies to provide basic coverage on an automobile. Though that regulatory limitation had some important consequences, it was easily obscured for marketing purposes. Many fire insurance companies (which were in existence long before the automobile and which were authorized to write the physical damage risks on the insured car) created wholly owned subsidiaries or otherwise affiliated themselves with companies that were authorized to write liability insurance. Then two contracts were written but were combined on the same policy form. Only the sophisticated policyholder would realize that there were two separate contracts and two insurers on the policy.

That particular regulatory limitation was long ago abandoned as counterproductive; today a single company may issue one contract containing all the relevant coverages for automobiles. Yet the traces of that limitation still exist in the separate companies created in an earlier regulatory era.

A. Insurance Institutions

1. Insurers

a. The Size of the Market

Some conception of the aggregate size of the various insurance markets will prove useful in understanding insurance law. The figures used here may not always be the very latest but will suffice to show the approximate magnitudes dealt with. The world's gross premiums in the direct insurance market (life and nonlife) reached $1,210 billion in 1989, compared to $498 billion in 1984. North America accounted for about 40 percent of the total, Europe 31 percent and Asia nearly 26 percent. Only "Modest Growth" Expected, Fin. Times, June 21, 1991. Eastern Europe, including the Soviet Union but excluding Yugoslavia and Bulgaria, accounted for less than 3.5 percent. Kirk, Swiss Re Sees "Hard Road" in Eastern Europe, Bus. Ins., Oct. 8, 1990, at 93. In earlier decades the U.S. insurance market greatly exceeded half the world market, but the recent rapid growth of the markets in Europe and on the Pacific Rim have reduced the American share, though its absolute size has continued to increase steadily. The Eastern European share, always small, declined from 1988 to 1989 in percentage terms while remaining about constant in nominal dollar terms. Id. Exchange rate changes alter the standings periodically, too. In 1986 North America accounted for 45.5 percent of the total world insurance market and 52 percent of the nonlife market, Europe about 29 percent and 31 percent, Japan about 20 percent and 11 percent, with all the rest of the world the remainder. Insurance Information Institute, Insurance Facts 1988-1989, at 17-18.

There were substantial increases in premiums in 1986 and 1987, undoubtedly in part because of the rate increases that resulted from the very tight market of the "crisis" years. It is some though not conclusive evidence of that growth that the world's largest broker had an increase in gross revenues of 31 percent from 1985 to 1986 and 19 percent from 1986 to 1987. In 1988 the cycle turned again toward a soft market and put a temporary damper on premium growth for 1988 and 1989, with less than a 5 percent increase in 1989 over 1988. Broker Growth Grounded, Bus. Ins., June 18, 1990, at 1. United States property and casualty insurance company premium income increased by 22 percent from 1984 to 1985 and 22.4 percent from 1985 to 1986, and by the smaller but still considerable amount of 9.5 percent from 1986 to 1987. Id. at 27.

Nonlife insurance accounted for about 52 percent of the world's premiums in 1986; life insurance accounted for the rest. Id. at 19.

Among insurers, at the end of 1987 the largest in assets was the Prudential Insurance Co. ($141 billion), with Nippon Life second ($123 billion), and Metropolitan Life third ($88 billion). As this suggests, the greatest accumulations of assets are in the life companies. Some combined groups are very large, too. Cigna, the result of the merger of the Connecticut General Life Insurance Co. with the Insurance Co. of North America, had $53.5 billion in assets. The Travelers had $46 billion. The pure nonlife companies, even the largest of them, fall considerably below those numbers. The Global Giants, Wall St. J., Sept. 23, 1988, at 19R.

The reason life companies dominate in terms of assets is that life insurance is a savings (or investment) vehicle as well as insurance. Nonlife companies are straight insurance operations. If the measure were premium volume the ranking would be considerably different, even among life companies, where in substantial part assets reflect the age of the book of business.

b. Classifications by Lines of Insurance Written

The institutions that provide insurance can be classified in a variety of ways. One such classification is rooted in regulatory restrictions. There have been important changes in these restrictions in recent history but they are still clearly discernible in the structure of the insurance business. For many decades the insurance business was classified under several main headings: life insurance (which included annuities), accident and sickness insurance (sometimes called "disability", sometimes "accident and health", sometimes just "health"), fire insurance, marine insurance, and "casualty" insurance. The last quotation marks suggest the questionable appropriateness of the term "casualty" — fire, shipwreck, and accidental death are also casualties, but those risks were covered by fire, marine, and accident insurance, not by casualty companies. "Casualty" was (and is) a catch-all word used in insurance to describe the kinds of insurance not otherwise classified, but it usually includes liability insurance, a major heading in its own right.

Until recent decades, three main kinds of primary or direct insurance *companies* sold the main classes of insurance: life insurance companies, fire and marine insurance companies, and casualty (or accident and indemnity) insurance companies. Accident and sickness (or disability or health) insurance was a minor line until after World War II. It was treated as a hybrid, and both life insurers and casualty insurers were authorized to write it. That remains true today, although in the meantime health insurance has become of overwhelming importance to our social arrangements. The life insurance companies captured much more of the health insurance business than did the casualty insurers. In addition, some important companies now exist for which health insurance is the main line of business or even the only line, such as Blue Cross/Blue Shield and HMOs, though some would deny that the latter are truly insurers. (There was a considerable period of time when the "Blues" strenuously resisted being called insurers, for reasons related to regulation.)

The division between "fire/marine" and "accident/indemnity" companies is no longer imposed by law and has become unimportant in the structure of the business, though it has left many traces in company names and relationships. The newly combined field has sometimes been designated as "fire/casualty," sometimes as "property/liability," and sometimes as "property/casualty." The last term seems the most used, but "property/liability" is more accurately descriptive, though incomplete.

In recent years some insurance executives have urged the elimination of the mandatory division between life and nonlife companies. The division is still important, however. For differing views on the issue at a time when the controversy was more lively than at present, see Kimball, All Lines Authority: Implications for Solidity, 11 Forum 433 (1976), and Stoddart, The All Lines Charter — Should the Walls Come Tumbling Down?, 11 Forum 449 (1976). These and other related articles were presented in a panel discussion at a meeting of the American Bar Association.

Life insurance differs in important ways from nonlife, partly because of its long-term character and partly because of the savings or investment function of life insurance. The differences result in regulatory problems of quite a different order, justifying the continued separation between life and nonlife business. Annuities, both fixed and variable, should be included with life insurance for this purpose (and for many others), though they are in a sense the converse of life insurance and are taxed differently. Variable annuities (and sometimes fixed annuities) are also securities for purposes of federal regulation of securities.

All of the classifications made thus far relate to primary or direct insurance companies. There are also reinsurance companies (as well as reinsurance departments of primary carriers).* Reinsurers may span the gap between life and nonlife insurance, reinsuring both. Reinsurance, immensely important to the functioning of the insurance business, is responsible for some of its most intransigent problems.

The net reinsurance premiums written by American reinsurers in the first nine months of 1990 were $10.7 billion dollars, an increase of 9.1 percent from 1989. The single largest company, General Re, accounted for over $2.0 billion of that. See McLeod, No Market Turn for Reinsurance: Better Results Not a Sign of Higher Sales, Bus. Ins., Apr. 22, 1991, at 3. A major share of the reinsurance purchased by American insurers is placed with offshore companies located mostly in London and in Europe but also in such places as Bermuda, the Bahamas, and the Channel Islands. Much of the "insurance crisis" of the mid-1980s was triggered by the reluctance (or inability) of reinsurers, especially in the London market, to provide backup protection to primary insurers through reinsurance. See London Reinsurance Capacity Shrinking, Bus. Ins., Nov. 11, 1985, at 23. Many reinsurers, especially new and inexperienced ones, have become insolvent.

Beyond the main categories mentioned briefly above, there are some categories of insurance of *relatively* minor importance, such as title insurance and political risk insurance, that do not fit neatly within the above classification. Mortgage guaranty is well-established; other forms of financial guaranty insurance are emerging. These lines of insurance are properly outside the major categories, although for statutory reporting purposes they are included in property/casualty insurance. They tend to be written by specialized companies; title and mortgage guaranty insurance are required to be. Current regulatory proposals would force all financial guaranty insurance to be written by monoline companies. Political risk insurance is written mainly by governments, though to a limited extent by large private insurers.

---

*Reinsurance issues seldom appear directly in reported judicial opinions because most controversies in reinsurance are settled by arbitration, but more and more reinsurance questions are appearing in the courts.

c.   The Legal Form of the Insurer

(1)   Stock Corporations

Insurers appear in many legal forms. The vast majority of insurance contracts are written by insurance corporations. Stock insurance corporations operate much like general business corporations, although most state insurance codes modify corporation law in important ways for insurers. Stock companies dominate the nonlife portion of the insurance business, yet some nonlife insurers like State Farm Mutual are very large indeed.

(2)   Mutual Corporations

Mutual corporations are owned in some sense by the policyholders, but it is a peculiar form of ownership. Its peculiarities are well stated in a perceptive article, Hetherington, Fact v. Fiction: Who Owns Mutual Insurance Companies?, 1969 Wis. L. Rev. 1068. Mutuals have been of relatively greater importance in life and health insurance than in property/liability insurance. While mutuals have a major share of the assets in life insurance they write less of the new business. The reason for their disproportionately large share of life insurance *assets* is that their business is older, on average, and has accumulated more cash values.

The leading life insurance mutuals, such as the Prudential, the Metropolitan, and the Equitable were originally stock corporations. Under pressure resulting in large part from the Armstrong investigation of 1906, which revealed a great deal of political corruption in some of the life companies (especially the Equitable), those three and other stock corporations underwent conversion to mutual companies.* This, rather than inherent advantages in the mutual form, accounts for the predominance of mutuals in the life insurance business. Indeed, under current statutory rules for the formation of mutuals, creation of new ones is difficult and even unlikely except in unusual situations. See the requirements for the formation of new mutuals in any state insurance code. It can be argued, however, that the unpredictability of interest rates over the long term makes the mutual form with fully participating policies the only "fair" way to sell life insurance.

There are important nonlife mutuals but, except in automobile and workers compensation insurance, they do not loom as large and important as do the life mutuals. Prominent examples on the nonlife side are State Farm Mutual, the Nationwide group (now including

---

*The Armstrong investigation had as Chief Counsel a young New York lawyer named Charles Evans Hughes. The investigation helped him to the governorship of New York, to the Supreme Court, and to a try for the Presidency of the United States.

Employers Mutual of Wausau which earlier was independently important), Liberty Mutual, the Hardware Dealers Mutuals (better known as the Sentry Group), and the Factory Mutuals. Almost without exception they originated either in tight markets or in markets in which the entrepreneurial companies misclassified risks or failed to see farreaching market possibilities. Their names often suggest the origins of the companies.

Existing commercial companies somehow did not see the possibilities inherent in fire prevention through engineering inspections and the use of sprinklers. The Factory Mutuals resulted. The commercial market also failed to see that rural drivers of cars imposed less risk on insurers than urban drivers. State Farm Mutual was one result, though it no longer limits its business to rural areas.

Often thinking they are creating something new, various industry groups are now engaging in *group self-insurance*. The term, by which the activity is frequently described, is a misnomer. Under new federal law, some of these groups are organizing as *risk retention groups*. These are nothing other than mutual insurers,* some of which may ultimately outgrow their original roles and serve broader markets. Many others, though, will become insolvent and disappear, or may disappear because the commercial market once again makes them irrelevant. They are much like many existing commercial mutuals were in their formative periods. Congress's authorization has not really created a new form of insurer, though it has enabled the new insurers to escape some of the rigors of state regulation; whether that is a good thing is a separate question.

Some groups of potential insurance buyers, feeling the need for similar organizations, have gone offshore to organize ordinary mutual (or sometimes stock) insurers in Bermuda, the Bahamas, and other places where regulation is less rigorous or more easily adapted to specialized needs. Many have developed during the recent insurance crises, though some of the new ones have also become dormant in the more recent relatively soft markets. Such evasion is reasonable enough in cases where the product is not sold in the general market, that is, when companies are formed by trade groups composed of sophisticated members solely to provide protection for themselves. State insurance laws for no good reason tend to be too rigid to accommodate such specialized needs.

In the past, many of these companies have been organized off-

---

*Most retention groups are composed of relatively small policyholders. But some mutuals have been formed by groups of very large corporations whose losses are expected to be rare. A nuclear disaster would be a good illustration. In such cases the premiums actually paid may be in the tens of millions of dollars per year, and large surpluses may be accumulated; yet because of the potentially enormous losses and the relatively small number of participants, assessability is still retained.

shore to reduce their tax burdens, although the Internal Revenue Service has sought such taxes as it could (usually large sums) from those insurers or their parents. In the early cases, the IRS succeeded against pure captives that wrote only the business of their noninsurance parents. Its recent efforts, however, to deny the tax deductibility of premiums paid to wholly owned insurers that also wrote substantial "unrelated" business were not successful. The matter remains unsettled.

For a commercial enterprise, the mutual has inherent disadvantages, despite what has frequently been called the "inherent mutuality of all insurance." There is little possibility of incentive compensation, at least in the usual form of stock options, though there may be some disagreement as to how serious a handicap that is. If additional capital is needed to expand the basic insurance business or to expand into related businesses in the era of integrated financial services markets, there are few ways for a mutual to do it. It is possible to issue subordinated notes as a form of capital instrument, but the market for them is likely to be thin because the downside risk for investors is large and the upside potential small. It is possible to form downstream subsidiaries in which a portion of the shares are sold to the public, but the market for those shares is apt to be thin, too. Still, such structures do exist, though regulatory restrictions on insurance company investments in subsidiaries puts serious constraints on the mutual. The commercial stock companies with which the mutual is competing can form upstream holding companies that are almost entirely free of the constraints of insurance regulation, though the insurance subsidiaries continue to be fully subject to that regulation. Those holding companies can go to the capital markets, use the proceeds to supplement the capital of their insurance subsidiaries, and form and capitalize wholly or partially owned subsidiaries to do all of the related (or even unrelated) business activity that interests them. The compensation of executives can be as creative as in any other business.

Subject to the constraints of the Insurance Holding Company Acts, which are substantial and nearly uniform throughout the country, insurance companies can be acquired by general corporations, which in turn may supply capital for the strengthening of the insurer in case of need. Sears, Roebuck formed Allstate and gave it a good capital base. Allstate has very nearly become more important than its parent. American Express was for a time the owner of Fireman's Fund; ITT is the owner of Hartford Fire. In the last two cases, the vicissitudes of the insurance cycle induced each parent to make a capital infusion into its subsidiary insurer. Conversely, there have also been instances when a noninsurance company acquired an insurer and stripped it of part of its surplus.

(3) Mutual to Stock Conversion

It is not surprising, then, that the possibility of mutual to stock conversion has become an important contemporary issue in insurance regulation. The general sentiment in the regulatory community favored such a conversion in principle, but remained troubled over how to protect the legitimate interests of the policyholder-owners, at which point it becomes important to reflect deeply on the nature of the ownership of mutuals and the techniques that might give such owners appropriate protection without making conversion impossible. The recent conversion of the Union Mutual Life Insurance Company of Portland, Maine to the stock form took place after the strenuous opposition of an organized group of its agents forced substantial changes in the plan of conversion.

Many large mutuals have considered conversion to the stock company form, but seem to have abandoned the thought after concluding that the gains were not worth the difficulties. Quite recently, however, there have been indications that the Equitable, one of the larger American life insurers, may reconvert to stock form.

(4) Reciprocals

In the nonlife insurance business there is another form of insurer called a *reciprocal*, which is unincorporated. Each member of a reciprocal is both an insurer and an insured, just as is true in a mutual (so long as it remains an assessable one). Unlike the mutual corporation, where the liability of each member as an insurer is joint and several, the liability of the member of the reciprocal is merely several. This makes a considerable difference, at least in theory, in the early stages of operation of the insurer when the members of both mutuals and reciprocals can be assessed if assets are not sufficient to pay claims, including ordinary commercial debts. There is also the theoretical problem of serving process on members of the reciprocal who are not present in the jurisdiction of suit. These two problems were solved decades ago for assessable reciprocals during the liquidations of insolvent ones. While still describing the liability of reciprocal members as several, courts have tended to *treat* the members as if their liability were joint and several. See Commonwealth ex rel. Schnader v. Keystone Indem. Exch., 338 Pa. 405, 11 A.2d 887 (1940). The problem in acquiring jurisdiction has sometimes been solved by a similarly effective tour de force; the reciprocal, though unincorporated, is treated as an entity for service of process. Long v. Sakleson, 328 Pa. 261, 195 A. 416 (1937). But see Tuck v. United Services Auto. Assn., 732 F. Supp. 100 (N.D. Okla. 1989), following a more traditional approach.

More important, in order to be commercially viable institutions both reciprocals and mutuals must accumulate enough surplus to be authorized to issue non-assessable policies, pursuant to contemporary insurance statutes. The amount required for that purpose will usually be the same as the amount required as capital and surplus for a comparable stock company. Once nonassessable policies are authorized, both mutuals and reciprocals can operate freely in the commercial market. They then differ from stock corporations mainly in that earning profits for the benefit of shareholders is not the central goal of the operation, while, at least nominally, providing insurance on the most favorable terms is. The larger a mutual or reciprocal becomes, however, the more completely its practices and its ethos become like those of its entrepreneurial counterparts. Ultimately, its management may wish to convert to the stock form!

Not being a corporation, the reciprocal has no board of directors to run it. Instead it is run under contract by a hired manager called an *attorney-in-fact*. The contract is a power of attorney which is at the same time an insurance policy. The attorney-in-fact is usually compensated by a percentage of the premiums and in fact is likely to be a corporation. It is legally separate from the insurers, who are the members, and is not liable on the insurance policies. For most purposes, however, including control of the enterprise, the attorney-in-fact *is* the insurer. In practical effect the nonassessable reciprocal is little different than a mutual with a management contract, under which a hired manager (natural person or corporation) manages the mutual and essentially has complete control of it through the contract. The manager or attorney-in-fact can run the business, is not liable on the insurance contracts, and may sometimes be able to exploit the policyholders for personal advantage (depending on the terms of the management contract or power of attorney).

This uncomplimentary view of the form (though not necessarily of the actual operation) of management contracts for both mutuals and reciprocals is reflected in the Wisconsin Insurance Code, which was primarily drafted by the author. See Wis. Stat. §§611.67, 618.23 (1987-1988). The drafters' comments on those sections can be found either in the session laws (1971 Wis. Laws ch. 260) or in West's Annotated Wisconsin Statutes. Foreign (that is, non-Wisconsin) reciprocals are admitted to do business in Wisconsin if they are judged by the insurance department to be sound, but no new reciprocals may be organized in Wisconsin. Management contracts for mutuals are forbidden.

This view of management contracts in general (though there is general agreement that abuses are possible and do occur) and of reciprocals is not universally held. Some insist that the latter are distinctive and make a valuable contribution to the insurance marketplace as a unique form of insurance enterprise. Whether they are distinctive or are really the equivalent of mutuals with management contracts, many of them have indeed been very successful in the marketplace and have been operated with integrity. Some very large and successful personal lines insurers, and especially automobile insurers, are reciprocals. The Farmers Group, for example, is basically the attorney-in-fact for three large reciprocals. For a long time it was a publicly held corporation. In 1988 it was acquired by British American Tobacco, U.S. (BATUS). The initial takeover attempt was hostile and was disapproved by various insurance commissioners under the Insurance Holding Company acts, but when the offer was increased to $5.2 billion the takeover was completed as a friendly one. In 1989, Farmers was a sticking point in the attempted takeover of British American Tobacco (the parent of BATUS) by Hoylake, a corporation created by a Goldsmith-Rothschild-Packer group for the purpose. Hoylake arranged to sell Farmers to a French insurance group, Axa-Midi, upon completion of the takeover of BAT, but after an adverse decision by the California Insurance Commissioner under the Insurance Holding Company Act in early 1990, Hoylake abandoned its efforts. In consequence Farmers remains a wholly owned subsidiary of British American Tobacco.

(5) Lloyd's

In general, neither partnerships nor natural persons may act as insurers, except as members of a mutual or a reciprocal. One important exception is found in the byzantine system of insurance known as Lloyd's. London is still the premier world market for commercial insurance; Lloyd's of London accounts for over half of the international commercial insurance business that comes to London. Its aggregated premium income was about $9 billion in 1990, which is less than many of the largest insurance companies but still substantial. Lloyd's itself is a market similar to the New York Stock Exchange. The Corporation of Lloyd's, governed by a 28-member council, operates the exchange. The Corporation is not an insurer but the manager of the external (that is, noninsurance) activities of the enterprise. The insurers (or "Underwriters at Lloyd's, London," as they are titled when they are sued) peaked in 1988 at 32,400 individuals, or *Names*, who stake their entire personal fortunes on the success of the insurance activities into which they enter. (About 6,000 have dropped out since.) The names are grouped into about 350 syndicates, of which each individual underwriter has a predetermined share. In the aggregate they have an underwriting capacity of perhaps $20-$22 billion. Alexander & Alexander, Industry Report, Vol. 4, No. 3 (1990); Lloyd's Capacity Now at $21 Billion, National Underwriter, Jan. 21, 1991 at 35; Lloyd's Capacity Grows, Bus. Ins., Mar. 11, 1991 at 1; The Lloyd's Mess: When Names Are Mud, The Economist, July 27, 1991 at 17. The syndicates constantly form, divide, merge, and disappear. An individual Name may be a member of more than one syndicate; most of them are not active participants in the business. The managers of the syndicates sit in stalls in "The Room" and receive proposals for insurance from Lloyds brokers representing the applicants for coverage.

The liability of each syndicate, and of each underwriter within the syndicate (like that of members of a reciprocal), is in theory several only, but that limitation is really never tested: A wide range of illogical but (in the British manner) workable protective devices give substantial assurance that all proven claims will be paid. Each Name must put up a personal guaranty fund and must limit premium writings in relation to that guarantee. (Paradoxically that rule makes underwriting capacity vary inversely with the adequacy of premium rates.) There is a Lloyd's Central Guaranty Fund that recently approximated £170 million. Great pride is taken in the asserted fact that no claimant with a justified claim has ever failed to be paid. (This is not to say that Lloyd's always pays claims that claimants — and sometimes others — think ought to be paid. Underwriters at Lloyds of London are defendants in innumerable lawsuits.) Because of the various protective devices, for practical purposes the liability of underwriters at Lloyd's might as well be joint and several. Although it is like the reciprocal in theoretically being subject only to several liability, the Lloyd's form is unlike the reciprocal in being an entrepreneurial form, not a mutual one.

About three fifths of the business of Lloyd's underwriters is written outside the United Kingdom, and most of it is denominated in dollars. Lloyd's is the United Kingdom's largest earner of invisible income. For policyholders holding dollar policies, any theoretical jurisdictional problems are solved neatly by a "service of suit" clause in the insurance policy, under which the underwriters agree to accept service in any jurisdiction in the United States, whether or not the jurisdiction has any connection with the policy or the claim. Policyholders of such dollar-denominated policies are protected against the exchange risk of fluctuations in the value of sterling by an American Trust Fund held in a New York bank which approximates in size the total dollar premium income of all Lloyd's underwriters for a year. Despite its byzantine character, Underwriters at Lloyd's, London constitute one of the great insurance enterprises of the world.

Reflecting its long history, the basic division of Lloyd's is between the marine and the non-marine market. The former has been relatively static in recent decades while the latter has grown rapidly. Lloyd's underwriters do not write "long-term" business, which for practical purposes means life insurance (and annuities).*

---

*Lloyd's has recently fallen on bad times, involving some unBritish bouts with corruption of major proportions in the management of some of the syndicates and among the Lloyd's brokerage firms, as well as some catastrophic losses, notably on United States liability business. There are also assertions that the operation of Lloyd's

A few American states permit the formation of "American Lloyds." A handful are still extant, mostly in Texas, but the Lloyd's model has not been notably successful on the western side of the Atlantic.

(6)　Exchanges

In an effort to capture some of the Lloyd's mystique as well as to solve some of the capacity problems of the American insurance market (especially for hard-to-place business), a movement has recently developed in the United States to create insurance exchanges much more like Lloyd's of London than are the American Lloyds. Three had made a start prior to the time of this writing. The underwriters are, in general, insurance companies or syndicates of companies that put up capital to participate in the exchange. In 1984, the New York Insurance Exchange wrote $350 million in premiums, the Insurance Exchange of the Americas in Miami wrote $62 million, and the Illinois Insurance Exchange wrote $15 million. The latter increased its volume to $205 million in 1989. Hoffman, Surplus Lines Battered, Not Beaten, Bus. Ins., Aug. 12, 1991, at 23. These are tiny shares of an enormous business. It is too soon to know whether exchanges will be successful in the long run, but the IEA ran into difficulty in the first part of 1987 and at least temporarily is not issuing policies. The New York Exchange had much recent trouble with insolvent syndicates, and is currently inoperative. Noises are heard from time to time, though not recently, about the establishment of similar exchanges elsewhere, but that development is likely to await the solution of the problems of the existing exchanges or the emergence of new market problems that can best be solved by institutions like the exchanges.

(7)　Pools and Syndicates

Insurance companies commit resources to pools and syndicates which operate as if they were independent corporations. They are used

---

has failed to keep pace with technological change. But the author finds it hard to doubt that Lloyd's will remain an important factor in the world insurance markets as long as any readers of this book will be practicing law, and that it will have solved its serious problems within a reasonable time. The contrary opinion exists, too, based on the expectation that one fallout of the recent troubles will be great difficulty in finding enough new Names to provide sufficient capital for the ever-increasing capital needs of the Lloyd's market. (One of the operating rules of Lloyd's Corporation imposes a limit on the amount of premium that can be written for a given amount of capital invested. Thus growth of the market requires a constant infusion of new capital.) For an extensive recent story detailing the Lloyd's problems, see The Lloyd's Mess: When Names Are Mud, The Economist, July 27, 1991, at 17.

when the ordinary structure of the market does not provide enough insuring capacity. An example is the American Hull Syndicate, which acts as underwriting manager for its member companies. The companies may write hull insurance outside their participation in the Syndicate only for coverage that the Syndicate has declined to write. Aircraft coverage, insurance of nuclear risks, and pollution liability are other examples of risks generally underwritten by pools. There are many more. Pools are very common in the reinsurance business.

(8)   Governments as Insurers

There are government insurers as well as private insurers. In the capitalist world, the oldest fire insurer extant is a state-owned and operated company, the *Hamburger Feuerkasse,* which is not only authorized to sell fire insurance in the *Land* (State — somewhat larger than the City) of Hamburg but has a total monopoly on that business. In the United States, there are some state monopolies in workers compensation, but there are also competitive state funds in workers compensation and, in Wisconsin, a competitive state life insurance fund. Some northern plains states have hail insurance funds. Pennsylvania created a Coal and Clay Mine Subsidence Insurance Fund, 1961 Pa. Laws 1068, 52 Pa. Cons. Stat. §§3201-3241 (1961). The state of Illinois has created a Grain Insurance Fund "to protect grain producers in the event of the financial failure of a grain dealer or grain warehouseman. . . ." Ill. Rev. Stat. ch. 114, par. 701 (1983). A few states have had savings bank insurance parallel to the FSLIC.

Important insurance activity is also carried on by the national government. Not to speak of Social Security, which was originally sold to the public as an insurance fund but which really is not one, there are federal government funds that have been regarded as true insurance funds. They include the Federal Deposit Insurance Corporation (FDIC), the former Federal Savings and Loan Insurance Corporation (FSLIC), and the Pension Benefit Corporation (PBC). Whether any of them can still properly be called an insurance fund has been placed in doubt by recent events, such as the handling of the Continental Illinois debacle by the FDIC, the savings and loan crisis that overwhelmed the FSLIC, and the negative capital position of the PBC if it were evaluated in the rigorous way a private insurer would be looked at by state insurance regulators. In its declining days FSLIC constituted little more than a golden pipeline from the United States Treasury to fortunate groups of beneficiaries (or investors) who would otherwise suffer considerable losses. (Some investors have even managed to make unconscionable profits out of the savings and loan crisis.) All three of the named federal agencies were vehicles for insurance-*like* purposes. The tragic (for the taxpayer) saga of the erstwhile FSLIC can best be followed daily in the pages of the Wall Street Journal or the New York Times. It is not likely to be concluded soon.

Nor do those massive government "insurance" enterprises stand alone. Federal government flood insurance has been important. There has long been a Federal Crop Insurance Corporation, which lost over $2 billion over the last decade. Yoo, Abolish Federal Crop Insurance Corp., But Not Its Programs, Panel Suggests, Wall St. J., July 14, 1989, at A3. Still another, relatively small but important in our foreign policy, is the Overseas Private Investment Corporation, which split off from the Agency for International Development in 1971. For recent word on its present role, see Hearn, U.S. Insurer Points to Eastern Europe, Chi. Tribune, Mar. 11, 1990, §7, at 5.

(9) Self-Insurers

Sometimes potential insureds *self-insure*, though if a potential insured has a large number of similar risks that are small in relation to the size of the enterprise, it may find it convenient *not* to insure but simply to pay losses out of current income. That practice is noninsurance, not self-insurance. Sometimes it is called *going bare*.

In some circumstances noninsurance may be a sensible practice because it eliminates the substantial costs of purchasing commercial insurance or of setting up the internal machinery needed to truly self-insure. It may be desirable for a company that goes bare to cap the potential for loss over a given time period by purchasing some kind of excess of loss insurance in the commercial market. Because of recent developments in the law of products liability, insurers increasingly *require* insureds to self-insure (or go bare) for a first layer ($1 million or more of products liability coverage in the case of a large manufacturer). The insurer then covers the next layer of exposure, usually *laying off* or reinsuring part of that. Further layers of excess insurance may also be purchased. The insured may then purchase a contract with an insurance company for administrative and claims adjustment services on the self-insured portion that to all intents and purposes appears as if there were a first-dollar insurance contract except that the insured pays the costs plus an administration fee. The contract is an insurance contract from which the coverage element has been removed by endorsement. Interesting legal problems can sometimes arise in which the scope of coverage in the next layer depends on whether the underlying contract is "insurance."

Going bare is an expression more often used for potential insureds who either have such difficulty obtaining insurance at a price they are willing to pay or suffer from such illusions about their invulnerability to suit because of the quality of their work (for example, a surgeon with great self-confidence) that they eschew the protection of insurance.

True self-insurance exists when the person engaged in the practice of paying its own losses as they occur actually sets up reserves in its accounts or has a *suspense account* on which it draws when losses materialize. That person in effect has an internal insurance-like operation. In that case, some kind of stop-loss protection is desirable and may quite possibly be obtained relatively cheaply. This kind of operation may sometimes be administered by an insurer for a fee. There is no good reason not to consider that practice to be a form of insurance.

Group self-insurance by groups of potential insureds with similar risks is not self-insurance at all but the creation of a mutual insurer, whether in corporate form, as a reciprocal, or as a risk retention group.

2. Intermediaries

Unlike insurers, which are not permitted to exist in the form of partnerships or sole proprietorships, those who act as intermediaries between insurers and insureds may operate in any legal form. All of the principal forms of legal organization are common. Intermediaries tend to be strictly regulated (at least in the statute books if not in fact) both as to qualifications and as to marketing practices considered important or troublesome.

a. Agents

Life insurers have traditionally marketed their products through natural persons who were captive agents working solely for a particular company. These agents were not usually empowered to bind the companies, and were therefore not agents in the ordinary legal sense. Instead, they were generally only solicitors: The actual binding of coverage was done by the company at its home or regional office. Some life companies have used general agents with broad binding power; in a defined geographical region they may be alter egos for the company. Nowadays there is a good deal of brokerage in the life insurance business: Persons representing the applicant place the business with any company that will write it. The company binds the coverage.

The nonlife insurance business has traditionally been organized in a different fashion. Under the so-called American Agency System, insurance agents (who are not necessarily natural persons) operate independent businesses and are true agents of insurance companies in the ordinary legal sense (they have binding power). They usually represent not one but many companies. The power to bind each company would be limited by contract except in the case of those general agents acting as alter egos for the company in a given area, geographical or substantive.

The latter agents would often be called *managing general agents*, or sometimes *underwriting managers*. These are not terms of art but more or less accurately describe what the contract says. The contracts are quite variable with respect both to the agent's actual authority and rate of compensation. Often such agents receive not only a straight commission as a percentage of premiums but also a contingent commission based on profits. Within the operation of a single company the rates of straight commissions might range from perhaps 10 percent to 35 percent, while the profit commission might vary from perhaps 15 percent to 30 percent of profits. The formulas for calculating profits are not uniform, and in recent years have tended to recognize the delayed determination of profit on liability business by providing for delay in calculation and payment until there is some likelihood that profit can be ascertained with reasonable accuracy.

For all types of agents, the company may sometimes be bound beyond the limits of actual authority under the doctrine of apparent authority. Nevertheless, under general doctrines of agency, an agent may not bootstrap himself into a position of binding power beyond that given by the company, though that power may be expanded quite unintentionally by the company's conduct.

Whenever independent agents represent many companies, they often owe (or at least feel) little loyalty to any particular one and tend to act more like brokers than agents. Their decisions are made with the interests of the buyer (or sometimes only their own interests) foremost.

In the middle of this century a revolution in marketing took place in the nonlife business with the rise of the so-called *direct writers* (an inaccurate but widely used term). These companies use employee agents, sometimes called *captive* or *exclusive agents*; enabling them to reduce distribution costs dramatically and as their competitors tell the story, to "cream the market" and make outsized profits. In truth, the companies involved in that revolution did quickly come to dominate the automobile insurance business. If they made large profits they were also able to reduce premiums for the targeted classes of business. State Farm Mutual has already been mentioned. In addition to its ability to exploit initially a special niche in the market, it also benefited from the marketing revolution and became the largest automobile insurer in the world. Allstate provides the paradigm case, however, with its use of over-the-counter selling in Sears stores.

b. Brokers

Brokers represent the applicant for insurance and, ideally, shop the market to find the best deals available for the client. Brokers are often compensated by commissions paid by the insurer, just as agents are, injecting into the relationship inherent conflict of interest problems. Brokers dominate the market for commercial lines of insurance, and agents dominate the market for the personal lines. Collective revenues of commercial insurance brokerages in 1990 was $12.8 billion. Largest Brokers' Revenues Grow Despite Stubborn Insurance Market. Bus. Ins., July 1, 1991 at 1. Marsh & McLennan (Marsh-Mac), the largest broker in the world, had gross revenues of nearly $2.8 billion in 1990. Alexander & Alexander, which is second, had gross revenues in 1990 of $1.4 billion. Id. In 1986 Marsh-Mac's gross revenues had been $1.83 billion, an increase of 31 percent from 1985. There was another increase of 19 percent to 1987. See Bus. Ins., Mar. 7, 1988, at 1; Bus. Ins., June 22, 1987, at 1. (The dramatic increases in those years reflected the tightening of the market and the increase of premiums after the devastatingly soft markets of the previous years). Alexander, which was already second in 1984, gained substantially on Marsh-Mac in 1985 by merging with Reed Stenhouse Cos., Ltd. of Toronto, but its later growth was less striking. Johnson & Higgins, which is third among American brokers, had gross revenues in 1990 of $833 million. Sedgwick James North America ranked fourth in the United States, with $529 million of revenues. The Sedgwick Group was third in the world, with $1.3 billion of gross revenues. The 1990 merger of Corroon & Black Corporation of New York and Willis Faber of London made that firm the fourth largest brokerage in the world, but its U.S. portion was still a little behind Sedgwick. Other brokers in the top ten are Frank B. Hall & Co., Rollins Burdick Hunter Co., Minet Holdings, Arthur J. Gallagher & Co., and Jardine Insurance Brokers, grossing from $443 million down to $127 million. After the top ten, the brokerages scale down fairly quickly. Number 100 had revenues in 1990 of about seven and a half million dollars. Burcke, The Going Stays Tough, Bus. Ins., July 1, 1991, at 31. The second tier have been growing more rapidly in percentage terms than the giants. By contrast with 1990, in 1984 Marsh-Mac was already over a billion dollars but number 100 was under a million. All along the line the growth has to a considerable extent been by acquisition and merger.

Insurance is in some respects a highly localized business, for in general it must operate where the clients are or come to shop: The largest American brokers are based in New York with offices everywhere, while the head offices of the smaller brokerage firms are found in diverse cities across the country. In other respects it is as international as any business can be. Many very large brokers are based in London. The location of the head offices of the largest brokerages in the world reflects in a rough way the distribution of the world market for placement of major commercial insurance. The degree of concentration in New York and London is startling.

Spinoffs and mergers can change relative rankings with surprising speed. The 1990 merger of Willis-Faber with Corroon & Black illustrates how quickly rankings can change, with the merged brokerage becoming fourth largest in the world, after Marsh & McLellan, Alexander & Alexander, and the Sedgwick Group. World rankings shift dramatically also when exchange rates shift. United States brokers do not loom as large on the world market now as they did in the days of the all-powerful dollar, though the effect of changing currency values is muted by the fact that the biggest brokers have revenues is most major currencies.

In recent decades, brokers have tended to acquire or create insurance companies, especially reinsurers and surplus lines companies,* as well as a wide range of service companies related to insurance.

The potential for self-dealing between brokers and subsidiary insurers is apparent, though the subtleties of some questionable transactions is extraordinary. Some scandals arising out of the abuse of such complex interrelationships at Lloyd's have erupted recently, leading to a demand by Lloyd's Corporation that all Lloyd's brokers divest themselves of their holdings of insurance companies. No determined effort to forbid broker control of insurers has yet been made in this country, though some have suggested it. The absence of comparable American scandals more likely represents the extreme difficulty of following audit trails (in a business where nothing happens except on paper) than superior American probity. A strong case could be stated for trying to compel brokers to truly shop the market for the benefit of their clients, which is only likely if (a) the client is as sophisticated about the insurance market as the broker, or (b) the broker is entirely free of conflict of interest. It is difficult to see how conflicts of interest can be eliminated except by divestment or by a rule forbidding all self-dealing, which would defeat the brokers' purpose in owning companies. On the other hand, there are tradeoffs in forcing divestment; brokers can make markets by creating their own, just as securities brokers make markets by dealing on their own account. In a tight market situation that may be an important advantage to buyers as well as to brokers. An alternative sometimes employed is for brokers to create and manage markets without owning them by organizing them in mutual or reciprocal form; that also has potential for abuse if the management contract gives effective control and the manager cannot be discharged without penalty. If the insureds are sufficiently sophisticated, it need not do so, of course; the new company can simply buy desired services

---

*Surplus or excess lines companies are unlicensed companies that, through specially licensed surplus lines brokers, sell types or amounts of insurance that cannot be placed with locally admitted companies. Surplus lines business is subject to a cycle opposite to the cycle of the general market. That is, when markets are tight, surplus lines companies do well; when markets are soft, surplus lines companies tend to retreat to special niches. If they do not, they are not apt to be around for another cycle.

from the brokers or their service subsidiaries. If the brokers are paid by commissions instead of by fees for services, there is an inevitable and obvious conflict of interest.

In addition to managing mutuals, brokers (through subsidiaries) have performed administrative services for self-insurers, provided loss prevention services, and organized and managed wholly owned captives, especially offshore in Bermuda and the Bahamas. One recent demand for information (by way of an interrogatory in litigation) directed to an offshore industry mutual named eight subsidiaries of a single one of the major brokers allegedly involved with the mutual and also included as unnamed subjects "any other" of the broker's subsidiaries or affiliates.

The insurance market can be very complex. An ordinary agent or broker may need to place some business with a surplus lines company, but the transaction cannot be direct. The local agent or broker goes to a specially licensed retail surplus lines broker, who may place the business through a wholesaler dealing in special programs (such as for long haul trucking, exterminators, asbestos removal companies, and so on). The wholesaler in turn may deal with a managing general agent for a company that may take all or a portion of the risk, perhaps laying most of it off to a pool of reinsurers through *treaty* reinsurance or to individual reinsurers on a *facultative* basis. There may be a reinsurance intermediary between the primary insurer and the reinsurer. See Chapter 9. Every participant in the chain of transactions including the original agent or broker may be a subsidiary of or affiliated with one of the major brokers.

No sharp line divides agents and brokers except for regulatory purposes. A person may act sometimes as a broker and sometimes as an agent, depending on the facts. In Rich Maid Kitchens v. Pennsylvania Lumbermens Mut. Ins. Co., 641 F. Supp. 297 (E.D. Pa. 1986), a person who was usually an agent was held to be acting as a broker, which made his testimony fatal to the insured's case. The discussion of the point is illuminating. Id. at 302-306.

Brokers and agents are sometimes called *insurance intermediaries*. The term is standard in England, though for some undiscernable reason many American insurance personnel strenuously resist its use. One exception to the resistance is with respect to reinsurance brokers. It is good terminology and not likely to be misunderstood, even if it is resisted.

c. Consultants

Another functionary who is sometimes called an intermediary, though with less justification, is the *consultant*. The consultant is a fee-compensated professional who gives advice that is theoretically unin-fluenced by any interest in the outcome. Life insurance agents sometimes call themselves consultants, which is a misnomer, for they have an interest in selling life insurance. There are few *true* consultants on insurance now in business, but some think the extensive use of consultants is a coming development. A recent advertisement received by the author contains the statement, "We Sell No Insurance . . . We Sell Insurance Expertise." If there are ways to ensure that in a particu-lar case a broker or agent is acting without the possibility of profiting from the sales following from the advice, it may be that the two functions can be appropriately engaged in by a single person, but prob-ably never in the same transaction.

B. Industry Organization

1. Regulatory Officials

Insurance is regulated mostly at the state level. The regulators are usually known as *Commissioners*, and operate as individuals, though insurance is regulated in Texas by a Board of Insurance Commission-ers. In a few states the regulator is called a *Director*, and in New York (and a few other places) the regulator is called *Superintendent*. In most states the Commissioner is a gubernatorial appointee, usually but not always for a term rather than at the governor's pleasure, managing a relatively independent agency, usually directly responsible to the gov-ernor to the extent that there is any political accountability. In a few states, the Insurance Department is structurally subordinate to a Department of Commerce or similar umbrella agency, though still rela-tively independent in operation. In a number of states, of which Flor-ida has been until recently the most notable, the Commissioner is an elected official; as a statewide office, the position is occasionally regarded as a plausible step toward the governorship. One Florida ex-Commissioner recently made an unsuccessful run for the United States Senate. The well-known initiative in California, Proposition 103, made the California Commissioner's office elective; the first election took place in 1990, and resulted in the election of an aggressive consumerist.

In an effort to make state regulation of a nationally operating industry viable, the commissioners and selected members of their staffs meet four times a year under the aegis of the National Associa-tion of Insurance Commissioners (NAIC). Opinions differ about the value and effectiveness of the work of the NAIC but the more extreme critics tend to ignore the limitations on all other human institutions, too.

2.   Trade Associations

Many trade associations in the insurance business exist to provide
vehicles for discussion of common problems and seek to influence
legislation and regulation at both the state and national levels, among
other purposes. The principal associations include the American Council of Life Insurance (located in Washington), representing most of the
life insurance companies of any substantial size; the American Insurance Association (recently moved from New York to Washington),
representing mostly the older eastern nonlife companies; the Alliance
of American Insurers (located in Chicago), representing mostly mutual
nonlife companies (under another name it formerly represented only
mutuals); the National Association of Independent Insurers (located in
Chicago), representing originally the companies in the forefront of the
marketing revolution of the 1950s and now representing many or even
most of the significant companies not belonging to the AIA or the
Alliance; and The Reinsurance Association of America, representing
the interests of reinsurers. A very few big companies are true indepen-
dents and belong to none of the above. Many other associations represent less substantial segments of the market, including those
representing state and local groups, as well as highly specialized ones.
   The Surety Association of America is one of the oldest trade
associations and represents several hundred companies, most of them
also members of other trade associations. It is primarily responsible for
the drafting of surety and fidelity contracts, including especially the
bankers blanket bond, or financial institution bond, which appears in
Chapter 4.

3.   Service Associations

Service organizations exist in numbers as well. Illustrative is the Insurance Services Office, which produces policy forms to recommend to
the industry and, in lines of insurance where rates are regulated, is
often designated by insurers to file rates for them. Recently the ISO
has been working for a number of years on a new comprehensive
general liability policy in "claims made" form which may significantly
change the market for liability insurance. That policy, which with
modifications resulting from the criticism of brokers, regulators, and
others, has now been generally approved by regulators and widely
though not universally adopted. See Chapter 5.
   The National Council on Compensation Insurance provides rate
making and filing services for the workers compensation field. Numerous other similar service organizations of greater or lesser importance
exist.

Consumers of the insurance product are not extensively organized, unlike the situation in some other countries, notably Germany. Some corporate consumers do belong to organizations. The Risk and Insurance Management Society, Inc. (RIMS) is the most important for industrial buyers of insurance.

The American Bankers Association, representing the buyers of the bankers blanket bond, has participated extensively in the preparation of successive drafts of that bond.

Until recently there has been almost no representation of ordinary consumers. There is now an increasing amount of it, and the organizations composing it make a great deal of noise. It is harder to judge how representative and how effective they are. In some states they may have some clout. See Weinstein, California Combat, Ins. Rev., Mar. 1988, at 44. A local group, the Insurance Consumer Action Network, was the principal (and successful) advocate of Proposition 103 in California in the fall of 1988. Proposition 103 made the office of Insurance Commissioner elective, cut automobile premium rates by 20 percent unless an insurer could show it would be made insolvent by the reduction, and other things. The California Supreme Court upheld the constitutionality of most of the Proposition, but held that the law must allow insurers to make a reasonable profit, which the Commissioner thereupon decided was 11.2%. There has been much subsequent discussion about that number. Until recently, rate hearings were being held by the California department of insurance to determine whether rates used by companies operating in California were excessive. As of this writing, the newly elected commissioner has frozen all rates and has declared his intention to reduce them as quickly as possible.

The complaint bureaus of the insurance departments are probably considerably more effective than consumer organizations in making insurers responsive to justified complaints by insureds. For a comprehensive study of complaint processing in one insurance department, see Whitford & Kimball, Why Process Consumer Complaints? A Case Study of the Office of the Commissioner of Insurance in Wisconsin, 1974 Wis. L. Rev. 639.

Most effective of all as protectors of ordinary consumers of insurance are the courts, at least in those instances where there is litigation, or where the results have been influenced by the results in litigated cases. See Chapter 1.

Table of Cases

Bibliography

A.B.A. Tort and Ins. Prac. Sec., Financial Institution Bond Litigation: A Case Study for Bankers, Sureties, Insurers, and Attorneys (1988)

Abraham, Distributing Risk: Insurance, Legal Theory, and Public Policy (1986)

———, Environmental Liability and the Limits of Insurance, 88 Colum. L. Rev. 942 (1988)

Alderman, A Transactional Guide to the U.C.C. (2d ed. 1983)

Alexander & Alexander, Industry Report, Vol. 4, No. 3 (1990)

Allen, Insurance Bad Faith Law, 13 Pac. L.J. 833 (Apr. 1982)

Alliance of American Insurers, 1986 Policy Kit for Students of Insurance 274 (1986)

American Council of Life Insurance, 1989 Life Insurance Fact Book Update

American Enterprise Institute for Public Policy Research, Renewal of the Price-Anderson Act (1985)

Andersen, Current Problems in Products Liability Law and Products Liability Insurance, 31 Ins. Coun. J. 436 (1964)

Ashley, Representation of the Insurer's Interests in an Environmental Damage Claim, 54 Def. Coun. J. 11 (1987)

Barbagallo, Violations of Antifraud Securities Laws and the Stockbrokers Blanket Bond, Form 14, 18 Forum 417 (1983)

Bean, The Accident Versus the Occurrence Concept, 440 Ins. L.J. 550 (Sept. 1959)

Beckman, Constitutional Issues in Insurance Claim Litigation, 22 Tort & Ins. L.J. 244 (1987)

Benktander & Fowler, Calculated Lag Factors — How Reliable Are Current Methods in a Trend Situation?, Best's Review 16 (April 1981)

Bergadano & Seymour, Duty of Defense Counsel to the Excess Insurance Carrier, 20 Forum 489 (1985)

Best, Defining Insurable Interest in Lives, 22 Tort & Ins. L.J. 104 (1986)

Bishop, New Cure for an Old Ailment: Insurance Against Directors and Officers Liability, 22 Bus. Law. 92 (1966)

Bixby, The Vendor-Vendee Problem: How Do We Slice the Insurance Pie?, 19 Forum 112 (1983)

Black & Skipper, Life Insurance (11th ed., 1987)

Blume, State and Federal No-Fault Automobile Insurance Developments, 12 Forum 586 (1977)

Brennan & Hanson, Misrepresentation in the Application as the Basis for Rescission of a Property Insurance Policy, 21 Tort & Ins. L.J. 451 (1986)

Brenner, Controversy Over Temporary Personal Insurance After 112 Years, No Signs Yet of an Early Peace, 22 Tort & Ins. L.J. 388 (1987)

Brown, Deterrence in Tort and No-Fault: The New Zealand Experience, 73 Cal. L. Rev. 976 (1985)

715

Brown & Romaker, *Cumis,* Conflicts and the Civil Code: Section 2860 Changes Little, 25 Cal. W. L. Rev. 45 (1988)

Butler & Freemon, The Innocent Coinsured: He Burns It, She Claims — Windfall or Technical Injustice?, 17 Forum 187 (1981)

Carter, Marketing a Jumbo Risk at Lloyd's and Managing It Thereafter, Address to the American Bar Association (July 1985)

Casey, Bad Faith in First Party Insurance Contracts — What's Next?, 8 U. Ark. Little Rock L.J. 237 (1985-1986)

Catenacci, *Sparks* Revisited: Sparks v. St. Paul Insurance Co., 23 Tort & Ins. L.J. 707 (1988)

Chesler, Rodburg & Smith, Patterns of Judicial Interpretation of Insurance Coverage for Hazardous Waste Site Liability, 18 Rutgers L.J. 9 (1986)

Chorley, Liberal Trends in Present-day Commercial Law, 3 Mod. L. Rev. 272 (1940)

Clarke, The Law of Insurance Contracts (1989)

Clifford & Iuculano, AIDS and Insurance: The Rationale for AIDS-related Testing, 100 Harv. L. Rev. 1806 (1987)

Cline, Defense of a Suicide Case, 16 Forum 726 (1981)

Clore, Suits Against Financial Institutions; Coverage and Considerations, 20 Forum 84 (1984)

Connally, Mortgagor-Mortgagee Problems and the Standard Mortgage Clause, 13 Forum 786 (1978)

Cozen & Bennett, Fortuity: The Unnamed Exclusion, 20 Forum 222 (1985)

Cross, The Community Property Law in Washington (Revised 1985), 61 Wash. L. Rev. 13 (1986)

Danzon, Medical Malpractice (1985)

Diehl, Professionalism in Reinsurance, Sigma 2 (Mar. 1981)

Dondanville, Defense Counsel Beware: The Perils of Conflicts of Interest, 18 Forum 62 (1982)

Dwyer & Barney, Analysis of Standard Mortgage Clause and Selected Provisions of the New York Standard Fire Policy, 19 Forum 639 (1984)

Farnham, Application Misrepresentation and Concealment in Property Insurance — The Elusive Elements of the Defense, 20 Forum 299 (1985)

————, The Untimely Demise of Policy Defenses — New Property Policies and the I.S.O., 14 Forum 177 (1978)

Fowler, Statutory Third-Party Unfair Practice Suits Following Settlement: The Impact of *Royal Globe*'s Conclusion Requirement, 22 Tort & Ins. L.J. 640 (1987)

Freeman, Tort Law Reform: Superfund/RCRA Liability as a Major Cause of the Insurance Crisis, 21 Tort & Ins. L.J. 517 (1986)

Gabriel, Standby Letters of Credit: Does the Risk Outweigh the Benefits?, 1988 Colum. Bus. L. Rev. 705

German & Gallagher, Allocation of the Duties of Defense Between Carriers Providing Coverage to the Same Insured, 47 Ins. Couns. J. 224 (1980)

Goble, The Moral Hazard Clauses of the Standard Fire Insurance Policy, 37 Colum. L. Rev. 410 (1937)

Gordon & Westendorf, Liability Coverage for Toxic Tort, Hazardous Waste Disposal and Other Pollution Exposures, 25 Idaho L. Rev. 567 (1988)

Greene & Serbein, Risk Management: Text and Cases (1978)

Gregory, Public Regulation of the Insurance Industry after *Barry* and *Royal Drug*: McCarran-Ferguson at the End of the Decade, 16 Forum 371 (1981)

Hecker & Goode, Wear and Tear, Inherent Vice, Deterioration, Etc.: The Multi-Faceted All-Risk Exclusions, 21 Tort & Ins. L.J. 634 (1986)

Henderson, Insurance Protection for Products Liability and Completed Operations — What Every Lawyer Should Know, 50 Neb. L. Rev. 415 (1971)

Hetherington, Fact v. Fiction: Who Owns Mutual Insurance Companies?, 1969 Wis. L. Rev. 1068

Hinsey, The New Lloyd's Policy Form for Directors' and Officers' Liability Insurance — An Analysis, 33 Bus. Law. 1961 (1978)

Hoens, When Can the Bankers Blanket Bond Be Rescinded for Fraud or Misrepresentation?, 16 Forum 1102 (1981)

Hoey, Property Insurance: Annual Survey of Property Insurance Law, 23 Tort & Ins. L.J. 405 (1988)

Holmes, A Conflicts-of-Interest Roadmap for Insurance Defense Counsel: Walking an Ethical Tightrope Without a Net, 26 Willamette L. Rev. 1 (1989)

Hook, Multiple Policy Period Losses Under First-Party Policies, 21 Tort & Ins. L.J. 393 (1986)

Hourihan, Insurance Coverage for Environmental Damages Claims, 15 Forum 551 (1980)

Houser et al., Comparative Bad Faith: The Two-Way Street Opens for Travel, 23 Idaho L. Rev. 367 (1986)

Houser & Kent, Concurrent Causation in First-Party Insurance Claims: Consumers Cannot Afford Concurrent Causation, 21 Tort & Ins. L.J. 573 (1986)

Howard, "Continuous Trigger" Liability: Application to Toxic Waste Cases and Impact on the Number of "Occurrences," 22 Tort & Ins. L.J. 625 (1987)

———, The Swan Song of a Dishonest Duck: A Prototype for Analyzing Coverage Under the Bankers Blanket Bond, 20 Loy. U. Chi. L.J. 81 (1988)

Ingram, The Friendly Fire Doctrine: Judicial Misconstruction Run Amok, 22 Tort & Ins. L.J. 312 (1987)

———, Triangular Reciprocity in the Duty to Settle Insurance Claims, 13 Pac. L.J. 859 (1982)

Insurance Information Institute, 1988-89 Property/Casualty Fact Book

Johnson, Construction and Application of Pollution Exclusion Clause in Liability Insurance Policy, 39 A.L.R.4th 1047 (1985)

Johnston, Corporate Indemnification and Liability Insurance for Directors and Officers, 33 Bus. Law. 1993 (1978)

Kahn, Looking for "Bodily Injury": What Triggers Coverage Under a Standard Comprehensive General Liability Insurance Policy?, 19 Forum 532 (1984)

———, The "Other Insurance" Clause, 19 Forum 591 (1984)

Keeton, Insurance Law Rights at Variance with Policy Provisions, 83 Harv. L. Rev. 961, 1261 (1970)

———, Liability Insurance and Responsibility for Settlement, 67 Harv. L. Rev. 1136 (1954)

———, Reasonable Expectations in the Second Decade, 12 Forum 275 (1976)

Keeton & Widiss, Insurance Law: Student Edition (1988)

Kennedy, The McCarran Act: A Limited "Business of Insurance" Antitrust Exemption Made Ever Narrower — Three Recent Decisions, 18 Forum 528 (1983)

Kenney, The Loan Receipt and Its Use by Insurers: Considerations and Suggestions, 10 Forum 920 (1975)

Kessler, Contracts of Adhesion — Some Thoughts About Freedom of Contract, 43 Colum. L. Rev. 629 (1943)

Kimball, All Lines Authority: Implications for Solidity, 11 Forum 433 (1976)

———, Historical Introduction to the Legal System (1966)

———, History and Development of the Law of State Insurer Insolvency Proceedings: An Overview, 1986 A.B.A. Natl. Inst. on Ins. Insolvency 10

———, Insurance and Public Policy (1960)

———, The Role of the Court in the Development of Insurance Law, 1957 Wis. L. Rev. 520

———, The Purpose of Insurance Regulation: A Preliminary Inquiry in the Theory of Insurance Law, 45 Minn. L. Rev. 471 (1961)

Kimball & Davis, The Extension of Insurance Subrogation, 60 Mich. L. Rev. 841 (1962)

Kimball & Denenberg, Mass Marketing of Property and Liability Insurance (1970)

Kimball & Heaney, Emasculation of the McCarran-Ferguson Act: A Study in Judicial Activism, 1985 Utah L. Rev. 1

Kimball & Pfennigstorf, Administrative Control of the Terms of Insurance Contracts: A Comparative Study, 40 Ind. L.J. 143 (1965)

———, Legislative and Judicial Control of the Terms of Insurance Contracts: A Comparative Study of American and European Practice, 39 Ind. L.J. 675 (1964)

King, Coverage Under Fidelity Bonds for Third Party Claims Not Involving Loss of Property, 13 Forum 507 (1978)

Knepper, Liability of Corporate Officers and Directors (3d ed. 1978)

Kornblum, Extracontract Actions Against Insurers: What's Ahead in the Eighties?, 19 Forum 58 (1983)

Kunzman, The Insurer as Surrogate Regulator of the Hazardous Waste Industry: Solution or Perversion?, 20 Tort & Ins. L.J. 469 (1985)

Landis & Rahdert, The Completed Operations Hazard, 19 Forum 570 (1984)

Leavenworth, L.U.S.T., Ins. Rev. 20 (Mar. 1987)

Lentz, Profit and the Potential Income Exclusion, 19 Forum 694 (1984)

Levine, Demonstrating and Preserving the Deterrent Effect of Punitive Damages in Insurance Bad Faith Actions, 13 U.S.F. L. Rev. 613 (1979)

Llewellyn, Book Review, 52 Harv. L. Rev. 700 (1939)

Lowenstein, The Price-Anderson Act: An Imaginative Approach to Public Liability Concerns, 12 Forum 594 (1977)

McCann & Hall, Innocent Spouse Doctrine — New Fire in an Old Issue, 51 Ins. Coun. J. 86 (1984)

McCarthy, CERCLA Cleanup Costs Under Comprehensive General Liability Insurance Policies: Property Damage or Economic Damage?, 56 Fordham L. Rev. 1169 (1988)

McGrath, The Superfund Insurance Dilemma: Defining the Super Risks and Rights of Comprehensive General Liability Policies, 21 Ind. L. Rev. 735 (1988)

Marrone, The Price-Anderson Act: The Insurance Industry's View, 12 Forum 605 (1977)

Meyers, Subrogation Rights and Recoveries, 9 Forum 83 (1973)

Mintel, Insurance Rate Litigation (1983)

Moelman, Deductibles Under Financial Institution Bonds: Conflicts and Obligations, 16 Forum 942 (1981)

Montgomery, The Alter Ego Type Defenses Reconsidered, 13 Forum 528 (1978)

Morris, C., Waiver and Estoppel in Insurance Policy Litigation, 105 U. Pa. L. Rev. 925 (1957)

Morris, J., Conflicts of Interest in Defending Under Liability Insurance Policies: A Proposed Solution, 1981 Utah L. Rev. 457

Murray, Conditions to Recovery Under the Bankers Blanket Bond, 50 Ins. Coun. J. 617 (1983)

NAC Re Corporation, Liability Bulletin, Jan. 15, 1991

National Advisory Panel on Insurance in Riot-Affected Areas, Meeting the Insurance Crisis of Our Cities (1968)

Nonna & Strassberg, Reinsurance Arbitration: Boom or Bust?, 22 Tort & Ins. L.J. 586 (1987)

North American Reinsurance Corp., Experiodica, Vol. 2, Nos. 1, 10, 12 (1964)

Note, A Critique of the Reasonable Expectations Doctrine, 56 U. Chi. L. Rev. 1461 (1989)

———, Financial Guaranty Insurance: Is It "The Business of Insurance?", 1988 Colum. Bus. L. Rev. 855 (1988)

———, Functional Value vs. Actual Cash Value in Partial Loss Settlements, 50 Ins. Coun. J. 332 (1983)

———, Insurance as Contract: The Argument for Abandoning the Ambiguity Doctrine, 88 Colum. L. Rev. 1849 (1988)

———, Insurance Settlements: An Insured's Bad Faith, 31 Drake L. Rev. 877 (1981-1982)

———, Insurer's Liability for Refusal to Settle: Beyond Strict Liability, 50 So. Cal. L. Rev. 751 (1977)

———, Mental Incapacity and Liability Insurance Exclusionary Clauses: The Effect of Insanity upon Intent, 78 Cal. L. Rev. 1027 (1990)

———, Reinsurance and Reinsurer Insolvency: The Problem of Direct Recovery by the Original Insured or Injured Claimant, 29 UCLA L. Rev. 872 (1982)

O'Connell, A Draft Bill to Allow Choice Between No-Fault and Fault-Based Auto Insurance, 27 Harv. J. of Legis. 143 (1990)

O'Connell & Joost, Giving Motorists a Choice Between Fault and No-Fault Insurance, 72 Va. L. Rev. 61 (1986)

Oettle & Howard, D & O Insurance: Judicially Transforming a "Duty to Pay" Policy into a "Duty to Defend" Policy, 22 Tort & Ins. L.J. 337 (1987)

————, *Zuckerman* and *Sparks*: The Validity of "Claims Made" Insurance Policies as a Function of Retroactive Coverage, 21 Tort & Ins. L.J. 659 (1986)

Oldham & Dillingham, Developments and Trends in Aviation Insurance, 21 Tort & Ins. L.J. 44 (1985)

Oshinsky, Comprehensive General Liability Insurance: Trigger and Scope of Coverage in Long-Term Exposure Cases, 17 Forum 1035 (1982)

Ostrager & Ichel, Should the Business Insurance Policy Be Construed Against the Insurer? Another Look at the Reasonable Expectations Doctrine, 33 Fed. Ins. Couns. Q. 273 (1983)

————, The Role of Bargaining Power Evidence in the Construction of the Business Insurance Policy: An Update, 18 Forum 577 (1983)

Palmer, Is There a Mystery to Mysterious, Unexplainable Disappearance Coverage?, 16 Forum 988 (1981)

Pasich, Insurance Coverage for the Asbestos Building Cases: There's More Than Property Damage, 24 Tort & Ins. L.J. 630 (1989)

Pfennigstorf, Insurance of Environmental Risks: Recent Developments, 1982 A.B.A. Envtl. L. Symp. 57, Research Contribution of the American Bar Foundation (1982, No. 1)

Pfennigstorf & Kimball, Employee Legal Service Plans: Conflicts Between Federal and State Regulation, Ch. 3 in Legal Service Plans: Approaches to Regulation 189 (Pfennigstorf & Kimball, eds. 1977)

Pollack, Medical Maloccurrence Insurance (MMI): A First-Party, No-Fault Insurance Proposal for Resolving the Medical Malpractice Controversy, 23 Tort & Ins. L.J. 552 (1988)

Poust, Coverage for Civil Rights Liability — A Great Opportunity for Insurers, 51 Ins. Couns. J. 55 (1984)

Priest, The Current Insurance Crisis and Modern Tort Law, 96 Yale L.J. 1521 (1987)

Property and Liability Insurance Handbook (1965)

Readey, Cancer Cases — The Achilles Heel of Credit Life Insurance, 50 Ins. Couns. J. 241 (1983)

Rejda, Principles of Insurance (1982)

Ring, Obtaining Insurance Proceeds Over a Suicide Defense, 16 Forum 743 (1981)

Rizk, Bank Directors' Liability to Fidelity Insurers: How "Bad" is Bad Faith?, 19 Forum 481 (1984)

Rynerson, Exclusion of Expected or Intended Personal Injury or Property Damage Under the Occurrence Definition of the Standard Comprehensive General Liability Policy, 19 Forum 513 (1984)

Saxon, Conflicts of Interest: Insurers' Expanding Duty to Defend and the Impact of "Cumis" Counsel, 23 Idaho L. Rev. 351 (1986-1987)

Schatz, The AIDS Insurance Crisis: Underwriting or Overreaching, 100 Harv. L. Rev. 1782 (1987)

Schauble, Garvey v. State Farm: California's New Approach to Concurrent Causation, 23 Idaho L. Rev. 419 (1986-1987)

Schroeder, Handling the Complex Fidelity or Financial Institution Bond Claim: The Liability of the Insured's Officers and Directors and Their D & O Carrier, 21 Tort & Ins. L.J. 269 (1986)

Shenefield, Insurance — The New Frontier of Deregulation, 14 Forum 679 (1981)

Shipstead and Thomas, Comparative and Reverse Bad Faith: Insured's Breach of Implied Covenant of Good Faith and Fair Dealing as Affirmative Defense or Counterclaim, 23 Tort & Ins. L.J. 215 (1987)

Skillern, The New Definition of Dishonesty in Financial Institution Bonds, 14 Forum 339 (1978)

Soderstrom, The Role of Insurance in Environmental Litigation, 11 Forum 762 (1976)

Stein, Construction Law, Appendix of Forms

Stewart, Profit Cycles in Property-Liability Insurance, Monograph 5 in Long & Randall, ed., 1 Issues in Insurance 273 (3rd ed. 1984)

Stockton, An Analysis of Insurable Interest Under Article Two of the Uniform Commercial Code, 17 Vand. L. Rev. 815 (1964)

Stoddart, The All Lines Charter — Should the Walls Come Tumbling Down?, 11 Forum 449
   (1976)
Stone, AIDS and the Moral Economy of Insurance, The American Prospect 62 (Spring 1990)
———, The Rhetoric of Insurance Law: The Debate over AIDS Testing, 15 Law & Social
   Inquiry 385 (1990)
Sullivan, The Trading Exclusion in the Broker's Blanket Bond, 15 Forum 297 (1979)
Sumner & Keller, The Science of Society (1927-1933)
Syverud, The Duty to Settle, 76 Va. L. Rev. 1113 (1990)

Theisen, Recent Developments in Private Rights of Action Under the Unfair Claims Settlement
   Practices Act, 23 Tort & Ins. L.J. 19 (1987)
Thornton, Extracontractual and Punitive Damage Liability of Insurers, Primary and Reinsur-
   ance Coverages, 13 Forum 754 (1978)
Tract & Henderson, Regulating Letters of Credit, Best's Review 40 (Feb. 1985)

Vance, Handbook on the Law of Insurance (Anderson 3d ed. 1951)
———, Friendly Fires, 1 Conn. B.J. 284 (1927)

Weiner & David, The Credit Union Discovery Bond and the Directors and Officers Policy:
   Elements of an Attorney's Conflict of Interest, 15 Forum 321 (1979)
Weinstein, California Combat, Ins. Rev., Mar. 1988, at 44
Weisbart, Extraterritorial Regulation of Life Insurance (1975)
Wendorff, The New Standard Comprehensive General Liability Insurance Policy, A.B.A. Sec.
   Ins., Neg. & Comp. L. Proc. 250 (1966)
Whitford & Kimball, Why Process Consumer Complaints? A Case Study of the Office of the
   Commissioner in Wisconsin, 1974 Wis. L. Rev. 639
Widiss, Life Insurance Applications and Interim Coverage Disputes: Revisiting Controversies
   About Conditional Binding Receipts, 75 Iowa L. Rev. 1097 (1990)
———, Uninsured and Underinsured Motorist Insurance (2d ed. 1985)
Willborn, Insurance, Public Policy, And Employment Discrimination, 66 Minn. L. Rev. 1003
   (1982)
Wilson, Nuclear Liability and the Price-Anderson Act, 12 Forum 612 (1977)
Wisner & Leo, Subrogation Rights of Surety on a Fidelity Bond Against Officers and
   Directors of Insured Corporation, 18 Forum 320 (1983)
Withers, Proximate Cause and Multiple Causation in First-Party Insurance Cases, 20 Forum
   256 (1985)
Witten, "Barn Burning" and What Can Be Done to Prevent It, 22 Tort & Ins. L.J. 511 (1987)
Works, Coverage Clauses and Incontestable Statutes: The Regulation of Post-Claim Underwrit-
   ing, 1979 U. of Ill. L. Forum 809

Index